Collins

CHEMISTRY

AQA A-level Year 2 Student Book

Andrew Clark
Lynn Bayley
Paolo Coppo

William Collins' dream of knowledge for all began with the publication of his first book in 1819.

A self-educated mill worker, he not only enriched millions of lives, but also founded a flourishing publishing house. Today, staying true to this spirit, Collins books are packed with inspiration, innovation and practical expertise. They place you at the centre of a world of possibility and give you exactly what you need to explore it.

Collins. Freedom to teach

HarperCollins Publishers
1 London Bridge Street
London SE1 9GF

HarperCollins Publishers
Macken House,
39/40 Mayor Street Upper,
Dublin 1, D01 C9W8, Ireland

Browse the complete Collins catalogue at
www.collins.co.uk

First edition 2016

10 9 8 7 6

ISBN 978-0-00-759763-5

Collins® is a registered trademark of HarperCollins Publishers Limited
www.collins.co.uk

A catalogue record for this book is available from the British Library

Commissioned by Emily Pither
Project managed by 4science
Edited by Ken Gadd and Douglas Meekison
Proofread by Heather Addison
Artwork and typesetting by Jouve
Cover design by We are Laura
Printed by Ashford Colour Ltd.

This book contains FSC™ certified paper and other controlled sources to ensure responsible forest management.

For more information visit: www.harpercollins.co.uk/green

Approval message from AQA

This textbook has been approved by AQA for use with our qualification. This means that we have checked that it broadly covers the specification and we are satisfied with the overall quality. Full details of our approval process can be found on our website.

We approve textbooks because we know how important it is for teachers and students to have the right resources to support their teaching and learning. However, the publisher is ultimately responsible for the editorial control and quality of this book.

Please note that when teaching the AS and A-Level Chemistry course, you must refer to AQA's specification as your definitive source of information. While this book has been written to match the specification, it cannot provide complete coverage of every aspect of the course.

A wide range of other useful resources can be found on the relevant subject pages of our website: aqa.org.uk

CONTENTS

TO THE STUDENT

The aim of this book is to help make your study of advanced chemistry interesting and successful. It includes examples of modern issues, developments and applications that reflect the continual evolution of scientific knowledge and understanding. We hope it will encourage you to study science further when you complete your course.

USING THIS BOOK

Chemistry is fascinating, but complex – underpinned by some demanding ideas and concepts, and by a great deal of experimental data ('facts'). This mass of information can sometimes make its study daunting. So don't try to achieve too much in one reading session and always try to keep the bigger picture in sight.

There are a number of features in the book to help with this:

- Each chapter starts with a brief example of how the chemistry you will learn has been applied somewhere in the world, followed by a short outline of what you should have learned previously and what you will learn through the chapter.
- Important words and phrases are given in bold when used for the first time, with their meaning explained. There is also a glossary at the back of the book. If you are still uncertain, ask your teacher or tutor because it is important that you understand these words before proceeding.
- Throughout each chapter there are many questions, with the answers at the back of the book. These questions enable you to make a quick check on your progress through the chapter.
- Similarly, throughout each chapter there are checklists of key ideas that summarise the main points you need to learn from what you have just read.
- Where appropriate, worked examples are included to show how important calculations are done.
- There are many assignments throughout the book. These are tasks relating to pieces of text and data that show how ideas have been developed or applied. They provide opportunities to apply the science you have learned to new contexts, practise your maths skills and practise answering questions about scientific methods and data analysis.
- Some chapters have information about the 'required practical' activities that you need to carry out during your course. These sections provide the necessary background information about the apparatus, equipment and techniques that you need to be prepared to carry out the required practical work. There are questions that give you practice in answering questions about equipment, techniques, attaining accuracy, and data analysis.

At the end of each chapter there are Practice Questions, which are exam-style questions including some past paper questions. There are a number of sections, questions, Assignments and Practice Questions that have been labelled 'Stretch and challenge', which you could try to tackle. In places these go beyond what is required for the specification but they will help you build upon the skills and knowledge you acquire and better prepare you for further study beyond advanced level.

Good luck and enjoy your studies. We hope this book will encourage you to study chemistry further when you complete your course.

PRACTICAL WORK IN CHEMISTRY

While they may not all wear white coats or work in a laboratory, chemists and others who use chemistry in their work carry out experiments and investigations to gather evidence. They may be challenging established chemical ideas and models or using their skills, knowledge and understanding to tackle important problems.

Chemistry is a practical subject. Whether in the laboratory or in the field, chemists use their practical skills to find solutions to problems, challenges and questions. Throughout this course you will learn, develop and use these skills.

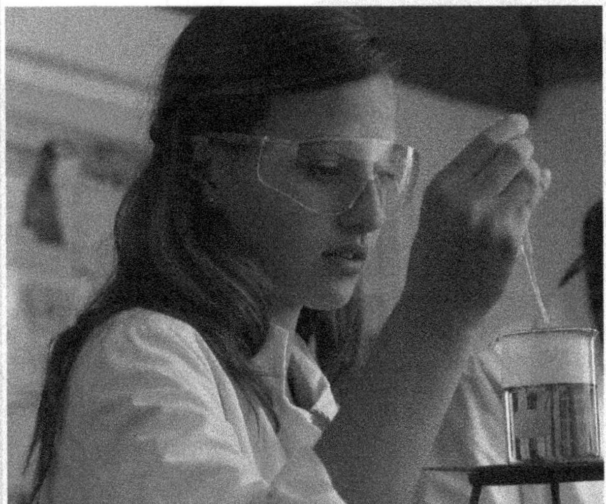

WRITTEN EXAMINATIONS

Your practical skills will be assessed in the written examinations at the end of the course. Questions on practical skills will account for about 15% of your marks. The practical skills assessed in the written examinations are:

Independent thinking

- solve problems set in practical contexts
- apply scientific knowledge to practical contexts

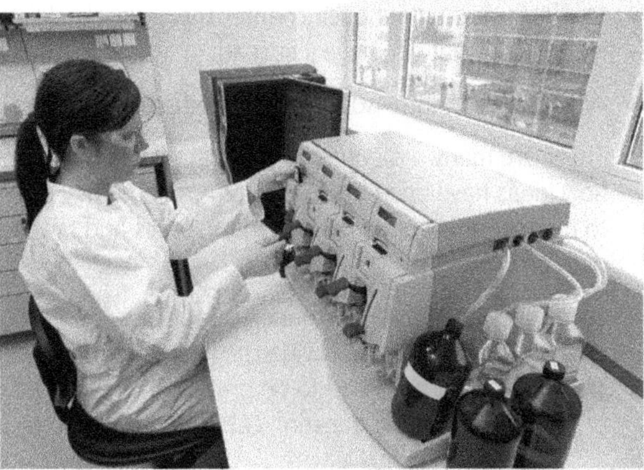

Figure 1 *Most chemists and others who use chemistry in their work spend time in laboratories. Many also use their practical skills outside of a laboratory.*

Use and application of scientific methods and practices

- comment on experimental design and evaluate scientific methods
- present data in appropriate ways
- evaluate results and draw conclusions with reference to measurement uncertainties and errors
- identify variables including those that must be controlled

Numeracy and the application of mathematical concepts in a practical context

- plot and interpret graphs
- process and analyse data using appropriate mathematical skills
- consider margins of error, accuracy and precision of data

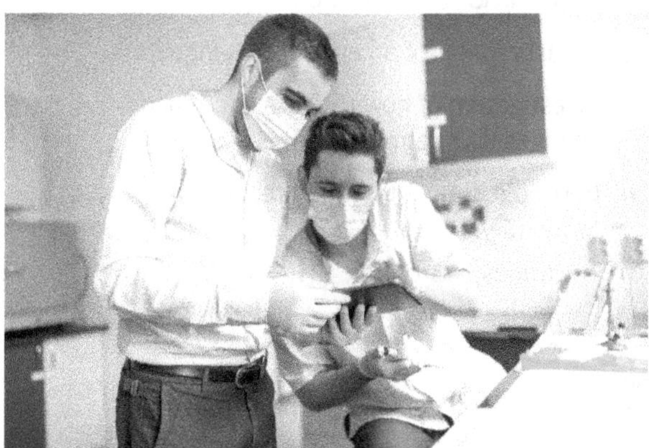

Figure 2 *Chemists record experimental data in laboratory notebooks. They also record, process and present data using computers and tablets.*

Instruments and equipment

- know and understand how to use a wide range of experimental and practical instruments, equipment and techniques appropriate to the knowledge and understanding included in the specification

Figure 3 *You will need to use a variety of equipment correctly and safely.*

Throughout this book there are questions and longer assignments that will give you the opportunity to develop and practise these skills. The contexts of some of the exam questions will be based on the 'required practical activities'.

ASSESSMENT OF PRACTICAL SKILLS

Some practical skills can only be practised when you are doing experiments. The following **practical competencies** will be assessed by your teacher:

- follow written procedures
- apply investigative approaches and methods when using instruments and equipment
- safely use a range of practical equipment and materials
- make and record observations and measurements
- research, reference and report findings

You must show your teacher that you consistently and routinely demonstrate the competencies listed above during your course. The assessment will not contribute to your A-level grade, but will appear as a 'pass' alongside your grade on the A-level certificate.

These practical competencies must be demonstrated by using a specific range of **apparatus and techniques**. These are:

- use appropriate apparatus to record a range of measurements (to include mass, time, volume of liquids and gases, temperature)
- use a water bath or electric heater or sand bath for heating
- measure pH using pH charts, or pH meter, or pH probe on a data logger
- use laboratory apparatus for a variety of experimental techniques including:
  - titration, using burette and pipette
  - distillation and heating under reflux, including setting up glassware using retort stand and clamps
  - qualitative tests for ions and organic functional groups
  - filtration, including use of fluted filter paper, or filtration under reduced pressure
- use a volumetric flask, including accurate technique for making up a standard solution
- use acid–base indicators in titrations of weak/strong acids with weak/strong alkalis

- purify:
  - a solid product by recrystallisation
  - a liquid product, including use of a separating funnel
- use melting point apparatus
- use thin-layer or paper chromatography
- set up electrochemical cells and measuring voltages
- safely and carefully handle solids and liquids, including corrosive, irritant, flammable and toxic substances
- measure rates of reaction by at least two different methods, for example:
  - an initial rate method such as a clock reaction
  - a continuous monitoring method.

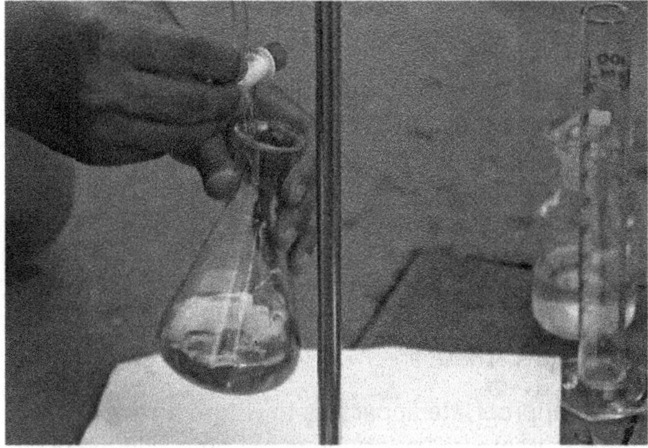

Figure 4 *Many chemists analyse material. They are called analytical chemists. Titration is a commonly used technique.*

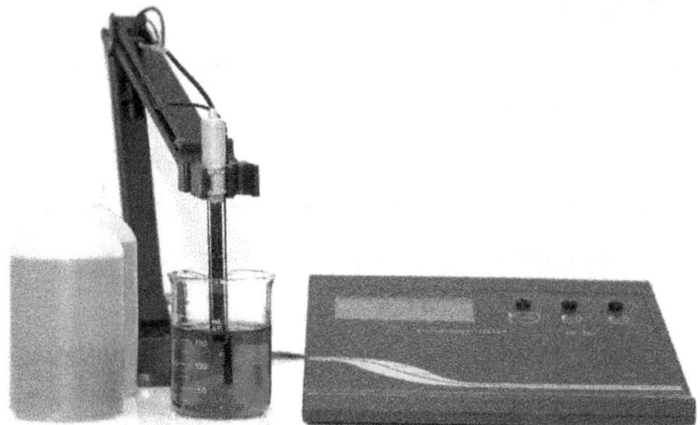

Figure 5 *pH probe*

REQUIRED PRACTICAL ACTIVITIES

During the A-level course you will need to carry out twelve **required practical** activities. These are the main sources of evidence that your teacher will use to award you a pass for your competency skills.

1. Make up a volumetric solution and carry out a simple acid–base titration
2. Measurement of an enthalpy change
3. Investigation of how the rate of a reaction changes with temperature
4. Carry out simple test-tube reactions to identify:
   - cations – Group 2, NH_4^+
   - anions – Group 7 (halide ions), OH^-, CO_3^{2-}, SO_4^{2-}
5. Distillation of a product from a reaction
6. Tests for alcohol, aldehyde, alkene and carboxylic acid
7. Measuring the rate of reaction:
   - by an initial rate method
   - by a continuous monitoring method
8. Measuring the EMF of an electrochemical cell
9. Investigate how pH changes when a weak acid reacts with a strong base and when a strong acid reacts with a weak base
10. Preparation of:
    - a pure organic solid and test of its purity
    - a pure organic liquid
11. Carry out simple test-tube reactions to identify transition metal ions in aqueous solution
12. Separation of species by thin-layer chromatography

Information about the apparatus, techniques and analysis of required practicals 1 to 6 are found in Student Book 1.

You will be asked some questions in your written examinations about these required practicals.

Practical skills are really important. Take time and care to learn, practise and use them.

1 THERMODYNAMICS

PRIOR KNOWLEDGE

You will have already studied some aspects of energy changes that happen during chemical reactions and whether they are exothermic or endothermic, and will have learned about enthalpy changes. This includes how to measure the amount of energy transferred and how to use known values to calculate other enthalpy changes using Hess's law. You have also learned about bond enthalpies (*see Chapter 7 of Year 1 Student Book*).

LEARNING OBJECTIVES

In this chapter you will learn about enthalpy changes and lattice energies. You will also learn how to calculate enthalpy changes using Born–Haber cycles (using known values for enthalpy of formation, ionisation energy, enthalpy of atomisation, bond enthalpy and electron affinity) and about enthalpy changes when compounds dissolve in water. You will learn about entropy and Gibbs free energy and how they influence the feasibility of chemical reactions.

(Specification 3.1.8)

What have hot mud packs got in common with self-heating cans for drinks and reusable hand warmers? They all use exothermic changes to heat things.

Self-heating cans have three compartments. One is for the drink, one contains water and the third contains calcium oxide. When the seal between the water and the calcium oxide is broken, the two come in contact and undergo an exothermic reaction. The energy released warms up the drink.

Hand warmers use the exothermic crystallisation of supercooled molten sodium ethanoate.

Hot mud facial packs contain clays that react exothermically with water. The energy released warms the skin, stimulates blood flow and opens the pores. By mixing cleansing oils with the clay, grease and dirt deep inside the pores can be removed, producing deep cleansing. Of course, the mixture should be safe for use on the skin and easy to remove.

You will probably know that enthalpy changes measure amounts of energy transferred to (exothermic) or from (endothermic) the surroundings of a reaction. You will have used Hess's law to calculate enthalpy changes. You will have learned that standard enthalpy changes are measured under standard conditions (usually temperature, 298 K and pressure, 100 kPa).

In this chapter you will extend your work on standard enthalpy changes, in particular those associated with the formation of ionic lattices. You will learn about entropy change and Gibbs free-energy change. This will help you to understand why some reactions are feasible but others are not.

1.1 ENTHALPY CHANGES AND IONIC LATTICES

Metals and nonmetals react to form ionic compounds. When just two elements are involved these are ionic compounds, for example sodium chloride, NaCl, sodium oxide, Na_2O, and magnesium oxide, MgO.

Ionic compounds form giant regular structures. These are called **lattices**. The regular arrangement of ions is reflected in the shape of the compounds' crystals. The strength of the bonding in a lattice is given by its lattice enthalpy.

Lattice enthalpies

There are two ways to define lattice enthalpy: the enthalpy of lattice formation and the enthalpy of lattice dissociation.

The **enthalpy of lattice formation** is the enthalpy change when one mole of a crystalline compound is formed from gaseous ions scattered an infinite distance apart (Figure 1). The enthalpy change for an ionic compound MX consisting of ions with single charges is represented as

$$M^+(g) + X^-(g) \rightarrow MX(s)$$

This is always an exothermic process.

The **enthalpy of lattice dissociation** is the enthalpy change when one mole of lattice is broken up to produce gaseous ions an infinite distance apart. For an ionic compound MX consisting of ions with single charges, this is represented as

$$MX(s) \rightarrow M^+(g) + X^-(g)$$

In other words, the process is the reverse of lattice formation. It is an endothermic process.

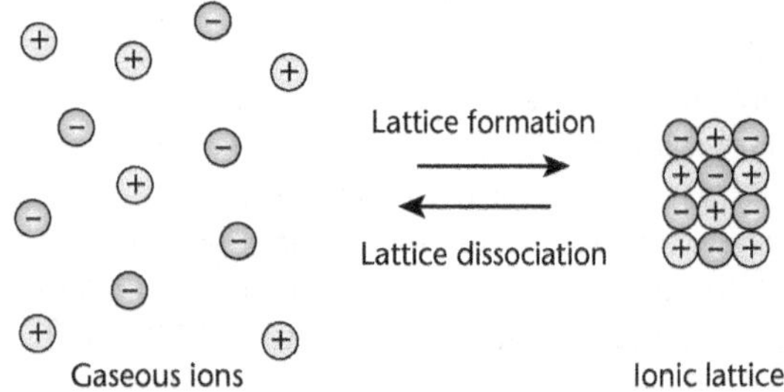

Figure 1 *Lattice formation and dissociation*

The value of a lattice enthalpy depends on:

- the charges on the ions
- the size of the ions
- the type of lattice formed (the pattern in which they pack together).

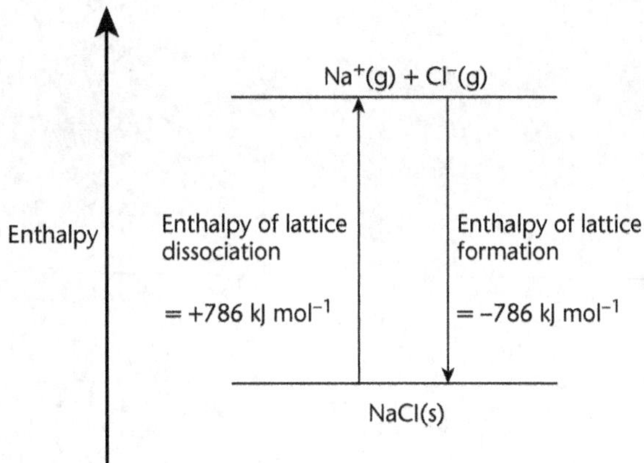

Figure 2 *A simple enthalpy diagram showing the lattice enthalpy of sodium chloride*

A larger exothermic enthalpy of lattice formation is favoured by a greater charge on the ions, smaller ions and a closer packing in the lattice.

QUESTIONS

1. Why does the enthalpy of lattice dissociation always have a positive value?

Using lattice enthalpies

Why are lattice enthalpies of interest? The main reason is to test our ideas of ionic bonding. Our simple model is one in which spherical ions of opposite charge pack together in a giant ionic lattice. By doing some mathematics, theoretical values for lattice enthalpies can be worked out.

A second reason is to increase our understanding of why some compounds do not exist. For example, why $MgCl_2$ and not MgCl or $MgCl_3$?

Lattice enthalpies cannot be measured directly (it is impossible to carry out experiments in which gaseous ions are spread out at infinite distances). However, they can be calculated from other experimental data using a special form of Hess's law called the Born–Haber cycle.

1.2 BORN–HABER CYCLES

As we have said, it is impossible to measure lattice enthalpies directly. But they can be calculated using **Born–Haber cycles**. To do this for an ionic compound you need these data:

- enthalpy of formation
- ionisation energy

- enthalpy of atomisation
- bond enthalpy
- electron affinity.

Enthalpy of formation

Like all enthalpy changes for reactions, the enthalpy of formation of a compound depends on the pressure and the temperature at which it is measured. In order to make comparisons between different sets of data, it is necessary to give the enthalpy changes under standard conditions, which are:

- temperature, 298 K.
- pressure, 100 kPa

In the equation for the enthalpy of formation, the states of matter (solid, liquid or gas) of the elements and the compound at 298 K and 100 kPa should be shown, for example

$$K(s) + \frac{1}{2}Cl_2(g) \rightarrow KCl(s)$$

The energy released during the formation of one mole of a compound from its elements in their standard states and under standard conditions is the **standard enthalpy of formation**, $\Delta_f H^\ominus$ (Table 1 and Figure 3).

Standard quantities at temperatures other than 298 K are sometimes given if it is more convenient for a particular reaction. $\Delta_f H^\ominus_{1000}$, for example, refers to a standard molar enthalpy change at a temperature of 1000 K. If no temperature is stated, it is assumed that the reference temperature is 298 K. So $\Delta_f H^\ominus$ on its own is the same as $\Delta_f H^\ominus_{298}$.

Compound	Equation	$\Delta_f H^\ominus$/ kJ mol^{-1}
Sodium chloride	$Na(s) + \frac{1}{2}Cl_2(g) \rightarrow NaCl(s)$	–411
Magnesium oxide	$Mg(s) + \frac{1}{2}O_2(g) \rightarrow MgO(s)$	–601
Calcium chloride	$Ca(s) + Cl_2(g) \rightarrow CaCl_2(s)$	–796
Sodium oxide	$2Na(s) + \frac{1}{2}O_2(g) \rightarrow Na_2O(s)$	–414

Table 1 Examples of standard enthalpies of formation

The value of lattice enthalpies of formation will be higher if:

- the ions are smaller (the smaller the ions, the more closely they can approach each other so the greater the force of attraction between oppositely charged ions)

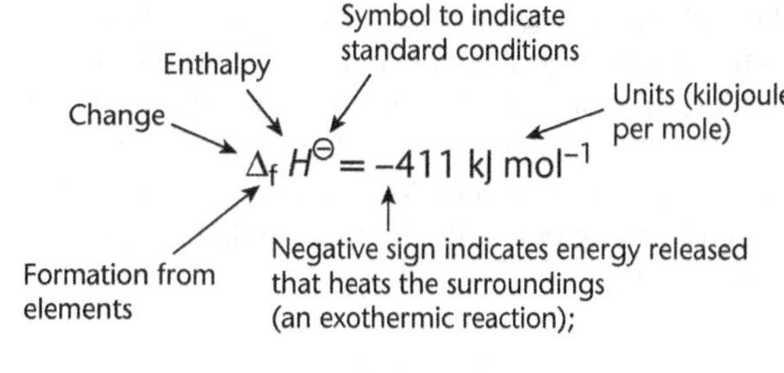

Figure 3 Standard enthalpy of formation of sodium chloride

- the ions have a greater charge (the higher the charge, the greater the force of attraction between oppositely charged ions).

QUESTIONS

2. What are the 'standard conditions' for a chemical reaction?
3. Use the correct symbols to write the standard enthalpy of formation of $CaCl_2$.

Ionisation energies

The enthalpy change when one mole of electrons is removed from one mole of gaseous atoms to produce singly charged ions is called the **first ionisation energy**:

$$M(g) \rightarrow M^+(g) + e^-$$

The enthalpy change when one mole of electrons is removed from one mole of singly charged ions to produce doubly charged ions is called the second ionisation energy:

$$M^+(g) \rightarrow M^{2+}(g) + e^-$$

and so on.

The symbol for ionisation energy is E_i.

Two examples:

Sodium

$Na(g) \rightarrow Na^+(g) + e^-$ 1st $E_i = +496$ kJ mol^{-1}

Magnesium

$Mg(g) \rightarrow Mg^+(g) + e^-$ 1st $E_i = +738$ kJ mol^{-1}

$Mg^+(g) \rightarrow Mg^{2+}(g) + e^-$ 2nd $E_i = +1451$ kJ mol^{-1}

Total enthalpy when $Mg^{2+}(g)$ is formed:

$Mg(g) \rightarrow Mg^{2+}(g) + 2e^-$ $E_i = +2189$ kJ mol^{-1}

The enthalpy change when an electron is removed from a full electron shell will always be much higher than the enthalpy change when an electron is removed from a partially full electron shell. Evidence from successive ionisation enthalpies can therefore be used to identify the group of the Periodic Table that an element is in.

QUESTIONS

4. a. Why is there such a difference in E_i (ionisation energy) between Mg^{2+} and Mg^{3+}?

   b. Explain why removing an electron from an atom is an endothermic process.

5. The successive ionisation enthalpies in kJ mol^{-1} for elements X, Y and Z are:

   X: 801, 2427, 3660, 25 026, 32 828

   Y: 1086, 2353, 4621, 6223, 37 832, 47 278

   Z: 1314, 3388, 5301, 7469, 10 989, 13 327, 71 337, 84 080.

   Giving your reasons, say which group of the Periodic Table each of the three elements is in.

Enthalpy of atomisation

The standard enthalpy of atomisation is the enthalpy change when one mole of gaseous atoms is formed from an element in its standard state.

Atomisation is always an endothermic process ($\Delta H^\ominus$ is positive) since chemical bonds are broken. The symbol $\Delta_{at}H^\ominus$ is used.

For example,

$Na(s) \rightarrow Na(g)$ $\quad \Delta_{at}H^\ominus = +107$ kJ mol^{-1}

$\frac{1}{2}Cl_2(g) \rightarrow Cl(g)$ $\quad \Delta_{at}H^\ominus = +121$ kJ mol^{-1}

The enthalpy of atomisation is related to the forces of attraction between atoms. In metals these forces are metallic bonds (electrostatic attraction of metal ions for delocalised electrons). In nonmetals they are covalent bonds (mutual electrostatic attraction of two nuclei of shared electrons).

Magnesium has a greater enthalpy of atomisation than sodium (Table 2) because the greater ionic charge (Mg^{2+} compared with Na^+) attracts the two delocalised electrons in the metallic lattice of magnesium more strongly. Aluminium has an even greater ionic charge (Al^{3+}) than magnesium, so its enthalpy of atomisation is even greater. Potassium has larger atoms than sodium and has more inner electron shells to screen the nucleus from the delocalised electrons. So the force of attraction is weaker and the enthalpy of atomisation is less than that for sodium.

Element	$\Delta_{at}H^\ominus$/ kJ mol^{-1}	Element	$\Delta_{at}H^\ominus$/ kJ mol^{-1}
lithium	+159	chlorine	+121
sodium	+107	bromine	+112
potassium	+89	iodine	+107
magnesium	+149	oxygen	+249
aluminium	+326	nitrogen	+472

Table 2 *Enthalpies of atomisation*

The enthalpies of atomisation for the halogens are quite similar because they all have single covalent bonds that are broken. The values decrease as the halogen atoms get larger, since the forces holding the atoms together are weaker. The values for oxygen and nitrogen are larger than for any of the halogens because atomising oxygen involves breaking a double bond and for nitrogen a triple bond.

QUESTIONS

6. Why is atomisation an endothermic process?

7. Explain why potassium has a higher $\Delta_{at}H^\ominus$ than rubidium.

Bond enthalpies of elements

The bond enthalpy is the enthalpy change when one mole of covalent bonds in a gaseous element is broken. It is often called the bond energy. These are not the same, but for our purposes they are interchangeable and you will see both terms being used. Energy is transferred from the surroundings to the gaseous element when covalent bonds are broken and, therefore, all bond enthalpies are endothermic.

Element	Bonding in molecule	*Bond enthalpy/* $kJ\,mol^{-1}$
chlorine	Cl–Cl	+242
bromine	Br–Br	+193
iodine	I–I	+151
oxygen	O=O	+498
nitrogen	N≡N	+944

Table 3 *Bond enthalpies*

QUESTIONS

8. Why do the bond enthalpy values of chlorine, bromine and iodine decrease with increasing atomic number?

For covalently bonded substances that are gases under standard conditions, the enthalpy of atomisation is half the bond dissociation enthalpy. For example,

$Cl_2(g) \rightarrow 2Cl(g)$ Bond enthalpy = +242 $kJ\,mol^{-1}$

$\frac{1}{2}Cl_2(g) \rightarrow Cl(g)$ $\Delta_{at}H^{\ominus}$ = +121 $kJ\,mol^{-1}$

However, the enthalpies of atomisation of bromine and iodine are more than half their bond dissociation enthalpies. This is because they are not gases in their standard state – bromine is a liquid and iodine is a solid. So, in addition to breaking bonds, there are changes of state:

$Br_2(g) \rightarrow 2Br(g)$ Bond enthalpy = +193 $kJ\,mol^{-1}$

$\frac{1}{2}Br_2(l) \rightarrow Br(g)$ $\Delta_{at}H^{\ominus}$ = +112 $kJ\,mol^{-1}$

$I_2(g) \rightarrow 2I(g)$ Bond enthalpy = +151 $kJ\,mol^{-1}$

$\frac{1}{2}I_2(s) \rightarrow I(g)$ $\Delta_{at}H^{\ominus}$ = +107 $kJ\,mol^{-1}$

Electron affinity

The enthalpy change when one mole of electrons is gained by one mole of gaseous atoms to produce singly charged ions is called the first electron affinity. Its symbol is E_{ea}.

For example, a gaseous chlorine atom can form a negative gaseous chloride ion:

$Cl(g) + e^- \rightarrow Cl^-(g)$ E_{ea} = −349 $kJ\,mol^{-1}$

Electron affinities can be exothermic for atoms on the right-hand side of the Periodic Table (the nonmetallic elements). These are atoms with a strong attractive force between their nuclei and outer electrons, produced by a relatively high nuclear charge for that period.

All ionisation energies are endothermic, but electron affinities may be endothermic or exothermic.

If one electron is added to an atom, energy may be released (exothermic). However, if more than one electron is added (to complete the outer shell), the second and third electron affinities are endothermic. This is because a negatively charged ion repels the electron and this repulsive force must be overcome.

Also, consider an atom and an ion with the same electronic configuration (Figure 4). Since the ion has a lower nuclear charge than the atom, the attraction of an electron by a nucleus of the ion is less than that of the nucleus of the atom.

These two factors cause many electron affinities to be endothermic. The second electron affinity is always endothermic because the electron (negatively charged) being pulled away is attracted by a positively charged ion.

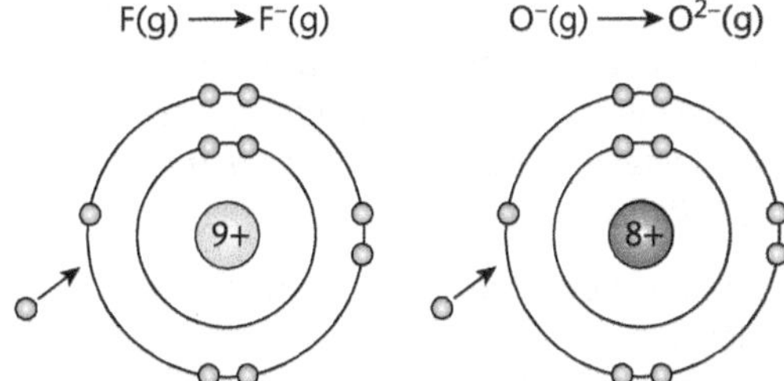

Figure 4 *$O^-(g)$ has a negative charge, but F(g) does not. Therefore $O^-(g)$ will repel electrons more than F(g). Furthermore, for $O^-(g) \rightarrow O^{2-}(g)$ there is a weaker attraction from the nucleus because the nuclear charge in $O^-(g)$ is less than in F(g) and $O^-(g)$ is larger than F(g).*

First electron added	1st E_{ea}/ $kJ\,mol^{-1}$	Second electron added	2nd E_{ea}/ $kJ\,mol^{-1}$
$H(g) \rightarrow H^-(g)$	−72	–	–
$F(g) \rightarrow F^-(g)$	−328	–	–
$Cl(g) \rightarrow Cl^-(g)$	−348	–	–
$Br(g) \rightarrow Br^-(g)$	−324	–	–
$I(g) \rightarrow I^-(g)$	−295	–	–
$N(g) \rightarrow N^-(g)$	−7	–	–
$P(g) \rightarrow P^-(g)$	−72	–	–
$O(g) \rightarrow O^-(g)$	−141	$O^-(g) \rightarrow O^{2-}(g)$	+798
$S(g) \rightarrow S^-(g)$	−200	$S^-(g) \rightarrow S^{2-}(g)$	+640

Table 4 *Electron affinities for some negative ions*

For the fluorine atom and the singly charged oxygen ion in Figure 4, the change in electronic structure is the same for each process. Fluorine has nine protons and oxygen has eight. At the same time, O^- is larger than F, so the force of attraction between the nucleus and the outer electrons is less in the O^- ion.

QUESTIONS

9. Explain why the first E_{ea} of sulfur is negative (−200 kJ mol^{-1}) but the second E_{ea} of sulfur is positive (+640 kJ mol^{-1}).

Born–Haber cycles

A Born–Haber cycle is a way to connect experimental data to lattice enthalpy, which cannot be measured directly. By applying Hess's law to the cycle, lattice enthalpies can be calculated.

Hess's law states that:

If a chemical change can occur by more than one route, then the overall enthalpy change for each route must be the same, provided that the starting and finishing conditions are the same.

You have already met some simple examples of energy cycles in *Chapter 7 of Year 1 Student Book*. Born–Haber cycles use the same principles but generally involve more steps.

The Born–Haber cycle for sodium chloride (Figure 5) shows the two routes from the elements sodium and chlorine to the compound sodium chloride.

For simplicity, the enthalpy changes are given as ΔH_1, ΔH_2 and so on, rather than by the full symbols.

Indirect route:

ΔH_1 for $Na(s) + \frac{1}{2}Cl_2(g) \rightarrow Na(g) + \frac{1}{2}Cl_2(g)$ is the enthalpy of atomisation of sodium, $\Delta_{at}H^{\ominus}[Na(s)]$.

ΔH_2 for $Na(g) + \frac{1}{2}Cl_2(g) \rightarrow Na^+(g) + \frac{1}{2}Cl_2(g) + e^-$ is the first ionisation energy of sodium, 1st E_i[Na].

ΔH_3 for $Na^+(g) + \frac{1}{2}Cl_2(g) \rightarrow Na^+(g) + Cl(g) + e^-$ is the enthalpy of atomisation of chlorine, $\Delta_{at}H^{\ominus}[Cl_2(g)]$.

ΔH_4 for $Na^+(g) + Cl(g) + e^- \rightarrow Na^+(g) + Cl^-(g)$ is the first electron affinity of chlorine, 1st E_{ea}[Cl].

ΔH_5 for $Na^+(g) + Cl^-(g) \rightarrow NaCl(s)$ is the enthalpy of lattice formation of sodium chloride, $\Delta_{latt}H^{\ominus}[NaCl(s)]$.

Direct route:

This is the reaction between solid sodium and gaseous chlorine:

ΔH_6 for $Na(s) + \frac{1}{2}Cl_2(g) \rightarrow NaCl(s)$ is the enthalpy of formation of sodium chloride, $\Delta_f H^{\ominus}[NaCl(s)]$.

From Hess's law,

sum of enthalpy changes in indirect route = enthalpy change by direct route

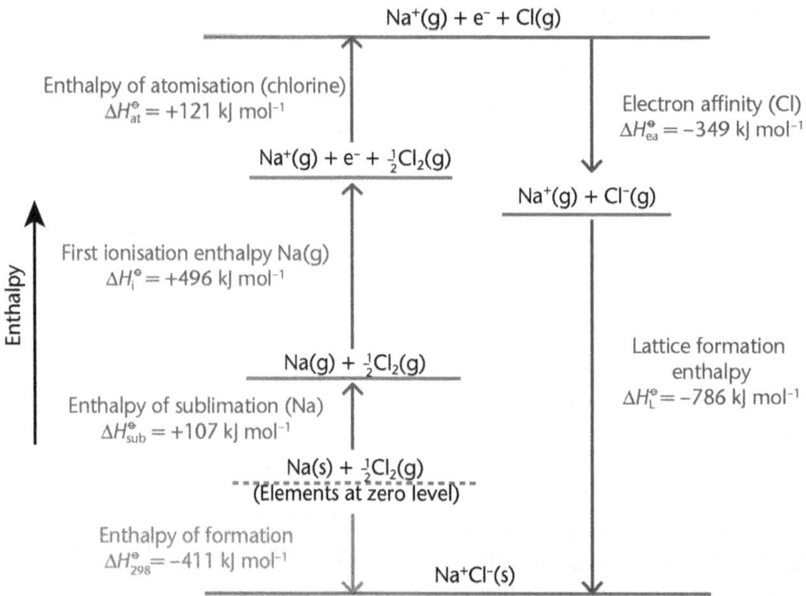

Figure 5 *Born–Haber cycle for sodium chloride*

$\Delta H_1 + \Delta H_2 + \Delta H_3 + \Delta H_4 + \Delta H_5 = \Delta H_6$

+107 + 496 + 121 + (–349) + (–786) = –411 (all values in kJ mol^{-1})

Born–Haber cycles are traditionally drawn with:

- the ionic solid on the lowest horizontal line
- positive ions, gaseous atoms of what will become negative ions, and electrons on the uppermost horizontal line
- electron affinity and lattice enthalpy on the right-hand side
- enthalpy of formation, enthalpy of atomisation and ionisation enthalpies on the left-hand side.

A Born–Haber cycle enables chemists to calculate:

- the enthalpy of lattice formation of an ionic compound from experimental data
- the enthalpy of formation of an ionic compound from a theoretical value for its enthalpy of lattice formation together with experimental data.

However, a Born–Haber cycle can be used to determine any missing value if the others are known.

The missing value represented by X in Figure 6 shows a change where two moles of gaseous chlorine atoms are converted to two moles of gaseous chloride ions with a charge of –1. Therefore, this change represents two times the electron affinity of chlorine.

This value can be calculated from the other values by adding or subtracting the enthalpy values shown in the cycle. The easiest way to work out which should be added and which should be subtracted is to draw a line around the outside of the cycle showing the alternative route from the gaseous chlorine atoms to the gaseous chloride ions (Figure 7). Any enthalpy changes which go in the same direction as this line should be added and any that go in the opposite direction should be subtracted.

$$2\Delta_{ea}H^{\ominus}(Cl) = -2\Delta H_{at}{}^{\ominus}(Cl) - \Delta H_{2nd\ IE}{}^{\ominus}(Mg) - \Delta H_{1st\ IE}{}^{\ominus}(Mg) - \Delta H_{at}{}^{\ominus}(Mg) + \Delta H_{at}{}^{\ominus}(Mg) + \Delta H_{IE}{}^{\ominus}(Cl)$$

$$2\Delta_{ea}H^{\ominus}(Cl) = -(+244) - (+1451) - (+738) - (+148) + (-641) + (+2524)$$

$$2\Delta_{ea}H^{\ominus}(Cl) = -698$$

$$\Delta_{ea}H^{\ominus}(Cl) = -349 \text{ kJ mol}^{-1}$$

QUESTIONS

10. Name these enthalpy changes:

a. $K(s) \rightarrow K(g)$

b. $O(g) + e^- \rightarrow O^-(g)$

c. $O^-(g) + e^- \rightarrow O^{2-}(g)$

d. $2K(s) + \frac{1}{2}O_2(g) \rightarrow K_2O(s)$

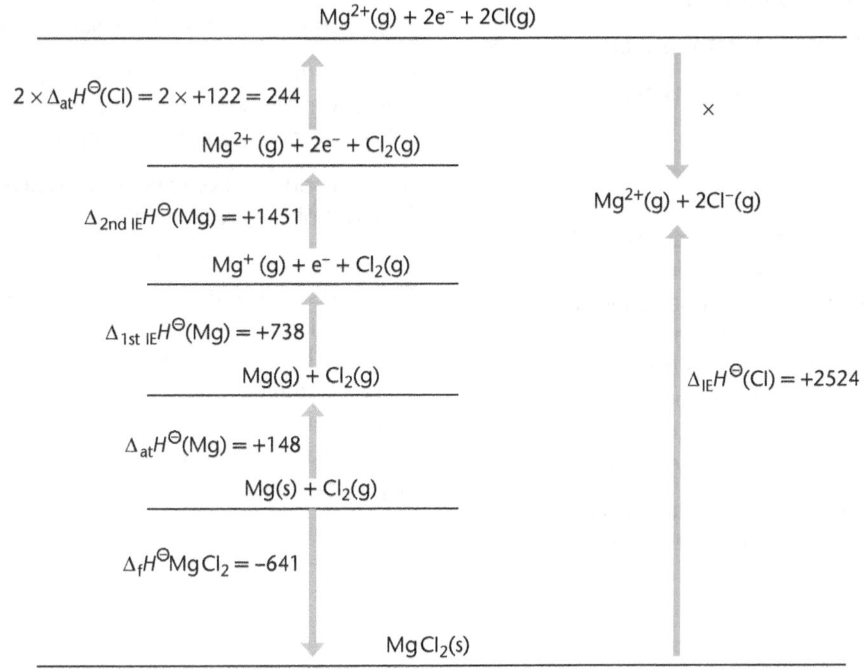

Figure 6 *Born–Haber cycle for magnesium chloride with a value missing*

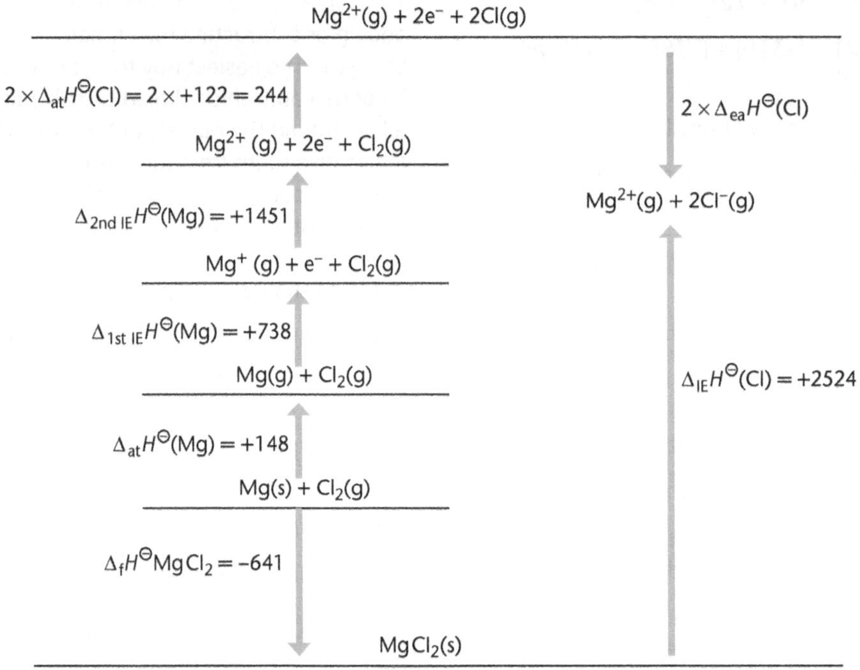

Figure 7 *The red line shows the cycle in Figure 6*

11. Calculate the energy change for the reaction $2NaHCO_3(s) \rightarrow Na_2CO_3(s) + CO_2(g) + H_2O(l)$, using the following data:

$\Delta_f H(CO_2(g)) = -393.5\ kJ\ mol^{-1}$

$\Delta_f H(H_2O(l)) = -285.8\ kJ\ mol^{-1}$

$\Delta_f H(Na_2CO_3(s)) = -1130.7\ kJ\ mol^{-1}$

$\Delta_f H(NaHCO_3(s)) = -950.8\ kJ\ mol^{-1}$

Born–Haber cycles and bonding

Theoretical values for lattice enthalpies can be calculated from Coulomb's law. Complete electron transfer is assumed to happen when ionic bonds form. The radii of the spherical ions that form are estimated. Then Coulomb's law is used to calculate the electrostatic forces of attraction between the oppositely charged ions as a function of the charges on the ions and the distance between them.

Agreement between values calculated using Born–Haber cycles and theoretical values provides evidence that the model of spherical ions packed together in a lattice and held together by electrostatic forces of attraction between the oppositely charged ions is a good one. This is the case for a number of ionic compounds: for example,

sodium chloride: lattice energy theoretical value = 766 kJ mol^{-1}; experimental value = 771 kJ mol^{-1}

However, there are also many examples where the differences between the theoretical and experimental values are significant. For example,

silver chloride: lattice energy theoretical value = 770 kJ mol^{-1}; experimental value = 905 kJ mol^{-1}

The explanation is that the bonding is not purely ionic. The bonds have some covalent character because the electron clouds surrounding the negative ions can be polarised by the positive ions. The degree of covalent character and polarisation is increased by having larger charges in either the negative or the positive ions, by having smaller positive ions, or by having larger negative ions.

ASSIGNMENT 1: BORN–HABER CYCLES AND NONEXISTENT COMPOUNDS

(PS 1.1, 3.2, MS 0.0, 2.1)

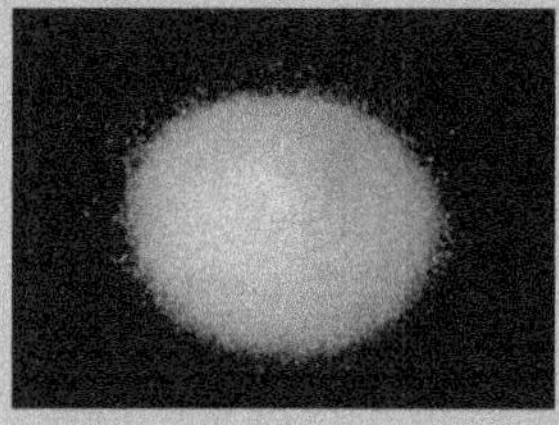

(a) (b)

Figure A1 (a) Powdered magnesium chloride; (b) crystals of magnesium chloride hexahydrate

Anhydrous magnesium chloride (Figure A1) has the formula $MgCl_2(s)$. No other chlorides of magnesium such as MgCl(s) or $MgCl_3(s)$ are known. Why?

Born–Haber cycles may be used to work out the enthalpy of formation of unknown ionic compounds. The data required are:

- the standard enthalpies of atomisation of the elements
- successive ionisation energies for the metal
- successive electron affinities for the nonmetal
- the lattice enthalpy, estimated from models, of the hypothetical compound.

The sign and magnitude of the calculated enthalpy of formation are a good indication of the stability of a compound. Stable compounds usually have high negative values. For example,

$Mg(s) + Cl_2(g) \rightarrow MgCl_2(s)$
$\Delta_f H^\ominus[MgCl_2(s)] = -642$ kJ mol^{-1}

In other words, stable compounds have enthalpies of formation that are highly exothermic.

Unstable compounds have enthalpies that are highly endothermic.

$Mg(s) \rightarrow Mg(g)$	$\Delta_{at}H^\ominus = +148$ kJ mol^{-1}
$Mg(g) \rightarrow Mg^+(g) + e^-$	1st $E_i = +738$ kJ mol^{-1}
$Mg^+(g) \rightarrow Mg^{2+}(g) + e^-$	1st $E_i = +1451$ kJ mol^{-1}
$Mg^{2+}(g) \rightarrow Mg^{3+}(g) + e^-$	1st $E_i = +7733$ kJ mol^{-1}
$\frac{1}{2}Cl_2(g) \rightarrow Cl(g)$	$\Delta_{at}H^\ominus = +121$ kJ mol^{-1}
$Cl(g) + e^- \rightarrow Cl^-(g)$	1st $E_{ea} = -349$ kJ mol^{-1}
$Mg^+(g) + Cl^-(g) \rightarrow MgCl(s)$	$\Delta_{latt}H^\ominus = -815$ kJ mol^{-1} (estimated from models)
$Mg^+(g) + 3Cl^-(g) \rightarrow MgCl_3(s)$	$\Delta_{latt}H^\ominus = -5540$ kJ mol^{-1} (estimated from models)

Table A1

Questions

A1. Using the thermodynamic data provided, calculate the standard enthalpy of formation of these two hypothetical compounds:

(a) MgCl(s)

(b) $MgCl_3(s)$.

A2. Explain why $MgCl_3(s)$ has never been made.

A3. During the reaction of magnesium with chlorine it seems likely that MgCl may form, but immediately disproportionate to $MgCl_2$ and Mg:

$$2MgCl(s) \rightarrow MgCl_2(s) + Mg(s)$$

Use Hess's law to determine the enthalpy change for this reaction.

KEY IDEAS

- The formation of compounds involves endothermic and exothermic reactions.
- An endothermic change occurs when forces must be overcome, e.g. during atomisation, ionisation or breaking up a lattice.
- An exothermic change occurs when forces of attraction operate, e.g. in the case of electron affinity or forming an ionic lattice.
- Born–Haber cycles can be used to calculate an unknown enthalpy; usually this is the lattice enthalpy.

1.3 SOLUBILITY AND ENTHALPY CHANGE

The process of dissolving

Water is an excellent solvent, dissolving a wide range of compounds. But why is it such a good solvent?

The covalent bonds in a water molecule are polar because of the electronegativity difference between oxygen and hydrogen. The overall effect is that the water molecule is polar (Figure 8).

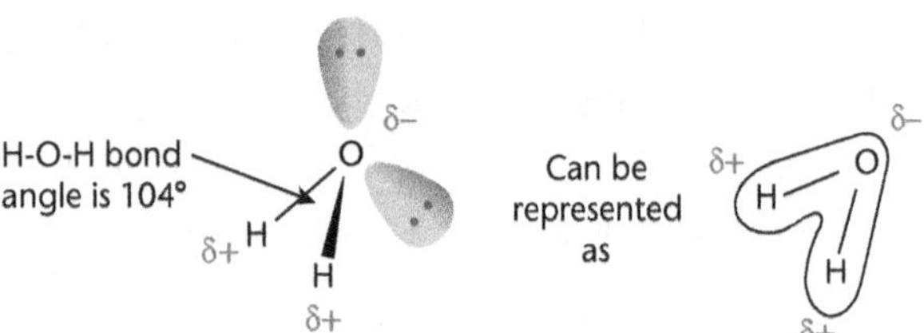

***Figure 8** Polarity in water molecules*

QUESTIONS

12. Explain why a water molecule is polar and the H–O–H bond angle is 104°.

The polar ends of the water molecules are attracted to the ions in the ionic lattice of a solid. Attractive forces between the water molecules and the ions in the lattice compete with the attractive forces between the ions in the lattice. Ions are surrounded and carried off into solution, helped further by the kinetic energy of the moving water molecules (Figure 9).

The ions become hydrated. Cations have a positive charge and are attracted to the negative end of the polar water molecules. Anions have a negative charge and are attracted to the positive end of the water molecules. As with the formation of any bond, the formation of bonds between water molecules and the cations and anions releases energy. It is an exothermic process.

QUESTIONS

13. Which atoms in a water molecule form bonds with cations and which form bonds with anions?

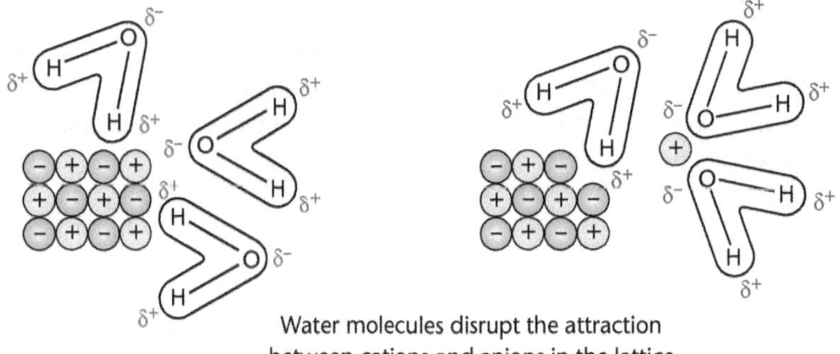

Anions surrounded by the δ^+ part of water molecules

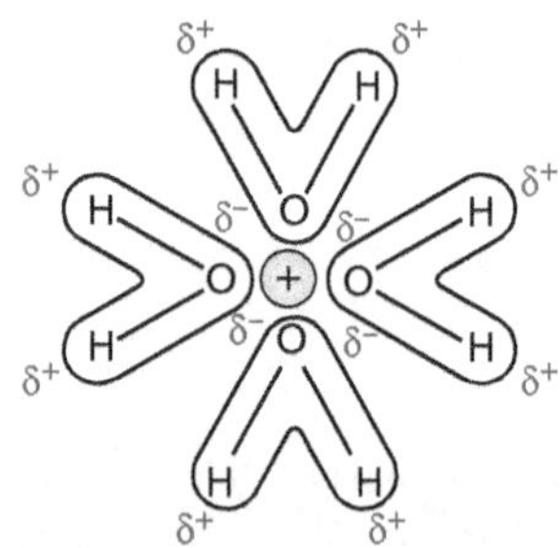

Cations surrounded by the δ^- part of water molecules

***Figure 9** Breaking down an ionic lattice by dissolving in water*

Water molecules surrounding the cations and anions hydrogen-bond to further water molecules, releasing more energy. When the ions move through the solution, the attached water molecules move with them. There is not a fixed number of these molecules, and the outer water molecules are held less strongly than those close to the ion. However, average values are sometimes given for the extent of hydration. Some examples are listed in Table 5.

Metal ion	Na^+	Mg^{2+}	Al^{3+}	K^+	Rb^+
Average hydration number	5	15	26	4	4

Table 5

Enthalpy of solution

When some compounds are put in water, there is a measurable enthalpy change. This is the enthalpy of solution. In this section we will consider only ionic compounds.

The enthalpy change may be exothermic or endothermic. For example:

- Sodium chloride dissolves in an excess of water, lowering the temperature of the water. This is an endothermic change. The enthalpy change is $+3.9\ kJ\ mol^{-1}$.
- Sodium hydroxide dissolves in an excess of water, raising the temperature of the water. This is an exothermic change. The enthalpy change is $-44.5\ kJ\ mol^{-1}$.

The enthalpy of solution is defined as:

the enthalpy change when one mole of an ionic compound dissolves in sufficient water to produce a solution of infinite dilution.

Enthalpy changes can be determined in the laboratory using calorimetry (*see Chapter 7 of Year 1 Student Book*). However, strictly speaking, to determine an enthalpy of solution would require making 'solution of infinite dilution', as the definition says. This is impossible, but we can get close enough because what it really means is that there is sufficient water present that adding any more does not cause a further enthalpy change; in other words there is no observable change in temperature.

Enthalpy of hydration

When an ionic compound dissolves in water a solution of hydrated cations and hydrated anions forms. For some compounds this is an exothermic process; for others it is endothermic. A thought experiment helps to explain why.

Imagine it was possible to break up an ionic compound into gaseous ions. The enthalpy change for this is the enthalpy of lattice dissociation (you learned earlier in this chapter how this can be determined using a Born–Haber cycle).

Now imagine that these gaseous ions dissolve in water to form hydrated ions (Figure 10). The enthalpy change for this is the enthalpy of hydration, which is defined as:

The enthalpy change when one mole of gaseous ions dissolves in sufficient water to produce a solution of infinite dilution.

The hydration of any gaseous ion is an exothermic process since bonds are being formed:

$M^{x+}(g) + aq \rightarrow M^{x+}(aq)$ $\qquad \Delta_{hyd}H$ is negative

$X^{y-}(g) + aq \rightarrow X^{y-}(aq)$ $\qquad \Delta_{hyd}H$ is negative

In these equations, 'aq' is taken to mean a large excess of water.

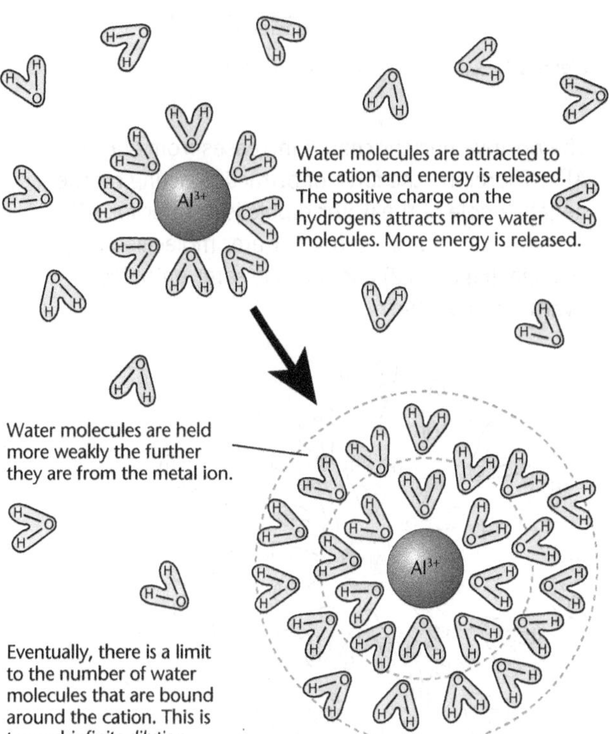

Water molecules are attracted to the cation and energy is released. The positive charge on the hydrogens attracts more water molecules. More energy is released.
Water molecules are held more weakly the further they are from the metal ion.
Eventually, there is a limit to the number of water molecules that are bound around the cation. This is termed infinite dilution.
Al3+

Figure 10 *Hydration of a cation*

QUESTIONS

14. Explain why water molecules In a hydrated ion are held less strongly the further they are from the metal ion.

The magnitude of the enthalpy of hydration depends on the strength of the bonds formed between the gaseous ion and water molecules. The smaller and more highly charged an ion is, the greater its enthalpy of hydration.

Consider the ions Na^+, Mg^{2+} and Al^{3+}. These cations all have the same electronic structure, but they have different charges and sizes (Figure 11).

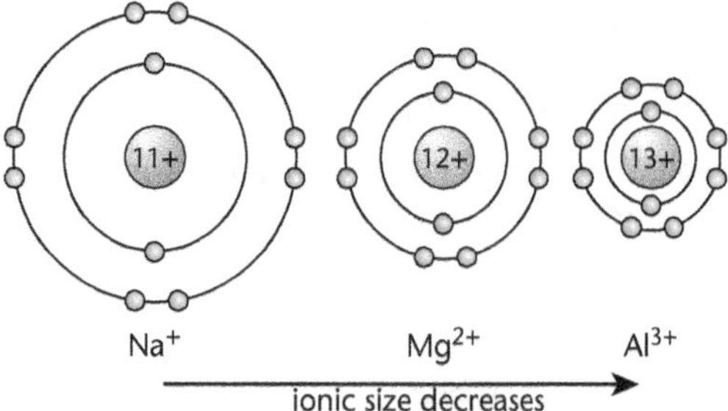

Figure 11 *Electronic configurations of cations*

The positive nuclear charge increases from Na^+ to Al^{3+}. Therefore, the force of attraction acting on the negative pole of the water dipole is greater for Al^{3+} than for Na^+. So Al^{3+} attracts water molecules very strongly (Figure 12) and has a greater enthalpy of hydration than Na^+.

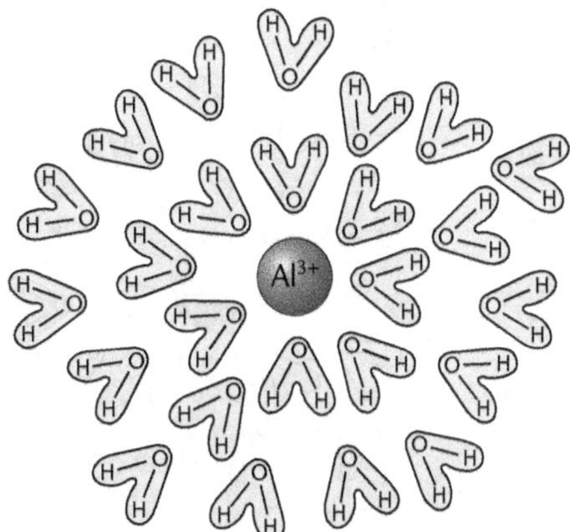

Figure 12 *Hydration of an Al^{3+} ion*

Cation	Na^+	Mg^{2+}	Al^{3+}	K^+	Rb^+
Enthalpy of hydration/ kJ mol^{-1}	−390	−1891	−4613	−305	−281
Anion	F^-	Cl^-	Br^-	I^-	OH^-
Enthalpy of hydration/ kJ mol^{-1}	−457	−381	−351	−307	−460

Table 6 *Some enthalpies of hydration*

For ions in the same period, the ionic charge increases and the ionic size decreases with increasing atomic number. As a result, the enthalpy of hydration increases significantly.

For ions in the same group – where ionic charge is constant and the ionic size increases down the group – there is a less dramatic change. The enthalpy of hydration decreases down the group – compare the values for Na^+, K^+ and Rb^+ in Table 6. Table 6 also shows that 2+ and 3+ ions have much larger hydration enthalpies than the 1+ ions. Ionic charge is a more significant factor than ionic size for producing larger hydration enthalpies.

Negative ions are also hydrated, but these attract the positive end of the water dipole (see Figure 9). The attraction of oppositely charged species will release energy and contribute to the overall value of the enthalpy of solution. Further data on the hydration enthalpies of some anions are listed in Table 6, and the lattice enthalpies and hydration enthalpies of some chlorides are listed in Table 7.

	NaCl	KCl	RbCl	$MgCl_2$	$SrCl_2$
Enthalpy of lattice/ kJ mol^{-1}	−780	−711	−691	−2258	−2156
Enthalpy of hydration/ kJ mol^{-1}	−771	−686	−662	−2653	−2323

Table 7 *Lattice enthalpies and enthalpies of hydration for various chlorides*

The immediate hydration spheres of some metal ions, especially transition metal ions, have a characteristic coordination number and geometry (see Figure 13, for example). In other words, those water molecules bonded directly to the metal ions have a characteristic geometry.

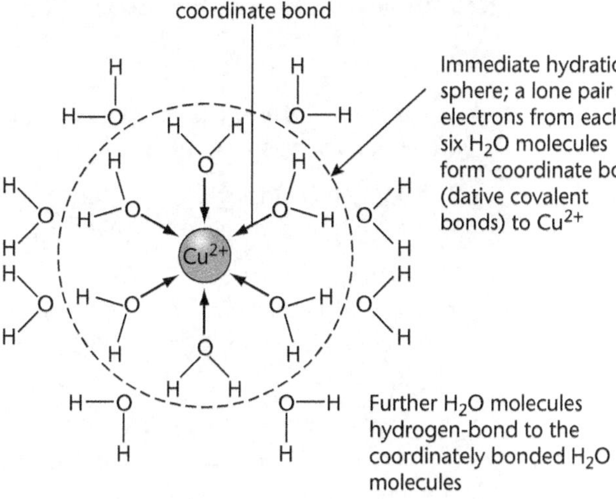

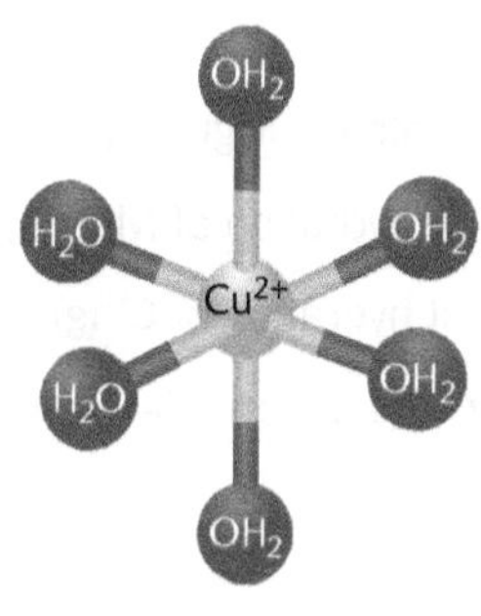

Figure 13 *Hydration of a Cu^{2+} ion. White anhydrous copper(II) sulfate dissolves in water exothermically. A blue solution forms owing to the presence of hydrated copper(II) ions.*

Using Hess's law and an enthalpy cycle

Enthalpies of solution can be estimated using lattice enthalpies and enthalpies of hydration. Figure 14 shows how enthalpy of solution, lattice enthalpy and enthalpies of hydration can be related in a cycle. In this example, dissolution of the ionic solid is an exothermic reaction.

QUESTIONS

15. Explain why an 'average hydration number' is given for a hydrated ion.

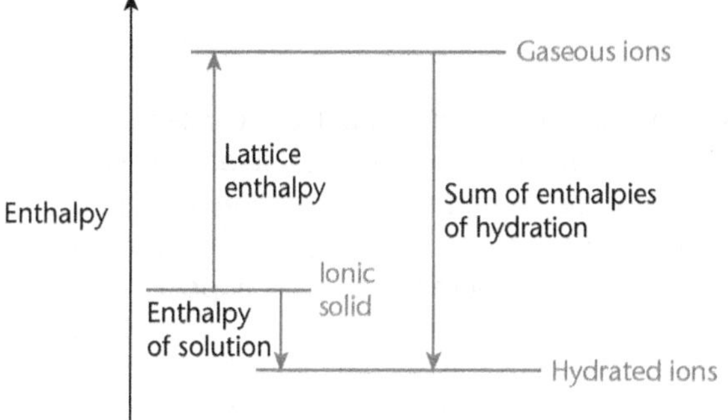

Figure 14 *An enthalpy cycle for enthalpy of solution, lattice enthalpy and enthalpy of hydration*

Using Hess's law,

enthalpy of solution = lattice enthalpy + sum of enthalpies of hydration of gaseous ions

Worked example

Calculate the enthalpy of solution of sodium chloride given:

- lattice enthalpy of NaCl(s) = 780 kJ mol^{-1}
- enthalpy of hydration of Na^+(g) = −390 kJ mol^{-1}
- enthalpy of hydration of Cl^-(g) = −381 kJ mol^{-1}

Equation for dissolution: $NaCl(s) + aq \rightarrow Na^+(aq) + Cl^-(aq)$

Enthalpy cycle:

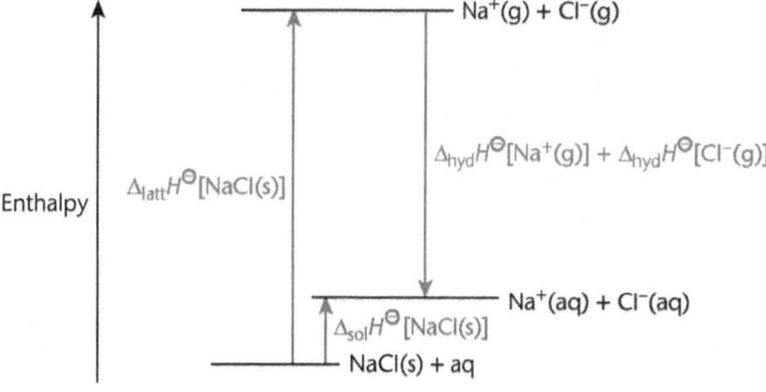

Using Hess's law,

$$\Delta_{sol}H^{\ominus}[NaCl(s)] = \Delta_{latt}H^{\ominus}[NaCl(s)] + \Delta_{hyd}H^{\ominus}[Na^+(g)] + \Delta_{hyd}H^{\ominus}[Cl^-(g)]$$

$\Delta_{latt}H^{\ominus}[NaCl(s)] = 780$ kJ mol^{-1}

$\Delta_{hyd}H^{\ominus}[Na^+(g)] = -390$ kJ mol^{-1}

$\Delta_{hyd}H^{\ominus}[Cl^-(g)] = -381$ kJ mol^{-1}

Therefore, $\Delta_{sol}H^{\ominus}[NaCl(s)] = 780 + (-390) + (-381) = 9$ kJ mol^{-1}

The dissolution of sodium chloride in water is endothermic.

Worked example

Calculate the enthalpy of solution of magnesium chloride given:

- lattice enthalpy of $MgCl_2(s) = 2526$ kJ mol^{-1}
- enthalpy of hydration of $Mg^{2+}(g) = -1891$ kJ mol^{-1}
- enthalpy of hydration of $Cl^-(g) = -381$ kJ mol^{-1}

Equation for dissolution: $MgCl_2(s) + aq \rightarrow Mg^{2+}(aq) + 2Cl^-(aq)$

Enthalpy cycle:

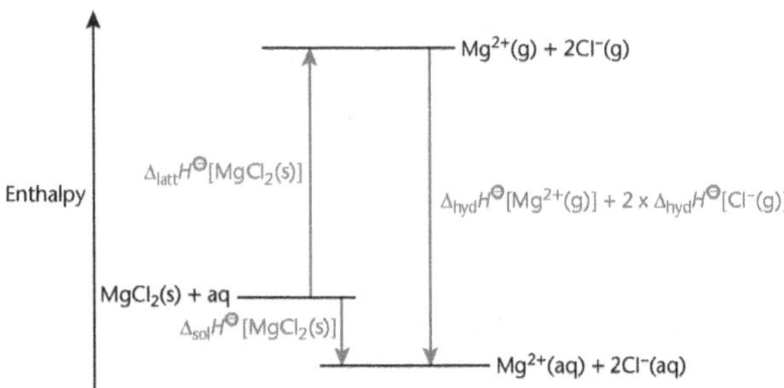

Using Hess's law,

$$\Delta_{sol}H^{\ominus}[MgCl_2(s)] = \Delta_{latt}H^{\ominus}[MgCl_2(s)] + \Delta_{hyd}H^{\ominus}[Mg^{2+}(g)] + (2 \times \Delta_{hyd}H^{\ominus}[Cl^-(g)])$$

$\Delta_{latt}H^{\ominus}[MgCl_2(s)] = 2526$ kJ mol^{-1}

$\Delta_{hyd}H^{\ominus}[Mg^{2+}(g)] = -1891$ kJ mol^{-1}

$\Delta_{hyd}H^{\ominus}[Cl^-(g)] = -381$ kJ mol^{-1}

Therefore, $\Delta_{sol}H^{\ominus}[MgCl_2(s)] = 2526 + (-1891) + (2 \times -381) = -127$ kJ mol^{-1}

The dissolution of magnesium chloride in water is exothermic.

QUESTIONS

16. Which of the enthalpies of solution of KCl, RbCl, $MgCl_2$ and $SrCl_2$ are:
   a. negative (exothermic)?
   b. positive (endothermic)?
   (See Table 7).

KEY IDEAS

- Water molecules are polar and are attracted to cations and anions.
- The hydration enthalpy of an ion is greater for an ion with a higher charge-to-size ratio.
- The enthalpy of hydration, $\Delta_{hyd}H^{\ominus}$, is the enthalpy change when one mole of gaseous ions is completely surrounded by water molecules, i.e. infinite dilution.
- If $\Delta_{hyd}H^{\ominus}$ is greater than $\Delta_{latt}H^{\ominus}$, energy will be released when ions are separated to form a solution.

1.4 ORDER, DISORDER AND ENTROPY

Some systems change spontaneously, and some change if they are triggered in some way. Some never appear to change. What is the explanation? What determines whether or not a change (physical or chemical) takes place?

Enthalpy changes are important – the more exothermic a change is, the more likely it is to happen. However, some endothermic changes also happen spontaneously. You have just seen, for example, that the dissolution of an ionic solid may be exothermic or endothermic. So there must be another factor to consider.

That factor is entropy.

Entropy

Order and disorder are important concepts in chemistry. In all natural physical and chemical changes, the system that is changing and its surroundings spontaneously go from an ordered state to a less ordered state. This happens regardless of whether the change is exothermic or endothermic. The degree of disorder in a system is called its **entropy**. As the disorder increases, so does the entropy value.

Some examples of changes that increase disorder are as follows.

When ice melts to form water, the process is endothermic:

$H_2O(s) \rightarrow H_2O(l) \qquad \Delta H^{\ominus}_{273\,K} = 6.01\ kJ\ mol^{-1}$

When water vaporises to form steam, the process is endothermic:

$H_2O(l) \rightarrow H_2O(g) \qquad \Delta H^{\ominus}_{373\,K} = 40.7\ kJ\ mol^{-1}$

Both changes happen spontaneously.

The particles of a substance are more ordered in solids, especially crystals, than they are in liquids. Similarly, particles of a substance are more ordered in liquids than they are in gases.

If a crystal melts, there is a dramatic change from an ordered state in the crystal to a disordered state in the liquid. If the liquid then changes to a gas, there is an even larger increase in disorder (Figure 15). So although both phase changes are endothermic, they happen spontaneously because each is accompanied by an increase in entropy.

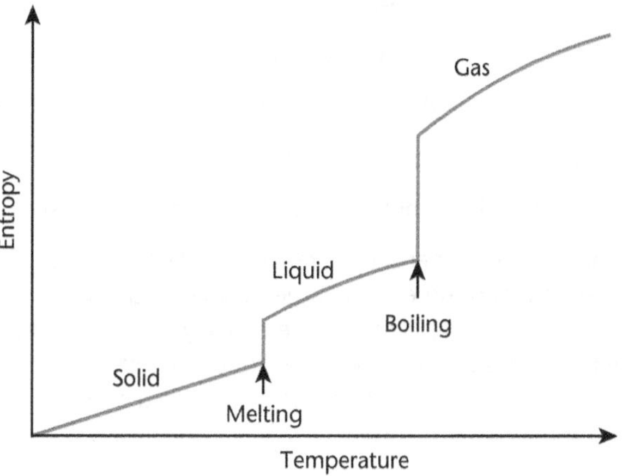

Figure 15 How the entropy of a substance varies with temperature and changes of state

Dissolution may be endothermic or exothermic. When a crystalline solid dissolves in water, it goes from a highly ordered state to a much more disordered state (Figure 16). The particles (ions or molecules) are released from their fixed positions in the lattice and move freely in solution. Whether the process is endothermic or exothermic, entropy always increases when a crystalline solid dissolves in water:

$NaOH(s) + aq \rightarrow Na^+(aq) + OH^-(aq)$
$\Delta_{sol}H^{\ominus} = -44.5\ kJ\ mol^{-1}$

$NH_4NO_3(s) + aq \rightarrow NH_4^+(aq) + NO_3^-(aq)$
$\Delta_{sol}H^{\ominus} = 25.7\ kJ\ mol^{-1}$

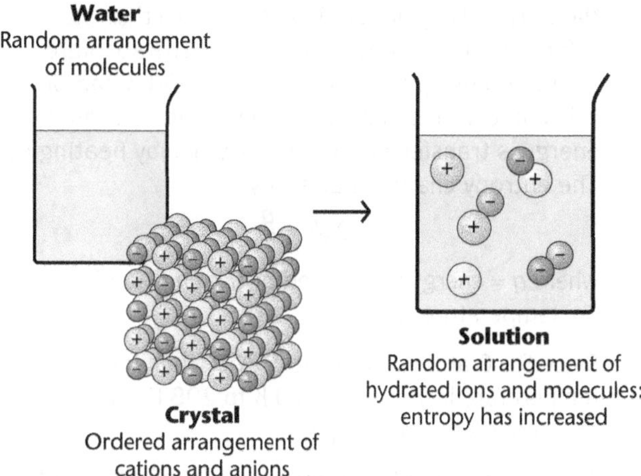

Figure 16 Modelling the dissolution of a crystalline solid in water

Any reaction that produces a gas from non-gaseous reactants, whether it is an endothermic or an exothermic change, leads to an increase in entropy:

$CaCO_3(s) \rightarrow CaO(s) + CO_2(g) \qquad \Delta H^{\ominus} = 179\ kJ\ mol^{-1}$

Figure 17 Dry solid nitrogen triiodide explodes when touched, even by a feather. It decomposes to nitrogen and iodine vapour: $2NI_3(s) \rightarrow N_2(g) + 3I_2(g)$, $\Delta H^{\ominus} = -290\ kJ\ mol^{-1}$. The exothermic reaction is accompanied by a huge increase in entropy.

Absolute entropy values

Entropy is a measure of the order or disorder in a system. It always decreases as the temperature of the system decreases.

It is not possible to calculate absolute enthalpy values, but only relative changes in enthalpy values from one system to another, $\Delta H^{\ominus}$. However, it is possible to calculate **absolute standard entropy** values $S^{\ominus}$ and use these to calculate standard entropy changes $\Delta S^{\ominus}$.

At absolute zero (0 K), particles in a crystalline lattice no longer jiggle about their positions in the lattice. They are static and a 'perfect' crystal is formed. Its entropy value is zero. The absolute standard entropy of a substance at 298 K can be calculated by measuring the temperature change as energy is transferred to the substance by heating it. The entropy change is given by

$$\Delta S^{\ominus} = \frac{q}{T}$$

where q = energy transferred by heating/J and T = temperature/K.

Since $S = 0$ at 0 K, the value of $\Delta S^{\ominus}$ when the temperature increases from 0 K to 298 K is the absolute standard entropy.

The units for standard entropy values are J K^{-1} mol^{-1}. Note that J is used, and not kJ as in enthalpy changes – this is because entropy values are quite small compared with values for enthalpy changes.

Calculating entropy changes $\Delta S^{\ominus}$

The entropy change during a chemical reaction is the difference between the total entropy values of the products and reactants. It can be calculated from standard entropy values such as the ones in Table 8.

	Substance	$S^{\ominus}$/J K^{-1} mol^{-1}
Gases	H_2(g)	131
	O_2(g)	205
	N_2(g)	192
	Cl_2(g)	223
	H_2O(g)	189
	HCl(g)	187
	NO_2(g)	240
Liquids	H_2O(l)	70
	HNO_3(l)	156
	C_2H_5OH(l)	161
Solids	$C(s)_{diamond}$	2.4
	$C(s)_{graphite}$	5.7
	$SiO_2(s)_{quartz}$	42
	NaCl(s)	72

Table 8 *Standard entropy values*

For example, consider the reaction between hydrogen and chlorine:

$H_2(g) + Cl_2(g) \rightarrow 2HCl(g)$

$\Delta S^{\ominus} = \Sigma S^{\ominus}_{products} - \Sigma S^{\ominus}_{reactants}$

(Note: Σ means 'sum of'.)

$\Sigma S^{\ominus}_{products} = 2 \times 187 = 374$ J K^{-1} mol^{-1}

$\Sigma S^{\ominus}_{reactants} = 131 + 223 = 354$ J K^{-1} mol^{-1}

$\Delta S^{\ominus} = 20$ J K^{-1} mol^{-1}

In the reaction between hydrogen and chlorine, all the molecules are in the gas phase and individually have quite high entropy values, but there is only a small increase in entropy ($\Delta S^{\ominus}$ is positive) when they react.

Now consider another example, the decomposition of nitric acid:

$4HNO_3(l) \rightarrow 4NO_2(g) + O_2(g) + 2H_2O(l)$

$\Delta S^{\ominus} = \Sigma S^{\ominus}_{products} - \Sigma S^{\ominus}_{reactants}$

$\Sigma S^{\ominus}_{products} = (4 \times 240) + 205 + (2 \times 70) = 1305$ J K^{-1}

$\Sigma S^{\ominus}_{reactants} = 4 \times 156 = 624$ J K^{-1}

$\Delta S^{\ominus} = 1305 - 624 = 681$ J K^{-1}

This is for 4 mol of HNO_3(l), and so for 1 mol

$\Delta S^{\ominus} = 170$ J K^{-1} mol^{-1} (to three significant figures)

There is a considerable increase in disorder in this reaction, and therefore a large positive entropy change (170 J K^{-1} mol^{-1}). The entropy value of liquid nitric acid is lower than the entropy value of the products, which include gases with molecules in a state of greater disorder.

System and surroundings

The entropy value of water vapour is 189 J K^{-1} mol^{-1} and the entropy value of liquid water is 70 J K^{-1} mol^{-1} (Table 8). If entropy must always increase, how can water vapour form liquid water (Figure 18)?

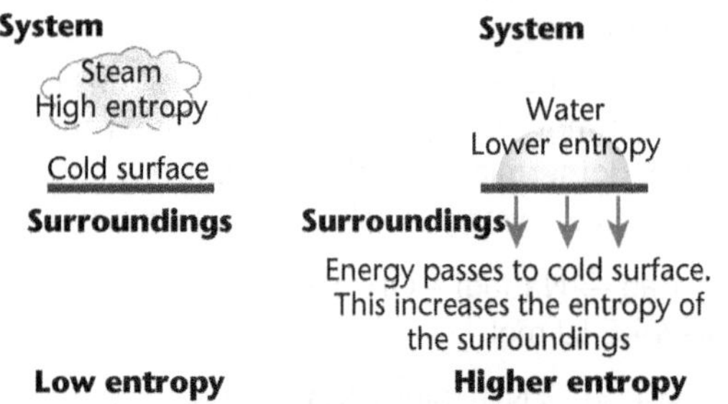

Figure 18 *Steam condensing on a cold surface*

$H_2O(g) \rightarrow H_2O(l)$

$\Delta S^\ominus_{system} = S^\ominus[H_2O(l)] - S^\ominus[H_2O(g)] = 70 - 189$

$= -119\ J\ K^{-1}\ mol^{-1}$

So there is a decrease in the entropy value of the system. However, we need to consider the system and its surroundings. When steam condenses, energy is transferred to the surroundings – the surface on which it has condensed, which in turn transfers it to the atmosphere and so on.

Condensation is an exothermic process. Energy is transferred to the surroundings. From this enthalpy change we can calculate the entropy increase in the surroundings. The value of this is 148 J K^{-1} mol^{-1}.

Using the equation

$$\Delta S^\ominus_{total} = \Delta S^\ominus_{system} + \Delta S^\ominus_{surroundings}$$

the total entropy change is

$$\Delta S^\ominus_{total} = -119 + 148 = 29\ J\ K^{-1}\ mol^{-1}$$

So the overall entropy increases.

An enthalpy change affects the entropy of the surroundings. Energy released in an exothermic reaction is absorbed by the surroundings and increases the entropy of the surroundings. Energy absorbed from the surroundings in an endothermic reaction decreases the entropy of the surroundings.

KEY IDEAS

- Entropy is a measure of the amount of disorder in a system.
- At 0 K, in a perfectly ordered crystal, the entropy value is zero.
- Entropy increases with increase in temperature.
- Entropy increases from solid to liquid to gas.
- If considered with the surroundings, entropy will always increase.

1.5 FEASIBILITY OF REACTIONS

Gibbs free energy

We often use the term **feasibility** to mean whether or not a physical or chemical change could take place spontaneously.

The feasibility depends on the combination of enthalpy and entropy changes. This is given by the equation

$$\Delta G = \Delta H - T\Delta S$$

where:

- ΔG = Gibbs free-energy change/kJ mol^{-1}
- ΔH = enthalpy change/kJ mol^{-1}
- ΔS = entropy change/kJ K^{-1} mol^{-1}
- T = temperature/K.

For standard conditions (298 K and 100 kPa), the equation is written in terms of the standard Gibbs free energy, enthalpy and entropy:

$$\Delta G^\ominus = \Delta H^\ominus - T\Delta S^\ominus$$

$\Delta H^\ominus$ and $\Delta S^\ominus$ depend slightly on temperature. However, because of the $T\Delta S$ term, $\Delta G^\ominus$ varies significantly with temperature. When doing calculations using $\Delta G^\ominus = \Delta H^\ominus - T\Delta S^\ominus$, we can assume as a reasonable approximation that $\Delta H^\ominus$ and $\Delta S^\ominus$ do not depend on temperature.

The magnitudes of entropy values are much smaller than those of enthalpy values. Enthalpy and free energy are quoted using kJ and entropy using J, so it is important in calculations to use compatible units (usually the entropy term is divided by 1000 to use kJ throughout).

Feasibility of change

For any system in which $\Delta G^\ominus$ is negative, change is feasible and spontaneous. Whether or not $\Delta G^\ominus$ is negative depends on the magnitudes of $\Delta H^\ominus$, $\Delta S^\ominus$ and T.

There are four scenarios:

- $\Delta H^\ominus$ is negative and $\Delta S^\ominus$ is positive: $\Delta G^\ominus$ is always negative regardless of the temperature. Change is feasible at all temperatures.
- $\Delta H^\ominus$ is negative and $\Delta S^\ominus$ is negative: $\Delta G^\ominus$ is negative only at temperatures below which $T\Delta S^\ominus$ is less than $\Delta H^\ominus$. Change is only feasible at these temperatures.
- $\Delta H^\ominus$ is positive and $\Delta S^\ominus$ is positive: $\Delta G^\ominus$ is negative only at temperatures above which $T\Delta S^\ominus$ is greater than $\Delta H^\ominus$. Change is only feasible at these temperatures.
- $\Delta H^\ominus$ is positive and $\Delta S^\ominus$ is negative: $\Delta G^\ominus$ is always positive regardless of the temperature. Change is not feasible at any temperature.

ASSIGNMENT 2: THE ENTROPY CHANGE WHEN WATER BOILS

(PS 1.1, 2.1, 3.2, MS 0.0, 2.1, 2.2)

A student is provided with:

- a 2.4 kW kettle, i.e. it transfers energy at a rate of 2.4 kilojoules per second (2.4 kJ s^{-1})
- a 1 dm^3 measuring cylinder
- water (note: 1 dm^3 of water is sufficient to cover the kettle's heating element completely)
- a balance upon which to weigh the kettle and water.

Procedure

1. Measure 1 dm^3 of water into the kettle, switch on and bring to the boil. Switch off and weigh the kettle and water.
2. Switch the kettle back on and boil the water for 100 seconds. The kettle has an automatic cutout that operates when the water boils, so the switch must be held down to keep the water boiling.
3. After 100 seconds, release the switch so that the kettle is turned off and boiling stops. Reweigh the kettle and water.

Results

Mass of kettle + water before boiling for 100 s = 2230 g.

Mass of kettle + water after boiling for 100 s = 2132 g.

Questions

A1. What mass of water, in grams, was poured into the kettle?

A2. What mass of water was lost owing to evaporation when the water was boiling for 100 seconds?

A3. How many moles of water were lost owing to evaporation when the water was boiling for 100 seconds?

A4. How much energy, in kJ, was transferred to the water during boiling?

A5. Calculate the enthalpy of vaporisation of water in kJ mol^{-1}.

A6. What is the boiling point of water in kelvin (K)?

A7. Using $\Delta S = \frac{\Delta H}{T}$, calculate the entropy of vaporisation of water in J mol^{-1} K^{-1}.

A8. How might the design of the experiment be improved?

$\Delta H^{\ominus}$ is negative and $\Delta S^{\ominus}$ is negative

Consider the formation of gaseous water from hydrogen and oxygen:

$$H_2(g) + \tfrac{1}{2}O_2(g) \rightarrow H_2O(g)$$

For this reaction,

$\Delta H^{\ominus} = -242$ kJ mol^{-1}

$\Delta S^{\ominus} = -147$ J K^{-1} mol^{-1} = -0.147 kJ K^{-1} mol^{-1}

$T = 298$ K

$\Delta G^{\ominus} = \Delta H^{\ominus} - T\Delta S^{\ominus}$

$= -242 - 298(-0.147) = -242 + 43.8$

$= -198$ kJ mol^{-1} (answer to three significant figures)

There is a decrease in entropy in changing from 1½ mol of gas molecules to 1 mol. However, $T\Delta S^{\ominus}$ (-43.8 kJ mol^{-1}) is less than the negative enthalpy term $\Delta H^{\ominus}$ (-242 kJ mol^{-1}), so overall $\Delta G^{\ominus}$ is negative. Even though the entropy decreases, the reaction is still feasible owing to the large negative enthalpy change.

$\Delta H^{\ominus}$ is positive and $\Delta S^{\ominus}$ is positive

When ammonium chloride dissolves in water there is an endothermic change. Entropy increases:

$NH_4Cl(s) + aq \rightarrow NH_4^+(aq) + Cl^-(aq)$

$\Delta H^{\ominus} = 14.4$ kJ mol^{-1}

$\Delta S^{\ominus} = 75.3$ J K^{-1} mol^{-1} = 0.0753 kJ K^{-1} mol^{-1}

$T = 298$ K

Figure 19 *The Hindenburg airship exploded in 1937 as a result of a spontaneous reaction between hydrogen and oxygen gases*

$\Delta G^\ominus = \Delta H^\ominus - T\Delta S^\ominus$

$= 14.4 - 298(0.0753) = 14.4 - 22.4$
$= -8.04$ kJ mol^{-1} (answer to three significant figures)

The reaction is endothermic, but the increase in entropy due to the breakdown of the ionic lattice and the formation of freely moving hydrated ions in solution makes $T\Delta S^\ominus$ sufficiently positive (22.4 kJ mol^{-1}) to overcome the positive enthalpy change (14.4 kJ mol^{-1}). So ammonium chloride dissolves spontaneously.

Now consider the chemical reaction between an acid and a solution of a hydrogen carbonate:

$$H^+(aq) + HCO_3^-(aq) \rightarrow H_2O(l) + CO_2(g)$$

The reaction is endothermic:

$\Delta H^\ominus = 13$ kJ mol^{-1}

$\Delta S^\ominus = 192$ J K^{-1} mol^{-1} $= 0.192$ kJ K^{-1} mol^{-1}

$T = 298$ K

$\Delta G^\ominus = \Delta H^\ominus - T\Delta S^\ominus$

$= 13 - 298(0.192) = 13 - 57.2 = -44.2$ kJ mol^{-1} (answer to three significant figures)

Although the reaction is endothermic, the increase in entropy (mainly due to the formation of a gaseous product, CO_2) makes $T\Delta S^\ominus$ sufficiently positive (57.2 kJ mol^{-1}) to overcome the positive enthalpy change (13 kJ mol^{-1}). So although the reaction is endothermic it happens spontaneously.

Temperature and change

A similar approach may be used to determine the temperature at which a change becomes feasible.

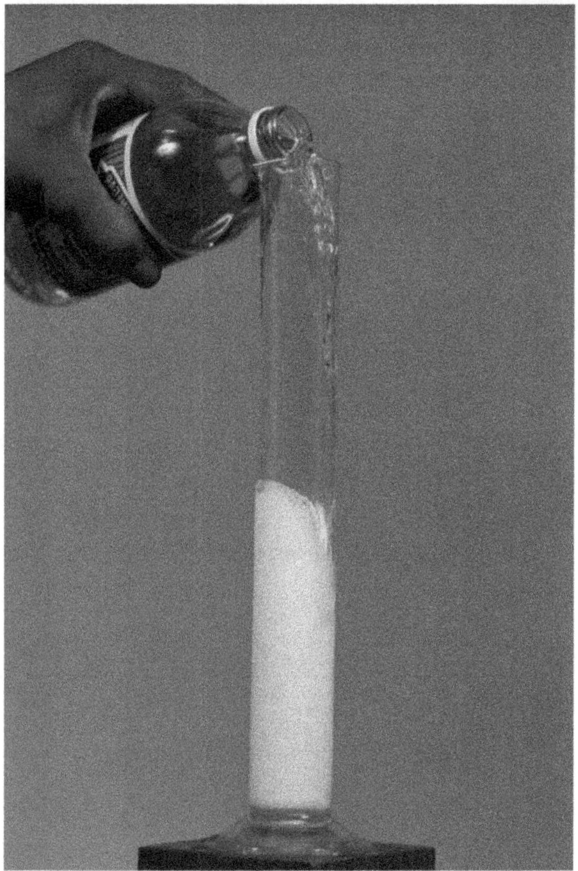

Figure 20 *A solution of sodium hydrogen carbonate reacts spontaneously with acids (in this case, ethanoic acid in household vinegar) to produce carbon dioxide. The reaction is endothermic.*

Consider the thermal decomposition of calcite (a crystalline form of calcium carbonate). The decomposition is endothermic:

$CaCO_3(s) \rightarrow CO_2(g) + CaO(s) \qquad \Delta H^\ominus = 179$ kJ mol^{-1}

The $S^\ominus$ values (J K^{-1} mol^{-1}) for the reactants and products are $CaCO_3$(s), 93; CaO(s), 40; and CO_2(g), 214.

Using $\Delta S^\ominus = \Sigma S^\ominus_{products} - \Sigma S^\ominus_{reactants}$,

$\Delta S^\ominus = (40 + 214) - 93$
$= 161$ J K^{-1} mol^{-1} $= 0.161$ kJ K^{-1} mol^{-1}

So this is another example of '$\Delta H^\ominus$ is positive and $\Delta S^\ominus$ is positive'.

At 298 K, we substitute the values for $\Delta H^\ominus$ and $\Delta S^\ominus$ into the equation

$\Delta G^\ominus = \Delta H^\ominus - T\Delta S^\ominus$

$= 179 - 298(0.161) = 131$ kJ mol^{-1}

Therefore, the thermal decomposition of calcium carbonate is not feasible at 298 K.

Yet we know that if calcite (calcium carbonate) is heated strongly it decomposes. So at what temperature does the thermal decomposition become feasible?

For the reaction to happen, $\Delta G^\ominus$ must be less than 0.

$$\Delta G^\ominus = \Delta H^\ominus - T\Delta S^\ominus$$

So if $\Delta G^\ominus = 0$, then

$$\Delta H^\ominus = T\Delta S^\ominus$$

and

$T = \Delta H^\ominus / \Delta S^\ominus$

$= 179/0.161 = 1110$ K (answer to three significant figures)

This means that the calcite must be heated above 1110 K. Remember, however, that this is the temperature at which the reaction becomes feasible. It gives no indication of the rate.

Determining ΔS and ΔH from a graph of ΔG versus T

The equation $\Delta G^\ominus = \Delta H^\ominus - T\Delta S^\ominus$ has the form $y = mx + c$, which means it is a straight-line graph with an intercept on the y-axis.

Here is a worked example.

$$2C(s) + O_2(g) \rightarrow 2CO(g)$$

Using the data in Table 9, $\Delta G^\ominus$ can be plotted against T. A straight-line graph is obtained (Figure 21), and from this the gradient of the line may be calculated to obtain the value of $\Delta S^\ominus$ and the intercept on the $\Delta G^\ominus$ axis found to obtain the value of $\Delta H^\ominus$.

T/K	400	600	800	1000	1200	1400	1600	1800
$\Delta G^\ominus$/kJ mol^{-1}	−300	−335	−370	−405	−440	−475	−505	−540

Table 9 *$\Delta G^\ominus$ and T for $2C(s) + O_2(g) \rightarrow 2CO(g)$*

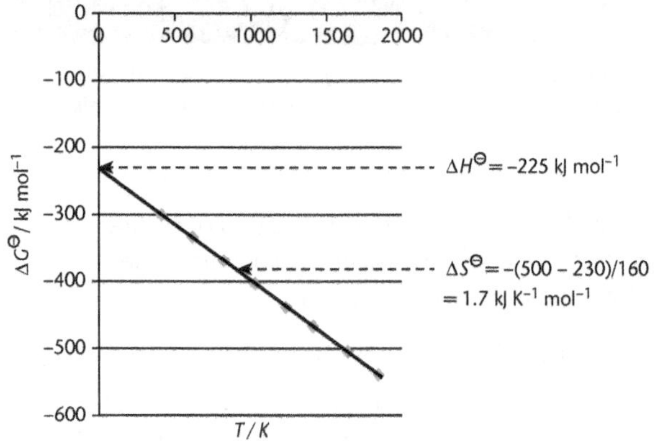

Figure 21 *Calculating $\Delta H^\ominus$ and $\Delta S^\ominus$ from a graph of $\Delta G^\ominus$ against T*

Kinetic barriers

There is a difference between feasibility and the rate at which a change takes place. Thermodynamics dictates feasibility, but kinetics and the energy barriers to effective collisions dictate how quickly change happens.

So even if a change has a negative $\Delta G^\ominus$ value, we still do not know how quickly that change will occur.

For example, diamond is thermodynamically less stable than graphite:

$C(s, diamond) + O_2(g) \rightarrow CO_2(g)$ $\Delta G^\ominus = -397$ kJ mol^{-1}

$C(s, graphite) + O_2(g) \rightarrow CO_2(g)$ $\Delta G^\ominus = -394$ kJ mol^{-1}

Using Hess's law, but with $\Delta G^\ominus$ values rather than $\Delta H^\ominus$ values:

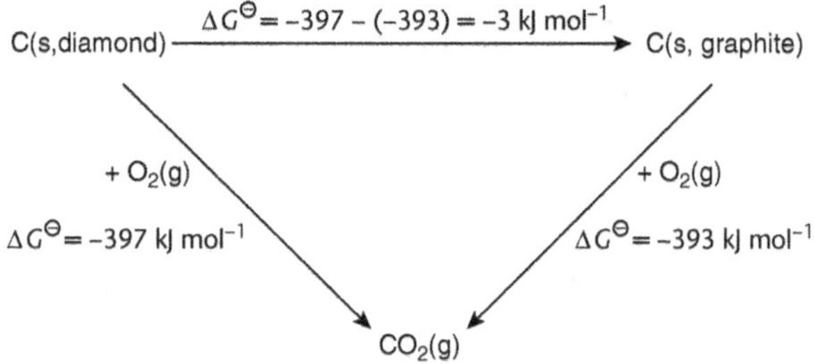

You can see that $\Delta G^\ominus$ for the change from diamond to graphite is negative (−3 kJ mol^{-1}) and therefore the change is feasible. So diamond should spontaneously revert to graphite, but in fact the reaction is infinitely slow, so it does not happen.

KEY IDEAS

- The feasibility of a process is determined by the standard Gibbs free energy, via $\Delta G^{\ominus} = \Delta H^{\ominus} - T\Delta S^{\ominus}$.
- If $\Delta G^{\ominus}$ is negative at a temperature T, the process will be spontaneous.
- A system is at equilibrium when $\Delta G^{\ominus}$ is zero.
- $\Delta H^{\ominus}$ and $\Delta S^{\ominus}$ can be determined using a graph of $\Delta G^{\ominus}$ versus T.
- Above or at 0 °C, $\Delta H^{\ominus} = +6.01$ kJ mol^{-1}, but $-\Delta S^{\ominus}$ is greater than or equal to 6.01 kJ mol^{-1}, so $\Delta G^{\ominus}$ is zero or negative; ice → water.
- Below or at 0 °C, $\Delta H^{\ominus} = -6.01$ kJ mol^{-1}, but $=T\Delta S^{\ominus}$ decreases by less than or equal to +6.01 kJ mol^{-1}, so $\Delta G^{\ominus}$ is zero or negative; water → ice.

ASSIGNMENT 3: LIMITING SPORTS INJURY DAMAGE

(PS 1.1, 1.2, 3.3, MS 0.0, 2.1)

Sports injuries such as muscle strains need to be cooled down to help prevent swelling. In most circumstances, a simple ice pack is enough to do the job, but storing ice in a 'first response box' – a large, portable first aid kit – would be impracticable. What sports coaches and physiotherapists need is a pack that can be stored at room temperature and will cool down when required.

Central Scientific have been asked to design a portable, easily used pack that cools 'on demand'. Dissolving a stable compound seemed the most promising method.

When ionic compounds are formed, a series of endothermic and exothermic processes takes place. These processes involved in making salts can be summarised in a Born–Haber cycle and can be used to calculate the relative stabilities of compounds.

$\Delta_{at}H^{\ominus}$[K(s)]	1st E_i[K(g)]	2nd E_i[K(g)]	$\Delta_{at}H^{\ominus}$[Cl_2(g)]	E_{ea}[Cl(g)]	$\Delta_{latt}H^{\ominus}$[KCl_2(s)]	$\Delta_{latt}H^{\ominus}$[KCl_2(s)]*
89	419	3051	122	−348	−2350	−711

* estimated value based on ionic lattice model

Table A1 *Enthalpy changes/kJ mol^{-1}*

Whether a compound dissolves or not depends largely upon the difference between the lattice enthalpy and the sum of the hydration enthalpies.

In an endothermic reaction, heat is drawn from the surroundings. If a cooling pack is applied to an injury, it will draw heat from that part of the body, so cooling it down. One compound that would produce a cooling effect on mixing with water is ammonium nitrate. The researchers' data book gave the enthalpy of solution for ammonium nitrate as +26.5 kJ mol^{-1}. This more endothermic reaction would produce a greater cooling effect than ammonium chloride would.

The development team consulted with medical staff to find out what temperature the pack had to cool down to. They recommended that a temperature of 1.5 °C should be maintained for at least 15 minutes. Central Scientific planned to make a pack weighing approximately 200 g, and this needed to cool down from 18 °C to 1.5 °C. The enthalpy change is given by the equation

$$\Delta H^{\ominus} = mc\Delta T$$

where m is the mass of the pack, c is the specific heat capacity and ΔT is the temperature change.

Questions

A1. Using data from the table, construct a Born–Haber cycle for:

a. KCl(s) to calculate the standard molar enthalpy of formation; define all the terms you use, and explain why each one is either exothermic or endothermic

b. KCl_2(s) to show why this compound will not be found naturally.

A2. Dissolving ammonium chloride in water produces a cooling effect. Draw a suitable enthalpy cycle and use the data below to calculate the enthalpy of solution, $\Delta_{sol}H^{\ominus}[NH_4Cl(s)]$:

$\Delta_{latt}H^{\ominus}[NH_4Cl(s)] = 705\ kJ\ mol^{-1}$

$\Delta_{hyd}H^{\ominus}[NH_4^+(g)] = -307\ kJ\ mol^{-1}$

$\Delta_{hyd}H^{\ominus}[Cl^-(g)] = -381\ kJ\ mol^{-1}$.

A3. Exothermic processes are favoured energetically, yet the above process is endothermic. Explain the idea of entropy and use it to explain why an endothermic process, such as dissolving ammonium chloride, can happen spontaneously.

A4. For a 200 g cooling pack, assuming a specific heat capacity of $4.2\ J\ g^{-1}\ K^{-1}$, calculate the enthalpy change that takes place.

A5. Calculate the number of moles of ammonium nitrate that will produce this amount of cooling.

PRACTICE QUESTIONS

1. Consider the incomplete Born–Haber cycle (Figure Q1) and the data in Table Q1.

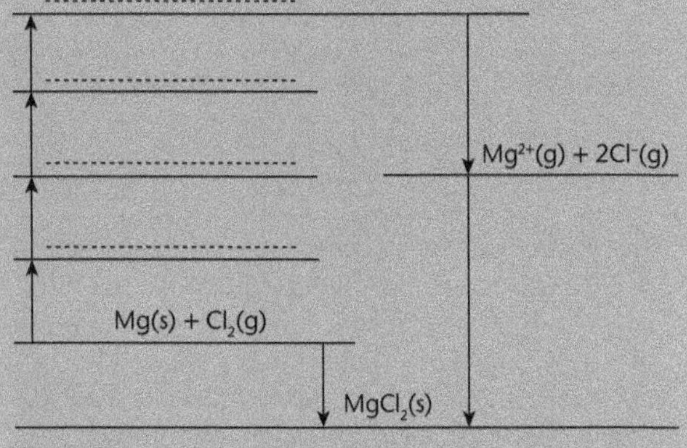

Figure Q1

Name of standard enthalpy change	Substance to which enthalpy change refers	Value of enthalpy change (kJ mol⁻¹)
Enthalpy of atomisation	chlorine	+121
Enthalpy of atomisation	magnesium	+150
Enthalpy of formation	magnesium chloride	–642
First Ionisation enthalpy	magnesium	+736
Electron affinity	chlorine	–364
Enthalpy of lattice formation	magnesium chloride	–2493

Table Q1

a. Complete the Born–Haber cycle above by writing the appropriate chemical formulae, with state symbols, on the dotted lines.

b. Use the cycle and the values given in the table to calculate the second ionisation enthalpy of magnesium.

c. The standard enthalpies of hydration of the Mg^{2+} and the Cl^- ions are $-1\,920$ kJ mol^{-1} and -364 kJ mol^{-1}, respectively. Use this information and data from the table in part a to calculate the enthalpy of solution of magnesium chloride.

d. The standard enthalpy of solution of ammonium chloride, $NH_4^+Cl^-$, is +15 kJ mol^{-1}.

i. Explain why ammonium chloride dissolves spontaneously in water even though this process is endothermic.

ii. A 2.0 g sample of ammonium chloride is dissolved in 50 g of water. Both substances are initially at 20 °C. Calculate the temperature change and the final temperature of the solution. Assume that the specific heat capacity of the solution is 4.2 J K^{-1} g^{-1}.

AQA June 2007 Unit 5 Question 1

2. Data for the following reaction, which represents the reduction of aluminium oxide by carbon, are shown in Table Q2.

$$Al_2O_3(s) + 3C(s) \rightarrow 2Al(s) + 3CO(g)$$

Substance	ΔH_f(kJ mol^{-1})	S(J K^{-1} mol^{-1})
Al_2O_3(s)	−1669	51
C(s)	0	6
Al(s)	0	28
CO(s)	−111	198

Table Q2

a. Calculate the values of $\Delta H^\ominus$, $\Delta S^\ominus$ and $\Delta G^\ominus$ for the above reaction at 298 K and suggest why this reaction is not feasible at 298 K.

b. Calculate the temperature above which this reaction is feasible. (If you have been unable to calculate values for $\Delta H^\ominus$ and $\Delta S^\ominus$ in part a you may assume that they are +906 kJ mol^{-1} and +394 J K^{-1} mol^{-1} respectively. These are not the correct values.)

c. The reaction between aluminium oxide and carbon to form aluminium and carbon monoxide does not occur to a significant extent until the temperature reaches a value about 1000 K above that of the answer to part b. Give one reason for this.

d. State the method used to reduce aluminium oxide on an industrial scale. Give the essential conditions for this industrial process.

AQA June 2007 Unit 5 Question 2

3. The sketch graph (Figure Q2) shows how the entropy of a sample of water varies with temperature.

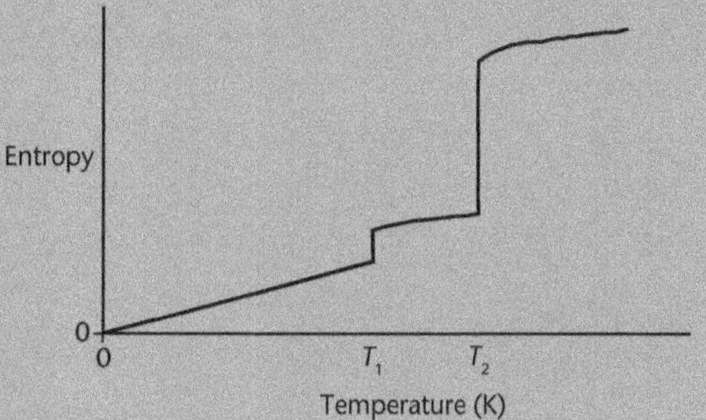

Figure Q2

a. Suggest why the entropy of water is zero at 0 K.

b. What change of state occurs at temperature T_1?

c. Explain why the entropy change, ΔS, at temperature T_2 is much larger than that at temperature T_1.

d. It requires 3.49 kJ of heat energy to convert 1.53 g of liquid water into steam at 373 K and 100 kPa.

i. Use these data to calculate the enthalpy change, ΔH, when 1.00 mol of liquid water forms 1.00 mol of steam at 373 K and 100 kPa.

ii. Write an expression showing the relationship between free-energy change, ΔG, enthalpy change, ΔH, and entropy change, ΔS.

iii. For the conversion of liquid water into steam at 373 K and 100 kPa, ΔG = 0 kJ mol^{-1}.

Calculate the value of ΔS for the conversion of one mole of water into steam under these conditions. State the units.

(If you have been unable to complete part d i you should assume that $\Delta H = 45.0$ kJ mol^{-1}. This is not the correct answer.)

AQA June 2006 Unit 5 Question 2

4. A Born–Haber cycle for the formation of calcium sulfide is shown in Figure Q3. The cycle includes enthalpy changes for all steps except Step F. (The cycle is not drawn to scale.)

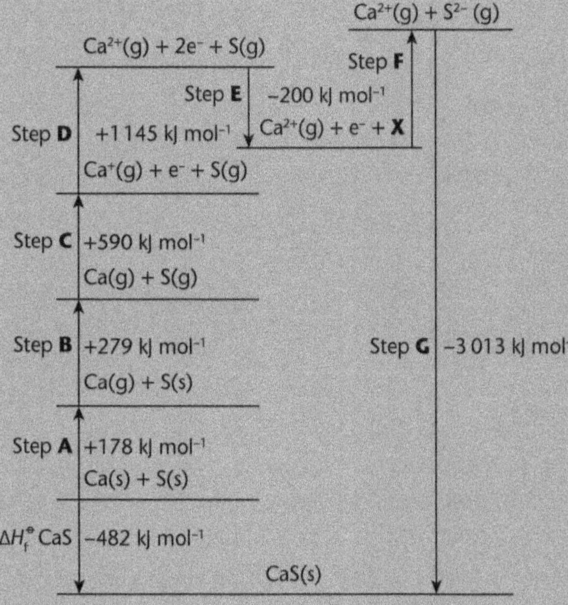

Figure Q3

a. Give the full electronic arrangement of the ion S^{2-}.

b. Identify the species X formed in Step E.

c. Suggest why Step F is an endothermic process.

d. Name the enthalpy change for each of the following steps.

   i. Step B

   ii. Step D

   iii. Step F

e. Explain why the enthalpy change for Step D is larger than that for Step C.

f. Use the data shown in the cycle to calculate a value for the enthalpy change for Step F.

AQA January 2005 Unit 5 Question 2

5. Table Q3 contains some entropy data relevant to the reaction used to synthesise methanol from carbon dioxide and hydrogen. The reaction is carried out at a temperature of 250 °C.

Substance	$CO_2(g)$	$H_2(g)$	$CH_3OH(g)$	$H_2O(g)$
Entropy ($S^\ominus$)/J K^{-1} mol^{-1}	214	131	238	189

Table Q3

$$CO_2(g) + 3H_2(g) \rightleftharpoons CH_3OH(g) + H_2O(g)$$
$$\Delta H = -49 \text{ kJ mol}^{-1}$$

a. Use this enthalpy change and data from Table Q3 to calculate a value for the free-energy change of the reaction at 250 °C. Give units with your answer.

b. Calculate a value for the temperature when the reaction becomes feasible.

c. Gaseous methanol from this reaction is liquefied by cooling before storage.

Draw a diagram showing the interaction between two molecules of methanol. Explain why methanol is easy to liquefy.

Specimen Paper 1 2015 Question 5

2 RATE EQUATIONS

PRIOR KNOWLEDGE

You will have already learned about rates of reactions, the factors that can affect the rate of a reaction and the energy changes that take place during a chemical reaction. You should know the shape of the Maxwell–Boltzmann distribution curve and be able to use this to explain the effects that temperature and catalysts have on the rate of the reaction (*see Chapter 8 of Year 1 Student Book*).

LEARNING OBJECTIVES

In this chapter you will learn how to recognise the order of a reaction, and construct and use equations to calculate the rate of a reaction. You will also understand how to use an equation linking the rate constant and temperature and how to use graphs and data to determine factors relating to rates.

(Specification 3.1.9)

Are you trying to reduce carbon emissions by taking the bus, using less electricity or recycling? The chemical industry is also trying to reduce its carbon emissions.

In the UK the chemical industry accounts for approximately £55 billion of sales annually through products such as medicines, paint, soap, fertilisers, plastics, dyes and artificial fibres.

In 2008 the government signed a legally binding agreement to reduce carbon emissions by 34% by 2020 and 80% by 2050 from the levels in 1990. This means that everyone, including you and the chemical industry, needs to do their part to cut down on energy usage.

Just like you, the chemical industry has been looking at renewable energy sources and recycling to reduce its emissions. However, the chemical industry also uses a large amount of fossil fuels to heat reactions to increase the rate of the reactions and make them fast enough to be profitable. Now industry is looking for ways to keep the same rate of reaction, but at lower temperatures so that it can save energy and meet carbon emission targets.

It is important to choose reaction conditions that will make the maximum amount of product in the smallest amount of time whilst keeping costs low. Knowing the rate of a reaction and being able to predict the change in the rate when the conditions are changed is important to be able to optimise the reaction conditions.

2.1 THE BASICS ABOUT RATES

The **rate** of a reaction is defined as the change in molar concentration of a substance (reactant or product) in a set time, usually one second. If a reaction takes place in solution or is a homogeneous gas reaction, the units of the rate of the reaction are always mol dm^{-3} s^{-1} (concentration per unit time).

$$\text{rate} = \frac{\text{change in concentration}}{\text{change in time}}$$

The concentration of a substance is represented by writing the formula of the substance inside square brackets; for example, the concentration of hydrogen ions would be written $[H^+]$. By measuring concentrations of substances at time intervals, at a fixed temperature, we can measure the rate of change of concentration of those substances. Figures 1 and 2 show how the change of concentration of a reactant or product in a reaction changes with time at that temperature. In Figure 1, the line is a curve because the reactant is being used up and its concentration decreases more slowly in each successive time interval. This is because, as the reaction proceeds, fewer reactant particles per unit volume are available for collisions, so the time taken for a given number of particles to react increases. The rate of reaction decreases and eventually it stops.

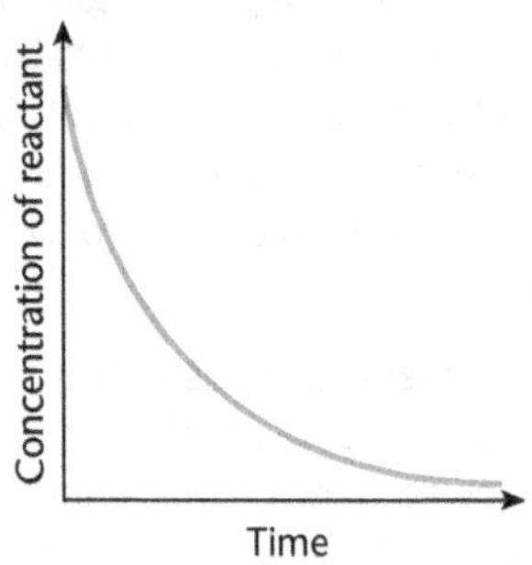

Figure 1 *The decrease in concentration of a reactant during a reaction*

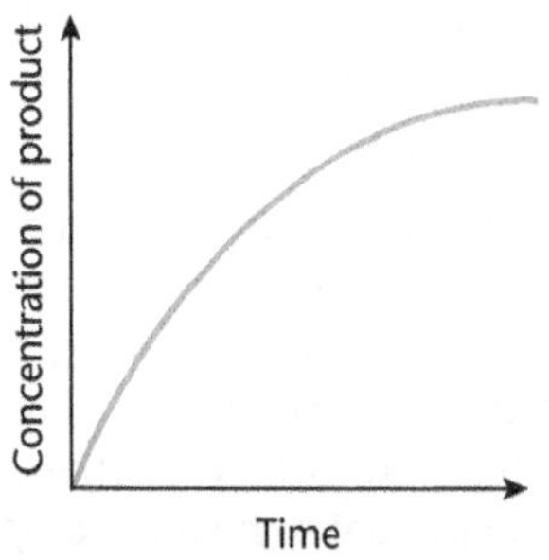

Figure 2 *The increase in concentration of a product during a reaction*

QUESTIONS

1. a. At what stage in a reaction is the reactant used up fastest?
   b. At what stage in a reaction is the formation of the product fastest?

2.2 ORDERS OF REACTIONS

At a fixed temperature, increasing the concentration of the reactants usually increases the rate of reaction. In some but by no means all reactions, doubling the concentration of a reactant (let us use A for the reactant in this example) doubles the number of particles of A with energies equal to or greater than the activation energy, and the reaction rate doubles. When you halve the concentration, the number of particles of A with the activation energy will halve, and the rate will be halved. In other words, the rate of reaction is proportional to the concentration of A, given by the expression

$$\text{rate} \propto \text{concentration of A}$$

By including a rate constant, k, we can replace the proportional sign by an equals sign, to give the rate equation

$$\text{rate} = k \times \text{concentration of A}$$

Using the symbol [A] for the concentration of A gives

$$\text{rate} = k[A]$$

The **order of reaction** is the proportionality of the rate to the concentration of reactants, where rate = $k[A]^x$ and x is the order.

'Rate = $k[A]$' is an example of a **first-order reaction**, which is defined as a reaction whose rate is proportional to the concentration of a reactant, and the reaction is said to be first order with respect to reactant A. The 'first' in these phrases comes from the power of the concentration of the reactant in the rate equation. The power is not written out above, since $[A]^1$ is the same as [A].

A reaction that is second order with respect to a reactant (let us use B for the reactant in this example) is one where the rate of the reaction is proportional to the concentration of the reactant squared:

$$\text{rate} = k[B]^2$$

If the concentration of B was doubled then the rate of the reaction would quadruple (22 = 2 × 2 = 4).

If the concentration of B was tripled then the rate would be multiplied by nine (32 = 3 × 3 = 9).

A reaction that is zero order with respect to a reactant (let us use C for the reactant in this example) is one where the rate of the reaction does not change when the concentration of the reactant changes. The value of any variable to the power zero equals one:

$$\text{rate} = k[\text{C}]^0$$

There can be more than one reactant that affects the rate of the reaction, and the individual effects on the rate can be combined to form a single equation called the overall rate equation. The overall order of the reaction is given by adding together the orders of reaction with respect to each reactant. For example, in the example rate = $k[\text{A}]^1[\text{B}]^2$ then $1 + 2 = 3$ and therefore the overall order is third order.

A general **rate equation** for two reactants is given as

$$\text{rate} = k[\text{A}]^m[\text{B}]^n$$

$$\text{Overall order of reaction} = m + n$$

The relationship between the rate of a reaction and the concentrations of the reactants is represented in the rate equation.

- If the rate is zero order with respect to a reactant then that reactant will not appear in the rate equation.
- If the rate is first order with respect to a reactant then the concentration of the reactant will appear in the rate equation.
- If the rate is second order with respect to a reactant then the concentration of the reactant squared will appear in the rate equation.
- k is the rate constant which appears in the rate equation.

For example, a reaction that is first order with respect to [A], zero order with respect to [B] and second order with respect to [C] will have the rate equation

$$\text{rate} = k[\text{A}][\text{C}]^2$$

It is important to note that the order of reaction with respect to each reactant and the overall reaction order must be determined from experimental data and cannot be derived from just writing down the stoichiometric or balanced equation.

KEY IDEAS

- The rate equation shows the proportionality of the rate to the concentrations of all of the reactants and takes the general form rate = $k[\text{A}]^m[\text{B}]^n$.
- The order of a reaction with respect to a single reactant shows the proportionality of the rate of the reaction to the concentration of that reactant and can be zero, first or second order.
- The overall order of a reaction is the sum of the orders of reaction for each reactant.

QUESTIONS

2. State the order of reaction with respect to *both* [A] *and* [B] for each of the following rate equations:
   a. Rate = $k[\text{B}]^2$
   b. Rate = $k[\text{A}][\text{B}]$
   c. Rate = $k[\text{A}]^2[\text{B}]$
   d. Rate = k
3. Construct the rate equations for the following reactions:
   a. First order with respect to [X], second order with respect to [Y].
   b. Zero order with respect to [H^+], second order with respect to [H_2O].
   c. Second order with respect to [A], second order with respect to [B], first order with respect to [C].
4. State the overall order of reaction for the following reactions shown by their rate equations:
   a. Rate = $k[\text{B}]^2$
   b. Rate = k
   c. Rate = $k[\text{A}][\text{B}]$
   d. Rate = $k[\text{OH}^-]$
   e. Rate = $k[\text{X}]^2[\text{Y}]$

2.3 THE RATE CONSTANT

The rate constant k is not affected by changes in the concentration or pressure of reactants. However, the rate constant for a reaction does vary with temperature. If the temperature increases, both the rate of reaction and the rate constant will increase.

Calculating the units of the rate constant

The rate constant for a chemical reaction can be calculated using the rate equation. It always has units, but the units depend on the rate equation. The units of k can be calculated by replacing each of the terms in the rate equation by their units and then cancelling out duplicated units. Remember, the rate of a reaction in solution always has the units of mol dm^{-3} s^{-1}.

Worked example

What are the units of k in the rate equation rate = $k[A][C]^2$?

Step 1

Rearrange the rate equation to make k the subject:

$$k = \frac{\text{rate}}{[A][C]^2}$$

Step 2

Insert the units for rate and concentration:

$$k \text{ units} = \frac{(\text{mol dm}^{-3}\text{ s}^{-1})}{(\text{mol dm}^{-3})(\text{mol dm}^{-3})^2}$$

Step 3

Cancel units that appear above and below the line:

$$k \text{ units} = \frac{(\text{mol dm}^{-3}\text{ s}^{-1})}{(\text{mol dm}^{-3})(\text{mol dm}^{-3})^2} = \frac{(\text{s}^{-1})}{(\text{mol dm}^{-3})^2}$$

$$= \frac{(\text{s}^{-1})}{(\text{mol}^2\text{ dm}^{-6})} = \text{s}^{-1}\text{ mol}^{-2}\text{ dm}^6$$

Step 4

Rearrange units so that s^{-1} comes at the end:

$$k \text{ units} = \text{mol}^{-2}\text{ dm}^6\text{ s}^{-1}$$

The units of the rate constant will always be the same for reactions with the same overall order of reaction.

Overall order of reaction $= n + m$	Rate equation: rate $= k \times$ [reactants]$^{n+m}$	Units of rate constant
0	rate $= k \times$ concn.^{0}	mol dm^{-3} s^{-1}
1	rate $= k \times$ concn.^{1}	s^{-1}
2	rate $= k \times$ concn.^{2}	mol^{-1} dm^3 s^{-1}
3	rate $= k \times$ concn.^{3}	mol^{-2} dm^6 s^{-1}

Table 1 *Summary of units for rate constants*

QUESTIONS

5. A chemical reaction has the equation rate = $k[A][B]$. When the reaction was carried out at 37 °C with a concentration of 0.1 mol dm^{-3} of both reactants the rate of the reaction was 5×10^{-4} mol dm^{-3} s^{-1}.
   a. Calculate the value of the rate constant k.
   b. Deduce the units of the rate constant k.
   c. State the effect on the rate constant of increasing the concentration of the reactants.
   d. State the effect on the rate constant of increasing the temperature.
6. The decomposition of hydrogen peroxide is second order with respect to hydrogen peroxide. Under standard conditions and a concentration of 1.2 mol dm^{-3} the rate of the reaction was 4.8×10^{-2} mol dm^{-3}.
   a. Write the rate equation for the reaction.
   b. Deduce the units of the rate constant k.
   c. Calculate the value of the rate constant k.

KEY IDEAS

- The rate constant is not affected by changes to the pressure or concentration of a reactant.
- The rate constant is affected by changes to the temperature.
- The units of the rate constant depend on the overall order of reaction.

2.4 GRAPHICAL DETERMINATION OF ORDER OF REACTION

The order of a reaction with respect to a reactant can sometimes be determined from the shape of a graph plotted of the concentration of the reactant against time as shown in Figure 3. The concentration of the reactant decreases over time in all types of reactions. In first- and second-order reactions the rate of the reaction is affected by the concentration of the reactant so, as the reactant is used up, the reaction becomes slower and the gradient decreases. In zero-order reactions the concentration of the reactant does not affect the rate, so the reaction continues at a constant rate with the gradient remaining steady.

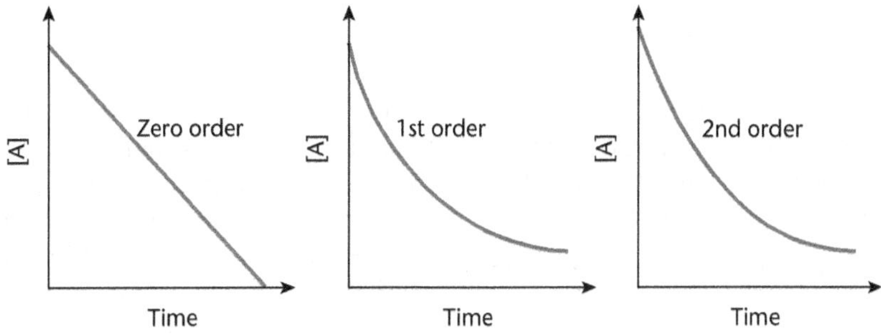

Figure 3 *Concentration of reactant plotted against time. The order of a reaction with respect to a product gives the same shaped curves, but inverted. In other words, concentration at the star of the reaction is zero.*

Zero order

For a reaction that is zero order with respect to a reactant, the rate constant k can be determined from the gradient of a graph of the concentration of that reactant against time.

Worked example

An example of a reaction that is zero order is the decomposition of ammonia to nitrogen on a hot tungsten wire:

$$2NH_3 \rightarrow N_2 + 3H_2$$

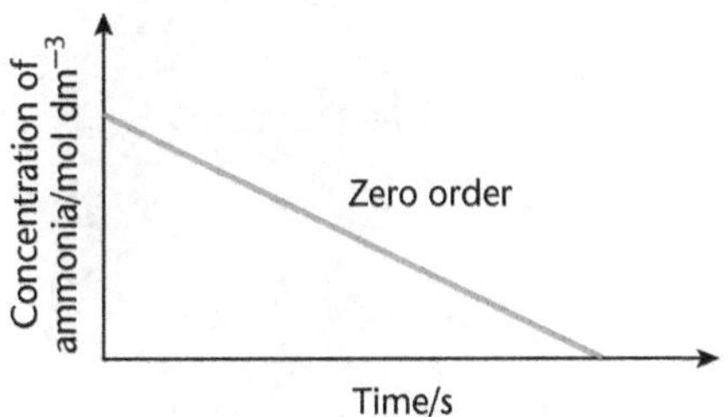

Consider that the straight line drawn on the graph has the general form $y = mx$. In this case y is the concentration of ammonia, $[NH_3]$, x is the time (t) and m is the gradient.

Substituting $[NH_3]$ and t in the equation shows that the equation for the line of best fit is

$$[NH_3] = mt$$

This can be rearranged to give

$$\frac{[NH_3]}{t} = m$$

You should recognise that $[NH_3]/t$ has the general form $[A]/t$ and represents the change in concentration of a reactant over time, which is the definition of a rate. The gradient, m, has a negative value as the concentration of the ammonia is decreasing. Since the gradient = – rate, the rate of reaction is –(–) and, therefore, it is positive.

As a zero-order reaction has the rate equation rate = k, the equation for the line of best fit becomes

$$\frac{[A]}{t} = \text{gradient} = -\text{rate} = -k$$

First and second order

Graphs of concentration against time can only be used to identify zero-order reactions. Similar plots for first- and second-order reactions do not have a straight line of best fit. Instead, curved graphs are obtained (Figure 4), which means that first- and second-order reactions cannot be distinguished from each other using a plot of concentration against time as the shapes are very similar.

To determine whether a reaction is first or second order, the rate must be determined at different concentrations of reactants and a graph of the rate must be plotted against concentration of one reactant. The shapes of the graphs are very distinctive (Figure 4).

The lines of best fit for a zero-order and a first-order reaction are both straight lines, but the gradient for a zero-order reaction is zero (horizontal line) whilst the gradient for a first-order reaction is positive. The line of best fit for a second-order reaction is a curve.

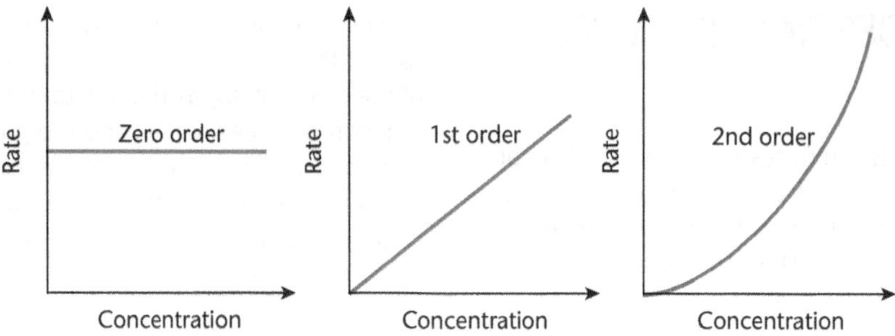

Figure 4 *Rate of reaction plotted against concentration of one reactant*

The graphs also allow rate constants to be determined. The gradient of the line of best fit for a first-order reaction is equal to k when the rate of reaction is plotted against concentration.

How do we plot a graph of concentration against rate? Two ways are:

- the continuous monitoring method
- the initial rate method.

Continuous monitoring method

If the concentration of a reactant remaining in a solution can be measured at set time intervals then a single reaction can monitored. We plot a graph of concentration against time and draw the line of best fit. We then choose a number of points on the line of best fit and draw tangents at each of them. The gradient of each tangent is used to determine the rate at that point. For each of our chosen points we now have the rate (tangent) and the concentration. The rate and the concentration of the reactant at each point are then drawn in another graph, which can be used to determine the order of reaction.

ASSIGNMENT 1: CONTINUOUS MONITORING TO DETERMINE RATE CONSTANT

(AT a, AT k, AT l, PS2.4, PS 3.1)

Esters such as methyl ethanoate hydrolyse in water to form an alcohol and a carboxylic acid:

$$CH_3COOCH_3 + H_2O \rightarrow CH_3COOH + CH_3OH$$

methyl ethanoate ethanoic acid methanol

The order of the reaction with respect to the ester is calculated by first finding its concentration at different stages in the reaction. One way to do this is to determine how much ester has been converted to the acid, and then to calculate the concentration of ester left in the mixture. *Small*, measured volumes of the reaction mixture are taken at different times and titrated against a standard alkali solution. This allows you to calculate how much acid has been produced and, therefore, the amount of ester that has been hydrolysed and the concentration of ester remaining in the reaction mixture at the different time points.

The results from a typical investigation of the hydrolysis of methyl ethanoate are shown in Table A1.

Figure A1 *The students are titrating the reaction mixture. The small sample that they are using is mixed with some ice to stop the reaction while they do the titration*

Time (min)	Ester concentration (mol dm^{-3})
0	0.200
5	0.134 = A
10	0.095
15	0.068 = B
20	0.046
25	0.034 = C

Table A1 *Results for the hydrolysis reaction of methyl ethanoate*

These results are plotted on the graph in Figure A2, which shows the typical declining curve for a first-order reaction. The rate at set time points is found by determining the slope of the curve at the tangent:

$$\text{rate} = \frac{\text{change in concentration}}{\text{time taken}} = \text{slope of curve}$$

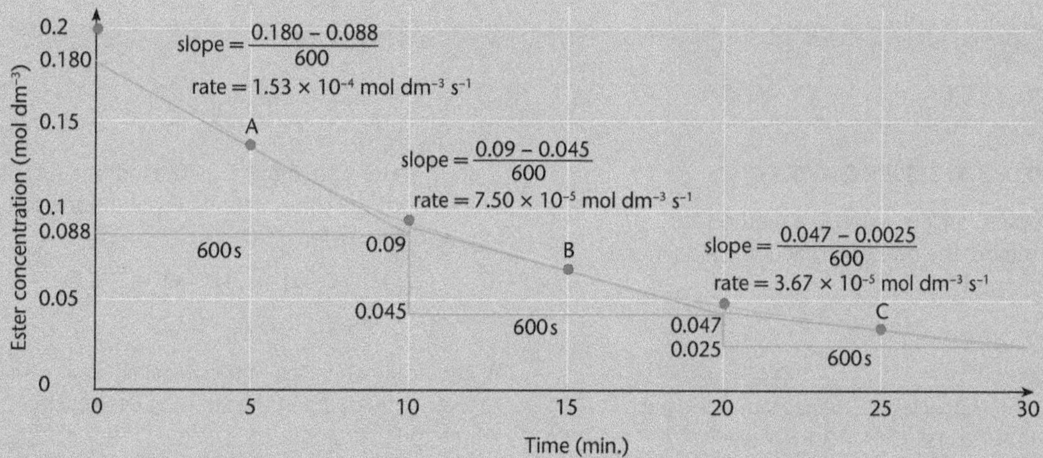

Figure A2 *Concentration of ester remaining in the mixture, plotted against time for the first-order reaction of the hydrolysis of methyl ethanoate*

Questions

A1. Which variables relating to the hydrolysis reaction of methyl ethanoate need to be controlled?

A2. What equipment should be used to remove the sample of reaction mixture for titration? Explain your answer.

A3. Suggest a suitable alkali for titrating the samples of reaction mixture.

A4. What are the risks associated with the alkali used for titration? What safety precautions should be taken when using substances with these types of risks?

A5. Plot a graph of ester concentration against time.

A6. (a) By drawing tangents to the curve calculate the rate of reaction at these ester concentrations (mol dm^3): 0.200, 0.150, 0.100, 0.050.

(b) Plot a graph of rate of hydrolysis against ester concentration against time. What does this tell you about the order of reaction?

(c) Calculate the gradient of the line of best fit. This gives the rate constant k for the hydrolysis of methyl ethanoate.

Initial rate method

In some reactions the concentration of a reactant remaining in solution cannot be continuously measured at set time intervals, perhaps because a sample cannot be taken without stopping or destroying the reaction. In this case we cannot use the previously described continuous monitoring method. Instead the reaction is carried out multiple times in separate experiments, each with a different starting concentration of a reactant. The rate of reaction is followed by measuring the amount or concentration of a product (not reactant). A graph of the amount of product against time is plotted for each experiment undertaken. As we know the initial concentration of the reactant for each different experiment, we measure the rate (the gradient of a tangent drawn to the line) for the first few seconds. This determines the initial rate of reaction for each experiment at the start, when the concentration of the reactant is known.

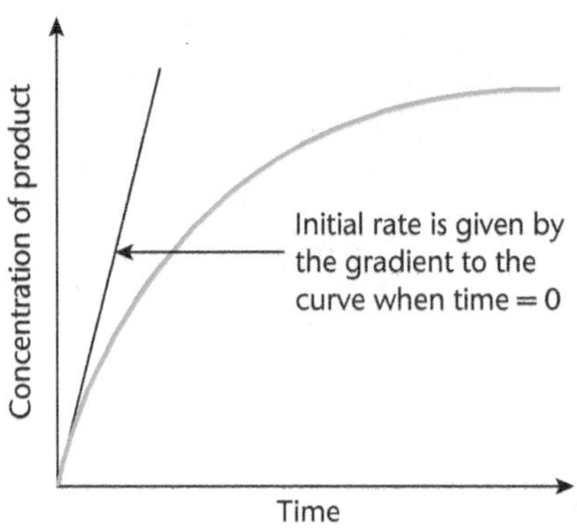
Concentration of product
Initial rate is given by the gradient to the curve when time = 0
Time

ASSIGNMENT 2: INITIAL RATE OF REACTION METHOD FOR DETERMINING ORDER OF REACTION

(MS 0.0, 3.1, 3.3, PS 2.4, 3.1)

The iodine clock reaction is a method for determining the rate of a reaction via an initial rate method.

Solution A	Solution B
Hydrogen peroxide (H_2O_2) 0.1 mol dm^{-3}	Potassium iodide (KI) 0.1 mol dm^{-3}
Sulfuric acid (H_2SO_4) 0.1 mol dm^{-3}	Sodium thiosulfate (Na_2SO_3) 0.01 mol dm^{-3}
	Starch

Table A1 *Solutions for Assignment 2*

When the solutions in Table A1 are combined the iodide ions (I^-) react with hydrogen peroxide (H_2O_2) to form water and iodine (I_2). The iodine reacts very quickly with the thiosulfate ($S_2O_3^{2-}$) to form iodide ions and sulfate ions (SO_4^{2-}):

$$H_2O_2 + 2I^- + 2H^+ \rightarrow I_2 + 2H_2O$$

$$2S_2O_3^{2-} + I_2 \rightarrow S_4O_6^{2-} + 2I^-$$

At the point where all of the thiosulfate ions have reacted, the iodine in the solution can react with the starch to form a dark blue colour. The time taken for the formation of the dark blue colour (Table A2) can be used to determine the initial rate of the reaction.

The amount of thiosulfate ions equals the number of moles of iodide ions that have been consumed when the solution changes colour. The initial rate of reaction can therefore be calculated from the change in concentration divided by the time taken.

Reaction number	Volume of solution A/cm^3	Volume of solution B/cm^3	Volume of water/cm^3	Time for blue colour to appear/s
1	50	50	0	25
2	40	50	10	31
3	30	50	20	41
4	20	50	30	62
5	10	50	40	104

Table A2 *Data for Assignment 2*

Questions

A1. Suggest how a light probe could be used to determine the time taken for the solution to change colour, and explain the advantages that this method could have over human observation with a stopwatch.

A2. What variables need to be controlled in this reaction?

A3. Calculate the concentration of thiosulfate and use this value to calculate the initial rate for each of the reactions.

A4. Calculate the concentration of hydrogen peroxide in each of the reactions.

A5. Plot a graph of rate against $[H_2O_2]$.

A6. What is the order of reaction with respect to $[H_2O_2]$?

KEY IDEAS

- The order of a reaction with respect to a reactant can be determined from the shape of a graph of concentration against time or rate against concentration.
- For a zero-order reaction, the graph of concentration of reactant against time gives a straight line of best fit with a gradient equal to $-k$.
- For a first-order reaction, the graph of rate against concentration of reactant gives a straight line of best fit with a gradient equal to k.
- The rate can be determined experimentally using a continuous monitoring method or an initial rate method.

2.5 NUMERICAL DETERMINATION OF ORDER OF REACTION

It is not always necessary to plot a graph to determine the order of a reaction with respect to a reactant. The order can also be determined from sets of data involving the initial rate of a reaction. Sometimes the data are very simple and it is easy to see by inspection what the order of the reaction is with respect to a reactant, as in Table 2.

Experiment	[X]/mol dm^{-3}	Initial rate of reaction/ mol dm^{-3} s^{-1}
1	0.1	2.0×10^{-4}
2	0.2	4.0×10^{-4}

Table 2 *Example of data on initial rate of a reaction*

In experiment 2, the concentration of [X] has doubled from experiment 1 and the initial rate of the reaction has also doubled; therefore this is a first-order reaction with respect to X. Rate = k[X].

In other cases the data may be more complicated, and you may need identify a suitable pair of experiments to compare from a long list and you may need to carry out calculations to find the multiplying factor.

Worked example

Work out the order of the reaction with respect to A from the data in Table 3.

Experiment	[A]/ mol dm^{-3}	[B]/ mol dm^{-3}	Initial rate of reaction/ mol dm^{-3} s^{-1}
1	0.2	0.2	1.28×10^{-4}
2	0.3	0.3	4.32×10^{-4}
3	0.5	0.3	1.20×10^{-3}

Table 3 *Data for worked example*

Step 1

Identify a pair of experiments where the concentration of the reactant you are looking at changes (in this case [A]) and the concentrations of the other reactants do not change (in this case [B]): see Table 3, experiments 2 and 3.

Experiments 1 and 2 are not suitable, because the concentrations of both reactant A and reactant B change. Experiments 2 and 3 have the same concentration of B and different concentrations of A, so we will use the data from these experiments to work out the order with respect to A.

Step 2

Work out what factor the concentration has increased or decreased by. In this example, $0.5 \div 0.3 = 1.667$.

Step 3

Work out what factor the rate has increased or decreased by. In this example, $(1.20 \times 10^{-3}) \div (4.32 \times 10^{-4}) = 2.778$.

Step 4

Compare the factors that the concentration and the rate have changed by:

- *Zero-order reactions*. The factor that the rate changes by is 0.
- *First-order reactions*. Both the concentration and the rate change by the *same* factor.
- *Second-order reactions*. The factor that the rate changes by is the factor that the concentration changes by *squared*.

In this example, the concentration has changed by ×1.67 and the rate has changed by ×2.78. As $1.667^2 = 2.778$, this reaction is second order with respect to A.

What do you do if there is no suitable pair of experiments?

Sometimes the data do not contain two experiments where the concentration of the reactant for which you are trying to work out the order of the reaction changes but the other concentrations remain constant. In this case we need to add a new line with hypothetical concentrations and calculate the rate for these concentrations, and then use the new line as though it were experimental data.

For example, the data in Table 4 show a reaction that is known to be first order with respect to Y, and you are asked to determine the order with respect to X.

We need to use a pair of experiments where only the concentration of X changes and not the concentration of Y, but this experiment was not carried out. However, we know the order of the reaction with respect to Y, so we can calculate what the rate would be if the concentration of Y changed. This means we can make a new line in the table for a hypothetical experiment where the concentrations used were suitable. The values of the concentrations for the new line are chosen so that there is a pair of experiments where the concentration of the reactant you are looking at changes (in this case [X]) and the concentrations of the other reactants do not change (in this case [Y]), as shown in Table 5.

Experiment	[X]/ mol dm^{-3}	[Y]/ mol dm^{-3}	Initial rate of reaction/ mol dm^{-3} s^{-1}
1	0.1	1.0	1.2×10^{-3}
2	0.2	2.0	9.6×10^{-3}

Table 4 *Data where there is no suitable pair of experiments*

Experiment	[X]/ mol dm^{-3}	[Y]/ mol dm^{-3}	Initial rate of reaction/ mol dm^{-3} s^{-1}
1	0.1	1.0	1.2×10^{-3}
2	0.2	2.0	9.6×10^{-3}
3	0.1	2.0	

Table 5 *Data with new line added*

The initial rate of reaction in the new line can be calculated from the order with respect to Y, which in this case is known to be first order. The concentration of [Y[doubles from experiment 1 to the new line, so the initial rate of reaction will also double as shown in Table 6.

Experiment	[X]/ mol dm^{-3}	[Y]/ mol dm^{-3}	Initial rate of reaction/ mol dm^{-3} s^{-1}
1	0.1	1.0	1.2×10^{-3}
2	0.2	2.0	9.6×10^{-3}
3 (theoretical)	0.1	2.0	$1.2 \times 10^{-3} \times 2$ $= 2.4 \times 10^{-3}$

Table 6 *Table 5 with calculated value added*

After the new line has been added, the order of the reaction with respect to X can be calculated normally.

QUESTIONS

7. The initial rate of reaction, *r*, of bromoethane with sodium hydroxide solution at different reactant concentrations is given in the table below:

$[CH_3CH_2Br]$/ mol dm^{-3}	$[OH^-]$/ mol dm^{-3}	*r*/mol dm^{-3} s^{-1}
0.01	0.02	8.60×10^{-8}
0.03	0.02	2.58×10^{-7}
0.03	0.06	7.74×10^{-7}
0.03	0.12	

a. Use the data to find the order of the reaction with respect to bromoethane and with respect to hydroxide ions.

b. Calculate the rate of the reaction for the final experiment in the table above.

8. Ethanal dimerises in dilute alkaline conditions to form compound A according to the equation

$$2CH_3CHO \rightarrow CH_3CH(OH)CH_2CHO$$

The following data were obtained in a study of the rate of the reaction:

$[CH_3CHO]$/ mol dm^{-3}	$[OH^-]$/ mol dm^{-3}	Initial rate of reaction (relative values)
0.1	0.015	1
0.2	0.015	2
0.4	0.030	8

a. Deduce the order of reaction with respect to ethanal.

b. Deduce the order of reaction with respect to hydrogen ions.

2.6 RATE-DETERMINING STEP

Many chemical reactions occur as a sequence of steps involving one or more intermediates, for example the reaction of HCN with ethanal by a nucleophilic addition mechanism:

Slow

Fast

$$H_3C{-}C(=O){-}H \;+\; :\overset{\ominus}{C}N \xrightarrow[\text{Step 1}]{\text{Slow}} H_3C{-}C(:\bar{O})(CN){-}H \;+\; H^+ \xrightarrow[\text{Step 2}]{\text{Fast}} H_3C{-}C(OH)(CN){-}H$$

If a reaction involves several steps and they all occur at different speeds, some will be faster than others and one will be the slowest. The reaction cannot go any faster than the slowest stage. The **rate-determining step**, or limiting step, is the slowest step in a series of intermediate stages and determines the overall rate of the chemical reaction.

In this reaction, the first step (reaction of CH_3CHO with CN^-) is slow and the second step (where the intermediate formed reacts with H^+) is fast. Although the concentration of H^+ will affect the rate of the fast reaction, this will have no effect on the overall rate of reaction since that is controlled by the slow step. Therefore $[H^+]$ has no effect on the overall rate of reaction and does not appear in the rate equation – the reaction is zero order with respect to H^+.

By experiment, the rate equation for this reaction is found to be

$$\text{rate} = k[CH_3CHO][HCN]$$

This rate equation can only be found experimentally.

Species which are involved in (or before) the rate-determining step have an effect on the overall rate of reaction and appear in the rate equation. Species which are involved in the reaction after the rate-determining step have no effect on the overall rate and do not appear in the rate equation.

This means that the rate equation can give us information about the mechanism of a chemical reaction.

KEY IDEAS

- The rate-determining step is the slowest step in a series of intermediate stages and will determine the overall rate of a chemical reaction.

QUESTIONS

9. A reaction between reactants C, D and E has two products, F and G. The reaction is known to proceed via an intermediate species X.
   $C + D + E \rightarrow F + G$ has the rate equation rate = $k[C][E]$

   Which of the following possibilities are consistent with this rate equation?

   1. $C + D \rightarrow X$ (fast) then $X + E \rightarrow F + G$ (slow)
   2. $C + E \rightarrow X$ (fast) then $X + D \rightarrow F + G$ (slow)
   3. $C + D \rightarrow X$ (slow) then $X + E \rightarrow F + G$ (fast)
   4. $C + E \rightarrow X$ (slow) then $X + D \rightarrow F + G$ (fast)

ASSIGNMENT 3: HYDROLYSIS OF HALOGENOALKANES

(MS 3.1, 3.3, 3.4, 3.5, PS 3.1)

Halogenoalkanes react with OH^- ions to produce alcohols in a nucleophilic substitution reaction. There are two possible mechanisms for this reaction, called the S_N1 and S_N2 mechanisms.

The S_N2 mechanism has two molecules involved in the rate-determining step, and the overall mechanism occurs in one step:

$$RBr + OH^- \xrightarrow{slow} ROH + Br^-$$

The S_N1 mechanism has one molecule involved in the rate-determining step, and the overall mechanism occurs in two steps:

$$RBr \xrightarrow{slow} R^+ + Br^- \xrightarrow[OH^-]{fast} ROH + Br^-$$

A1. A chemist investigated the reaction of the halogenoalkane 2-bromo-2-methylpropane (C_4H_9Br) with sodium hydroxide and recorded the data in the next column:

Experiment number	Initial $[C_4H_9Br]$/ mol dm^{-3}	Initial $[OH^-]$/ mol dm^{-3}	Initial rate/mol dm^{-3} s^{-1}
1	2.5	1.25	0.001
2	2.5	2.50	0.001
3	1.25	2.50	0.0005
4	1.25	1.25	0.0005

a. Deduce the order of reaction with respect to C_4H_9Br and OH^-, explaining your reasoning.

b. Write the rate equation for the reaction.

c. Calculate a value for the rate constant (including units).

d. Does this reaction proceed via an S_N1 or S_N2 mechanism? Explain your reasoning.

A2. Another chemist investigated the reaction between the halogenoalkane 1-bromobutane and sodium hydroxide. They recorded how the concentration of OH^- varied with time and recorded the following data:

Time (s)	0	150	350	650	900	1200	1400
$[OH^-]$ /mol dm^{-3}	0.241	0.195	0.155	0.118	0.099	0.084	0.077

a. Use these data to plot a graph of [OH^-] versus time.

b. Measure the gradient at five different points on your graph to determine the rate at those points.

c. Plot a graph of rate versus [OH^-] and hence state the order of reaction with respect to OH^-.

d. Does this reaction have an S_N1 or an S_N2 mechanism? Explain your reasoning.

2.7 EFFECT OF TEMPERATURE ON RATE OF REACTION

Svante Arrhenius was a Swedish scientist who worked in the late 19th and early 20th century and was awarded the Nobel Prize in Chemistry in 1903. He worked on many different areas of chemistry and you have already met some of the theories that he developed, such as ions carrying electric current in solution.

He also developed an equation that linked the rate constant, temperature and the activation energy of a reaction. This equation was named the Arrhenius equation after him and is shown in Figure 5.

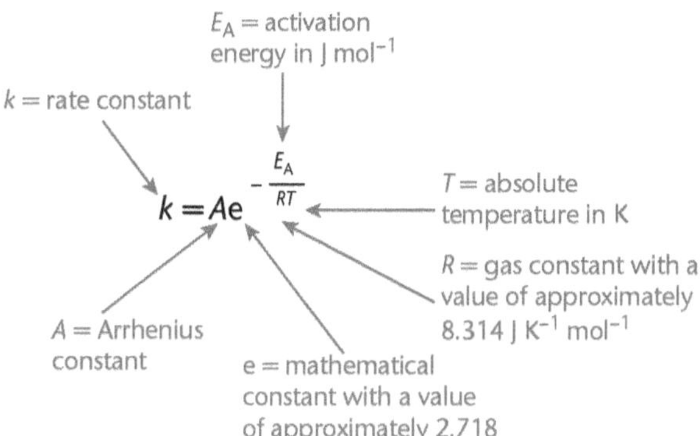

Figure 5 *The Arrhenius equation*

The natural logarithm, ln, of each side of the Arrhenius equation can be taken to give the logarithmic form:

$$\ln k = \ln A - \frac{E_A}{RT}$$

Plotting a graph of ln k against $1/T$ gives a line of best fit where the gradient is equal to $-E_A/R$ and the intercept is equal to ln A.

Values of k and T can be used to calculate the activation energy for a reaction.

Worked example

An example of data and a graph which allow the calculation of the activation energy of a reaction is shown in Table 7 and Figure 6.

T/°C	T/K	k/s^{-1}	ln k	$1/T$ (/K^{-1})
0	273	1.80×10^{-4}	-8.626	0.00366
30	303	2.70×10^{-3}	-5.916	0.00330
60	333	3.00×10^{-2}	-3.507	0.00300
90	363	2.60×10^{-1}	-1.347	0.00276

Table 7 *Data for determining activation energy from temperature and rate constants*

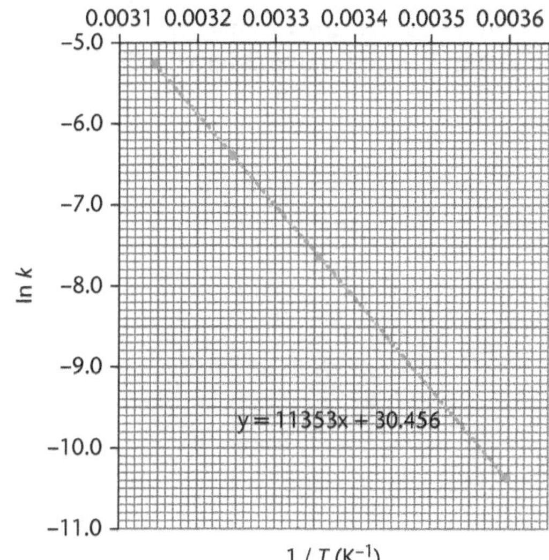

Figure 6 *A graph of ln k plotted against 1/T can be used to determine the activation energy*

$$\text{gradient} = -7996.5 = -\frac{E_A}{R}$$

$$E_A = -7996.5 \times -8.31$$

$$E_A = 664151 \text{ J mol}^{-1}$$

$$E_A = 66.4 \text{ kJ mol}^{-1}$$

KEY IDEAS

- The Arrhenius equation can be used to calculate values relating to the temperature, rate constants and activation energy of a reaction.

QUESTIONS

10. The logarithmic form of the Arrhenius equation is

$$\ln k = \ln A - \frac{E_A}{RT}$$

At 25 °C a reaction has a rate constant of 3.4 mol dm^{-3} s^{-1} and a pre-exponential factor, *A*, of 9.0 mol dm^{-3} s^{-1}.

a. Calculate the activation energy of the reaction using 8.31 J K^{-1} mol^{-1} as the value of the gas constant *R*.

b. Using the activation energy calculated in part a, calculate the rate constant at a temperature of 400 K.

11. The temperature and rate constants for a zero-order reaction are shown in Table 8. These data can be used to determine the activation energy of the reaction using the logarithmic form of the Arrhenius equation,

$$\ln k = \ln A - \frac{E_A}{RT}$$

T	k/s^{-1}
278	3.1×10^{-5}
298	4.7×10^{-4}
308	1.7×10^{-3}
318	5.2×10^{-3}

Table 8 *Temperature and rate constants for a zero-order reaction*

a. Calculate values of ln *k* and 1/*T* for all of the values shown in Table 8.

b. Plot a graph of ln *k* against 1/*T*.

c. Determine the activation energy of the reaction from the graph.

REQUIRED PRACTICAL 7: APPARATUS AND TECHNIQUES

Measuring the rate of reaction by an initial rate method and a continuous monitoring method

(AT a, AT k, AT l)

Doing experiments to determine the rate constant of a reaction gives you the opportunity to show that you can:

- use appropriate apparatus to record a range of measurements
- safely and carefully handle liquids
- measure rates of reaction by at least two different methods.

Apparatus

As seen in *Chapter 8 of the Year 1 Student Book*, there are a number of ways to monitor the rate of a reaction depending on the changes that can be measured. You may want to recap the different types of changes that can be monitored and the apparatus used to measure these changes.

When the rate of a reaction and the rate constants are to be calculated, it is important to measure accurately the quantities that may affect the rate. There is a wide variety of apparatus that can be used to measure volumes, and it is important to select the correct apparatus for the task. This selection will depend on how accurate the measurement needs to be, the volume required and the type of substance being measured.

Apparatus	Description	Use when...
Volumetric pipette	Long glass tube, open at both ends, with a wider bulb area in the middle. A single graduation mark is located at a fixed volume in the narrower range. Volumetric pipettes can measure volumes of solutions very accurately. Standard sizes of volumetric pipettes are 5, 10, 25, 50 and 100 cm^3.	You need to dispense accurately a set amount of a solution that corresponds to one of the standard sizes of volumetric pipettes.
Burette	Long, thin glass tube, open at the top with a tap at the bottom. Graduation marks are typically located every 0.2 cm^3. Can measure volumes accurately.	You are dispensing a set amount of a solution but it is a nonstandard volume (e.g. 7.5 cm^3) or you are finding out the volume that is required (e.g. titration).
Gas syringe	Glass barrel with graduation marks and a tightly fitting piston that can move inside the barrel. Gas syringes can measure volumes of gases accurately.	You are measuring the volume of a gas.
Measuring cylinder	Glass or plastic tube with a sealed base and stand. Large number of graduation marks depending on size. Volumes cannot be measured accurately enough for analytical chemistry.	You are dispensing a set volume of solution but the measurement does not need to be accurate.
Pasteur pipette	Glass tube tapered to a narrow point, fitted with a rubber bulb at the top. Volumes cannot be measured accurately enough for analytical chemistry.	You are dispensing a small amount of solution but the measurement does not need to be accurate.

Technique

To carry out the acid/thiosulfate reaction eye protection must be worn. The technique used will depend on the nature of the reaction and the analytical method used to measure and monitor changes.

The continuous monitoring method can only be used if the concentration of the reactant being studied can be measured in a nondestructive way as the reaction progresses. It only requires one reaction to be carried out; the rate at different times, and therefore different concentrations, can be determined.

The initial rate method requires a number of reactions to be carried out with a different concentration of reactant in each reaction.

Here are some important considerations when using either of these methods:

- All variables that may affect the rate need to be controlled, for example total volume of solution, temperature, particle size and concentration of other reactants.
- You will need to consider how you can measure quantities and variables as accurately as possible.
- You may need to decide how often to take samples and/or measurements and this may involve carrying out trial runs to determine sensible values.
- For the initial rate method, you may also need to decide what concentrations of reactant to test and how you will evaluate the rate at each concentration. This could involve measuring the time taken for an event to occur or measuring a variable at set time intervals and plotting a graph.

QUESTIONS

P1. Hydrogen peroxide reacts with iodide ions to form iodine. The thiosulfate ion immediately reacts with iodine as shown below. The 'iodine clock' experiment can be used to determine the effect of a change in the concentration of iodide ions on the reaction between hydrogen peroxide and iodide ions:

$H_2O_2(aq) + 2H^+(aq) + 2I^-(aq) \rightarrow I_2(aq) + 2H_2O(l)$

$2S_2O_3^{2-}(aq) + I_2(aq) \rightarrow 2I^-(aq) + S_4O_6^{2-}(aq)$

When the I_2 produced has reacted with all of the limited amount of thiosulfate ions present, excess I_2 remains in solution. Starch is added to the mixture, and reaction of the excess of iodine forms a dark blue-black colour.

By varying the concentration of I^-, you can determine the order of reaction with respect to I^- ions.

a. Does this experiment use the continuous monitoring method or the initial rate method?

b. Suggest suitable apparatus for measuring:

   i. exactly 10 cm^3 of sodium thiosulfate solution

   ii. exactly 25 cm^3 of sulfuric acid solution

   iii. approximately 1 cm^3 of starch solution

   iv. exactly 15 cm^3 of potassium iodide solution.

c. Why does the starch solution not need to be measured accurately?

d. Explain how a light meter could be used in this experiment to monitor the reaction.

P2. You are asked to determine the rate constant for the reaction between magnesium and hydrochloric acid.

a. Write an equation for the reaction.

b. Suggest which chemical species, (either reactant or product), would be most suitable to use to monitor the rate of the reaction.

c. State the variables that would need to be controlled.

d. Describe the experimental procedure that you would use to collect data.

e. Explain how you would use the data collected to calculate the rate constant of the reaction.

PRACTICE QUESTIONS

1. 2-Bromo-2-methylpropane, $(CH_3)_3CBr$, and sodium hydroxide react together according to the following equation:
$(CH_3)_3CBr + OH^- \rightarrow (CH_3)_3COH + Br^-$.

The following data give the results of three experiments used to determine the rate equation for the reaction at 25 °C.

Experiment	Initial $[(CH_3)_3CBr]$ /mol dm^{-3}	Initial $[OH^-]$ /mol dm^{-3}	Initial rate of reaction/ mol dm^{-3} s^{-1}
1	1.0×10^{-3}	2.0×10^{-1}	3.0×10^{-3}
2	2.0×10^{-3}	2.0×10^{-1}	6.0×10^{-3}
3	2.0×10^{-3}	4.0×10^{-1}	6.0×10^{-3}

From these results it can be deduced that the rate equation is Rate = $k[(CH_3)_3CBr]$.

a. Show how the data can be used to deduce that the reaction is first order with respect to $(CH_3)_3CBr$.

b. Show how the data can be used to deduce that the reaction is zero order with respect to OH^-.

c. Calculate a value for the rate constant at this temperature and state its units.

d. Calculate the initial rate of reaction when the initial concentration of $(CH_3)_3CBr$ is 4.0×10^{-3} and the initial concentration of OH^- is 1.0×10^{-1}.

2. The initial rate of reaction between substances **A** and **B** was measured in a series of experiments and the following rate equation was deduced: Rate = $k[A][B]^2$.

a. Complete the table of data below for the reaction between **A** and **B**.

Experiment	Initial [A] /mol dm^{-3}	Initial [B]/mol dm^{-3}	Initial rate of reaction /mol dm^{-3} s^{-1}
1	0.020	0.020	1.2×10^{-4}
2	0.040	0.040	
3		0.040	2.4×10^{-4}
4	0.060	0.030	
5	0.040		7.2×10^{-4}

b. Using the data for Experiment 1, calculate a value for the rate constant k and state its units.

3. The initial rate of reaction between substances **X** and **Y** was measured in a series of experiments and the following rate equation was deduced:

Rate = $k[X]^2[Y]$

a. Complete the table of data below for the reaction between **X** and **Y**.

Experiment	Initial [X] /mol dm^{-3}	Initial [Y] /mol dm^{-3}	Initial rate of reaction /mol dm^{-3} s^{-1}
1	3.0×10^{-2}	4.0×10^{-2}	1.6×10^{-5}
2	6.0×10^{-2}	4.0×10^{-2}	
3	3.0×10^{-2}		6.4×10^{-5}
4		16.0×10^{-2}	1.6×10^{-5}

b. Using data for Experiment 1, calculate a value from the rate constant k and state its units.

c. State the effect on the rate constant k of increasing the temperature.

d. State the effect on the rate constant k of increasing the concentration of Y at a fixed temperature.

4. The initial rate of the reaction between compounds **X** and **Y** was measured in a series of experiments at a fixed temperature. The following rate equation was deduced:

$$\text{rate} = k[\mathbf{X}]^2[\mathbf{Y}]^0$$

a i. Complete the table of data below for the reaction between **X** and **Y**.

Experiment	Initial [X] (mol dm^{-3})	Initial [Y] (mol dm^{-3})	Initial rate (mol dm^{-3})
1	1.20×10^{-3}	3.30×10^{-3}	2.68×10^{-4}
2	1.20×10^{-3}	6.60×10^{-3}	
3	2.40×10^{-3}	6.60×10^{-3}	
4		9.90×10^{-3}	8.04×10^{-4}

ii. Using the data for Experiment 1, calculate a value for the rate constant, k, and deduce its units.

b. Sketch a graph to show how the value of the rate constant, k, varies with temperature.

AQA January 2008 Unit 4 Question 6

5. a. The rate equation for the reaction between compounds **C** and **D** is:

$$\text{rate} = k[\mathbf{C}][\mathbf{D}]^2$$

i. In an experiment where the initial concentration of **C** is 0.15 mol dm^{-3} and the initial concentration of **D** is 0.24 mol dm^{-3}, the initial rate of reaction is 0.65 mol dm^{-3} s^{-1} at a given temperature. Calculate a value for the rate constant, k, at this temperature and deduce its units.

ii. The reaction between **C** and **D** is repeated in a second experiment at the same temperature, but the concentrations of both **C** and **D** are half of those in part **a i.** Calculate the initial rate of reaction in this second experiment.

b. The following data were obtained in a series of experiments on the rate of the reaction between compounds **E** and **F** at a constant temperature.

Experiment	Initial concentration of E (mol dm^{-3})	Initial concentration of F (mol dm^{-3})	Initial rate (mol dm^{-3})
1	0.24	0.64	0.80×10^{-2}
2	0.36	0.64	1.80×10^{-2}
3	0.48	0.32	3.20×10^{-2}

i. Deduce the order of reaction with respect to **E**.

ii. Deduce the order of reaction with respect to **F**.

AQA June 2007 Unit 4 Question 4

6. a. The following data were obtained by studying the reaction between compounds **A**, **B** and **C** at a constant temperature.

Experiment	Initial concentration of A (mol dm^{-3})	Initial concentration of B (mol dm^{-3})	Initial concentration of C (mol dm^{-3})	Initial rate (mol dm^{-3} s^{-1})
1	0.20	0.10	0.40	0.80×10^{-3}
2	0.20	0.40	0.40	3.20×10^{-3}
3	0.10	0.80	0.40	1.60×10^{-3}
4	0.10	0.30	0.20	0.60×10^{-3}

i. Deduce the order of reaction with respect to **A**.

ii. Deduce the order of reaction with respect to **B**.

iii. Deduce the order of reaction with respect to **C**.

b. The rate equation for the reaction between compounds **D** and **E** at a given temperature is:

$$\text{rate} = k[\mathbf{D}]^2[\mathbf{E}]$$

The initial rate of reaction is 8.36 $\times 10^{-4}$ mol dm^{-3} s^{-1} when the initial concentration of **D** is 0.84 mol dm^{-3} and the initial concentration of **E** is 1.16 mol dm^{-3}.

Calculate a value for the rate constant, k, at this temperature and deduce its units.

AQA January 2007 Unit 4 Question 1

7. The hydrolysis of methyl propanoate was studied in acidic conditions at 25 °C and the rate equation was found to be:

$$\text{rate} = k[CH_3CH_2COOCH_3][H^+]$$

a. Use the data below to calculate the value of the rate constant, k, at this temperature. Deduce its units.

b. The reaction in part **a** was repeated at the same temperature, but water was added so that the volume of the reaction mixture was doubled. Calculate the initial rate of reaction under these conditions.

Initial rate of reaction (mol dm^{-3} s^{-1})	Initial concentration of methyl propanoate (mol dm^{-3})	Initial concentration of hydrochloric acid (mol dm^{-3})
1.15×10^{-4}	0.150	0.555

8. This question involves the use of kinetic data to deduce the order of a reaction and calculate a value for a rate constant.

The data in Table Q1 were obtained in a series of experiments on the rate of the reaction between compounds **A** and **B** at a constant temperature.

Experiment	Initial concentration of A (mol dm^{-3})	Initial concentration of B (mol dm^{-3})	Initial rate (mol dm^{-3} s^{-1})
1	0.12	0.26	2.10×10^{-4}
2	0.36	0.26	1.89×10^{-3}
3	0.72	0.13	3.78×10^{-3}

Table Q1

a. Show how these data can be used to deduce the rate expression for the reaction between **A** and **B**.

The data in Table Q2 were obtained in two experiments on the rate of the reaction between compounds **C** and **D** at a constant temperature.

Experiment	Initial concentration of C (mol dm^{-3})	Initial concentration of D (mol dm^{-3})	Initial rate (mol dm^{-3} s^{-1})
4	1.9×10^{-2}	3.5×10^{-2}	7.2×10^{-4}
5	3.6×10^{-2}	5.4×10^{-2}	To be calculated

Table Q2

b. Use the data from experiment **4** to calculate a value for the rate constant, k, at this temperature. Deduce the units of k.

c. Calculate a value for the initial rate in experiment **5**.

d. The rate equation for a reaction is

$$\text{rate} = k[\mathbf{E}]$$

Explain qualitatively why doubling the temperature has a much greater effect on the rate of the reaction than doubling the concentration of **E**.

e. A slow reaction has a rate constant $k = 6.51 \times 10^{-3}$ mol^{-1} dm^3 at 300 K.

Use the equation $\ln k = \ln A - E_a/RT$ to calculate a value, in kJ mol^{-1}, for the activation energy of this reaction.

The constant $A = 2.57 \times 10^{10}$ mol^{-1} dm^3.

The gas constant $R = 8.31$ J K^{-1} mol^{-1}.

AQA 2015 Specimen Paper 2 Question 1

3 EQUILIBRIUM CONSTANTS

PRIOR KNOWLEDGE

You will have already learned about reversible reactions, chemical equilibria and how changes to reaction conditions affect the position of an equilibrium. You should be able to write an equation for an equilibrium constant and use the equation to calculate values for the equilibrium constant K_c (see Chapter 9 of Year 1 Student Book).

LEARNING OBJECTIVES

In this chapter you will learn about equilibria in gaseous reactions and how to calculate values relating to these experiments, including partial pressures, mole fractions and equilibrium constants K_p.

(Specification 3.1.10)

An adult body normally has about 5 dm^3 of blood, but people who live at high altitudes, where the air contains less oxygen, may have up to 6.9 dm^3. Many athletes train at high altitude so that their bodies adapt to a lower oxygen concentration by producing extra blood. When they run at lower altitudes they have a greater supply of oxygen.

Damaged cells also need a supply of oxygen for repair, so the body needs to maintain its flow of oxygen to all parts of the body. In the case of a serious accident or, indeed, an operation, there may be considerable blood loss and tissues can die. In these cases a blood transfusion may be necessary.

Our bodies use oxygen to break down glucose and release energy. The reaction produces carbon dioxide and water. Both oxygen and carbon dioxide can bond reversibly to haemoglobin in our blood, depending on their concentrations in the tissue fluids and blood.

The concentration of blood oxygen is high in the arteries from our lungs, where haemoglobin bonds preferentially to oxygen and carries it to the body's cells. Oxygen is used during metabolism (chemical reactions that happen in cells). Its concentration in blood and tissues decreases and oxygen dissociates from haemoglobin (Hb). When the carbon dioxide concentration is high, as it is in blood leaving active muscles, carbon dioxide bonds to haemoglobin and is carried back to our lungs, where it dissociates, diffuses into the lungs and is breathed out:

$$\text{Hb} + \text{O}_2 \underset{\text{in tissues}}{\overset{\text{in lungs}}{\rightleftharpoons}} \text{HbO}_2 \qquad \text{Hb} + \text{CO}_2 \underset{\text{in lungs}}{\overset{\text{in tissues}}{\rightleftharpoons}} \text{HbCO}_2$$

How effectively oxygen is transported and released depends upon the strength of the bond between the haemoglobin and the oxygen molecule. Scientists have found that the release of oxygen is triggered by the presence of hydrogen carbonate ions, HCO_3^-, in cells.

The processes of bonding of oxygen and carbon dioxide molecules to haemoglobin are **dynamic equilibrium** reactions. The position of equilibrium shifts to respond to our bodies' needs.

3.1 DYNAMIC EQUILIBRIA

In *Chapter 9 of the Year 1 Student Book* we saw that many reactions go more or less to completion (Figure 1). In other words, all the reactants are used up to make the products of the reaction. To all intents and purposes these reactions are not reversible.

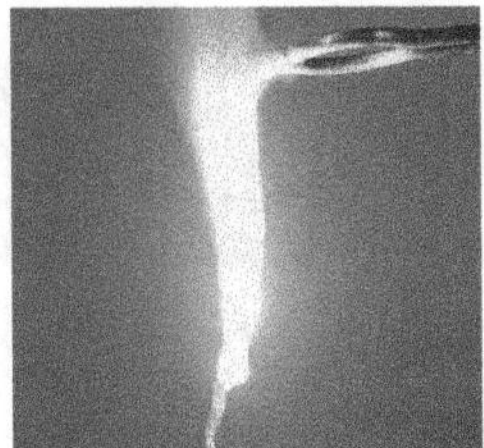

Figure 1 *The reaction between magnesium and oxygen is not reversible*

However, many other reactions do not go to completion. After a while there appears to be no further change, yet if the reaction mixture is analysed there are still significant amounts of reactants as well as products in the reaction mixture.

The reaction mixture has reached a position of dynamic equilibrium. Reactants are still being changed into products, but as fast as that happens the reverse reaction (products → reactants) is also happening. An analogy might help.

Imagine somebody walking up a down-going escalator. If they walk at the same speed as the escalator steps are coming down, they neither go up nor down. The person and escalator are moving at the same speed, but in opposite directions. They are in dynamic equilibrium.

Iodine and hydrogen

The reaction between hydrogen and iodine is an example of a reversible reaction. At room temperature, hydrogen is a gas and iodine is a solid, but at temperatures over 457 K and at 101 kPa pressure, iodine is also a gas.

If equimolar quantities of the reactants are heated to 600 K and the two gases are sealed in a container, they combine and form hydrogen iodide:

$$H_2(g) + I_2(g) \rightarrow 2HI(g)$$

If 1 mol $H_2(g)$ reacted to completion with 1 mol $I_2(g)$, it would produce 2 mol HI(g).

However, no matter how long the mixture is kept at 600 K, there is always some hydrogen and iodine present in the container – the reaction does not go to completion (Figure 3).

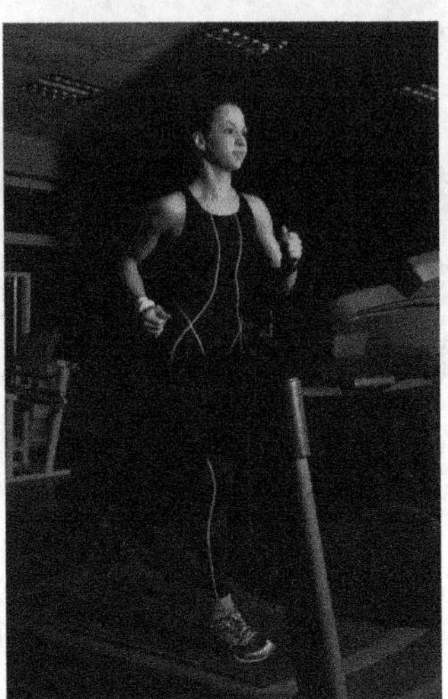

Figure 2 *This runner is running at the same speed as the treadmill, but in the opposite direction. She and the treadmill are in dynamic equilibrium.*

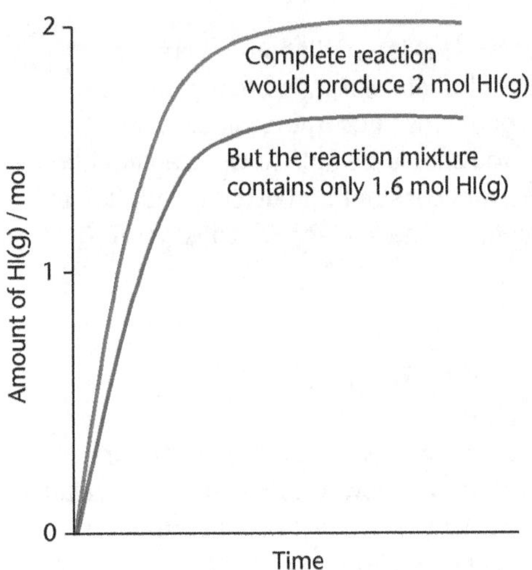

Figure 3 *At 600 K in a sealed container 1 mol $H_2(g)$ and 1 mol $I_2(g)$ produce a final reaction mixture containing 0.2 mol $H_2(g)$, 0.2 mol $I_2(g)$ and 1.6 mol HI(g). The reaction does not go to completion. It reaches a position of dynamic equilibrium.*

As the product HI(g) is formed in the reaction, it decomposes to form gaseous hydrogen and gaseous iodine again, so the forward and reverse reactions are happening at the same time:

$$H_2(g) + I_2(g) \rightarrow 2HI(g)$$

$$2HI(g) \rightarrow I_2(g) + H_2(g)$$

At equilibrium the concentrations of reactants and products do not change, because the rates of the forward and reverse reactions are equal. A position of dynamic equilibrium is reached. We show this using the equilibrium sign '$\rightleftharpoons$':

$$H_2(g) + I_2(g) \rightleftharpoons 2HI(g)$$

At 600 K all reactants and products are in the same phase. A reaction in which only one phase is present is described as **homogeneous**. The reaction of hydrogen and iodine in the gas phase is called a homogeneous equilibrium.

If there is a mixture of phases, then the reaction is **heterogeneous**. The thermal decomposition of calcium carbonate is an example. In an open system, the carbon dioxide produced can escape and the reaction goes to completion. However, in a sealed container (a closed system) a dynamic heterogeneous equilibrium is established:

Open system $CaCO_3(s) \rightarrow CaO(s) + CO_2(g)$

Closed system $CaCO_3(s) \rightleftharpoons CaO(s) + CO_2(g)$

3.2 EQUILIBRIUM CONSTANT FOR HOMOGENEOUS GASEOUS REACTIONS

K_c and concentration

In *Chapter 9 of the Year 1 Student Book* we looked at the equilibrium constant in terms of the equilibrium concentrations of reactants and products. This equilibrium constant has the symbol K_c.

For the general reversible reaction

$$aA + bB \rightleftharpoons cC + dD$$

the equilibrium constant K_c is given by

$$K_c = \frac{[C]^c[D]^d}{[A]^a[B]^b}$$

Remember:

- The right-hand side of the equation goes on the top line, and the left-hand side goes on the bottom line.
- The square brackets indicate concentrations, in mol dm^{-3}, in the equilibrium mixture.
- The value of K_c depends on the temperature of the equilibrium mixture, and therefore the temperature should always be stated.
- Knowing K_c enables us to predict how a reaction will behave when the concentrations of reactants or products are changed.

K_p and pressure

In the case of homogeneous gaseous reactions, the quantities of reactants and products are often given in terms of pressure rather than concentration. The equilibrium mixture exerts a total pressure on the walls of its sealed container. The quantities of reactants and products are expressed as partial pressures, which when added together make up the total pressure.

The partial pressures of all of the gases in a system add up to the total pressure (Dalton's law):

$$P_{total} = P_A + P_B + P_C + \ldots$$

where P_{total} is the total pressure of the gaseous mixture, and P_A, P_B, P_C etc. are the partial pressures of the gases A, B, C and so on that make up the mixture.

The **mole fraction** x of a substance is the number of moles of the substance divided by the total number of moles in the mixture:

$$x_A = \frac{\text{moles of A}}{\text{total number of moles}}$$

The sum of all the mole fractions of reactants and products in an equilibrium reaction mixture is always 1.

To a good approximation, all gases obey the ideal gas law, $PV = nRT$. Therefore, in a mixture of gases the mole fraction of each gas equals its partial pressure divided by the total pressure:

$$x_A = \frac{P_A}{P_{total}}$$

This equation may be rearranged to allow the partial pressure to be calculated when the mole fraction and total pressure are known:

$$P_A = x_A \times P_{total}$$

QUESTIONS

1. The total pressure of a mixture of three gases A, B and C is 200 Pa. The partial pressure of A is 40 Pa. Calculate the mole fraction of A.
2. The mole fraction of gas X in a mixture of two gases X and Y is 0.12. Calculate the ratio of the partial pressures of X and Y.
3. Z is a gas in a mixture made up of several gases. Its partial pressure is 30 kPa and its mole fraction is 0.15. Calculate the total pressure of the mixture.

The equation for the equilibrium constant of a gaseous reaction is written in the same way as the equation for a reaction that takes place in solution, with products on the top and reactants on the bottom. However, while square brackets are used to show concentrations of reactants and products in solution, the symbol *P* is used for partial pressures of reactants and products in the gas phase.

For the reaction $H_2(g) + I_2(g) \rightleftharpoons 2HI(g)$, the equilibrium constants are written as

$$K_c = \frac{[HI]^2}{[H_2][I_2]}$$

and

$$K_p = \frac{P_{(HI)}{}^2}{P_{(H_2)}P_{(I_2)}}$$

Units of K_p

The values used to calculate K_p are the partial pressures of the gases and not concentrations, mole fractions or any other values.

The units of partial pressure are usually pascals (Pa) or kilopascals (kPa); 1000 Pa = 1 kPa.

The units of K_p can be calculated by replacing each of the terms in the equation by their units and then cancelling out duplicated units.

Worked example

$$N_2(g) + 3H_2(g) \rightleftharpoons 2NH_3(g)$$

What are the units of K_p in the equation

$$K_p = \frac{P_{(NH_3)}{}^2}{P_{(N_2)}P_{(H_2)}{}^3}$$

where the partial pressures are given in kPa?

Insert the units for the partial pressures:

$$K_p\text{units} = \frac{\text{kPa} \times \text{kPa}}{\text{kPa} \times \text{kPa} \times \text{kPa} \times \text{kPa}}$$

Cancel units that appear above and below the line:

$$K_p \text{ units} = \frac{\cancel{\text{kPa} \times \text{kPa}}}{\cancel{\text{kPa} \times \text{kPa} \times} \text{kPa} \times \text{kPa}}$$

Rearrange units:

$$K_p \text{ units} = \text{kPa}^{-2}$$

QUESTIONS

4. Write equations for the equilibrium constant K_p for the following reactions:
   a. $CO_2(g) + NO(g) \rightleftharpoons CO(g) + NO_2(g)$
   b. $N_2O_4(g) \rightleftharpoons 2NO_2(g)$
   c. $2H_2(g) + O_2(g) \rightleftharpoons 2H_2O(g)$
   d. $CH_4(g) + O_2(g) \rightleftharpoons CO_2(g) + 2H_2O(g)$

5. Thermal cracking takes place at very high temperatures and pressures. In one example of a thermal cracking procedure, temperatures of 750 °C and pressures of 7500 kPa are used. These reaction conditions result in the production of very light fractions, such as the reaction where ethane is broken down into ethene and hydrogen:

   $C_2H_6(g) \rightleftharpoons C_2H_4(g) + H_2(g)$

   Assuming that ethane, ethene and hydrogen are the only substances in the reaction mixture, calculate the following:

   a. The partial pressure of ethene if the partial pressure of ethane is 3000 kPa and the partial pressure of hydrogen is 2500 kPa.
   b. The partial pressure of ethane if the mole fraction of ethane is 0.15.
   c. The mole fraction of hydrogen if the partial pressure of hydrogen is 1500 kPa.
   d. The mole fraction of ethane if the mole fraction of ethene is 0.2 and the mole fraction of hydrogen is 0.2.
   e. The partial pressure of hydrogen if the mole fraction of ethane is 0.3 and the mole fraction of ethene is 0.15.

6. The Haber process involves the reaction of nitrogen and hydrogen to produce ammonia:

   $N_2(g) + 3H_2(g) \rightleftharpoons 2NH_3(g)$

   Nitrogen and hydrogen were placed in a sealed reaction vessel and the mixture was allowed to reach equilibrium.

   At equilibrium the reaction vessel had a total pressure of 7500 kPa and contained 1.0 moles of nitrogen, 3.0 moles of hydrogen and 2.0 moles of ammonia.

a. Calculate the partial pressures of each of the reactants and products in the reaction vessel at equilibrium.

b. Calculate the equilibrium constant K_p.

c. State the units of the equilibrium constant K_p.

KEY IDEAS

- K_p is the equilibrium constant for a reaction in the gas state, using the partial pressures of the component gases.
- The sum of the partial pressures of gases in a mixture equals the total pressure.
- The partial pressure of a gas in a mixture can be calculated using the mole fraction of the gas multiplied by the total pressure.

3.3 CALCULATIONS INVOLVING K_p

In *Chapter 9 of the Year 1 Student Book* you learned how K_c for an equilibrium reaction can be calculated. The same method may be used to calculate K_p for a homogeneous gaseous equilibrium reaction from partial pressures. Here are two worked examples.

Worked example (MS 1.1, 2.2, 2.3)

Calculate K_p for the reaction between methane and hydrogen sulfide.

Step 1. The reaction is

$CH_4(g) + 2H_2S(g) \rightleftharpoons CS_2(g) + 4H_2(g)$

$$K_p = \frac{P_{(CS_2)}P_{(H_2)}{}^4}{P_{(CH_4)}P_{(H_2S)}{}^2}$$

Step 2. The partial pressure of each reactant and product at equilibrium at 298 K is shown in Table 1.

Substance	Partial pressure at equilibrium/kPa
$CH_4(g)$	0.20
$H_2S(g)$	0.25
$CS_2(g)$	0.52
$H_2(g)$	0.10

Table 1 *Partial pressures of reactants and products in worked example*

Substituting in the equation,

$$K_p = \frac{(0.52)(0.10)^4}{(0.20)(0.25)^2} \qquad \text{Units } \frac{\text{kPa} \times \text{kPa}^4}{\text{kPa} \times \text{kPa}^2} = \text{kPa}^2$$

$= 0.00416 \text{ kPa}^2$

$= 0.0042 \text{ kPa}^2$

(can only be given to two significant figures because of the limits of the partial pressures used).

Worked example (MS 1.1, 2.2, 2.3)

K_p for the reaction

$N_2(g) + 3H_2(g) \rightleftharpoons 2NH_3(g)$

is 3.1×10^{-4} kPa^{-2} at 400 °C

Calculate the partial pressure of NH_3 if $P_{N_2} = 220$ kPa and $P_{H_2} = 125$ kPa.

Step 1. The equation for K_p is

$$K_p = \frac{P_{(NH_3)}{}^2}{P_{(N_2)}P_{(H_2)}{}^3}$$

Step 2. Substituting in the equation,

$$3.1 \times 10^{-4} = \frac{P_{(NH_3)}{}^2}{220 \times 125^3}$$

$P_{NH_3}{}^2 = 3.1 \times 10^{-4} \times 220 \times 125^3$

$P_{NH_3} = \sqrt{(3.1 \times 10^{-4} \times 220 \times 125^3)} = \sqrt{0.00042}$
$= 365$ kPa

(to three significant figures because of the limits of the data used).

Here is an alternative method for calculating equilibrium constants. It is often called the ICE method. Both of these methods will work for both K_c and K_p, and you should use whichever method suits you.

In the ICE method, a table is made that describes:

- the amount of each substance initially (I)
- the change (C) in the amount of substance when the reaction occurs X times
- the amount of each substance at equilibrium (E).

Worked example

1.0 moles of nitrogen and 3.0 moles of hydrogen were sealed into a container. After the mixture had reached equilibrium, at a pressure of 300 kPa, the remaining amount of nitrogen was 0.4 moles.

$N_2(g) + 3H_2(g) \rightleftharpoons 2NH_3(g)$

Step 1. Construct an ICE table with a separate column for each substance. The stoichiometry of the reaction is accounted for in the 'change' and must be ignored at all other times to avoid counting it more than once.

	N_2	H_2	NH_3
Initial			
Change			
Equilibrium			

Step 2. Insert all known values of initial amounts of substances. The values must be in moles, not partial pressures (this is calculated later). Assume that there is no product in the initial reaction mixture.

	N_2	H_2	NH_3
Initial	1.0	3.0	0.0
Change			
Equilibrium			

Step 3. Use the stoichiometry of the reaction to show the changes in amounts of substance.

If X moles of nitrogen are used up, then from the stoichiometry of the equation $3X$ moles of hydrogen are used up and $2X$ moles of ammonia are produced. The signs '−' and '+' are used to show decreases and increases, respectively, in the amounts of substances.

	N_2	H_2	NH_3
Initial	1.0	3.0	0.0
Change	$-X$	$-3X$	$+2X$
Equilibrium			

Step 4. Use the initial values and changes to produce an equation containing X to show the equilibrium amounts of each substance.

	N_2	H_2	NH_3
Initial	1.0	3.0	0.0
Change	$-X$	$-3X$	$+2X$
Equilibrium	$1.0 - X$	$3.0 - 3X$	$0 + 2X$

Step 5. Solve for the value of X using the data provided for the equilibrium amount of one substance.

The data given tell you that amount of nitrogen at equilibrium was 0.4 moles. Therefore,

$1.0 - X = 0.4$

$X = 0.6$ moles.

Step 6. Calculate equilibrium numbers of moles of each substance.

	N_2	H_2	NH_3
Initial	1.0	3.0	0.0
Change	$-X$	$-3X$	$+2X$
Equilibrium	$1.0 - 0.6 = 0.4$	$3 - (3 \times 0.6) = 1.2$	$0 + (0.6 \times 2) = 1.2$

Step 7. Calculate the partial pressure of each substance using the total pressure multiplied by the mole fraction (moles of substance/total number of moles).

Total number of moles at equilibrium = 0.4 + 1.2 + 1.2 = 2.8 moles

Partial pressure of nitrogen = mole fraction × total pressure = $\frac{0.4}{2.8} \times 300 = 42.857$ kPa

Partial pressure of hydrogen = mole fraction × total pressure = $\frac{1.2}{2.8} \times 300 = 128.571$ kPa

Partial pressure of ammonia = mole fraction × total pressure = $\frac{1.2}{2.8} \times 300 = 128.571$ kPa

Step 8. Use the partial pressures to calculate the equilibrium constant:

$$K_p = \frac{P_{(NH_3)}{}^2}{P_{(N_2)}P_{(H_2)}{}^3} = \frac{128.571^2}{128.571^3 \times 42.857}$$

$$= 1.814 \times 10^{-4}\ \text{kPa}^{-2}$$

The value of K_p needs to be rounded to two significant figures as the least accurate measurements are the initial values of the numbers of moles, which are given to two significant figures, so this is the maximum confidence that the final value can be reported to:

$K_p = 1.8 \times 10^{-4}\ \text{kPa}^{-2}$ at the temperature of the reaction.

QUESTIONS

7. 1.0 mole of hydrogen and 2.0 moles of fluorine were sealed into a container. After the mixture had reached equilibrium, at a pressure of 1.5×10^6 Pa, 0.3 moles of hydrogen fluoride were formed.
   a. Write an equation to show the reaction between hydrogen and fluorine.
   b. Calculate the mole fraction of hydrogen fluoride at equilibrium.
   c. Calculate K_p.

Stretch and challenge

8. Two moles of carbon monoxide and 1 mole of oxygen were placed in a sealed container. The reaction was allowed to reach equilibrium and a final pressure of 300 kPa was recorded, with carbon dioxide having a partial pressure of 100 kPa.
   a. Write an equation to show the reaction between carbon monoxide and oxygen.
   b. Calculate K_p.
   (Hint: you will need to calculate the total number of moles by forming and writing an equation that you can solve in terms of *x*.)

3.4 EFFECT OF CHANGING REACTION CONDITIONS

Changes in concentration or pressure do not affect the value of K_p. Neither does the use of a catalyst.

However, changing the temperature of the system changes the equilibrium position and the value of the equilibrium constant.

Le Chatelier's principle predicts that, if the temperature is changed, the reaction will try to minimise the effect of the change. If the temperature is increased, the reaction will try to remove heat from the system, so it will move in the endothermic direction.

For example, the reaction between nitrogen and hydrogen to produce ammonia is exothermic:

$$N_2(g) + 3H_2(g) \rightleftharpoons 2NH_3(g)$$

$$\Delta H^\ominus = -92 \text{ kJ mol}^{-1}$$

$$K_p = \frac{P_{(NH_3)}{}^2}{P_{(N_2)}P_{(H_2)}{}^3}$$

Increasing the temperature drives the equilibrium to the left (the endothermic direction – the dissociation of ammonia), decreasing the yield of ammonia.

Figure 4 shows the effect of pressure and temperature on the percentage of ammonia produced at equilibrium in the Haber process. Note that the percentage yield reduces with higher temperatures and increases with higher pressures.

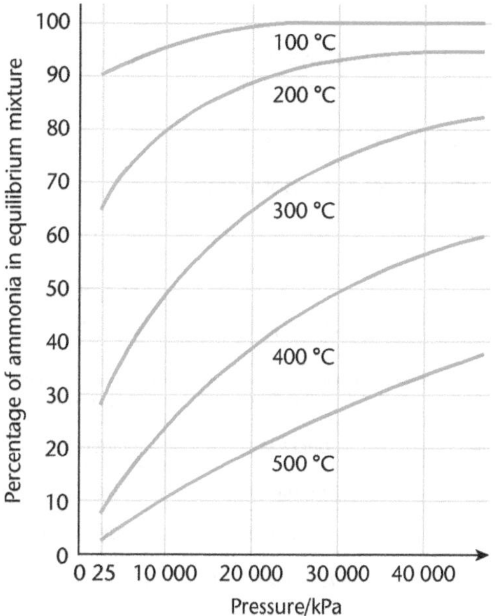

Figure 4 *Effect of changing temperature on the percentage of ammonia in the equilibrium mixture*

Figure 4 shows that there is a much higher percentage of ammonia in the equilibrium mixture at 100 °C than at 500 °C. Increasing the pressure has very little effect at 100 °C but has considerable effect at higher temperatures. The rate of reaction at 100 °C is very low, so ammonia is manufactured at 450 °C and 20 000 kPa, and a catalyst is used to increase the rate.

Although the percentage yield increases with higher pressure, the equilibrium constant does not change when the pressure changes. This is because the pressure is used in the calculation of the equilibrium constant and the increased yield is cancelled out by the increased pressure.

Using a catalyst will also not change the equilibrium constant, as it affects only the rate at which the reaction mixture reaches equilibrium and not the actual position of the equilibrium. A summary of the effect of changing the reaction conditions on rates, yields and equilibrium constants is shown in Table 3.

Change in reaction conditions	Effect on rate	Effect on rate constant	Effect on yield	Effect on equilibrium constant
increased pressure or concentration	increase	no change	depends on stoichiometry	no change
increased temperature	increase	increase	depends on enthalpy change	depends on enthalpy change
addition of catalyst	increase	increase	no change	no change

Table 2 *Effect of changing reaction conditions*

The reaction used nowadays to produce the hydrogen required for ammonia synthesis is

$CH_4(g) + H_2O(g) \rightleftharpoons CO(g) + 3H_2(g)$

$\Delta H^{\ominus} = +206\ \text{kJ mol}^{-1}$ (endothermic)

The production of hydrogen is an endothermic process, so raising the temperature will drive the equilibrium to the right – the endothermic direction – thus increasing the equilibrium yield of hydrogen. The effects of temperature change on a reaction are summarised in Table 3.

Reaction	Change in temperature	Effect on equilibrium constant	Shift in equilibrium position	Effect on equilibrium yield of product
exothermic	increase	decrease	left	decrease
exothermic	decrease	increase	right	increase
endothermic	increase	increase	right	increase
endothermic	decrease	decrease	left	decrease

Table 3 *Effect of changing temperature on equilibrium*

ASSIGNMENT 1: ATMOSPHERIC POLLUTION

(PS 1.2, 3.2)

In the reaction

$N_2(g) + O_2(g) \rightleftharpoons 2NO(g)$

$K_p = 4 \times 10^{-31}$ at 20 °C (293 K), but at the combustion temperature inside a car engine, typically 800 °C (approximately 1100 K), $K_p = 8 \times 10^{-9}$.

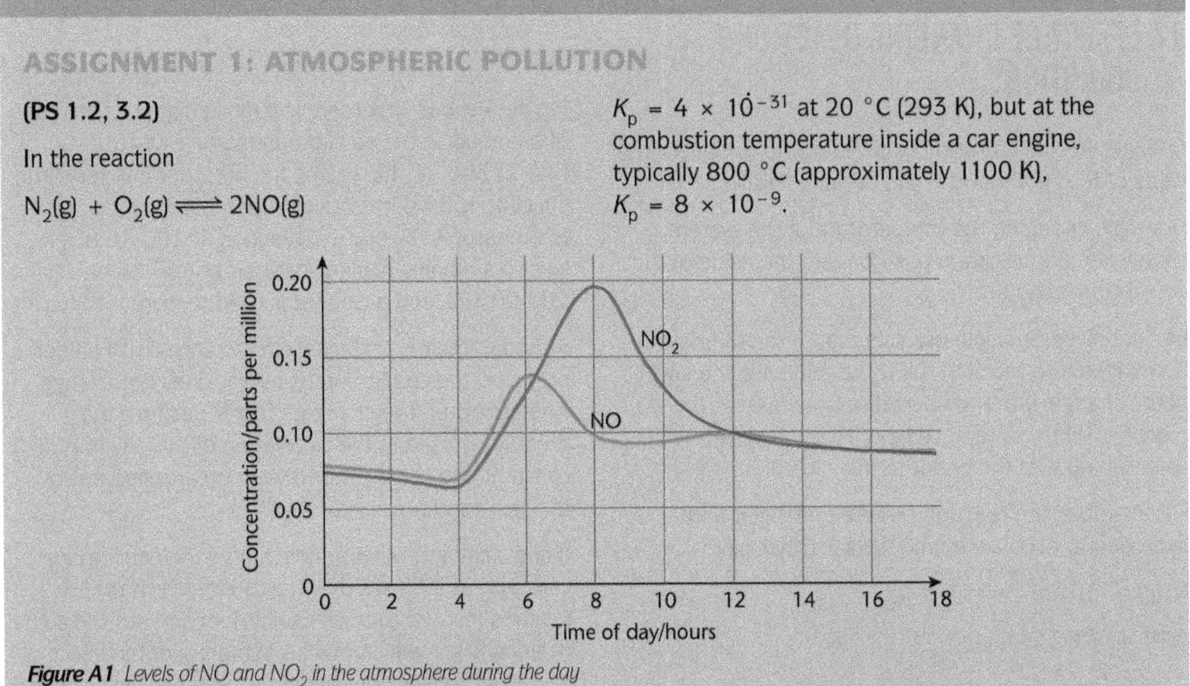

Figure A1 *Levels of NO and NO_2 in the atmosphere during the day*

Nitrogen monoxide from petrol combustion reacts with atmospheric oxygen to give nitrogen dioxide. This gas forms the brown haze seen over polluted towns and cities, such as São Paulo, shown in the top part of Figure A2. Nitrogen dioxide causes respiratory problems and acid rain.

Questions

A1. Is this reaction likely to happen at normal room temperature? Explain your reasoning.

A2. The temperature of the spark that ignites the fuel/air mixture is about 2500 K. At this temperature, how does the value of K_p change? How will this affect the yield of NO(g)?

A3. Is the reaction endothermic or exothermic? Explain your answer using the change in the value of the equilibrium constant.

A4. Explain in detail the shape of the graph for the production of NO and NO_2 in Figure A1.

A5. Many EU countries have introduced or are introducing Low Emission Zones (LEZ) for some diesel and petrol vehicles. Give your opinion about these moves, supporting your arguments with sound scientific, financial or libertarian evidence.

Figure A2 Top, brown haze in São Paulo; bottom, a London 'Low Emission Zone' sign

PRACTICE QUESTIONS

1. Under suitable conditions, the equilibrium represented as follows was established:

$2CH_4(g) \rightleftharpoons 3H_2(g) + C_2H_2(g)$
$\Delta H^\ominus = +377\ \text{kJ mol}^{-1}$

a. Write an expression for the equilibrium constant, K_p, for this reaction.

b. At a given temperature, the equilibrium mixture contained 0.44 mol of methane, 0.28 mol of hydrogen and 0.12 mol of ethyne (C_2H_2) in a container with a pressure of 200 kPa.

Calculate the partial pressures of the three gases and the value of K_p under these conditions and deduce its units.

c. State the effect of an increase in temperature on the position of this equilibrium and on the value of K_p for this reaction.

d. State the effect of an increase in pressure on the position of this equilibrium and on the value of K_p for this reaction.

Adapted from AQA January 2008 Unit 4 Question 3 (a–d)

2. a. The diagram in Figure Q1 shows the effect of temperature and pressure on the equilibrium yield of the product in a gaseous equilibrium.

i. Use the diagram to deduce whether the forward reaction involves an increase or a decrease in the number of moles of gas. Explain your answer.

ii. Use the diagram to deduce whether the forward reaction is exothermic or endothermic. Explain your answer.

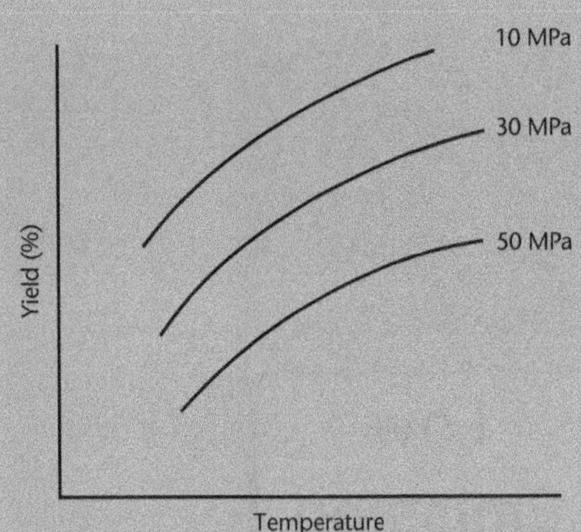

Figure Q1

b. When a 0.218 mol sample of hydrogen iodide was heated in a flask, the following equilibrium was established at 700 K and 350 kPa.

$H_2(g) + I_2(g) \rightleftharpoons 2HI(g)$

The equilibrium mixture was found to contain 0.023 mol of hydrogen.

i. Calculate the number of moles of iodine and the number of moles of hydrogen iodide in the equilibrium mixture.

ii. Write an expression for K_p for the equilibrium.

iii. Calculate the value of K_p at 700 K.

Adapted from AQA June 2006 Unit 4 Question 3

3. Tetrafluoroethene, C_2F_4, is obtained from chlorodifluoromethane, $CHClF_2$, according to the equation:

$2CHClF_2(g) \rightleftharpoons C_2F_4(g) + 2HCl(g)$
$\Delta H^\ominus = +128\ kJ\ mol^{-1}$

a. A 1.0 mol sample of $CHClF_2$ is placed in a container of volume 18.5 dm^3 and heated.

When equilibrium is reached, the mixture contains 0.20 mol of $CHClF_2$.

i. Calculate the number of moles of C_2F_4 and the number of moles of HCl present at equilibrium.

ii. Write an expression for K_p for the equilibrium.

iii. Calculate a value for K_p and give its units.

b. i. State how the temperature should be changed at constant pressure to increase the equilibrium yield of C_2F_4.

ii. State how the total pressure should be changed at constant temperature to increase the equilibrium yield of C_2F_4.

AQA January 2005 Unit 4 Question 5 (a–b)

4. At high temperatures, PCl_5 dissociates according to the following equation.

$PCl_5(g) \rightleftharpoons PCl_3(g) + Cl_2(g)$
$\Delta H^\ominus = +93\ kJ\ mol^{-1}$

A 2.60 mol sample of PCl_5 is placed in a sealed container and heated to a fixed temperature. At equilibrium, 1.40 mol of PCl_5 remain unreacted. The total pressure in the container is 125 kPa.

a. Calculate the number of moles of Cl_2 and the total number of moles of gas present in the equilibrium mixture.

b. Calculate the mole fraction of PCl_5 and the mole fraction of Cl_2 in the equilibrium mixture.

c. i. Write a general expression for the partial pressure of a gas, in a mixture of gases.

ii. Calculate the partial pressure of PCl_5 and the partial pressure of Cl_2 in the equilibrium mixture.

d. Write an expression for the equilibrium constant, K_p, for this reaction.

e. i. State the effect, if any, on the value of K_p of adding more PCl_5 at a constant temperature.

ii. State the effect, if any, on the value of K_p of increasing the temperature of the container.

f. In a further experiment, a second sample of PCl_5 is heated to a different temperature.

In the equilibrium mixture produced at this temperature, the partial pressure of PCl_5 is 36.9 kPa and the partial pressure of Cl_2 is 42.6 kPa. Calculate a value for the equilibrium constant, K_p, for this reaction at this temperature and give its units.

AQA January 2007 Unit 4 Question 2

4 ACIDS AND BASES

PRIOR KNOWLEDGE

You should be able to calculate concentrations, moles and volumes of species in a titration. You should be able to carry out a titration experiment.

LEARNING OBJECTIVES

In this chapter you will learn how to describe Brønsted–Lowry acids and bases and define pH. You will also learn how to calculate the pH of acidic and basic solutions and carry out calculations using acid dissociation constants. You will learn about pH curves, titrations and indicators.

(Specification 3.1.12)

Diabetes affects about one person in 20 in the UK. If not controlled, the disease can reduce the pH of the blood, making it more acidic. This can result in a coma or even death. The most common cause of diabetes in young people is a deficiency of the hormone insulin. Medical staff in hospitals need to have an understanding of the chemistry of the metabolic reactions involved in order to treat the disease effectively.

Lack of insulin means that glucose, an energy store, is not provided for muscles. Fat has to be used as an alternative energy source, and its metabolism causes the muscles to tire. When fat is broken down, metabolites can form, including propanone and weak acids such as ethanoic acid and lactic acid. This is called diabetic ketoacidosis and its symptoms include nausea, vomiting, thirst, increased heart rate and decreased blood pressure.

The treatment for diabetes is improving all the time, and now insulin pumps with a slow release mechanism are being used more widely. These have advantages over injections, which give periodic boosts to the insulin level. Also, the way insulin is produced is different and advances in genetic engineering have meant that insulin derived from cattle or pigs has been removed.

4.1 THEORIES OF ACIDS AND BASES

Arrhenius theory of acids and bases

In 1884, the Swedish chemist Arrhenius described an acid as a substance that contains hydrogen and releases hydrogen ions when it dissolves in water.

Hydrogen chloride dissolves in water to produce hydrochloric acid. Hydrochloric acid is a solution of hydrogen ions and chloride ions in water:

$$HCl(g) \rightarrow H^+(aq) + Cl^-(aq)$$

Hydrochloric acid is an example of a **strong acid** – an acid that dissociates (ionises) fully in water. There are no molecules of hydrogen chloride present.

Ethanoic acid dissolves in water to produce a solution of hydrogen ions and ethanoate ions in water. The mixture also contains ethanoic acid molecules. This is often represented using two equations:

$$CH_3COOH(l) + aq \rightarrow CH_3COOH(aq)$$

$$CH_3COOH(aq) \rightleftharpoons CH_3COO^-(aq) + H^+(aq)$$

Ethanoic acid is an example of a **weak acid** – an acid that does not dissociate fully in water. The solution is an equilibrium mixture that contains ethanoic acid molecules, hydrogen ions and ethanoate ions.

Arrhenius's theory also states that a base is a substance that reacts with H^+ to form water. An example of a reaction with an insoluble base is

$$MgO(s) + 2HCl(aq) \rightarrow MgCl_2(aq) + H_2O(l)$$

or, in its ionic form,

$$MgO(s) + 2H^+(aq) \rightarrow Mg^{2+}(aq) + H_2O(l)$$

An example of a reaction with a soluble base is

$$NaOH(aq) + HCl(aq) \rightarrow NaOH(aq) + H_2O(l)$$

or, in its ionic form,

$$OH^-(aq) + H^+(aq) \rightarrow H_2O(l)$$

(sodium hydroxide solution is a 1:1 ratio of sodium ions and hydroxide ions).

A hydrogen ion, H^+, is simply a proton. Chemists realised that this could not exist independently in aqueous solution. Instead, it forms a bond with a water molecule to form a hydronium ion ($H_3O^+(aq)$) (Figure 1). This is represented by the equation in Figure 1.

So, the reactions described previously may be shown as

$$HCl(aq) + H_2O(l) \rightarrow H_3O^+(aq) + Cl^-(aq)$$

$$CH_3COOH(aq) + H_2O(l) \rightleftharpoons H_3O^+(aq) + CH_3COO^-(aq)$$

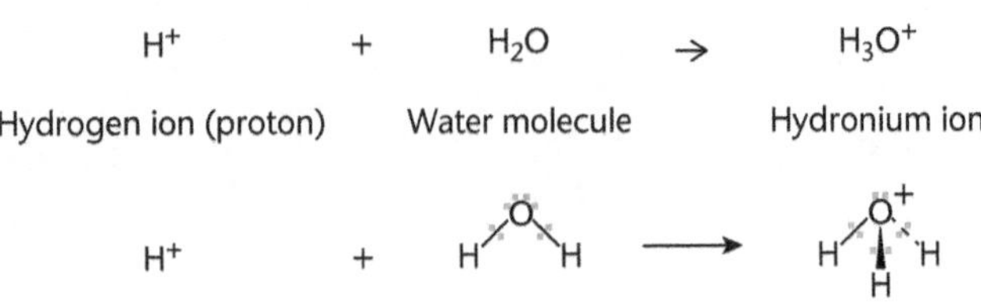

Figure 1 *The proton is bonded through a lone pair on a water molecule to give a pyramidal hydronium ion*

and the general reaction of an acid with an alkali is written

$$H_3O^+(aq) + OH^-(aq) \rightarrow 2H_2O(l)$$

However, when writing equations for the reactions of acids with bases, the less precise H^+ is often used rather than H_3O^+ for simplicity.

The importance of H_3O^+ is that it explains, for example, why solutions of hydrogen chloride in solvents such as methylbenzene that cannot form a bond with H^+ therefore do not have any acidic properties.

Brønsted–Lowry acids and bases

In 1923 the Danish scientist Johannes Brønsted and the British chemist Thomas Lowry adapted the Arrhenius theory of acid–base behaviour to give a wider definition that described the behaviour of acids and bases in both aqueous and non-aqueous reactions. They defined an acid as follows:

An **acid** is a substance that donates protons in a reaction; it is a **proton donor**.

Their theory says that when an acid donates protons, another substance must accept the protons. This substance is a base, and it behaves oppositely to an acid. They defined a base as follows:

A **base** is a substance that accepts protons in a reaction; it is a **proton acceptor**.

So the Brønsted–Lowry definitions apply to a wider range of acid–base reactions, not just those that take place in aqueous solutions.

The reaction between hydrochloric acid and ammonia (Figure 2) is an acid–base reaction which can occur in (a) aqueous solution and (b) the gas phase:

$$\text{(a) } HCl(aq) + NH_3(aq) \rightarrow NH_4^+(aq) + Cl^-(aq)$$

or, ionically,

$$H^+(aq) + NH_3(aq) \rightarrow NH_4^+(aq)$$

$$\text{(b) } HCl(g) + NH_3(g) \rightarrow NH_4^+Cl^-(s)$$

In both (a) and (b), HCl has donated H^+ and NH_3 has accepted H^+:

$$NH_3 + H^+ \rightarrow NH_4^+$$

The Brønsted–Lowry theory also covers reactions in non-polar solvents.

$$HCl + NH_3 \rightarrow NH_4^+ + Cl^-$$

Figure 2 *The Brønsted–Lowry acid–base reaction of hydrochloric acid and ammonia*

Figure 3 *When the stoppers from hydrochloric acid and ammonia bottles are held near each other, white fumes of ammonium chloride are produced*

The aqueous and gaseous reactions are both Brønsted–Lowry acid–base reactions, but only the aqueous reaction is an Arrhenius acid–base reaction. This illustrates the application of the Brønsted–Lowry theory to a wider range of reactions.

You will also meet the Lewis theory of acids and bases in later chapters when looking at situations that do not involve protons at all. Substances that act as an acid or base according to the Lewis theory are defined specifically as a Lewis acid or Lewis base. A substance that is referred to as just an acid or base can be assumed to be an acid or base according to the Brønsted–Lowry definitions.

Ionic equations

In aqueous solution, an acid and a base react to form a salt and water only. This is a **neutralisation reaction**. The base accepts one or more hydrogen ions (protons) from the acid:

$$HCl(aq) + NaOH(aq) \rightarrow NaCl(aq) + H_2O(l)$$

This equation does not show what happens to the ions in the solution. When we rewrite it showing all the ions present, some ions appear on both sides of the equation. The above is a reaction of a strong acid with a strong base, so all the reactant species are fully dissociated:

$$H^+(aq) + Cl^-(aq) + Na^+(aq) + OH^-(aq) \rightarrow Na^+(aq) + Cl^-(aq) + H_2O(l)$$

Because sodium ions and chloride ions appear on both sides of the equation, we can say that the sodium ions and chloride ions do not take part in the reaction. They are **spectator ions**. Omitting them allows us to write a simplified equation, the **ionic equation**, for the neutralisation reaction:

$$H^+(aq) + OH^-(aq) \rightarrow H_2O(l)$$

Other strong acids and strong bases (Table 1) react similarly, and they can all be represented by the ionic equation for water.

Strong acids	Strong bases
Hydrochloric acid, HCl	Sodium hydroxide, NaOH
Sulfuric acid, H_2SO_4	Potassium hydroxide, KOH
Nitric acid, HNO_3	

Table 1 *Strong acids and strong bases*

QUESTIONS

1. Write full equations and ionic equations for the reactions between:
   a. hydrochloric acid and potassium hydroxide solution
   b. sulfuric acid and sodium hydroxide solution.
2. a. Explain why methane does not act as a hydrogen ion (proton) donor, but methanoic acid, HCOOH, does.
   b. Write an equation to show how methanoic acid ionises in water.

3. Identify the acids and bases in the following reactions:
   a. $CuO(s) + H_2SO_4(aq) \rightarrow CuSO_4(aq) + H_2O(l)$
   b. $NH_4^+(aq) + OH^-(aq) \rightarrow NH_3(aq) + H_2O(l)$
   c. $CH_3COO^-(aq) + H_3O^+(aq) \rightarrow CH_3COOH(aq) + H_2O(l)$.

KEY IDEAS

- The Brønsted–Lowry theory is used to provide the definitions of acids and bases.
- An acid is a substance that donates protons in a reaction.
- A base is a substance that accepts protons in a reaction.

4.2 DISSOCIATION AND pH

Strong and weak acids

An acid dissociates in water to form hydrogen ions (or, more correctly, hydronium ions) and negative ions. A dynamic equilibrium is established between the nondissociated acid molecules and these ions.

For an acid with one ionisable hydrogen,

$$HA(aq) \rightleftharpoons H^+(aq) + A^-(aq)$$

The negative ion, $A^-(aq)$, acts as a base because it recombines with the hydrogen ion, $H^+(aq)$, to re-form the acid molecule, $HA(aq)$. The negative ion is called the conjugate base of the acid.

Similarly, when a base such as $NH_3(g)$ reacts with $H^+(aq)$ to form $NH_4^+(aq)$, the positive ion that forms is referred to as the conjugate acid.

Some examples are shown in Table 2. Note that in the last example, the right-hand side shows that the same species can act both as an acid and as a base. Pure water will always contain some hydrogen ions and hydroxide ions: it is amphoteric, and can be described as self-protonating.

In all acid dissociation reactions, an equilibrium is established between the species involved. Acids that dissociate completely in solution are known as strong acids. Those that only partially dissociate are known as weak acids.

Do not confuse 'strong' and 'weak' with 'concentrated' and 'dilute'. When describing an acid, 'strong' and 'weak' refer to the extent of dissociation (or ionisation) of molecules at equilibrium. 'Concentrated' and 'dilute' refer to the amount of acid in solution.

$$\text{Hydrochloric acid: } HCl(g) \rightarrow H^+(aq) + Cl^-(aq)$$

$CH_3COOH(l)$ ethanoic acid donates proton	+	$OH^-(aq)$ base accepts proton	$\rightleftharpoons$	$CH_3COO^-(aq)$ ethanoate ion: conjugate base accepts proton	+	$H_2O(l)$ conjugate acid donates proton
$HCl(g)$ acid donates proton	+	$NH_3(g)$ base accepts proton	$\rightleftharpoons$	NH_4^+ conjugate acid donates proton	+	$Cl^-(s)$ conjugate base accepts proton
$HCl(g)$ acid donates proton	+	$H_2O(l)$ base accepts proton	$\rightleftharpoons$	$H_3O^+(aq)$ conjugate acid donates proton	+	$Cl^-(aq)$ conjugate base accepts proton
$H_3O^+(aq)$ acid donates proton	+	$CO_3^{2-}(aq)$ base accepts proton	$\rightleftharpoons$	$HCO_3^-(aq)$ conjugate acid donates proton	+	$H_2O(l)$ conjugate base accepts proton
$H_3O^+(aq)$ acid donates proton	+	$NH_3(aq)$ base accepts proton	$\rightleftharpoons$	$NH_4^+(aq)$ conjugate acid donates proton	+	$H_2O(l)$ conjugate base accepts proton
$H_3O^+(aq)$ acid donates proton	+	$OH^-(aq)$ base accepts proton	$\rightleftharpoons$	$H_2O(l)$ conjugate acid donates proton	+	$H_2O(l)$ conjugate base accepts proton

Table 2 *Examples of acid dissociation reactions*

In aqueous solution, HCl molecules dissociate into hydrogen ions, H^+, and chloride ions, Cl^-. The equilibrium lies so far to the right that all HCl molecules are ionised. It is said to be a strong acid.

Ethanoic acid: $CH_3COOH(aq) \rightleftharpoons CH_3COO^-(aq) + H^+(aq)$

In contrast, at the same concentration only a small proportion of CH_3COOH molecules dissociate. The equilibrium lies well to the left and, therefore, ethanoic acid is a weak acid. Most acids are weak acids. When these dissociate and an equilibrium is set up, significant amounts of all the molecules and ions are present.

Hydrogen ion concentration

We could use the hydrogen ion concentration as a measure of acidity, but when the concentration of $H^+(aq)$ is very small, the numbers can be cumbersome to work with. So instead scientists use a log scale, which makes the numbers easier to handle. This is the **pH scale**.

The pH of a solution is $-\log_{10}$ of the molar hydrogen ion concentration in that solution:

$$pH = -\log_{10}[H^+]$$

Because pH values are logarithms, they have no units.

Calculating pH of strong acids from concentrations

Strong acids dissociate completely. If we know their concentrations we simply use

$$pH = -\log_{10}[H^+]$$

where, for a strong acid, $[H^+]$ is equal to the concentration of the acid.

pH indicators (Figure 4) may be used to obtain an approximate value for the pH of a solution. A more accurate and precise measure may be obtained using a pH meter.

Moving up or down the pH scale by one unit means that the hydrogen ion concentration changes by a factor of 10 (Table 3).

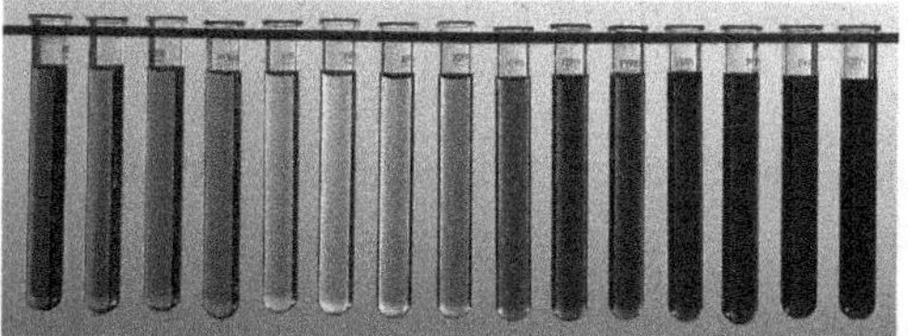

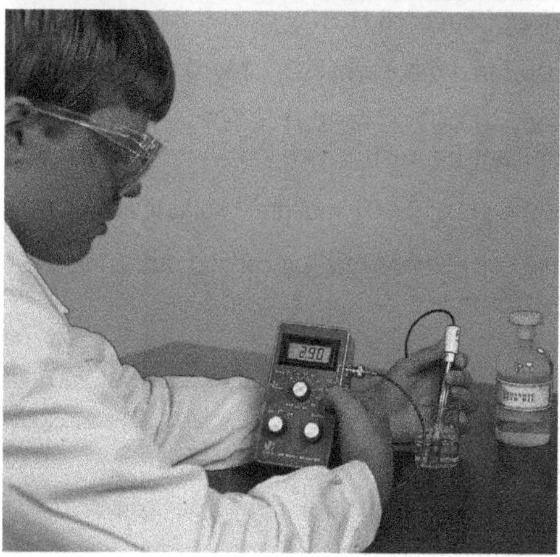

Figure 4 The changing colour of chemical indicators gives a rough measure of the pH of a solution. A more accurate and precise value can be obtained using a pH meter.

$[H^+]$/mol dm^{-3}	pH
10^{-4}	4
10^{-5}	5
10^{-6}	6
10^{-7}	7
10^{-8}	8
10^{-9}	9

Table 3 Comparison of $[H^+]$ values with corresponding pH values. Note that the pH is the power to which 10 is raised to give $[H^+]$, and the sign is changed.

Worked example 1

(a) Calculate the pH of a solution of 0.100 mol dm^{-3} hydrochloric acid.

Since hydrochloric acid is a strong acid,

$[H^+] = 0.100$ mol dm^{-3} and $[Cl^-] = 0.100$ mol dm^{-3}

$pH = -\log_{10} 0.1 = -(-1) = 1$

Therefore, the pH of 0.100 mol dm^{-3} hydrochloric acid is 1.

(b) Calculate the pH of a solution of 0.001 mol dm^{-3} hydrochloric acid.

Since hydrochloric acid is a strong acid,

$[H^+] = 0.001$ mol dm^{-3} and $[Cl^-] = 0.001$ mol dm^{-3}

$pH = -\log_{10} 0.001 = -(-3) = 3$

Therefore, the pH of 0.001 mol dm^{-3} hydrochloric acid is 3.

(c) Calculate the pH of a solution of 0.015 mol dm^{-3} hydrochloric acid.

Since hydrochloric acid is a strong acid,

$[H^+] = 0.015$ mol dm^{-3} and $[Cl^-] = 0.015$ mol dm^{-3}

$pH = -\log_{10} 0.015 = -(-1.82) = 1.82$
(to 2 significant figures)

Therefore, the pH of 0.015 mol dm^{-3} hydrochloric acid is 1.8.

(d) Calculate the pH of a solution of 0.001 mol dm^{-3} sulfuric acid.

Since sulfuric acid is a strong acid and 2 moles of H^+ are produced from each H_2SO_4,

$[H^+]$ = 0.002 mol dm^{-3} and $[SO_4^{2-}]$ = 0.001 mol dm^{-3}

pH = $-\log_{10}$ 0.002 = −(−2.7) = 2.7
(to 2 significant figures)

Therefore, the pH of 0.001 mol dm^{-3} sulfuric acid is 2.7.

The reverse calculations may be carried out using the rearranged formula

$$[H^+] = 10^{-pH}$$

Worked example 2

(a) Calculate the concentration of hydrochloric acid with pH = 2.

$$[H^+] = 10^{-pH}$$
$$= 10^{-2} = 0.01 \text{ mol dm}^{-3}$$

Therefore, the concentration of a solution of hydrochloric acid with pH = 2 is 0.01 mol dm^{-3}.

(b) Calculate the concentration of sulfuric acid with pH = 2.

$$[H^+] = 10^{-pH}$$
$$= 10^{-2} = 0.01 \text{ mol dm}^{-3}$$

But 2 moles of H^+ are produced from each H_2SO_4.

Therefore, the concentration of sulfuric acid with pH = 2 is 0.01/2 = 0.005 mol dm^{-3}.

QUESTIONS

4. Calculate the pH of:
   a. 0.2 mol dm^{-3} nitric acid (remember – nitric acid is a strong acid and is fully ionised in aqueous solution)
   b. a solution with $[H^+]$ = 1.2 × 10^{-2} mol dm^{-3}
   c. a solution with $[H^+]$ = 6.7 × 10^{-5} mol dm^{-3}.
5. What is the pH of a 2.0 mol dm^{-3} solution of hydrochloric acid?

KEY IDEAS

- Strong acids dissociate completely in water.
- Weak acids dissociate partially in water.
- pH = $-\log_{10}[H^+]$.
- For a strong acid $[H^+]$ = concentration of acid.

4.3 ACID DISSOCIATION CONSTANTS

Figure 5 *The vinegar commonly put on chips is a dilute solution of ethanoic acid in water. Some vinegars are colourless. Others are brown owing to colouring agents such as caramel.*

The strength of a weak acid is determined by the position of the equilibrium. If the equilibrium lies to the left, the acid is weak (less dissociated); the further to the right the equilibrium lies, the stronger the acid is (more dissociated).

Remember: a strong acid is one that fully dissociates in water.

As with other equilibria, the dissociation of weak acids and, therefore, their strength can be described using equilibrium constants. These are called acid dissociation constants, K_a.

Dissociation constants are calculated in a similar way to equilibrium constants for reversible reactions, with products (right-hand side of equation) divided by reactants (left-hand side).

Consider this equilibrium between the undissociated acid and ethanoate ions in aqueous solution:

$CH_3COOH(aq) + H_2O(l) \rightleftharpoons CH_3COO^-(aq) + H_3O^+(aq)$

ethanoic acid ethanoate ion

The extent of dissociation is given by the equilibrium constant, K_c, for the process:

$$K_c = \frac{[CH_3COO^-(aq)][H_3O^+(aq)]}{[CH_3COOH(aq)][H_2O(l)]}$$

The units for concentrations cancel out, so K_c has no units.

Since water is in a vast excess we make the assumption that its concentration remains constant. This allows us to give an expression for K_a:

$$K_a = \frac{[CH_3COO^-(aq)][H_3O^+(aq)]}{[CH_3COOH(aq)]}$$

For the units for K_a, we insert the units for the terms into the expression for the dissociation constant. Where the acid releases one hydrogen ion only, the units are

$$\frac{mol\,dm^{-3} \times mol\,dm^{-3}}{mol\,dm^{-3}} = mol\,dm^{-3}$$

We can also simplify the appearance of the expression to

$$K_a = \frac{[CH_3COO^-][H^+]}{[CH_3COOH]}$$

For ethanoic acid, a weak acid, K_a is 1.76×10^{-5} mol dm^{-3}.

We can now give a general expression for the dissociation constant K_a of any weak acid, of general formula HA:

$$HA(aq) \rightleftharpoons H^+(aq) + A^-(aq)$$

$$K_a = \frac{[H^+][A^-]}{[HA]}$$

where all concentrations are those at equilibrium and the units are mol dm^{-3}.

QUESTIONS

6. Write an expression for the acid dissociation constant of butanoic acid, $CH_3(CH_2)_2COOH$.

For every H^+ produced on dissociation of HA, one A^- is also produced. In other words, in the equilibrium mixture,

$$[H^+] = [A^-]$$

This means we can rewrite the expression for K_a as

$$K_a = \frac{[H^+]^2}{[HA]}$$

The less an acid dissociates, the smaller the value, while the stronger the acid, the higher is the value of its dissociation constant (Table 4).

Acid	K_a/mol dm^{-3}
HF	5.6×10^{-4}
HNO_2	4.7×10^{-4}
HCOOH	1.6×10^{-4}
C_6H_5COOH	6.5×10^{-5}
CH_3COOH	1.7×10^{-5}
C_2H_5COOH	1.3×10^{-5}
HClO	3.7×10^{-8}
HCN	4.9×10^{-10}

Table 4 *Dissociation constants of some common acids*

The values of the acid dissociation constant can have a very large range and it can be helpful to use a logarithmic scale for K_a in the same way as for $[H^+]$:

$$pK_a = -\log_{10} K_a$$

This can be rearranged so that K_a can be calculated from a pK_a value (this is similar to calculating $[H^+]$ from pH):

$$K_a = 10^{-pKa}$$

The smaller the value of K_a, the greater the value of pK_a and the weaker the acid.

Worked examples

(a) The acid dissociation constant of ethanoic acid is 1.7×10^{-5} mol dm^{-3}. Calculate its pK_a.

$pK_a = -\log_{10} K_a = -\log_{10}(1.7 \times 10^{-5}) = -(-4.8) = 4.8$

Therefore, the pK_a of ethanoic acid is 4.8.

(b) The acid dissociation constant of hydrogen cyanide solution (sometimes called prussic acid) is 4.9×10^{-5} mol dm^{-3}. Calculate its pK_a.

$pK_a = -\log_{10} K_a = -\log_{10}(4.9 \times 10^{-5}) = -(-9.3) = 9.3$

Therefore, the pK_a of hydrogen cyanide solution is 9.3.

(c) The pK_a of hydrofluoric acid is 3.25. Calculate its acid dissociation constant.

$K_a = 10^{-pKa} = 10^{-3.25} = 5.62 \times 10^{-4}$ mol dm^{-3}

Therefore, the acid dissociation constant of hydrofluoric acid is 5.62×10^{-4} mol dm^{-3}.

Calculating pH from K_a values for weak acids

We can calculate the pH of a solution of a weak acid from the following information:

- $HA(aq) \rightleftharpoons H^+(aq) + A^-(aq)$
- $[H^+] = [A^-]$
- $K_a = \frac{[H^+][A^-]}{[HA]} = \frac{[H^+]^2}{[HA]}$
- the concentration of the weak acid
- the value of its dissociation constant.

Worked example

Lactic acid forms in muscle cells if insufficient oxygen reaches the muscles during exercise:

$CH_3CH(OH)COOH(aq) \rightleftharpoons H^+(aq) + CH_3CH(OH)COO^-(aq)$

The concentration of lactic acid is typically 0.01 mol dm^{-3} and its dissociation constant, K_a, is 1.288×10^{-4} mol dm^{-3}.

$$K_a = \frac{[H^+][CH_3CH(OH)COO^-]}{[CH_3CH(OH)COOH]}$$

Rearranging this equation gives

$[H^+]^2 = [CH_3CH(OH)COOH(aq)] \times K_a$

Substituting the values given above,

$[H^+]^2 = 0.01 \times 1.288 \times 10^{-4}$
$= 1.288 \times 10^{-5}$ mol^2 dm^{-6}

$[H^+] = \sqrt{(1.288 \times 10^{-5})} = 3.589 \times 10^{-3}$ mol dm^{-3}

The pH of the solution can be found using

$pH = -\log_{10}[H^+]$
$= -\log_{10}(3.589 \times 10^{-3}) = 2.44$

QUESTIONS

7. a. A solution has a pH of 5.49. What is the value of $[H^+]$?
   b. What is the hydrogen ion concentration in a solution of pH 2.75?
8. Calculate the pH of 0.01 mol dm^{-3} propanoic acid. The acid dissociation constant of propanoic acid is 1.34×10^{-5} mol dm^{-3}.
9. Calculate the pH of a 0.150 mol dm^{-3} benzenecarboxylic acid solution (pK_a for benzenecarboxylic acid is 4.20).
10. Calculate the concentration of a solution of pentanoic acid with pH 3.56 (pK_a for pentanoic acid is 4.86).

So far, we have looked at monoprotic acids, acids that have just one ionisable hydrogen. However, many acids can release more than one H^+ ion.

Sulfuric (VI) acid, H_2SO_4, is an example of a diprotic acid. It is a strong acid that dissociates completely in water.

Sulfurous acid (H_2SO_3, also called sulfuric(IV) acid) is a weak diprotic acid. It only partially dissociates in water. Two equilibria are established in solution, and each has an equilibrium constant:

$H_2SO_3(aq) + H_2O(l) \rightleftharpoons HSO_3^-(aq) + H_3O^+(aq)$
$K_{a1} = 1.5 \times 10^{-2}$ mol dm^{-3}

$HSO_3^-(aq) + H_2O(l) \rightleftharpoons SO_3^{2-}(aq) + H_3O^+(aq)$
$K_{a2} = 6.2 \times 10^{-8}$ mol dm^{-3}

KEY IDEAS

- The strength of an acid is defined in terms of its acid dissociation constant.
- A weak acid dissociates only slightly in water, and has a small dissociation constant.
- A strong acid dissociates fully in water, and has a large dissociation constant.

ASSIGNMENT 1: LACTIC ACID IN THE BLOOD

(PS 1.1, 3.2; MS 0.0, 0.1)

Figure A1 *High levels of lactic acid in the blood can cause painful cramps*

Lactic acid can reach high levels in healthy people, especially after strenuous exercise. This results in painful cramps. Lactic acid can also reach high levels in some diabetic patients.

Where does the lactic acid come from?

We store energy in our bodies in the form of glucose. If there is sufficient oxygen available, aerobic respiration takes place, producing carbon dioxide and water and releasing energy. Aerobic respiration is a series of enzyme-controlled reactions that release the energy that was stored in carbohydrates and lipids during photosynthesis and make it available to living organisms. For example, the oxidation of glucose may be summarised by the equation

$$C_6H_{12}O_6 + 6O_2 \rightarrow 6CO_2 + 6H_2O$$

If there is insufficient oxygen, for example when somebody has been exercising very hard, anaerobic respiration happens. Again this is a complex series of chemical reactions, the first few of which are the same as in aerobic respiration. However, without oxygen, the later reactions are different and result in the formation of lactic acid. The anaerobic respiration of glucose may be summarised by the overall equation

$$C_6H_{12}O_6 + 6O_2 \rightarrow 2C_3H_6O_3$$

Energy is released. Remember, however, that this equation summarises a series of enzyme-controlled chemical reactions.

Questions

A1. The molecular formula of lactic acid is $C_3H_6O_3$. Its structural formula is $CH_3CH(OH)COOH$ and its displayed formula is

```
    H   H
    |   |      O
H — C — C — C //
    |   |      \
    H   OH      OH
```

Lactic acid is a weak acid.

Write an equation to represent the chemical equilibrium when lactic acid is dissolved in water.

A2. Write a general ionic equation for the reaction between an aqueous solution of lactic acid and an alkali.

A3. The pK_a of lactic acid is 3.86. What is its acid dissociation constant, K_a? (Remember to give the correct units.)

A4. Typically, normal levels of lactic acid in blood are:

venous blood: 0.5–2.2 mmol dm^{-3}

arterial blood: 0.5–1.6 mmol dm^{-3}

(1 mmol = 0.001 mol = 1×10^{-3} mol)

Calculate the pH range of aqueous solutions of lactic acid at the concentrations found in blood.

A5. The human body controls blood pH and keeps it within the range 7.35–7.45.

a. How do your calculated pH values for aqueous lactic acid compare with the pH of blood?

b. Return to this assignment when you have learned about buffers and explain the difference.

4.4 THE IONIC PRODUCT OF WATER

Water dissociates, but only to a very small extent:

$$H_2O(l) \rightleftharpoons H^+(aq) + OH^-(aq)$$

The equilibrium constant, K_c, is

$$K_c = \frac{[H^+][OH^-]}{[H_2O]}$$

Since undissociated water molecules are present in vastly greater numbers than the ions, we can assume that $[H_2O]$ is a constant (just as we did for calculations of K_a).

This gives us the expression for the ionic product of water, K_w:

$$K_w = [H^+][OH^-]$$

At 298 K, K_w is 10^{-14} mol^2 dm^{-6}.

We can calculate the pH of pure water, using the fact that it contains equal numbers of hydrogen ions and hydroxide ions:

$$[H^+] = [OH^-]$$

At 298 K, from K_w,

$$K_w = [H^+][OH^-] = [H^+]^2 = 10^{-14}\ \text{mol}^2\ \text{dm}^{-6}$$

$$[H^+] = 10^{-7}\ \text{mol dm}^{-6}$$

(To get the square root of a power, divide the power by 2.)

$$\text{pH} = -\log_{10}[H^+]$$

$$= -\log_{10} 10^{-7} = 7$$

The pH of pure water is 7 at 298 K, but changes when the temperature changes (Table 5). This is because the ionisation of water is an endothermic process:

$$H_2O \rightarrow H^+ + OH^- \rightarrow \Delta H \text{ is positive}$$

Temperature/°C	$-\log_{10} K_w$	K_w/mol dm^{-3}	$[H^+]$	pH
0	14.94	1.15×10^{-16}	3.39×10^{-8}	7.47
20	14.17	6.76×10^{-16}	8.22×10^{-8}	7.09
25	14.00	1.00×10^{-14}	1.00×10^{-7}	7.00
30	13.83	1.48×10^{-14}	1.22×10^{-7}	6.91
40	13.54	2.88×10^{-14}	1.70×10^{-7}	6.77
50	13.26	5.50×10^{-14}	2.35×10^{-7}	6.63
60	13.02	9.55×10^{-14}	3.09×10^{-7}	6.51

Table 5 *The pH of pure water at different temperatures*

When the temperature is changed, the position of the equilibrium shifts to oppose the change (Le Chatelier's principle). This changes the values of $[H^+]$ and $[OH^-]$ and therefore the value of K_w. The pH of water is altered and is not exactly 7 at different temperatures. Despite this, the solution is still neutral because the concentration of hydroxide ions equals the concentration of hydrogen ions.

KEY IDEAS

- $K_w = [H^+][OH^-]$
- For pure water, $[H^+] = [OH^-]$ and therefore $K_w = [H^+]^2$.

QUESTIONS

11. Define a 'neutral solution'.

12. Use Le Chatelier's principle to explain why:

a. the concentration of hydrogen ions increases when the temperature increases

b. the pH decreases when the temperature increases.

4.5 pH OF STRONG BASES

When a strong base is dissolved in water it produces hydroxide ions. For example,

$$NaOH(s) + aq \rightarrow Na^+(aq) + OH^-(aq)$$

To calculate the pH of an alkaline solution we need to:

Step 1. Calculate the concentration of hydroxide ions, OH^-.

Step 2. Use the ionic product of water, K_w, to calculate the concentration of hydrogen ions, H^+.

Step 3. Calculate the pH from the hydrogen ion concentration.

Worked example

Calculate the pH of a 0.01 mol dm^{-3} sodium hydroxide solution.

Sodium hydroxide dissociates completely.

Each mole of NaOH produces 1 mole of OH^-.

Therefore, in 0.01 mol dm^{-3} sodium hydroxide solution the concentration of OH^- is 0.01 mol dm^{-3}.

$$[H^+][OH^-] = 10^{-14}$$

$[OH^-] = 10^{-2}$ mol dm^{-3} (putting it in standard form)

Therefore,

$$\left[H^+\right] = \frac{10^{-14}}{\left[OH^-\right]} = \frac{10^{-14}}{10^{-2}} = 10^{-12}$$

$$pH = -\log_{10}[H^+] = -\log_{10} 10^{-12} = -(-12) = 12$$

So, the pH of 0.01 mol dm^{-3} sodium hydroxide solution is 12.

QUESTIONS

13. Calculate the pH of the following solutions:
    a. 0.15 mol dm^{-3} KOH
    b. 0.05 mol dm^{-3} NaOH
    c. 0.20 mol dm^{-3} $Ba(OH)_2$.

14. Calculate the concentrations of the following basic solutions:
    a. NaOH with pH 14.30
    b. KOH with pH 13.70
    c. $Ba(OH)_2$ with pH 12.50.

4.6 ACID–BASE TITRATIONS

In a typical titration, an alkaline solution is gradually added to an acid solution (or an acid to an alkali) of known volume or concentration containing an indicator.

As the alkali is added to the acid (or the acid to the alkali), the pH changes. A change in indicator colour signals the end point of the titration and corresponds to the mixing of the stoichiometric amounts shown in the equation for the reaction. Changes in pH at points before and after the end point can be measured using a pH meter.

If a base is added to an acid, the pH rises as the acid is neutralised. However, the pH change is not directly proportional to the amount of alkali added. This is seen clearly when a graph of measured pH against quantity of solution added is plotted. This produces a plot known as a pH curve.

REQUIRED PRACTICAL: APPARATUS AND TECHNIQUES

(AT a, AT c, AT d, AT k)

pH changes for reactions of a weak acid with a strong base and a strong acid with a weak base

This practical gives you the opportunity to show that you can

- use appropriate apparatus to record volume of liquids
- use laboratory apparatus for a titration, using burette and pipette
- use acid–base indicators in titrations of weak/strong acids with weak/strong alkalis
- safely and carefully handle solids and liquids, including corrosive, irritant, flammable and toxic substances. As a strong base is being used it will be necessary to wear eye protection to carry out this titration.

You may find it useful to read through the required practical 'Carry out a simple acid–base titration' in *Chapter 2 of the Year 1 Student Book*.

Apparatus

To investigate the changes in pH that happen when a weak acid reacts with a strong base or a strong acid reacts with a weak base, you need to be able to measure volumes of liquids accurately and to measure the pH of a solution. The apparatus needed (Figure P1) is:

- a pipette to transfer an accurately measured volume of liquid
- a burette to measure accurately any volume within its capacity
- a pH meter to measure pH
- a magnetic or mechanical stirrer.

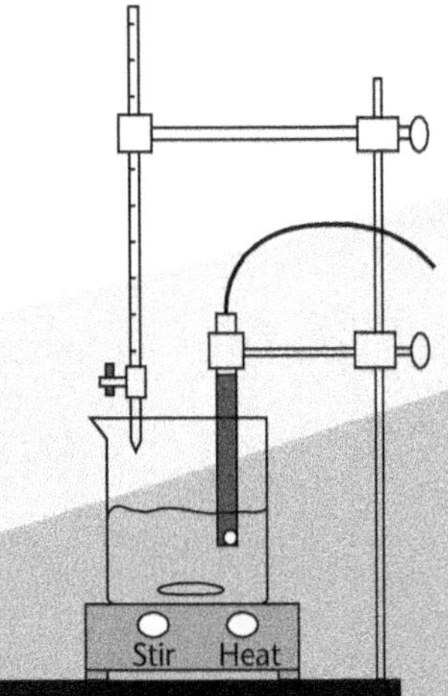

Figure P1 *Apparatus for carrying out a pH titration*

Technique

The technique used to monitor pH changes here is a pH titration. Unlike the case in other titrations, the pH is measured after the addition of a known amount of acid to a base or a known amount of base to an acid.

The technique is illustrated here by the reaction of a strong base with a weak acid (where the concentrations of both are known).

1. Calibrate (standardise) the pH meter using solutions of known pH (the meters usually come with the necessary instructions).
2. Use a pipette to measure the required volume of the weak acid into a beaker (for notes on using a pipette, see *Chapter 2 of the Year 1 Student Book*).
3. Set up a magnetic or mechanical stirrer to mix the contents of the beaker when base is added. If such a stirrer is not available, the solution can be stirred with a stirring rod after each addition, before the pH is measured.
4. Fill the burette with the strong base that will be added to the acid (for notes on using a burette, see *Chapter 2 of the Year 1 Student Book*).
5. Measure the pH of the weak acid.
6. Now add 1.0 cm^3 quantities of the base to the acid, stirring between additions and measuring the pH before adding the next quantity of base. Continue adding until there is no further change in pH.
7. Plot a graph of pH against volume of base added.

QUESTIONS

P1. Explain what it means to calibrate any apparatus or instrument such as a pH meter.

P2. Explain why:

a. a pipette is used to measure the required volume of the weak acid into a beaker

b. a burette is used to measure quantities of the strong base.

P3. Explain how a pH titration could be used to determine the concentration of a weak base.

Shapes of pH curves

When an acid is added to a base or a base is added to an acid, the pH of the solution changes. A graph of pH against the volume of acid or base is called a pH curve.

All the pH curves shown in Figures 6–10 apply to titrations involving a monobasic acid with a monoacidic base, in which only one hydrogen ion is donated. The first solution in each figure caption is in the beaker, and the second is added from the burette.

Strong acid with strong base

Strong-acid–strong-base curves look like the ones in Figures 6 and 7. They are simply mirror images of each other, depending upon whether the solution in the flask is an acid or a base. Strong-acid–strong-base curves are typical of reactions such as

$$HCl(aq) + NaOH(aq) \rightarrow NaCl(aq) + H_2O(l)$$

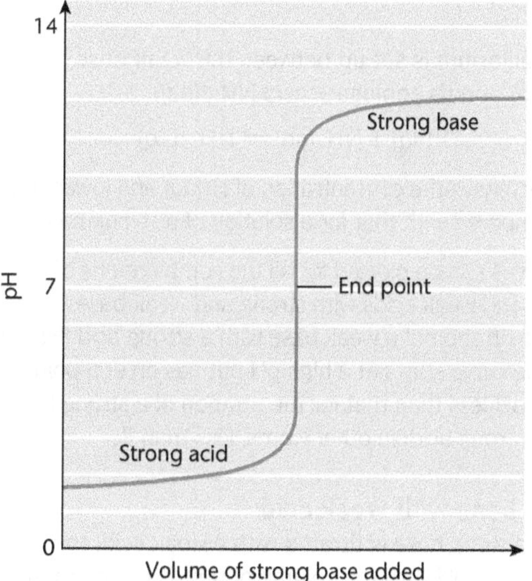

Figure 6 Titration of a strong acid with a strong base

Strong acids and strong bases are fully dissociated. When a strong base is added to a strong acid (Figure 6):

- Initially, when a small volume of $OH^-(aq)$ is added to the acid, the proportion of $H^+(aq)$ removed is quite small compared with the total amount of $H^+(aq)$ present. The increase in pH is very small.
- As more $OH^-(aq)$ is added, the proportion of $H^+(aq)$ being removed each time relative to the total amount increases, so there is a greater increase in pH.
- The change becomes greater when the end point is close.
- The graph then shows a very steep rise, and at the end point the pH is 7 (the pH of pure water at 25 °C).

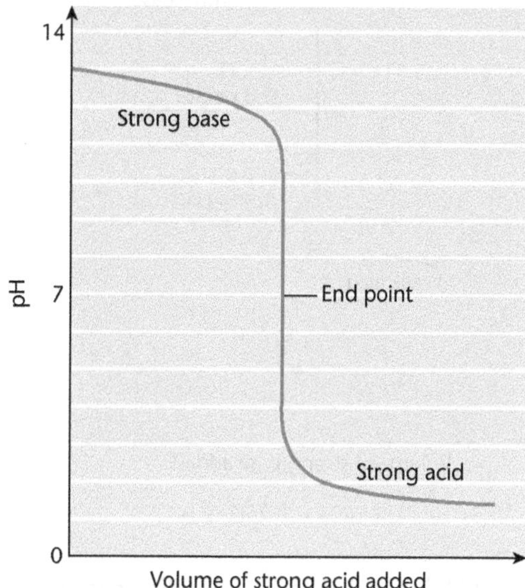

Figure 7 Titration of a strong base with a strong acid

When a strong acid is added to a strong base (Figure 7):

- Initially, when a small volume of $H^+(aq)$ is added to the acid, the proportion of $OH^-(aq)$ removed is quite small compared with the total amount of $OH^-(aq)$ present. The decrease in pH is very small.
- As more $H^+(aq)$ is added, the proportion of $OH^-(aq)$ being removed each time relative to the total amount increases, so there is a greater decrease in pH.
- The change becomes greater when the end point is close.
- The graph then shows a very steep drop, and at the end point the pH is 7 (the pH of pure water).

Weak acid with strong base

The pH curve for the titration of a weak acid with a strong base (Figure 8) differs from the curve in Figure 6.

Consider ethanoic acid reacting with sodium hydroxide:

$$CH_3COOH(aq) + NaOH(aq) \rightarrow Na^+(aq) + CH_3COO^-(aq) + H_2O(l)$$

- The pH curve starts at a higher pH value, since the weak acid is only slightly dissociated, producing a low $[H^+]$ at equilibrium.

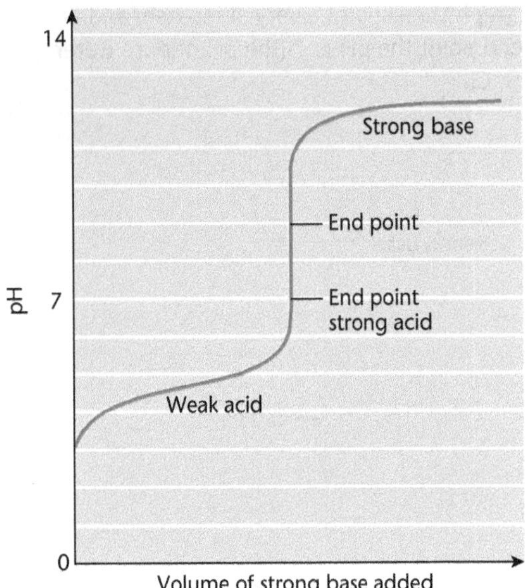

Figure 8 Titration of a weak acid with a strong base

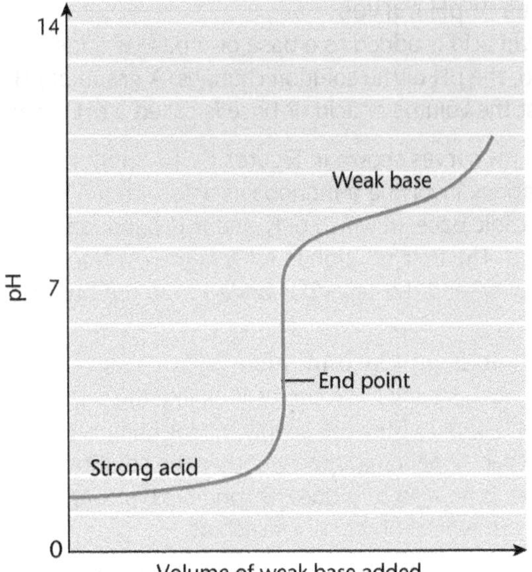

Figure 9 Titration of a strong acid with a weak base

- $CH_3COO^-(aq)$ acts as a weak conjugate base and recombines with $H^+(aq)$ to form $CH_3COOH(aq)$. The greater $[CH_3COO^-(aq)]$ is, the greater is the tendency to do this. This resistance to change in $[H^+]$, despite the increasing acid concentration, is called buffering action and will be discussed later.

In the titration of strong and weak monobasic acids, where the number of moles of acid is the same, the total number of $H^+(aq)$ that react will be the same. This is because although the acid only partially dissociates, as $H^+(aq)$ reacts with $OH^-(aq)$, more acid dissociates (Le Chatelier's principle). Eventually, all the available hydrogens are released to react with a stoichiometrically equivalent amount of base. Therefore, strong and weak acids give the same quantities in a calculation, but the pH at the end point for weak-acid–strong-base titrations has a higher value than for strong-acid–strong-base titrations: it is greater than 7. After the end point, the curve follows the pattern for a strong-acid–strong-base titration.

The pH curve for the titration of a strong base with a weak acid is the mirror image, and the pH at the end point is still greater than 7.

Strong acid with weak base

For a strong-acid–weak-base titration, the curve (Figure 9) follows the pattern for a strong acid initially, but the end point is at a pH of less than 7. The reaction between $HCl(aq)$ and $NH_3(aq)$ shows this:

$$HCl(aq) + NH_3(aq) \rightarrow NH_4^+(aq) + Cl^-(aq)$$

An equilibrium is set up between the weak base $NH_3(aq)$ and its conjugate acid $NH_4^+(aq)$:

$$H^+(aq) + NH_3(aq) \rightleftharpoons NH_4^+(aq)$$

This increases the concentration of $H^+(aq)$ and lowers the pH compared with that for a solution of a strong base.

pH curves can be plotted for all the combinations of strong and weak acids with strong and weak bases. For the titration of a weak base with a strong acid (Figure 10), the curve starts at a high pH but has an end point with a pH less than that for the titration of a strong base with a strong acid: in other words, less than 7.

Weak base with weak acid

When a weak base is titrated with a weak acid, the variation in pH with the volume of titre is more gradual, and it is not possible to detect an accurate end point (Figure 11). A pH meter should therefore be used.

Indicators and acid–base titrations

Acid–base indicators are solutions of compounds that have different colours below and above a specific concentration of $H^+(aq)$.

Indicators are weak acids (usually written HIn) where the dissociated form, In^-, and the undissociated form, HIn, have different colours. There is an equilibrium for this reaction:

$$HIn \rightleftharpoons H^+ + In^-$$

If acid is added or is neutralised by a base during a titration, then $[H^+]$ changes. This affects the indicator

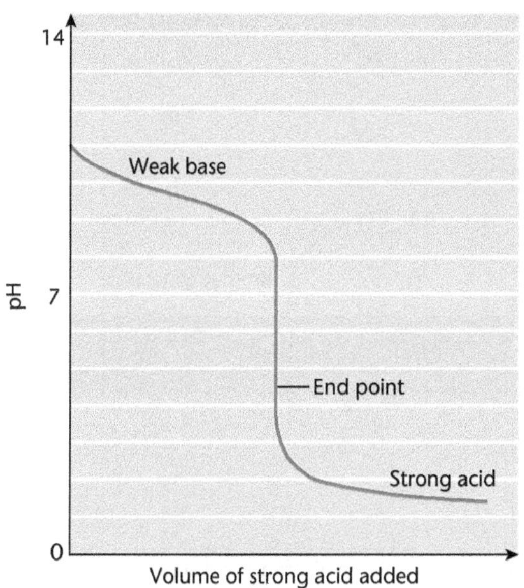

Figure 10 Titration of a weak base with a strong acid

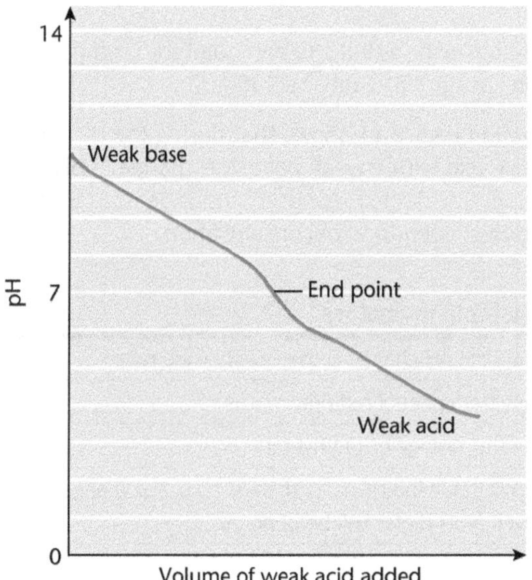

Figure 11 Titration of a weak base with a weak acid

equilibrium. The indicator should change colour over a narrow pH range. The most significant change in $[H^+]$ in a titration is at the end point, so the indicator should change colour when there is this large change in pH. The colour of at least one form of the indicator needs to be fairly intense, so that only two or three drops are needed to give a clearly visible change without significantly affecting $[H^+]$ itself.

When the concentrations of the acid and base forms of the indicator are equal, this is referred to as the end point of the titration.

Choosing indicators for titrations

Different indicators change colour at different pH values (Table 6). This property can be used to select a suitable indicator for a particular titration. A suitable indicator must change colour in the pH range that corresponds to the steep part of the pH curve, where there is a marked change in the pH and the indicator will change colour completely. The best way to do this is to look at the pH curve for the particular titration and choose an indicator where the pH range of activity for that indicator matches the end point of the titration (see Figures 12 and 13).

For the titration of a strong acid with a strong base, any of the indicators in Table 6 would be suitable, because the steep part of the pH curve runs from pH 2 to pH 12 and all the indicators fall in this range.

For a weak acid being titrated with a strong base, the pH at the end point is 8.8. This applies, for example, for a titration of 0.1 mol dm^{-3} ethanoic acid with 0.1 mol dm^{-3} sodium hydroxide. An indicator such as methyl orange changes colour in the pH range 2.9–4.0 and would not be suitable since it would change colour before the end point was reached. The most suitable indicator in the list is phenolphthalein, which changes colour between pH 8.2 and 10.0.

Indicator	Colour in acid (HIn)	Colour in alkali (In^-)	pH range for colour change
methyl orange	red	yellow	2.9–4.0
methyl red	red	yellow	4.2–6.3
litmus	red	blue	5.0–8.0
bromothymol blue	yellow	blue	6.0–7.6
phenol red	yellow	red	6.6–8.0
thymol blue	yellow	blue	9.1–9.6
phenolphthalein	colourless	purple	8.2–10.0
alizarin yellow	yellow	red	10.1–12.0

Table 6 Colour changes for some indicators

The pH at the end point of the titration of a strong base with a strong acid is 7, so again any indicator would be suitable. For a weak base with a strong acid, for example 0.1 mol dm^{-3} aqueous ammonia with 0.1 mol dm^{-3} hydrochloric acid, the pH at the end point is 5.2, so methyl red (pH range 4.2–6.3) would be the most suitable.

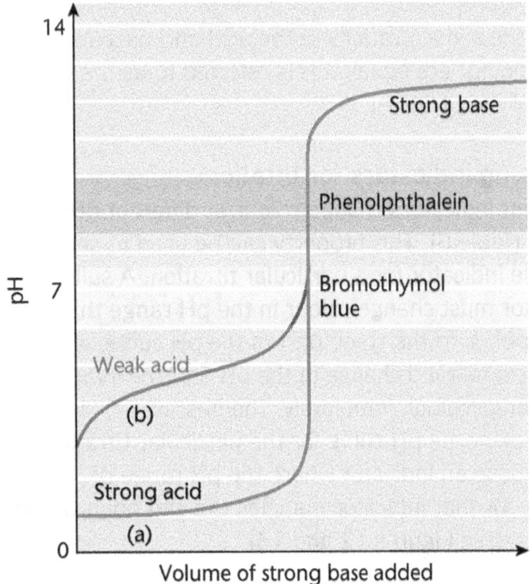

Figure 12 *Titration curves for (a) a strong acid with a strong base and (b) a weak acid with a strong base*

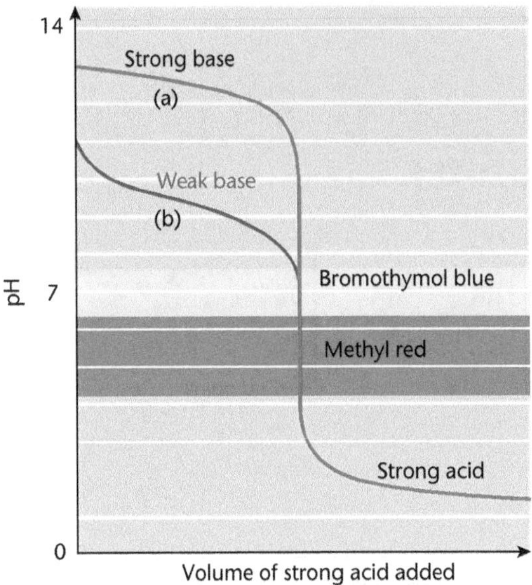

Figure 13 *Titration curves for (a) a strong base with a strong acid and (b) a weak base with a strong acid*

Table 7 shows the pH at the end point for a range of titrations using 1 mol dm^{-3} solutions.

The curve in Figure 11 shows that during the titration of a weak acid with a weak base, the change in pH is so gradual that such a reaction cannot be used in the quantitative estimation of concentration.

Acid	Base	pH range at end point	Suitable indicators
HCl (strong)	NaOH (strong)	3–11	any: the pH change is over a very wide range
CH_3COOH (weak)	NaOH (strong)	7–11	any from phenol red downwards
HCl (strong)	NH_3 (weak)	3–7	methyl orange or methyl red
CH_3COOH (weak)	NH_3 (weak)	no sharp change	no suitable indicator, as there is no sharp change; even a pH meter will be of no use

Table 7 *pH at end point for a range of titrations using 1 mol dm^{-3} solutions*

QUESTIONS

15. a. Choose a suitable indicator for the following titrations (use Tables 6 and 7 to help you):
    i. adding ammonia (a weak base) to nitric acid (a strong acid)
    ii. adding potassium hydroxide (a strong base) to ethanoic acid (a weak acid)
    iii. adding ammonia to ethanoic acid.

    b. Sketch the pH curve for each titration.

4.7 BUFFER SOLUTIONS

A solution that can resist a change in pH when small amounts of acid or base are added is called a buffer.

There are many different buffers, but they all work according to the same principle. Generally, buffers contain either:

- a weak acid and a large amount of a strong-base salt of the acid (an acid buffer), e.g. ethanoic acid with sodium ethanoate, or
- a weak base and a large amount of a strong-acid salt of the base (an alkaline buffer), e.g. ammonia with ammonium chloride.

A mixture of ethanoic acid, CH_3COOH, and ethanoate, CH_3COO^-, has a buffering action. Ethanoic acid partially dissociates in water. Sodium ethanoate, CH_3COONa, dissolves and dissociates completely in water:

$$CH_3COOH(aq) \rightleftharpoons CH_3COO^-(aq) + H^+(aq)$$

$$CH_3COONa(aq) \rightarrow CH_3COO^-(aq) + Na^+(aq)$$

An acid buffer normally contains relatively high concentrations of both the undissociated acid and the acid anion (the conjugate base). The acid dissociation constant is given by

$$K_a = \frac{[CH_3COO^-(aq)][H^+(aq)]}{[CH_3COOH(aq)]}$$

The presence of ethanoate ions pushes the ethanoic acid equilibrium towards undissociated acid:

$$CH_3COOH(aq) \leftleftarrows CH_3COO^-(aq) + H^+(aq)$$

The equilibrium is driven to the left by $CH_3COO^-(aq)$ present in large amounts from $CH_3COONa(aq)$.

- If acid is added to the buffer, the equilibrium adjusts as $H^+(aq)$ combines with some of the large amount of $CH_3COO^-(aq)$ to give more undissociated acid:

  $$CH_3COOH(aq) \leftleftarrows CH_3COO^-(aq) + H^+(aq)$$

  The position of equilibrium shifts to the left.

- If alkali is added to the buffer, the equilibrium adjusts as $OH^-(aq)$ reacts with $H^+(aq)$, neutralising it, while some of the large amount of $CH_3COOH(aq)$ present dissociates to give more $H^+(aq)$:

  $$CH_3COOH(aq) \rightrightarrows CH_3COO^-(aq) + H^+(aq)$$

  The position of equilibrium shifts to the right.

The buffer maintains the equilibrium reaction and the pH remains steady, except in the presence of large quantities of acid or alkali. K_a remains constant throughout.

K_a can be used to show that $[H^+]$ remains fairly constant:

$$K_a = \frac{[CH_3COO^-(aq)][H^+(aq)]}{[CH_3COOH(aq)]}$$

$$[H^+(aq)] = K_a \times \frac{[CH_3COOH(aq)]}{[CH_3COO^-(aq)]}$$

If both $[CH_3COOH(aq)]$ and $[CH_3COO^-(aq)]$ are large, then small changes in these concentrations will not affect the overall ratio significantly, so $[H_3O^+(aq)]$ remains fairly constant.

If equal amounts of salt and acid are present (half-neutralisation) in the buffer, then $[CH_3COO^-(aq)] = [CH_3COOH(aq)]$ and

$$K_a = \frac{[CH_3COO^-(aq)][H^+(aq)]}{[CH_3COOH(aq)]} = [H^+(aq)]$$

(since $[CH_3COO^-(aq)] = [CH_3COOH(aq)]$)

Therefore, for the buffer,

$$K_a = [H^+(aq)]$$

and

$$pK_a = pH$$

QUESTIONS

16. a. Explain how an NH_3/NH_4Cl buffer works.
    b. Calculate the pH of a propanoic acid/sodium propanoate buffer containing 0.2 mol dm^{-3} salt and 0.05 mol dm^{-3} acid, where $K_a = 1.3 \times 10^{-5}$.
17. Calculate the pH of a buffer made by mixing 25.0 cm^3 of 2.0 mol dm^{-3} propanoic acid, $K_a = 1.34 \times 10^{-5}$, with 20.0 cm^3 of 1.5 mol dm^{-3} sodium propanoate.

ASSIGNMENT 2: STORING CARBON DIOXIDE

(PS 1.1, 3.2; MS 0.0, 0.1)

Much of the carbon dioxide we release into the atmosphere from the combustion of fuels is absorbed by dissolving in the oceans. It is thought that as much as 35–50% is absorbed in this way. As the amount of CO_2 in the atmosphere rises, more of the gas reacts with seawater to produce hydrogen carbonate ions and hydrogen ions, increasing the acidity of the surface layer of water.

An equilibrium is set up (see Figure A1). If the amount of CO_2 in the atmosphere increases, more will dissolve:

$$CO_2(g) \rightleftharpoons CO_2(aq)$$

Some CO_2 reacts with water and is removed from the equilibrium. More dissolves to maintain the equilibrium.

The oceans are effective at controlling the pH, as they act as a giant buffer solution. They will release or absorb $H^+(aq)$ as the conditions change. We can regard dissolved carbon dioxide as carbonic acid – a weak acid:

$$CO_2(aq) + H_2O(l) \rightleftharpoons H_2CO_3(aq) \rightleftharpoons H^+(aq) + HCO_3^-(aq)$$

A high concentration of H_2CO_3 is available. HCO_3^- is available in almost limitless supply. Therefore, this reaction acts as a buffer:

$$HCO_3^-(aq) \rightleftharpoons H^+(aq) + CO_3^{2-}(aq)$$

Any removal of H^+ or CO_3^{2-} ions from solution will cause more CO_2 to dissolve (the equilibria are shifted to the right). As a result, through time, many marine organisms have evolved to build protective shells of insoluble calcium carbonate. Hence shells provide another way of mopping up carbon dioxide and keeping the composition of the atmosphere constant:

$$Ca^{2+} + CO_3^{2-} \rightarrow CaCO_3(s)$$

The atmospheric level of carbon dioxide has risen from about 280 ppm in pre-industrial times to about 380 ppm today, and it is still rising. If CO_2 emissions continue as at present, then the pH of the oceans is predicted to drop by approximately 0.5 units by 2100, giving a threefold increase in the concentration of H^+ ions since pre-industrial times. The average pH has dropped from 8.3 to 8.1. Climate change may be veering out of control before we understand the consequences, say scientists studying the world's oceans.

Atmospheric CO_2 has risen well above 2000 ppm several times in the past 300 million years. Ken Caldeira (Figure A3) says this has never pushed the ocean pH below 7.5 because carbonate rocks on the seafloor act as a natural buffer, limiting seawater's acidity. But that process takes 10 000 years or so, and there is not enough time to deal with the more rapid changes caused by human activity.

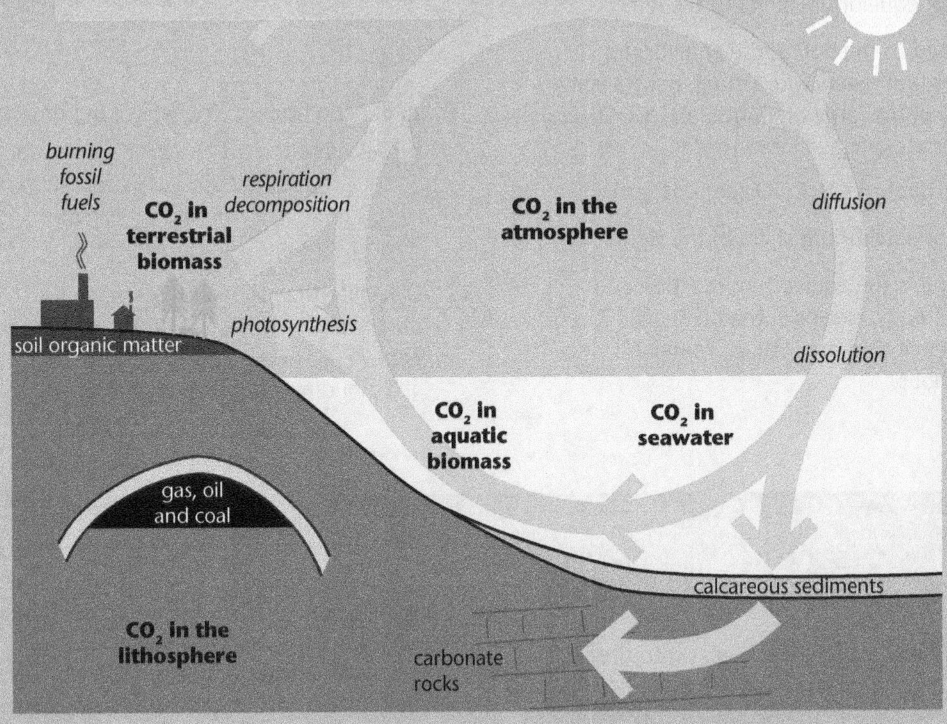

Figure A1 The carbon cycle

Lowering the pH of seawater ultimately results in a decrease in the concentration of CO_3^{2-}. It is not clear yet what such a dramatic change in acidity would do to ocean life. But acidity tends to dissolve carbonate, so the most vulnerable creatures will be those with calcium carbonate shells or exoskeletons, such as corals, molluscs and some algae. Meanwhile, satellite measurements of chlorophyll levels in the open ocean show that primary productivity – the amount of new biomass being produced from carbon dioxide by photosynthesis – has dropped sharply in the past couple of decades. As increasingly large amounts of CO_2 become absorbed in the oceans, then their ability to act as a buffer is lessened.

Figure A2 *Change in the acidity of the oceans will affect sea life*

Figure A3 *'We are changing the chemistry of the ocean and we don't know what it's going to do', says Ken Caldeira, a climate specialist at Lawrence Livermore National Laboratory in California*

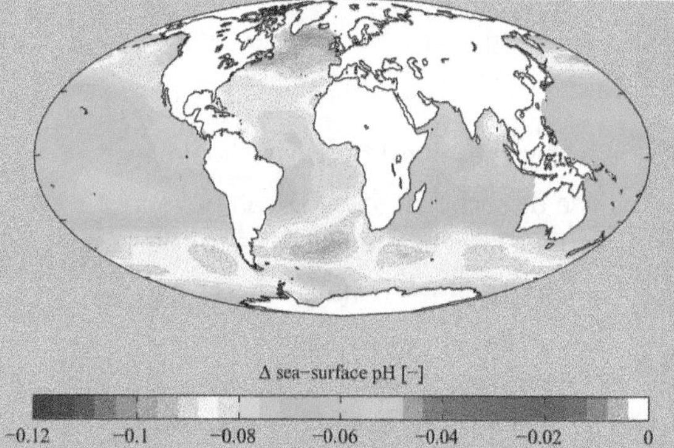

Figure A4 *Change in sea-surface pH caused by anthropogenic CO_2 between the 1700s and the 1990s*

There are other, indirect effects. In the oceans, metals can be in either complexed or free dissolved forms and the equilibrium is pH dependent. Decreasing the pH of the oceans is anticipated to result in an increase in the concentration of free metals, some of which are believed to be toxic. Predicting the impact of this change is highly problematic, though, with the role of trace elements in aquatic biochemical processes still an area of ongoing research.

Clearly, much more research is needed, and the key questions that may need to be addressed include:

- How will CO_2 absorption by the oceans be affected in the future by current absorption and by increased global temperatures?
- Do climate change models need to be addressed with regard to changes in rates of CO_2 absorption?
- What research needs to be done to identify the effects on marine life?

Summary

Increased emissions of carbon dioxide (CO_2) are causing the oceans to become more acidic.

To date, the oceans have absorbed approximately half of the carbon emitted into the environment by human activity.

The ability of the oceans to continue to absorb carbon dioxide is not well understood.

Increasing acidity due to carbon dioxide could have a significant impact on many marine organisms, specifically calcifying organisms and larger aquatic animals. The effects of ocean acidification on these and other organisms are not completely known.

Questions

Stretch and challenge

A1. Prepare a report for a committee, an article or podcast for a science magazine, or a PowerPoint presentation to summarise issues concerning the possible effects of climate change on the oceans.

You can use the article plus your own research to present your arguments. You should explain the underlying chemistry involved.

You should present any arguments for change and further research, and highlight areas of scientific uncertainty.

PRACTICE QUESTIONS

1. Give all values of pH to two decimal places.
   a. The dissociation of water can be represented by the following equilibrium:
      $H_2O(l) \rightleftharpoons H^+(aq) + OH^-(aq)$
      i. Write an expression for the ionic product of water, K_w.
      ii. The pH of a sample of pure water is 6.63 at 50 °C. Calculate the concentration in mol dm^{-3} of H^+ ions in this sample of pure water.
      iii. Deduce the concentration in mol dm^{-3} of OH^- ions in this sample of pure water.
      iv. Calculate the value of K_w at this temperature.
   b. At 25 °C the value of K_w is 1.00×10^{-14} mol^2 dm^{-6}. Calculate the pH of a 0.136 mol dm^{-3} solution of KOH at 25 °C.

   AQA January 2008 Unit 4 Question 1

2. Give all values of pH to two decimal places. The acid dissociation constant, K_a, for propanoic acid has the value 1.35×10^{-5} mol dm^{-3} at 25 °C:

$$K_a = \frac{[H^+][CH_3CH_2COO^-]}{[CH_3CH_2COOH]}$$

   a. Calculate the pH of a 0.169 mol dm^{-3} solution of propanoic acid.
   b. A buffer solution contains 0.250 mol of propanoic acid and 0.190 mol of sodium propanoate in 1 000 cm^3 of solution. A 0.015 mol sample of solid sodium hydroxide is then added to this buffer solution.
      i. Write an equation for the reaction of propanoic acid with sodium hydroxide.
      ii. Calculate the number of moles of propanoic acid and of propanoate ions present in the buffer solution after the addition of the sodium hydroxide.
      iii. Hence, calculate the pH of the buffer solution after the addition of the sodium hydroxide.

   AQA January 2008 Unit 4 Question 2

3. When answering this question, assume that the temperature is 298 K and give all pH values to two decimal places. The acid dissociation constant, K_a, of propanoic acid, CH_3CH_2COOH, has the value 1.35×10^{-5} mol dm^{-3}:

$$K_a = \frac{[H^+][CH_3CH_2COO^-]}{[CH_3CH_2COOH]}$$

   a. Calculate the pH of a 0.550 mol dm^{-3} solution of propanoic acid.
   b. A buffer solution is formed when 10.0 cm^3 of 0.230 mol dm^{-3} aqueous sodium hydroxide is added to 30.0 cm^3 of 0.550 mol dm^{-3} aqueous propanoic acid.
      i. Calculate the number of moles of propanoic acid originally present.
      ii. Calculate the number of moles of sodium hydroxide added.
      iii. Hence, calculate the number of moles of propanoic acid present in the buffer solution.
      iv. Hence, calculate the pH of the buffer solution.

   AQA June 2007 Unit 4 Question 3

4. In this question, give all pH and pK_a values to two decimal places.
   a. Hydrochloric acid is described as a strong Brønsted–Lowry acid.
      i. State what is meant by the term *Brønsted–Lowry acid*.
      ii. State why hydrochloric acid is described as *strong*.
   b. A sample of hydrochloric acid contains 7.05×10^{-3} mol of hydrogen chloride in 50 cm^3 of solution.
      i. Calculate the concentration, in mol dm^{-3}, of this hydrochloric acid.
      ii. Write an expression for the term *pH*.
      iii. Calculate the pH of this hydrochloric acid.
      iv. When water is added to this 50 cm^3 sample of acid the pH increases. Calculate the total volume of the solution when the pH becomes exactly 1.00.

c. The value of the acid dissociation constant, K_a, for the weak acid HX is 6.10×10^{-5} mol dm^{-3} at 25 °C.

i. Write an expression for the acid dissociation constant, K_a, for the acid HX.

ii. Calculate the pH of a 0.255 mol dm^{-3} solution of HX at 25 °C.

d. A given volume of a buffer solution contains 6.85×10^{-3} mol of the weak acid HY and 2.98×10^{-3} mol of the salt NaY. The pH of the buffer solution is 3.78.

i. Calculate the value of pK_a for the acid HY at this temperature.

ii. State and explain the effect on the pH of the buffer solution when a small amount of hydrochloric acid is added.

AQA January 2007 Unit 4 Question 3

5. a. A sample of hydrochloric acid has a pH of 2.34. Write an expression for pH and calculate the concentration of this acid.

b. A 0.150 mol dm^{-3} solution of a weak acid, HX, also has a pH of 2.34.

i. Write an expression for the acid dissociation constant, K_a, for the acid HX.

ii. Calculate the value of K_a for this acid and state its units.

iii. Calculate the value of pK_a for the acid HX. Give your answer to two decimal places.

c. A 30.0 cm^3 sample of a 0.480 mol dm^{-3} solution of potassium hydroxide was partially neutralised by the addition of 18.0 cm^3 of a 0.350 mol dm^{-3} solution of sulfuric acid.

i. Calculate the initial number of moles of potassium hydroxide.

ii. Calculate the number of moles of sulfuric acid added.

iii. Calculate the number of moles of potassium hydroxide remaining in excess in the solution formed.

iv. Calculate the concentration of hydroxide ions in the solution formed.

v. Hence calculate the pH of the solution formed. Give your answer to two decimal places.

AQA June 2006 Unit 4 Question 3

6. Give all pH values to two decimal places.

a. i. Write expressions for the ionic product of water, K_w, and for pH.

ii. At 318 K, the value of K_w is 4.02×10^{-14} mol^2 dm^{-6} and hence the pH of pure water is 6.70. State why pure water is not acidic at 318 K.

iii. Calculate the number of moles of sodium hydroxide in 2.00 cm^3 of 0.500 mol dm^{-3} aqueous sodium hydroxide.

iv. Use the value of K_w given above and your answer to part **a iii** to calculate the pH of the solution formed when 2.00 cm^3 of 0.500 mol dm^{-3} aqueous sodium hydroxide are added to 998 cm^3 of pure water at 318 K.

b. At 298 K, the acid dissociation constant, K_a, for propanoic acid, CH_3CH_2COOH, has the value 1.35×10^{-5} mol dm^{-3}.

i. Write an expression for K_a for propanoic acid.

ii. Calculate the pH of 0.125 mol dm^{-3} aqueous propanoic acid at 298 K.

c. Sodium hydroxide reacts with propanoic acid as shown in the following equation:

$$NaOH + CH_3CH_2COOH \rightarrow CH_3CH_2COONa + H_2O$$

A buffer solution is formed when sodium hydroxide is added to an excess of aqueous propanoic acid.

i. Calculate the number of moles of propanoic acid in 50.0 cm^3 of 0.125 mol dm^{-3} aqueous propanoic acid.

ii. Use your answers to part **a iii** and part **c i** to calculate the number of moles of propanoic acid in the buffer solution formed when 2.00 cm^3 of 0.500 mol dm^{-3} aqueous sodium hydroxide are added to 50.0 cm^3 of 0.125 mol dm^{-3} aqueous propanoic acid.

iii. Hence calculate the pH of this buffer solution at 298 K.

AQA January 2006 Unit 4 Question 2

7. a. Titration curves labelled **A**, **B**, **C** and **D** for combinations of different acids and bases are shown in Figure Q1. All solutions have a concentration of 0.1 mol dm^{-3}.

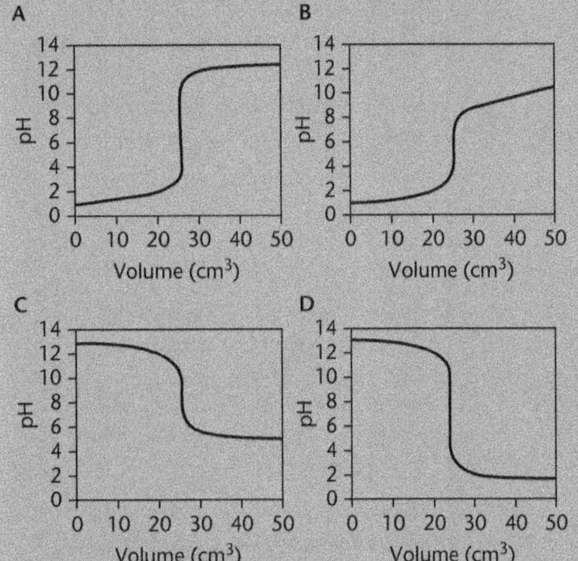

Figure Q1

i. From **A**, **B**, **C** and **D**, select the curve produced by the addition of:

- ammonia to 25 cm^3 of hydrochloric acid
- ethanoic acid to 25 cm^3 of sodium hydroxide
- sodium hydroxide to 25 cm^3 of hydrochloric acid.

ii. A table of acid–base indicators and the pH ranges over which they change colour is shown below. From the table, select an indicator which could be used in the titration which produces curve **A** but not in the titration which produces curve **B**.

Indicator	pH range
Thymol blue	1.2 — 2.8
Bromophenol blue	3.0 — 4.6
Methyl red	4.2 — 6.3
Cresolphthalein	8.2 — 9.8
Thymolphthalein	9.3 — 10.5

b. i. Write an expression for the term *pH*.

ii. A solution of potassium hydroxide has a pH of 11.90 at 25 °C. Calculate the concentration of potassium hydroxide in the solution.

c. The acid dissociation constant, K_a, for propanoic acid has the value of 1.35 × 10^{-5} mol dm^{-3} at 25 °C:

$$K_a = \frac{[H^+][CH_3CH_2COO^-]}{[CH_3CH_2COOH]}$$

In each of the calculations below, give your answer to two decimal places.

i. Calculate the pH of a 0.117 mol dm^{-3} aqueous solution of propanoic acid.

ii. Calculate the pH of a mixture formed by adding 25 cm^3 of 0.117 mol dm^{-3} aqueous solution of sodium propanoate to 25 cm^3 of a 0.117 mol dm^{-3} aqueous solution of propanoic acid.

AQA June 2005 Unit 4 Question 2

8. This question concerns the weak acid, ethanoic acid, for which the acid dissociation constant, K_a, has a value of 1.74 × 10^{-5} mol dm^{-3} at 25 °C:

$$K_a = \frac{[H^+][CH_3COO^-]}{[CH_3COOH]}$$

In each of the calculations below, give your answer to two decimal places.

a. Calculate the pH of a 0.150 mol dm^{-3} solution of ethanoic acid.

b. A buffer solution is prepared by mixing a solution of ethanoic acid with a solution of sodium ethanoate.

i. Explain what is meant by the term *buffer solution*.

ii. Write an equation for the reaction which occurs when a small amount of hydrochloric acid is added to this buffer solution.

c. In a buffer solution, the concentration of ethanoic acid is 0.150 mol dm^{-3} and the concentration of sodium ethanoate is 0.100 mol dm^{-3}.

i. Calculate the pH of this buffer solution.

ii. A 10.0 cm^3 portion of 1.00 mol dm^{-3} hydrochloric acid is added to 1 000 cm^3 of this buffer solution. Calculate the number of moles of ethanoic acid and the number of moles of sodium ethanoate in the solution after addition of the hydrochloric acid. Hence, find the pH of this new solution.

AQA January 2005 Unit 4 Question 8

9. The pH curve shown in Figure Q2 was obtained when a 0.150 mol dm^{-3} solution of sodium hydroxide was added to 25.0 cm^3 of aqueous solution of weak monoprotic acid, HA.

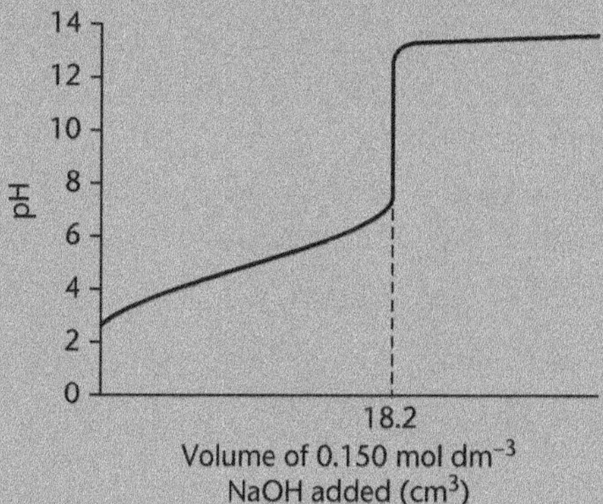

Figure Q2

a. Use the information given to calculate the concentration of the acid.

b. i. Write an expression for the acid dissociation constant, K_a, for HA.

ii. Write an expression for pK_a.

iii. Using your answers to parts **b i** and **b ii**, show that when sufficient sodium hydroxide has been added to neutralise half of the acid: pH of the solution = pK_a for the acid HA.

c. Explain why dilution with a small volume of water does not affect the pH of a buffer solution.

AQA June 2005 Unit 5 Question 2(a–c)

10. Chromium(III) ions are weakly acidic in aqueous solution as shown by the following equation:

$$[Cr(H_2O)_6]^{3+}(aq) \rightleftharpoons [Cr(H_2O)_5(OH)]^{2+}(aq) + H^+(aq)$$

The value of K_a for this reaction is 1.15×10^{-4} mol dm^{-3}.

Calculate the pH of a 0.500 mol dm^{-3} solution of $[Cr(H_2O)_6]^{3+}(aq)$.

AQA June 2007 Unit 5 Question 3(c)

11. Ammonium chloride, when dissolved in water, can act as a weak acid as shown by the following equation.

$$NH_4^+(aq) \rightleftharpoons NH_3(aq) + H^+(aq)$$

Figure Q3 shows a graph of data obtained by a student when a solution of sodium hydroxide was added to a solution of ammonium chloride. The pH of the reaction mixture was measured initially and after each addition of the sodium hydroxide solution.

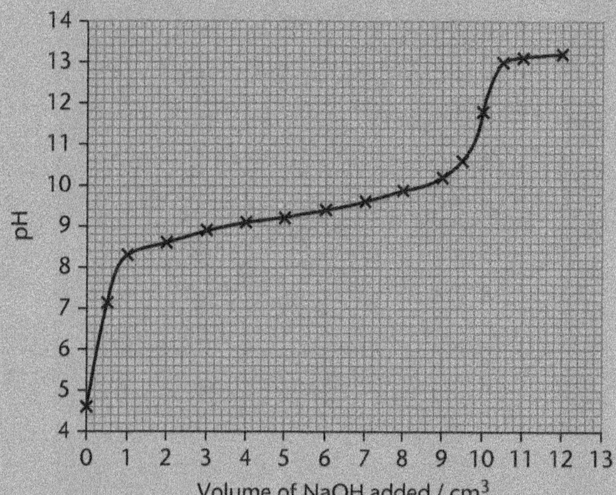

Figure Q3

a. Suggest a suitable piece of apparatus that could be used to measure out the sodium hydroxide solution. Explain why this apparatus is more suitable than a pipette for this purpose.

b. Use information from the curve in Figure Q3 to explain why the end point of this reaction would be difficult to judge accurately using an indicator.

c. The pH at the end point of this reaction is 11.8.

Use this pH value and the ionic product of water, $K_w = 1.0 \times 10^{-14}$ mol^2 dm^{-6}, to calculate the concentration of hydroxide ions at the end point of the reaction.

d. The expression for the acid dissociation constant for aqueous ammonium ions is:

$$K_a = \frac{[NH_3][H^+]}{[NH_4^+]}$$

The initial concentration of the ammonium chloride solution was 2.00 mol dm^{-3}.

Use the pH of this solution, before any sodium hydroxide had been added, to calculate a value for K_a.

e. A solution contains equal concentrations of ammonia and ammonium ions. Use your value of K_a from part **d** to calculate the pH of this solution. Explain your working. (If you were unable to calculate a value for K_a you may assume that it has the value 4.75×10^{-9} mol dm^{-3}. This is **not** the correct value.)

Specimen Paper 1 2015 Question 6

12. Ethanedioic acid is a weak acid. Ethanedioic acid acts, initially, as a monoprotic acid.

$$HO-\overset{\overset{O}{\|}}{C}-\overset{\overset{O}{\|}}{C}-OH \rightleftharpoons HO-\overset{\overset{O}{\|}}{C}-\overset{\overset{O}{\|}}{C}-O^- + H^+$$

a. Use the concept of electronegativity to justify why the acid strengths of ethanedioic acid and ethanoic acid are different.

b. A buffer solution is made by adding 6.00×10^{-2} mol of sodium hydroxide to a solution containing 1.00×10^{-1} mol of ethanedioic acid ($H_2C_2O_4$). Assume that the sodium hydroxide reacts as shown in the following equation and that in this buffer solution, the ethanedioic acid behaves as a monoprotic acid.

$$H_2C_2O_4(aq) + OH^-(aq) \rightarrow HC_2O_4^-(aq) + H_2O(l)$$

The dissociation constant K_a for ethanedioic acid is 5.89×10^{-2} mol dm^{-3}.

Calculate a value for the pH of the buffer solution.

Give your answer to the appropriate number of significant figures.

Specimen Paper 3 2015 Question 4

5 OPTICAL ISOMERISM

PRIOR KNOWLEDGE

You will have already studied some organic chemistry and should understand the naming systems used to describe organic compounds, be able to use different types of formulae to represent molecules and have learned about structural isomerism and stereoisomerism, including compounds containing a carbon–carbon double bond (see *chapter 5 of Year 1 Student Book*).

LEARNING OBJECTIVES

In this chapter you will learn about a type of stereoisomerism called optical isomerism. You will be able to identify molecules which exhibit this type of isomerism and be able to recognise and draw individual isomers (enantiomers) of these structures.

(Specification 3.3.7)

Most of us at some point in our lives have accidentally tried to put a glove on the wrong hand. It just doesn't work. A left-handed glove is meant for a left hand, and a right-handed glove for a right hand. This is an example of 'chirality' (Figure 1).

If you describe the parts of the hands then they sound the same – the thumb is connected to the first finger, which is connected to the middle finger and so on. However, it is not possible to overlay your hands so they are in exactly the same position. Whenever the

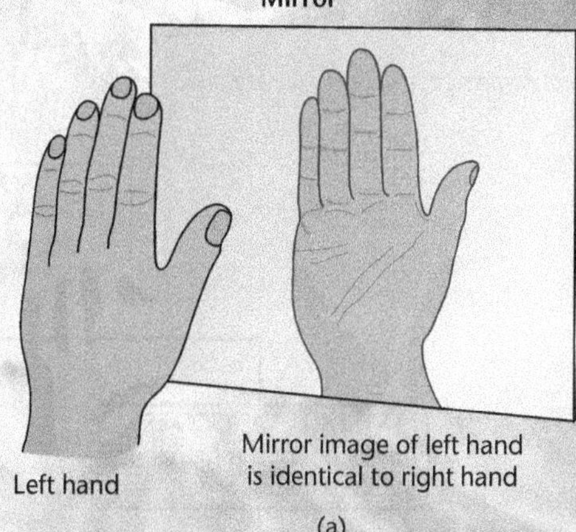

Figure 1 *Left and right hands are examples of chirality*

fingers match up the palm and back of the hand are in the wrong places. The mirror image of a chiral object cannot be superimposed upon itself.

Chirality is all around us both in nature and in everyday life. A spiral exhibits chirality and the rotation must be either clockwise or anticlockwise. The shells of many marine organisms are chiral and in fact the majority of known shells exist as one form only. Everyday objects exhibit chirality as well, such as screws and golf clubs.

Chirality has important consequences in chemistry and the chemistry of life. Proteins, carbohydrates and DNA are all chiral molecules and this affects how molecules interact with biological systems, explaining why certain drugs work, how enzymes can recognise their substrates, and even our senses of taste and smell.

5.1 CHIRALITY AND OPTICAL ISOMERISM

Optical isomerism is a form of stereoisomerism displayed by molecules that contain an asymmetric carbon atom. An asymmetric carbon atom is one that has four different atoms or groups bonded to it.

Any molecule that has an asymmetric carbon atom can exist in one of two forms. The two forms are non-superimposable mirror images of one another. They are called **optical isomers** or **enantiomers** (Figure 2).

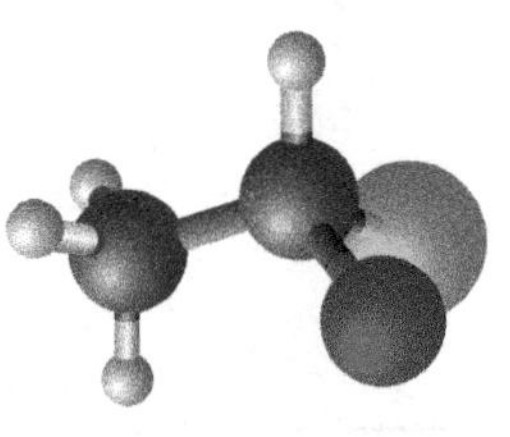

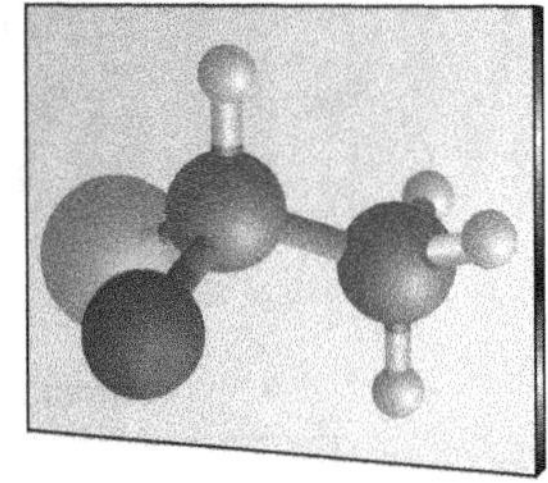

Figure 2 *Optical isomers of 1-chloro-1-fluoroethane*

Stereoisomers are isomers that have the same molecular formula and structural formula but different arrangements in space of the atoms from which they are made. You should be familiar with one type of stereoisomerism called *E–Z* isomerism. This is a form of stereoisomerism displayed by alkenes. The relationship between different types of isomers is shown in Figure 3.

The carbon atom bonded to four different atoms or groups is called a **chiral** carbon atom and the molecule is said to have a chiral centre. Chirality is a property of three-dimensional objects. Every object has a mirror image. If the mirror image is not superimposable on the original object, then that object is chiral. Objects which have symmetry, such as a sphere, are not chiral, as their mirror images are identical, but other objects (such as your hands) are chiral.

While we can recognise chiral molecules from their displayed formula shown in two dimensions, we

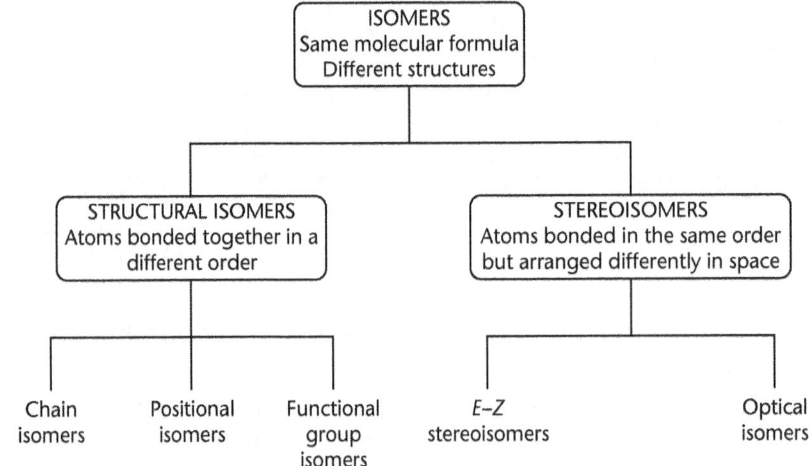

Figure 3 *Different types of structural isomers and stereoisomers and how they relate to one another*

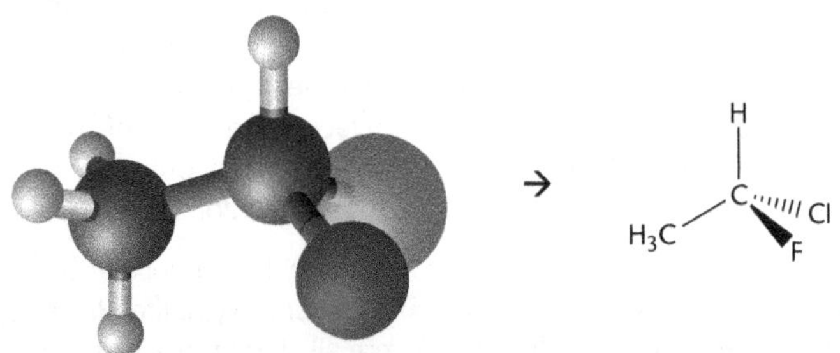

- A bond shown as a solid line is used for bonds that lie in the plane of the paper.
- A bond shown as a wedge is used for bonds that come forwards out of the page towards the viewer.
- A bond shown as a dashed line or dashed wedge is used for bonds that go backwards out of the page away from the viewer.

Figure 4 *3D representation of molecules*

can only show the difference between a pair of enantiomers properly by a three-dimensional drawing. Figure 4 shows how we draw a three-dimensional representation of a chiral molecule.

We can draw the enantiomer of a chiral molecule simply by imagining the reflection of it in a mirror. We can illustrate this by looking at the two enantiomers of lactic acid, $CH_3CH(OH)CO_2H$ (Figure 5).

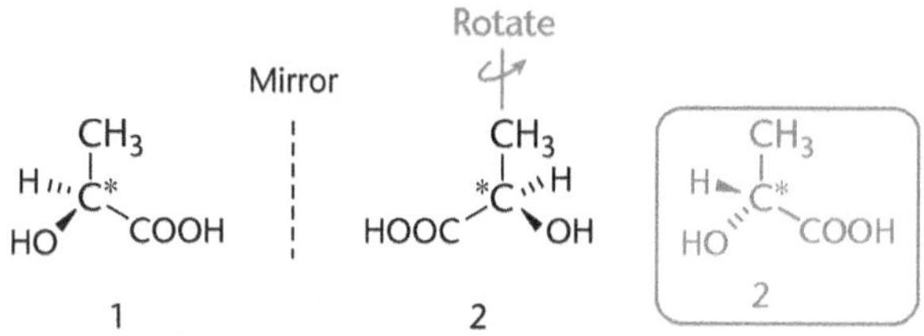

Rotate

Mirror

CH_3 H C* HO COOH 1 | CH_3 *C H HOOC OH 2 | CH_3 H C* HO COOH 2

Figure 5 *Enantiomers of lactic acid*

Lactic acid is a naturally occurring molecule that is found in sour milk. It is also produced in our muscles when we exercise. It contains a chiral centre, shown by the asterisk. Only enantiomer **1** is found in our muscles. In order to draw the other enantiomer of **1** you draw its reflection in a mirror to give enantiomer **2**. These isomers are not superimposable. It is easier to visualise this if you rotate enantiomer **2** 180° around the axis shown in Figure 5. Now it is easy to see that structures **1** and **2** are different. In enantiomer **1** the alcohol group is facing out of the paper but in enantiomer **2** it is facing into the page.

QUESTIONS

1. Draw each of the molecules below, identify the chiral carbon atom in each molecule and circle it.

   a. H–C(H)(H)–C(H)(OH)–C(H)(H)–C(H)(H)–H

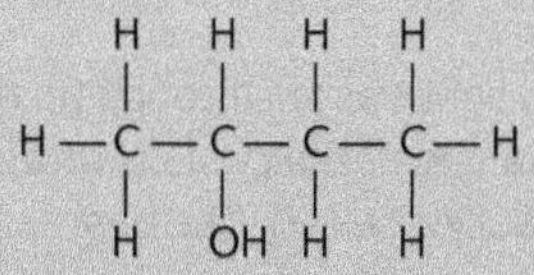

   b. H–C(H)(H)–C(CH₃ above: H–C–H with H; CH₃ below: H–C–H with H)–C(H)(H)–C(H)(H)–C(F)(Br)–H

   c. O=C ring: C, CH_2, CH_2, CH_2, CH_2, CH with CH_3

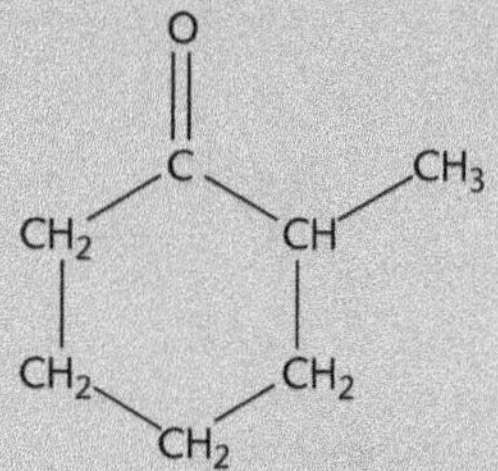

   d. H_3C–C(CH_3)(CH_3)–C(=O)–C(CH_3)(H)–C(H)(H)–C(H)=CH_2

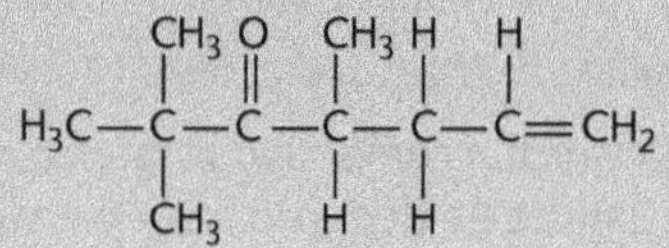

2. Draw each of the molecules shown below and state whether they would show optical isomerism or not. If the molecule does show optical isomerism, mark the chiral centre with an asterisk (*).

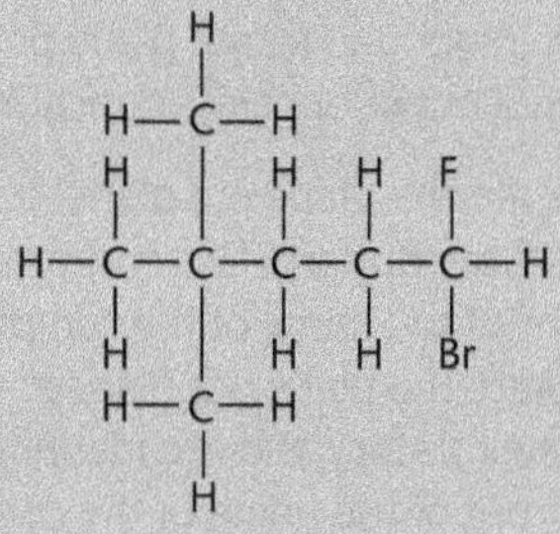

   a. CH_2ClBr

   b. $CH_3CHClBr$

   c. (benzene ring)–C(=O)–CH_3

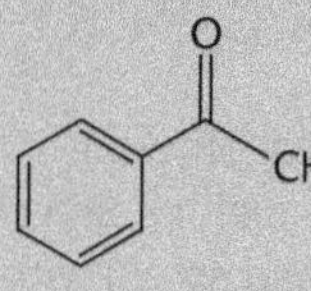

   d. (benzene ring)–CH(OH)–CH_3

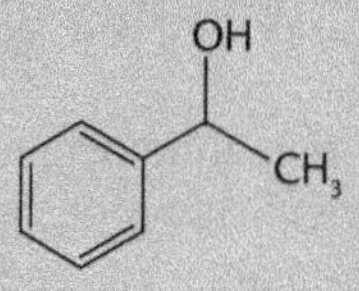

3. Draw three-dimensional representations of BOTH enantiomers for each of the following compounds.

   a. H–C(H)(H)–C(H)(Cl)–C(H)(H)–C(H)(H)–H

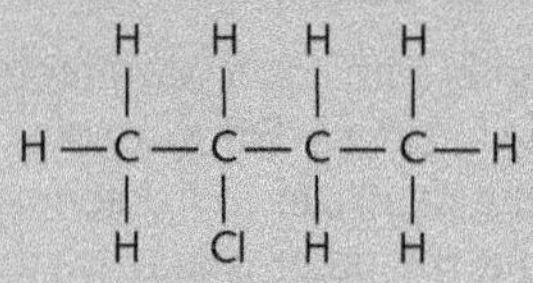

   b. butan-2-ol

   c. Cl (skeletal structure: CH(Cl) with CH₃, CH₂–CH=CH₂)

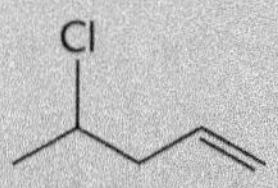

   d. 2-aminopropanoic acid

Stretch and challenge

4. An alkane has the molecular formula C_7H_{16}. It has nine structural isomers. One of the structural isomers is 2,3-dimethylpentane and this compound also displays optical isomerism.
   a. In total how many of the structural isomers of the alkane C_7H_{16} display optical isomerism?
   b. Draw both enantiomers of 2,3-dimethylpentane in skeletal form.

5. Cholesterol is an essential molecule for animals. Its main role is in building cell membranes. How many chiral carbon centres are there in cholesterol? Mark the chiral centres with an asterisk (*).

HO

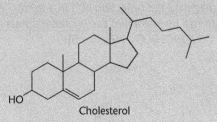

Cholesterol

KEY IDEAS

- A carbon atom attached to four different atoms or groups is called a chiral carbon atom.
- Molecules with chiral carbon atoms exhibit optical isomerism.
- Optical isomers (or enantiomers) are mirror images of one another.
- Mirror images of chiral molecules are not superimposable.

5.2 PROPERTIES OF OPTICAL ISOMERS

Pairs of enantiomers have identical physical and chemical properties (such as melting and boiling points, infrared spectra, and so on) with two exceptions:

- They interact differently with plane polarised light (hence the term optical isomers); this is referred to as a difference in optical activity.
- They interact differently with other asymmetric molecules, especially enzymes. For example, one enantiomer of the painkiller ibuprofen has a therapeutic effect, but the other is inactive.

Optical activity

Light travels in straight lines, transferring energy from place to place by electromagnetic waves. These are transverse waves that vibrate in all possible planes at right angles to the direction in which the wave is travelling. When passed through a polariser, all the waves are absorbed except for those vibrating in one particular plane, as shown in Figure 6. The light is then said to be plane polarised.

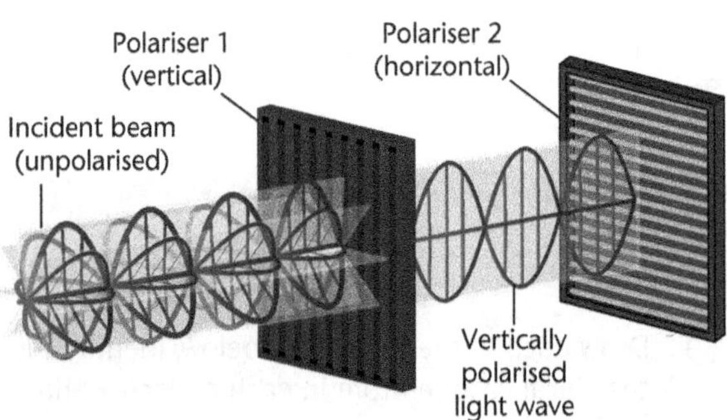

***Figure 6** Plane polarised light*

When plane polarised light passes through an optically active compound the angle of the plane is rotated either clockwise (+) or anticlockwise (−). The degree by which the plane is rotated is called the optical rotation. Optical isomers of the same compound rotate plane polarised light by equal amounts but in opposite directions.

Enantiomers that rotate the plane of polarised light clockwise are dextrorotatory. This is shown by putting D-(+)- in front of the name of the compound. Enantiomers that rotate the plane of polarised light anticlockwise are laevorotatory and are identified by putting L-(−)- in front of the name of the compound (Figure 7).

Optical rotation = +15° (+)-butan-2-ol (or d-butan-2-ol)

Optical rotation = −15° (-)-butan-2-ol (or l-butan-2-ol)

***Figure 7** Dextrorotatory and laevorotatory forms of butan-2-ol*

The direction in which a compound rotates plane polarised light cannot be deduced from the structure. It has to be determined experimentally using a polarimeter as illustrated in Figure 8.

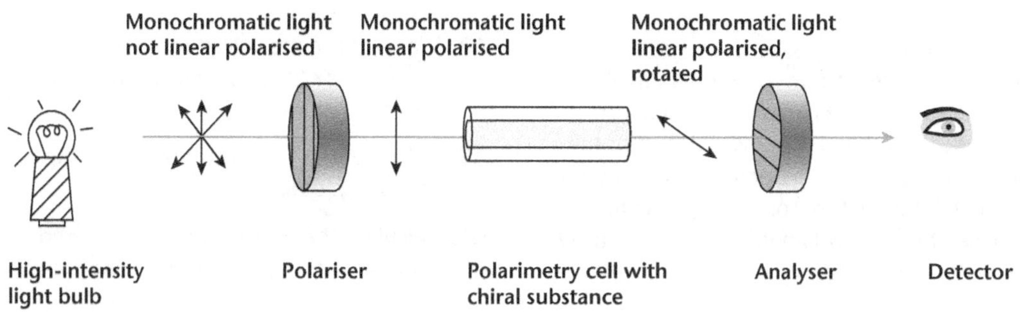

Figure 8 *A simple polarimeter*

ASSIGNMENT 1: USING POLARIMETRY IN CHEMICAL ANALYSIS

(AT a, AT k, PS 1.2)

Polarimetry is often used by the pharmaceutical and food industries to measure the purity of chiral molecules. Sucrose is a sugar that is optically active and contains many chiral centres. In chemistry, the term sugar is a generalised name for a group of carbohydrates with the general formula $C_nH_{2n}O_n$. There are a wide range of compounds with this formula, including glucose, galactose and fructose. The sugar commonly used to sweeten food and drink is actually just one of the molecules from this family, sucrose, which contains one molecule of glucose linked to one molecule of fructose. Almost all plants contain sucrose but commercially available sugar comes from sugar cane or sugar beet (Figure A2).

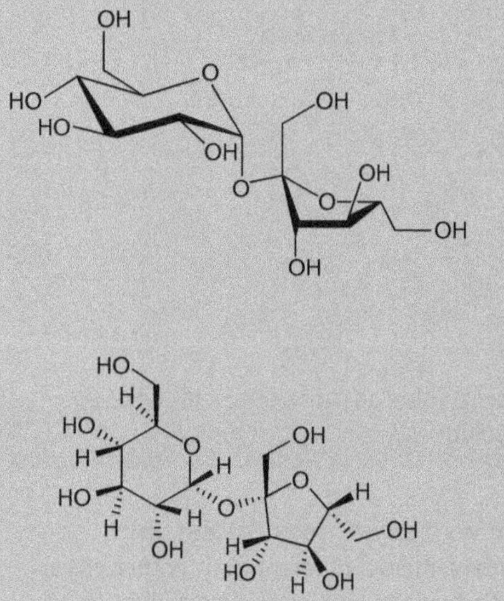

Figure A2 *Sucrose is the name of the sugar compound found in table sugar*

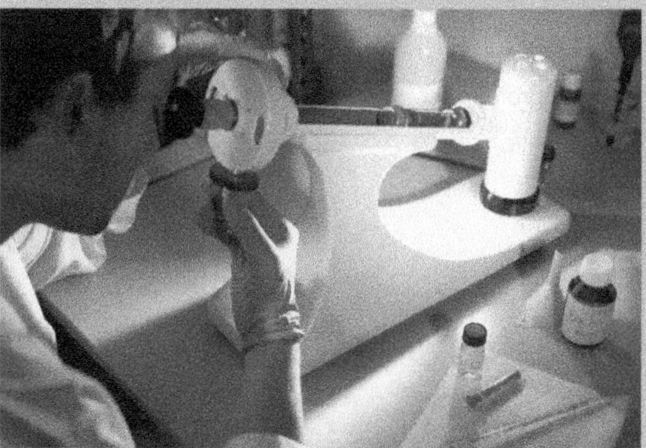

Figure A1 *This chemist is using a polarimeter to analyse a sample*

The theory

A solution of an optically active compound rotates the plane of polarised light, but how much it does so depends on (a) the concentration of the compound in the solution and (b) the distance that the light travels through the solution (the path length).

The specific optical rotation relates the measured optical rotation, the concentration of the solution and the path length to allow the comparison of different solutions:

$$\text{Specific optical rotation} = \frac{\text{observed rotation}}{\underset{(\text{g dm}^{-3})}{\text{concentration}} \times \underset{(\text{dm})}{\text{path length}}}$$

A chemist wanted to use this effect to analyse solutions of sucrose.

The experiment

5.0000 g of sucrose were weighed on an analytical balance (4 decimal places) and placed in a 100 cm^3 volumetric flask. Distilled water was added to the volumetric flask to make up a solution with a total volume of 100 cm^3. 10 cm^3 of the sugar solution was removed from the volumetric flask and placed in a cell with a path length of 1 dm.

A polarimeter was used to determine the actual rotation of the plane of polarised light of the sample.

The process was repeated from the beginning five times.

The results

Sample	Measured rotation / °
1	+3.33
2	+3.34
3	+3.32
4	+3.48
5	+3.33

Questions

A1. Why is a volumetric flask used to make up the solutions?

A2. Which of the measured rotations is anomalous? Suggest why this anomalous result may have occurred.

A3. Calculate the concentration of the sugar solution in g dm^{-3}.

A4. Calculate the average of the measured rotations and use the average measured rotation to determine the specific optical rotation of sucrose.

A4. Which enantiomer of sucrose is present in the solution?

Stretch and challenge

A5. Comment on the magnitude of the values measured for the specific rotation and the effect that this may have on the percentage errors caused by the instrument precision. How could the experiment be amended to reduce the percentage errors?

A6. How many chiral centres are there in sucrose?

A7. If the measured rotation of a solution of sucrose was found to be 15°, what would be the concentration of the solution in g dm^{-3}?

Interaction with asymmetric molecules

Optical isomers interact differently with other chiral molecules, particularly biological molecules such as proteins and enzymes. For example, the nonsteroidal anti-inflammatory painkiller ibuprofen (Figure 9) contains a chiral centre, but the dextrorotatory isomer was found to be far more biologically active than the laevorotatory isomer. The reason why different enantiomers often exhibit different biological properties will be explored in depth in *chapter 11 of the Year 2 Student Book*.

H
O
OH
dextrorotatory ibuprofen

H
O
OH
laevorotatory ibuprofen

Figure 9 *Ibuprofen isomers*

ASSIGNMENT 2: IDENTIFYING OPTICAL ISOMERS IN CITRUS FRUIT

Citrus fruits are able to cross-breed between species and most of the citrus fruits that we commonly use, including oranges and lemons, are actually cross-breeds of the four wild-breeding species key lime, pomelo, citron and mandarin. The familiar citrus smell from many of these fruits comes primarily from the compound limonene. This compound is chiral as shown in Figure A1. The D enantiomer creates the smell of oranges and the L enantiomer creates the smell of lemons. D-(+)-limonene has a specific optical rotation of +102°.

l-(−)-limonene
lemon

d-(+)-limonene
orange

Figure A1 *Enantiomers of limonene*

A new cross-breed of oranges and lemons called 'oramon' was developed and analysed. The essential oil was extracted from the peel using steam distillation. The essential oil was found to contain mostly a mixture of the *l*- and d-isomers of limonene and have an optical rotation of 0°.

Questions

A1. State the expected specific optical rotation of *l*-(−)-limonene found in lemons.

A2. Explain why the optical rotation of 'oramon' oil is 0°.

A3. State the instrument used to determine the optical rotation of 'oramon' oil.

A4. Suggest techniques that could have been used in the analysis to find out that the essential oil contained mostly limonene.

A5. Explain why the techniques used to deduce the compound present in the essential oil cannot also be used to find out which enantiomers are present.

KEY IDEAS

- Enantiomers have the same chemical and physical properties apart from their interactions with plane polarised light and with other chiral molecules.
- Enantiomers rotate the plane of polarised light by the same amount but in opposite directions.
- A polarimeter is used to measure the optical rotation of an enantiomer.

5.3 SYNTHESIS OF OPTICAL ISOMERS

Compounds that show optical isomerism can be synthesised from starting materials that do not show optical isomerism. For example, butan-2-ol can be formed by the reaction of but-1-ene with sulfuric acid followed by the addition of water. But-1-ene does not show any form of stereoisomerism but butan-2-ol does show optical isomerism.

However, chiral molecules produced during chemical reactions often contain a 50:50 mixture of the two enantiomers. This is called a **racemic mixture** or a **racemate** and occurs when there is an equal chance of forming each enantiomer during the chemical reaction. We often obtain racemic mixtures when we do addition reactions on a planar double bond (C = C or C = O), because the reaction can occur with equal probability from either side of the plane.

For example, ethanal undergoes nucleophilic addition with hydrogen cyanide to form chiral 2-hydroxypropanenitrile (Figure 10). The reaction mixture produced will be the racemate because there is a 50:50 chance of the cyanide nucleophile bonding to either side of the planar molecule. Attack at one side produces one enantiomer; attack at the other side produces the other.

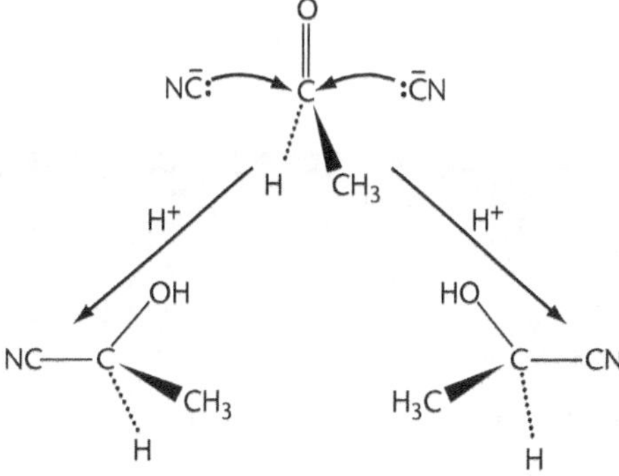

Figure 10 *Racemate formed by nucleophilic addition of hydrogen cyanide to ethanal*

The enantiomers in a racemate both rotate the plane of polarised light but the rotation effects of each isomer are equal and opposite and therefore cancel out. If we test a sample and find that it does not produce an optical rotation effect, then either it is not chiral or it consists of a 50:50 mixture of two enantiomers.

ASSIGNMENT 3: CHIRAL DRUGS

(MS 4.1, 4.2, 4.3, PS 1.2)

Penicillamine is a drug that is used to treat a number of conditions. It was first used in 1964 to treat rheumatoid arthritis and has also been used to treat a rare genetic disease where copper accumulates in the body and cannot be excreted, called Wilson's disease. Only the dextrorotatory form, D-penicillamine, is biologically active, with the laevorotatory form, L-penicillamine, being toxic to the body. Another example of a chiral drug molecule is naproxen, a nonsteroidal anti-inflammatory drug (NSAID) which is used similarly to ibuprofen to relieve pain and to reduce inflammation. Like ibuprofen, only the D-enantiomer is responsible for its biological activity. However, unlike ibuprofen, the L-enantiomer of naproxen is toxic.

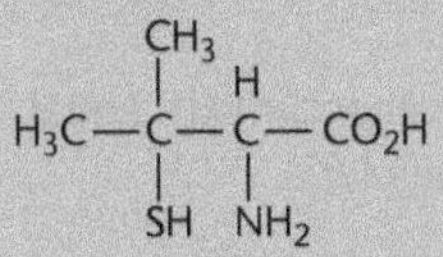

CH$_3$ H
H$_3$C—C—C—CO$_2$H
SH NH$_2$

Penicillamine

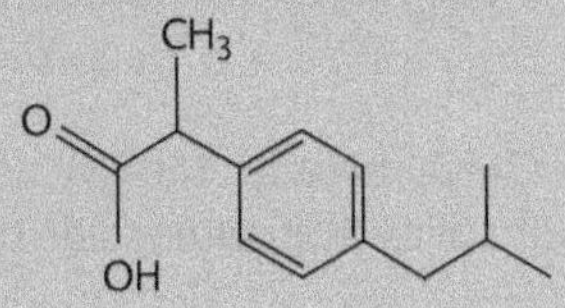

CH$_3$ O OH

Ibuprofen

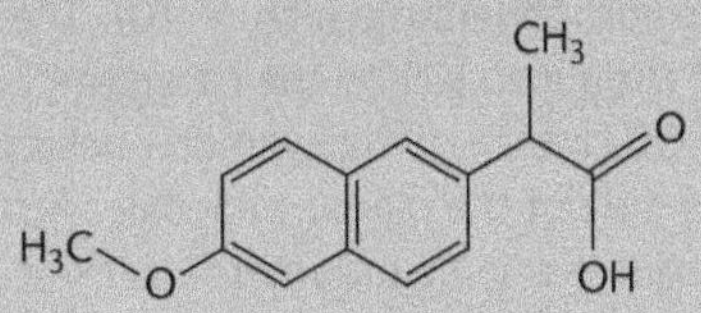

CH$_3$ O H$_3$C O OH

Naproxen

Figure A1

A racemic mixture is always produced from addition reactions to planar C = C and C = O bonds. In recent years a new branch of chemistry called 'asymmetric synthesis' has been developed which concerns itself with the production of single enantiomers only – this type of chemistry can be very expensive and time-consuming to undertake.

Questions

A1. For each of the chiral drugs, identify the chiral carbon atom by circling it.

A2. Draw a three-dimensional representation of both enantiomers of penicillamine. What type of isomerism are you illustrating?

A3. Ibuprofen is sold as a racemate. What does this mean?

Stretch and challenge

A4. Both ibuprofen and naproxen are nonsteroidal anti-inflammatory drugs which are used for the treatment of pain. What are the chemical similarities between the two drugs?

A5. Why is ibuprofen sold as a racemate but naproxen is sold as the d-isomer?

KEY IDEAS

- A 50:50 mixture of enantiomers is known as a racemate or a racemic mixture.
- The optical rotation of a racemic mixture is always zero.
- When chiral molecules are synthesised by the addition of reagents to planar alkenes or carbonyl groups the products form a racemic mixture.
- A racemic mixture is formed because there is equal likelihood of the reagent attaching from above or below the planar bond.

PRACTICE QUESTIONS

1. a. Deduce the number of monochloroisomers formed by isooctane.

   b. Draw the structure of the monochloro-isomer that exists as a pair of optical isomers.

   AQA Specimen Paper 2, 2015, Question 3.5

2. The tripeptide shown in Figure Q1 is formed from the amino acids glycine, threonine and lysine.

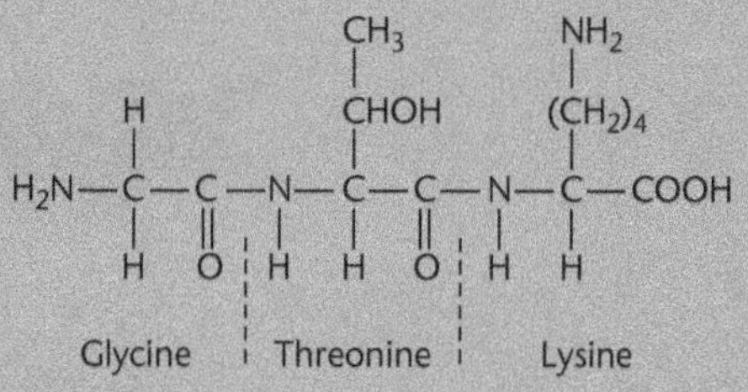

```
                    CH3           NH2
                    |             |
         H          CHOH          (CH2)4
         |          |             |
   H2N—C—C—N—C—C—N—C—COOH
         |  ||   |  |  ||   |  |
         H  O  ¦ H  H  O  ¦ H  H
                ¦           ¦
     Glycine    ¦ Threonine ¦   Lysine
```

Figure Q1

Draw a separate circle around each of the asymmetric carbon atoms in the tripeptide in Figure Q1.

AQA Specimen Paper 2, 2015, Question 6.1

3. But-1-ene reacts with a reagent of the form HY to form a saturated compound.

   Explain how three isomeric products are formed when HY reacts with but-1-ene.

   AQA Specimen Paper 2, 2015, Question 12.3

4. Phenylalanine exists as a pair of stereoisomers. State the meaning of the term stereoisomers. Explain how a pair of stereoisomers can be distinguished.

   AQA Chemistry, January 2012, Question 7(e)

Multiple choice

5. What property leads to a compound showing optical isomerism?

   A. Restricted rotation around a double bond

   B. Four different atoms or groups attached to a carbon atom

   C. Planar C = C or C = O bond

   D. 50 : 50 ratio of enantiomers

6. Which compound is optically active?

   A. $CH_3CH_2CH(OH)CH_3$

   B. $CH_3CH_2CH(OH)CH_2CH_3$

   C. $CH_3CH_2C(CH_3)(OH)CH_3$

   D. $CH_3CH_2CH_2CH_2OH$

7. How many of the position isomers of dichlorobutane show optical isomerism?

   A. One

   B. Two

   C. Three

   D. Four

8. Which of the following will be different for optical isomers of a compound?

   A. Infrared spectrum

   B. Rotation of plane polarised light

   C. Reaction with a non-chiral compound

   D. Melting point

9. The reaction of but-1-ene with hydrogen bromide produces a mixture of three products. The overall reaction mixture does not rotate the plane of polarised light. Which statement explains this observation?

   A. There are equal amounts of all three products present.

   B. One compound is optically inactive and the enantiomers of the other compound are present in a 50 : 50 ratio.

   C. The products are not optically active.

   D. There is restricted rotation around the C = C bond in but-1-ene.

6 ALDEHYDES AND KETONES

PRIOR KNOWLEDGE

You will already have studied how curly arrows can be used to show reaction mechanisms in organic chemistry and the rules for naming hydrocarbons. You should also be familiar with the oxidation of primary and secondary alcohols to give aldehydes and ketones, as well as optical isomerism (see *chapters 5 and 14 of Year 1 Student Book and chapter 5 of Year 2 Student Book*).

LEARNING OBJECTIVES

In this chapter you will learn about the structures and reactions of aldehydes and ketones. You will be able to understand the oxidation and reduction products of aldehydes and ketones as well as identify their nucleophilic addition reactions.

(Specification 3.3.8)

What is responsible for the flavour of your vanilla ice cream? The flavour of vanilla is due to the aldehyde vanillin, an organic compound that can be extracted from the vanilla bean. Nowadays, however, most vanillin is synthesised in the laboratory.

Vanillin is an aldehyde. Aldehydes and ketones have a variety of uses but many are found in essential oils used as flavourings or perfumes. The characteristic taste of cinnamon is due to the aldehyde cinnamaldehyde. Recently, cinnamaldehyde has been found to have medical uses, including promoting blood circulation and blood vessel dilation, and potentially anti-tumour activity. It has also been used as a

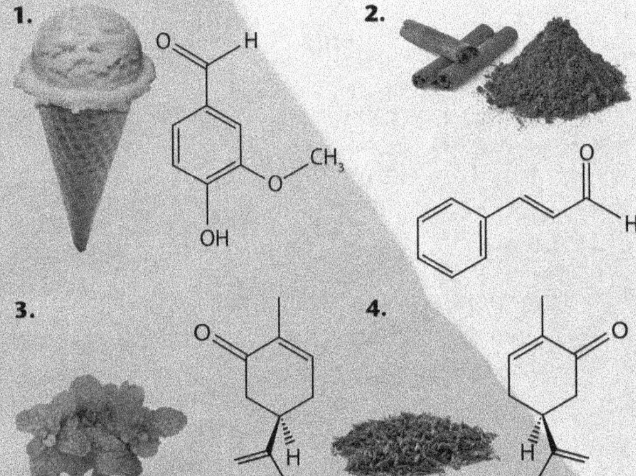

Figure 1 *Structures of some naturally occurring aldehydes and ketones: 1. vanillin, 2. cinnamaldehyde, 3. L-carvone (spearmint) and 4. D-carvone (caraway)*

fungicide. Another volatile aldehyde that contains an alkene is citronellal, the main component of citronella oil. It is often used in fragrances, owing to its lemony smell, but is also used in candles, where it acts as an insect repellent in the surrounding area. On the other hand, the aldehyde nonanal, which humans excrete through their skin, is known to attract mosquitoes. Our noses contain smell receptors that can often differentiate molecules that contain chiral centres. The ketone carvone exists in both D and L chiral forms. D-Carvone is found in oil of caraway and is responsible for the caraway smell, while its enantiomer L-Carvone smells of spearmint. Monkeys and other mammals have also been shown to differentiate the enantiomers of carvone, suggesting that many mammals share evolutionary principles of odour perception. Aldehydes and ketones can also be used industrially. Propan-2-one (also known as acetone) is an important industrial solvent that can be found in nail varnish remover.

6.1 ALDEHYDES AND KETONES

Aldehydes and ketones contain the **carbonyl group** (>C=O). They differ in that aldehydes have a carbon atom and a hydrogen atom bonded to the carbon of the carbonyl group, while ketones have two carbon atoms bonded to the carbon of the carbonyl group (Figure 2). This means that the carbonyl group is always situated at the end of a carbon chain in aldehydes, but somewhere within a carbon chain in ketones. The simplest possible aldehyde is called methanal (old name: formaldehyde). In a methanal molecule two hydrogens are bonded to the carbon of the carbonyl group.

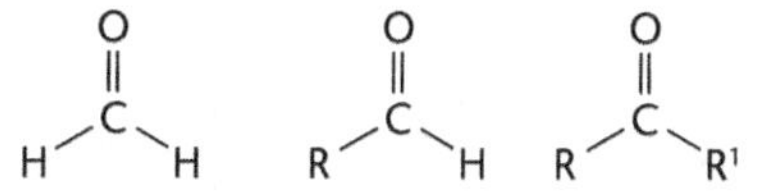

Methanal (formaldehyde) Aldehyde Ketone

R, R[1] = Different alkyl goups

Figure 2 General structures of aldehydes and ketones. In some ketones two of the same alkyl groups may be attached to the carbonyl group (R = R[1]).

Aldehydes can be prepared from the oxidation of primary alcohols, while ketones are prepared by oxidation of secondary alcohols (Figure 3).

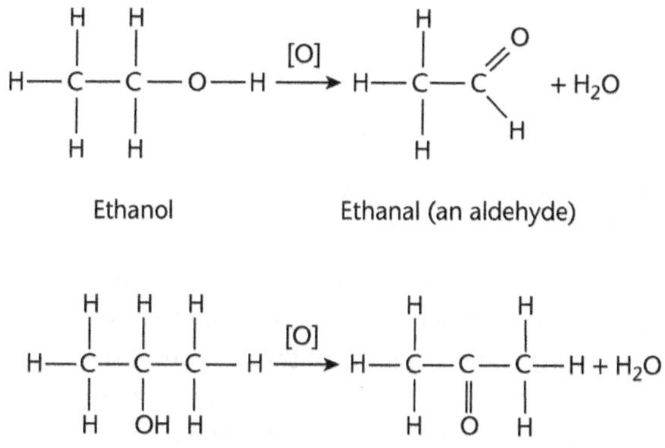

Ethanol $\xrightarrow{[O]}$ Ethanal (an aldehyde) $+ H_2O$

Propan-2-ol $\xrightarrow{[O]}$ Propanone (a ketone) $+ H_2O$

Figure 3 Preparation of aldehydes and ketones by oxidation of alcohols

Nomenclature of aldehydes and ketones

For aldehydes we identify the longest carbon chain that the carbonyl group is part of and modify the parent alkane name by removing the terminal *-e* and replacing it with *-al*. For ketones we replace the *-e* with *-one* and number the carbon chain to give the carbonyl carbon atom the lowest possible number. Common names are still sometimes used, and these are shown in brackets in Figure 4.

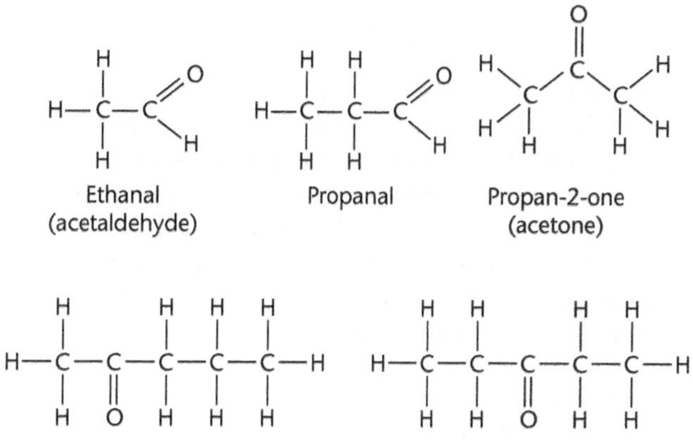

Ethanal (acetaldehyde) Propanal Propan-2-one (acetone)

Pentan-2-one Pentan-3-one

Figure 4 The names and structures of some simple aldehydes and ketones

Worked example 1

Name this molecule:

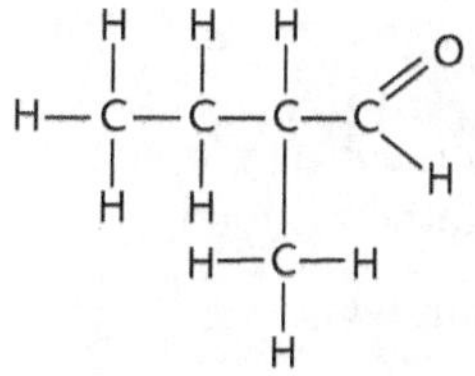

The aldehyde group gives the suffix *-al* to the name. The longest carbon chain is four carbon atoms long, giving the last element of the compound name as butanal. The methyl group is on the second carbon of the chain and so this is 2-methyl butanal.

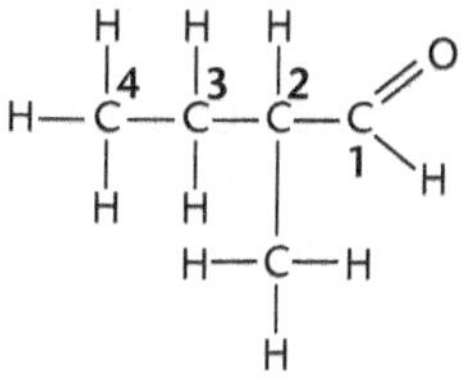

Worked example 2

Name this molecule:

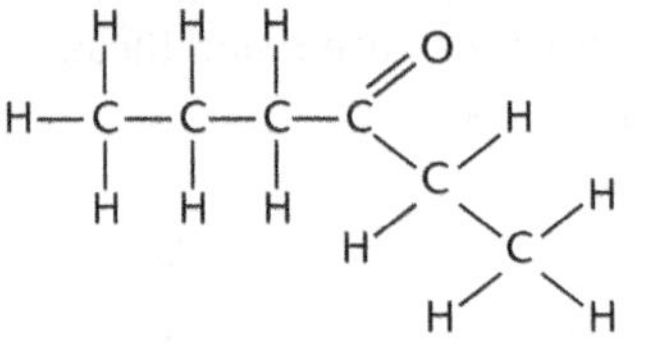

The ketone group gives the suffix *-one* to the name. The longest carbon chain is six carbon atoms long giving the last element of the compound name as hexanone. The carbonyl group could be on the third or the fourth carbon depending upon which way you counted along the chain, but the correct position should be named with the lowest number, so this is hexan-3-one, or 3-hexanone.

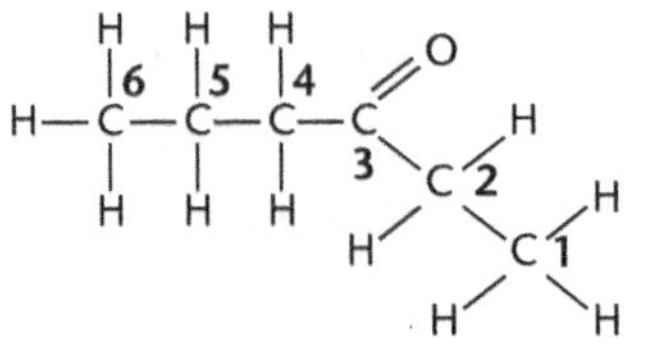

KEY IDEAS

- Aldehydes have a carbon atoms and a hydrogen atom bonded to carbon of a carbonyl group.
- Ketones have two carbon atoms bonded to carbon of a carbonyl group.

6.2 REACTIONS OF ALDEHYDES AND KETONES

Nucleophilic addition reactions

The more electronegative oxygen in the C = O group attracts the shared electrons more strongly than the carbon, resulting in this bond being polar. Therefore, the carbon is prone to attack by nucleophiles, which have lone pairs of electrons available for bonding (Figure 5). This is called a nucleophilic addition reaction. Owing to their similarity, aldehydes and ketones often react in similar ways, particularly in nucleophilic addition reactions.

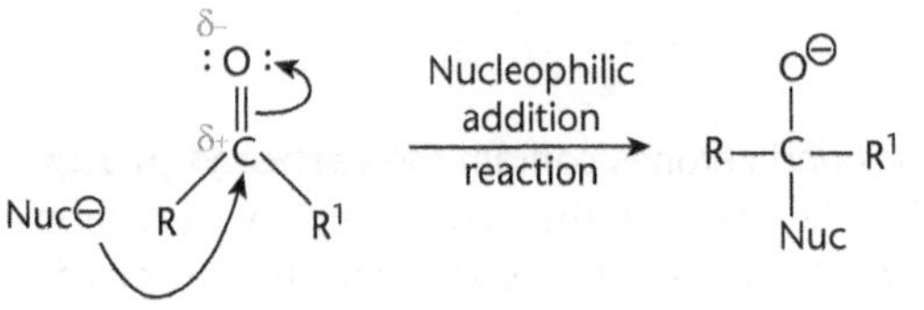

Figure 5 *Nucleophilic additions to aldehydes and ketones*

Addition of hydrogen cyanide to both aldehydes and ketones gives hydroxynitriles and is an example of a nucleophilic addition reaction (Figure 6). Hydrogen cyanide is an acid and is ionised to give hydrogen ions (H^+) and the reactive nucleophilic cyanide ion ($:CN^-$), which is the nucleophile.

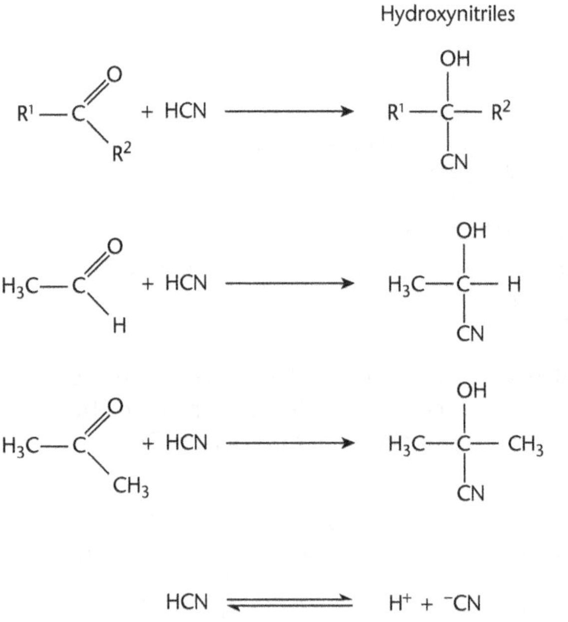

Figure 6 *The formation of hydroxynitriles by the addition of HCN to aldehydes and ketones*

The mechanism of the reaction is shown in Figure 7. Step 1 is the addition of the nucleophile CN^- to the partially positive carbon of the carbonyl group. The lone pair of electrons on CN^- forms a bond with the C of the >C = O group and one of the shared electron pairs in the C = O bond moves to the oxygen, leaving one remaining shared pair between C and O (i.e. a single covalent bond). In step 2, the negatively charged oxygen atom reacts to form a covalent bond with a hydrogen ion, forming the hydroxynitrile product. Hence an addition reaction results and, overall, the reaction mechanism is called a **nucleophilic addition across the C = O bond**.

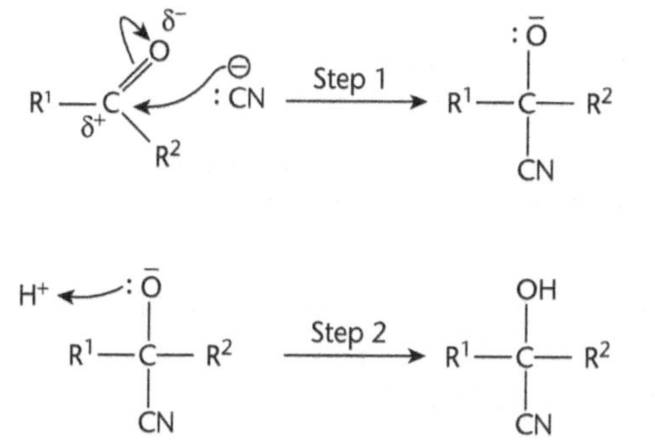

Figure 7 *The mechanism of nucleophilic addition of cyanide to aldehydes and ketones*

In practice we often use the ionic compound potassium cyanide, KCN, as a source of nucleophilic cyanide ion ($:CN^-$), followed by an acid such as sulfuric or hydrochloric acid (Figure 8). The mechanism for the reaction is the same as with HCN (Figure 7), but the reaction is easier. The reaction using potassium cyanide is faster and avoids using the highly toxic compound hydrogen cyanide, although potassium cyanide is also toxic. Hydrogen cyanide is a very weak acid and the degree of ionisation in solution, to produce hydrogen ions (H^+) and the reactive nucleophilic cyanide ions ($:CN^-$), is very small (K_a for HCN = 4.0×10^{-10} mol dm^{-3}) (see *chapter 4 of Year 2 Student Book*).

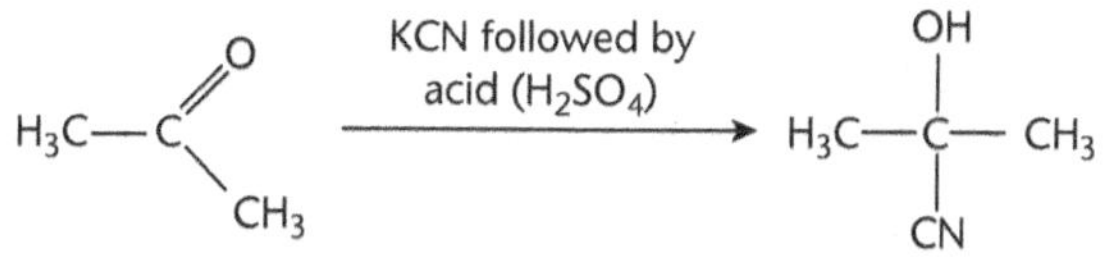

Figure 8 *Formation of hydroxynitriles by the addition of KCN to aldehydes and ketones.*

The carbonyl bond is planar in shape, so the cyanide nucleophile has an equal likelihood of attacking from either side of the molecule. This means that when the product is chiral a racemic mixture will be formed (Figure 9) (see *chapter 5 of Year 2 Student Book*).

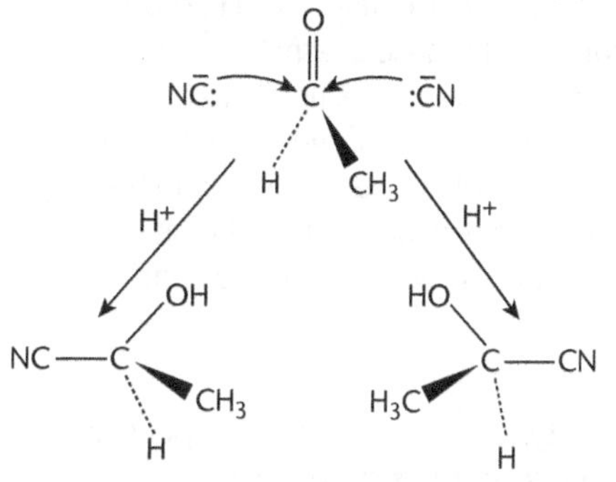

Figure 9 *The formation of a racemic mixture during nucleophilic addition of HCN to an aldehyde*

QUESTIONS

1. Write equations to show the reaction of hydrogen cyanide with:
   a. propanal
   b. butanone
   c. hexan-2-one
2. Name the organic products from Question 1.
3. Which of the products from Question 1 contain a chiral centre? Draw the structures of the optical isomers concerned.

ASSIGNMENT 1: THE FORMATION OF ALPHA HYDROXYACIDS VIA NUCLEOPHILIC ADDITION TO ALDEHYDES

(AT k)

You do not need to remember the details of this assignment but you could be asked to apply your knowledge to unfamiliar situations. Alpha hydroxyacids (AHAs) are molecules that contain an alcohol group next to a carboxylic acid group. In recent years, AHAs have become important in the cosmetic industry, particularly in anti-wrinkle creams. Naturally occurring AHAs include lactic acid, malic acid and citric acid. Lactic acid contains a chiral centre and in animals is found as the L-enantiomer. In humans, lactic acid is a product of metabolism and is produced when we exercise. It is possible to make lactic acid in the laboratory from ethanal via a two-stage process shown

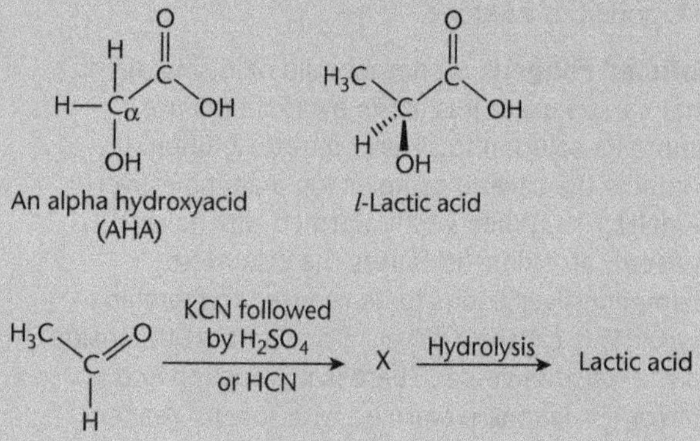

An alpha hydroxyacid (AHA)

l-Lactic acid

Figure A1 *Structure of alpha hydroxyacids and a laboratory synthesis of lactic acid. The product is a racemic mixture of the D- and L-lactic acid.*

in Figure A1. In the first stage, reaction of ethanal with either HCN or KCN followed by H_2SO_4 gives compound X, which upon hydrolysis gives lactic acid.

Hydrogen cyanide is a colourless gas that smells of bitter almonds and is extremely toxic (100 parts per million can quickly cause death). The gas is also highly flammable, so great care needs to be exercised when using cyanides. Like hydrogen cyanide, the crystalline solid potassium cyanide is also extremely toxic to humans and exposure by inhalation or by absorption through the skin can lead to death.

Questions

A1. Name the type of reaction that happens in the first stage of the synthesis when HCN is used as the reagent.

A2. Identify the intermediate X in the reaction of ethanal with HCN.

A3. Draw a curly arrow mechanism to illustrate the formation of the intermediate X using HCN.

A4. Hydrolysis of X furnishes lactic acid. Is this product identical to the naturally occurring lactic acid found in animals?

A5. Would you expect the reaction to be faster if potassium cyanide followed by acid was used instead of HCN? Explain your answer.

A6. What safety precautions would you take if you were undertaking a reaction with potassium cyanide in the laboratory and why?

Redox reactions

Oxidation reactions

Like alcohols, aldehydes can be oxidised with acidified potassium dichromate(VI) solution to give carboxylic acids (see *chapter 15 of Year 1 Student Book*). It is much more difficult to oxidise ketones. They can be oxidised only by very strong oxidising agents. This gives us a good way to distinguish between aldehydes and ketones.

A sample of a compound known to be an aldehyde or ketone is treated with **Fehling's solution** (a mild oxidising agent). Fehling's solution is blue (see Figure 12) because it contains copper(II) complex ions in alkaline solution. When the solution is warmed with an aldehyde, the aldehyde is oxidised to a carboxylic acid and blue copper(II) ions are reduced to a brick-red precipitate of copper(I) oxide. There is no reaction, and no colour change of Fehling's solution if it is added to a ketone.

Tollens' reagent is another mild oxidising agent that can be used. It is made by adding dilute ammonia solution to silver(I) nitrate solution. It contains the silver(I) complex ion diamminesilver(I), $[Ag(NH_3)_2]^+$. When gently warmed with Tollens' reagent, an aldehyde causes the colourless diamminesilver(I) ions to be reduced to metallic Ag(0). This causes a 'silver mirror' to coat the inside of the reaction vessel. There is no reaction and no mirror if a ketone is warmed with Tollens' reagent.

$$\mathrm{RCHO} + 2Cu^{2+}(aq) + 4OH^- \xrightarrow{2[O]} \mathrm{RCOOH} + Cu_2O(s) + 2H_2O$$

Blue (Cu²⁺) → Brick red (Cu₂O)

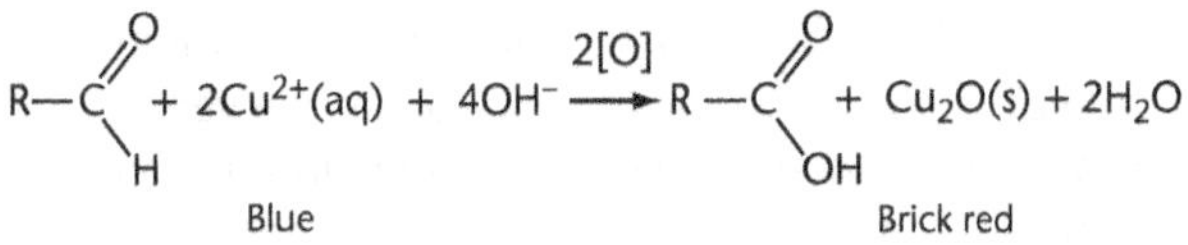

Figure 10 The oxidation of aldehydes with Fehling's solution

$$\mathrm{RCHO} + 2[Ag(NH_3)_2]^+(aq) + 2OH^- \xrightarrow{[O]} \mathrm{RCOOH} + 2Ag(s) + 4NH_3 + H_2O$$

Colourless → Silver

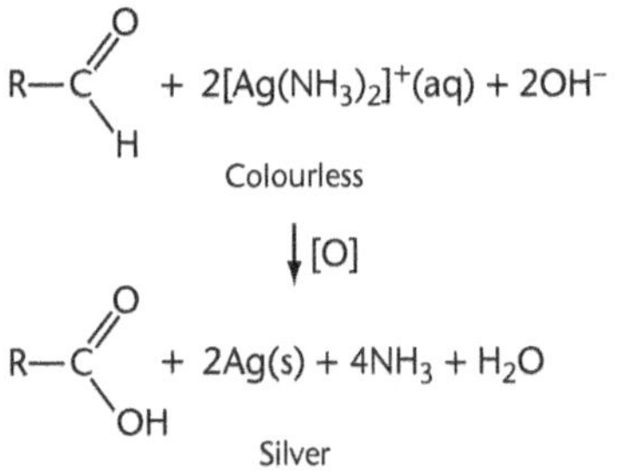

Figure 11 The oxidation of aldehydes with Tollens' reagent

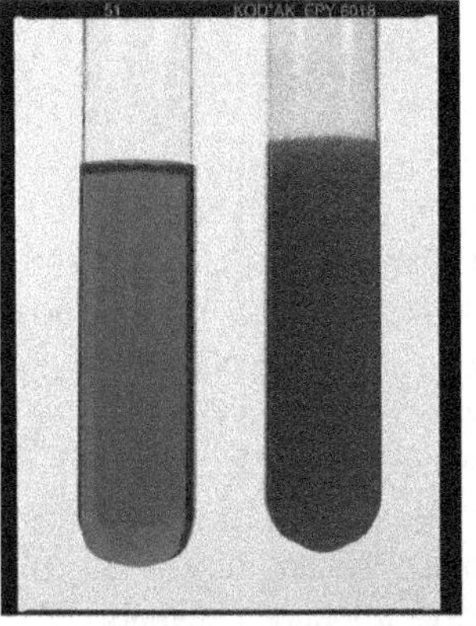

Figure 12 The Fehling's and Tollens' tests for aldehydes. The copper(II) complex ion gives Fehling's solution its blue colour; after an aldehyde is oxidised, the copper(II) ion is reduced to brick-red Cu_2O (left). The silver(I) complex ion in Tollens' reagent is reduced by an aldehyde to metallic silver (right).

Table 1 summarises the possible oxidation reactions of alcohols, aldehydes and ketones.

Oxidising agent	Primary alcohol	Secondary alcohol	Tertiary alcohol	Aldehyde	Ketone
Acidified potassium dichromate(VI)	✓	✓	✗	✓	✗
Fehling's solution	✗	✗	✗	✓	✗
Tollens' reagent	✗	✗	✗	✓	✗

Table 1 *Oxidation of alcohols, aldehydes and ketones*

Reduction reactions

The oxidation reactions used to make aldehydes and ketones (described earlier in this section) can be reversed with a strong reducing agent, i.e. lithium tetrahydridoaluminate ($LiAlH_4$, in a non-aqueous solvent) or sodium tetrahydridoborate ($NaBH_4$, in alcohol or water solution). These agents, represented by [H] in Figure 12, reduce aldehydes to primary alcohols and ketones to secondary alcohols. Carboxylic acids can also be reduced to primary alcohols because they are first reduced to aldehydes.

Acids and aldehydes

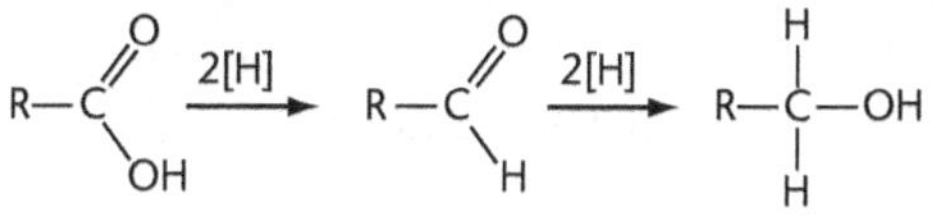

R—C(=O)OH —2[H]→ R—C(=O)H —2[H]→ R—CH₂—OH

Acid Aldehyde Primary alcohol

Ketones

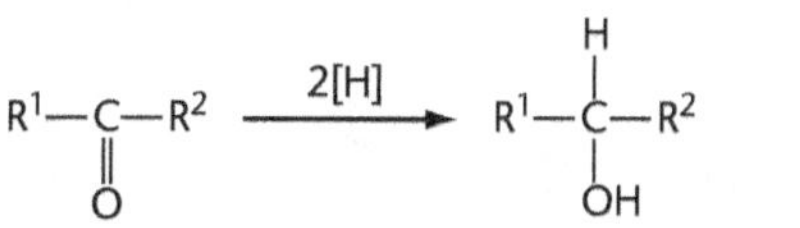

R^1—C(=O)—R^2 —2[H]→ R^1—CH(OH)—R^2

Ketone Secondary alcohol

Figure 13 *Reduction reactions of acid, aldehydes and ketones*

The reductions of aldehydes and ketones to alcohols are nucleophilic addition reactions. $NaBH_4$ is a source of the hydride ion, $:H^-$, which is a nucleophile. The mechanism for this process is shown in Figure 14. As with the addition of the cyanide anion, the first step is nucleophilic addition to the carbonyl group. The second step is the formation of the alcohol. In this case the H^+ can be provided by the water or by an added acid.

1 $:H^-$ + R^1—C(=O)—R^2 ⟶ R^1—CH(O^-)—R^2

Aldehydes: $R^1 = H$, R^2 = alkyl group (though for methanal it is H)

Ketones: R^1 and R^2 = alkyl groups (may or may not be the same alkyl group)

2 R^1—CH(O^-)—R^2 + H—O—H ⟶ R^1—CH(OH)—R^2 + $:\bar{O}H$

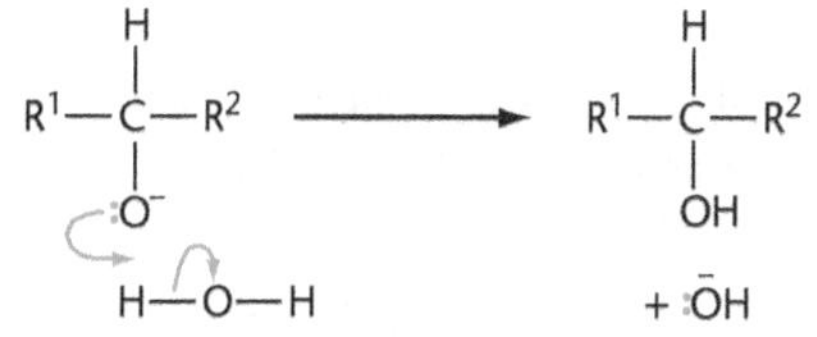

Figure 14 *The mechanism of $NaBH_4$ reduction of aldehydes and ketones*

QUESTIONS

4. Draw the products obtained from reduction of the following molecules:
   a. propanal
   b. pentan-2-one
   c. butanoic acid.
5. Butanone and butanal can be reduced to butan-2-ol and butan-1-ol, respectively.
   a. Suggest a reagent that could carry out the reduction of butanone and butanal.
   b. Hydride ions are produced by the reagent. Give a symbol for a hydride anion.
   c. Write the equations for the reductions of butanone and butanal using [H] as the reducing agent.
   d. What role do hydride anions carry out in the reduction? Use you answer to suggest an alternative name for reduction reactions of aldehydes and ketones.
6. Draw the curly arrow mechanism for the reduction of propanal with $NaBH_4$ in water using H^- to represent the nucleophile.

ASSIGNMENT 2: FLAVOURINGS AND ODOURS

(AT k)

Aldehydes and ketones are commonly responsible for both the taste and the odour of food. For example, aldehydes that contain six carbon atoms, such as hexanal, are often described as imparting a 'grassy' or 'green' smell and have been shown to be important in providing the fresh aroma of green beans. Research has shown that the amount of hexanal found in nectarines decreases as the fruit matures. Longer-chain aldehydes, such as (*E,Z*)-2,6-nonadienal, containing other functional groups such as alkenes, are responsible for the smell of cucumbers, and others such as (*E,E*)-2,4-decadienal for roast chicken (Figure A1).

Questions

A1. The typical aroma of chocolate is due to 5-methyl-2-phenyl-2-hexenal. Draw the structure of this molecule.

A2. Draw the structure of the product obtained from the reaction of 5-methyl-2-phenyl-2-hexenal with $NaBH_4$. What type of reaction is this?

Stretch and challenge

A3. Aldehydes containing five carbon atoms are found in cooked foods. How many of the isomers of $C_5H_{10}O$ are aldehydes, and how many isomers are ketones? Are any of the isomers chiral? If so, highlight the chiral centres with an asterisk.

A4. Draw the chiral product of reduction of the ketone shown below with $NaBH_4$. Why does the reaction give a racemic mixture?

O $\xrightarrow[H_2O]{NaBH_4}$?

A5. The reductions of ALL aldehydes with $NaBH_4$ do not generate chiral centres. Why is this? You should use the reduction of any aldehyde to illustrate your reasoning.

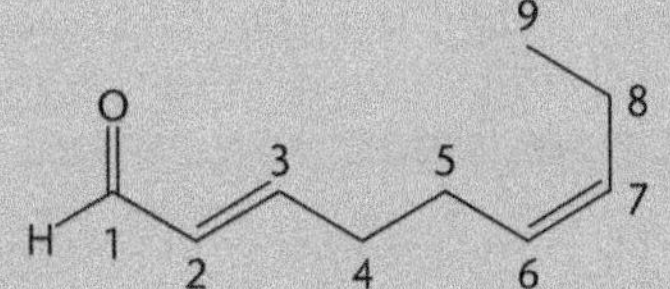

Cucumber smell
(E, Z)-2,6-nonadienal

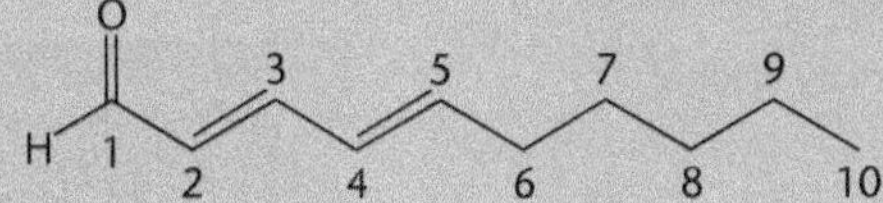

Roast chicken smell
(E, E)-2,4-decadienal

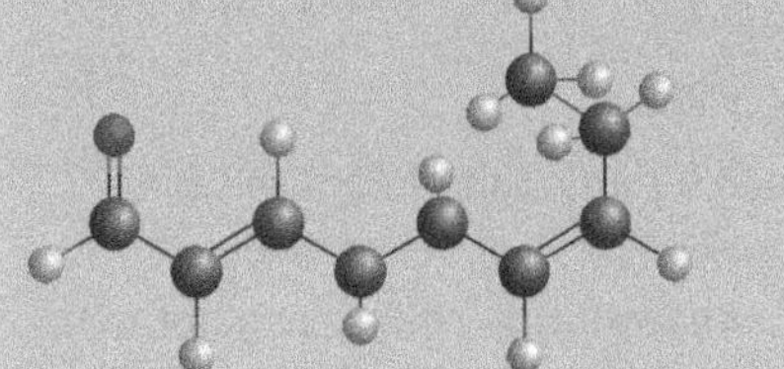

Figure A1 Structures of some odour chemicals

KEY IDEAS

- Aldehydes can be oxidised to carboxylic acids.
- Ketones are not oxidised readily.
- Fehling's and Tollens' tests distinguish aldehydes from ketones.
- Aldehydes can be reduced to primary alcohols and ketones can be reduced to secondary alcohols.
- Aldehydes and ketones undergo nucleophilic addition reactions with cyanide anions and hydride ions.
- For some aldehydes and ketones, nucleophilic addition can give rise to a chiral centre and occurs so as to give a racemic mixture of products.

PRACTICAL ACTIVITY: APPARATUS AND TECHNIQUES

(PS 2.2, AT b, AT d, AT k)

Distinguishing aldehydes and ketones by using Tollens' reagent and Fehling's solution

This practical activity gives you the opportunity to show that you can:

- Use a water bath for heating.
- Use laboratory apparatus to undertake qualitative tests for organic functional groups.
- Safely and carefully handle solids and liquids including corrosive, irritant, flammable and toxic substances.

Apparatus

Qualitative tests using Fehling's solution and Tollens' reagent are used to confirm the presence of the aldehyde functional group in a molecule. They are therefore useful tools in distinguishing between aldehydes and ketones. If the sample is a liquid then only a few drops are normally required for the test. Solid samples must be dissolved in deionised water and the solution tested. Guidance is usually given about the quantities of solid and water to use. Sometimes warming is necessary to dissolve the sample.

Generally, the tests are carried out in a clean test tube or boiling tube (contamination could lead to a false result). For the same reason, dropping pipettes used to transfer liquids must be clean. It may be necessary to warm the mixture of sample and reagent. This is best done by resting the test tube in a beaker of warm water. Since most organic compounds are flammable, heating with naked flames should be avoided.

Technique

Fehling's solution

Fehling's solution should be freshly prepared as it is unstable. This can be done by mixing two solutions: Fehling's A (an aqueous solution of copper(II) sulfate, typically about 0.3 mol dm^{-3}) and Fehling's B (a colourless solution of sodium hydroxide and potassium sodium tartrate). These are usually provided. Care should be taken and goggles should be worn when handling both solutions to avoid spillages as copper sulfate is harmful and sodium hydroxide is corrosive at the concentration used in the test. Mix about 1 cm^3 of each solution in a test tube and ensure reaction by gently swirling the test tube. Different pipettes should be used for each solution to avoid contamination. The solution should form the characteristic blue colour of Fehling's test solution, which contains a Cu(II) complex ion. Add a few drops of the sample to the reagent, swirling the tube gently. Warm the reaction in a water bath (at approximately 60 °C) for a few minutes to speed up the reaction. If an aldehyde is present the Cu(II) is reduced to Cu(I) in the form of insoluble brick-red Cu_2O, which precipitates out of solution.

Tollens' reagent

Tollens' reagent is normally prepared before the test is required. Eye protection should be worn and the room should be well ventilated. To prepare it three aqueous solutions are needed: silver nitrate, sodium hydroxide and ammonia. Silver nitrate solution is a relatively low-hazard substance, but it can stain the skin. Both aqueous sodium hydroxide and aqueous ammonia are irritants and corrosive. Tollens' reagent is prepared by using a dropping pipette to add sodium hydroxide solution to silver nitrate solution in a clean test tube. A light brown precipitate of silver oxide, Ag_2O, is formed, which dissolves when aqueous ammonia solution is added. The Tollens' solution of $[Ag(NH_3)_2]^+(aq)$ should be colourless.

Place about 2 cm^3 of the sample being tested in a clean test tube and add about 5 cm^3 of the Tollens' solution using a pipette. After a few minutes a silver precipitate or silver mirror is formed if an aldehyde was present in the test sample. While the reaction will take place at room temperature, sometimes it is helpful to stand the test tube in a hot water bath to increase the rate of the reaction. Your instructions or teacher will state the temperature of the water bath.

QUESTIONS

P1. You have been given five white crystalline solids and are asked to identify which are aldehydes and which are ketones. Write a set of instructions detailing how to do this.

P2. Predict the colour and the oxidation state of copper observed when the following compounds are added to Fehling's solution.

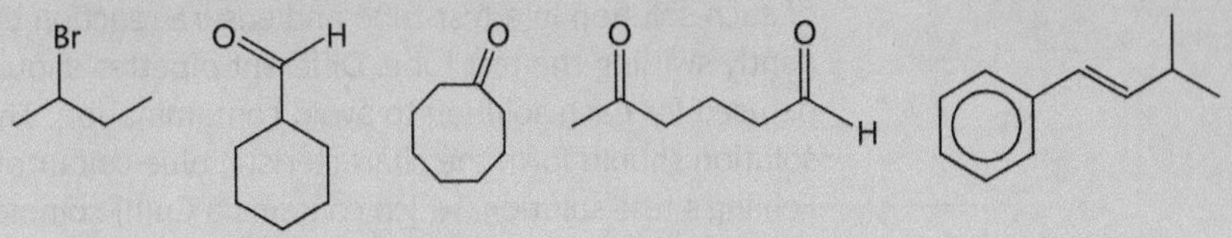

P3. When the Fehling's test is undertaken, the organic compound is warmed with the Fehling's reagent. How might you heat the reaction?

P4. You are working at a fragrance company. Two old bottles of fragrances have been found but the labels have faded and are now unreadable. It is known, however, that the two bottles contain the compounds shown here. You do not have access to any spectroscopic equipment.

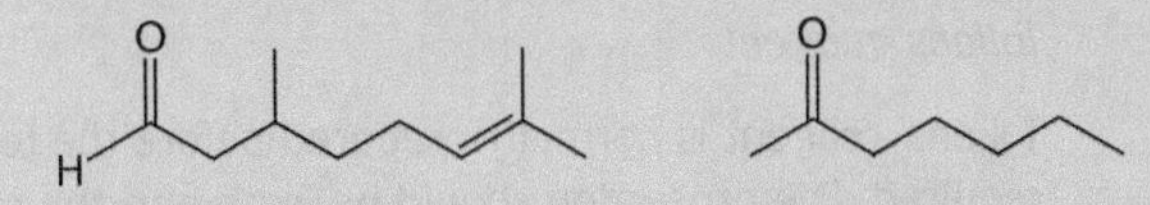

a. Name a chemical test that you could undertake to identify the two compounds.

b. What apparatus would you need to undertake the test?

c. How would you undertake the test in a laboratory?

d. Explain how the test works and what you would observe.

It turns out that the aldehyde has the smell of lemons, while the ketone, heptan-2-one, smells of blue cheese. (It might have been quicker to smell the bottles!)

P5.

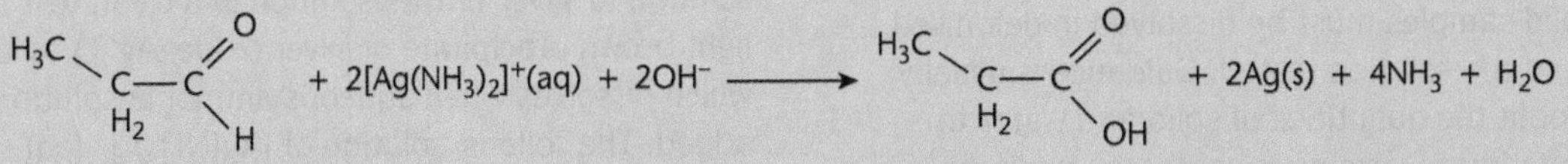

$$H_3C{-}CH_2{-}CHO + 2[Ag(NH_3)_2]^+(aq) + 2OH^- \longrightarrow H_3C{-}CH_2{-}COOH + 2Ag(s) + 4NH_3 + H_2O$$

Tollens' reagent ($[Ag(NH_3)_2]^+$) is made by mixing silver nitrate solution, $AgNO_3(aq)$, with aqueous sodium hydroxide, NaOH(aq), and ammonia, $NH_3(aq)$:

a. How many cubic centimetres of 2 M aqueous NH_3 solution are required to completely react with 5 cm^3 of 1 M $AgNO_3$ solution?

b. How many grams of Ag(0) will be produced if 1.0 g of propanone is added to 10 cm^3 of 2 M Tollens' reagent, $[Ag(NH_3)_2]^+(aq)$?

c. Assuming a complete reaction, how many grams of Ag(0) will be produced if an excess of Tollens' reagent is added to 0.05 mole of n-nonanal?

PRACTICE QUESTIONS

1. Butanone is reduced in a two-step reaction using $NaBH_4$ followed by dilute hydrochloric acid.
   a. Write an overall equation for the reduction of butanone using [H] to represent the reductant.
   b. By considering the mechanism of the reaction, explain why the product has **no** effect on plane polarised light.

   AQA Specimen Paper 2, 2015, Question 11

2. Which alcohol could **not** be produced by the reduction of an aldehyde or ketone?
   a. 2-methylbutan-1-ol
   b. 2-methylbutan-2-ol
   c. 3-methylbutan-1-ol
   d. 3-methylbutan-2-ol.

   AQA Specimen Paper 3, 2015, Question 29

3. Two isomeric ketones are shown in Figure Q1:

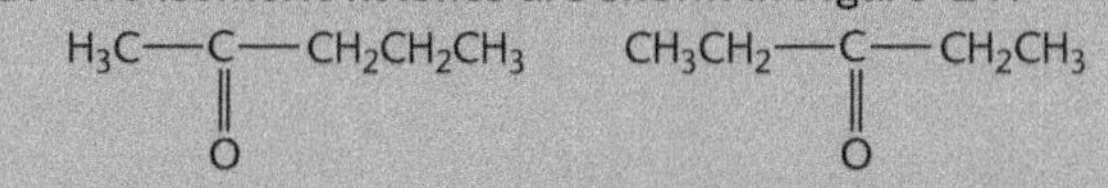

   Q: $H_3C—C(=O)—CH_2CH_2CH_3$

   R: $CH_3CH_2—C(=O)—CH_2CH_3$

   Figure Q1

   a. Name and outline a mechanism for the reaction of compound **Q** with HCN and name the product formed.
   b. Some students were asked to suggest methods to distinguish between isomers **Q** and **R**. One student suggested testing the optical activity of the products formed when **Q** and **R** reacted separately with HCN. By considering the optical activity of these products formed from **Q** and **R**, explain why this method would not distinguish between **Q** and **R**.

   AQA Chemistry, January 2010, Question 4a–b

3. Consider the reaction of propanal with HCN.
   a. Write an equation for the reaction of propanal with HCN and name the product.
   b. Name and outline a mechanism for the reaction of propanal with HCN.
   c. The rate-determining step in the mechanism in part b. involves attack by the nucleophile. Suggest how the rate of reaction of propanone with HCN would compare with the rate of reaction of propanal with HCN. Explain your answer.

   AQA Chemistry, January 2011, Question 6b

4. The reducing agent in this conversion is $NaBH_4$:

   $H_3C—C(=O)—CH_2CH_3 \longrightarrow H_3C—CH(OH)—CH_2CH_3$

   a. Name and outline a mechanism for the reaction.
   b. By considering the mechanism of this reaction, explain why the product formed is optically inactive.

   AQA Chemistry, January 2013, Question 7c

5. Lactic acid, $CH_3CH(OH)COOH$, is formed in the human body during metabolism and exercise. This acid is also formed by the fermentation of carbohydrates such as sucrose, $C_{12}H_{22}O_{11}$. A molecule of lactic acid contains an asymmetric carbon atom. The lactic acid in the body occurs as a single enantiomer. A racemic mixture (racemate) of lactic acid can be formed in this two-stage synthesis:

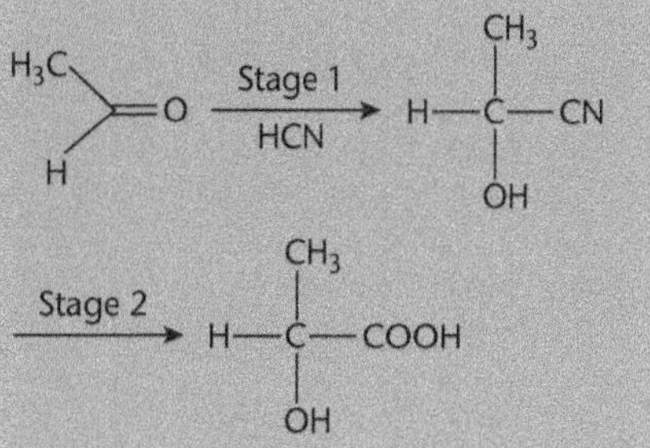

   $H_3C(H)C{=}O \xrightarrow[\text{HCN}]{\text{Stage 1}} H—C(CH_3)(OH)—CN \xrightarrow{\text{Stage 2}} H—C(CH_3)(OH)—COOH$

   Name and outline a mechanism for stage 1.

   AQA Chemistry, June 2013, Question 5b

6. The carbonyl compound CH_3CH_2CHO reacts very slowly with HCN.
   a. Name and outline a mechanism for the reaction of CH_3CH_2CHO with HCN.

b. The reaction in part a. produces a pair of enantiomers.

i. Draw the structure of each enantiomer to show how they are related to one another.

ii. State and explain how you could distinguish between the two enantiomers.

c. Give the IUPAC name of the product of the reaction in part a.

d. In practice KCN rather than HCN is added to the carbonyl compound. Given that K_a for HCN = 4.0×10^{-10} mol dm^{-3}, suggest why the reaction with HCN is very slow.

AQA Chemistry, June 2014, Question 5

7 CARBOXYLIC ACIDS AND DERIVATIVES

PRIOR KNOWLEDGE

You will already have studied the reactions of aldehydes and ketones and be familiar with the curly arrow mechanisms of their nucleophilic addition reactions. You learned about acids and bases and chemical equilibria (see *chapter 9 of Year 1 Student Book and chapters 4 and 6 of Year 2 Student Book*).

LEARNING OBJECTIVES

In this chapter you will learn about the structures and reactions of carboxylic acids and esters and the formation of their derivatives. You will be able to outline the mechanism of the nucleophilic addition–elimination reactions of acyl chlorides with water, alcohols, ammonia and primary amines. In addition, you will learn about the uses of esters in the formation of plasticisers, soaps and biodiesel.

(Specification 3.3.9)

Carboxylic acid groups are found in polymers, food additives, cosmetics, dietary supplements and many drugs. Many naturally occurring biological molecules, such as amino acids, also contain a carboxylic acid group. Citric acid, for example, is a tricarboxylic acid found in citrus fruits, and is an important preservative and flavouring. The functional group can be easily transformed into esters and amides, which themselves have a large number of uses. Esters are found in biodiesel, lipids, cell membranes, fragrances and flavourings, while amides are the main components of polymers such as nylon and proteins as well as pharmaceutical drugs such as paracetamol.

Carboxylic acids with long-chain alkyl groups are called **fatty acids**. Esters formed from naturally occurring fatty acids are used in the biofuel industry and are produced from animal fats or vegetable oils, such as rapeseed, palm or soybean oil. Esters of fatty acids have been used as renewable feedstocks to make plastics and polymers to replace those made from petrochemical feedstocks.

7.1 CARBOXYLIC ACIDS AND DERIVATIVES

As described in *chapter 6 of Year 2 Student Book*, carboxylic acids are produced when primary alcohols or aldehydes are oxidised. The simplest four carboxylic acids are listed in Table 1. Vinegar is an aqueous solution of ethanoic acid (also known as acetic acid), and ethanoic acid is responsible for the vinegary taste of wine that has been oxidised by exposure to air. The carboxylic acid butanoic acid has the characteristic smell of vomit. Carboxylic acids with low relative molecular masses are volatile.

The functional group of carboxylic acids is –COOH.

In chemistry, a 'derivative' is a molecule that is made from a similar compound by a chemical process.

Carboxylic acids with fewer than six carbon atoms per molecule are water-soluble. This is because water molecules can hydrogen-bond with the functional group. In aqueous solution they are only slightly ionised, to give low concentrations of hydronium ions and alkanoate ions (often called carboxylate ions) (Figure 1).

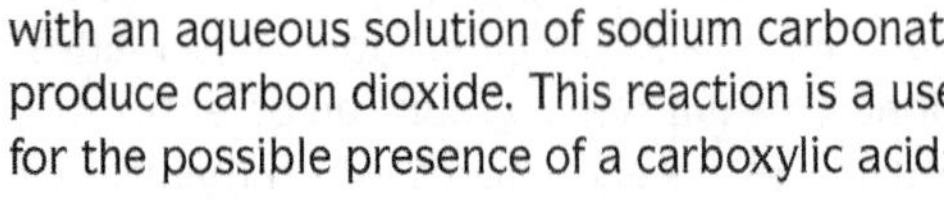

$$R{-}C(=O)OH + H_2O \rightleftharpoons R{-}C(=O)O^- + H_3O^+$$

Figure 1 *Ionisation of carboxylic acids in water*

This partial ionisation in solution means that carboxylic acids are **weak acids**. Nevertheless, the concentration of hydrogen ions is sufficient to react with an aqueous solution of sodium carbonate and produce carbon dioxide. This reaction is a useful test for the possible presence of a carboxylic acid:

$$2RCOOH + CO_3^{2-} \rightarrow 2RCOO^- + CO_2 + H_2O$$

methanoic acid	HCOOH	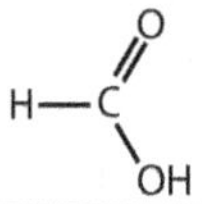 H–C(=O)OH
ethanoic acid	CH_3COOH	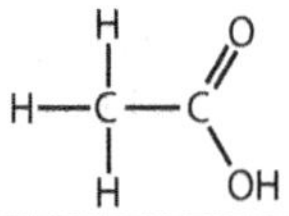 H_3C–C(=O)OH
propanoic acid	CH_3CH_2COOH	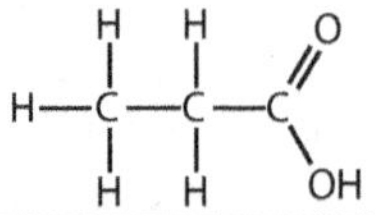 H_3C–CH_2–C(=O)OH
butanoic acid	$CH_3CH_2CH_2COOH$	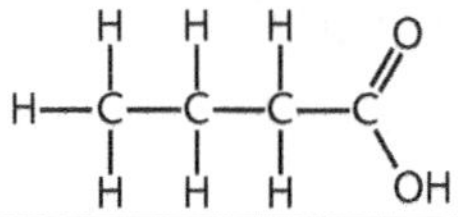 H_3C–CH_2–CH_2–C(=O)OH

Table 1 *Structures of the first four carboxylic acids*

QUESTIONS

1. The values for the acid dissociation constant K_a (see *chapter 3 of Year 2 Student Book*) of some carboxylic acids are:
   - ethanoic acid 2.0×10^{-5} mol dm^{-3}
   - benzene carboxylic acid 1.0×10^{-5} mol dm^{-3}
   - methanoic acid 1.0×10^{-4} mol dm^{-3}.

   Use these data to place 0.1 mol dm^{-3} solutions of these acids in order of increasing pH.

Common derivatives of carboxylic acids are acyl chlorides, acid anhydrides, esters and amides (Figure 2).

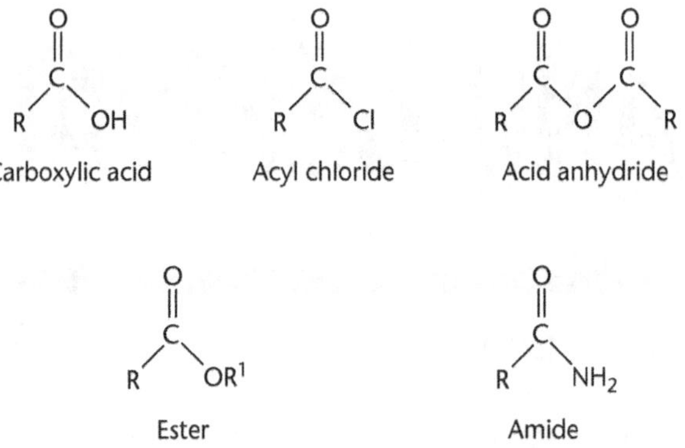

Carboxylic acid: R–C(=O)–OH; Acyl chloride: R–C(=O)–Cl; Acid anhydride: R–C(=O)–O–C(=O)–R; Ester: R–C(=O)–OR[1]; Amide: R–C(=O)–NH_2

Figure 2 *The names and structures of carboxylic acid derivatives*

IUPAC nomenclature of carboxylic acids, esters and amides

Carboxylic acids are named from the parent alkane by replacement of the suffix with *-oic acid*. For esters, identify the chain that contains the carbonyl group and the one directly attached to the oxygen atom. List the group attached to the oxygen first and introduce the suffix *-oate* to the parent chain containing the C=O. For amides, it is similar. For amides derived from ammonia add the suffix *-amide*, while for those derived from primary amines first list the nitrogen substituent and reinforce the fact that it is bonded to the nitrogen atom by incorporating the prefix *N*-. These rules are illustrated in Figure 3.

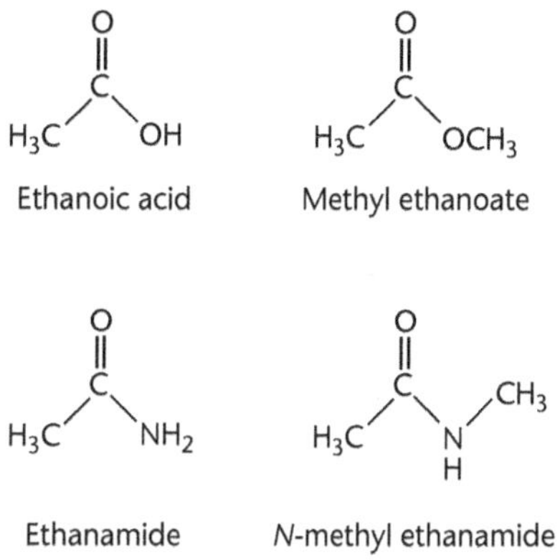

$H_3C-C(=O)-OH$ Ethanoic acid

$H_3C-C(=O)-OCH_3$ Methyl ethanoate

$H_3C-C(=O)-NH_2$ Ethanamide

$H_3C-C(=O)-NH-CH_3$ *N*-methyl ethanamide

Figure 3 *The names and structures of ethanoic acid and some derivatives*

Worked example 1

Name this molecule:

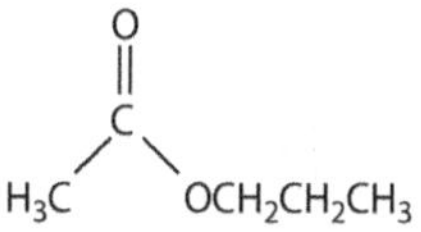

$H_3C-C(=O)-OCH_2CH_2CH_3$

The ester group gives the suffix *-oate* to the name. The longest carbon chain containing the C=O group is two carbon atoms long, giving the ester group the suffix 'ethanoate'. The group attached to the oxygen of the ester is a propyl group and so the ester is called propyl ethanoate.

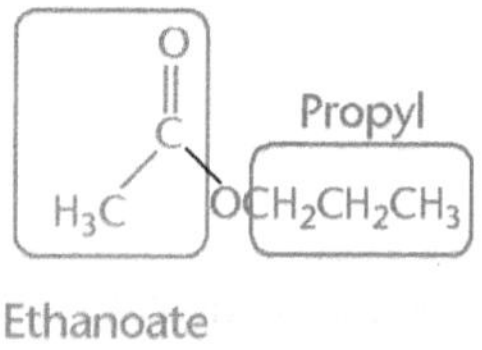

Propyl: $CH_2CH_2CH_3$; Ethanoate: $H_3C-C(=O)-O$

Worked example 2

Name this molecule:

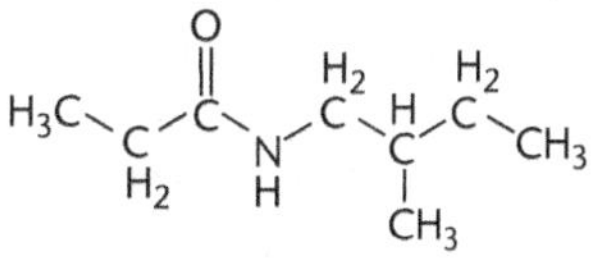

$H_3C-CH_2-C(=O)-NH-CH_2-CH(CH_3)-CH_2-CH_3$

The amide group gives the suffix *-amide* to the name. The longest carbon chain containing the carbonyl group is three carbon atoms long, giving the amide group the suffix 'propanamide'. The group attached to the nitrogen of the amide is a 2-methylbutyl group, so the amide is called *N*-2-methylbutyl propanamide. The alkyl group after '*N*' is the group that is attached to the nitrogen in amide.

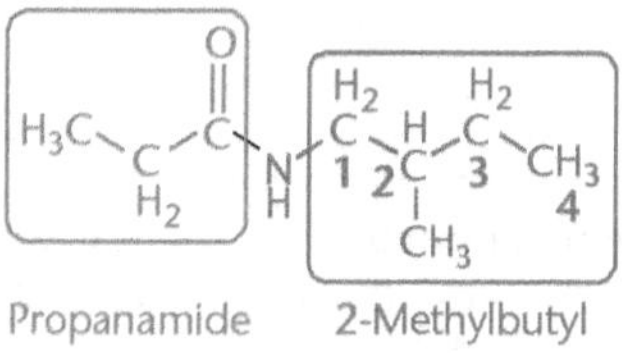

Propanamide: $H_3C-CH_2-C(=O)-$; 2-Methylbutyl: $-CH_2(1)-CH(CH_3)(2)-CH_2(3)-CH_3(4)$

QUESTIONS

2. Draw the structures of:
   a. propyl butanoate
   b. *N*-butyl ethanamide
   c. *N*-ethyl butanamide
   d. 2-methyl-5-chloro-pentanamide.

7.2 ESTERS

Preparation of esters

An ester is formed when an alcohol and a carboxylic acid react together in the presence of a concentrated, strong acid catalyst (e.g. sulfuric acid or hydrochloric acid). The general equation for this type of reaction is shown in Figure 4.

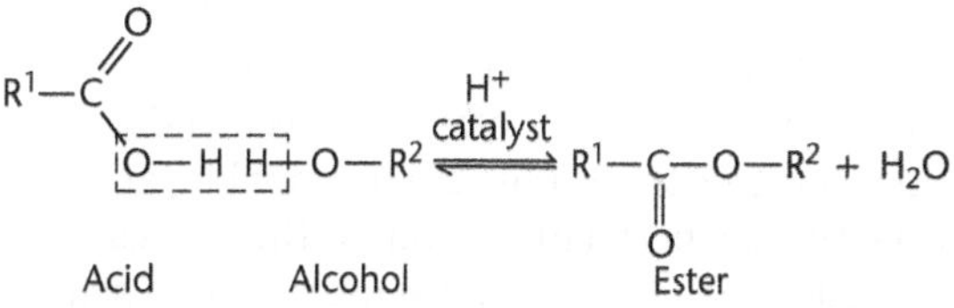

$$R^1-C(=O)-OH + H-O-R^2 \underset{\text{catalyst}}{\overset{H^+}{\rightleftharpoons}} R^1-C(=O)-O-R^2 + H_2O$$

Acid | Alcohol | Ester

Figure 4 *The synthesis of esters from carboxylic acids and alcohols*

Radioactive labelling studies have shown that in most cases the C–O bond in the acid breaks rather than the C–O bond in the alcohol. Table 2 gives some examples of ester formation.

This reaction is often referred to as an **esterification**. It is an example of a **condensation reaction** since a small molecule (H_2O) is eliminated from two carbon-based molecules that form a larger molecule. Such reactions are vitally important in the production of natural and artificial polymers, as we will see in *chapter 10 of Year 2 Student Book*.

Acid	+ methanol gives:	+ ethanol gives:
Ethanoic acid $CH_3-C(=O)OH$	Methyl ethanoate $CH_3-C(=O)-O-CH_3$	Ethyl ethanoate $CH_3-C(=O)-O-CH_2CH_3$
Propanoic acid $CH_3CH_2-C(=O)OH$	Methyl propanoate $CH_3CH_2-C(=O)-O-CH_3$	Ethyl propanoate $CH_3CH_2-C(=O)-O-CH_2CH_3$

Table 2 *Ester structures*

QUESTIONS

3. Write an equation for the reaction of butanoic acid with propan-1-ol, and name the organic product.

QUESTIONS

4. Draw the skeletal structure of the carboxylic acid and alcohol components required to prepare the principal esters responsible for the smell of rum, banana and peach.

Banana

Rum

Peach

Ester formation reactions are reversible, and produce relatively low yields of esters. The equilibrium can be shifted towards the product if water is distilled from the reaction mixture as it is formed or if a large excess of alcohol is used. Higher yields of esters are obtained by reacting the alcohol with the acyl chloride or acid anhydride instead of the carboxylic acid. These reactions are also called **acylations** and will be discussed later.

Uses of esters

Like aldehydes and ketones, esters are important chemicals in the fragrances and flavourings industry. They tend to be used more often, however, and have a fruitier, sweeter smell. They are responsible for many flower scents and fruit flavours. The artificial fruit flavours (e.g. cherry, banana, pear) used in some confectionery products are mixtures of synthetic esters. Some of these are shown in Table 3. Aromas and tastes are often due to complex mixtures of different esters; the aroma of coffee is thought to be due to over 100 different esters.

Ester	Essence
ethyl methanoate	raspberry
ethyl butanoate	pineapple
ethyl ethanoate	pear drops
2-pentyl ethanoate	pear

Table 3 *Ester fragrances*

The sweet or fruity smell of an ester can be used as a test for the presence of an alcohol or carboxylic acid. If we suspect that the compound being investigated is an alcohol, it can be warmed with a carboxylic acid such as ethanoic acid in the presence of concentrated sulfuric acid (a catalyst). Excess acid with its pungent, vinegary smell can be removed by adding warm aqueous sodium carbonate solution. If the remaining mixture has a sweet smell of an ester, this confirms the presence of an alcohol. The warmth of the solution then causes the ester to evaporate, and the sweet smell is easily detected.

Esters are also used as **plasticisers**, additives mixed into polymers to increase the flexibility of the polymer. Poly(chloroethene), better known as PVC (see *chapter 14 in Year 1 Student Book*), is a strong, rigid polymer suitable for making drainpipes and guttering.

Figure 5 Esters flavour the sweets in this Turkish sweet shop

However, when treated with up to 18% by mass of an appropriate plasticising ester, it can be made into cling film, which is used as food wrapping.

PVC consists of very long polymer chains. The carbon–chlorine bond is strongly polar and there is considerable intermolecular attraction between the polymer chains (Figure 6). PVC is therefore a strong, rigid plastic. Plasticiser molecules penetrate between the polymer chains and increase the distance between the chains. The polar effects of the carbon–chlorine bond are weakened and the rigidity of the three-dimensional structure is reduced (Figure 7). As a result, the polymer chains can slide over each other and the resulting plastic is soft and pliable, as cling film must be.

The ester originally used as a plasticiser in cling film was di(2-ethylhexyl) adipate (commonly called DEHA). DEHA is an ester of 2-ethylhexan-1-ol and adipic acid (hexanedioic acid). Such plasticised PVC is also used to make imitation leather for car seats, shoes, briefcases and so on. Over time the plasticiser evaporates, causing the 'leather' to lose its flexibility and crack.

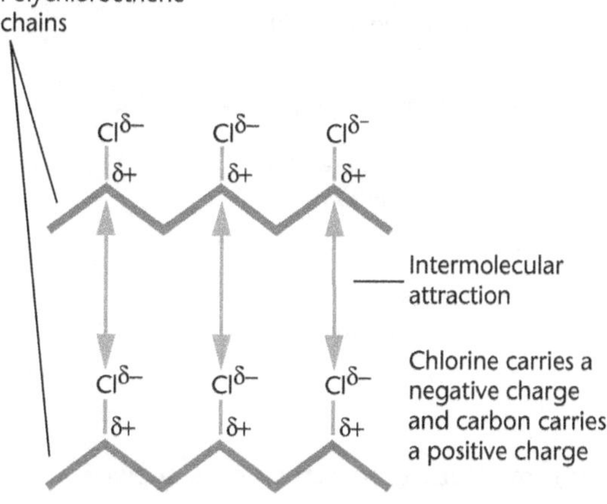
Polychloroethene chains
$Cl^{\delta-}$
$\delta+$
Intermolecular attraction
Chlorine carries a negative charge and carbon carries a positive charge
The dipoles in the carbon–chlorine bonds attract adjacent polymer chains

Figure 6 Intermolecular forces in PVC

Polychloroethene chains
Plasticiser molecules
Distance too great for intermolecular forces to be effective

Figure 7 The addition of a plasticiser reduces rigidity

Esters are also commonly used as solvents for organic compounds. A common solvent is ethyl ethanoate, which is relatively cheap, with low toxicity. Its volatility (its boiling point is 77 °C) makes it ideal as a solvent in glues, fragrances and nail varnishes (Figure 8). The ingredients are dissolved in the ester, which evaporates in air and leaves the scent or varnish behind. Ethyl ethanoate is also thought to be partially responsible for the fruity smell found in wines as it can be formed by the reaction of ethanol with ethanoic acid.

Figure 8 The volatile esters used as solvents in nail varnish quickly evaporate in the air

QUESTIONS

5. a. Draw the structural formula of 2-ethylhexan-1-ol.
   b. Draw the structure of 1,6-hexanedioic acid (adipic acid).
   c. Hence write an equation for the formation of DEHA (di(2-ethylhexyl) adipate).

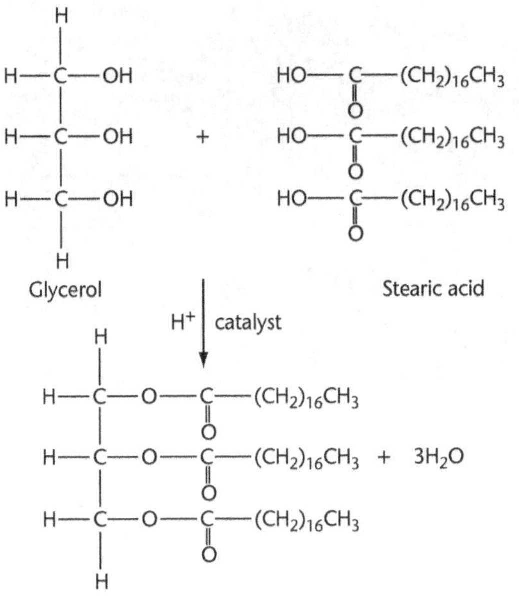

Naturally occurring fats and oils, such as animal fat and olive oil, are esters called triglycerides. They are the tri-esters of glycerol (propane-1,2,3-triol) and fatty acids (long-chain hydrocarbon carboxylic acids), such as stearic acid (*n*-octadecanoic acid). Reaction of 1 mole of glycerol with 3 moles of a fatty acid in the presence of an acid catalyst leads to the triglyceride via an esterification reaction in which 3 moles of water are eliminated.

Glycerol + Stearic acid ($3\ HO{-}C(=O){-}(CH_2)_{16}CH_3$) $\xrightarrow{H^+\ \text{catalyst}}$ triglyceride + $3H_2O$

Figure 9 *The synthesis of a triglyceride from glycerol and stearic acid*

ASSIGNMENT 1: FATTY ACIDS AND TRIGLYCERIDES

(PS 1.1, PS 1.2)

The melting points of some fatty acids are shown below. Naturally occurring fatty acids normally have an even number of carbon atoms, typically between 14 and 24. Fatty acids that contain *unbranched* groups are called saturated fatty acids and their melting point increases as the number of carbons increases owing to the increased van der Waals interactions between the linear chains. Introducing one, two or three *cis* (*Z*) C = C double bonds into the chain significantly lowers the melting point of the fatty acid.

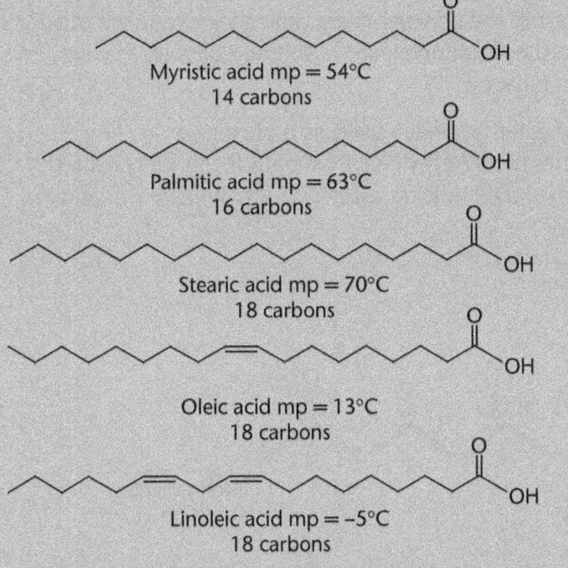

Figure A1 *The structures of some fatty acids and their melting points*

Oleic acid, an unsaturated fatty acid, contains one C = C double bond and is the main component of olive oil. The *cis* C = C double bonds introduce a kink into the chains, meaning that in the solid state the molecules cannot pack as efficiently. Consequently the van der Waals forces between molecules are weaker, resulting in a lower melting point.

Olive oil is a triglyceride. It is the **tri-ester** of glycerol (propane-1,2,3-triol) and two fatty acids, oleic acid and palmitic acid. It is a liquid at room temperature. Its structure is shown in Figure A2.

Trimyristin is a fat found in nutmeg. Its structure is also shown in Figure A2.

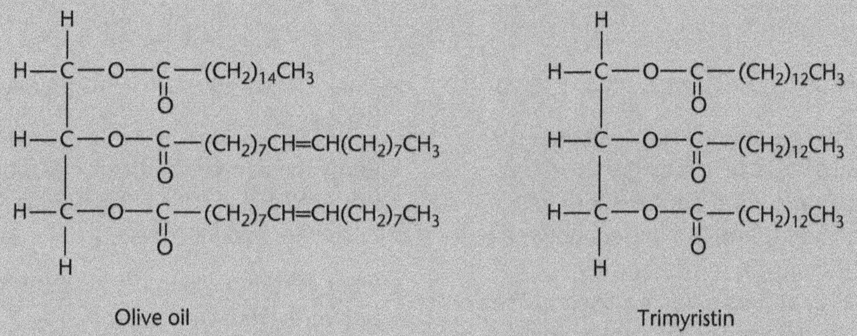

$$\begin{array}{l} \text{H} \\ | \\ \text{H—C—O—C(=O)—(CH}_2)_{14}\text{CH}_3 \\ | \\ \text{H—C—O—C(=O)—(CH}_2)_7\text{CH=CH(CH}_2)_7\text{CH}_3 \\ | \\ \text{H—C—O—C(=O)—(CH}_2)_7\text{CH=CH(CH}_2)_7\text{CH}_3 \\ | \\ \text{H} \end{array}$$

Olive oil

$$\begin{array}{l} \text{H} \\ | \\ \text{H—C—O—C(=O)—(CH}_2)_{12}\text{CH}_3 \\ | \\ \text{H—C—O—C(=O)—(CH}_2)_{12}\text{CH}_3 \\ | \\ \text{H—C—O—C(=O)—(CH}_2)_{12}\text{CH}_3 \\ | \\ \text{H} \end{array}$$

Trimyristin

Figure A2 *The structures of olive oil and trimyristin*

Questions

A1. Write an equation for the formation of trimyristin from glycerol.

A2. What ratio of reagents (glycerol and fatty acids) would be required to make synthetic olive oil?

Stretch and challenge

A3. Using your answer to Question A2, are there any other products that might theoretically be formed when you react the fatty acids with glycerol in the esterification process? Give the structural formulae of the other possible products.

A4. The main fatty acid found in animal fat is stearic acid (octadecanoic acid), while the main component of olive oil is oleic acid. Why do you think animal fat is a solid while olive oil is a liquid at room temperature?

A5. Predict whether trimyristin would be a solid or a liquid at room temperature, giving reasons.

Hydrolysis of esters

The reverse of an esterification reaction is called hydrolysis. The ester is hydrolysed by the action of water to re-form the acid and the alcohol (Figure 10). Such a hydrolysis requires heating and a strong acid or alkali such as sulfuric acid or sodium hydroxide catalyst. The acid-catalysed hydrolysis reaction is normally carried out with an excess of water to drive the equilibrium to the desired carboxylic acid.

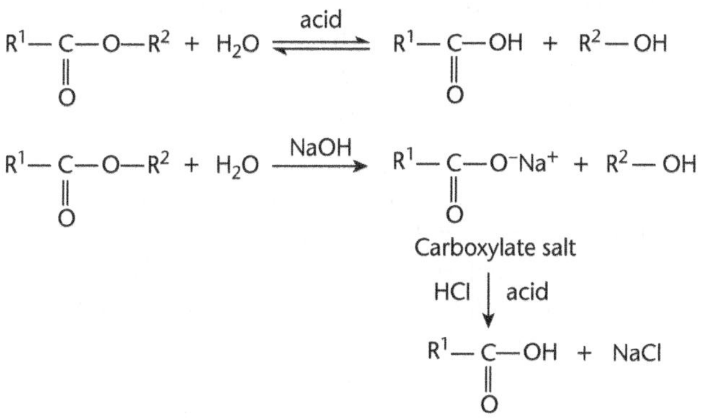

$$R^1\text{—C(=O)—O—}R^2 + H_2O \overset{\text{acid}}{\rightleftharpoons} R^1\text{—C(=O)—OH} + R^2\text{—OH}$$

$$R^1\text{—C(=O)—O—}R^2 + H_2O \xrightarrow{\text{NaOH}} R^1\text{—C(=O)—O}^-\text{Na}^+ + R^2\text{—OH}$$

Carboxylate salt

$$\downarrow \text{HCl acid}$$

$$R^1\text{—C(=O)—OH} + \text{NaCl}$$

Figure 10 *Hydrolysis of esters catalysed by acid and base*

In alkaline hydrolysis, an excess of sodium hydroxide is used. The carboxylic acid that forms reacts with excess alkali to form a carboxylate salt. This reaction continually removes the carboxylic acid from the equilibrium mixture. The alkaline solution containing the carboxylate salt is neutralised with hydrochloric acid to give a high yield of the carboxylic acid.

QUESTIONS

6. Naming the products, write equations for the hydrolysis of:
   a. ethyl ethanoate by hot concentrated sulfuric acid solution
   b. methyl propanoate by hot sodium hydroxide solution.

ASSIGNMENT 2: HYDROLYSIS OF METHYL BENZOATE TO GIVE BENZOIC ACID

(AT b, AT c, AT d, AT g, AT h, AT k PS 2.1, 2.3)

Food additives are compounds that enhance the taste and flavour of food or act as preservatives. In the European Union, food additives are given E-numbers to identify them. E-numbers between E200 and E299 are given to preservatives. Benzoic acid (E210) and its salts are used in the food industry as preservatives as they inhibit the growth of mould. Benzoic acid (C_6H_5COOH, IUPAC name benzene carboxylic acid) can be synthesised in the laboratory by hydrolysis of the ester methyl benzoate ($C_6H_5COOCH_3$). The following set of instructions was provided to carry out the base-catalysed hydrolysis of methyl benzoate to benzene carboxylic acid in the laboratory.

- Add 4 g of methyl benzoate to a round-bottomed flask and add 20 cm^3 of 2 mol dm^{-3} NaOH(aq) and 20 cm^3 of ethanol.
- Add a few anti-bumping granules and then fit a water-cooled condenser to the flask.
- Heat the flask until the contents boil and then heat for a further 30 minutes.
- Allow the contents of the flask to cool, remove the condenser and carefully pour the solution into a 250 cm^3 beaker.
- POINT A: Measure the pH with litmus paper.
- POINT B: Carefully add 2.0 mol dm^{-3} HCl(aq) until the solution is acidic as tested by litmus paper. (At this stage solid benzene carboxylic acid C_6H_5COOH, crystallises out).
- Filter off the solid benzene carboxylic acid from the solution.
- Purify the benzene carboxylic acid by recrystallisation from hot water (use the minimum amount of water).
- Filter off the purified benzene carboxylic acid and dry under reduced pressure.
- Measure the melting point of the benzene carboxylic acid (the melting point should be between 121 and 123 °C).

Questions

A1. Write an equation for the reaction of methyl benzoate with aqueous sodium hydroxide.

A2. How many moles of methyl benzoate and NaOH were used?

A3. Why were anti-bumping granules and a water-cooled condenser added to the flask?

A4. What colour would you expect red litmus paper to indicate at POINT A?

A5. What is the purpose of adding HCl (aq) to the mixture, and what colour would you expect litmus paper to indicate after the addition?

A6. Why, when you are undertaking the recrystallisation, should the minimum amount of hot water be used?

A7. The melting point of the purified material was determined to be 115–123 °C. What conclusions can you draw from this information?

Soaps

Soaps are carboxylate salts of long-chain carboxylic acids (**fatty acids**). They are made by hydrolysing naturally occurring fat and oil triglycerides.

Soap is manufactured by boiling fats and oils in aqueous sodium hydroxide. The process also called **saponification** (Figure 11). After the boiling is complete, sodium chloride is added to precipitate the soap. Since the hydrolysis is done under alkaline conditions, the product is a mixture of glycerol and the salts of the fatty acids, soaps. Glycerol is a useful by-product of soap manufacture that has extensive uses in pharmaceutical and cosmetic preparations.

Soaps are **anionic detergents**. The polar negatively charged carboxyl group of a soap is attracted to water. It is hydrophilic. The long, non-polar hydrocarbon chains are attracted to oil rather than water. They are hydrophobic.

Dirt, oil and grease consist mainly of non-polar organic molecules that do not dissolve in water. Therefore, oil forms a thin film on the water's surface. When soap or detergent molecules are added, they accumulate at the oil/water interface, with the polar 'head' of the soap interacting with the water layer and the non-polar hydrocarbon chain interacting with the non-polar organic oil. When the mixture is stirred or shaken,

$$\begin{array}{l} H_2C-O-C(=O)-R \\ HC-O-C(=O)-R \\ H_2C-O-C(=O)-R \end{array} + 3NaOH \longrightarrow \begin{array}{l} H_2C-OH \\ HC-OH \\ H_2C-OH \end{array} + 3R-C(=O)-O^-Na^+$$

a soap

e.g. $R = C_{17}H_{35}$

e.g. $R = C_{17}H_{35}COONa$, sodium stearate

Figure 11 *Base-catalysed hydrolysis of a triglyceride gives a soap by saponification*

the oil breaks up into tiny droplets (**emulsification**) and is dispersed throughout the water. The droplets are stable because the 'outside' is made up of polar carboxyl groups interacting favourably with water, and the 'inside' is made up of the hydrocarbon segments of the soap interacting with the grease.

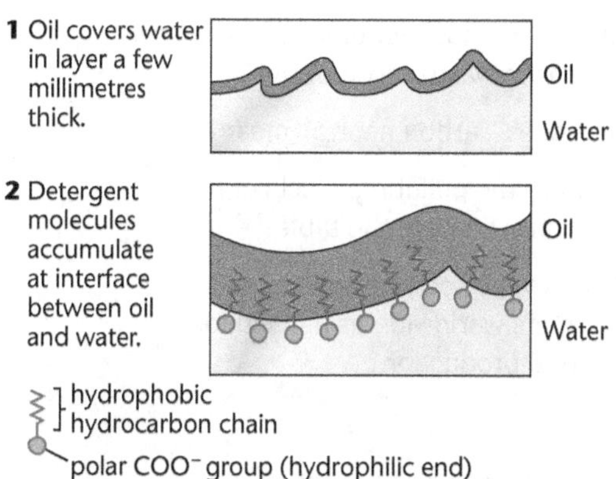
1 Oil covers water in layer a few millimetres thick.
Oil
Water
2 Detergent molecules accumulate at interface between oil and water.
Oil
Water
hydrophobic hydrocarbon chain
polar COO^- group (hydrophilic end)

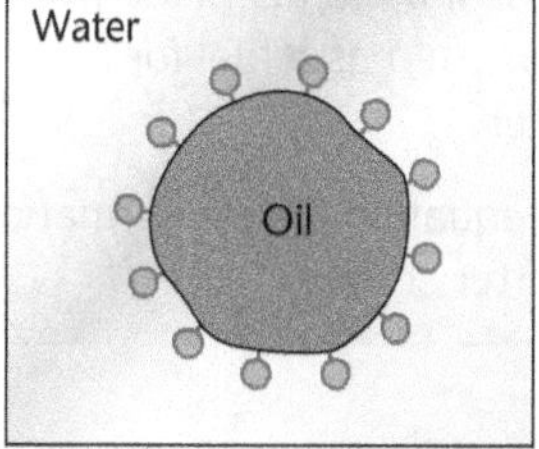
3 Oil breaks up into droplets that can mix with water. The emulsified oil can now be dispersed and broken down much more easily.
Water
Oil

Figure 12 *How a soap breaks up oil into droplets by emulsification*

The sodium salts (soaps) may be converted to free fatty acids by adding a strong acid such as hydrochloric acid:

$$CH_3-(CH_2)_{16}-C(=O)-O^-Na^+ + H_3O^+ \longrightarrow CH_3-(CH_2)_{16}-C(=O)-OH + Na^+ + H_2O$$

Sodium stearate — Stearic acid

Figure 13 *Reaction of a soap with a strong acid generates the carboxylic acid*

Remember, carboxylic acids are weak acids, so addition of hydrogen ions moves the equilibrium to the right, producing the insoluble fatty acid. This is why it can be a mistake to mix soap-based cosmetics with others based on citric acid products – slimy fatty acids may precipitate!

Biodiesel formation

Biodiesel, which can be used in normal diesel engines, is made from renewable vegetable oils rather than non-sustainable petrochemicals. We refer to biodiesel as a 'green' fuel. Natural triglyceride oils are converted to esters of methanol, which makes them less viscous. Biodiesel made, for example, from rapeseed oil is produced by **transesterification**. The triglyceride is converted into the less viscous methyl ester (rape methyl ester, or RME) using a sodium hydroxide catalyst and methanol. The transesterification is reversible, so an excess of methanol is used to drive the equilibrium to the right. Under optimum conditions this process can produce a 98% yield.

$$\begin{array}{l} H_2C-O-C(=O)-R^1 \\ HC-O-C(=O)-R^2 \\ H_2C-O-C(=O)-R^3 \end{array} + \underset{\text{methanol}}{CH_3OH} \underset{}{\overset{NaOH}{\rightleftharpoons}} \begin{array}{l} H_3CO-C(=O)-R^1 \\ H_3CO-C(=O)-R^2 \\ H_3CO-C(=O)-R^3 \end{array} + \begin{array}{l} H_2C-OH \\ HC-OH \\ H_2C-OH \end{array}$$

Rapeseed oil — Biodiesel esters — Glycerol

Figure 14 *The reaction for the preparation of biodiesel from a triglyceride and methanol using a catalyst*

ASSIGNMENT 3: BIODIESEL AND BIOFUEL

(PS 1.2)

The plants that make biodiesel use CO_2 from the atmosphere to grow, so burning biodiesel provides less CO_2 pollution overall than burning petrochemicals. There are also economic advantages to using biofuel: farmers can grow cash crops on, for example, set-aside land. The resulting fuels are called first-generation biofuels and are made from edible oils. However, the use of agricultural land or of increased deforestation to grow fuel crops such as rapeseed oil or palm oil leads to a decrease in the amount of land available to grow food or to destruction of our environment. Consequently, work is being undertaken to use waste vegetable oils from industry (second-generation biofuels) or natural oils derived from algae and microbes (third-generation biofuels).

Emission data vary depending on the biofuel and engine used. However, the following data are typical for the use of 100% biofuel in a diesel engine.

Type of emission	Change in emissions (%) when biofuel replaces mineral diesel
particulates (non-carcinogenic)	−47
carbon monoxide	−48
nitrogen oxides	+10
greenhouse gases	−80
sulfur oxides	−100

Questions

A1. Cocoa butter is a waste product from chocolate manufacture. The structure of its triglyceride is shown below. Write an equation for the formation of a methanol-derived biodiesel from cocoa butter (you can abbreviate the three chains as R^1, R^2 and R^3).

$$\begin{array}{l} H_2C{-}O{-}C({=}O){-}(CH_2)_{14}CH_3 \\ \;| \\ HC{-}O{-}C({=}O){-}(CH_2)_7CH{=}CH(CH_2)_7CH_3 \\ \;| \\ H_2C{-}O{-}C({=}O){-}(CH_2)_{16}CH_3 \end{array}$$

Cocoa butter

Figure A1 *The structure of cocoa butter*

A2. Which 'generation' of biofuel is biodiesel made from waste cocoa butter?

A3. What does 'carbon neutral' mean?

A4. What are the polluting effects of the emissions shown in the table?

A5. What are the social disadvantages of farmers worldwide using land for biodiesel production?

Stretch and challenge

A6. What potential problems do you think might arise if a biofuel made from saturated esters was used as a fuel for a car during a cold winter?

A7. Write an equation for the formation of a cocoa butter soap.

KEY IDEAS

- Esters can be produced by the reaction between an alcohol and a carboxylic acid using an acid catalyst.
- Esters are commonly used as solvents, flavourings and plasticisers.
- Fats and oils are naturally occurring tri-esters formed between glycerol (propane-1,2,3-triol) and long-chain fatty acids.
- Fats and oils are hydrolysed to soaps by boiling with aqueous sodium hydroxide.
- Biodiesel (a mixture of methyl esters of fatty acids) is prepared from vegetable oils and methanol using a catalyst.

REQUIRED PRACTICAL ACTIVITY 10B: APPARATUS AND TECHNIQUES

(MS 4.1, PS 2.3, PS 4.1, AT b, AT d, AT g, AT k)

Preparation of a pure organic liquid

This practical activity gives you the opportunity to show that you can:

- Use a water bath or electric heater or sand bath for heating.
- Use laboratory apparatus for a variety of experimental techniques.
- Purify a liquid product, including use of a separating funnel.
- Safely and carefully handle solids and liquids.

Apparatus

The apparatus used will depend upon the organic liquid being prepared. However, many organic liquids are prepared by refluxing a mixture of two or more reagents. The term 'reflux' refers to the process of carrying out a reaction, sometimes with a solvent, where the reagents are boiled for a set period of time. Therefore, a suitable heating source, a round-bottomed flask and a condenser are needed. Attaching a water condenser prevents volatile reagents, solvents or products from boiling away. Vapour condenses in the tube and drips back into the reaction vessel (Figure P1). Normally, the glassware has Quikfit™ ground glass joints so that a good connection is made. The apparatus is set up differently from that involved in a normal distillation in that the condenser is positioned vertically in the flask (Figure P1). Unlike in a normal distillation (see *section 3 in chapter 15 of Year 1 Student Book*), a thermometer is NOT needed. It is essential that the condenser is left open to the atmosphere, otherwise a pressure build-up will occur.

Figure P1 *Apparatus showing how a condenser is attached to a flask for a reaction under reflux*

For many preparations of esters, the apparatus may be taken apart after reflux and assembled for distillation (see *section 3 in chapter 15 of Year 1 Student Book*), enabling the liquid product to be obtained by distillation. This product may need purifying. A separating funnel can be used for this.

A separating funnel is used to separate two different immiscible liquids, typically an organic liquid and an aqueous solution. Two layers form, with the denser liquid at the bottom of the funnel. This bottom layer can then be separated from the upper layer by opening the tap and carefully allowing the bottom layer to run out. When using a separating funnel, you will also require a stopper for the funnel and two clean beakers to collect the two different layers. You will need to hold the funnel either in a clamp stand or in a separating funnel ring (see Figure P2).

Separating funnels come in different sizes. The size to choose will depend upon the amount of liquid that will be added to the funnel (see *section 3 in chapter 15 of Year 1 Student Book*). You should not fill a separating funnel more than half-full.

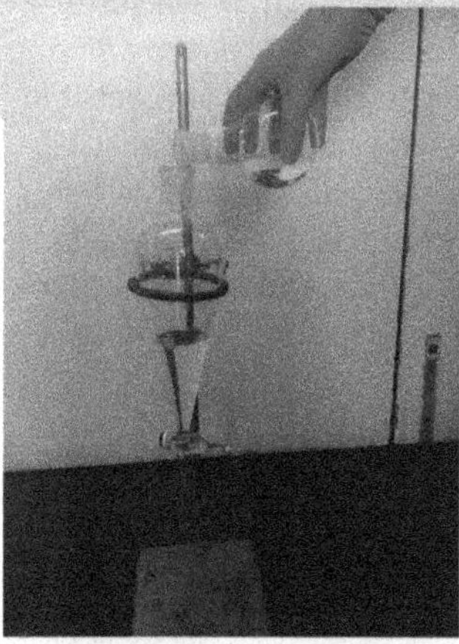

Figure P2 *Filling a separating funnel*

Techniques

Use an appropriate-sized flask and ensure that the reaction mixture occupies less than one-third of the flask's volume. Make sure that the condenser is attached to the water supply with the water entering the condenser at the bottom and exiting at the top. The flask can then be heated using a water bath. Always add anti-bumping granules to the flask to ensure smooth boiling of the contents. Make sure all joints in the apparatus are secure so that volatile chemicals do not escape during the reaction. Once the reaction is finished, wait for the apparatus to cool before dismantling it. Care must be taken when decoupling the condenser from the flask as on occasion it may be difficult to remove. Impure products can be partially purified at this stage by reconfiguring the apparatus for distillation and collecting appropriate fractions, or further purification may involve separation of components using a separating funnel.

When two immiscible liquids need to be separated, a separating funnel is used. To use a separating funnel correctly, make sure that the tap is freely movable but does not leak. For safety, and to avoid the loss of reagents, have a clean beaker positioned under the flask at all times.

Ensure that the tap of the separating funnel is closed and carefully pour the two liquids to be separated into the funnel (Figure P2). If it is necessary to mix the two liquids, place the stopper into the top of the separating funnel and then, making sure that the tap is closed, hold the stopper onto the funnel and invert the whole separating funnel a number of times. Open the tap to allow any build-up of gas to escape (Figure P3). Make sure to close the tap before the funnel is inverted again. Clamp the separating funnel to a stand or place it in a separating funnel ring and wait for the immiscible layers to separate. Make sure you can identify which is the aqueous layer and which is the organic layer. If unsure, add a few cubic centimetres of water and observe which layer increases in size. This layer will be the aqueous layer.

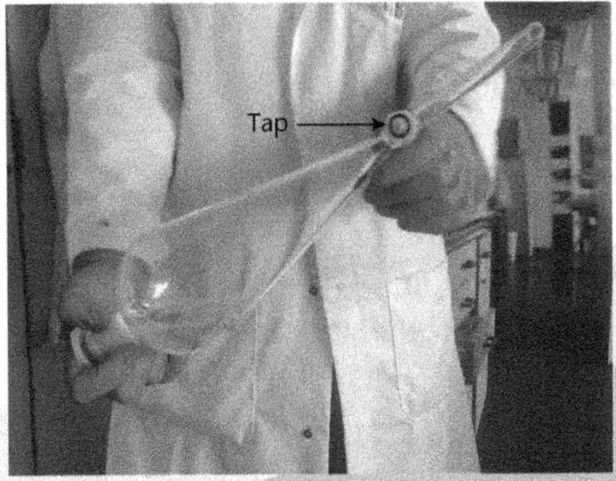

Figure P3 *Opening the tap of a separating funnel to allow any build-up of gas to escape*

If the two layers are of different colours, it is easy to see the interface between them. If they are both clear it might be more difficult (Figure P4), but if you hold a blank piece of white paper behind the funnel the interface will become apparent. To separate the denser layer from the top layer, open the tap carefully and allow the bottom layer to drain into a clean, labelled beaker. When the bottom layer is nearly all drained, slow down the rate of drainage by partially closing the tap in order to avoid accidently draining a little of the top layer as well. Normally, the top layer is the organic layer containing the product (organic compounds are normally less dense than water). Drain the top layer into a second clean beaker. The organic layer may still contain a small amount of water, and in order to remove any last traces of water a solid drying agent is added to the beaker (typically anhydrous sodium sulfate or anhydrous magnesium sulfate) and the mixture stirred vigorously. If the organic liquid is to be purified further (e.g. by distillation), then the dried liquid can be decanted off the drying agent into a clean round-bottomed flask for distillation. Alternatively, the drying agent can be removed by filtration to provide the organic product.

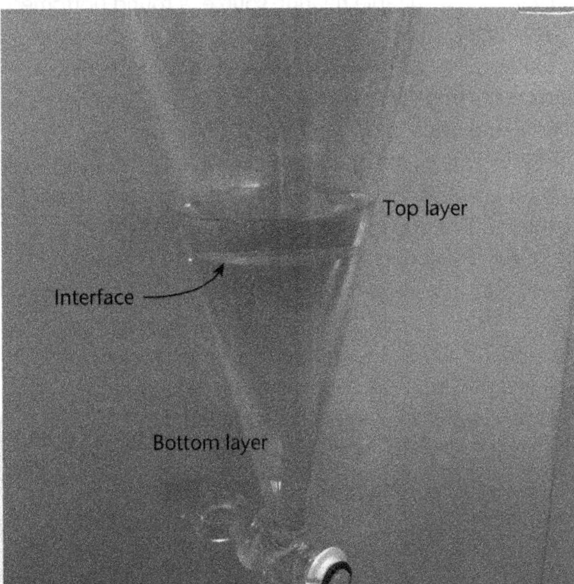

Figure P4 *Two immiscible layers can be seen in the separating funnel*

QUESTIONS

P1. When a reaction is conducted under reflux, why must the reflux condenser be open to the atmosphere?

P2. A reaction mixture was heated under reflux. After the reaction, the heating source was removed. Why was it necessary to keep the apparatus set up with the water running in the condenser until the flask and its contents had cooled?

P3. Suggest a problem that might arise if the joint between the condenser and the round-bottomed flask was found to be leaking.

P4. In a separating funnel, the top layer of two immiscible liquids contained the product. When separating it from the bottom layer in a separating funnel, a student failed to close the tap quickly enough and half of the top layer was lost into the beaker containing the denser layer. What could the student do to ensure that no loss of product occurred?

P5. A mixture of ethyl ethanoate and ethanoic acid was poured into a separating funnel. Aqueous sodium carbonate was added and the separating funnel stoppered and inverted five times. Each time the funnel was inverted, the tap was opened and a hissing sound of gas escaping was heard, before the tap was closed.

a. What caused the hissing sound of gas escaping?

b. What was the purpose of adding aqueous sodium carbonate to the separating funnel?

c. After shaking with aqueous sodium carbonate, what chemical(s) are in the top layer?

d. After separation of the top layer, anhydrous calcium chloride was added to it. What was the purpose of the addition of anhydrous calcium chloride?

P6. How are insoluble impurities removed from a liquid?

Stretch and challenge

P7. When separating two immiscible layers in a separating funnel, why is it important to remove the stopper from the separating funnel before opening the tap to drain the bottom layer?

7.3 ACYLATION

Acyl groups (Figure 15) can be built into many molecules using acyl chlorides or acid anhydrides (acylating agents). Acyl chlorides and acid anhydrides (Figure 16) are derivatives of carboxylic acids. Acyl chlorides are derived from carboxylic acids by substitution of the –OH group by a chlorine atom. Acid anhydrides are derived by substitution of the –OH group by an alkanoate. Acid chlorides are named by identifying the parent hydrocarbon chain and adding the suffix *-oyl chloride*, while symmetrical anhydrides utilise the suffix *-oic anhydride*. Hence, the acyl chloride and acid anhydride of ethanoic acid are ethanoyl chloride and ethanoic anhydride, respectively.

Ethanoyl Propanoyl

Figure 15 *Acyl groups*

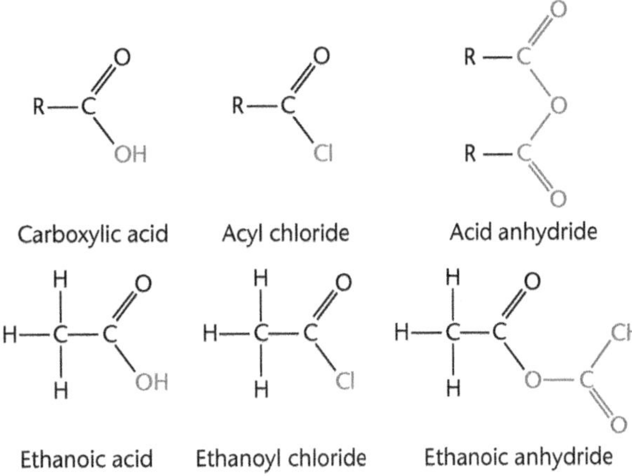

Figure 16 *Ethanoic acid derivatives*

> **QUESTIONS**
>
> **7.** Draw either a displayed formula or skeletal structure of:
>
> a. butanoyl chloride
>
> b. butanoyl anhydride
>
> c. 2-methyl-4-chloropentanoyl chloride.

Synthesis of acids, esters and amides via nucleophilic addition–elimination reactions

Reactions in which acyl groups are introduced into molecules are called acylations. Acylation reactions have many uses, for example in the pharmaceutical and textile industries. Acylation reactions are used to make drugs such as aspirin and textiles such as cellulose acetate. Reaction of acyl chlorides with water or alcohols is normally a fast, exothermic process producing carboxylic acids or esters, respectively, along with rapid generation of plumes of highly corrosive hydrogen chloride gas.

In general, acid anhydrides make better acylating agents than acyl chlorides (Figure 17). The anhydrides are cheaper to produce and, as they are less reactive, their reactions can be more easily controlled. For example, the industrial processes to produce aspirin and cellulose acetate use ethanoic anhydride rather than ethanoyl chloride. For acyl chlorides the by-product is hydrogen chloride, but for acid anhydrides the by-product is the less corrosive carboxylic acid.

The reactions of acylating agents with ammonia and primary amines produce amides and *N*-substituted amides, respectively (Figure 18). Because the by-products of the reactions are acidic (namely hydrogen chloride or a carboxylic acid), two moles of ammonia or amine are required for each mole of

HCl + R^1COOR^2 ← (R^2OH) — Acyl chloride — (H_2O) → R^1COOH + HCl

R^1COOH + R^1COOR^2 ← (R^2OH) — Acyl anhydride — (H_2O) → R^1COOH + R^1COOH

Figure 17 *Nucleophilic acylation reactions*

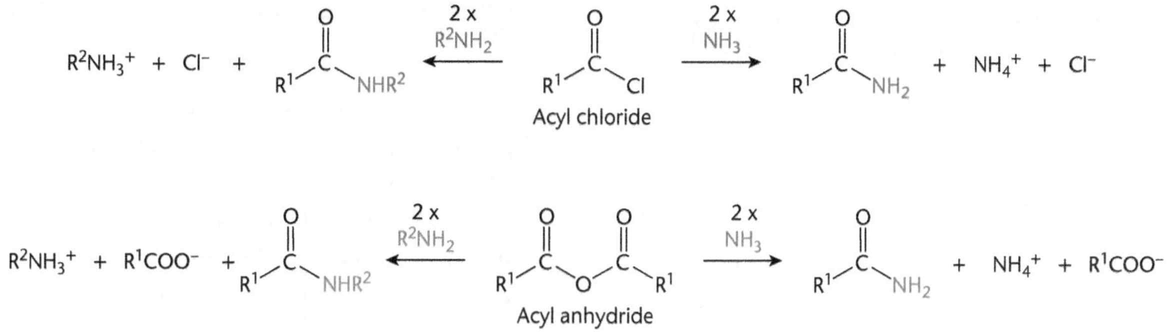

$R^2NH_3^+$ + Cl^- + $R^1C(=O)NHR^2$ ← (2 x R^2NH_2) $R^1C(=O)Cl$ (Acyl chloride) → (2 x NH_3) $R^1C(=O)NH_2$ + NH_4^+ + Cl^-

$R^2NH_3^+$ + R^1COO^- + $R^1C(=O)NHR^2$ ← (2 x R^2NH_2) $R^1C(=O)OC(=O)R^1$ (Acyl anhydride) → (2 x NH_3) $R^1C(=O)NH_2$ + NH_4^+ + R^1COO^-

Figure 18 *Nucleophilic acylation reactions with ammonia and amines*

acylating agent. The first acts as the nucleophile, while the second acts as a base and reacts with the generated acid. We will learn more about the basicity of ammonia and amines in *chapter 9 of Year 2 Student Book*.

The nucleophilic addition–elimination mechanism

All acylation reactions are examples of a nucleophilic addition–elimination mechanism. All of the nucleophiles (:NucH) here have lone pairs associated with either an oxygen atom or a nitrogen atom, and contain a hydrogen atom directly bonded to that oxygen atom (H_2O, ROH) or nitrogen atom (NH_3, RNH_2). Both acyl chlorides and acid anhydrides react readily with such nucleophiles. The electronegative oxygen atoms (in anhydrides) and/or chlorine atoms (in acyl chlorides) polarise the bonds towards the carbon atom of the acyl group. Carbon is the positive end of the polar bond and is exposed to attack by the nucleophiles.

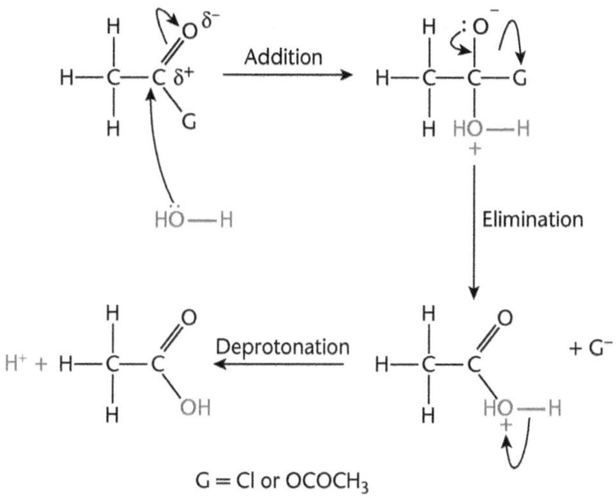

Addition

Elimination

Deprotonation

H^+ + CH_3COOH ... + G^-

G = Cl or $OCOCH_3$

Figure 19 *General nucleophilic addition–elimination mechanism with water*

The addition–elimination reaction occurs in four stages (Figure 19):

1. *Attraction*: the δ+ carbon atom of the polar C=O bond attracts the lone pair of a nucleophile.
2. *Addition*: the lone pair of the nucleophile molecule forms a new bond to the carbon atom and the C=O bond breaks, producing a saturated ion that has both positive and negative charges.
3. *Elimination*: the C–Cl of the acyl chloride or the C–O of the anhydride breaks, with the electron pair liberating a chloride ion (Cl^-) or ethanoate ion (CH_3COO^-) as, simultaneously, the C=O bond re-forms.
4. *Deprotonation*: the new compound is formed by removal of an H^+. With ammonia or amine nucleophiles two moles of ammonia or amine are required: one acts as the nucleophile, while the other reacts with the acid produced in an acid–base reaction.

The nucleophile is said to be acylated, i.e. an acyl group has replaced a hydrogen atom in the nucleophile.

This general mechanism is illustrated further for two specific examples, the formation of ethanamide from ethanoyl chloride with ammonia as the nucleophile and of methyl ethanoate from ethanoic anhydride with methanol as the nucleophile (Figures 20 and 21).

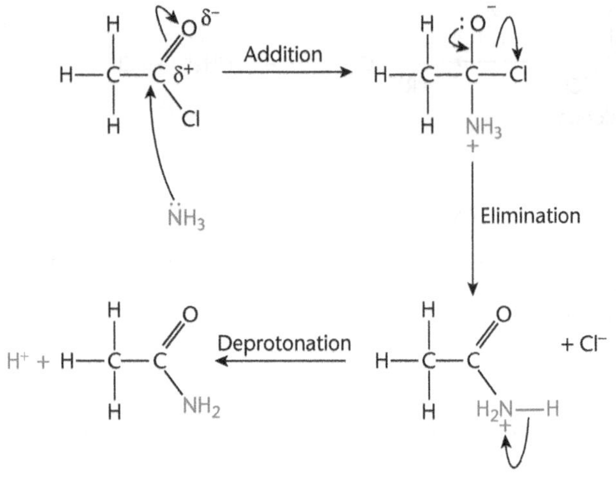

Figure 20 Mechanism for the formation of ethanamide

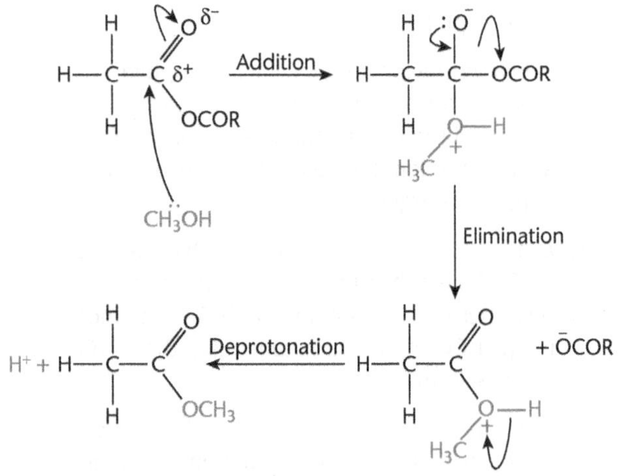

Figure 21 Mechanism for the formation of methyl ethanoate

QUESTIONS

8. Give the name and structure of the principal organic products from each of the following reactions:
   a. ethanoic anhydride with water
   b. propanoyl chloride with ammonia
   c. butanoic anhydride with ethylamine (aminoethane).

9. For each of the reactions in Question 8, write an equation and draw the mechanism of the reaction.

10. What would you observe if you added ethanoyl chloride to 5 cm^3 of (a) water, (b) ethanol and (c) ammonia in a beaker?

KEY IDEAS

- Acylation reactions can be carried out using acyl chlorides or acid anhydrides.
- Industrial acylation reactions are usually carried out using acid anhydrides.
- Nucleophilic molecules containing :N–H or :O–H bonds are readily acylated.
- Acylation occurs via a nucleophilic addition–elimination mechanism.
- Acylation reactions are used in a wide variety of industrial processes.

REQUIRED PRACTICAL ACTIVITY 10A: APPARATUS AND TECHNIQUES

(PS 2.1, PS 2.3, PS 4.1, AT a, AT b, AT d, AT g, AT h, AT k)

Preparation of an organic solid and a test of its purity

This practical activity gives you the opportunity to show that you can:

- Use appropriate apparatus to record a range of measurements.
- Use a water bath or electric heater or sand bath or Bunsen burner for heating.
- Use laboratory apparatus for a variety of experimental techniques.
- Purify a solid by recrystallisation.
- Use a melting point apparatus.
- Safely and carefully handle solids and liquids.

Apparatus

If the reaction needs to be heated, it may be carried out under reflux using a condenser. After the reaction is complete, the solid product is normally isolated either by removal of the solvent by distillation or by pouring the crude solution into water and filtering off the precipitated product under reduced pressure (Figure P1).The solid product is then purified by recrystallisation.

Solid products and impurities will have different solubilities in different solvents. The impurities may not be soluble in a solvent in which the product dissolves. In this case a hot saturated solution of the product is filtered through a hot filter paper and funnel and the solution is cooled until crystallisation occurs. If the impurities have a greater solubility in the solvent than the product then it is also possible to obtain the pure product by recrystallisation, and in this case the pure compound is filtered from the solution, normally by suction filtration. The solvent for recrystallisation is chosen so that the product is highly soluble in the hot solvent but poorly soluble at room temperature. It may be necessary to use a mixture of two solvents.

A source of heating such as a hotplate or water bath is needed and a container for the hot solvent such as a boiling tube, beaker or conical flask. Ice may be required if crystallisation does not occur at room temperature. A glass rod may also be required to induce crystallisation.

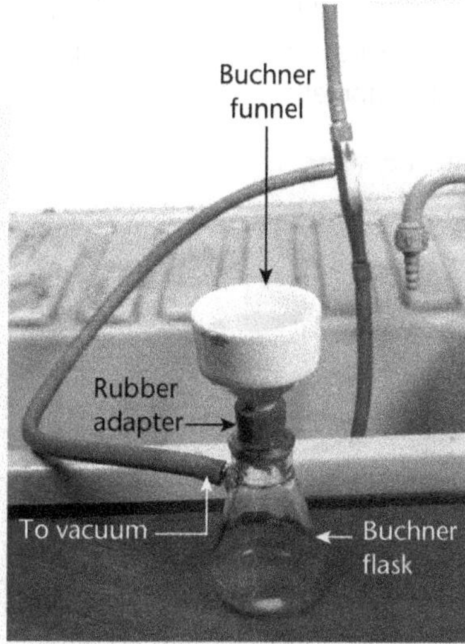

Figure P1 *Filtration under reduced pressure*

Filtration of recrystallised samples is easily achieved by filtration under reduced pressure (sometimes called suction filtration or vacuum filtration). A Buchner flask, Buchner funnel and filter paper are used and a vacuum is required (Figure P1). A Buchner funnel is a ceramic funnel that contains a number of holes. It is placed into the Buchner flask along with a flexible rubber adapter and a filter paper. The adapter ensures a seal when a vacuum is applied to the side arm of the Buchner flask. For safety, ensure the Buchner flask is clamped to a clamp stand (via the neck). You will need to have a thick walled rubber tube to connect the flask to a vacuum source.

The purity of a solid can be determined by measuring its melting point. The result can then be compared with the published value reported in data books. Pure compounds exhibit melting points at precise temperatures, whereas impure compounds exhibit melting points over a range of temperatures. Melting points can be measured using a commercial 'melting point apparatus' (Figure P2). A sample of the solid is placed in a thin capillary 'melting point' tube. The tube is placed onto a heating block and the temperature of the block raised slowly. The sample is observed and the temperature range of melting noted. Some commercial melting point apparatuses require a thermometer to be inserted along with the sample. Alternatively, the melting point tube and sample can be attached to a thermometer by a small rubber band, with the sample aligned with the mercury bulb of the thermometer. Both the thermometer and the sample are immersed in an oil bath, which is slowly heated and the temperature of the melting sample is read off from the thermometer.

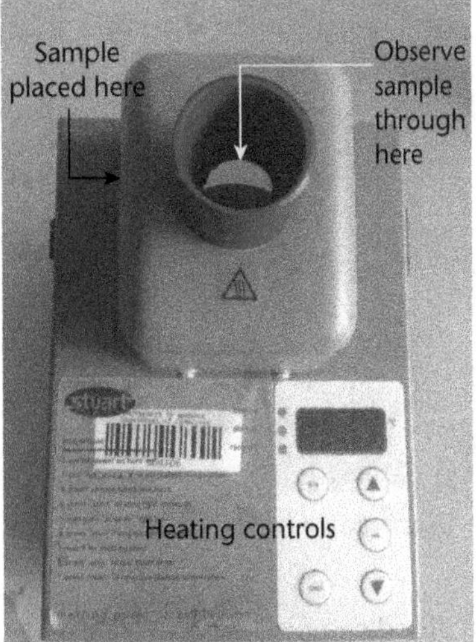

Figure P2 *Commercial melting point apparatus*

Techniques

There are different methods for recrystallising samples depending upon the type of impurities that need to be removed. You will normally be instructed which solvent or solvents are required. If the chosen solvent has a boiling point less than 90 °C then you can use a water bath for heating the solvent.

Removing impurities that are more soluble than the product in a solvent

Heat the required amount of solvent to a few degrees below its boiling point in a conical flask or a boiling tube by immersion in a water bath or on a hotplate. Add the solid to the hot solvent (still maintain heating) and swirl until the solid dissolves. If you have not been told how much solvent to use, then you will need to determine the minimum amount yourself. Heat the solvent in a boiling tube and place the solid in another boiling tube or conical flask. Add a few cubic centimetres of the hot solvent to your solid and swirl. Place both containers in the water bath to ensure the solvent remains hot in both. If the solid has not completely dissolved, repeat the addition of a few cubic centimetres of hot solvent until it does.

Remove the solution from the heat and allow it to cool to room temperature. As the saturated solution cools, crystallisation occurs, but the impurities remain in solution. Alternatively, the hot solution may be added to another solvent before cooling is allowed. A greater yield may be obtained by cooling in ice. Occasionally crystallisation does not occur upon cooling, in which case initiate crystallisation by carefully scratching the side of the container with a glass rod. This produces microscopic particles of glass, which act as nucleating sites for crystallisation.

Removing impurities that are insoluble in a solvent

If you have made a hot saturated solution of the product but there is still insoluble material, this can be separated by filtration through a hot filter funnel (Figure P3). A funnel and its filter paper are heated by placing them in a beaker in which a small amount of the same solvent as used in the recrystallisation is boiling. The filter paper should be saturated with the solvent before filtration occurs. The vapour of the boiling solvent heats the funnel and paper. The saturated solution is then filtered and the filtrate allowed to cool in the normal manner to induce crystallisation (see above).

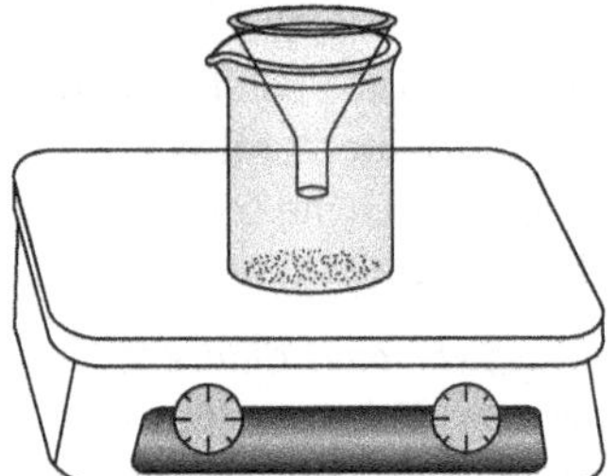

Figure P3 *Filtration through a hot filter funnel*

Filtration

Clamp the Buchner flask by the neck to a stand. Add the rubber adapter to the neck and place the Buchner funnel into the adapter. Place a filter paper in the funnel. Make sure all the holes are covered and no creases are visible in the filter paper. Attach the side arm of the Buchner flask, via a thick walled rubber tube, to a vacuum source. Turn on the vacuum. Carefully swirl the mixture of crystals and solvent to be filtered to ensure no crystals are stuck on the side of the glassware, and pour into the funnel. The vacuum will suck the solvent through very quickly. Wash the crystals with a very small amount of cold solvent. Leave the crystals under vacuum until they are dry. Carefully pull off the rubber hose attached to the Buchner flask BEFORE you turn off the vacuum. Remove the crystals from the funnel, place on a watch glass and record the mass.

Assessing purity by melting point

The solid to be analysed should be crushed to a powder either in a pestle and mortar or on a watch glass or filter paper. A spatula may be used to crush the solid. Push the powder carefully into the capillary tube by placing the opening of the tube in the powder (Figure P4a). Sometimes the powder gets stuck at the open end of the tube and does not fall to the bottom (the sealed end). If this is the case, hold the tube with the sealed end at the bottom and gently tap the bottom of the tube on the bench (take care not to break the delicate tube). Make sure about 3–4 mm of the sample is located in the tube, and make two further samples in this way. Place one tube in your heating apparatus, make sure you can easily observe the sample, increase the temperature and observe at what temperature the solid melts into a liquid (this will be over a range of temperatures). Let the heating apparatus cool to about 20 °C below the original observed melting point. Then repeat the process with the second and third samples, but slow the rate of heating (2–3 °C a minute) as you near the first observed melting point. This will allow you to get a more accurate value for the melting point of the solid.

Push open end of capillary carefully into powder
(a)

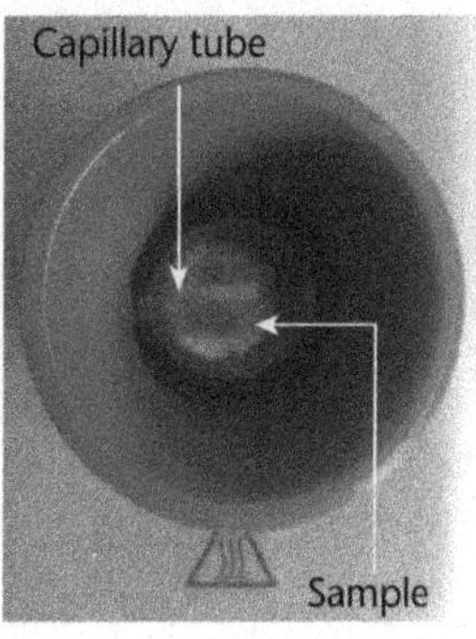
Capillary tube
Sample
(b)

Figure P4 *(a) Loading a melting point capillary with sample. (b) Observing the sample in a melting point apparatus.*

QUESTIONS

P1. What properties should a solvent have if it is to be used to purify a contaminated solid compound by the technique of recrystallisation?

P2. Why is it important to use the minimum of hot solvent when undertaking a recrystallisation?

P3. Two compounds, compound A and compound B, are present in a mixture. The solubilities of the two compounds at 20 °C and 90 °C in water are shown. The mixture contains 10 g of A and 1 g of B.

Compound	Solubility at 20 °C / g 100 cm^{-3}	Solubility at 90 °C / g 100 cm^{-3}
A	0.2	20.0
B	2.5	54.5

a. What is the minimum amount of water necessary to completely dissolve all of compound A in the mixture at 90 °C?

b. Assuming the amount of water calculated in part (a), how much compound A would remain in solution at 20 °C?

c. What is the maximum amount of compound A that could be recovered by recrystallising the mixture? Will the compound be pure?

P4. Why should you heat the sample slowly when recording its melting point?

ASSIGNMENT 4: SYNTHESIS AND PURIFICATION OF ASPIRIN

(PS1.1)

$$HOC_6H_4COOH \text{ (salicylic acid)} + (CH_3CO)_2O \rightarrow CH_3COOC_6H_4COOH \text{ (aspirin)} + CH_3COOH$$

Aspirin is the most widespread drug used to treat inflammation, fever and pain. In low doses it is also used to thin the blood and its long-term use has been recommended for people with a high risk of developing blood clots. It is not as popular as ibuprofen for the treatment of pain because it has been shown to be more likely to lead to gastrointestinal bleeding. It has also been shown to be beneficial in lowering the risk of various cancers. Commercially aspirin is prepared by the acylation of salicylic acid with ethanoic anhydride.

Students were given the following instructions to make a sample of aspirin.

Add 10 cm^3 of ethanoic anhydride to 6.0 g of salicylic acid in a conical flask. Add five drops of concentrated sulfuric acid and heat the flask on a water bath at 60 °C for 20 minutes.

Allow the mixture to cool and add 75 cm^3 of water. Stir the mixture with a glass rod. A white precipitate should form. Filter the precipitate under reduced pressure. Add the crude aspirin to 15 cm^3 of ethanol in a boiling tube. Heat the tube in a water bath at 75 °C until the aspirin has dissolved. Pour the solution into about 30 cm^3 of cold water. Filter the white crystals under reduced pressure, washing with a little ice-cold water.

Dry the crystals. Measure the mass obtained and determine the melting point of the purified aspirin.

Questions

A1. The students obtained 6.1 g of purified aspirin. Calculate the percentage yield of aspirin from the experiment.

A2. Give three reasons why the manufacture of aspirin uses ethanoic anhydride as the acylating agent, rather than ethanoyl chloride.

A3. Calculate the atom economy for the synthesis of aspirin using (a) ethanoyl chloride, and (b) ethanoic anhydride. Which has greater atom economy?

A4. Provide written instructions on how to prepare a sample for a melting point analysis.

Stretch and challenge

A5. During the recrystallisation, why was the ethanol solution containing the product poured into cold water?

PRACTICE QUESTIONS

1. **a.** Write an equation for the reaction between ethanoyl chloride and dimethylamine. Name and outline the mechanism of this reaction.

   b. Aspirin is manufactured by the reaction of 2-hydroxybenzenecarboxylic acid with ethanoic anhydride. Write an equation for this reaction and give two reasons why ethanoic anhydride, rather than ethanoyl chloride, is used.

   NEAB, CH06, March 1998, Question 3

2. 1,4-Diaminobenzene is an important intermediate in the production of polymers such as Kevlar® and also of polyurethanes, used in foam seating. A possible synthesis of 1,4-diaminobenzene from phenylamine is shown in Figure Q1 on the next page.

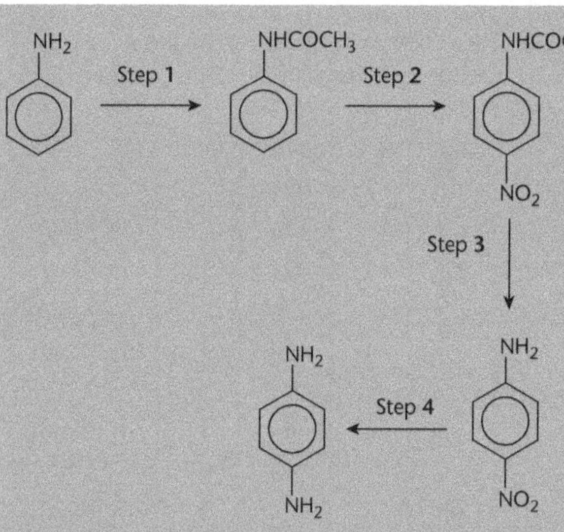

NH2 →(Step 1) NHCOCH3 (benzene ring) →(Step 2) NHCOCH3 / NO2 (para) →(Step 3) NH2 / NO2 (para) →(Step 4) NH2 / NH2 (para)

Figure Q1

a. A suitable reagent for step **1** is CH_3COCl. Name and draw a mechanism for the reaction in step **1**.

b. The product of step **1** was purified by recrystallisation as follows.

The crude product was dissolved in **the minimum quantity of hot water** and the hot solution was filtered through a hot filter funnel into a conical flask. This filtration removed any insoluble impurities. The flask was **left to cool to room temperature**.

The crystals formed were filtered off using a Buchner funnel and a clean cork was used to **compress the crystals in the funnel. A little cold water was then poured through the crystals.**

After a few minutes, the crystals were removed from the funnel and weighed. A small sample was then used to find the melting point.

Give reasons for these practical steps:

i. The minimum quantity of hot water was used.

ii. The flask was cooled to room temperature before the crystals were filtered off.

iii. The crystals were compressed in the funnel.

iv. A little cold water was poured through the crystals.

c. The melting point of the sample in part (b) was found to be slightly lower than a data-book value. Suggest the most likely impurity to have caused this low value and an improvement to the method so that a more accurate value for the melting point would be obtained.

d. In an experiment starting with 5.05 g of phenylamine, 4.82 g of a purified product were obtained in step **1**. Calculate the percentage yield in this reaction. Give your answer to the appropriate number of significant figures.

AQA Specimen Paper 2, 2015, Question 9

3. The tri-ester, **T**, shown below, is found in palm oil. When **T** is heated with an excess of sodium hydroxide solution, the alcohol glycerol is formed together with a mixture of three other products as shown in this equation:

$$\begin{array}{l} CH_2OOC(CH_2)_{14}CH_3 \\ | \\ CHOOC(CH_2)_7CH{=}CH(CH_2)_7CH_3 + 3NaOH \\ | \\ CH_2OOC(CH_2)_{12}CH_3 \\ \quad\quad T \end{array} \longrightarrow \begin{array}{l} CH_2OH \\ | \\ CHOH \\ | \\ CH_2OH \\ \text{Glycerol} \end{array} + \begin{array}{c} CH_3(CH_2)_{14}COONa \\ + \\ CH_3(CH_2)_7CH{=}CH(CH_2)_7COONa \\ + \\ CH_3(CH_2)_{12}COONa \end{array}$$

a. Give the IUPAC name for glycerol.

b. Give a use for the mixture of sodium salts formed in this reaction.

c. When **T** is heated with an excess of methanol, glycerol is formed together with a mixture of methyl esters.

i. Give a use for this mixture of methyl esters

ii. One of the methyl esters in the mixture has the IUPAC name methyl (*Z*)-octadec-9-enoate.

(*continued*)

Draw two hydrogen atoms on the diagram below to illustrate the meaning of the letter *Z* in the name of this ester:

iii. One of the other methyl esters in the mixture has the formula $CH_3(CH_2)_{12}COOCH_3$. Write an equation for the complete combustion of one molecule of this ester.

AQA Chemistry, January 2010, Question 5

4. Name and outline a mechanism for the reaction of $CH_3CH_2NH_2$ with CH_3CH_2COCl. Name the amide formed.

AQA Chemistry, January 2010, Question 9a

5. Esters have many important commercial uses such as solvents and artificial flavourings in foods.

   Esters can be prepared in several ways including the reactions of alcohols with carboxylic acids, acid anhydrides, acyl chlorides and other esters.

   a. Ethyl butanoate is used as a pineapple flavouring in sweets and cakes. Write an equation for the preparation of ethyl butanoate from an acid and an alcohol. Give a catalyst for the reaction.
   b. Butyl ethanoate is used as a solvent in the pharmaceutical industry. Write an equation for the preparation of butyl ethanoate from an acid anhydride and an alcohol.
   c. Name and outline a mechanism for the reaction of CH_3COCl and CH_3OH to form an ester.
   d. Write an equation to show the formation of biodiesel from this ester, which occurs in vegetable oils:

$CH_2OOCC_{17}H_{31}$
|
$CHOOCC_{17}H_{33}$
|
$CH_2OOCC_{17}H_{29}$

AQA Chemistry, June 2010, Question 7a–d

6. This question is about the primary amine $CH_3CH_2CH_2NH_2$. The amine $CH_3CH_2CH_2NH_2$ reacts with CH_3COCl. Name and outline a mechanism for this reaction. Give the IUPAC name of the organic product.

AQA Chemistry, June 2013, Question 8a

7. Esters are produced by the reaction of alcohols with other esters and by the reaction of alcohols with carboxylic acids.

   a. The esters which make up biodiesel are produced industrially from the esters in vegetable oils.

      i. Complete the equation for this formation of biodiesel.

$CH_2OOCC_{17}H_{35}$ $C_{17}H_{35}COOCH_3$
|
$CHOOCC_{17}H_{31}$ + $\rightleftharpoons$ $C_{17}H_{31}COOCH_3$ +
|
$CH_2OOCC_{17}H_{29}$ $C_{17}H_{29}COOCH_3$

      ii. Write an equation for the complete combustion of $C_{17}H_{35}COOCH_3$.

AQA Chemistry, January 2013, Question 3a

8. Nucleophiles such as alcohols can react with CH_3COCl. The ion CH_3COO^- can act as a nucleophile in a similar way. State the meaning of the term *nucleophile*. Draw the structure of the organic product formed by the reaction of CH_3COO^- with CH_3COCl.

AQA Chemistry, January 2013, Question 8b

9. a. i. Complete this equation for the preparation of aspirin using ethanoic anhydride by writing the structural formula of the missing product:

COOH, OH (benzene ring) + $H_3C—C(=O)—O—C(=O)—CH_3$ ⟶ COOH, O—C(=O)—CH_3 (benzene ring) +

      ii. Suggest a name for the mechanism for the reaction in part (i).

      iii. Give two industrial advantages, other than cost, of using ethanoic anhydride rather than ethanoyl chloride in the preparation of aspirin.

   b. Complete the following equation for the reaction of one molecule of benzene-1,2-dicarboxylic anhydride (phthalic anhydride) with one molecule of methanol by drawing the structural formula of the single product.

(phthalic anhydride) + CH_3OH ⟶

AQA Chemistry, January 2012, Question 4c–d

8 AROMATIC CHEMISTRY

PRIOR KNOWLEDGE

You will already have studied the structure and bonding in alkenes and their addition reactions. You will also be familiar with curly arrow mechanisms (see *chapter 9 of Year 1 Student Book and chapters 3, 5 and 14 of Year 2 Student Book*).

LEARNING OBJECTIVES

In this chapter you will learn about the structure, bonding and stability of benzene and other aromatic molecules. You will be able to outline the electrophilic substitution reactions for nitration and acylation of benzene.

(Specification 3.3.10)

The word 'aromatic' is used in normal conversation to describe various fragrant and perfumed smells. In chemistry, however, 'aromatic' is used to define molecules that contain the benzene ring. Benzene was first isolated by Michael Faraday in 1825. The benzene ring is found in compounds used, for example, in many drugs, pesticides, polymers, explosives and dyes.

The first synthetic dye to contain a benzene ring, mauvine, was made in 1856. A few years later, the compound 2,4,6-trinitrotoluene (TNT) was manufactured as a yellow dye by nitration of toluene (methylbenzene) but its main use quickly changed to that of an explosive. Today, the molecules of many common painkillers (aspirin, paracetamol, ibuprofen, codeine and morphine) contain the benzene ring. Aromatic chemistry is important.

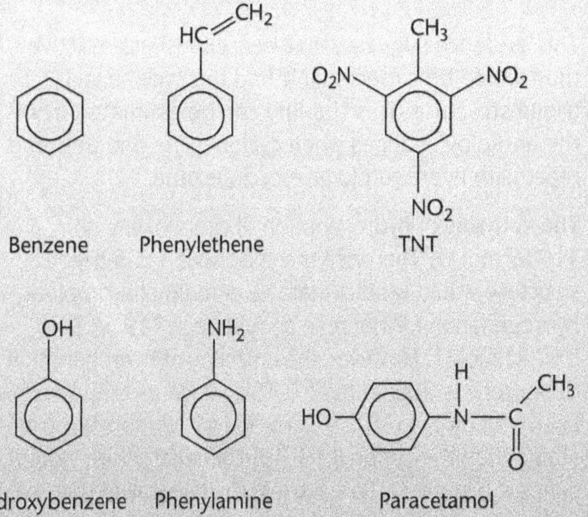

Benzene

HC=CH_2 — Phenylethene

CH_3, O_2N, NO_2, NO_2 — TNT

OH — Hydroxybenzene

NH_2 — Phenylamine

HO—N(H)—C(=O)—CH_3 — Paracetamol

Figure 1 *Some common aromatic molecules*

8.1 THE STRUCTURE OF BENZENE

The molecular formula of benzene was determined in 1834 to be C_6H_6. Thirty-one years later August Kekulé, a German organic chemist, proposed a hexagonal structure with alternating single and double carbon–carbon bonds. This structure suggests that benzene should react like an unsaturated alkene, but it does not undergo the reactions characteristic of alkenes. For example, unlike alkenes, benzene does not react with an aqueous solution of bromine, but instead requires vigorous conditions with a catalyst (Figure 2).

Theoretical Kekulé structure
IUPAC name
cyclohexa-1,3,5-triene

Modern structure of benzene

Br_2 →

Br_2 → No reaction

Figure 2 Kekulé structure of benzene and difference in reactivity between an alkene and benzene

This evidence suggests that benzene is less reactive than would be expected if it had the cyclohexa-1,3,5-triene structure. This stability can be estimated from the enthalpy changes when cyclohexene and benzene react with hydrogen to give cyclohexane.

The enthalpy of hydrogenation of cyclohexene is 119 kJ mol^{-1}. Therefore the cyclohexa-1,3,5-triene structure would predict that the enthalpy of complete hydrogenation for benzene should be $-119 \times 3 =$ 357 kJ mol^{-1}. However, the enthalpy of hydrogenation of benzene is 208 kJ mol^{-1}. This indicates that benzene is 149 kJ mol^{-1} (357 − 208 = 149 kJ mol^{-1}) more stable than the cyclohexa-1,3,5-triene structure would suggest (Figure 3). This extra stability is called the **delocalisation energy** of benzene.

The cyclic structure of a benzene molecule was confirmed by X-ray diffraction. However, *all* the carbon–carbon bond lengths in benzene were found to be 0.140 nm. The Kekulé structure (the theoretical compound cyclohexa-1,3,5-triene) would have three C–C single bonds (0.154 nm) and three C = C double bonds (0.134 nm) (Figure 4). The actual length (0.140 nm) was about halfway between the lengths of a single and a double carbon–carbon bond.

Cyclohexene + H_2 → Cyclohexane $\Delta H^\circ = -119$ kJ mol^{-1}

Benzene + $3H_2$ → Cyclohexane $\Delta H^\circ = -208$ kJ mol^{-1}

Figure 3 The hydrogenation of cyclohexene and benzene

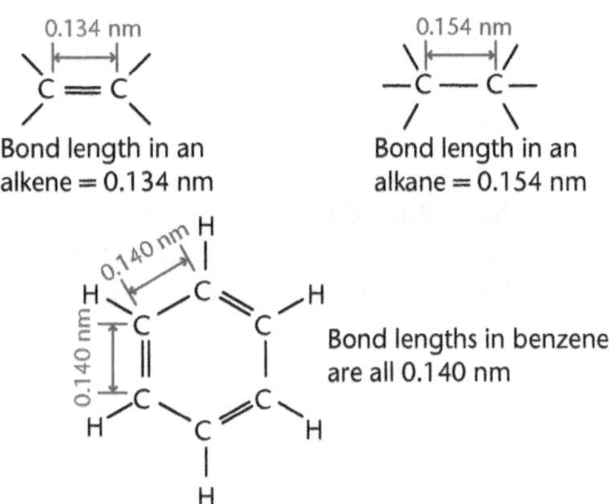

Figure 4 Bond lengths in benzene

The currently accepted structure of a benzene molecule is shown in Figure 5. Each carbon has three single bonds with its two adjacent carbon atoms and one hydrogen. These are σ-bonds. Its fourth bonding electron is shared in a pi (π)-bond. The π-bonds of the six carbon atoms overlap and the six electrons are shared in a doughnut-shaped electron cloud above and below the plane of the flat hexagon of carbon atoms. The electrons in these π-orbitals are said to be **delocalised**. This is what makes benzene more stable than the theoretical compound cyclohexa-1,3,5-triene and explains its delocalisation energy. Consequently, we represent benzene as shown in Figure 5, with six carbon–carbon bonds of the same length and a delocalised doughnut of electron density.

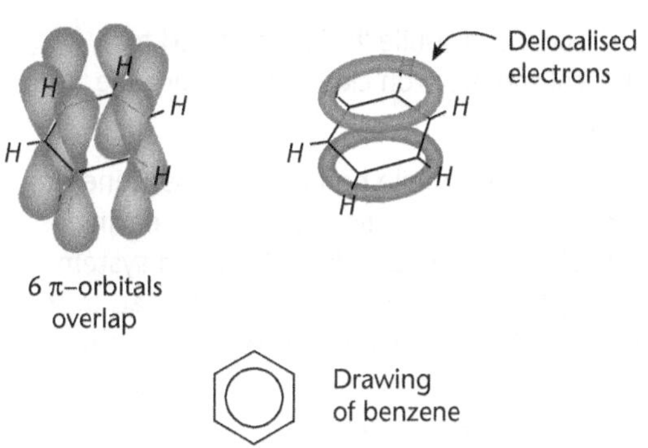

Figure 5 Currently accepted structure of benzene showing delocalised electron cloud

QUESTIONS

1. Give two examples of reactions you would expect if benzene did contain double bonds.
2. Provide three pieces of evidence that suggest that the Kekulé structure of benzene was not correct.

KEY IDEAS

- The benzene molecule (C_6H_6) is a planar regular hexagon.
- Benzene does not contain alternating C–C and C = C double bonds and so does not react in a similar manner to alkenes such as ethene.
- The structure of the benzene molecule has six delocalised electrons.
- Delocalisation of electrons increases the stability of the benzene molecule.
- The delocalisation of electrons accounts for the observed same carbon–carbon bond length for each bond.

8.2 NAMING AROMATIC COMPOUNDS

Benzene can:

- form the root of the name, such as in methylbenzene, nitrobenzene, chlorobenzene and benzenecarboxylic acid
- be regarded as a substituent, in which case the C_6H_5 group is known as the phenyl group.

Sometimes compounds may be called by more than one name, and many benzene derivatives are still known by old names (Figure 6). If a benzene ring has two or more substituents then we use numbers to describe the positions of the groups, making sure we give the lowest possible numbers to the substituents.

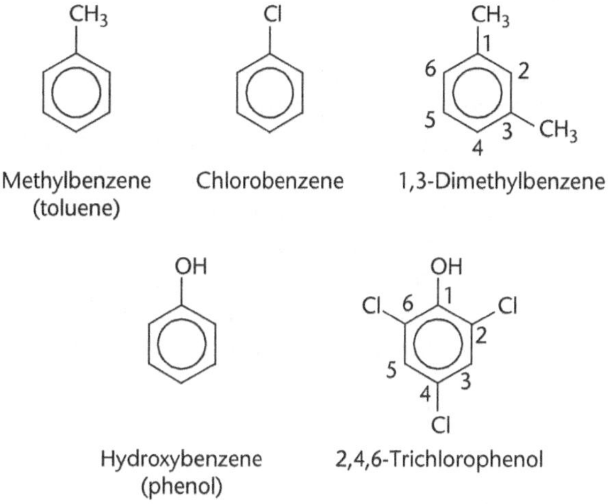

Methylbenzene (toluene) | Chlorobenzene | 1,3-Dimethylbenzene

Hydroxybenzene (phenol) | 2,4,6-Trichlorophenol

Figure 6 Some aromatic molecules, with other common names in brackets

QUESTIONS

3. Name these compounds:

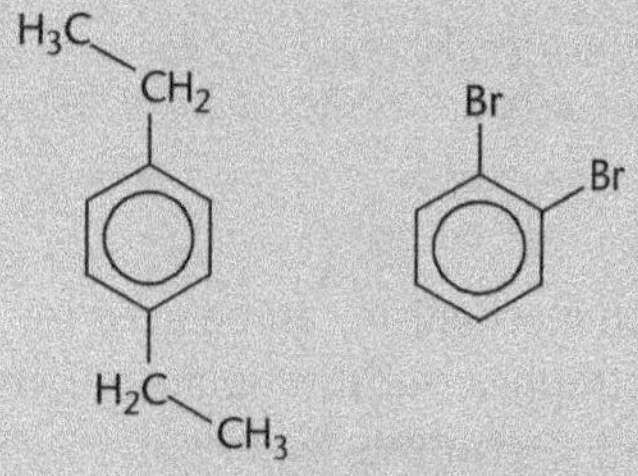

4. Draw these compounds:
   a. 1-hydroxy-4-methylbenzene
   b. 1,3,5-triiodobenzene
   c. 4-nitrophenol.

8.3 THE REACTIONS OF BENZENE

The electrophilic substitution mechanism

The main reactions of benzene involve the replacement of one or more of the six hydrogen atoms by halogen atoms or a functional group. The hydrogen atom is said to be 'substituted' by the halogen atom or functional group and so these are called substitution reactions (Figure 7).

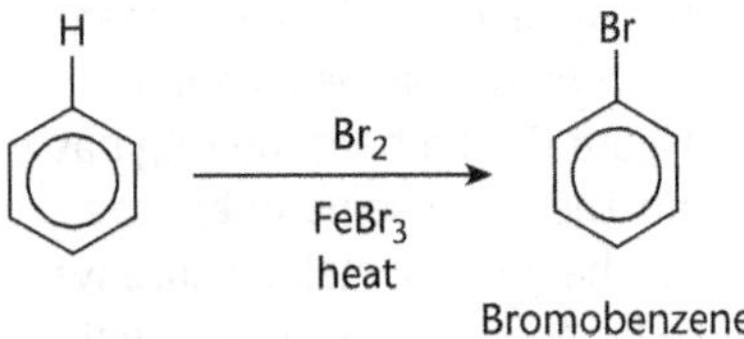

Figure 7 *A substitution reaction of benzene*

Because the delocalised electrons are a region of *high* electron density, substitution reactions generally involve reaction with a positively charged ion or the positive end of a polar molecule that can accept electrons to form new covalent bonds. These are called **electrophiles**, so this type of reaction is more fully described as electrophilic substitution (Figure 8), as opposed to electrophilic additions, which are the characteristic reactions of alkenes studied in *chapter 14 of Year 1 Student Book*. The stable nature of the benzene ring is why substitution and not addition occurs.

H
HNO_3, H_2SO_4,
50 °C
NO_2^+
NO_2
+ H^+
Nitrobenzene
Reacting electrophile produced from the reaction of HNO_3 and H_2SO_4

Figure 8 *An electrophilic substitution of benzene. The electrophile NO_2^+ is prepared by the reaction of concentrated nitric and sulfuric acids.*

One general reaction mechanism can be used to describe all the electrophilic substitution reactions of benzene and benzene derivatives (Figure 9).

- *Step 1.* The electrophile 'E^+' is attracted to the delocalised electron cloud of the benzene ring structure.
- *Step 2.* The electrophile bonds to the benzene ring via two of the six delocalised electrons, leaving a positively charged partially delocalised system containing four delocalised electrons spread over five carbon atoms. This temporarily causes the loss of the natural stability of the six-electron delocalised benzene system.
- *Step 3.* In order to regain the delocalisation energy of the benzene ring, an H^+ ion is lost by breaking the C–H bond. The electrons from this bond re-form the stable delocalised six-electron system.

Several different types of electrophiles (E^+) react with benzene (Figure 10). These electrophiles cannot simply be added to benzene to give the required reaction. They have to be produced in the reaction mixture by mixing appropriate reagents. The reaction conditions are generally severe: we have to use heat, concentrated reagents and catalysts to make these reactions take place. This is because of the high stability (low reactivity) of the delocalised benzene structure.

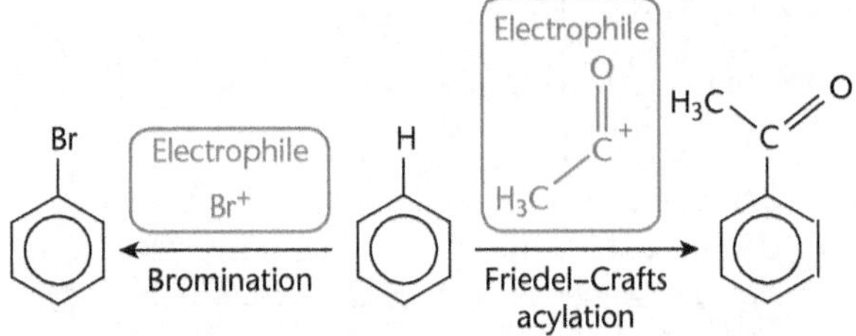

Figure 10 *Electrophilic substitution of benzene with the Br^+ electrophile (which is formed by the reaction of bromine and iron(III) bromide) and the $CH_3C{=}O^+$ electrophile (which is formed by the reaction of ethanoyl chloride and aluminium trichloride)*

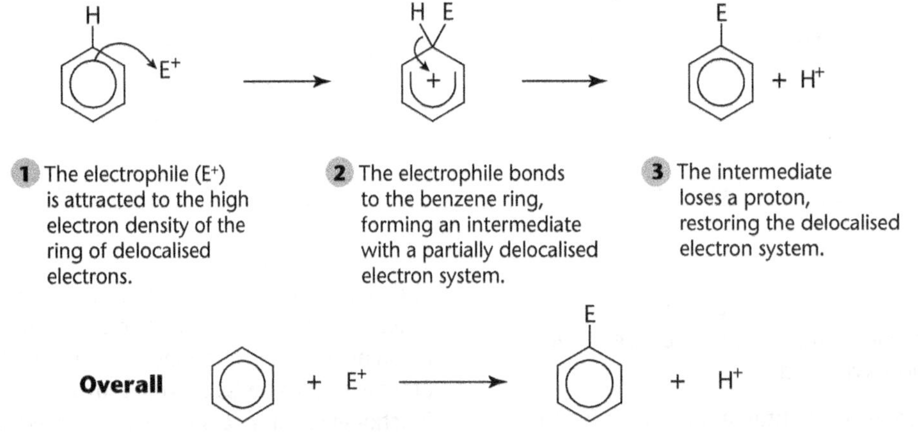

H
E^+
H E
E
+ H^+
1 The electrophile (E^+) is attracted to the high electron density of the ring of delocalised electrons.
2 The electrophile bonds to the benzene ring, forming an intermediate with a partially delocalised electron system.
3 The intermediate loses a proton, restoring the delocalised electron system.
Overall
+ E^+
E
+ H^+

Figure 9 *The mechanism for electrophilic substitution of benzene*

Nitration of benzene

When benzene undergoes nitration a nitro group, $-NO_2$, replaces one of the hydrogen atoms. The electrophile is the nitronium ion, NO_2^+, which is generated by mixing concentrated nitric acid and concentrated sulfuric acid and heating to 50 °C. The concentrated sulfuric acid donates a proton to nitric acid. This produces an intermediate, $[H_2NO_3]^+$, which decomposes to yield the electrophilic nitronium ion as shown in Figure 11. The concentrated sulfuric acid also acts as a catalyst in the reaction, as it is regenerated when the HSO_4^- ion reacts with the H^+ ion released in the last step of the reaction mechanism.

$$H_2SO_4 + HNO_3 \rightleftharpoons [H_2NO_3]^+ + HSO_4^-$$

$$\text{then } [H_2NO_3]^+ \rightleftharpoons NO_2^+ + H_2O$$

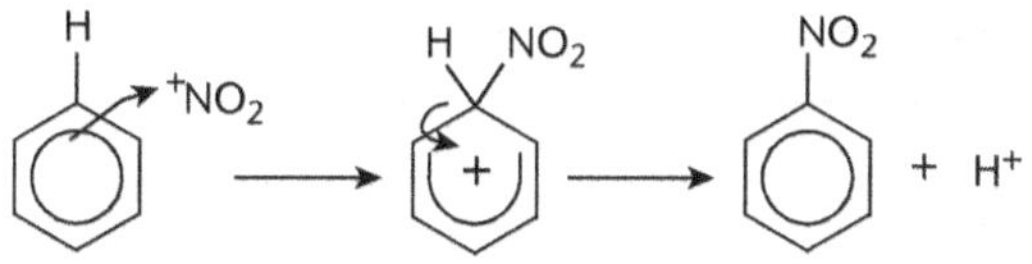

H, $^+NO_2$ → H NO_2 (+) → NO_2 + H^+

Figure 11 The synthesis of nitrobenzene from benzene

Reduction of nitrobenzene

The nitration of benzene and other related aromatic compounds is an important industrial reaction. The nitro group can be reduced to an amine group. Aromatic amines are used widely in the dye and other industries. Reduction can be achieved using iron or tin with concentrated hydrochloric acid or, alternatively, catalytic hydrogenation can be carried out with nickel and hydrogen gas. These reagents are represented as [H] in Figure 12.

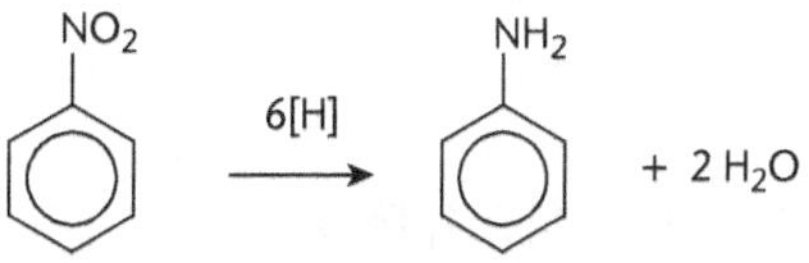

NO_2 —6[H]→ NH_2 + $2\,H_2O$

Figure 12 Reduction of the nitro group

QUESTIONS

5. Draw the three possible isomeric products from the reaction of ethylbenzene with nitric acid and sulfuric acid and name them.

ASSIGNMENT 1: EXPLOSIVES

(PS 1.1, PS 1.2)

The well-known explosive TNT was widely used by armed forces, especially during the First World War, and is still used to demolish buildings and bridges and for blasting in mines and quarries. Its full IUPAC name is 2-methyl-1,3,5-trinitrobenzene. 'TNT' comes from its old name – 2,4,6-trinitrotoluene. TNT is made by nitrating methylbenzene using concentrated nitric and sulfuric acids at a temperature of over 120 °C. The process proceeds via the mononitro (**A**) and dinitro (**B**) compounds (Figure A1).

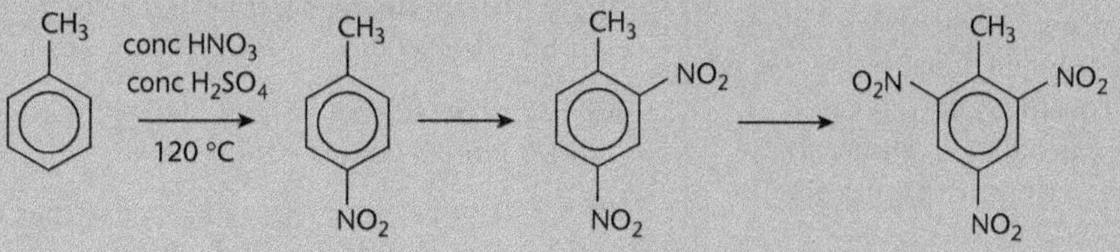

CH_3 —conc HNO_3, conc H_2SO_4, 120 °C→ CH_3, NO_2 (Compound A) → CH_3, NO_2, NO_2 (Compound B) → CH_3, O_2N, NO_2, NO_2 (**TNT**)

Figure A1 The synthesis of TNT

Questions

A1. Name compound **A**, that is the product of the mononitration of methylbenzene.

A2. State the type of reaction involved in the nitration process to give compound **A**.

A3. Give the reaction mechanism for the formation of compound **A**.

Stretch and challenge

A4. The mononitration of methylbenzene to give compound **A** occurs more easily than the mononitration of benzene. Does this suggest that the methyl group increases or decreases the electron density in the benzene ring?

A5. The second and third nitrations of methylbenzene give compound **B** and TNT, respectively, but occur much less easily than the first nitration to give **A**. Does this suggest that a nitro group increases or decreases the electron density in the benzene ring?

ASSIGNMENT 2: SYNTHESIS OF METHYL 3-NITROBENZOATE

(AT b, AT d, AT g, AT h, PS 2.1, PS 2.3, PS 4.1)

The following set of instructions was provided to carry out the nitration of methyl benzoate in the laboratory:

Care must be taken when using concentrated acids as they are corrosive. Ethanol is flammable. Methyl benzoate is harmful.

1. Add 8 cm^3 of concentrated sulfuric acid to a conical flask, and then carefully add 4.0 g of methyl benzoate.
2. Cool the conical flask using an ice bath to between 0 and 10 °C.
3. Make a nitrating solution by adding 3 cm^3 of concentrated nitric acid to a boiling tube and then carefully adding a further 3 cm^3 of concentrated sulfuric acid dropwise with a pipette.
4. Cool the boiling tube of the nitrating mixture in an ice bath.
5. Add the nitrating solution slowly, dropwise, to the solution of methyl benzoate while constantly stirring the mixture. During the addition, ensure the temperature of the reaction mixture does not exceed 20 °C.
6. After addition is complete, leave the reaction mixture for 15 minutes.
7. Pour the reaction mixture onto approximately 15 cm^3 of ice and, after the ice has melted, filter the solid by filtration under reduced pressure.
8. Recrystallise the solid from the minimum amount of hot ethanol.
9. Filter off the purified methyl-3-nitrobenzoate and dry under reduced pressure.
10. Measure the melting point of the product.

Questions

A1. Write an equation for the reaction of methyl benzoate with concentrated sulfuric acid and concentrated nitric acid to give methyl-3-nitrobenzoate.

A2. This reaction is an example of an electrophilic substitution. What is the electrophile in the reaction? Draw equations for its formation.

A3. What safety precautions would you take before carrying out the synthesis?

A4. What size of conical flask would you suggest using? Give your reasons.

A5. Why were the reagents cooled in ice before use?

A6. What would you use to add the nitrating solution to the conical flask?

A7. (a) Why, when you are undertaking the recrystallisation, should the minimum amount of hot ethanol be used?

(b) How would you heat the ethanol?

A8. What is the purpose of measuring the melting point of the recrystallised material?

KEY IDEAS

- Benzene is nitrated by concentrated nitric acid in the presence of concentrated sulfuric acid.
- Nitration of benzene is an electrophilic substitution reaction, with the electrophile being the nitronium ion (NO_2^+).
- Some commercial explosives are made by nitrating aromatic compounds.
- The nitro group of aromatic compounds can be reduced to an amine group using tin and hydrochloric acid or nickel and hydrogen.
- Aromatic amines are used in the dye industry.

Friedel–Crafts acylation of benzene

The Friedel–Crafts reaction was developed in 1877 by the French chemist Charles Friedel and the American chemist James Mason Crafts. It is an electrophilic substitution reaction of benzene or some other aromatic compound with an acyl chloride, using a catalyst such as aluminium chloride or iron(III) chloride (Figure 13).

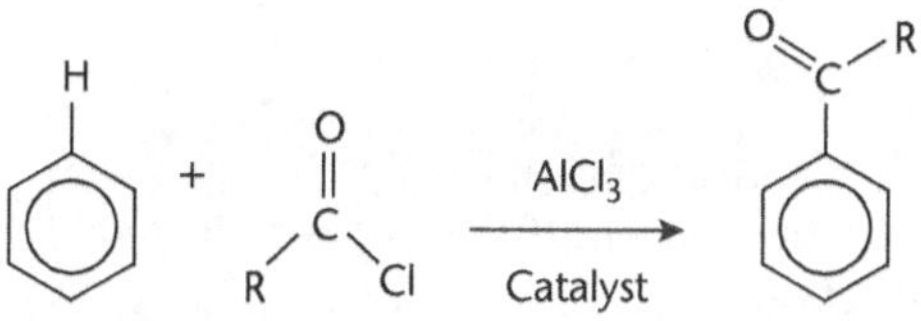

H O AlCl3 Catalyst R Cl O R C

Figure 13 The Friedel–Crafts acylation

$AlCl_3$ and $FeCl_3$ can form a dative covalent bond with a lone pair of electrons from the chlorine of the acyl chloride. Compounds which can 'accept' a lone pair of electrons and form a dative covalent bond are called **Lewis acids**.

This weakens the C–Cl bond, which breaks and forms the acyl carbocation (an electrophile) and $[AlCl_4]^-$. The electrophile is attracted to the delocalised electron cloud of the benzene ring (Figure 8). H^+ is released and reacts with the $[AlCl_4]^-$ to produce HCl and re-form the $AlCl_3$ catalyst (Figure 14). As with the other electrophilic substitution reactions, a catalyst is required, and heating to a temperature of about 80 °C. It is also essential to ensure that the reaction mixture is completely free of water because $AlCl_3$ and $FeCl_3$ react vigorously with water.

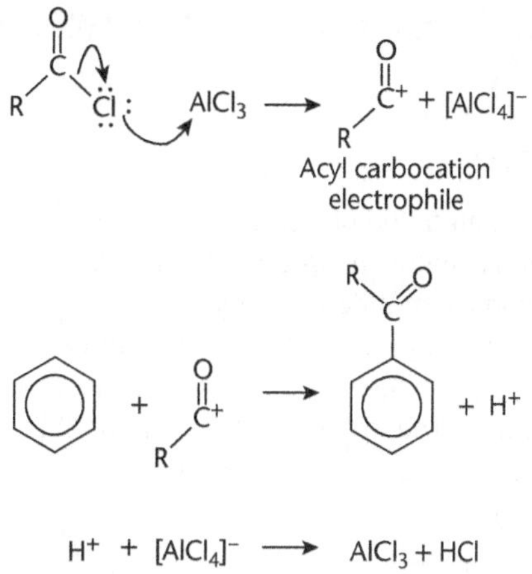

R–C(=O)–Cl: + $AlCl_3$ ⟶ R–C^+=O + $[AlCl_4]^-$

Acyl carbocation electrophile

benzene + R–C^+=O ⟶ R–C(=O)–C₆H₅ + H^+

$H^+ + [AlCl_4]^- \longrightarrow AlCl_3 + HCl$

Figure 14 The Friedel–Crafts acylation mechanism

The ketone functional group can be reduced to an alkane using nickel and hydrogen gas or zinc and concentrated HCl, or to an alcohol using sodium borohydride (Figure 15).

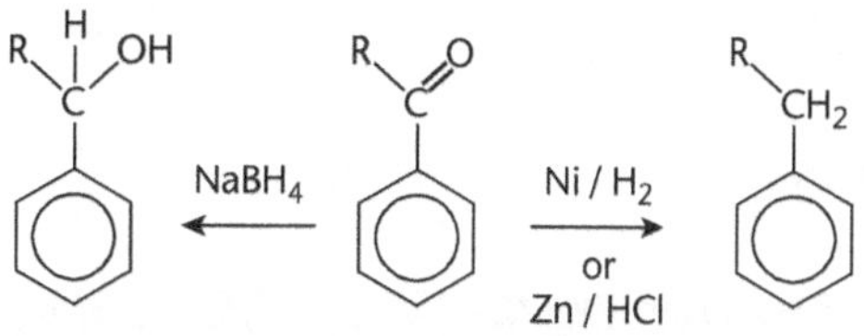

R H OH ← $NaBH_4$ — R C O — Ni / H_2 or Zn / HCl → R CH_2

Figure 15 Reduction of aromatic ketones

QUESTIONS

6. Suggest reagents to carry out these reactions:

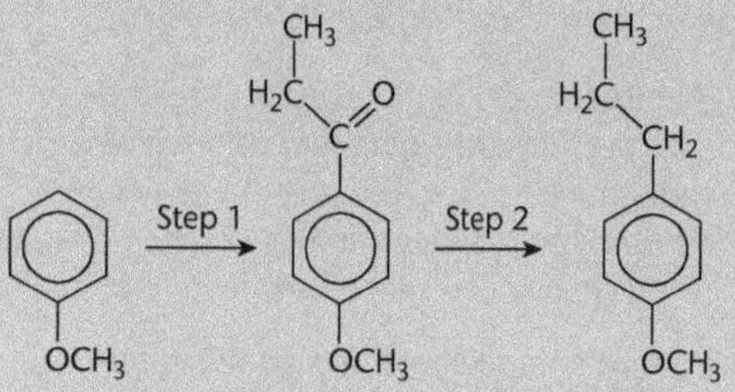

OCH_3 —Step 1→ CH_3 H_2C C O OCH_3 —Step 2→ CH_3 H_2C CH_2 OCH_3

7. What type of reaction is step 1?
8. What is the electrophile in step 1? Draw a mechanism to show how the electrophile is formed.

ASSIGNMENT 3: SYNTHESIS OF IBUPROFEN

(PS 1.1, PS 2.1)

Ibuprofen is a common painkiller and anti-inflammatory that is in a group of painkillers called nonsteroidal anti-inflammatory drugs (NSAIDs). It is normally used for mild pain but can also be used to treat a fever and swellings caused by sprains and strains. The first few steps in a possible synthesis of ibuprofen are shown in Figure A1.

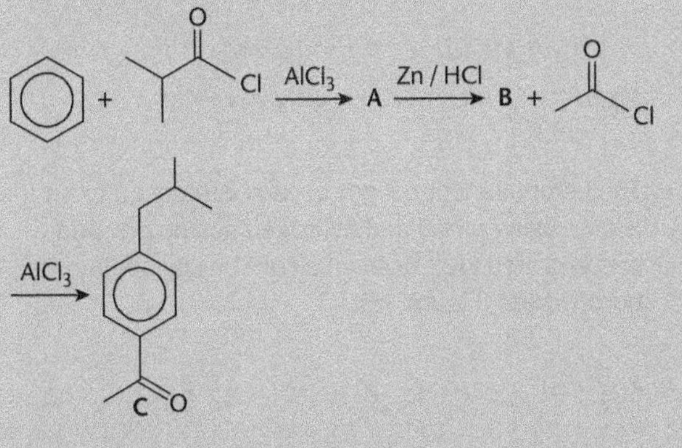

Figure A1 *The first three steps of a synthesis of ibuprofen*

Questions

A1. What is a Lewis acid?

A2. Draw the structure of the product **A** of the reaction between benzene and 2-methylpropanoyl chloride in the presence of anhydrous aluminium chloride.

A3. Draw the reaction mechanism for the formation of **A**.

A4. Draw and name structure **B**. What type of reaction is the formation of **B** from **A**?

A5. Suggest other reagents that might be used to prepare **B** from **A**.

A6. If 1.34 g of **B** was reacted with 0.79 g of ethanoyl chloride and a 75% yield of **C** was obtained, how many grams of **C** were isolated?

A7. What precautions should you take when using ethanoyl chloride in a reaction?

A8. If **A** is a liquid, suggest how you would purify it.

KEY IDEAS

- Friedel–Crafts acylations use acyl halides and are catalysed by $AlCl_3$ or $FeCl_3$.
- The Friedel–Crafts acylation is an electrophilic substitution reaction where the electrophile is the acyl carbocation.

PRACTICE QUESTIONS

1. Benzene reacts with propanoyl chloride in the presence of aluminium chloride. Write equations to show the role of aluminium chloride as a catalyst in this reaction. Outline a mechanism for this reaction of benzene.

2. 1,4-Diaminobenzene is an important intermediate in the production of polymers such as Kevlar and also of polyurethanes, used in foam seating. A possible synthesis of 1,4-diaminobenzene from phenylamine is shown in Figure Q1.

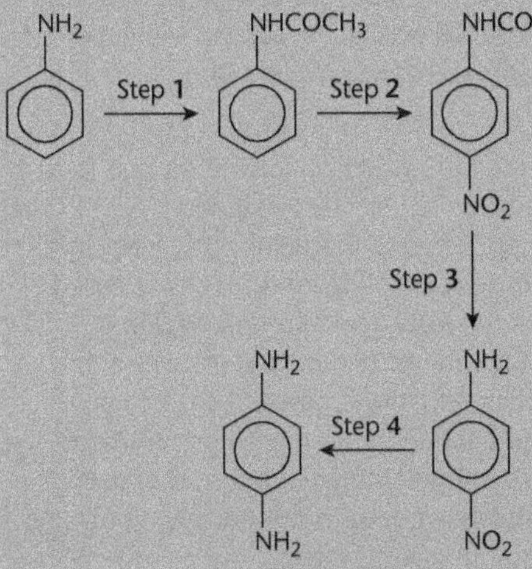

Figure Q1

a. A reagent for step **2** is a mixture of concentrated nitric acid and concentrated sulfuric acid, which react together to form a reactive intermediate. Write an equation for the reaction of this intermediate in step **2**.

b. Name the mechanism for the reaction in step **2**.

c. Suggest the type of reaction occurring in step **3**.

d. Identify the reagents used in step **4**.

AQA Specimen Paper 2, 2015, Question 9, parts 4–8

3. Three isomers of $C_6H_4(NO_2)_2$ are shown in Figure Q2:

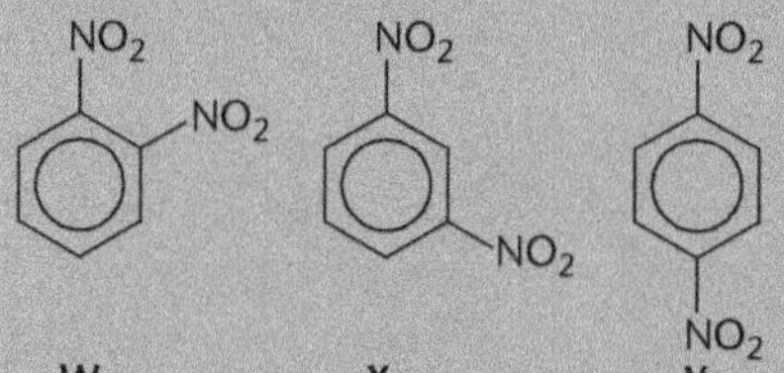

W X Y

Figure Q2

a. Isomer **X** is prepared from nitrobenzene by reaction with a mixture of concentrated nitric acid and sulfuric acid. The two acids react to form an inorganic species that reacts with nitrobenzene to form **X**.

i. Give the formula of this inorganic species formed from the two acids and write an equation to show its formation.

ii. Name and outline a mechanism for the reaction of this inorganic species with nitrobenzene to form **X**.

b. Isomer **Y** is used in the production of the polymer Kevlar. **Y** is first reduced to the diamine shown in Figure Q3:

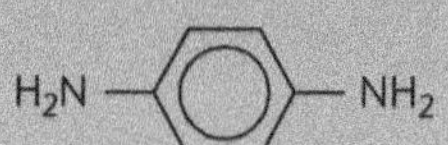

H_2N—C₆H₄—NH_2

Figure Q3

Identify a suitable reagent or mixture of reagents for the reduction of **Y** to form this diamine. Write an equation for this reaction using [H] to represent the reducing agent.

AQA Chemistry, January 2010, Question 8b–c

4. Consider compound **P** shown in Figure Q4 that is formed by the reaction of benzene with an electrophile.

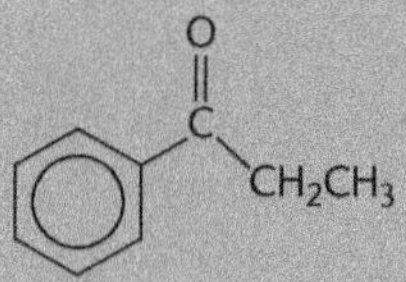

P

Figure Q4

a. Give the two substances that react together to form the electrophile and write an equation to show the formation of this electrophile.

b. Outline a mechanism for the reaction of this electrophile with benzene to form **P**.

c. Compound **Q** is an isomer of **P** that shows optical isomerism. **Q** forms a silver mirror when added to a suitable reagent. Identify this reagent and suggest a structure for **Q**.

AQA Chemistry, June 2010, Question 8a–c

5. The hydrocarbons benzene and cyclohexene are both unsaturated compounds. Benzene normally undergoes substitution reactions, but cyclohexene normally undergoes addition reactions.

a. The molecule cyclohexatriene does not exist and is described as hypothetical. Use the following data to state and explain the stability of benzene compared with the hypothetical cyclohexatriene.

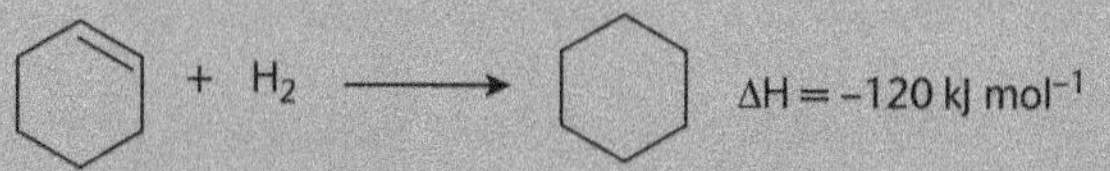

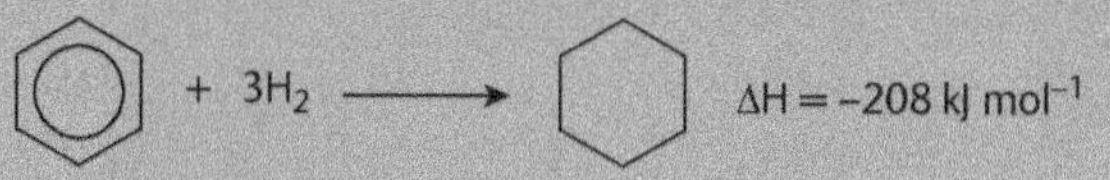

cyclohexene + H_2 → cyclohexane $\Delta H = -120\ \text{kJ mol}^{-1}$

benzene + $3H_2$ → cyclohexane $\Delta H = -208\ \text{kJ mol}^{-1}$

b. Benzene can be converted into amine **U** by the two-step synthesis shown below.

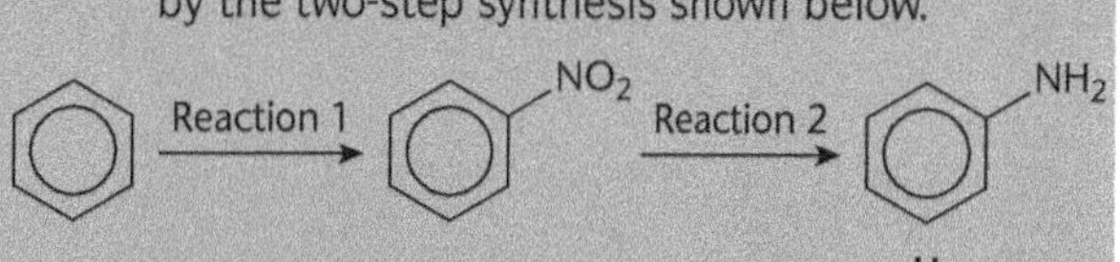

benzene —Reaction 1→ nitrobenzene (NO_2) —Reaction 2→ **U** (NH_2)

The mechanism of Reaction **1** involves attack by an electrophile.

(countined)

Give the reagents used to produce the electrophile needed in Reaction **1**.

Write an equation showing the formation of this electrophile.

Outline a mechanism for the reaction of this electrophile with benzene.

AQA Chemistry, June 2011, Question 8a–b

6. Many aromatic nitro compounds are used as explosives. One of the most famous is 2-methyl-1,3,5-trinitrobenzene, originally called trinitrotoluene or TNT. This compound, shown below, can be prepared from methylbenzene by a sequence of nitration reactions.

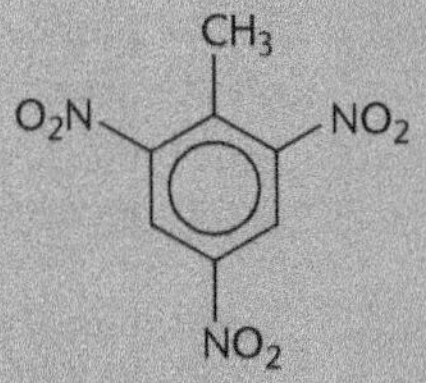

CH_3

O_2N NO_2

NO_2

a. The mechanism of the nitration of methylbenzene is an electrophilic substitution.

   i. Give the reagents used to produce the electrophile for this reaction.

   ii. Write an equation or equations to show the formation of this electrophile.

   iii. Outline a mechanism for the reaction of this electrophile with methylbenzene to produce 4-methylnitrobenzene.

AQA Chemistry, January 2012, Question 9a

7. Each of the following conversions involves reduction of a starting material.

a. Consider this conversion:

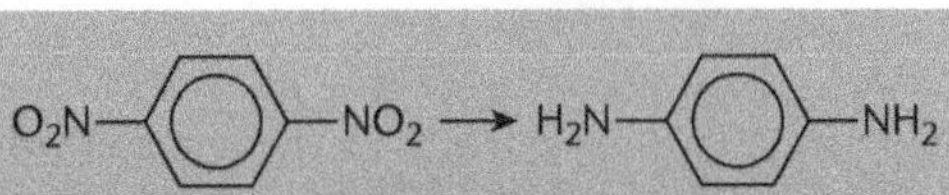

O_2N–⟨benzene ring⟩–NO_2 → H_2N–⟨benzene ring⟩–NH_2

Identify a reducing agent for this conversion.

Write a balanced equation for the reaction using molecular formulae for the nitrogen-containing compounds and [H] for the reducing agent.

Draw the repeating unit of the polymer formed by the product of this reaction with benzene-1,4-dicarboxylic acid.

b. Consider this conversion:

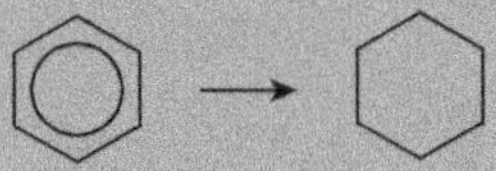

⟨benzene⟩ → ⟨cyclohexane⟩

Identify a reducing agent for this conversion.

State the empirical formula of the product.

State the bond angle between the carbon atoms in the starting material and the bond angle between the carbons in the product.

c. The reducing agent in the following conversion is $NaBH_4$.

$$H_3C-C(=O)-CH_2CH_3 \longrightarrow H_3C-CH(OH)-CH_2CH_3$$

   i Name and outline a mechanism for the reaction.

   ii By considering the mechanism of this reaction, explain why the product formed is optically inactive.

AQA Chemistry, January 2013, Question 7

9 AMINES

PRIOR KNOWLEDGE

You will already have studied acids and bases. You will also be familiar with the curly arrow mechanisms of nucleophilic addition–elimination reactions and the nitration of benzene (see *chapters 4, 7 and 8 of Year 2 Student Book*).

LEARNING OBJECTIVES

In this chapter you will learn about the structure, base properties, reactions and preparation of amines. You will be able to outline the nucleophilic reactions of amines and be able to explain the difference in base strength of different amines.

(Specification 3.3.11)

Many molecules needed for biological processes contain an amine group. These include amino acids, DNA and RNA. Dopamine is a neurotransmitter (a molecule that enables communication between nerve cells). As the name suggests, it contain an amine group. Levels of dopamine in the brain have been linked to Parkinson's disease and schizophrenia.

Acetylcholine is another neurotransmitter, but in this compound the amine group is in the form of a quaternary ammonium salt.

Some synthetic molecules with similar structures to dopamine can also affect the brain. Methamphetamine is an illegal, addictive drug. It is an antidepressant and a central nervous system stimulant. Amine drugs are also used in medicine. Benzedrex®, a nasal decongestant, is used to treat allergic rhinitis.

Alkaloids are naturally occurring amines found in plants. Examples are morphine (an analgesic), strychnine (a poison), quinine (an anti-malarial drug), omacetaxine (an anti-cancer drug) and caffeine (a stimulant).

The amines 1,4-diaminobutane (putrescine) and 1,5-diaminopentane (cadaverine) are produced when dead bodies decompose. They get their common names from 'putrefy', meaning to rot and decay, and 'cadaver', the medical name for a corpse.

Diamines are also important chemicals in the polymer industry, with 1,6-diaminohexane being one part of the important polymer nylon-6,6.

9.1 AMMONIA, AMINES AND QUATERNARY AMMONIUM SALTS

Structure and nomenclature

An ammonia molecule has a nitrogen atom bonded to three hydrogen atoms. The nitrogen atom also has a lone pair of electrons. Repulsion between the pairs of electrons (three bonding pairs and one lone pair) means that an ammonia molecule is tetrahedral (Figure 1). The lone pair on the nitrogen atom is responsible for the two main properties of ammonia and amines: their tendency to act as nucleophiles and their action as Brønsted–Lowry bases.

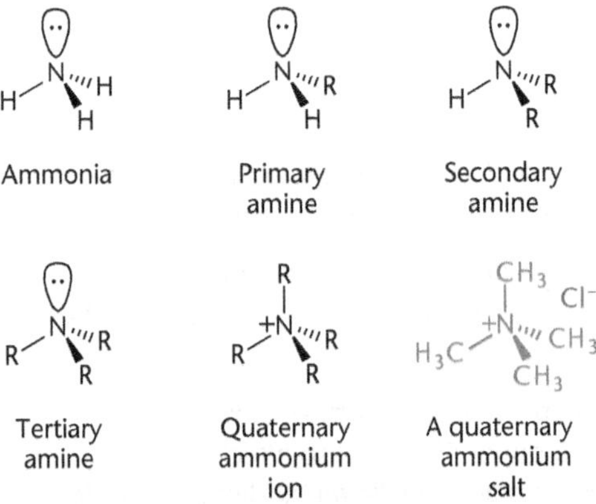

Figure 1 *The structures of ammonia, amines and quaternary ammonium salts*

There are three classes of amines: primary, secondary and tertiary. Amines are derived from ammonia when one, two or all three hydrogen atoms are replaced by alkyl or aryl groups to make primary, secondary or tertiary amines, respectively. As with ammonia, the shape of all of these molecules is tetrahedral.

Quaternary ammonium ions are produced from tertiary amines when the nitrogen atom's lone pair of electrons forms a dative (coordinate) bond to a carbocation to form a fourth hydrocarbon group (Figure 2). Hence, a quaternary ammonium ion is like an ammonium ion (NH_4^+) where alkyl or aryl groups have replaced all four hydrogens. Like ammonium salts, $NH_4^+X^-$, quaternary ammonium salts, $NR_4^+X^-$ are crystalline, ionic solids (Figure 1).

Ammonium ion

Tetramethylammonium ion, a quaternary ammonium ion

Figure 2 *The bonding in ammonium and quaternary ammonium salts*

Primary amines are named by identifying the longest hydrocarbon chain and adding the suffix 'amine'. For secondary and tertiary amines, first we must identify the longest hydrocarbon chain attached to the nitrogen as for primary amines. Then we identify the other smaller hydrocarbon groups attached to the nitrogen and list these at the beginning of the name. The prefix *N*- is used to show that the smaller groups are attached to the main chain via the nitrogen atom (Figure 3).

2-aminopropane
a primary amine.
The nitrogen is bonded to one alkyl group.

N-Methylpropylamine
a secondary amine.
The nitrogen is bonded to two alkyl groups.

N,N-Dimethylethylamine
a tertiary amine.
The nitrogen is bonded to three alkyl groups.

Figure 3 *Nomenclature of primary, secondary and tertiary amines*

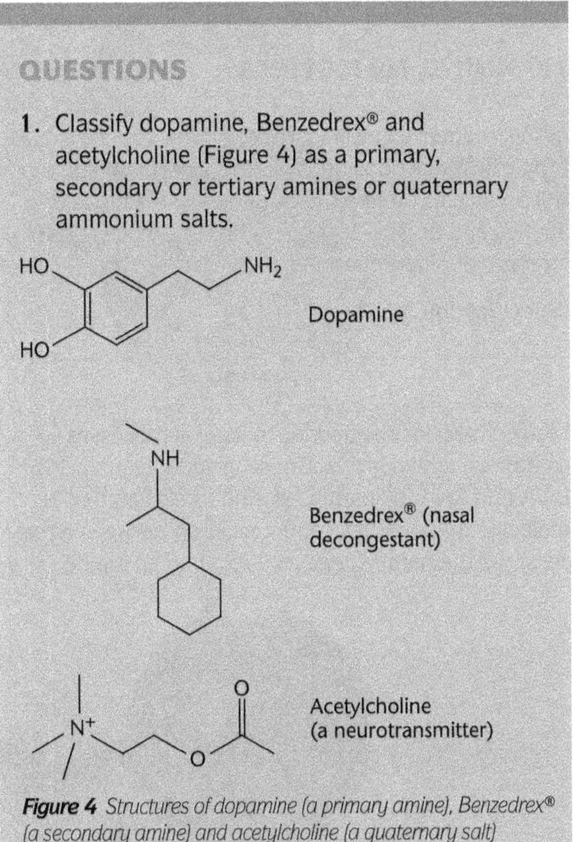

QUESTIONS

1. Classify dopamine, Benzedrex® and acetylcholine (Figure 4) as a primary, secondary or tertiary amines or quaternary ammonium salts.

Figure 4 *Structures of dopamine (a primary amine), Benzedrex® (a secondary amine) and acetylcholine (a quaternary salt)*

2. Draw the structures of:
   a. *N*-ethylbutylamine
   b. *N*-ethyl-*N*-methylpropylamine
   c. *N*,*N*-dimethylbutylamine.
3. Name these structures:
   a. $CH_3CH_2C(CH_3)_2CH_2NHCH_3$
   b. $CH_3CH_2N(CH_2CH_3)CH_2CH_3$ (as drawn: $H_3C-CH_2-N(CH_2-CH_3)-CH_2-CH_3$ with branch H_3C-CH_3)

Stretch and challenge

4. Name this structure:
   NH_2 on C2 of a pent-3-ene chain

9.2 BASIC PROPERTIES OF AMMONIA AND AMINES

In aqueous solution, ammonia and amine molecules can accept a proton from a water molecule, producing an ammonium ion (NH_4^+) and a substituted ammonium ion ($R\text{–}NH_3^+$), respectively, and a hydroxide (OH^-) ion (Figure 5). The solution is alkaline because of the OH^- ions. Ammonia and amine molecules can accept protons because the lone pair of electrons on the nitrogen atom is available to form a dative (coordinate) bond with a proton. However, the reactants and products are in equilibrium (Figure 5). Therefore, ammonia and amines are weak bases.

$$R\text{—}NH_2\text{:} + H\text{—}O\text{—}H \rightleftharpoons [R\text{—}NH_3]^+ + [\text{:}OH]^-$$

R = H, alkyl or aryl

Figure 5 *Formation of a substituted ammonium ion and hydroxide ion in aqueous solution*

The position of the equilibrium is an indication of the strength of the amine as a base. Table 1 compares the pH of 1 mol dm^{-3} solutions of some amines. Sodium hydroxide is a strong base. It ionises completely in aqueous solution to give a solution of pH 14. Ammonia and amines do not fully ionise in water and the pH of their solutions is less than 14. They are all weak bases. Alkyl amines are slightly stronger bases than ammonia, but aryl amines are weaker.

1 mol dm^{-3} of base	$[OH^-]$ / mol dm^{-3}
sodium hydroxide	1
ethylamine	0.022
methylamine	0.021
ammonia	0.0043
phenylamine	0.000021

Table 1 *Comparison of different amines as bases. When an amine dissolves in water, an equilibrium is established and the solution contains hydroxide ions (see Figure 5).*

Alkyl groups push electron density away from the alkyl group towards the amine group. Because of this, the electron density on the nitrogen atom increases, increasing its ability to accept a proton (Figure 6).

Figure 6 *Factors affecting electron density of the nitrogen lone pair and, therefore, the base strength of the amine*

In aromatic amines, overlap occurs between the lone pair on the nitrogen and the delocalised electron system of the benzene ring, and the nitrogen lone pair is delocalised towards the benzene ring. The electron density on the nitrogen atom is lowered and this reduces the ability of nitrogen to accept a proton (Figure 6).

This difference in base strength accounts for the need to use dilute acid to dissolve aromatic amines in water. According to Le Chatelier's principle, acid removes OH^- and shifts the position of equilibrium (Figure 5) to the right. The amine dissolves because it is converted to its ionic salt.

QUESTIONS

5. Draw the acid–base reaction of butylamine with water. Predict whether the pH of a 1 mol dm^{-3} aqueous solution of butylamine would be more acidic or basic than the same concentration of phenylamine in water. Why is this?

KEY IDEAS

- Amines and quaternary ammonium salts are derived from ammonia.
- There are three types of amine: primary, secondary and tertiary.
- Ammonia and amines act as bases because of the lone pair of electrons on the nitrogen atom.
- Aliphatic primary amines are stronger bases than ammonia.
- Aromatic primary amines are weaker bases than ammonia.

9.3 NUCLEOPHILIC PROPERTIES OF AMINES

Preparing primary aliphatic amines

Ammonia and amines have a lone pair of electrons and this makes these compounds nucleophiles. Primary aliphatic amines can be prepared by the **nucleophilic substitution** of the halogen atom in a halogenoalkane with ammonia (Figure 7). Excess ammonia is dissolved in ethanol and heated with the halogenoalkane in a sealed vessel. Using a sealed vessel leads to an increased pressure, which increases the rate of reaction. The halogenoalkane must have the same number of carbon atoms as the required amine product and the halogen atom(s) must be positioned on the carbon atom(s) to which the amino group(s) need to be bonded. The nucleophilic substitution reaction involves three stages:

- *Stage 1*. The lone pair on the nitrogen atom of the ammonia molecule is attracted to the δ+ charge on the carbon atom of the polar carbon–halogen bond.
- *Stage 2*. The lone pair forms a covalent bond between the nitrogen atom and the carbon atom and the carbon–halogen bond is broken (with the halogen leaving with the electron pair). This is the nucleophilic substitution.
- *Stage 3*. The amine is released from the intermediate salt by the removal of a proton by a base. This base can be added to the reaction mixture (e.g. aqueous sodium hydroxide) or the excess of ammonia can act as the base.

The overall reaction is a nucleophilic substitution of the halogen atom in the halogenoalkane by ammonia.

1 Attraction of ammonia's lone pair to δ+ charge on carbon atom of the polar carbon–halogen bond (R is alkyl group)

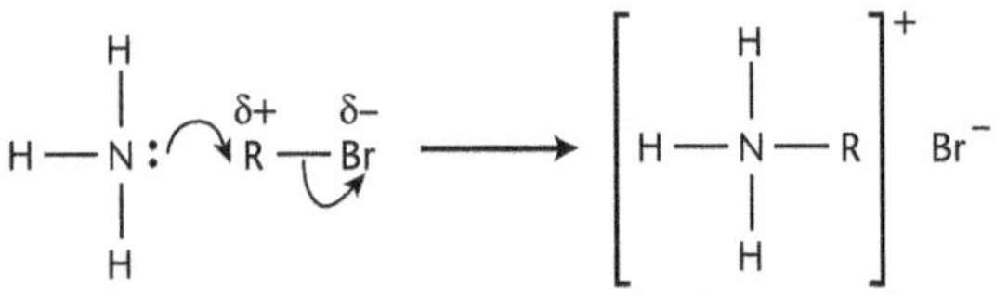

$$H_3N: + \overset{\delta+}{R}-\overset{\delta-}{Br} \longrightarrow [H_3N-R]^+ \; Br^-$$

2 Covalent bond forms between nitrogen and carbon, with release of bromide ion. An alkylammonium salt is produced.

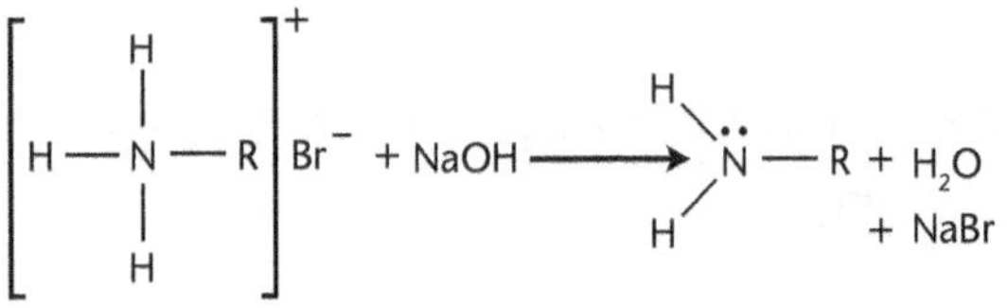

$$[H_3N-R]^+ Br^- + NaOH \longrightarrow H_2\ddot{N}-R + H_2O + NaBr$$

3 Amine released by adding alkali to alkylammonium salt.

Figure 7 *Reaction between ammonia and a halogenoalkane*

QUESTIONS

6. Which halogenoalkane would react with ammonia to produce:
   a. ethylamine?
   b. 1-methylethylamine?
   c. hexane-1,6-diamine?

Chloro- and bromoalkanes are preferred as sources of the hydrocarbon groups because they are more readily available than iodoalkanes and are more reactive than fluoroalkanes. For example, 2-phenylethylamine (or 1-amino-2-phenylethane), the primary amine responsible for the common yearning for chocolate, can be made by reacting 1-bromo-2-phenylethane with excess ethanolic ammonia (Figure 8).

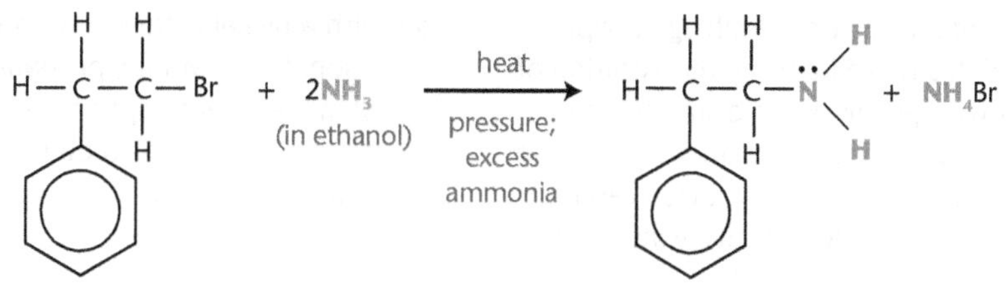

heat; pressure; excess ammonia

$C_6H_5CH_2CH_2Br + 2NH_3$ (in ethanol) → $C_6H_5CH_2CH_2NH_2 + NH_4Br$

2-Phenylethylamine (1-amino-2-phenylethane)

Figure 8 *Reaction between ammonia and 1-bromo-2-phenylethane*

However, this method does not give high yields, because it is not possible to guarantee that only one of the ammonia's hydrogens will be substituted in the alkylation reaction. Like ammonia, all amines have a lone pair of electrons. This allows further nucleophilic substitution by the halogenoalkane (Figure 9). Because alkyl groups push electron density towards the nitrogen, the product of each successive alkylation is a better nucleophile than the starting material. As a result, mixtures of primary, secondary and tertiary amines and quaternary ammonium salts are always produced.

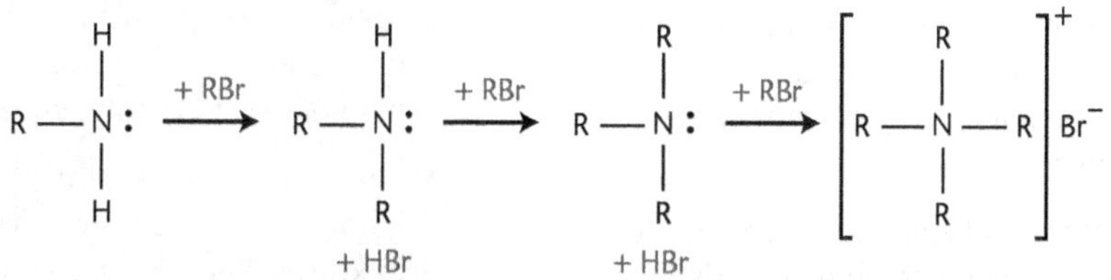

$RNH_2 \xrightarrow{+RBr} R_2NH + HBr \xrightarrow{+RBr} R_3N + HBr \xrightarrow{+RBr} [R_4N]^+Br^-$

Primary, Secondary, Tertiary, Quaternary ammonium salt

Figure 9 *Successive replacement of hydrogens by alkyl groups in aliphatic amines*

We can adjust the composition of the initial reaction mixture to favour either the primary amine or the quaternary ammonium salt. Excess ammonia favours the production of primary amines because it is less likely that a second halogenoalkane molecule will react with a primary amine when there are very many unreacted ammonia molecules still available. Quaternary ammonium salts will be favoured if an excess of the halogenoalkane is used. This ensures that each ammonia molecule will react with four halogenoalkane molecules.

Despite this, the production of primary amines from halogenoalkanes is often not efficient because mixtures containing secondary and tertiary amines and quaternary ammonium salts are inevitably produced.

A different approach is to introduce the $-NH_2$ group indirectly into a molecule. The first step is to reflux an appropriate halogenoalkane with a solution of potassium cyanide dissolved in a mixture of water and ethanol. The lone pair of the cyanide ion ($:CN^-$) allows nucleophilic substitution of the halogen atom and puts a cyanide group (–CN) into the organic molecule. Organic compounds with a cyanide group are called nitriles. For example, refluxing bromoethane with potassium cyanide yields propanenitrile (Figure 10). The reaction is useful in organic syntheses because it increases the length of the carbon chain by one carbon atom.

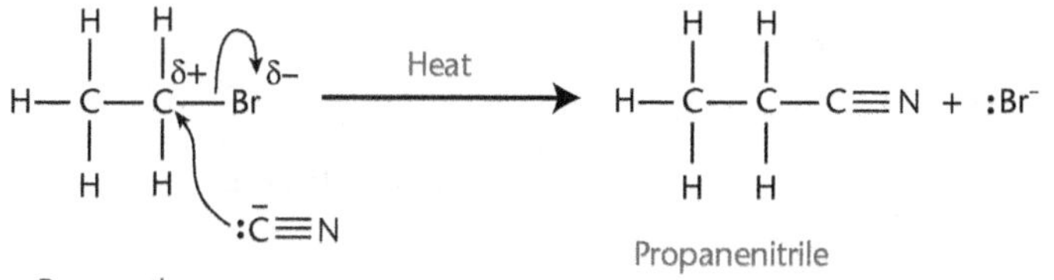

$CH_3CH_2^{\delta+}-Br^{\delta-} + :\bar{C}\equiv N \xrightarrow{\text{Heat}} CH_3CH_2-C\equiv N + :Br^-$

Bromoethane

Propanenitrile (a new C–C bond has formed, extending the carbon chain)

Figure 10 *Nucleophilic substitution of bromoethane by cyanide ions*

The nitrile group contains a carbon–nitrogen triple bond. Reduction of this triple bond by the addition of two molecules of hydrogen gives the primary amine in good yield. The reduction can be achieved by using lithium tetrahydridoaluminate, $LiAlH_4$, dissolved in dry ether, followed by hydrolysis. Alternatively, hydrogen gas with a nickel catalyst can bring about the reduction. For example, propanenitrile is reduced to propylamine (1-aminopropane) (Figure 11). Aliphatic primary amines can also be made by reducing nitro compounds and amides.

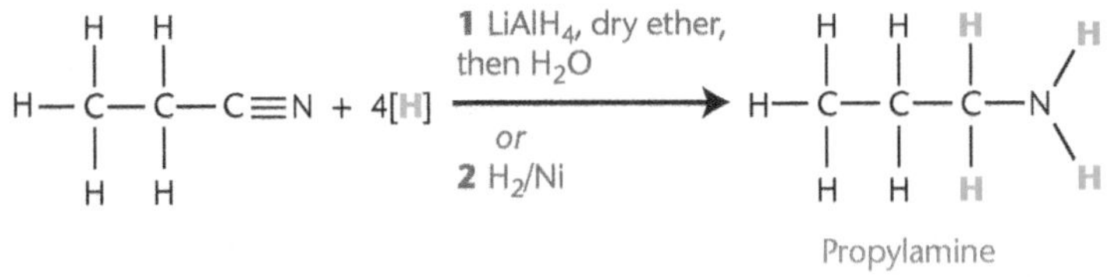

$$CH_3CH_2C{\equiv}N + 4[H] \xrightarrow[\text{or } \mathbf{2}\ H_2/Ni]{\mathbf{1}\ LiAlH_4\text{, dry ether, then } H_2O} CH_3CH_2CH_2NH_2$$

Propylamine

Figure 11 *Reduction of propanenitrile to propylamine*

QUESTIONS

7. Give the names and structures of the other amines that could be produced when trying to make ethylamine using bromoethane and ammonia.
8. What reactants and conditions are required to make tetraoctylammonium chloride from ammonia?
9. Devise a reaction sequence to prepare 2-methylbutylamine (or 1-amino-2-methylbutane), stating which halogenoalkane you will use.
10. Can 2-propylamine be prepared by making and reducing a nitrile? If it can, give the equations. If it cannot, explain why not.

KEY IDEAS

- Amines and quaternary ammonium salts can be produced by nucleophilic substitution of ammonia with a halogenoalkane.
- The production of primary amines from halogenoalkanes is not efficient because mixtures of secondary and tertiary amines and quaternary ammonium salts are also produced.
- Primary aliphatic amines are best produced by the reduction of nitriles.

ASSIGNMENT 1: SYNTHESIS OF AN AMIDE

(PS 1.1, PS 1.2)

You are a chemist in a pharmaceutical company. Computerised studies of the receptor sites for a nasal decongestant and the shapes and structures of potentially active compounds have led researchers to the idea that amide **D** might be an effective drug. You have used two different methods to prepare **D**, shown in Figure A1.

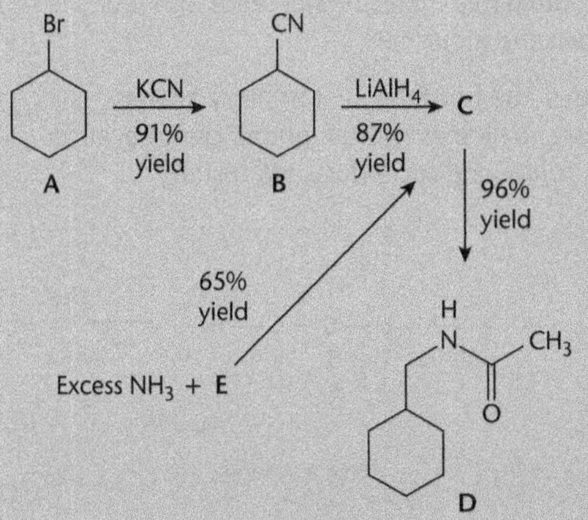

A (bromocyclohexane) → KCN, 91% yield → B (cyclohexanecarbonitrile) → $LiAlH_4$, 87% yield → C → 96% yield → D

Excess NH_3 + E → 65% yield → C

D: cyclohexylmethyl–NH–C(=O)–CH_3

Figure A1 *The synthesis of amide **D***

Questions

A1. Draw the mechanism for the formation of **B** from **A** with potassium cyanide. What type of mechanism is this?

A2. Predict the product **C** obtained from reaction of **B** with $LiAlH_4$. Name the type of reaction.

A3. Suggest reagents to carry out the reaction of **C** to give **D**. Draw the mechanism of the reaction.

A4. An alternative method for the synthesis of **C** was attempted. Draw the structure of and name the halogenoalkane **E** that would be required to react with excess ammonia to give **C**.

Stretch and challenge

A5. Why do you think the yield of the reaction of **E** and excess ammonia is quite low?

A6. If you were responsible for commercialising a synthesis of **D**, which route would you choose? What factors would influence your decision and what information would you need to finalise your choice?

A7. Why do you think that the functional groups present and the structure and shape of a molecule are key to its potential as a pharmaceutical drug?

Preparing primary aromatic amines

Primary aromatic amines are compounds with an $-NH_2$ functional group directly bonded to the benzene ring. The simplest example is phenylamine (Figure 12). The methods used to make aliphatic amines do not work for aromatic amines. For example, reacting chlorobenzene with ethanolic ammonia does not produce a reasonable yield of phenylamine.

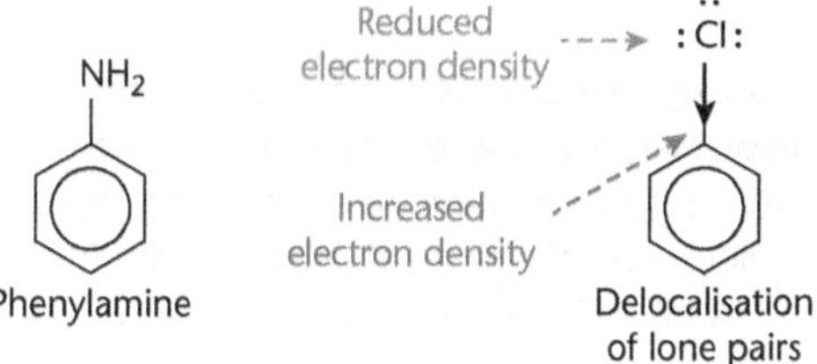

Figure 12 *Delocalisation of lone pairs in chlorobenzene*

There are two reasons why halogenobenzenes do not react strongly with ammonia:

1. The nitrogen atom in ammonia is nucleophilic, but benzene usually reacts with electrophiles (see *Chapter 8*) – the high electron density of the delocalised electron cloud of the benzene ring repels nucleophiles such as ammonia.
2. The aromatic ring is an electron-attracting group. The lone pairs of the halogen atom are delocalised towards the benzene ring (Figure 12). This has the effect of shortening and strengthening the C–Cl bond, making it less reactive than in an aliphatic halogenoalkane.

$$C_6H_6 + HNO_3 \xrightarrow[50\,^\circ C]{H_2SO_4} C_6H_5NO_2 + H_2O$$

$$C_6H_5NO_2 + 6[H] \xrightarrow[\text{then NaOH (aq)}]{Sn / HCl} C_6H_5NH_2 + 2H_2O$$

Figure 13 *Preparation of phenylamine from benzene*

Phenylamine is made by nitrating benzene with concentrated nitric acid and sulfuric acid at 50 °C (see *Chapter 8*). The nitro group is then reduced to a primary amine group using an acid together with a metal (Figure 13). On an industrial scale, scrap iron and hydrochloric acid are used, but tin and hydrochloric acid are used in the laboratory. Since excess acid is present, the initial product is the protonated form of phenylamine, $C_6H_5NH_3^+Cl^-$. The amine is released by addition of a base such as sodium hydroxide. This removes the proton from the $C_6H_5NH_3^+$ ion. The reduction can also be achieved using hydrogen gas and a nickel catalyst.

The conversion of aromatic nitro compounds to aromatic amines is of huge importance in the dye industry. It is used to introduce primary amine groups into a wide variety of aromatic molecules used for making dyes or into dye molecules themselves, causing changes in colour and ability to bond to fabrics.

QUESTIONS

11. Indicate whether the reaction sequences below will work well or poorly, and explain your answers.

a.

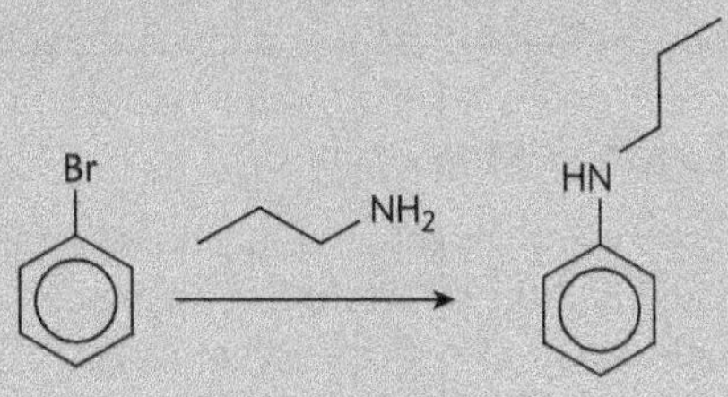

b.

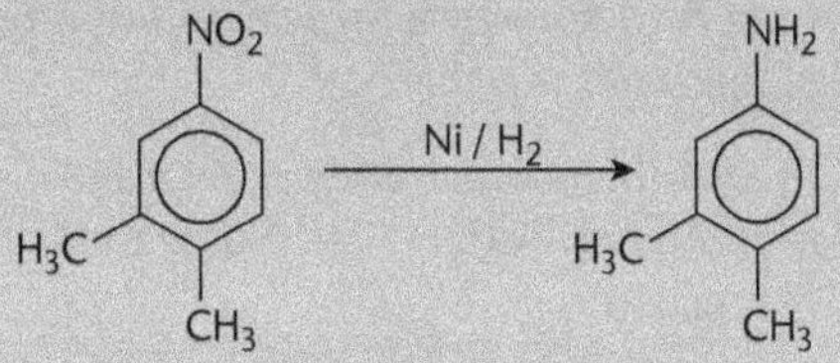

c.

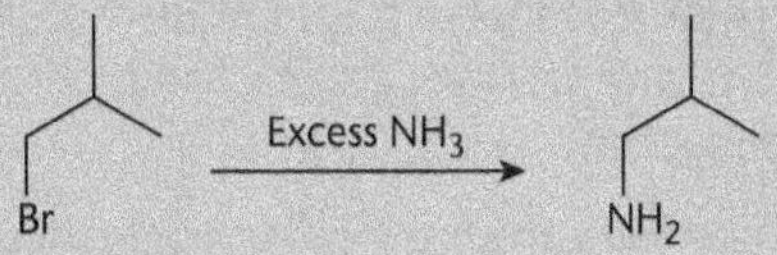

d.

KEY IDEAS

- Methods used to make aliphatic amines do not work for aromatic amines.
- Primary aromatic amines are prepared from aromatic nitro compounds via reduction.

ASSIGNMENT 2: PREPARATION OF AN AZO DYE

(PS 1.1)

You do not need to remember the details of this assignment but you could be asked to apply your knowledge to unfamiliar situations. Dyes are compounds that change the colour of a material. They can be natural or synthetic. A common class of synthetic dye is that of **azo dyes**, which contain an aromatic group and an **azo** group (N = N). The two aromatic rings and the azo group together make up the **chromophore**, which gives rise to the colour of the dye. The N = N double bond in the chromophore allows the delocalised electrons of one benzene ring to be extended into the second ring. The delocalised electrons in the chromophore can absorb certain wavelengths of visible light and the light not absorbed gives rise to the observed colour.

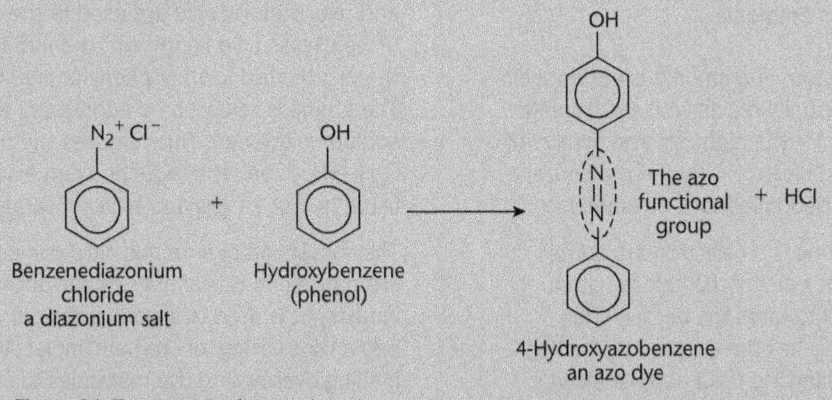

Figure A1 The synthesis of an azo dye

Azo dyes are made by reacting an aromatic diazonium salt with another aromatic molecule such as hydroxybenzene (phenol) or phenylamine (aniline) in a **coupling** reaction (Figure A1). The diazonium salt is unstable and in aqueous solution decomposes at temperatures above 5 °C. It is prepared from an aromatic amine by reacting with nitrous acid (HNO_2) made in situ by the reaction of sodium nitrite and aqueous hydrochloric acid at low temperature (between 0 and 5 °C).

$$NaNO_2 + HCl \xrightarrow{0\text{–}5\,°C} HNO_2 + NaCl$$

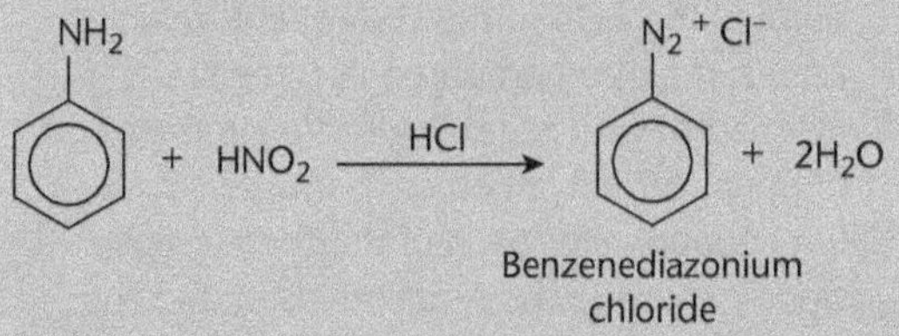

$$C_6H_5NH_2 + HNO_2 \xrightarrow{HCl} C_6H_5N_2^+Cl^- + 2H_2O$$

Benzenediazonium chloride

Figure A2 The synthesis of benzenediazonium chloride using nitrous acid

An important property of any dye is that it should be colour-fast, because it must not be easily washed from the material that it is colouring. Other functional groups can be attached to the aromatic rings of an azo dye that help to bond the dye to a material. The synthesis of an azo dye is shown in Figure A3.

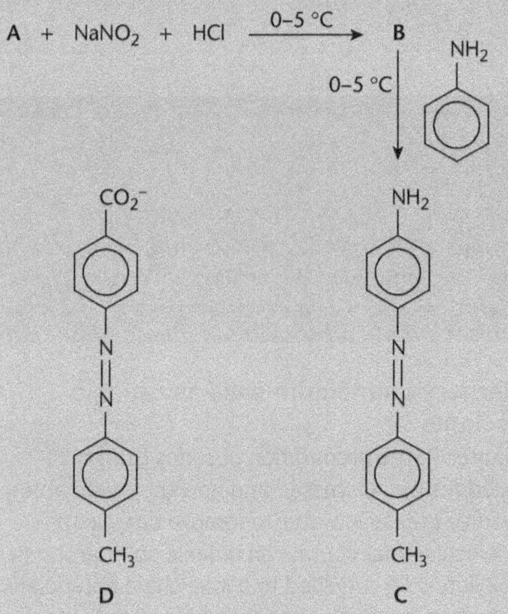

$$A + NaNO_2 + HCl \xrightarrow{0\text{–}5\,°C} B$$

B reacts with phenylamine (NH_2) at 0–5 °C to give C.

D: CO_2^- – benzene ring – N=N – benzene ring – CH_3

C: NH_2 – benzene ring – N=N – benzene ring – CH_3

Figure A3 The synthesis of an azo dye

A1. Draw the product **A** arising from reacting 4-nitromethylbenzene with iron and hydrochloric acid. Draw the balanced equation for the reaction using [H] to represent the reducing agent.

A2. Reaction of compound **A** with sodium nitrite and hydrochloric acid gives molecule **B**.

a. Write an equation showing how sodium nitrite and hydrochloric acid react together.

b. Why is it important to carry out the coupling reaction below 5 °C?

c. Give the name and structure of compound **B**.

A3. Reaction of **B** with phenylamine gives the yellow azo dye molecule **C**. Why is this molecule coloured?

Stretch and challenge

A4. The amine group in **C** is used to help bond the dye to a fabric. How might this work?

A5. The azo dye **D** bonds more strongly to a fabric than **C**. Suggest a possible reason.

A6. Methyl yellow (or butter yellow), shown below, is used as a pH indicator. It was used as a food additive until it was found to cause liver cancer. Propose a synthesis of methyl yellow from benzene and *N,N*-dimethylaniline. You should list all the reagents that you would use and draw any intermediate compounds.

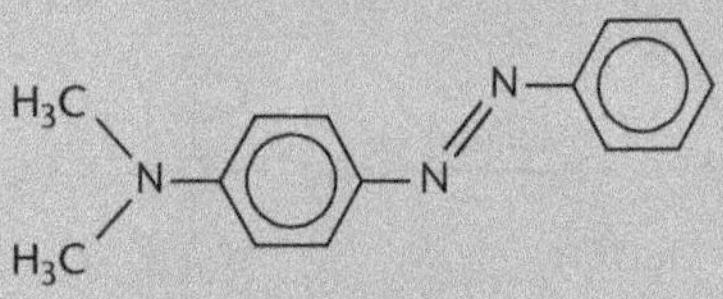

$(H_3C)_2N$ – benzene ring – N=N – benzene ring

Methyl yellow

Nucleophilic addition–elimination reactions of ammonia and primary amines

Another important reaction of ammonia and primary amines is with acyl chlorides and acid anhydrides to give amides. The by-products of the reactions are acidic (HCl and a carboxylic acid, respectively) and, therefore, two moles of ammonia or amine are required for each mole of acyl chloride or acid anhydride. The first acts as the nucleophile, while the second acts as a base and reacts with the generated acid.

This general mechanism is illustrated for two specific examples, the formation of ethanamide from ethanoyl chloride with ammonia as the nucleophile (Figure 14), and *N*-phenyl ethanamide from ethanoic anhydride with phenylamine as the nucleophile (Figure 15).

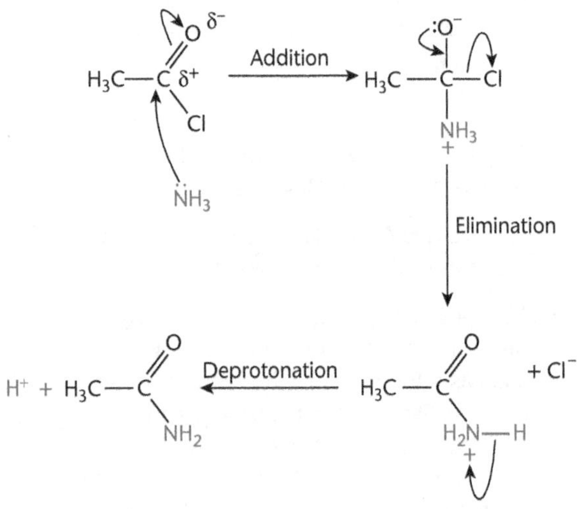

Figure 14 *Mechanism for the formation of ethanamide*

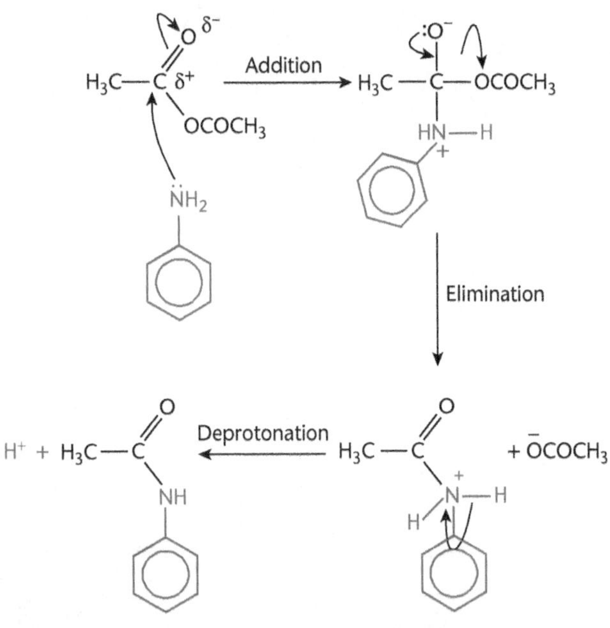

Figure 15 *Mechanism for the formation of N-phenylethanamide*

QUESTIONS

12. Paracetamol is a common painkiller mainly used to treat headaches. Using the IUPAC naming system, paracetamol is known as 4-hydroxy-(*N*-ethanoylphenylamine). Draw the full structure of paracetamol.

Stretch and challenge

13. A molecule of similar structure to another is called an analogue. An analogue of paracetamol, phenacetin (see below), was used as a painkiller from 1887 but was banned in 1983 in the USA due to toxicity issues. It can be prepared in three steps from ethoxybenzene. Suggest a synthesis of phenacetin from ethoxybenzene. Write full equations for each of the three steps, clearly showing the reagents used and the products obtained.

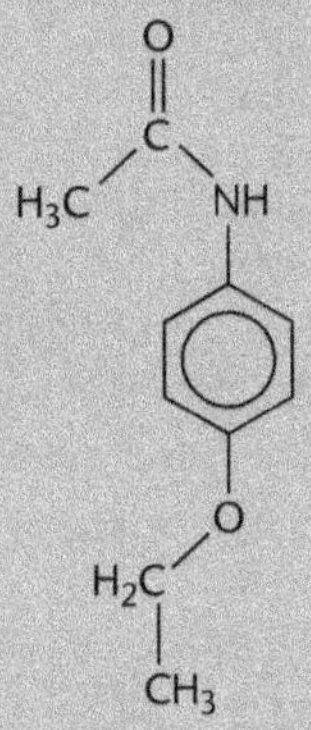

KEY IDEAS

- Acylation reactions of ammonia and primary aliphatic or aromatic amines with acyl chlorides or acid anhydrides give amides via a nucleophilic addition–elimination mechanism.

Quaternary ammonium salts as cationic surfactants

In Chapter 7, the preparation of soaps from triglycerides was discussed and how they were able to dissolve grease in water to remove dirt. Soaps are molecules that contain an anionic polar group (a carboxylate salt) attached to a long-chain non-polar hydrocarbon group and are examples of **anionic detergents** or **anionic surfactants**. Consequently, soaps are often described as containing a polar 'head' and a non-polar, long 'tail' (Figure 16). It is possible also to make cationic detergents, where the polar head is positively charged. These are called **cationic surfactants**.

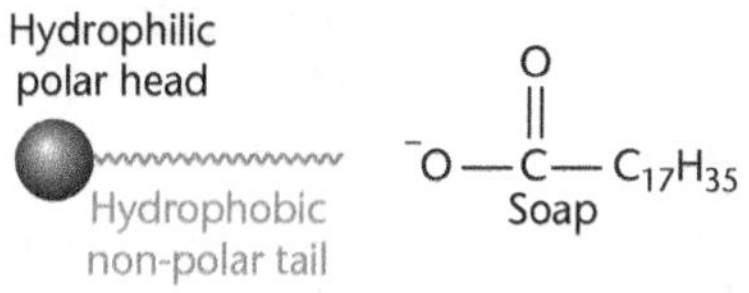

Figure 16 *A typical anionic detergent or soap. The 'heads' dissolve in water and the 'tails' dissolve grease, thus solubilising the grease in aqueous solution.*

Quaternary ammonium salts can be manufactured using long-chain (e.g. C_{12}) halogenoalkanes (Figure 17). Many surfaces are negatively charged, such as those of glass, hair, fibres, metals and plastics. These compounds can be used as cationic surfactants because the positive charge on the nitrogen atom of the quaternary ammonium ion is attracted to the negatively charged surfaces. They are used in fabric conditioners, leather softeners, sewage flocculants (for bringing particles to the surface), corrosion inhibitors, hair conditioners, anti-static agents and emulsifiers. Some quaternary ammonium salts with shorter carbon chains are also used in disinfectants, where they combine surfactant action with germicidal properties.

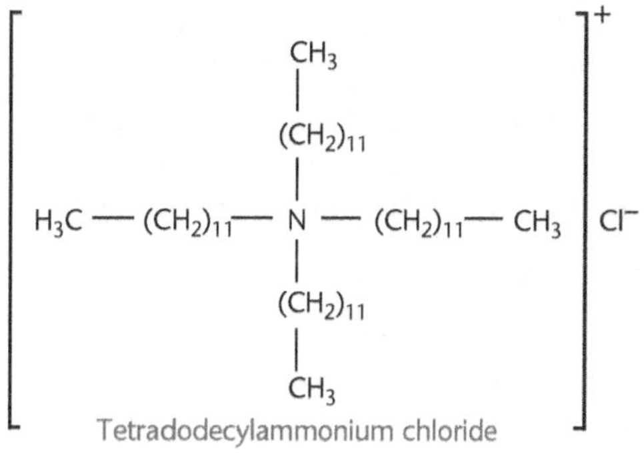

Figure 17 *A typical cationic detergent, a quaternary salt*

PRACTICE QUESTIONS

1. How many secondary amines have the molecular formula $C_4H_{11}N$?

AQA Chemistry Specimen Paper 2015, Question 31

2. a. Name the compound $(CH_3)_2NH$.
   b. $(CH_3)_2NH$ can be formed by the reaction of an excess of CH_3NH_2 with CH_3Br. Name and outline a mechanism for this reaction.
   c. Name the type of compound produced when a large excess of CH_3Br reacts with CH_3NH_2. Give a use for this type of compound.
   d. Draw the structures of the two compounds formed in the reaction of CH_3NH_2 with ethanoic anhydride.

AQA Chemistry, January 2006, Unit 4, Question 5

3. The reaction scheme in Figure Q1 shows the formation of two amines, **K** and **L**, from methylbenzene.

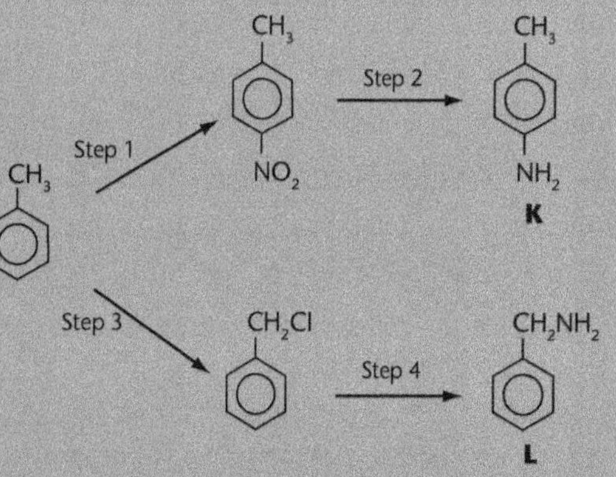

Figure Q1

a. i. Give the reagents needed to carry out Step 1. Write an equation for the formation from these reagents of the inorganic species which reacts with methylbenzene.
   ii. Name and outline a mechanism for the reaction between this inorganic species and methylbenzene.

b. Give a suitable reagent or combination of reagents for Step 2.

c. i. Give the reagent for Step 4 and state a condition to ensure that the primary amine is the major product.

ii. Name and outline the mechanism for Step 4.

d. Explain why amine **K** is a weaker base than ammonia.

e. Draw the structure of the organic compound formed when a large excess of bromomethane reacts with amine **L**.

f. Draw the structure of the organic compound formed when ethanoyl chloride reacts with amine **L** in an addition-elimination reaction.

AQA Chemistry, January 2005, Unit 4, Question 1

4. a. Name and outline the mechanism for the reaction of $CH_3CH_2NH_2$ with CH_3CH_2COCl. Name the amide formed.

b. Halogenoalkanes such as CH_3Cl are used in organic synthesis. Outline a three step synthesis of $CH_3CH_2NH_2$ starting from methane. Your first step should involve the formation of CH_3Cl.

In your answer, identify the product of the second step and give reagents and conditions for each step. Equations and mechanisms are not required.

AQA Chemistry, January 2010, Question 9

5. Ammonia and ethylamine are examples of weak Brønsted–Lowry bases.

a. State the meaning of the term *Brønsted–Lowry* base.

b. i. Write an equation for the reaction of ethylamine ($CH_3CH_2NH_2$) with water to form a weakly alkaline solution.

ii. In terms of this reaction, state why the solution is **weakly** alkaline.

c. State which is the stronger base, ammonia or ethylamine. Explain your answer.

d. Give the formula of an organic compound that forms an alkaline buffer solution when added to a solution of ethylamine.

e. Explain qualitatively how the buffer solution in part (d) maintains an almost constant pH when a small amount of hydrochloric acid is added to it.

AQA Chemistry, January 2012, Question 3

6. The reactions of molecules containing the chlorine atom are often affected by other functional groups in the molecule. Consider the reaction of CH_3CH_2COCl and $CH_3CH_2CH_2Cl$ with ammonia.

a. For the reaction of CH_3CH_2COCl with ammonia, name and outline the mechanism and name the product.

b. For the reaction of $CH_3CH_2CH_2Cl$ with **excess** ammonia, name and outline the mechanism and name the product.

c. Suggest **one** reason why chlorobenzene (C_6H_5Cl) does not react with ammonia under normal conditions.

AQA Chemistry, January 2012, Question 10

7. The question is about the primary amine $CH_3CH_2CH_2NH_2$.

a. The amine $CH_3CH_2CH_2NH_2$ reacts with CH_3COCl. Name and outline a mechanism for this reaction. Give the IUPAC name of the organic product.

b. Isomers of $CH_3CH_2CH_2NH_2$ include another primary amine, a secondary amine and a tertiary amine.

i. Draw the structure of these **three** isomers. Label each as primary, secondary or tertiary.

ii. Use table 1 to explain how you would use infrared spectra in the range outside the fingerprint region to distinguish between the secondary amine and the tertiary amine.

Bond	Wavenumber / cm^{-1}
N—H (amines)	3300–3500
O—H (alcohols)	3230–3550
C—H	2850–3300
O—H (acids)	2500–3000
C≡N	2220–2260
C=O	1680–1750
C=C	1620–1680
C—O	1000–1300
C—C	750–1100

Table 1 *Infrared absorption data*

c. The amine $CH_3CH_2CH_2NH_2$ can be prepared by two different routes.

Route **A** is a two-stage route and starts from CH_3CH_2Br.

Route **B** is a one-stage process and starts from $CH_3CH_2CH_2Br$.

i. Give the reagents and conditions for both stages in Route **A** and the single stage in Route **B**.

ii. Give **one** disadvantage of Route **A** and **one** disadvantage of Route **B**.

AQA Chemistry, June 2013, Question 8

8. Imipramine has been prescribed as an antidepressant. The structure of imipramine is:

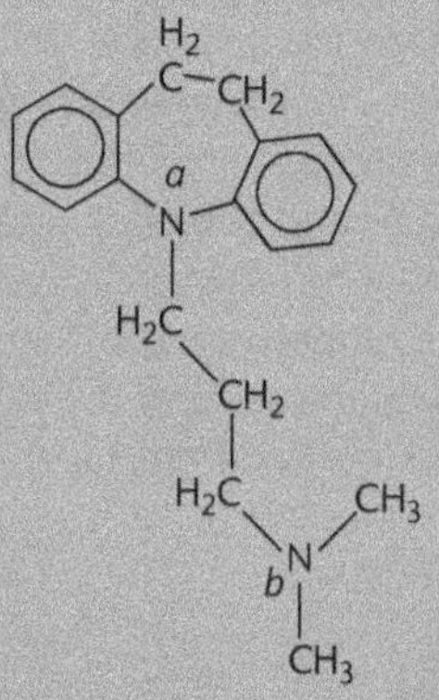

The medicine is normally supplied as a salt. The salt is formed when one mole of imipramine reacts with one mole of hydrochloric acid. Suggest why the nitrogen labelled *b* is more likely to be protonated than the nitrogen atom labelled *a* when the salt is formed.

AQA Chemistry, June 2013, Question 9a

9. Cetrimide is used as an antiseptic:

$[CH_3(CH_2)_{15}\overset{+}{N}(CH_3)_3]\ \overset{-}{Br}$

Cetrimide

a. Name this type of compound. Give the reagent that must be added to $CH_3(CH_2)_{15}NH_2$ to make cetrimide and state the reaction conditions.

b. Name the type of mechanism involved in this reaction.

AQA Chemistry, June 2014, Question 7b

10. One of the monomers used in the synthesis of Kevlar is:

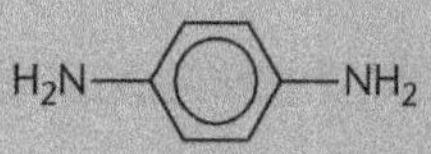

a. An industrial synthesis of this monomer uses a two-stage process starting from compound **X** (see below).

i. Suggest why the reaction of ammonia with **X** in Stage **1** might be considered unexpected.

ii. Suggest a combination of reagents for the reaction in Stage **2**.

iii. Compound **X** can be produced by the nitration of chlorobenzene. Give the combination of reagents for this nitration of chlorobenzene. Write an equation or equations to show the formation of a reactive intermediate from these reagents.

iv. Name and outline a mechanism for the formation of **X** from chlorobenzene and the reactive intermediate in question (iii).

AQA Chemistry, June 2014, Question 4b

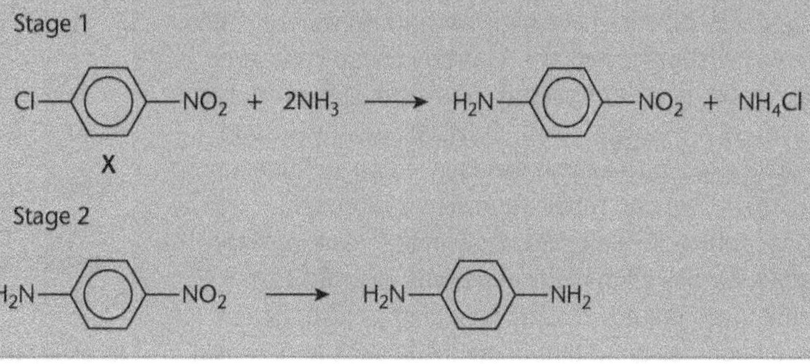

Stage 1

Stage 2

10 POLYMERS

PRIOR KNOWLEDGE

You will already have studied addition polymers (see *section 3 in chapter 14 of Year 1 Student Book*) and you should also be familiar with the chemistry of carboxylic acids, esters, amines, amides and aromatic compounds (see *chapters 7, 8 and 9 of Year 2 Student Book*).

LEARNING OBJECTIVES

In this chapter you will learn about the structure, synthesis and properties of condensation polymers. You will learn about biodegradable polymers and the advantages and disadvantages of different methods for disposal of polymers. You will be able to explain why polyesters and polyamides can be hydrolysed but polyalkenes cannot.

(Specification 3.3.12)

In 2013, 300 million tonnes of polymers (often called plastics) were produced globally. Each polymer has its own specific properties that determine its applications. In general, plastics have high strength-to-weight ratios, are easily shaped and are relatively cheap compared with wood, glass and metals. Some familiar everyday polymers are poly(ethene), poly(styrene), nylon and Kevlar®. Recent research has focused on self-healing polymers that can repair themselves if broken. Applications of self-healing polymers in coatings and paints, as well as in medical devices, are currently being investigated. Biodegradable organic polymers have been designed that allow the growth of new skin, muscles, bones and other organs in the laboratory.

Nature makes use of polymers. Materials such as collagen and keratin are natural proteins (polymers of amino acids), while wood, cotton and cellulose are polymeric sugars. At least 10–20 million tonnes of waste plastic ends up in the oceans annually, so the design of sustainable materials and of biodegradable polymers from renewable plant-based sources is important. The Ford Motor Company used soybean oil to make the polymeric foam in the seats of the Ford Mustang, and polylactic acid (derived from sugar cane) is used in 3-D printing.

10.1 TYPES OF POLYMERS

Poly(ethene) and nylon are two well-known polymer materials that illustrate the two general types of polymer. Poly(ethene) is an example of an **addition polymer**, produced by repeated addition reactions of ethene **monomers** (Figure 1). You have learned about addition polymers at AS level (see *chapter 14 of Year 1 Student Book*).

$$n\,H_2C{=}CH_2 \longrightarrow \left[\!-CH_2-CH_2-\right]_n$$

Figure 1 *The addition polymerisation of ethene*

Nylon is an example of a **condensation polymer**. A condensation reaction links two organic molecules together with the elimination of a small molecule (such as water, methanol or hydrogen chloride).

In order to allow repeated condensation reactions and so build up a polymeric structure, the monomers used for condensation polymers must be **bifunctional**.

This means they must contain two functional groups, one at each end of the molecule. For most synthetic polymers, condensation occurs between two different monomers, one containing two carboxylic acid (–COOH) functional groups and the other containing either two alcohol (–OH) groups to make a polyester or two amine ($-NH_2$) groups to make a polyamide.

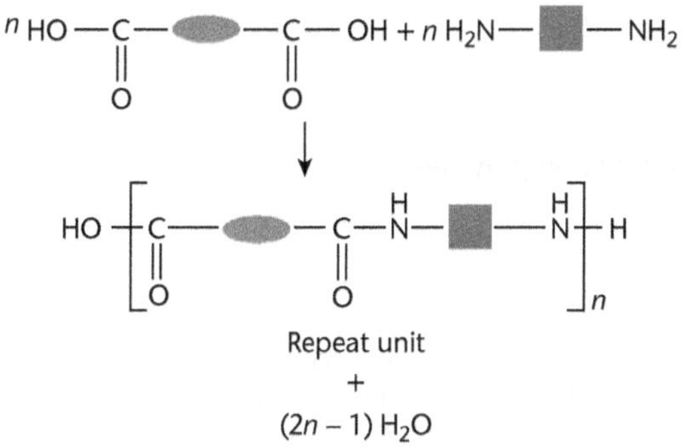

$$n\,HO{-}\underset{\underset{O}{\|}}{C}{-}\bullet{-}\underset{\underset{O}{\|}}{C}{-}OH + n\,H_2N{-}\blacksquare{-}NH_2 \longrightarrow HO\left[\underset{\underset{O}{\|}}{C}{-}\bullet{-}\underset{\underset{O}{\|}}{C}{-}\overset{H}{N}{-}\blacksquare{-}\overset{H}{N}\right]_n H + (2n-1)\,H_2O$$

Repeat unit

Figure 2 *The condensation polymerisation to form nylon and water*

Typical condensation reactions involve the reaction of carboxylic acids, acyl chlorides and methyl esters with alcohols to give an ester and water, hydrochloric acid and methanol, respectively (Figure 3).

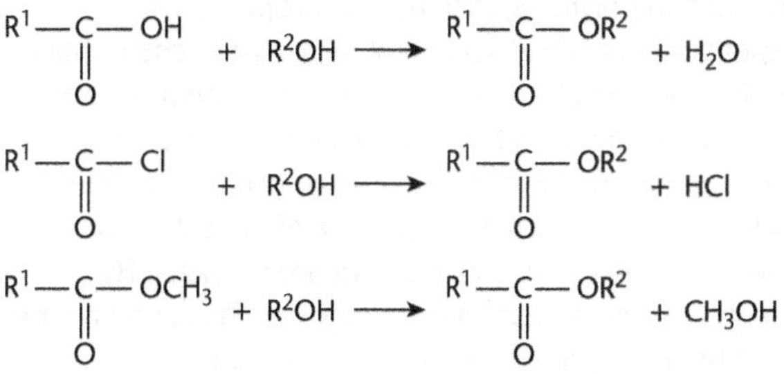

$$R^1{-}\underset{\underset{O}{\|}}{C}{-}OH + R^2OH \longrightarrow R^1{-}\underset{\underset{O}{\|}}{C}{-}OR^2 + H_2O$$

$$R^1{-}\underset{\underset{O}{\|}}{C}{-}Cl + R^2OH \longrightarrow R^1{-}\underset{\underset{O}{\|}}{C}{-}OR^2 + HCl$$

$$R^1{-}\underset{\underset{O}{\|}}{C}{-}OCH_3 + R^2OH \longrightarrow R^1{-}\underset{\underset{O}{\|}}{C}{-}OR^2 + CH_3OH$$

Figure 3 *Condensation reactions to produce esters*

Replacing the alcohol with an amine generates amides from carboxylic acids or acyl chlorides via a condensation reaction (Figure 4).

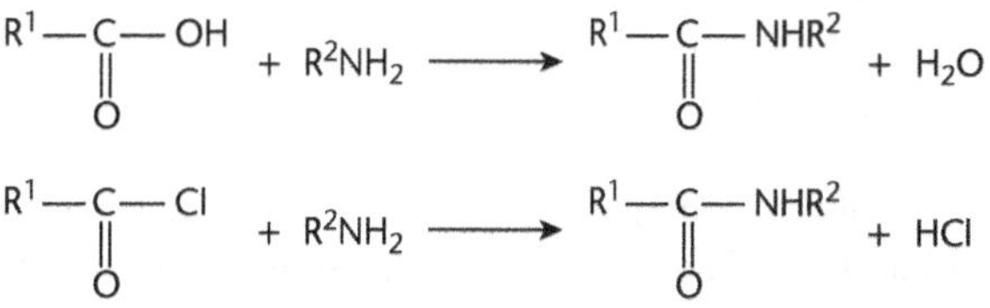

$$R^1{-}\underset{\underset{O}{\|}}{C}{-}OH + R^2NH_2 \longrightarrow R^1{-}\underset{\underset{O}{\|}}{C}{-}NHR^2 + H_2O$$

$$R^1{-}\underset{\underset{O}{\|}}{C}{-}Cl + R^2NH_2 \longrightarrow R^1{-}\underset{\underset{O}{\|}}{C}{-}NHR^2 + HCl$$

Figure 4 *Condensation reactions to produce amides*

10.2 CONDENSATION POLYMERS

A condensation polymer is produced by repeated condensation reactions between monomers (Figure 2). Natural condensation polymers are all formed by elimination of water. Condensation polymers can be identified because the monomers are linked by ester or amide bonds.

Examples of bifunctional monomers are shown in Figure 5.

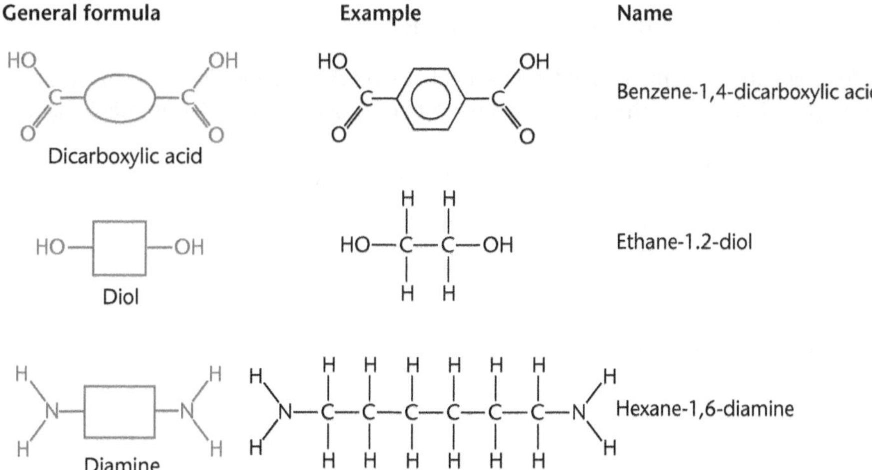

Figure 5 *Monomers with two functional groups used in condensation reactions*

In addition polymers, such as poly(propene), the repeating unit is that section of the polymer chain that is added sequentially every time a further monomer adds. In Figure 6 the repeat unit is highlighted in blue; it is the smallest section of the molecule that can be identified in the repeat pattern. Polymers are often written with the repeat unit surrounded by square brackets. By identifying the repeat unit in a polymer chain, you will be able to identify the monomer it came from.

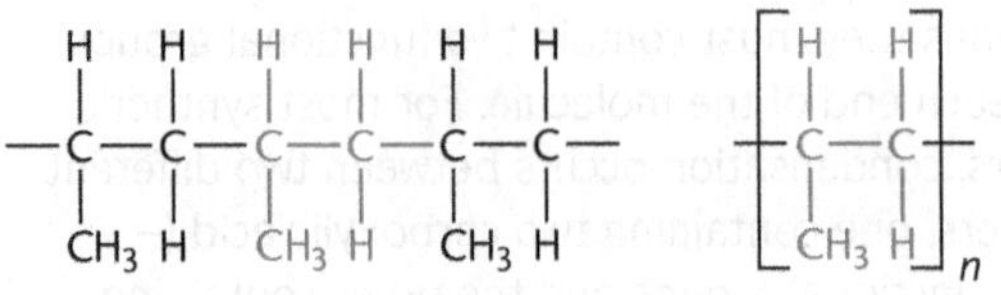

Repeat unit in blue

Figure 6 *The addition polymerisation to form poly(propene)*

Worked example 1

Identify the repeating unit and hence the monomer in the following addition polymer:

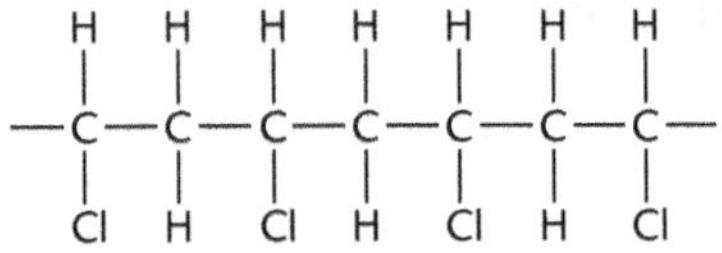

The smallest repeating section of the molecule is highlighted in blue below. The monomer is derived from this section and is chloroethene.

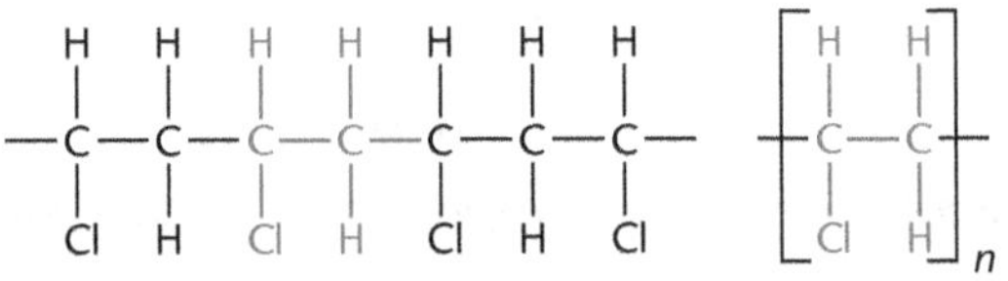

Repeat unit in blue

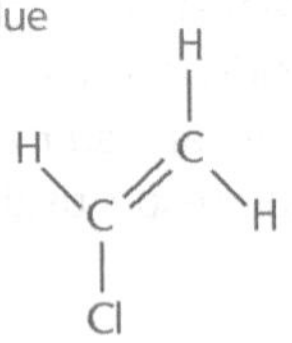

Monomer

As with addition polymers, for condensation polymers look for the smallest repeating unit. Because condensation polymers contain ester or amide linkages and are often made by reacting two different monomers together, the monomers can be identified by imagining breaking the molecule at these points.

Worked example 2

Identify the repeat unit and hence the monomers in the following condensation polymer:

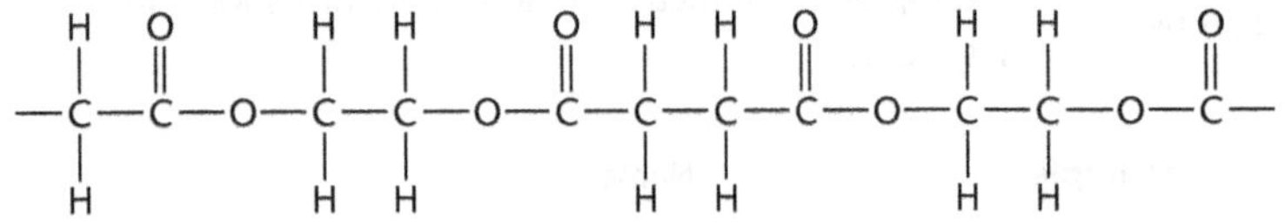

Here the shortest repeating fragment is highlighted in blue. As the polymer is linked by an ester group it is a condensation polymer made from the two monomers ethane-1,2-diol and 1,4-butandioic acid.

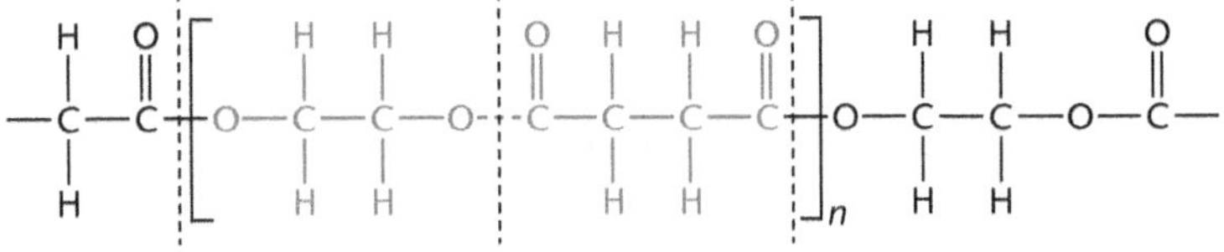

..... break at these points to identify monomers

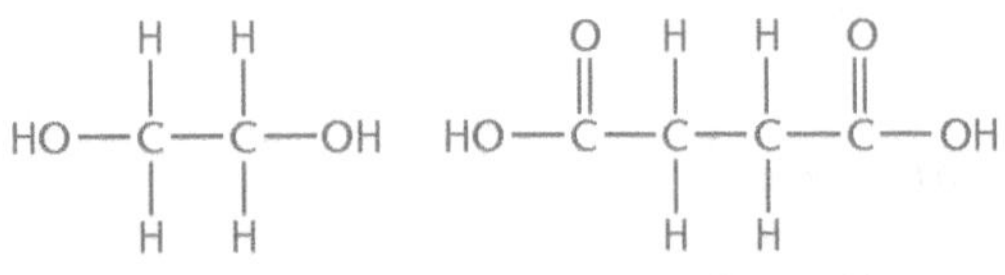

Ethane-1.2-diol

1,4-Butandioic acid

QUESTIONS

1. Identify the repeat unit in the following polymers. Draw the repeating unit and identify the monomers used to make the polymers.

a.

b.

c.

d.

Polyesters

A polyester is a polymer produced by linking together monomers via ester linkages. If the alcohol has two –OH groups and the organic acid has two –COOH groups, then the ester that is formed will still contain an –OH group at one end and a –COOH group at the other. Further esterification reactions are still possible and the molecule will increase in size to eventually give a polyester (Figure 7).

Terylene is one of the trade names for the polyester made by linking 1,4-benzenedicarboxylic acid and the alcohol ethane-1,2-diol. Another name for this polyester is poly(ethylene)terephthalate (or PET), which is derived from the old name for 1,4-benzenedicarboxylic acid (terephthalic acid) (Figure 8).

Repeated condensation reactions occur between the –COOH groups of 1,4-benzenedicarboxylic acid molecules and the –OH groups of ethane-1,2-diol molecules (Figure 9). A high temperature is required to drive the equilibrium towards the polymer.

The polyester is thermoplastic, which means it can be repeatedly heated to soften and melt it and

Organic acid with two acid groups (a dicarboxylic acid)

Alcohol with two hydroxy groups (a diol)

One ester linkage formed, but acid and alcohol groups still available

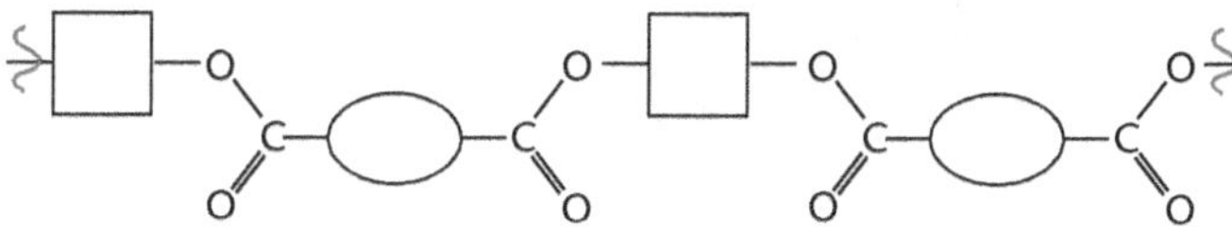

Many ester linkages can form, producing a polyester

Figure 7 *General scheme showing the production of a polyester*

Figure 8 *PET is an ideal material for carbonated drinks bottles as it is light, tough and water resistant and won't shatter when dropped*

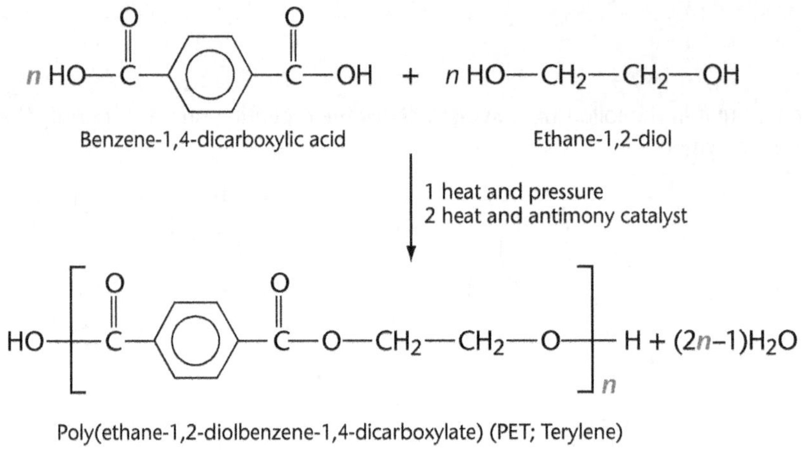

$$n\,HO-\overset{O}{\overset{\|}{C}}-C_6H_4-\overset{O}{\overset{\|}{C}}-OH \;+\; n\,HO-CH_2-CH_2-OH$$

Benzene-1,4-dicarboxylic acid   Ethane-1,2-diol

1 heat and pressure
2 heat and antimony catalyst

$$HO-\left[\overset{O}{\overset{\|}{C}}-C_6H_4-\overset{O}{\overset{\|}{C}}-O-CH_2-CH_2-O\right]_n-H + (2n-1)H_2O$$

Poly(ethane-1,2-diolbenzene-1,4-dicarboxylate) (PET; Terylene)

Figure 9 *Condensation reaction to form poly(ethylene)terephthalate (PET) – a polyester*

cooled to solidify it. A thermoplastic polymer can be extruded to form fine fibres for use in artificial fabrics, or be blow-moulded into fizzy drinks bottles and other containers.

It is also possible to produce thin films of PET. These films are used extensively for packaging, especially for food, helping to keep it fresh and free from contamination. It can also be used for making windsurfer sails, flexible printed circuit boards and cable insulation.

Polyamides

The best-known example of an artificial polyamide is nylon. The brand name 'Nylon' was created in the 1930s by the DuPont chemical company in America. It followed the discovery of how to make the polymer by one of their employees, Wallace Carothers. Nylon proved to be a very acceptable, cheap substitute for silk. There are several types of nylon. Nylon-6,6 (Figure 10) is one. The 6,6 refers to the fact that each of the two monomers (a diamine and a dicarboxylic acid) contains six carbon atoms. Hence, the diamine is hexane-1,6-diamine and the dicarboxylic acid is 1,6-hexandioic acid.

The reaction between an amine group and a carboxylic acid group to form an amide link is slow and the equilibrium established contains a significant proportion of unreacted amine and acid. Consequently, the dicarboxylic acid is usually first converted to hexane-1,6-dioyl chloride by reaction with thionyl chloride, $SOCl_2$ (Figure 11). This diacyl chloride reacts with the diamine much faster and, because of the evolution of hydrogen chloride, the equilibrium shifts almost entirely towards the polymer product (Figure 12).

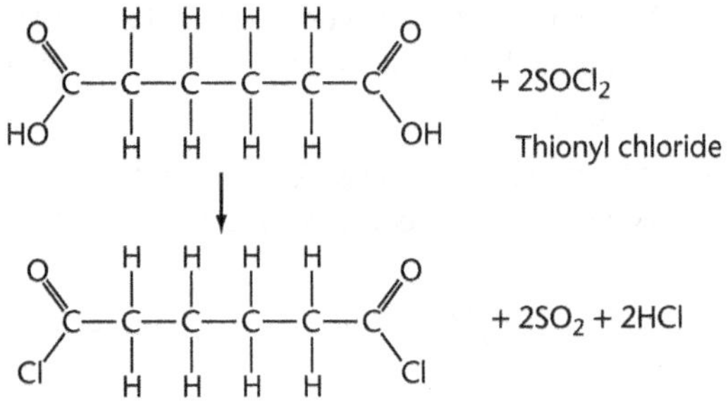

$$HOOC-(CH_2)_4-COOH + 2SOCl_2 \text{ (Thionyl chloride)} \longrightarrow ClOC-(CH_2)_4-COCl + 2SO_2 + 2HCl$$

Figure 11 *Converting 1,6-hexandioic acid to hexane-1,6-dioyl chloride*

$$\left[-\overset{O}{\overset{\|}{C}}-CH_2-CH_2-CH_2-CH_2-\overset{O}{\overset{\|}{C}}-\overset{H}{N}-CH_2-CH_2-CH_2-CH_2-CH_2-CH_2-\overset{H}{N}-\right]_n$$

this can be also written as

$$\left[-\overset{O}{\overset{\|}{C}}-(CH_2)_4-\overset{O}{\overset{\|}{C}}-\overset{H}{N}-(CH_2)_6-\overset{H}{N}-\right]_n$$

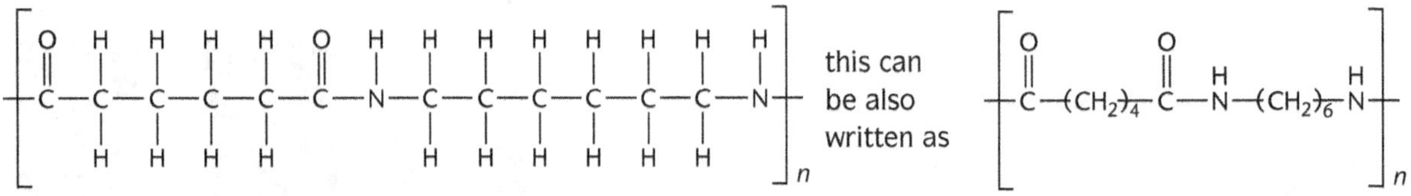

Figure 10 *The structure of nylon-6,6 showing the repeat unit*

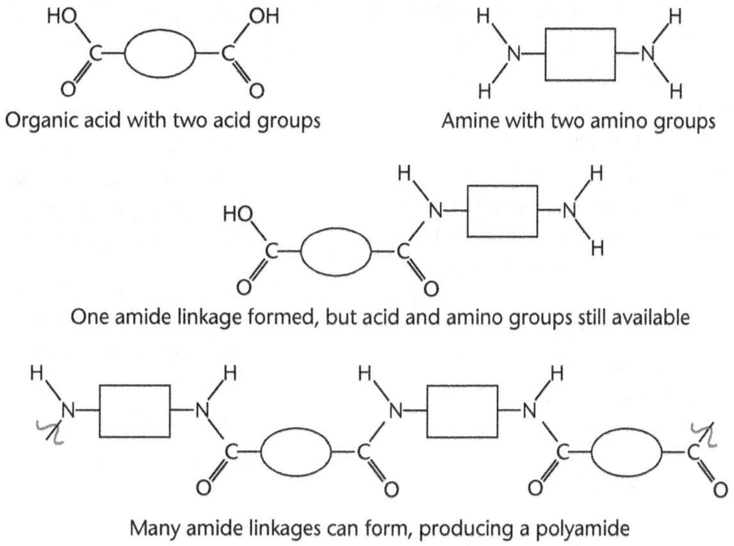

Organic acid with two acid groups

Amine with two amino groups

One amide linkage formed, but acid and amino groups still available

Many amide linkages can form, producing a polyamide

Figure 12 *Production of a polyamide*

Condensation polymers such as nylon-6,6 are long-chain molecules which can be drawn out at room temperature to form fibres. During this process the linear molecules align and become increasingly linked by hydrogen bonds between adjacent chains. This causes the strength of the fibre to increase during the drawing process (Figure 13).

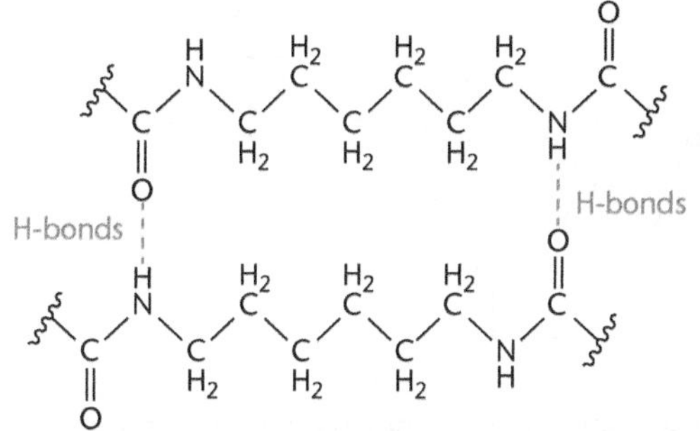

Condensation polymers of naturally occurring amino acids

Figure 13 *H-bonds between nylon-6,6 chains increase the strength of the fibres*

Since its use as a substitute for silk, nylon has found many other applications. It is used to make ropes, twines, Velcro®, machinery parts and a wide range of clothing. In clothing and carpets, natural fibres such as cotton or wool are often mixed with nylon to make them last longer (Figure 14).

Figure 14 *Nylon rope is used by rock climbers*

Polyamides can also be prepared by the condensation of amino acids. Amino acids are bifunctional compounds that contain both an amine and a carboxylic acid in the same molecule (see chapter 11 of Year 2 Student Book). Heating the naturally occurring amino acid glycine generates the condensation polymer polyglycine (Figure 15). Proteins are condensation polymers of naturally occurring amino acids.

$$n\,H_2N{-}CH_2{-}COOH \xrightarrow{\text{Heat}} H_2N{-}CH_2{-}CO{-}[NH{-}CH_2{-}CO]_n{-}OH + nH_2O$$

Glycine amino acid

Polyglycine

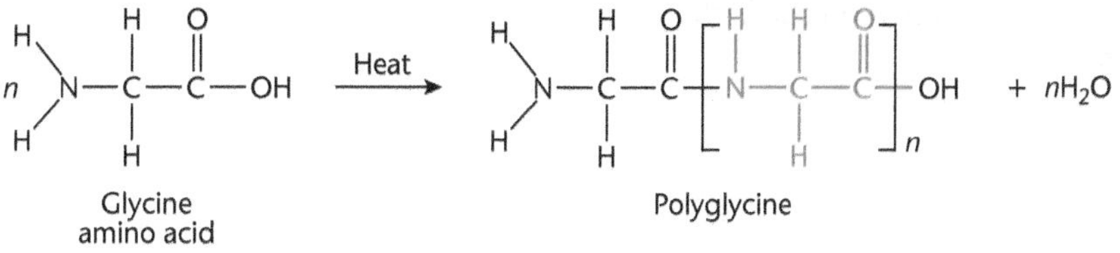

Figure 15 *Synthesis of polyglycine by heating the amino acid glycine*

Biodegradability of polyesters and polyamides

Simple esters and amides can be hydrolysed by reaction with either aqueous acids or bases into carboxylic acids and alcohols (in the case of esters) or amines (in the case of amides) (see *chapter 7 of Year 2 Student Book*). Unlike addition polymers, where the links between monomers are carbon–carbon bonds, condensation polymers are linked by ester or amide linkages and so can undergo hydrolysis. Under the action of acid catalysts or bacterial enzymes the amide and ester links in polyamides and polyesters can be hydrolysed into smaller fragments (Figures 16 and 17). In other words, unlike polyalkenes, condensation polymers will biodegrade when placed in landfill sites.

Hydrolysis here

Bacterial enzymes | Hydrolysis

Figure 16 *Biodegradation of a polyester with a bacterial enzyme*

Hydrolysis here

Hydrolysis

Figure 17 *Biodegradation of a polyamide by hydrolysis*

If you spill dilute acid onto a garment made of nylon, then the amide links can be hydrolysed and the polymer chain broken into smaller fragments. This leads to a hole in the fabric. Hydrolysis reactions can take place at any of the ester or amide linkages in a polymer and you can eventually produce the original monomers.

QUESTIONS

2. Nylon-6,4 is made from hexane-1,6-diamine and a dicarboxylic acid. Give the structure of the dicarboxylic acid used to make this form of nylon and the structure of nylon-6,4, showing the repeat unit.

3. For each of the following monomers, draw the polymer produced from the monomer. State whether the polymer is a condensation or addition polymer and highlight the repeat unit.

   a. H_3C CH_2 C

   b. HO–⬡–OH + CO_2H CO_2H

   c. O Cl Cl O + NH_2 NH_2

   d.

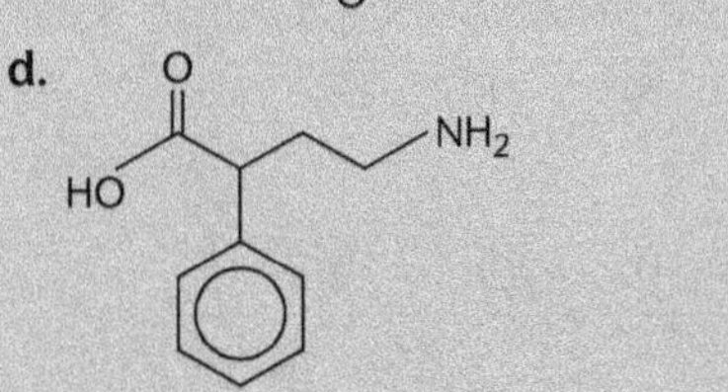

4. Ester and amide bonds react with water in the presence of an acid catalyst.

   a. Write equations for such reactions for ethyl ethanoate and *N*-ethylethanamide.

   b. What type of reaction is involved in both of these reactions?

   c. Why is this reaction important from the point of view of biodegradability?

ASSIGNMENT 1: SYNTHESIS OF NYLON

(AT k, PS 1.2)

These instructions were provided to prepare a nylon polymer:

1. Make up a solution of 2.2 g of hexane-1,6-diamine in 50 cm^3 of water.
2. Make up a second solution of 1.5 g of decandioyl dichloride in 50 cm^3 of cyclohexane.
3. Place 5 cm^3 of the hexane-1,6-diamine solution in a 25 cm^3 beaker.
4. Carefully add 5 cm^3 of the acyl chloride solution to the top of the hexane-1,6-diamine solution. It is important to do this in such a way that the solutions do not mix.
5. At the interface of the two solutions nylon will be formed. Using tweezers, carefully pick up the nylon film and wrap it around a glass rod.
6. Without breaking the nylon thread, rotate the glass rod slowly to remove a nylon fibre.
7. After you have extracted as much nylon as you can, wash it with water.

Questions

A1. What hazards are associated with:

- **a.** hexane-1,6-diamine?
- **b.** decandioyl dichloride?
- **c.** cyclohexane?

A2. What safety precautions are necessary when undertaking the experiment?

A3. What is the concentration (in mol dm^{-3}) of the solution of:

- **a.** hexane-1,6-diamine?
- **b.** decandioyl dichloride in cyclohexane?

A4. Name the nylon that is produced and draw the repeat unit of the polymer.

A5. What small molecule is eliminated during the condensation polymerisation?

Stretch and challenge

A6. Theoretically, what mole ratio of hexane-1,6-diamine and hexane-1,6-dioyl dichloride is required to make a polymer of nylon-6,6?

A7. Why do you think an excess of hexane-1,6-diamine is used in the experiment?

A8. Why is it necessary to wash the nylon fibre with water before it is used to make fabrics?

ASSIGNMENT 2: KEVLAR® AND NOMEX®: TOUGH POLYAMIDES

A group of polymers called **aramids** are aromatic polyamides. They are very tough and lightweight and are used to make bulletproof vests, fireproof suits, puncture-resistant bicycle tyres and reinforced concrete. Nomex® (made from 1,3-benzenediamine and 1,3-benzenedicarboxylic acid) and Kevlar® (made from 1,4-benzenediamine and 1,4-benzenedicarboxylic acid, Figure A1) are the two best-known examples of aramids. This general name derives from the fact that they involve benzene rings (from **ar**enes) linked via **amid**e bonds.

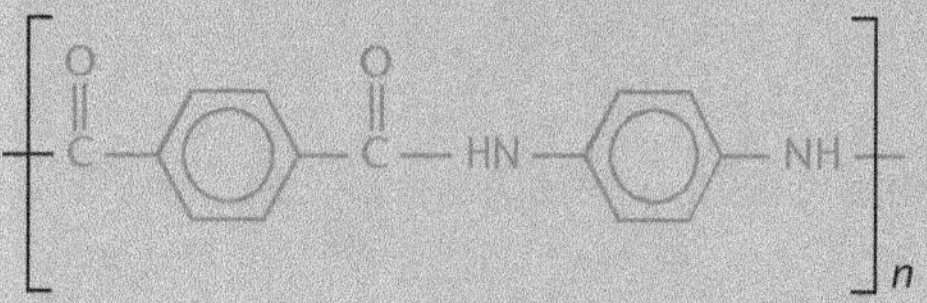

Figure A1 *Structure of Kevlar®, an aramid, showing the repeating unit*

Weight for weight, Kevlar® fibre is five times stronger than steel and much stronger than nylon-6,6. The rigid aromatic rings in aramids impart greater strength than the more flexible hydrocarbon chains in nylons. The linear Kevlar® chains can align with each other so that each chain has multiple hydrogen bond interactions with its neighbours. The hydrogen bonds occur between a polarised amide NH group on one chain with a polarised C = O on another (Figure A2). This forms a large, tough, flat two-dimensional sheet. These flat sheets stack upon one another, providing a very strong material. Unlike most plastics, Kevlar® does not melt but decomposes around 450 °C.

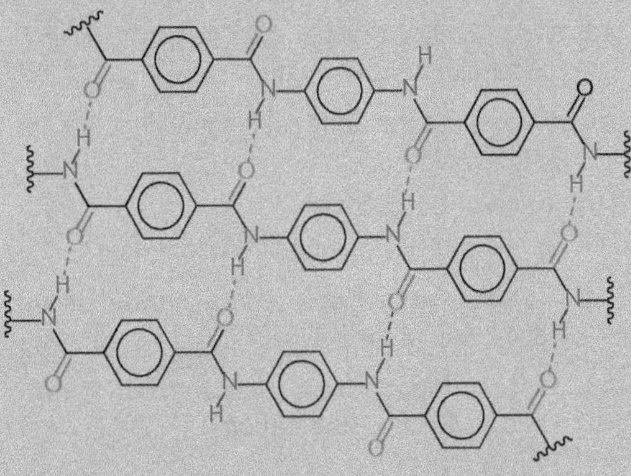

Figure A2 *The rigid aromatic rings and H-bond interactions between linear chains of Kevlar® are responsible for its strength*

Questions

A1. Draw the structures of the monomers used to make the aramid Nomex®.

A2. Draw the structure of Nomex® and show the repeat unit of the polymer.

A3. What type of intermolecular force will occur between Kevlar® polymer chains?

A4. Draw a diagram to show this type of intermolecular force in nylon-6,6.

A5. Why are aramids stronger than nylons?

Stretch and challenge

A6. Suggest which will have the higher melting point, Kevlar® or Nomex®? Explain your reasoning.

KEY IDEAS

- Condensation polymers include polyesters and polyamides.
- Condensation polymers are derived from monomers that have two functional groups.
- Condensation polymers are biodegradable because the links are hydrolysable.
- Proteins are naturally occurring condensation polymers.
- Polyamides such as Kevlar® are very strong because of intermolecular H-bonding between polymer chains.

Disposal of polymers

There are three main ways of disposing of polymers: landfill, incineration and recycling (Figure 18). All three have advantages and disadvantages (Table 1). Landfill is a well-established method for disposal of waste. The UN Environment Programme has estimated that 22–43% of global plastic ends up in landfill. While condensation polymers will slowly degrade, addition polymers will not. In addition, landfill sites produce methane (a greenhouse gas) that can be released into the atmosphere. If the landfill site is not well maintained, toxic chemicals can leach into the neighbouring environment.

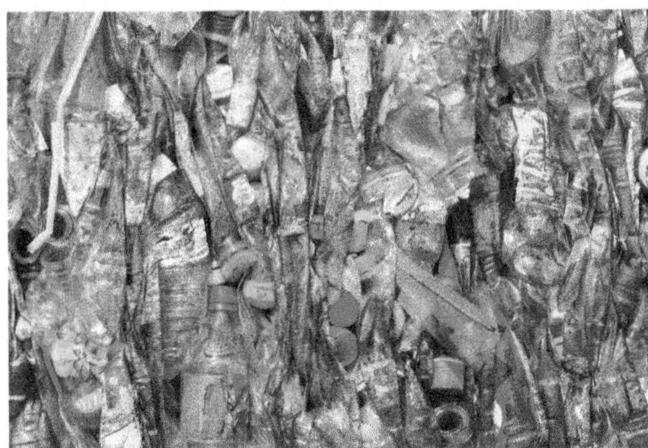

Figure 18 *Waste plastics can be burned in incinerators, sent to landfill or recycled*

Another widely used method of disposal is incineration. Most types of polymers will generate a lot of energy when burned. This energy can be used to generate electricity to power local areas. Incineration plants take up less space than landfill sites. However, large amounts of CO_2 gas are released into the atmosphere and the incineration of certain polymers generates toxic gases.

Theoretically, recycling is environmentally more preferable. Two approaches to recycling involve chemical or mechanical reprocessing. In chemical reprocessing a polymer is chemically depolymerised to its constituent monomers. These monomers can be reused to regenerate the original polymer in a new application. However, this can often be more expensive or require more energy than the original procedure.

Mechanical reprocessing is generally cheaper than chemical reprocessing and can involve cleaning, grinding, remelting and remoulding materials. However, remoulding requires pure materials, and efficient collection and sorting of different types of plastics from each other are required. The costs of collection, transportation, sorting (often by hand) and the removal of contaminants such as dyes and labels all add to the cost of recycling and are a major disadvantage.

Method of disposal	Advantages	Disadvantages
Landfill	Buried at specific contained site Biodegradable polymers will slowly degrade	Limited land available Gas emissions Slow degradation of plastics Leaching of toxic compounds
Incineration	Less space than landfill Energy released from burning can generate electricity Prevents build-up of polymers in the environment	Increase in CO_2 (greenhouse gas) Toxic gas emissions to atmosphere Particulates
Recycling	Reduction of waste going to landfill Reuse and conservation of precious hydrocarbon resources	Collection, sorting, separating and remoulding all require energy Expensive

Table 1 *Ways of disposing of polymers*

QUESTIONS

5. Explain the benefits of recycling plastics over landfill and incineration.

6. Current research is focused on preparing condensation polymers where the monomers are obtained from plants. What advantages would polymers produced in this way have over petrochemical-derived condensation polymers? Are there any disadvantages of making polymers this way?

PRACTICE QUESTIONS

1. An isomer of **Q** which has the structure shown below is polymerised to form the biodegradeable polymer known as PHB.

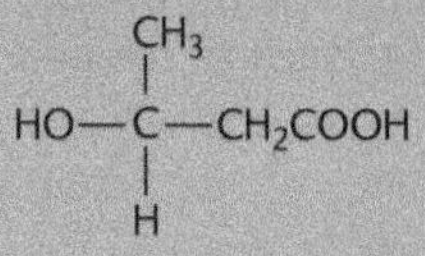

$$\mathrm{HO{-}\underset{\large H}{\overset{\large CH_3}{\underset{|}{\overset{|}{C}}}}{-}CH_2COOH}$$

Figure Q1

Draw the repeating unit of the polymer PHB.

Suggest a reason why the polymer is biodegradeable.

AQA, June 2005, Unit 4, Question 3c

2. Repeating units of two polymers, **P** and **Q**, are shown in figure Q2.

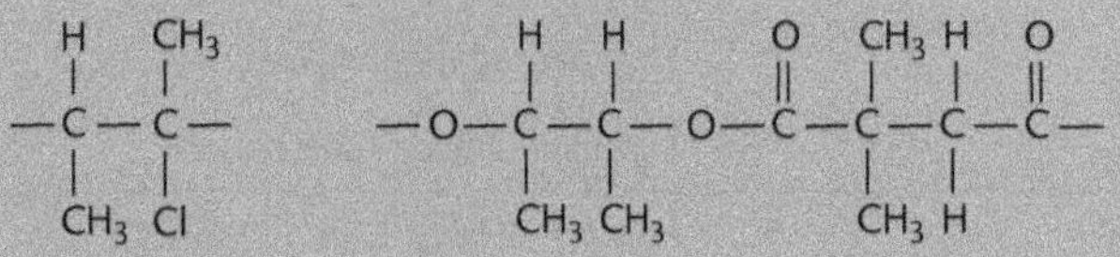

P: $-\underset{CH_3}{\overset{H}{C}}-\underset{Cl}{\overset{CH_3}{C}}-$

Q: $-O-\underset{CH_3}{\overset{H}{C}}-\underset{CH_3}{\overset{H}{C}}-O-\overset{O}{\overset{\|}{C}}-\underset{CH_3}{\overset{CH_3}{C}}-\underset{H}{\overset{H}{C}}-\overset{O}{\overset{\|}{C}}-$

Figure Q2

a. Draw the structure of the monomer used to form polymer **P**. Name the type of polymerisation.

b. Draw the structures of the **two** compounds that react together to form polymer **Q**.

c. Suggest an environmental advantage of polymer **Q** over polymer **P**.

AQA Chemistry Specimen Paper 2015, Paper 2, Question 7

3. Isomer **Y** is used in the production of the polymer Kevlar. **Y** is first reduced to the diamine shown in Figure Q3.

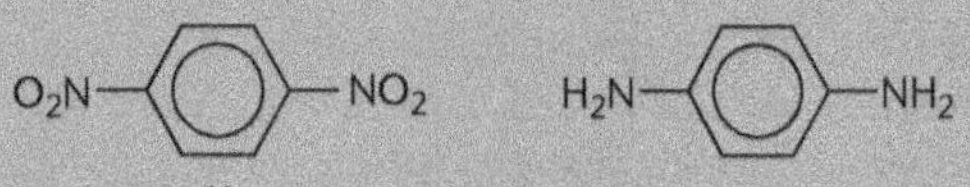

$O_2N-C_6H_4-NO_2$ (**Y**) $\quad H_2N-C_6H_4-NH_2$

Figure Q3

Identify a suitable reagent or mixture of reagents for the reduction of **Y** to form this diamine. Write an equation using [H] to represent the reducing agent.

This diamine is then reacted with benzene-1,4-dicarboxylic acid to form Kevlar. Draw the repeating unit of Kevlar.

Kevlar can be used as the inner lining of bicycle tyres. The rubber used for the outer part is made of polymerised alkenes.

State the difference in the biodegradability of Kevlar compared to that of rubber made from polymerised alkenes.

Use your knowledge of bonding in these polymer molecules to explain this difference.

AQA Chemistry, January 2010, Question 8c

4. Draw the repeat unit of the polyester Terylene that is made from benzene-1,4-dicarboxylic acid and ethane1,2-diol. Although Terylene is biodegradable, it is preferable to recycle objects made from Terylene.

Give **one** advantage and **one** disadvantage of recycling objects made of Terylene.

AQA Chemistry A2, June 2010, Question 7e

5. The amide or peptide bond is found in synthetic polyamides and also in naturally-occurring proteins.

a. i. Draw the repeating unit of the polyamide formed by the reaction of propanedioic acid with hexane-1,6-diamine.

ii. In terms of the intermolecular forces between the polymer chains, explain why polyamides can be made into fibres suitable for use in sewing and weaving, whereas polyalkenes usually produce fibres that are too weak for this purpose.

AQA Chemistry, June 2011, Question 4a

6. Common substances used in everyday life often contain organic compounds.

   a. State an everyday use for each of the following compounds.

      i. $CH_3(CH_2)_{16}COO^-Na^+$

      ii. $CH_3(CH_2)_{19}COOCH_3$

      iii. $[C_{16}H_{33}N(CH_3)_3]^+Br^-$

   b. The following structures are repeating units of two different condensation polymers. For each example, name the type of condensation polymer. Give a common name for a polymer of this type.

      i.

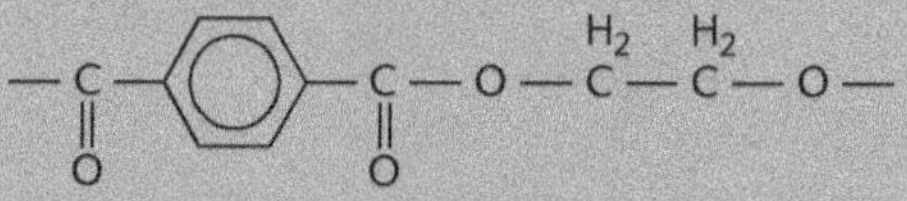

```
                        H2  H2
 —C—⟨benzene⟩—C—O—C—C—O—
  ||            ||
  O             O
```

      ii.

```
  H              H  O               O
  |              |  ||              ||
 —N—⟨benzene⟩—N—C—⟨benzene⟩—C—
```

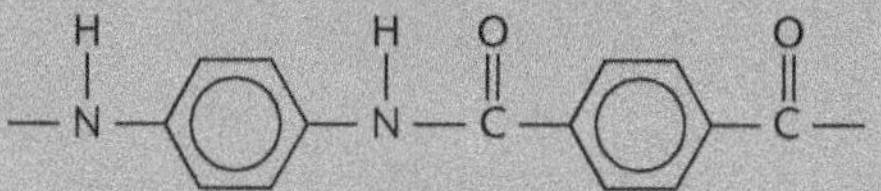

      iii. Explain why the polymer in part b.ii. has a higher melting point than the polymer in part b.i.

AQA Chemistry, January 2012, Question 8a–b

7. Acyl chlorides and acid anhydrides are important compounds in organic synthesis.

   a. Outline a mechanism for the reaction of CH_3CH_2COCl with CH_3OH and name the organic product formed.

   b. A polyester was produced by reacting a diol with a diacyl chloride. The repeating unit of the polymer is shown in Figure Q7.

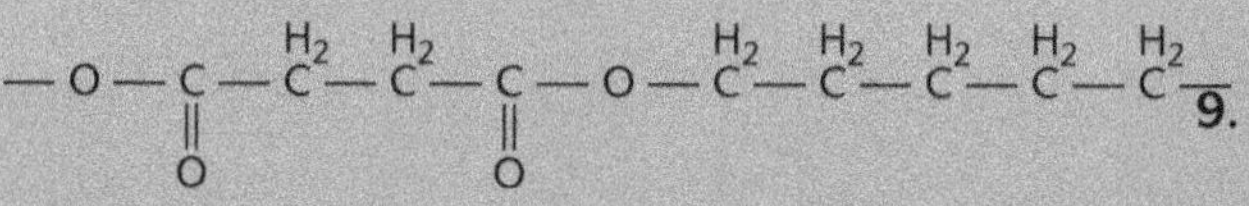

```
          H2  H2             H2  H2  H2  H2  H2
 —O—C—C—C—C—O—C—C—C—C—C—
     ||          ||
     O           O
```

Figure Q7

      i. Name the diol used.

      ii. Draw the displayed formula for the diacyl chloride used.

      iii. A shirt was made from this polyester. A student wearing the shirt accidently splashed aqueous sodium hydroxide on a sleeve. Holes later appeared in the sleeve where the sodium hydroxide had been. Name the type of reaction that occurred between the polyester and aqueous sodium hydroxide. Explain why the aqueous sodium hydroxide reacted with the polyester.

AQA Chemistry, June 2012, Question 4a–b

8. The repeating unit in Figure Q8a represents a polymer

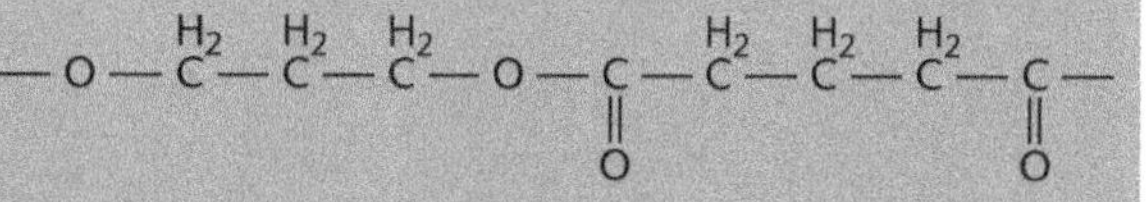

```
      H2  H2  H2              H2  H2  H2
 —O—C—C—C—O—C—C—C—C—C—
                  ||                  ||
                  O                   O
```

Figure Q8a

   a. i. Name this type of polymer

      ii. Give the IUPAC name for the alcohol used to prepare this polyester.

   b. The repeating unit in Figure Q8b represents a polyalkene co-polymer. The co-polymer is made from two different alkene monomers.

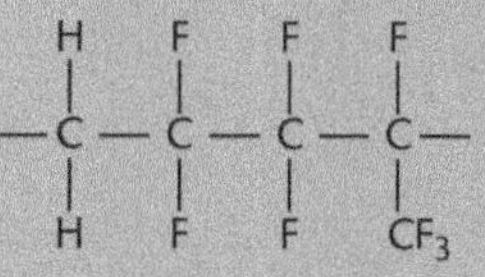

```
  H   F   F   F
  |   |   |   |
 —C—C—C—C—
  |   |   |   |
  H   F   F   CF3
```

Figure Q8b

      i. Name the type of polymerisation occurring in the formation of this co-polymer.

      ii. Draw the structure of each alkene monomer.

AQA Chemistry, January 2013, Question 4b–c

9. Kevlar is a polymer used in protective clothing. The repeating unit within the polymer chain of Kevlar is shown in Figure Q9.

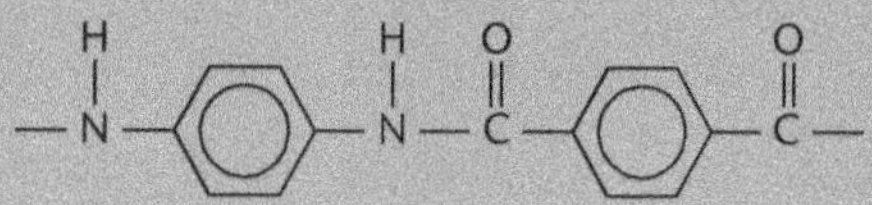

```
  H              H  O               O
  |              |  ||              ||
 —N—⟨benzene⟩—N—C—⟨benzene⟩—C—
```

Figure Q9

Name the strongest type of interaction between polymer chains in Kevlar.

AQA Chemistry, June 2014, Question 4a

Multiple choice

10. Which compound can polymerise by reaction with itself?

a. $NH_2CH_2CH_2NH_2$

b. $CH_3CH_2CONH_2$

c. $HOOCCH_2COOH$

d. NH_2CH_2COCl

AQA Chemistry Specimen Paper 2015, Paper 3, Question 33

11. What functional group is present in nylon-6,6?

a. Ester

b. Amide

c. Ether

d. Amine

12. Which of these statements about disposal of polymers in landfill sites is false?

a. There are limited landfill sites available.

b. Condensation polymers will slowly biodegrade in a landfill site.

c. There are no gas emissions from a landfill site.

d. There is a danger of toxic chemicals escaping into the environment.

13. Which of the following is an addition polymer?

a. Poly(ethene)

b. Nylon-6,6

c. Kevlar®

d. PET

11 AMINO ACIDS, PROTEINS AND DNA

PRIOR KNOWLEDGE

You will already have studied catalysts (*see Chapter 4 of Year 1 Student Book*), the behaviour of acids and bases, and the different types of intermolecular forces between molecules (*chapters 3 and 8 of Year 2 Student Book*). You will also be familiar with the chemistry of carboxylic acids and their derivatives, and that of polymers (*chapters 7 and 10 of Year 2 Student Book*).

LEARNING OBJECTIVES

In this chapter you will learn about the structure and properties of amino acids, proteins and DNA. You will understand how enzymes and the anticancer drug cisplatin work. You will be able to draw the structures of amino acids at different pH, identify different types of structure in proteins and explain why enzymes can interact differently with pairs of enantiomers. You will also understand how intermolecular forces lead to the structure of DNA and how drug molecules can prevent DNA replication.

(Specification 3.3.13)

Proteins are biological polymers made from amino acids. The immune system's antibodies are proteins designed to recognise foreign cells and pathogens. They can be prepared in the laboratory, and many new drugs seek to use antibody therapy to treat cancer or kill bacteria resistant to antibiotics. Our muscles are made up of fibres which include the proteins myosin and actin. Enzymes (nature's catalysts) are proteins that control growth and various bodily functions. Proteins can be used to transport molecules around an organism. The protein haemoglobin is able to carry and deliver oxygen in animals. Protein-based receptors are often the targets for drugs but can be so specific that only one enantiomer of a drug might be active. The instructions on how to make proteins are encoded in an organism's DNA. Understanding the chemistry of proteins and DNA will allow us to cure many diseases of today in the future.

Figure 1 *The 3D chemical structure of haemoglobin, a protein responsible for oxygen transport in the blood*

11.1 AMINO ACIDS

Amino acids are bifunctional molecules (molecules with two functional groups) that contain both an amino ($-NH_2$) functional group and carboxylic acid ($-COOH$) functional groups. The structure of alanine (2-aminopropanoic acid), a naturally occurring amino acid, is shown in Figure 2. Alanine is a 2-amino acid, where the amino group is bonded to the carbon atom adjacent to the carboxylic acid group (carbon atom 2 in the chain). 2-amino acids may also be called α-amino acids.

Side chain H_3C – C(H)(α)(NH_2) – C(=O)OH

Alanine
2-Aminopropionic acid

H_2N–CH$_2$–CH$_2$–CH$_2$–C(=O)OH

GABA
A neurotransmitter

Figure 2 *The structure of alanine, a 2-amino acid (or α-amino acid), and GABA, a 4-amino acid*

The side chain of the naturally occurring 2-amino acids may be represented by R (Figure 3). It may be a simple group such as $-H$, in the amino acid glycine, or $-CH_3$, in alanine (Figure 2). It can also be a much more complex group such as $-CH_2C_6H_5$, in phenylalanine, or $-CH_2COOH$, in aspartic acid. Table 1 shows the 20 different R groups that give rise to the 20 biologically active 2-amino acids in humans.

Side chain R – C(H)(NH_2) – C(=O)OH

Figure 3 *The general structure of a 2-amino acid*

Apart from glycine (R = H, 2-aminoethanoic acid), all naturally occurring α-amino acids exist as optical isomers (enantiomers) because the central carbon atom in these amino acids is bonded to four different groups (Figure 4). This form of stereoisomerism was discussed in chapter 5 of Year 2 Student Book. Only the L-isomers occur naturally in proteins.

Amino acid	Abbreviation	R group (side chain)
glycine	Gly	$-H$
alanine	Ala	$-CH_3$
valine	Val	$-CH(CH_3)_2$
leucine	Leu	$-CH_2CH(CH_3)_2$
isoleucine	Ile	$-CH(CH_3)CH_2CH_3$
serine	Ser	$-CH_2OH$
threonine	Thr	$-CH(OH)CH_3$
lysine	Lys	$-CH_2CH_2CH_2CH_2NH_2$
arginine	Arg	$-CH_2CH_2CH_2NHC(NH)NH_2$
histidine	His	$-CH_2-C{=}CH$ (imidazole ring: N, NH, C–H)
aspartic acid	Asp	$-CH_2COOH$
asparagine	Asn	$-CH_2CONH_2$
glutamic acid	Glu	$-CH_2CH_2COOH$
glutamine	Gln	$-CH_2CH_2CONH_2$
proline	Pro	(whole structure) H_2C–C(H)–C(=O)OH; H_2C, NH, C–H ring
phenylalanine	Phe	$-CH_2-C_6H_5$ (benzene ring)
tyrosine	Tyr	$-CH_2-C_6H_4-OH$
tryptophan	Trp	$-CH_2-C{=}CH$–NH (indole ring with benzene ring)
methionine	Met	$-CH_2CH_2SCH_3$
cysteine	Cys	$-CH_2SH$

Table 1 *The naturally occurring amino acids*

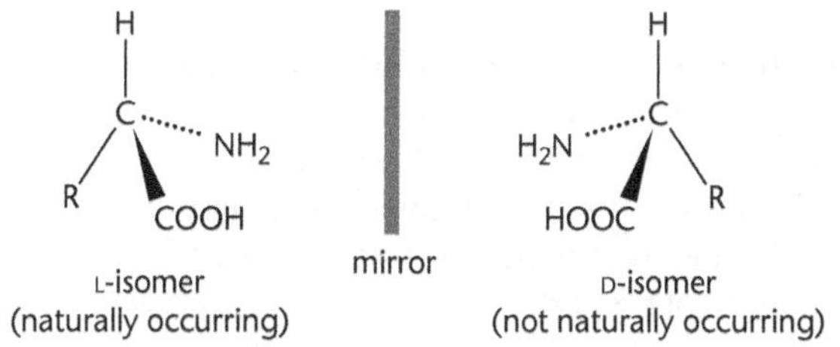

H
C NH₂ R COOH — mirror — H₂N C R HOOC

L-isomer (naturally occurring) D-isomer (not naturally occurring)

Figure 4 Enantiomers of amino acids

QUESTIONS

1. Draw the general structure for:
   a. an α-amino acid
   b. a 5-amino acid.
2. Give the IUPAC name for GABA.
3. Why does glycine (R = H, 2-aminoethanoic acid) not have optical isomers?
4. Draw the two enantiomers of serine (2-amino-3-hydroxypropanoic acid).
5. How many asymmetric carbon atoms (chiral centres) are there in threonine (2-amino-3-hydroxybutanoic acid)?
6. Which isomer of phenylalanine (2-amino-3-phenylpropanoic acid) is naturally occurring?

Acid–base properties of amino acids

The –COOH group is weakly acidic and tends to donate its proton to water, while the $-NH_2$ group is weakly basic and tends to accept a proton from water via the nitrogen lone pair. An amino acid therefore has the ability to act as both a weak acid and a weak base.

When dissolved in a highly acidic solution, the amino acid is protonated to its corresponding cation (Figure 5). Similarly, when dissolved in a highly alkaline solution, the amino acid exists as its corresponding anion. Consequently, at some intermediate pH value, it exists simultaneously as both an anion and a cation. Such an ion is called the zwitterion of the amino acid.

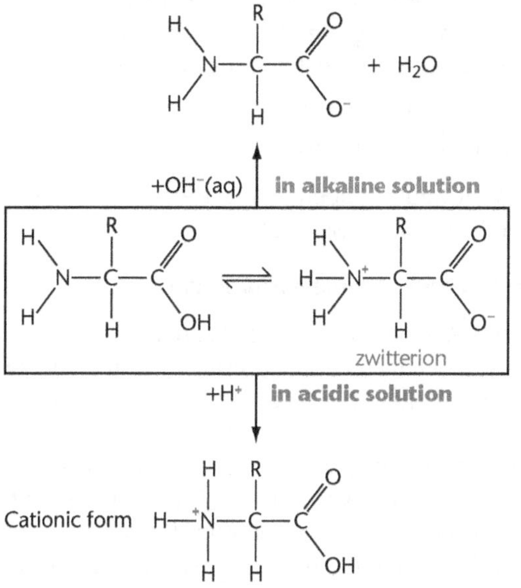

+ H_2O

+OH⁻(aq) in alkaline solution

zwitterion

+H⁺ in acidic solution

Cationic form

Figure 5 pH-dependent equilibria shown by amino acids

In solution, the zwitterion exists at a unique pH value for each different amino acid. This unique value is referred to as the amino acid's **isoelectric pH**; for example, the isoelectric pH for glycine is 6.1, while for cysteine it is 5.0.

Zwitterions also exist in the crystalline form of the amino acid. The electrostatic attraction between the oppositely charged parts of the ion accounts for the relatively high melting-point values of amino acids. For example, even the smallest amino acid molecule, glycine, is a crystalline solid at room temperature, whereas the corresponding amine ($CH_3CH_2CH_2NH_2$, m.p. 190 K) and acid (CH_3CH_2COOH, m.p. 252 K) *of similar molecular size* are both liquids.

ASSIGNMENT 1: SEPARATION OF AMINO ACIDS BY ELECTROPHORESIS

(PS 1.1)

Electrophoresis is an important separation technique in molecular biology. It can be used in the detection of abnormal proteins and in studying DNA during DNA profiling.

The charge on an amino acid is positive below its isoelectric pH and negative above it. This property makes it possible to separate mixtures of amino acids in an electric field using a technique called **electrophoresis**. In this technique, a mixture of amino acids is added to a gel at a specific pH (using buffers) and an electric current is applied. Positively charged amino acids migrate through the gel towards the negative electrode (cathode) and negatively charged amino acids migrate towards the positive electrode (anode).

Questions

A1. State whether glycine subjected to an electric field would migrate towards a positive or a negative electrode if first dissolved in:

a. dilute hydrochloric acid

b. dilute sodium hydroxide.

A2. What would happen to a zwitterion under the influence of an electric field?

Essential and non-essential amino acids

Alanine (2-aminopropanoic acid) and aspartic acid (1-carboxy-2-aminopropanoic acid) are non-essential amino acids. They are called 'non-essential' because we do not need to eat proteins made from them, as our bodies can make them from other nutrients in a balanced diet. However, lysine (2,6-diaminohexanoic acid) is one of the eight amino acids that are *essential*. We cannot synthesise them, so they must be eaten regularly.

A3. Use the IUPAC names and the information in Table 1 to draw the full structures of alanine, aspartic acid and lysine.

A4. All three of the amino acids mentioned here can exist as optical isomers (enantiomers). Draw three-dimensional diagrams to represent the optical isomers of lysine. Outline the differences in their chemical and physical properties.

A5. By comparing their structures, explain why equimolar solutions of lysine, alanine and aspartic acid would produce solutions of decreasing pH.

A6. Draw the structures of the molecules or ions that would be present if:

a. alanine were placed in a pH 1 buffer solution

b. alanine were placed in a pH 11 buffer solution

c. alanine were placed in a buffer solution of pH equal to the isoelectric point of alanine.

Stretch and challenge

A7. A student is required to separate a mixture of glycine (isoelectric pH 6.1), cysteine (isoelectric pH 5.0) and asparagine (isoelectric pH 5.4). Name an experiment to do this, identifying an appropriate pH to conduct your experiment.

KEY IDEAS

- Naturally occurring 2-amino acids have similar structures, differing only in the group R.
- All naturally occurring 2-amino acids (except glycine) have a chiral carbon atom and occur as the L-isomer.
- Amino acids have acidic properties due to the –COOH group and basic properties due to the $-NH_2$ group.
- At the isoelectric pH the amino acid exists as a zwitterion.

11.2 PROTEINS

A protein is a **condensation polymer** of amino acids. The $-NH_2$ group of one amino acid can undergo a condensation reaction with the –COOH group of another amino acid, eliminating a water molecule and forming a **dipeptide**. The amide group (–CONH–) that links the two amino acids is called a peptide link and the C–N bond within this group is called the peptide bond (Figure 6).

Figure 6 *The green box highlights the peptide link and the green bond the peptide bond*

The dipeptide we obtain from this reaction has an amino group at one end of the molecule (the amino terminus) and a carboxylic acid group at the other (the carboxyl terminus). The structures of peptides can be written using abbreviations (see Table 1); for example HOOC-Gly-Ala-NH_2 indicates that the glycine is bonded to the alanine via its amine leaving the carboxylic acid free, and the alanine is bonded to the glycine via its acid leaving its amine group free.

The primary structure of a protein

Condensation reactions of the 20 naturally occurring amino acids can occur repeatedly (Figure 7). The result is a protein (a polyamide or polypeptide). The length ranges from 20 to more than 10 000 amino acids bonded together to form a continuous chain via repeated peptide links. The order (sequence) of amino acids in the chain of the protein is called its **primary structure**.

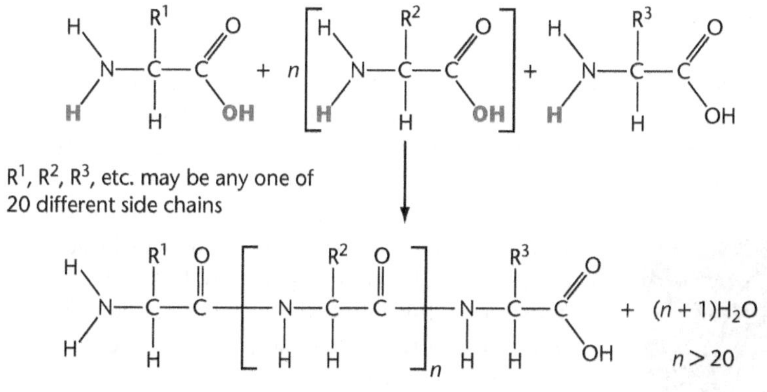

R^1, R^2, R^3, etc. may be any one of 20 different side chains

$+ (n+1)H_2O$

$n > 20$

Figure 7 Polypeptide (protein) formation via sequential condensation reactions

QUESTIONS

7. Draw the structures of the two different dipeptides that may be produced by condensing glycine (2-aminoethanoic acid) with alanine (2-aminopropanoic acid).

The secondary structure of a protein

A protein chain has many N–H and C = O groups along its length. Hydrogen bonds can form between an N–H group from one peptide link and a C = O group from another peptide link four amino acids further down the protein chain to form an **α-helix** (Figure 8). This is an example of a **secondary structure** of a protein. The helical shape is held in place by a regular pattern of hydrogen bonds. In an α-helix all the R groups attached to the protein are pointed towards the outside of the helix. The helix itself is elastic and flexible (like a spring). Keratin, the protein that makes up human hair, contains α-helices and each hair can support about 100 g before it will break.

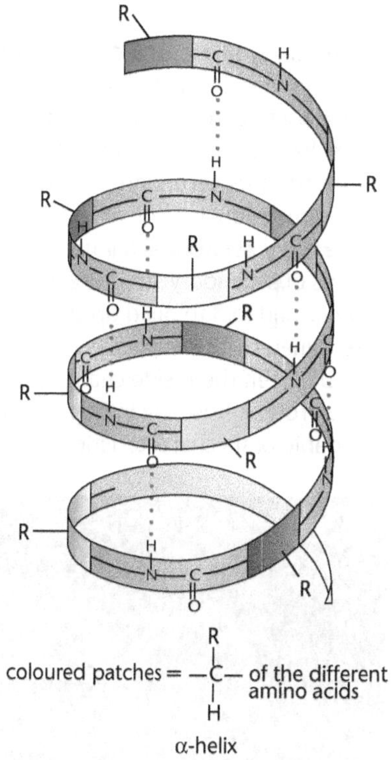

coloured patches = –C(R)(H)– of the different amino acids

α-helix

Figure 8 The α-helix, a three-dimensional secondary structure of a protein

Another type of secondary protein structure is called the **β-pleated sheet**. In this case two or more parallel regions of the protein can line up so that hydrogen bonds form between an N–H group from one peptide link and a C = O group from another peptide link much further along the chain in another parallel region (Figure 9). Many parallel strands can interact side by side, leading to a flat sheet-like structure. This type of arrangement is similar to the interaction between chains in polymeric nylons (see *chapter 10 of Year 2 Student Book*).

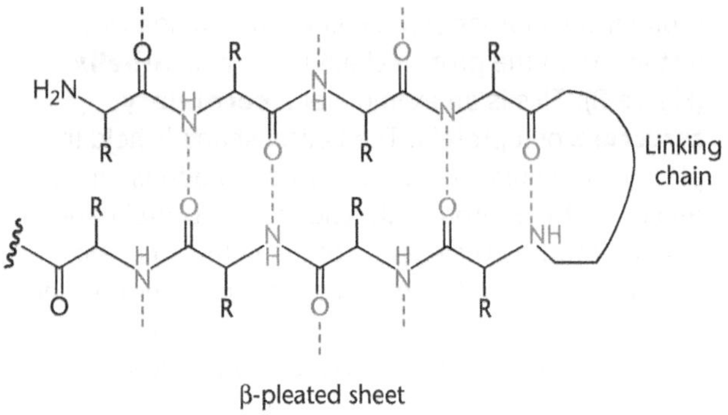

β-pleated sheet

Figure 9 *The β-pleated sheet, a secondary structure of a protein*

The tertiary structure of a protein

A protein may be made up of different regions of secondary structure; it may have some regions of α-helix and other regions of β-sheets. No matter what its secondary structure is, the overall three-dimensional shape of the whole protein is called its **tertiary structure** (Figure 10). How the different regions of secondary structure interact with one another and fold to build up the tertiary structure is determined by the various electrostatic or covalent links between the R side chains of amino acid residues in the protein. It is only in this form that the structure is capable of its characteristic biochemical functions.

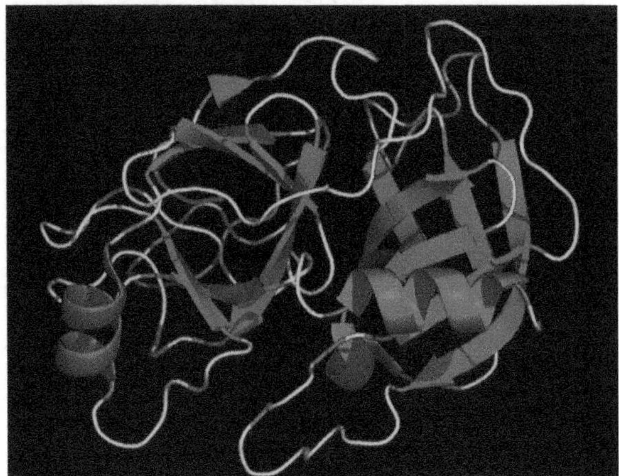

Figure 10 *This protein is made up of different regions of α-helices (highlighted in red) and β-pleated sheets (highlighted in blue). The overall three-dimensional structure is the tertiary structure of the protein.*

If a protein contains cysteine amino acids that are positioned close in space then the side-chain –SH groups can react together to form a strong S–S disulfide bridge (called a cystine link). This covalent bond helps fix the tertiary structure of the protein and can be seen in Figure 11. The S–S bond can be broken if the protein is heated, reduced or treated with base and this can cause the collapse of the biologically active tertiary structure. In this case the protein is said to be **denatured** and may not be biologically active.

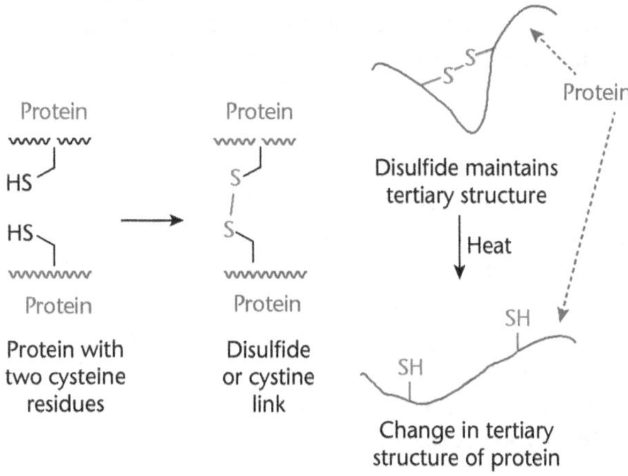

Figure 11 *Cysteine residues can form disulfide bridges, which are important in maintaining tertiary structure*

Ionic interactions and hydrogen-bonding interactions between the R groups of the side chains of amino acids also contribute to the overall tertiary structure of a protein. For example, a protonated lysine side chain could interact via an electrostatic ionic interaction with a deprotonated glutamic acid side chain close to it in space (Figure 12). If the pH changed, then this interaction could be broken. This is why many proteins are biologically active over a very narrow pH range.

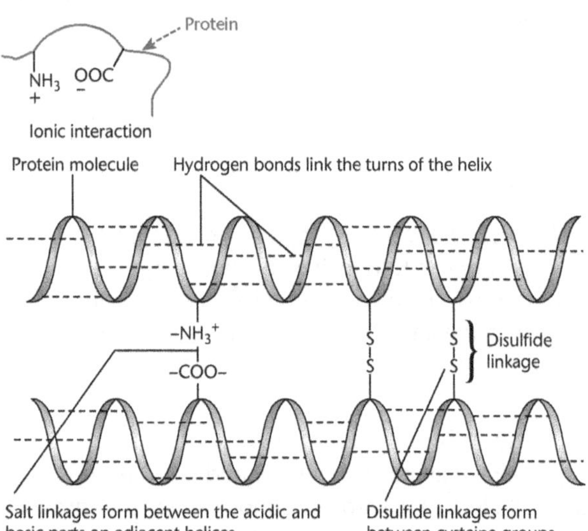

Figure 12 *Ionic interactions and disulfide linkages between amino acid side chains in proteins can be important in maintaining tertiary structure*

QUESTIONS

8. Define what is meant by the primary structure of a protein.
9. What type of bonding interaction is responsible for the formation of an α-helix?
10. Define what is meant by the tertiary structure of a protein. What role does the amino acid cysteine play in maintaining the tertiary structure of a protein?

Hydrolysis of peptide bonds

Whenever we digest proteins, our bodies break up the protein chains. This process can also be achieved in the laboratory by heating a protein with 5 mol dm^{-3} hydrochloric acid for about 24 hours. The secondary and tertiary structures of the protein are rapidly broken down, causing the polyamide chain to unravel. The chain is then hydrolysed at each of the peptide links and liberates the component amino acids (Figure 13).

Dipeptide

$$H_2N-CH(R^1)-CO-NH-CH(R^2)-COOH + H_2O \xrightarrow[\text{heat for 24 hours}]{5\ \text{mol dm}^{-3}\ \text{HCl;}} H_2N-CH(R^1)-COOH + H-NH-CH(R^2)-COOH$$

Polypeptide

$$H_2N-[CH(R)-CO-NH]_n-CH(R)-COOH + nH_2O \longrightarrow (n+1)\ H_2N-CH(R)-COOH$$

Figure 13 *Hydrolysis of the peptide link*

Using thin layer chromatography to identify amino acids

We can use this hydrolysis reaction as the first stage in determining the structure of a protein. The amino acids formed during the hydrolysis can be counted and identified using **thin-layer chromatography** (TLC). Chromatography is a technique that allows us to separate mixtures of compounds (see *chapter 13 of Year 2 Student Book*). A small spot of a mixture is added near to the bottom of a TLC plate and the plate is dipped into a solvent, making sure the spot is above the solvent line. As the solvent moves up the TLC plate different amino acids move up the plate at different rates. The TLC plate is removed when the solvent has nearly reached the top of the plate and the compounds are revealed using an appropriate technique.

The most common approach to revealing the amino acids is to spray the plate with an ethanol solution of ninhydrin. Ninhydrin reacts with the amine groups of the amino acids and produces a blue–purple colour. Once the amino acids have been visualised, a retention factor (R_f) can be calculated for each amino acid and used to identify the amino acid composition of the protein by comparison with known data (Figure 14).

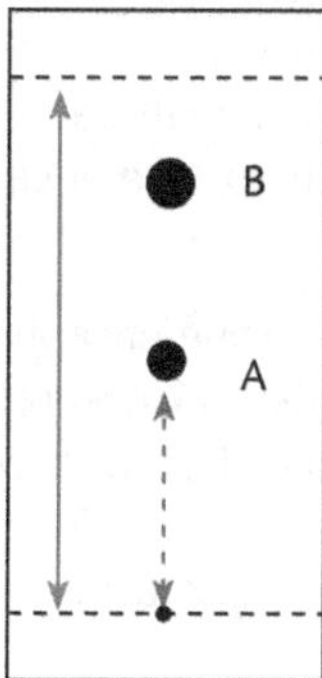

$$R_f\ (\text{spot A}) = \frac{\text{Distance moved by compound A}}{\text{Distance moved by solvent}}$$

Figure 14 *A thin-layer chromatography plate showing two compounds. Different amino acids have different retention factors (R_f values) in a particular solvent, allowing identification of mixtures*

QUESTIONS

11. The R_f values of pure glycine, alanine and valine were obtained by experiment and found to be as follows: glycine, R_f = 0.36; alanine, R_f = 0.42; and valine, R_f = 0.75. A dipeptide was heated with 5 mol dm^{-3} HCl for 24 hours and the mixture of the two α-amino acids obtained was analysed by TLC. The plate is shown here:

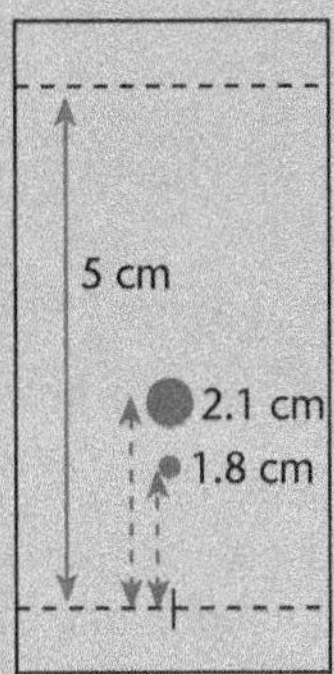

a. Identify the two amino acids. Explain your reasoning.

b. What is the purpose of the 5 mol dm^{-3} HCl?

c. How might you reveal the amino acids on the TLC plate?

ASSIGNMENT 2: DETERMINING THE STRUCTURE OF THE PAINKILLER LEUCINE ENCEPHALIN

The naturally occurring oligopeptide (a peptide with fewer than 20 amino acids) known as leucine encephalin contains five amino acids. This molecule was discovered in the 1970s during an investigation into how the pain-killing properties of morphine and codeine worked. Research showed that these molecules fit into brain receptor sites, in a sense imitating the role of the brain's own pain-suppressing molecules, of which leucine encephalin is just one example.

When hydrolysed, leucine encephalin releases four different amino acids, which were shown to be glycine (Gly), tyrosine (Tyr), phenylalanine (Phe) and leucine (Leu) in the ratio 2 : 1 : 1 : 1. The structures of these amino acids were given earlier in Table 1.

Questions

A1. What conditions could be used to carry out the hydrolysis?

A2. Which amino acids released from leucine encephalin would not be optically active? Explain your answer.

When partially hydrolysed using a shorter reaction time, apart from the individual amino acids, the following dipeptides and tripeptides are identified:

A HOOC-Tyr-Gly-NH_2

B HOOC-Phe-Leu-NH_2

C HOOC-Gly-Gly-Phe-NH_2

A3. Which of these are dipeptides and which are tripeptides?

A4. Showing all atoms and all bonds, draw the structures of the molecules (a) **A** and (b) **C**.

Stretch and Challenge

A5. Using the structures of the dipeptides and tripeptides obtained by partial hydrolysis deduce the order of the five amino acids in the leucine encephalin chain. Explain your reasoning. Hint: The order of the amino acids found in the dipeptides and tripeptides A, B and C will be the same as in leucine encephalin.

ASSIGNMENT 3: THE CHEMISTRY OF HAIR

Human hair contains a protein called α-keratin. The amino acid cysteine makes up 14% of the structure of α-keratin, and the main secondary structure in α-keratin is the α-helix (Figure A1). H-bonding between α-helices helps give structure to hair. It is possible to straighten curly hair by wetting it and then stretching and heating it. It is also possible to straighten hair chemically.

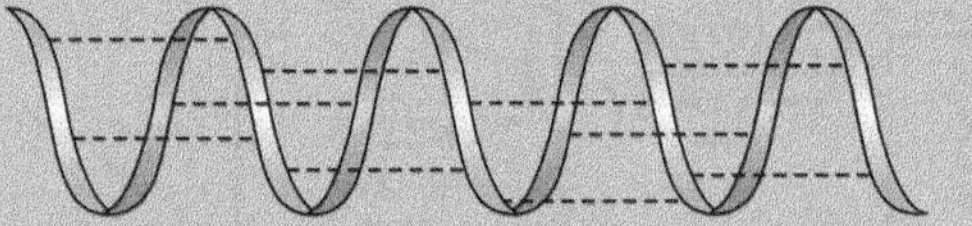

Figure A1 A keratin protein showing the α-helix and hydrogen bonds (dotted lines)

Questions

A1. What is the primary structure of a protein?

A2. 'A protein α-helix is like a spring'. Do you think this statement is justified? What are your reasons?

A3. Name two types of secondary structure found in proteins.

A4. What role might cysteine play in the structure of hair?

A5. Explain chemically what is happening when curly hair is wetted and stretched.

KEY IDEAS

- Proteins are sequences of amino acids joined by condensation reactions by means of peptide links.
- When proteins are hydrolysed, the peptide links are broken and the constituent amino acids are formed.
- The order of α-amino acids in a protein is called the primary structure.
- Hydrogen bonding between the N–H and C=O groups of the peptide bonds in a protein can lead to regions of α-helix or β-pleated sheet structure. These are called secondary structures.
- The overall 3D shape of the protein is called the tertiary structure. This structure is required for biochemical activity.
- Hydrogen bonding, ionic interactions and disulfide bonds formed between two cysteine side chains maintain the tertiary structure of the protein.

11.3 ENZYMES

At AS level you learned that a catalyst speeds up the rate of a reaction without being used up or chemically changed during the process (see chapter 8 of Year 1 Student Book). A catalyst provides an alternative route for a reaction, via one or more intermediates. The catalysed route has a lower activation energy. The rate of reaction increases because the activation energy is lowered, allowing more reactants to have sufficient energy to react (Figure 15). Enzymes are proteins that catalyse specific chemical reactions, often by a factor of 10^6–10^{12} times. This allows enzymes to catalyse biological reactions under the conditions found in living cells (in humans, 37 °C and around pH 7).

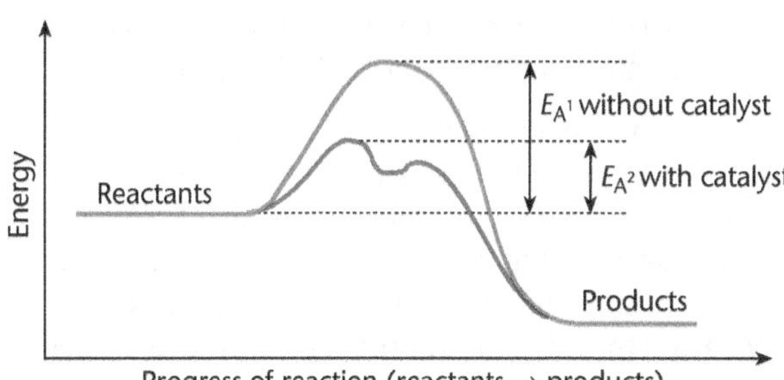

Figure 15 Energy profiles for a catalysed and an uncatalysed reaction

Catalysts are specific, though the same catalysts may catalyse more than one reaction. Aluminium trichloride, for example, catalyses the reaction of many different aromatic molecules with many different acyl chlorides. Enzymes are very specific, however. The enzyme DOPA decarboxylase catalyses the loss of carbon dioxide from L-DOPA but not from its enantiomer D-DOPA (Figure 16).

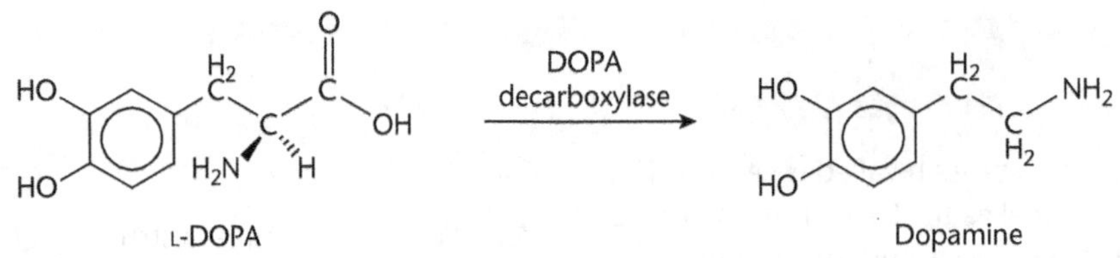

DOPA decarboxylase

L-DOPA

Dopamine

Figure 16 Unlike most catalysts, enzymes catalyse very specific reactions

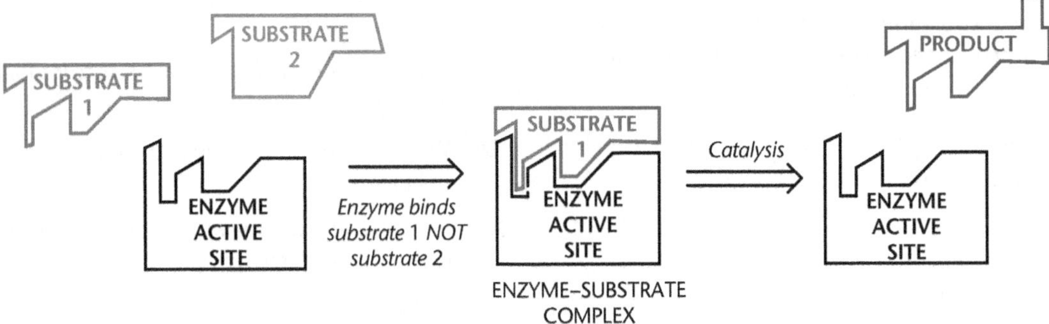

Figure 17 The lock and key hypothesis of binding of a substrate to an enzyme active site

The reactant in an enzyme-catalysed reaction is called the **substrate**. Most enzymes are large molecules compared with their substrates. The reaction of the substrate takes place at the **active site** of the enzyme. The active site is normally a cleft or hole in the protein in which the substrate can fit (Figure 17). The substrate enters the active site to produce the **enzyme–substrate complex**. The substrate is said to be bound to the active site. The enzyme then catalyses the reaction of the substrate to give the product and ejects the product from the active site. The enzyme is then free to bind another substrate and start the process again.

The enzyme, being a protein, will have a three-dimensional tertiary structure and it is this structure that gives the active site its unique shape. Only molecules that have the right shape can fit into the active site. This is known as the **lock and key hypothesis**. This is one of the reasons why enzymes only catalyse specific reactions.

The side chains in the amino acids that make up the enzyme active site play an important role in the attraction and bonding of the substrate to the enzyme. The side chains may contain –OH groups that can hydrogen-bond to the substrate, or ionic groups such as $-NH_3^+$ or $-COO^-$ which can attract the substrate by electrostatic forces. Amino acids that contain hydrocarbon side chains can also contribute to bonding of the substrate by van der Waals forces. The substrate must have the correct functional groups displayed in the correct orientation in space to be capable of interacting with the side chains of the active site efficiently (Figure 18).

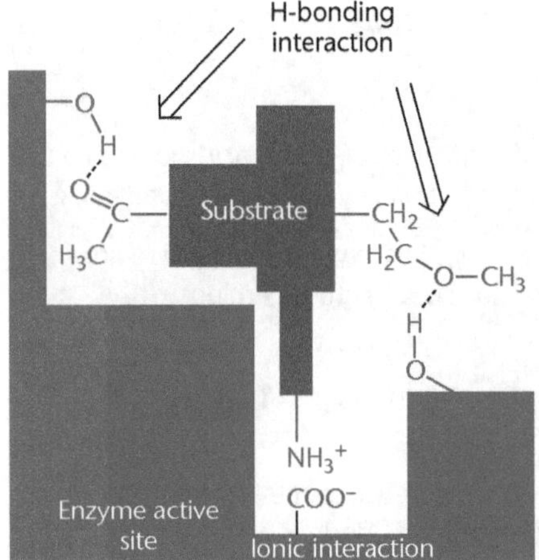

Figure 18 The functional groups of the substrate can interact with the amino acid side-chain functional groups in the active site via H-bonding, ionic interactions or van der Waals forces. The combined bonding interactions lead to the binding of the substrate to the enzyme active site.

Enzymes are chiral molecules, as they are made from *l*-amino acids. An important consequence of this is that enantiomers of chiral substrates can interact differently with the active sites of enzymes. In the example in Figure 19, the *l*-lactic acid can bind strongly with the enzyme shown because each of the three groups interacts in the correct way with the active site; however, d-lactic acid cannot orientate itself to bind correctly. This is an example of a **stereospecific** active site, an active site that will only bind one enantiomer of a racemate. This explains why one enantiomer of the drug ibuprofen, the d-isomer, is far more active as a painkiller than its enantiomer and why it is important to evaluate both enantiomers of new drugs for their efficacy.

A molecule that binds to an enzyme active site and decreases its activity is called an **enzyme inhibitor**. Many drugs that treat disease are enzyme inhibitors. If the activity of an essential enzyme in an organism, such as a bacterium, can be decreased then the organism may die. Similarly, if a disease is caused by an imbalance in enzyme activity, then an enzyme inhibitor might restore the balance and treat the disease. Many drugs act as enzyme inhibitors by blocking the active site of the enzyme. This stops the natural substrate from binding and affects the organism. For an inhibitor to be active it must bind more strongly to the active site than the natural substrate does (Figure 20).

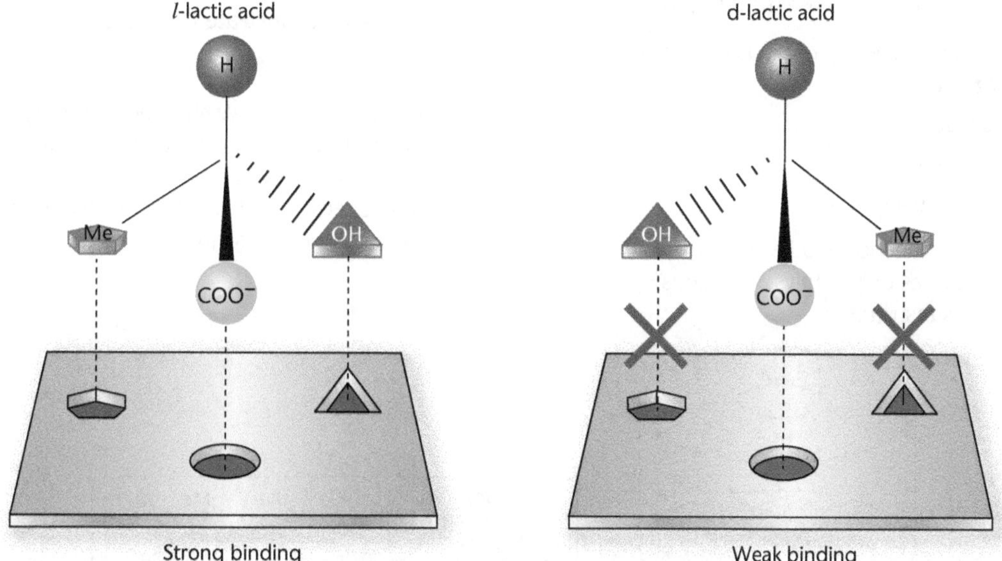

Figure 19 *Different enantiomers of lactic acid binding to the active site in L-lactate dehydrogenase. Binding is stronger for the natural substrate, L-lactic acid, than for D-lactic acid because the molecule has the correct 3D-structure to fit into the enzyme binding site. The yellow area is a schematic representation of the binding site of the L-lactate dehydrogenase enzyme.*

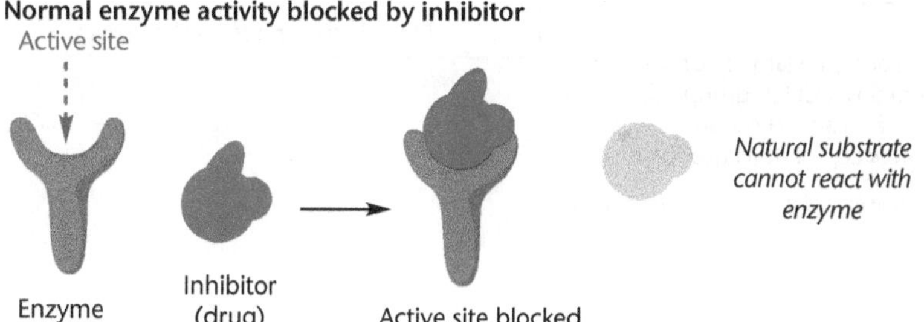

Figure 20 *An enzyme inhibitor binds to the active site of the enzyme more strongly than the natural substrate does and blocks the natural substrate from reacting to give product*

To design a drug which acts as an enzyme inhibitor, it is necessary to know the three-dimensional structure as well as the amino acid side chains present in the enzyme active site. Then a molecule of the correct shape with appropriate functional groups to block the active site must be synthesised. Sophisticated computer programs allow chemists to predict the shape of enzymes and drugs and to highlight potential drug targets. Drugs are often similar in structure to the natural substrates that they inhibit. This is not surprising, as the drug must bind to the active site of the enzyme to inhibit the substrate binding.

QUESTIONS

12. What is an enzyme?

13. How do catalysts increase the rate of a reaction?

14. Define the following terms as they relate to enzymes:

a. substrate

b. active site

c. enzyme inhibitor.

15. How does the lock and key hypothesis explain why enzymes only catalyse reactions of specific substrates?

16. Name *two* types of intermolecular interactions that could be responsible for the binding of a substrate to an enzyme.

Stretch and challenge

17. Figure 21 is an illustration of a stereospecific active site of an enzyme. Using the substrate shown as an example, explain why a stereospecific binding site can only bond to one enantiomeric form.

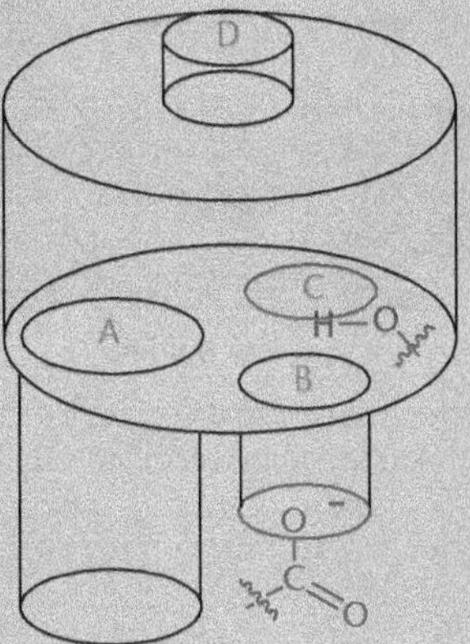

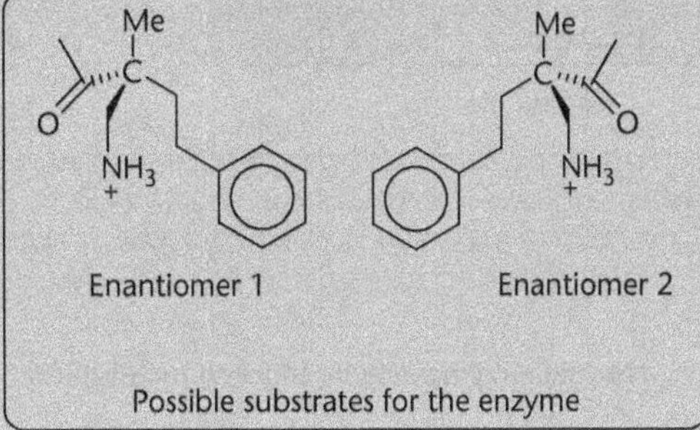

A. Can accept a large hydrocarbon
B. Contains a COO^- group
C. Contains an OH group
D. Can accept a small group only

Figure 21 *Illustration showing an active site of an enzyme*

ASSIGNMENT 4: THE DRUGS THALIDOMIDE AND POMALIDOMIDE

Thalidomide (Figure A1) was marketed as a sedative drug in 1957 and given to pregnant women to treat morning sickness. Unfortunately, it was later discovered to be responsible for babies being born with deformities, normally in their limbs. It was withdrawn in 1962. When a molecule affects physiological development it is called a teratogen. Thalidomide contains a chiral carbon atom. Laboratory tests showed that it was the laevorotatory enantiomer that caused problems and the dextrorotatory isomer was an effective sedative.

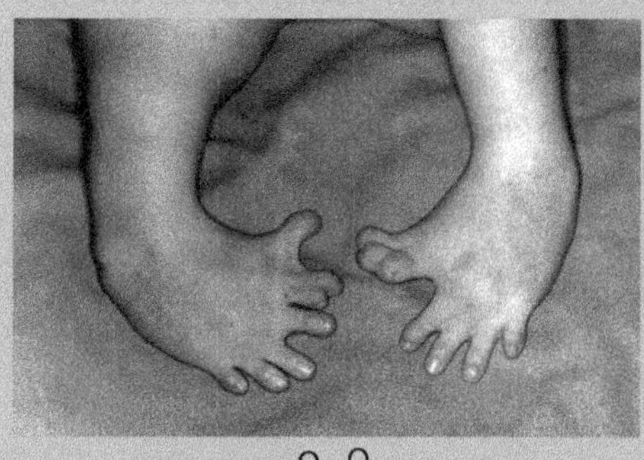

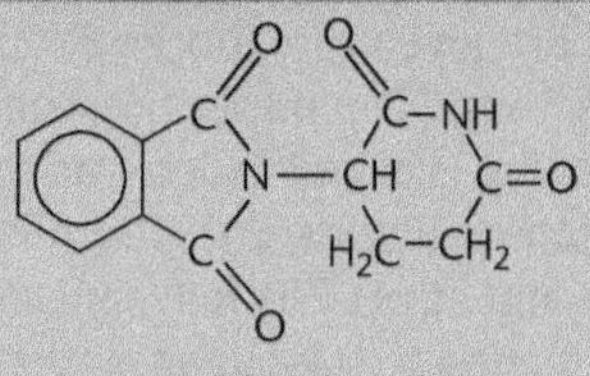

Thalidomide

Figure A1 *Thalidomide caused birth defects in babies whose mothers were prescribed the drug for morning sickness when pregnant*

Although it is still not yet known how thalidomide causes birth defects, the latest evidence suggests it inactivates an enzyme called cereblon that is responsible for limb development in embryos. An X-ray structure determination of thalidomide bound to this protein has identified the active site.

Questions

A1. Identify the chiral centre in thalidomide and draw both enantiomers.

A2. Assuming the drug is bound to the active site of an enzyme, highlight the atom(s) in thalidomide that could interact with the active site as:

a. H-bond donors

b. H-bond acceptors.

A3. Assuming that a serine residue was identified to be in the active site of the enzyme, hypothesise what type of intermolecular interaction it might have with thalidomide.

A4. Why do you think the two different enantiomers have different biological effects?

Recently, thalidomide has been shown to be active in treating leprosy and multiple myeloma (a cancer of the white blood cells). A number of other drugs similar in structure (analogues) have been prepared. Pomalidomide (Figure A2) was licensed for use in treating multiple myeloma in 2013.

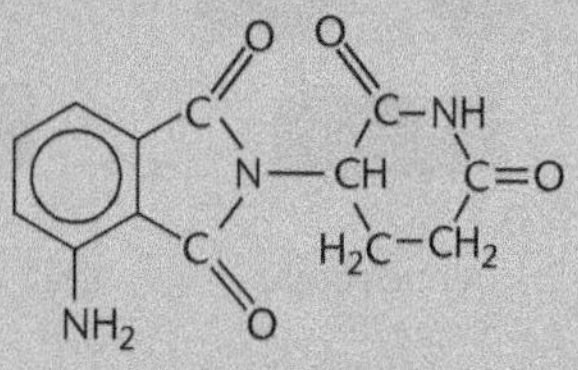

Pomalidomide

Figure A2 *Structure of pomalidomide, used to treat multiple myeloma*

Stretch and challenge

A5. Suggest a reason why pomalidomide has similar biological activity to thalidomide.

A6. How might the extra amine group in pomalidomide interact with an active site in an enzyme?

A7. What precautions would you advise a female cancer patient being treated with pomalidomide to take during treatment?

KEY IDEAS

- Enzymes are proteins that act as biological catalysts. They work by providing an alternative reaction pathway of lower activation energy.
- Enzymes work by binding substrates in an active site. The size and orientation of amino acid side chains in the active site determine how the substrate will bind.
- The substrate can bind to the active site by hydrogen bonding, ionic bonding or van der Waals forces.
- An active site that binds one enantiomer of a racemate is a stereospecific active site.
- A molecule that binds to an enzyme active site and decreases its activity is called an enzyme inhibitor.
- Many drugs that treat disease are enzyme inhibitors.

11.4 DEOXYRIBONUCLEIC ACID

Deoxyribonucleic acid (DNA) is an organic polymer that records genetic information. It is made up of two polymer strands held together by H-bonding. It has a double helical shape. The monomers that make up DNA are called **nucleotides**. Each nucleotide consists of three components linked together, a phosphate, a sugar and a base (Figure 22).

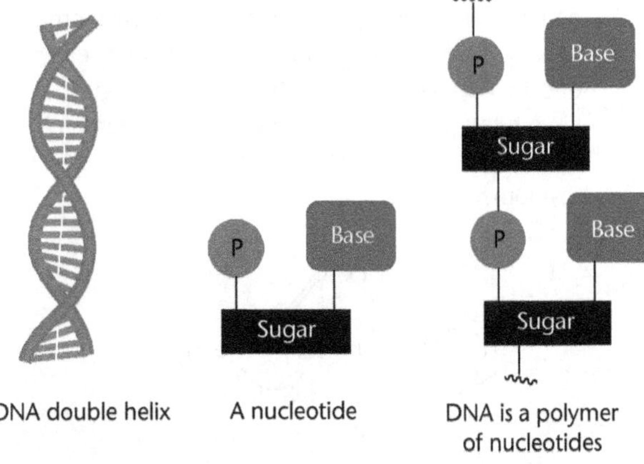

Figure 22 *DNA is a polymer made up of nucleotides linked through a phosphate group (P)*

The sugar in DNA is **2-deoxyribose**, and is a modified version of the sugar ribose (used in RNA) missing a hydroxyl group at the 2 position. In DNA, 2-deoxyribose is numbered as shown in Figure 23. The phosphate is attached to the 5 position of 2-deoxyribose and the base is attached to the 1 position.

There are four different bases that can be bonded to the sugar to make four different nucleotides. The bases are thymine, cytosine, adenine and guanine and are given the abbreviations T, C, A and G, respectively. The nucleotide containing the base adenine is called 2-deoxyadenosine 5-monophosphate (Figure 24). The phosphate is a diprotic acid and at pH 7 is fully ionised. The four bases are attached to the sugar by the nitrogen atoms shown in blue.

The polymer DNA is made up by the linking of nucleotides via the phosphate at the 5 position of one nucleotide and the hydroxyl group at the 3 position of a different nucleotide. This produces a **polynucleotide** with a backbone of sugars and phosphates and with the various bases attached to the backbone (Figure 25).

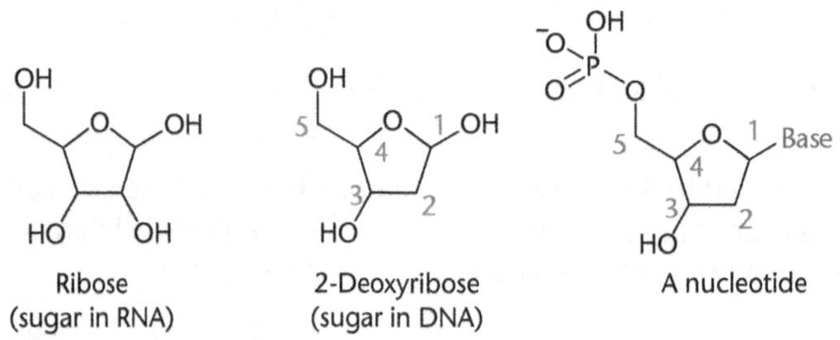

Ribose (sugar in RNA)

2-Deoxyribose (sugar in DNA)

A nucleotide

Figure 23 *The sugars in RNA and DNA are ribose and 2-deoxyribose, respectively*

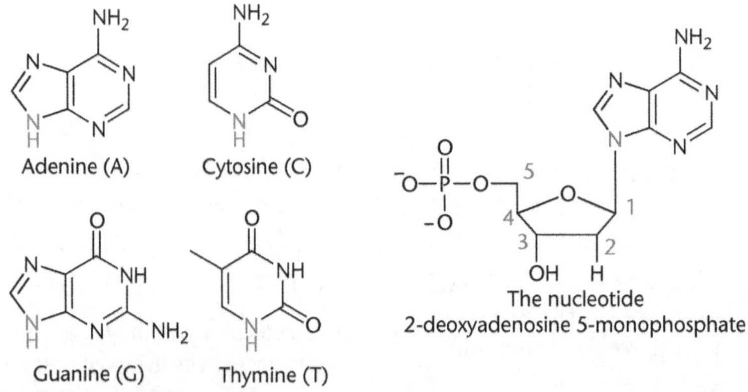

Adenine (A)

Cytosine (C)

Guanine (G)

Thymine (T)

The nucleotide 2-deoxyadenosine 5-monophosphate

Figure 24 *The four bases found in DNA and their abbreviations*

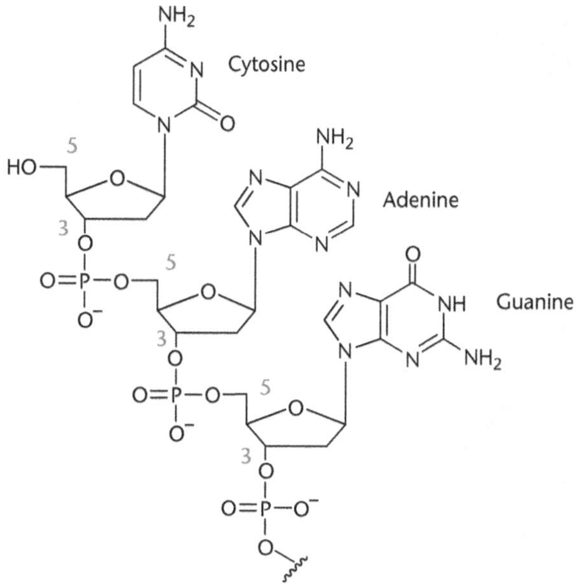

Figure 25 *A portion of a DNA molecule showing the phosphate linkages between nucleotides*

The double-helix shape of DNA, first postulated by the chemists James Watson and Francis Crick in 1953, is formed as a result of H-bonding between bases in one polynucleotide strand and bases in a second strand (called the **complementary strand**). The H-bonding is very specific, with the base adenine only H-bonding with the base thymine, and guanine only H-bonding with cytosine. This is because these **base pairs** fit exactly in terms of size and shape, forming strong H-bonding interactions. The AT base pair makes two H-bonds, while the GC base pair makes three H-bonds (Figure 26).

A single polynucleotide strand of DNA can be represented by writing the order of the bases starting with the end that contains the free 5 carbon and ending with the end that contains the 3 position. The complementary strand that makes the double helix runs in the opposite direction (Figure 27).

When a cell divides, a copy of its DNA must be made. DNA replicates itself by first unwinding the double helix (this is catalysed by an enzyme). Next, complementary nucleotides can bind to the two unwound chains, ultimately leading to two copies of the original DNA molecule (Figure 28).

Watson and Crick, together with Maurice Wilkins, were awarded the Nobel Prize for their work. Dr Rosalind Franklin played a significant role on the discovery of the structure of DNA, but her contribution was only acknowledged after her death.

The adenine thymine (AT) base pair

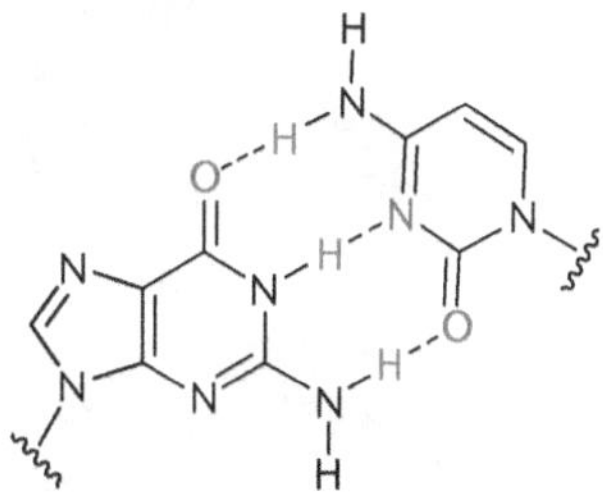

The guanine cytosine (GC) base pair

Figure 26 *H-bonding between the base pairs AT and GC*

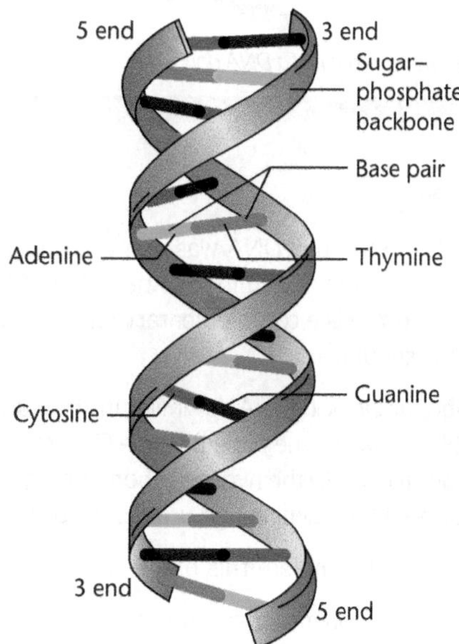

Figure 27 *H-bonding between the base pairs AT and GC leads to the formation of the DNA double helix from two complementary strands of polymeric nucleotides*

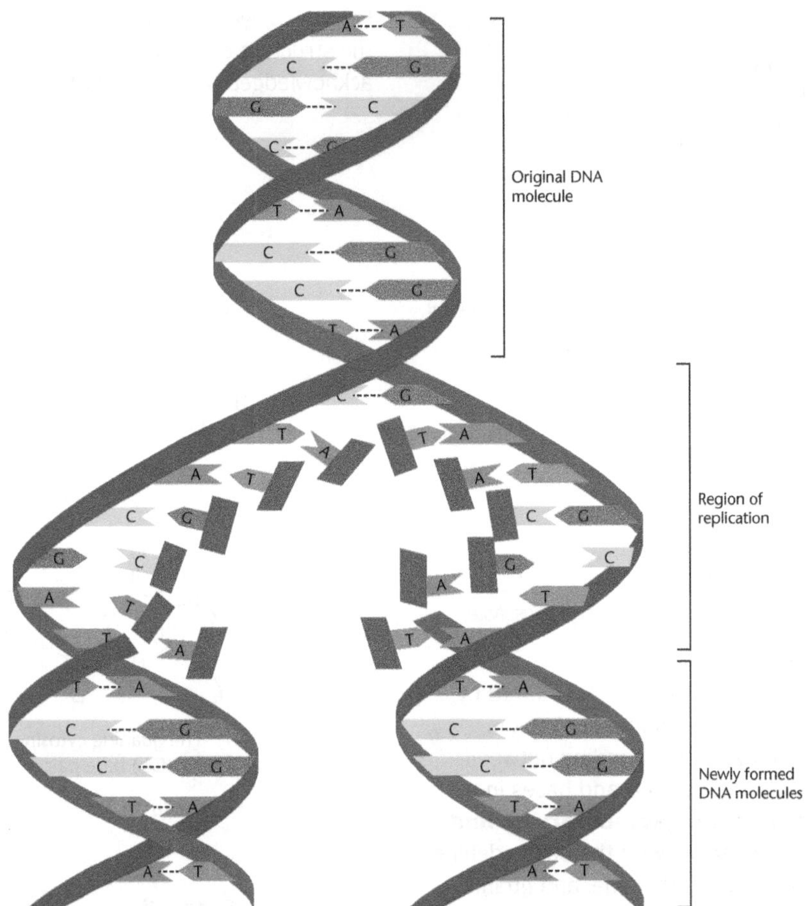

Figure 28 The replication of a DNA double helix

QUESTIONS

18. A short strand of DNA was prepared. The structure was determined to be 5-AGGTCCAC-3. Write down the complementary strand of this DNA sequence.

19. Ribonucleic acid (RNA) is similar in structure to DNA; however, the base thymine (T) is replaced by uracil (U). Draw the hydrogen bond interactions between the adenine and uracil base pair.

20. Copy and complete this paragraph:

    DNA is a polymer made up of_________ monomers. The monomers contain the elements carbon, hydrogen, oxygen _________ and_________ A nucleotide contains three components: a sugar, a _________ and a _________The sugar in DNA is _________ and it contains _________ carbon atoms. The complementary base to adenine is _________ and it forms a base pair via _________ H-bonds.

KEY IDEAS

- DNA is an organic polymer made from nucleotides.
- Nucleotides consist of a phosphate group attached to the 5 carbon of 2-deoxyribose and a base attached to the 1 position.
- Four nucleotides make up DNA, differing only in the base. The four bases are adenine, guanine, cytosine and thymine.
- H-bonding between the complementary base pairs adenine/thymine and guanine/cytosine on separate chains is responsible for the double-helix structure of DNA.
- Owing to base pairing, the sequence of bases on one strand of DNA dictates the sequence on the second strand.

11.5 ACTION OF ANTICANCER DRUGS

The use of drugs to treat cancer is known as **chemotherapy**. A number work by targeting cells that divide rapidly, a characteristic of cancer cells. However, other cells such as those that make up the gastrointestinal tract, hair follicles and bone marrow also replicate quickly. Consequently, many anticancer drugs can have side effects such as nausea, hair loss and susceptibility to infection. Because cancer cells divide rapidly, drugs which affect cell division by binding to DNA and stop replication can be used in cancer treatment.

Cisplatin (*cis*-diamminedichloridoplatinum(II)) is an anticancer drug that is used to treat a number of different cancers (Figure 29). It was first licensed in 1978 to treat ovarian and testicular cancer. The isomer transplatin does not have significant anticancer activity.

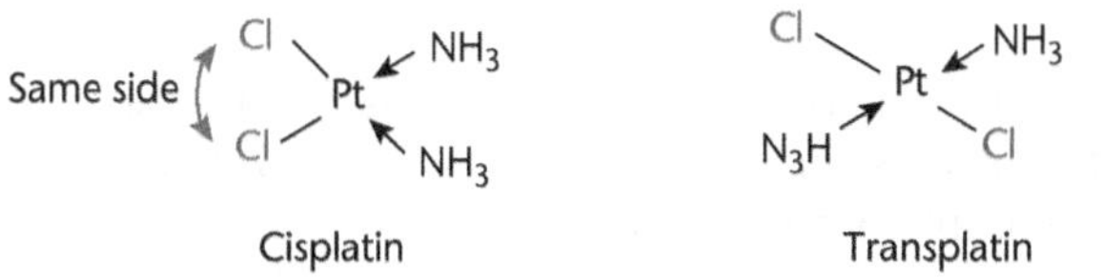

Same side

Cisplatin　　Transplatin

Figure 29 *Cisplatin has the chlorides on the same side of the molecule (similarly to the way in which a cis alkene has substituents on the same side of the double bond; see* *chapter 5 of Year 1 Student Book**)*

When cisplatin enters a cell, one of the chlorides is initially replaced by water and then by one of the nitrogen atoms of a guanine base in DNA. This forms a nitrogen–platinum bond and fixes the drug to one strand of the DNA double helix. The second chloride is then lost from the platinum atom in the same way and this allows a second guanine base to bind (Figure 30). This distorts the shape of the DNA and prevents replication (Figure 30).

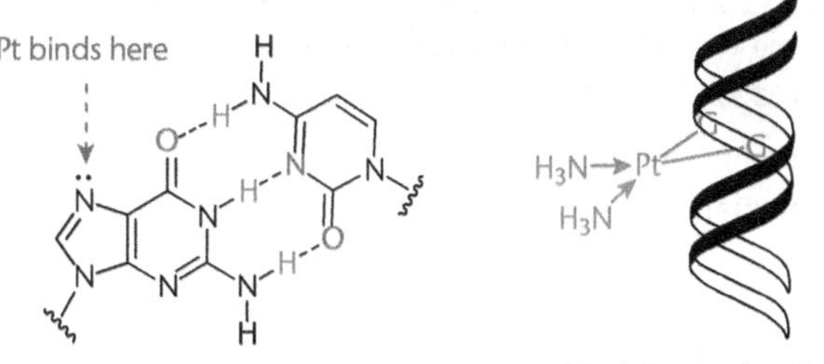

The guanine–cytosine (GC) base pair　　Cisplatin reacts with two guanine bases, each labelled G

Figure 30 *Cisplatin will bind to the nitrogen atom of a guanine base in a DNA strand. This can happen twice, anchoring the drug onto the DNA and changing the shape of the DNA.*

QUESTIONS

21. Draw the product from the reaction of cisplatin with one mole of water.

22. Figure 31 shows how cisplatin can bind to two guanine residues on the same strand of a DNA double helix. Suggest *one* other way the cisplatin might bind to guanine bases in a DNA double helix.

Some of the side effects of cisplatin, such as nausea, can be treated with other medications. Other side effects include kidney damage and nerve damage as the drug may affect the action of other molecules, such as enzymes, in the body. To minimise damage to healthy cells, chemotherapy doses are given in small quantities at regular intervals to allow the body to recover.

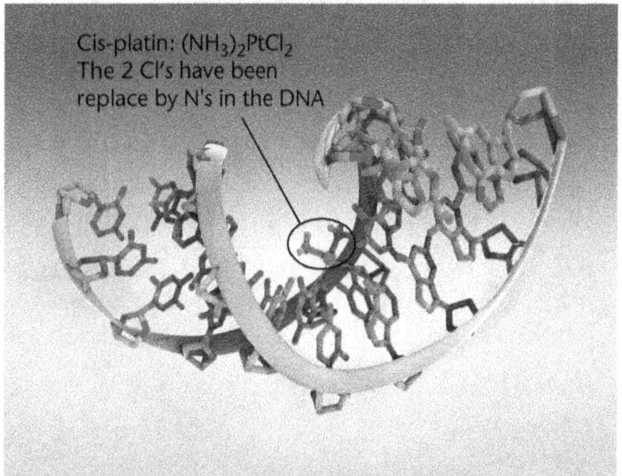

Figure 31 *Computer image showing the structure of a molecule of cisplatin (centre) coordinated to a section of DNA. Cisplatin slows the growth of the cancer by damaging the DNA in the cancerous cells, preventing them from dividing.*

QUESTIONS

23. Two new platinum drugs, carboplatin and oxaliplatin, are being used successfully to treat cancer. What structural features do they share with cisplatin? Using this knowledge, hypothesise what features are important for drug action.

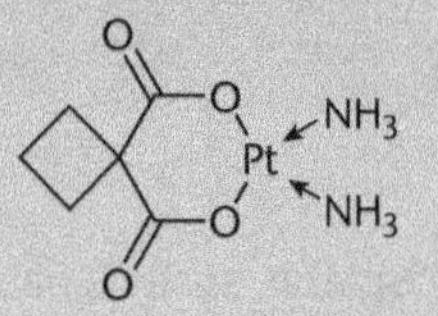

Carboplatin 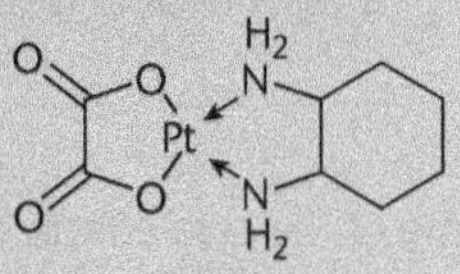 Oxaliplatin

24. Different patients often experience different levels of side effects when taking cisplatin. How might a physician try and minimise side effects? What are the long-term consequences for patients with very severe side effects?

ASSIGNMENT 5: AZIDOTHYMIDINE (AZT), AN ANTIVIRAL DRUG

In 1987 azidothymidine (AZT) (Figure A1) was licensed for the treatment of HIV/AIDS. It was the first drug available to treat HIV infection. The drug works by affecting the process that is responsible for the DNA replication of HIV. In the body, AZT is phosphorylated.

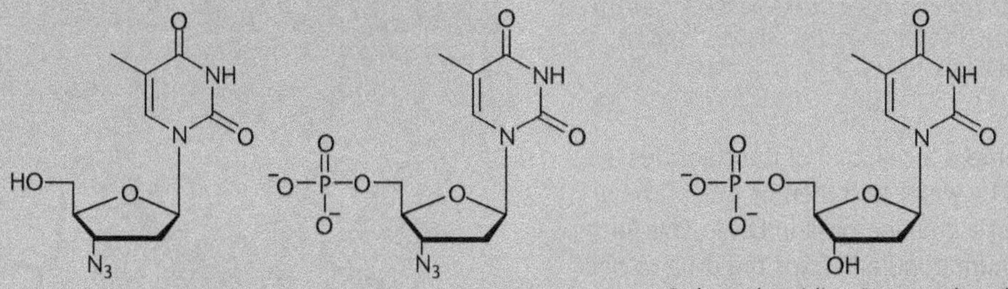

AZT Monophosphorylated AZT 2-deoxythymidine-5-monophosphate

Figure A1 *Structures of AZT and the nucleotide 2-deoxythymidine-5-monophosphate*

Questions

A1. What is the main difference in structure between monophosphorylated AZT and 2-deoxythymidine-5-monophosphate?

A2. During viral DNA replication, AZT can be incorporated into the growing DNA strand. By only drawing the base part of the structure, show how AZT can form a base pair with adenine and suggest why it gets incorporated into the growing DNA strand.

A3. As soon as AZT has been incorporated into the viral DNA the replication stops. Suggest a reason for this.

A4. Would you predict that AZT would be toxic to human cells? Justify your answer.

KEY IDEAS

- Cisplatin prevents DNA replication by reacting with the guanine bases in DNA.
- Cancer cells replicate faster than many healthy cells, so cisplatin can be used to selectively kill cancer cells.
- Side effects of cisplatin can include damage to healthy fast-dividing cells such as bone marrow, hair follicles and intestinal cells.
- Drugs can have side effects because they can interact with other biological molecules and not just those they have been designed to interact with.

PRACTICE QUESTIONS

1. Figure Q1 shows a representation of the arrangement of some amino acids in a portion of a protein structure in the form of an α-helix.

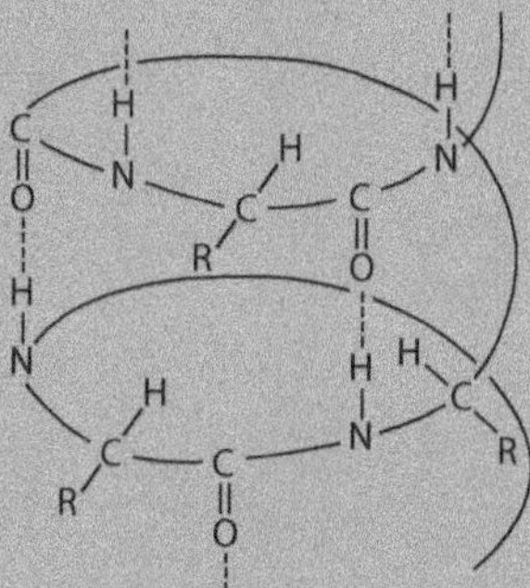

Figure Q1

   a. Name the type of protein structure in Figure Q1.

   b. Explain the origin of the interaction represented by the dotted lines in Figure Q1.

AQA Chemistry Specimen Paper 2015 Paper 2 Question 5

2. The polymerase chain reaction (PCR) is a laboratory technique that makes many copies (amplification) of DNA, and is often used in forensic science when a larger sample of DNA is required for tests. In this technique, the double helix of DNA is first broken into single strands and then short sequences of complementary nucleotides are added; these sequences are called primers. The primers are designed to be complementary to the ends of the two strands. Then the four nucleotide monomers are added together with an enzyme (a polymerase) that attaches them to the end of the primers. The single strands of DNA act as a template along which a new complementary strand is built up. The cycle is then repeated until enough sample is obtained.

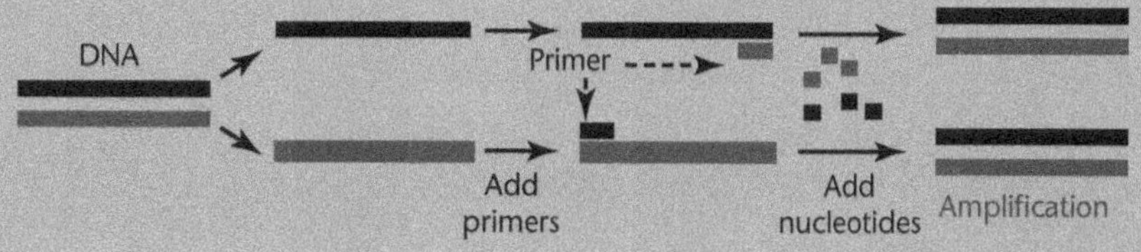

(*continued*)

a. DNA is a polymer made up of nucleotides. What is a nucleotide? What three components make up its structure?

b. Draw the structure of 2-deoxyribose. How does it differ from the structure of ribose?

c. The first step involves heating the DNA to 95 °C. What types of bonds are broken during this step? Why is it necessary to heat to such a high temperature?

d. A primer consisting of 10 nucleotides was designed to be complementary to the DNA fragment AGAGTACGTT. What is the sequence of the primer?

3. The anticancer drug cisplatin operates by reacting with the guanine in DNA. Figure Q2 shows a small part of a single strand of DNA. Some lone pairs are shown.

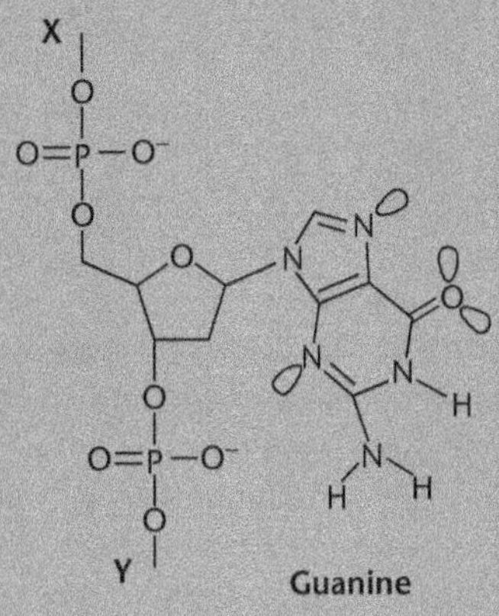

Guanine

Figure Q2

a. The DNA chain continues with bonds at X and Y. State the name of the sugar molecule that is attached to the bond at X.

b. Messenger RNA is synthesised in cells in order to transfer information from DNA. The bases in one strand of DNA pair up with the bases used to synthesise RNA. Figure Q3 shows two bases used in RNA.

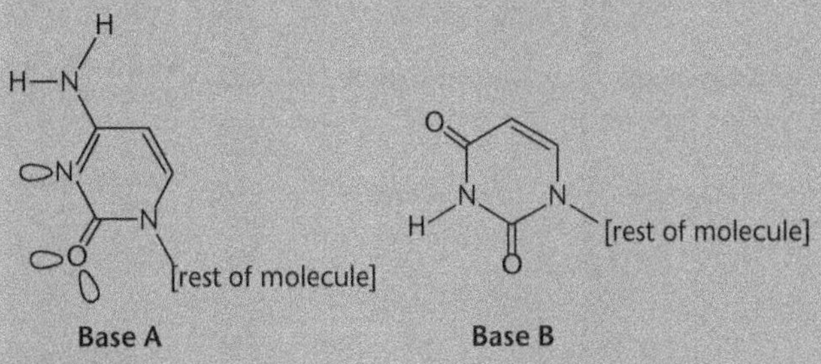

Base A　　Base B

Figure Q3

Suggest which of the bases **A** and **B** forms a pair with guanine in Figure Q2 when messenger RNA is synthesised. Explain how the base that you have chosen forms a base pair with guanine.

c. Cisplatin works because one of the atoms of guanine can form a co-ordinate bond with platinum, replacing one of the ammonia or chlorine ligands. Another atom on another guanine can also form a co-ordinate bond with the same platinum by replacing another ligand.

In Figure Q2, draw a ring around an atom in guanine that is likely to bond to platinum.

d. An adverse effect of cisplatin is that it also prevents normal healthy cells from replicating. Suggest one way in which cisplatin can be administered so that this side effect is minimised.

AQA Chemistry Specimen Paper 2015
Paper 2 Question 8

4. a. The structure of the amino acid *alanine* is shown here:

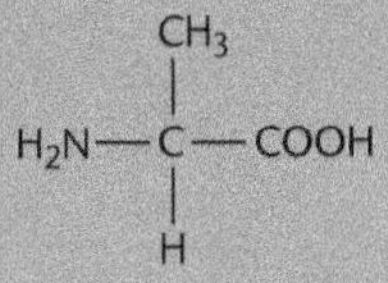

$H_2N—C(CH_3)(H)—COOH$

i. Draw the structure of the zwitterion formed by *alanine*.

ii. Draw the structure of the organic product formed in each case from *alanine* when it reacts with:

- CH_3OH in the presence of a small amount of concentrated sulfuric acid
- Na_2CO_3
- CH_3Cl in a 1 : 1 mole ratio.

b. The amino acid *lysine* is shown here:

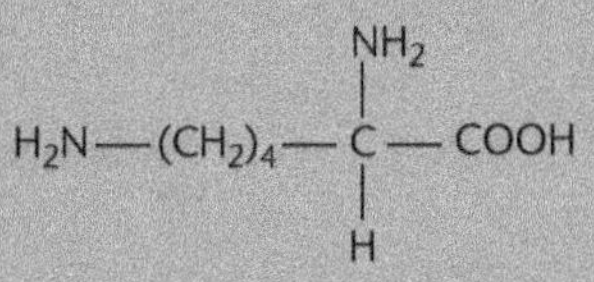

$H_2N—(CH_2)_4—C(NH_2)(H)—COOH$

Draw the structure of the *lysine* species present in a solution at low pH.

c. The amino acid *proline* is shown here:

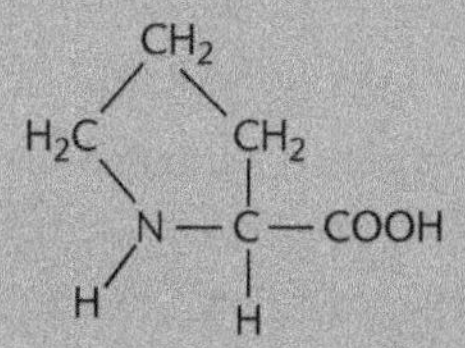

Draw the structure of the dipeptide formed from two *proline* molecules.

AQA June 2007 Unit 4 Question 5

5. a. Draw the structure of the species present in solid aminoethanoic acid, H_2NCH_2COOH.

b. Explain why the melting point of aminoethanoic acid is much higher than that of hydroxyethanoic acid, $HOCH_2COOH$.

AQA January 2006 Unit 4 Question 6(b–c)

6. The structure of the D-isomer of 2,6-diaminohexanoic acid (lysine) is shown in Figure Q4:

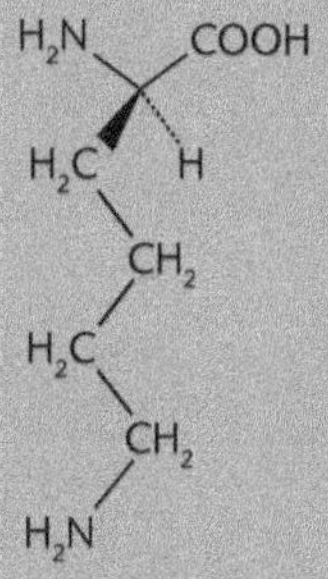

Figure Q4

Draw the structure of L-lysine next to that of the D-isomer in Figure Q4.

Copy and complete the structures in Figure Q5 to show the main species of lysine present in aqueous solution at pH 2, pH 7 and pH 11.

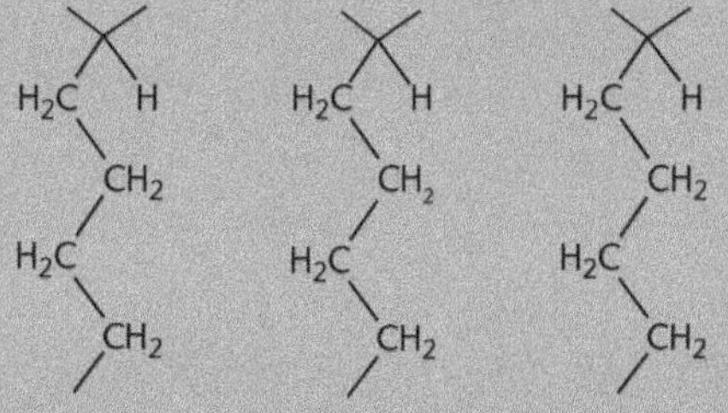

pH 2 pH 7 pH 11

Figure Q5

NEAB June 1998, Chapter 9 Question 4(a–b)

7. The structural formulae of three amino acids are shown here:

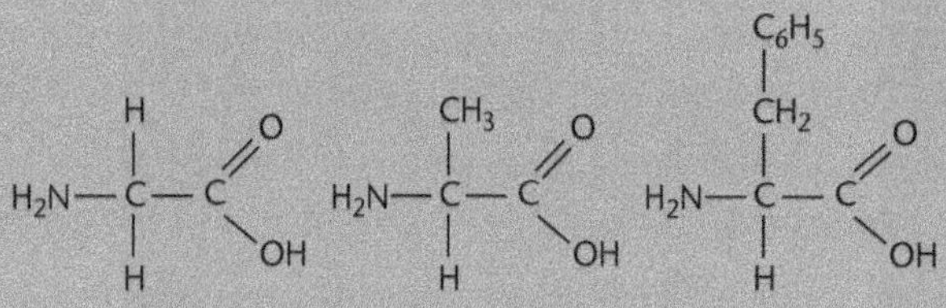

Glycine Alanine Phenylalanine

a. Explain why alanine and phenylalanine have optical isomers, but glycine does not.

Amino acids can react both with acids and with bases and are also capable of forming zwitterions.

b. Write equations for the reactions between:

i. phenylalanine and hydrochloric acid

ii. alanine and sodium hydroxide.

The isoelectric point is described in terms of the pH at which an amino acid forms its zwitterions. The isoelectric point is different for each amino acid.

c. i. The isoelectric point for glycine is at pH = 5.97. Draw the zwitterion formed by glycine at this point.

ii. Draw the ions that would be formed at pH = 5.75 by alanine (isoelectric point = 6.01) and phenylalanine (isoelectric point = 5.48).

Glycine and alanine can react together to form the dipeptide shown here:

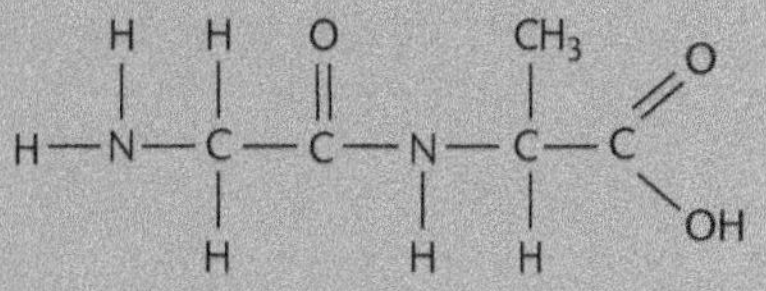

d. A different dipeptide can be formed from the reaction between glycine and alanine. Draw its displayed formula.

Multiple choice

8. Select the correct facts about proteins:

a. Proteins are addition polymers.

b. Proteins contain an amide functional group.

(continued)

c. All naturally occurring α-amino acids contain a chiral carbon atom.

d. Enzymes are proteins.

9. If an amino acid is dissolved in aqueous hydrochloric acid it will exist as:

a. a cation

b. an anion

c. a neutral molecule

d. a zwitterion.

10. Which statements about the structure of DNA are true?

a. The sugar in DNA is ribose.

b. H-bonding between base pairs is responsible for the double-helix structure.

c. Cisplatin binds to DNA through thymine groups.

d. DNA is a polymer of nucleotide monomers.

12 ORGANIC SYNTHESIS

PRIOR KNOWLEDGE

You will already have studied the organic chemistry and reactions of many different functional groups. You will have studied alkanes, alkenes, halogenoalkanes and alcohols (see chapters 5, 6 and 13–15 of Year 1 Student Book) and the chemistry of aldehydes, ketones, carboxylic acid derivatives, aromatic molecules, amines, amino acids and polymers (chapters 6–10 of Year 2 Student Book). You will also be familiar with the concept of isomerism, including optical isomerism (chapter 5 of Year 2 Student Book).

LEARNING OBJECTIVES

Using the reactions you have already studied you will learn how to devise a synthesis, with up to four steps, for any organic molecule. You will be able to explain why synthetic routes that involve fewer steps, have high atom economy and use non-hazardous chemicals and solvents are preferred.

(Specification 3.3.14)

Taxol, a natural product marketed under the name paclitaxel, is used to treat ovarian, breast, lung and pancreatic cancers. It was isolated from the bark of the Pacific yew tree, an endangered species. Not enough taxol could be prepared for clinical trials and so there was a need for organic chemists to devise a synthesis of this molecule. In 1988 a French chemist, Pierre Potier, found a way to make taxol from another widely occurring natural product, 10-deacetylbaccatin. In 1994, a different synthesis was announced, starting from ethyl propanoate. Although taxol is now prepared by a different route, Potier's method illustrates how organic synthesis can solve crucial problems such as preparing a much-needed drug and saving an endangered species. The ability to devise and evaluate a multistage synthesis of an organic molecule is an important skill that is in great demand.

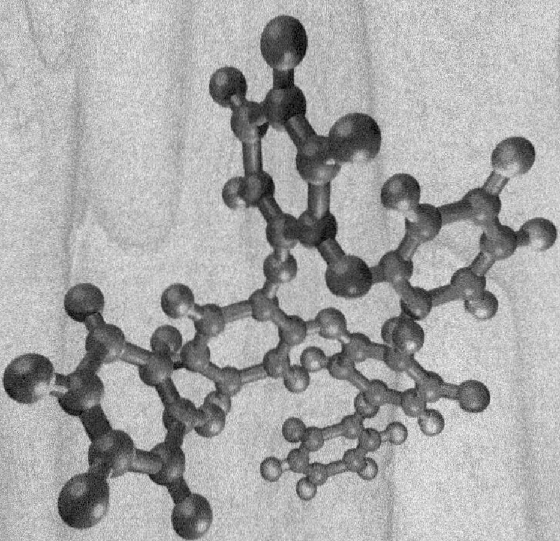

Figure 1 *The structure of the naturally occurring anticancer drug taxol, which was isolated from the Pacific yew tree*

12.1 MULTISTEP ORGANIC SYNTHESIS

There are more than seven million known organic compounds. The majority of these have been synthesised in a laboratory. On a day-to-day basis it is necessary to prepare drugs, polymers, dyes and other organic materials in an economic and environmentally sustainable way. Organic synthesis is the science of making organic molecules which cannot be sourced in sufficient quantities naturally, normally via multistep sequences of reactions. Synthesis can also be used to confirm the structure of a molecule deduced using chemical testing and spectroscopy. Once it has been synthesised, if the spectroscopic data match then the structure has been confirmed.

In a multistep synthesis each step will have a molar yield. The overall yield of the synthesis is given by multiplying each individual percentage together and finally multiplying by 100. For example,

$$A \xrightarrow{\quad 70\%\ \text{yield} \quad} B \xrightarrow{\quad 20\%\ \text{yield} \quad} C$$

Overall yield = (70/100) x (20/100) x 100 = 14%

QUESTIONS

1. In a three-stage process, the molar yields of the individual stages are 50%, 40% and 75%. What is the overall molar percentage yield?

Different functional groups are related to each other by organic reactions. The interconnections between the more significant synthetic reactions you have learned are shown in Figure 2.

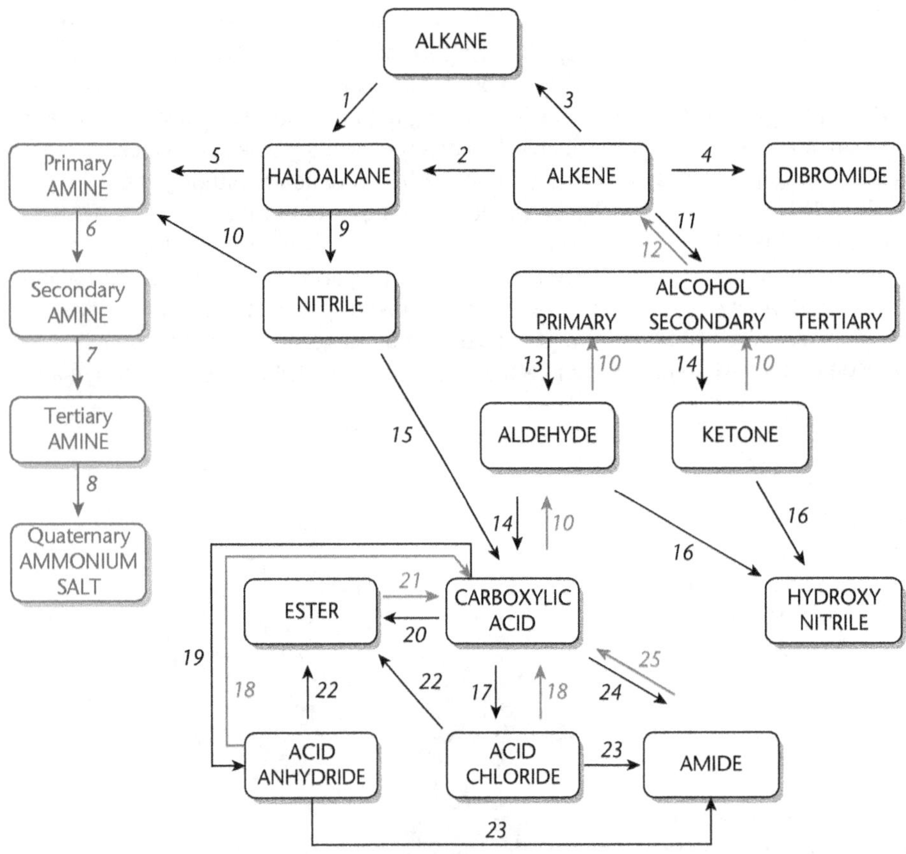

Figure 2 *The interconnections between different functional groups (continued)*

	Reaction type	Reactants and reaction conditions
1	Free-radical substitution	Halogen with UV light to initiate
2	Electrophilic addition	Aqueous HBr (gives bromoalkane)
3	Reduction	H_2 and Ni
4	Electrophilic addition	Aqueous Br_2
5	Nucleophilic substitution	Excess concentrated NH_3 in ethanol solvent; heat
6	Nucleophilic substitution	Halogenoalkane in ethanol solvent; heat
7	Nucleophilic substitution	Excess halogenoalkane in ethanol solvent; heat
8	Nucleophilic substitution	Large excess of halogenoalkane in ethanol; heat
9	Nucleophilic substitution	KCN in ethanol; heat
10	Reduction	$LiAlH_4$ in ethoxyethane solvent
11	Electrophilic addition – hydration	Catalytic H_2SO_4 in water
12	Elimination – dehydration	Concentrated H_2SO_4; heat
13	Partial oxidation	$K_2Cr_2O_7$ and dilute H_2SO_4; distil
14	Full oxidation	Excess $K_2Cr_2O_7$ and dilute H_2SO_4
15	Hydrolysis	Heat with dilute H_2SO_4
16	Nucleophilic addition	Concentrated solution of HCN and acidification
17	Nucleophilic substitution	PCl_5 or $SOCl_2$
18	Nucleophilic substitution – hydrolysis	H_2O
19	Nucleophilic substitution	P_2O_5
20	Nucleophilic substitution – condensation	Alcohol with concentrated H_2SO_4
21	Nucleophilic substitution – hydrolysis	Aqueous NaOH; heat and then dilute acid
22	Nucleophilic substitution – condensation	Alcohol and a base
23	Nucleophilic substitution – condensation	Ammonia or amine
24	Nucleophilic substitution – dehydration	Amine and heat
25	Nucleophilic substitution – hydrolysis	5 mol dm^{-3} HCl; heat for 24 hours

Figure 2 *The interconnections between different functional groups*

Owing to delocalisation effects in aromatic molecules, functional groups bonded directly to a benzene ring are likely to behave differently from those bonded to saturated structures. This is often an important consideration when selecting reactions to achieve a particular synthesis (Figure 3).

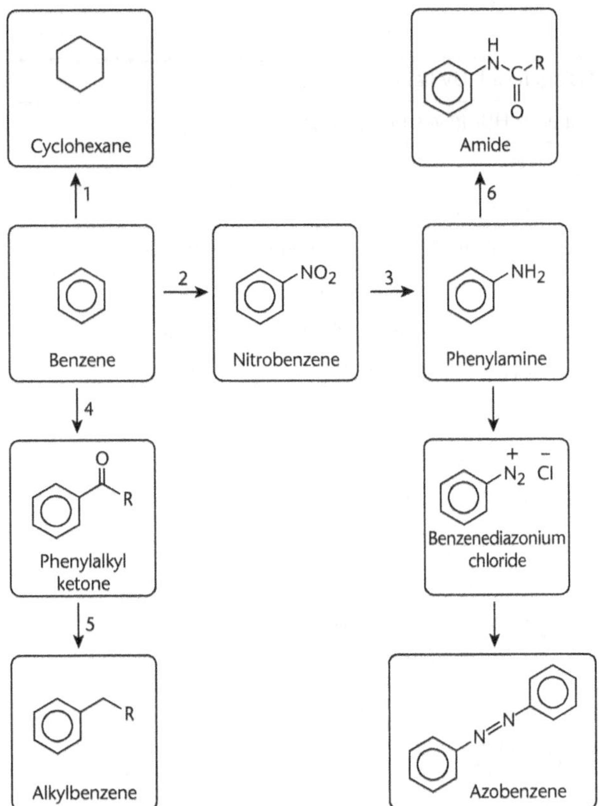

	Reaction type	Reactants and reaction conditions
1	Reduction	H_2 + Ni catalyst at 150 °C
2	Electrophilic substitution (nitration)	Concentrated H_2SO_4 + concentrated. HNO_3 at 50 °C
3	Reduction	Sn + concentrated HCl followed by NaOH
4	Electrophilic substitution (Friedel–Crafts)	Acyl chloride + $AlCl_3$; heat
5	Reduction	Zn + concentrated HCl
6	Nucleophilic substitution (acylation)	Acyl chloride

Figure 3 *The interconnections between different functional groups*

In organic synthesis, the molecule that we wish to prepare is called the **target molecule** and the chemicals used at the start of the synthesis are known as **starting materials**.

QUESTIONS

2. State the reagent(s) and conditions needed to achieve each of the following conversions. Write equations for the reactions that occur.
   a. $CH_3CH_2CH(OH)CH_3$ to $CH_3CH_2COCH_3$
   b. $CH_3CH_2CH_2OH$ to $CH_3CH_2CH_2OCOCH_3$
   c. $CH_3CH_2CH_2CH_2OH$ to $CH_3CH_2CH=CH_2$
   d. $CH_3CH_2CH_2COOH$ to $CH_3CH_2CH_2CH_2OH$
   e. CH_3CH_2Br to $CH_3CH_2NH_2$
3. State the reagent(s) and conditions needed to achieve each of the following two-step conversions:
   a. An alkene to a ketone.
   b. An alkane to a primary amine.
   c. A halogenoalkane to a carboxylic acid.

When devising a synthesis of a target molecule, it is often easier to work backwards from the target molecule to arrive at the starting materials using your knowledge of what carbon groups need to be 'joined' and what functional groups need to be created.

Worked example

How would you prepare the molecule **A** (Figure 4) from bromocyclohexane?

A

Figure 4 *Structure of A*

The target molecule **A** contains an extra carbon atom compared with cyclohexane. Amines can be made by the reduction of nitriles with $LiAlH_4$. The reaction of KCN in ethanol as solvent with a halogenoalkane increases the number of carbon atoms by one.

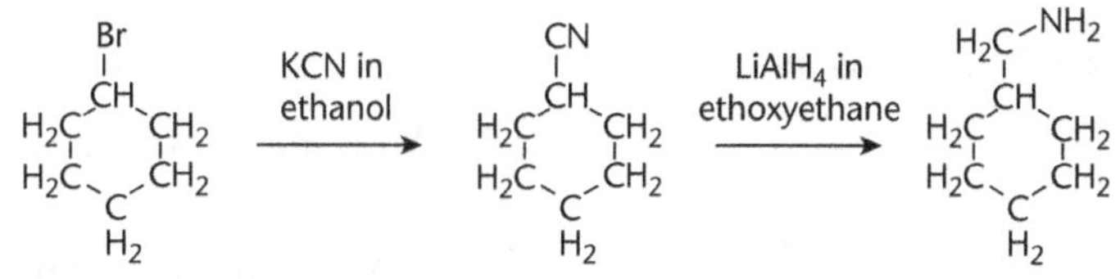

Bromocyclohexane —(KCN in ethanol)→ cyanocyclohexane —($LiAlH_4$ in ethoxyethane)→ A

Figure 5 *Two-step synthesis of A. First step is nucleophilic substitution. Second step is hydrogenation.*

QUESTIONS

4. Devise reaction schemes for each of the following syntheses:
   a. propanone from propene
   b. ethyl ethanoate from ethanol
   c. aminobenzene from benzene.

Stretch and challenge

5. There are two routes to make carboxylic acids from alkenes (each with three steps). Using ethene as an example, devise reaction schemes for each of these routes. Name the final product for each route.

Often there are a number of potential reaction pathways which could deliver a target molecule. When designing such a synthesis, many factors will influence your final choice of pathway. These include:

- the availability and cost of a suitable starting material from which the target molecule can be synthesised
- the number of stages needed to convert the starting material to the target molecule
- whether more than one product is formed during any stage, resulting in the need to purify a mixture
- the number and cost of any separation and purification processes required
- the percentage yield that can be expected from the overall process
- the mass of the desired product divided by the mass of reactants used, often expressed as a percentage
- the atom economy of the overall process
- the amount of waste generated from the overall process
- whether toxic or hazardous chemicals and solvents are required
- additional problems involved in scaling the synthesis to manufacturing proportions, particularly special designs for chemical plant and safety considerations.

QUESTIONS

6. Define atom economy.
7. Two potential syntheses of a target molecule **D** have been proposed (Figure 6).

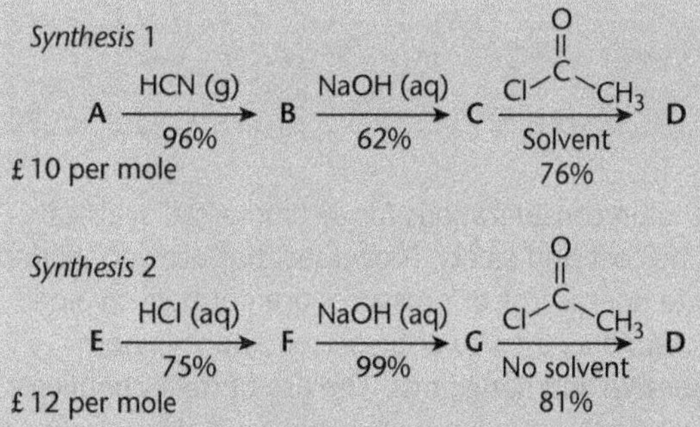

Synthesis 1

A (£10 per mole) —HCN (g), 96%→ B —NaOH (aq), 62%→ C —CH_3COCl, Solvent, 76%→ D

Synthesis 2

E (£12 per mole) —HCl (aq), 75%→ F —NaOH (aq), 99%→ G —CH_3COCl, No solvent, 81%→ D

Figure 6 *Two different syntheses of molecule D*

   a. Based upon the overall percentage yield, which synthesis is more efficient?
   b. Assuming the only difference in cost between the two syntheses is in the price of the starting materials **A** and **E**, which synthesis is more cost-efficient?
   c. Based upon safety considerations alone, which synthesis would you assess as being less hazardous and why?
   d. Which synthesis would you recommend and why?

8. Examine the reaction scheme in Figure 7.

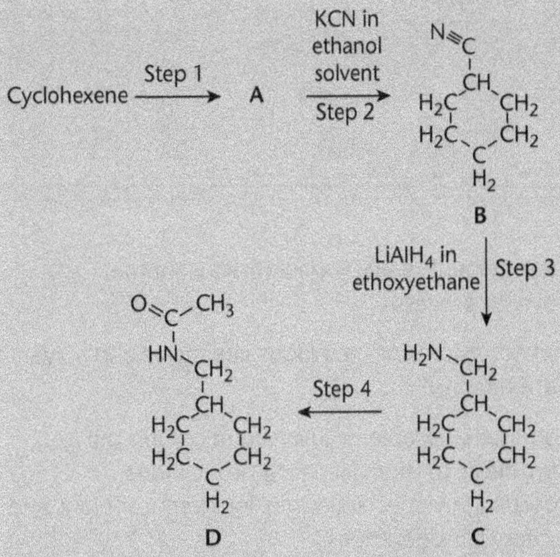

Cyclohexene —Step 1→ A —(KCN in ethanol solvent, Step 2)→ B (cyclohexane bearing $C \equiv N$: $N \equiv C$–CH with H_2C, CH_2, H_2C, CH_2, C H_2 ring)

B —(LiAlH₄ in ethoxyethane, Step 3)→ C (H_2N–CH_2–CH ring: H_2C, CH_2, H_2C, CH_2, C H_2)

C —Step 4→ D ($O{=}C$–CH_3, HN–CH_2–CH ring: H_2C, CH_2, H_2C, CH_2, C H_2)

Figure 7 Proposed synthesis of molecule D

a. Draw the structure of compound **A**.

b. Give the reagents required for step 1.

c. Name the type of reaction in step 3.

d. Reaction of **C** with ethanoyl chloride gives **D**. Outline a curly arrow mechanism for the reaction.

Stretch and challenge

9. The synthesis of a polymer **E** is shown in Figure 8.

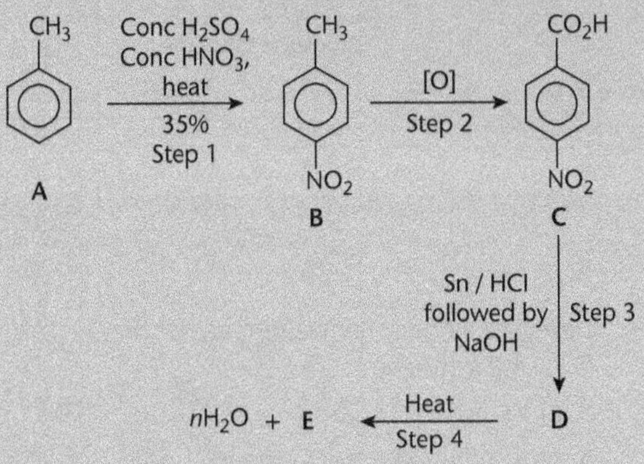

A (methylbenzene, CH_3) —(Conc H_2SO_4, Conc HNO_3, heat, 35%, Step 1)→ B (CH_3, NO_2) —([O], Step 2)→ C (CO_2H, NO_2)

C —(Sn / HCl followed by NaOH, Step 3)→ D

D —(Heat, Step 4)→ nH_2O + E

Figure 8 Proposed synthesis of a polymer

a. Give the IUPAC name of the product of step 1.

b. Nitration of methylbenzene **A** gives a low yield of **B**. Suggest a reason for this.

c. Name the mechanism for step 1.

d. Give a structure for compound **D**. Name the type of reaction in step 3.

e. Draw the structure of the polymer **E** produced from heating **D**, showing the repeat unit.

f. Is polymer **E** an addition or condensation polymer?

The main considerations for a commercial synthesis will be cost and safety. Processes that use very high or low temperatures or pressures are normally avoided if possible as the use of these conditions is both expensive and dangerous. The use of toxic chemicals and solvents must be minimised as these will be hazardous and will incur disposal and separation costs. If solvents must be used then non-flammable, easily recyclable and non-toxic ones should be considered.

ASSIGNMENT 1: SYNTHESIS OF A NEW DRUG

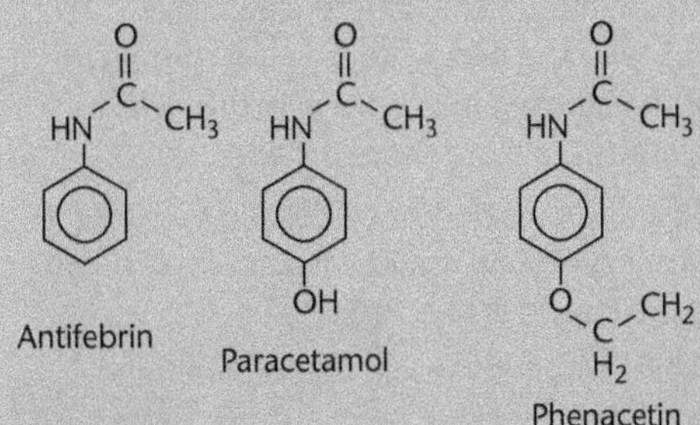

Figure A1 Structures of some painkillers

Antifebrin (Figure A1) is a painkiller that was first used in 1886. Very soon it was found to be toxic, and phenacetin was developed as a replacement. This was used until 1983, when it too was banned as it was found to increase the risk of developing cancer. Paracetamol was first marketed in 1950 and is still used today. The structures of all three drugs are similar and both antifebrin and phenacetin react with enzymes in the body, producing paracetamol.

You work in a pharmaceutical company and have been given the task of testing a number of molecules for their ability to replace paracetamol in the marketplace. Your first target is molecule **E** in Figure A2.

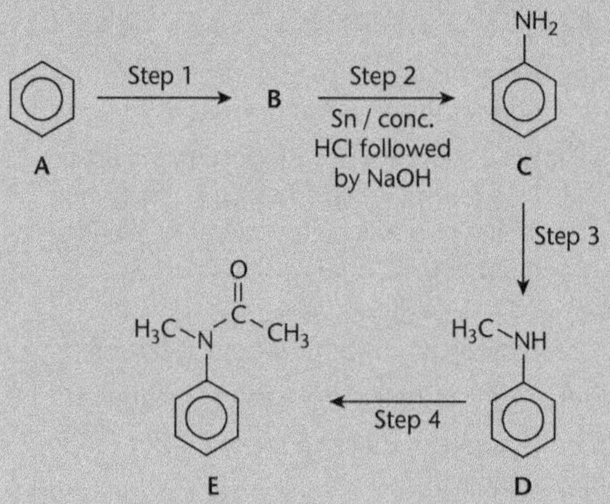

Figure A2 A proposed four-step synthesis of a new drug

The second target compound, **F** (Figure A3), has structural features similar to both paracetamol and ibuprofen.

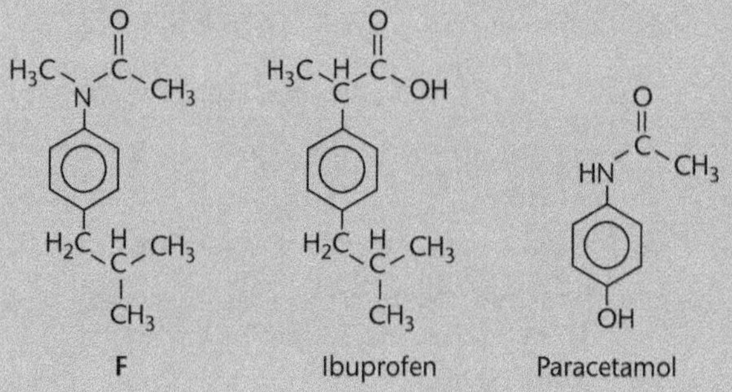

Figure A3 Structures of ibuprofen and other molecules

Questions

A1. Suggest a structure for the product of step 1.

A2. For step 1, give reagents and conditions, and name and draw the mechanism.

A3. Give the IUPAC name of the product of step 2.

A4. Give the IUPAC name of the product of step 3.

A5. For step 3, give reagents and conditions.

A6. In step 4, the product **E** can be prepared by acylating **D** with either ethanoyl chloride or ethanoic anhydride. Which of these reagents is more likely to be used industrially and why?

A7. State whether ibuprofen and compounds **F** and **G** (Figure A4) exhibit optical isomerism. For those that do, circle the chiral carbon atom.

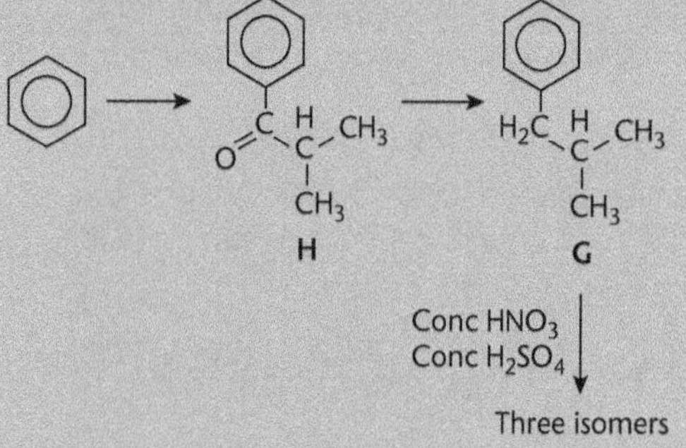

Figure A4 See Questions A8–A10

A8. Name the reagents needed for the formation of **H** from benzene.

A9. Reaction of **G** with concentrated nitric acid and concentrated sulfuric acid gives a mixture of three isomers. Draw the structures of each isomer.

A10. Draw the curly arrow mechanism for the formation of 4-nitro-2-methylpropylbenzene from 2-methylpropylbenzene, **G**. What is the electrophile in the reaction? How is it formed?

KEY IDEAS

- A synthesis should be designed to minimise the use of hazardous chemicals and solvents.
- A synthesis should have as few steps as possible and a high atom economy to minimise waste.

PRACTICE QUESTIONS

1. The compound $(CH_3CH_2)_2NH$ can be made from ethene in a three step synthesis as shown here:

$$\text{ethene} \xrightarrow{\text{Step 1}} F \xrightarrow{\text{Step 2}} G \xrightarrow{\text{Step 3}} (CH_3CH_2)_2NH$$

   a. Name the compound $(CH_3CH_2)_2NH$.

   b. Identify compounds **F** and **G**.

   c. For the reactions in Steps **1**, **2** and **3**:
      - Give a reagent or reagents.
      - Name the mechanism.

   Balanced equations and mechanisms using curly arrows are **not** required.

   d. Identify one organic impurity in the product of step 3 and give a reason for its formation.

AQA January 2011 Question 7

2. Chemists have to design synthetic routes to convert one organic compound into another.

CH_3CH_2-CHO —Step 1 (HCN)→ $CH_3CH_2-CH(OH)-CN$

—Step 2→ $CH_3CH_2-CH(Br)-CN$

—Step 3→ $CH_3CH_2-CH(NH_2)-CN$

—Step 4→ $CH_3CH_2-CH(NH_2)-COOH$

X

   a. Name and outline a mechanism for Step **1**.

   b. Give the IUPAC name of the product in Step **2**.

   c. For Step **3**, give the reagent, give a necessary condition and name the mechanism.

   d. At room temperature, the amino acid **X** exists as a solid.

      i. Draw the structure of the species present in the solid amino acid.

      ii. With reference to your answer to part (d)(i), explain why the melting point of the amino acid **X** is higher than the melting point of $CH_3CH_2CH_2(OH)COOH$.

   Propanone can be converted into 2-bromopropane by a three step synthesis.

   Step 1: propanone is reduced to compound **L**.

   Step 2: compound **L** is converted into compound **M**.

   Step 3: compound **M** reacts to form 2-bromopropane.

   Deduce the structures of **L** and **M**.

   For each of the three steps, suggest a reagent that could be used and name the mechanism.

   Equations and curly arrows are **not** required.

AQA January 2012 Question 11

3. A possible synthesis of the amino acid **X** is shown here:

   a. There are many structural isomers of **X**, $CH_3CH_2CH(NH_2)COOH$.

      i. Draw a structural isomer of **X** that is an ethyl ester.

      ii. Draw a structural isomer of **X** that is an amide and also a tertiary alcohol.

      iii. Draw a structural isomer of **X** that has an unbranched carbon chain and can be polymerised to form a polyamide.

   b. Draw the structure of the tertiary amine formed when **X** reacts with bromoethane.

AQA June 2012 Question 5

13 NMR AND CHROMATOGRAPHY

PRIOR KNOWLEDGE

You will already have studied how to use various analytical techniques to identify functional groups and learned how to use mass spectrometry and infrared spectroscopy to confirm the structure of a molecule (*see chapters 11 and 16 of Year 1 Student Book*).

LEARNING OBJECTIVES

In this chapter you will build on these analytical techniques by understanding how nuclear magnetic resonance (NMR) can be used to identify molecules. You will be able to use ^{1}H and ^{13}C NMR spectra to suggest possible structures for molecules. You will also learn how different forms of chromatography can be used to purify and identify components of a mixture.

(Specification 3.3.15 and 3.3.16)

Magnetic resonance imaging (MRI) enables nuclear magnetic resonance (NMR) to generate three-dimensional images. MRI scanners are powerful tools for medical diagnosis. These scanners provide fast and accurate diagnosis of a very wide range of illnesses by observing the varying water content of living tissues.

NMR spectroscopy has been used by chemists regularly since the 1950s. Utilising the magnetic properties of atomic nuclei, NMR helps chemists to deduce molecular structures by pinpointing and counting the positions of atoms, such as hydrogen atoms, in molecules. It is one of the most powerful spectroscopic techniques for confirming the structure of molecules. In recent years, the sensitivity of NMR instruments has increased so that very large proteins and enzymes can have their structures accurately determined from milligram quantities. Modern NMR spectrometers utilise superconducting electromagnets cooled to 4 K with liquid helium.

Figure 1 *A laboratory technician placing plant extracts in an NMR spectrometer for analysis. The NMR spectrometer uses the same technology as MRI scanners in hospitals.*

13.1 NUCLEAR MAGNETIC RESONANCE SPECTROSCOPY

Spectroscopic methods involve making observations of how molecules are affected when subjected to electromagnetic radiation. In nuclear magnetic resonance (known as NMR or n.m.r.) spectroscopy the part of the electromagnetic spectrum that is used is the radio frequency region (Figure 2).

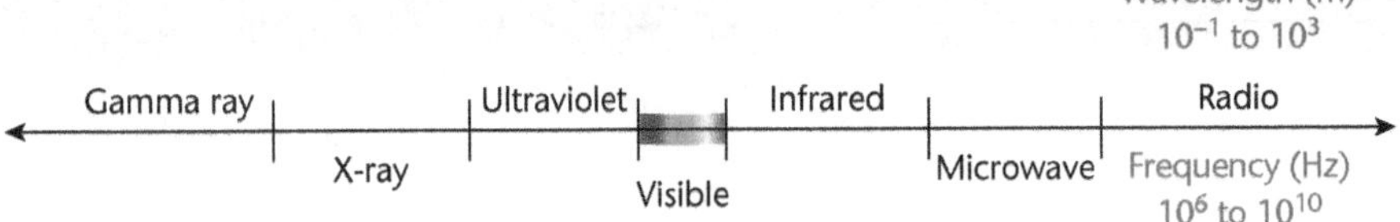

Figure 2 *NMR spectroscopy uses the radio frequency region of the electromagnetic spectrum*

The nuclei of some atoms (such as ^{1}H and ^{13}C but not ^{12}C) have a property known as **nuclear spin**. Nuclei that possess spin have their own **magnetic field**, and can be considered to behave as if they are small bar magnets (Figure 3). In an external magnetic field these bar magnets can align either with the external field (lower-energy state) or opposite to it (higher-energy state) (Figure 4).

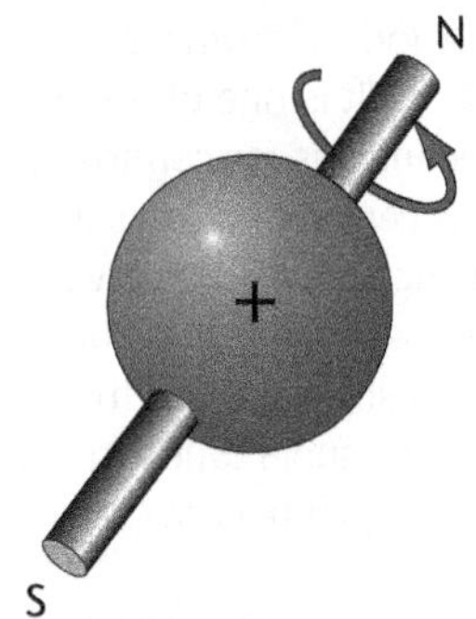

Figure 3 *A nucleus with spin can be considered as if it was a small bar magnet*

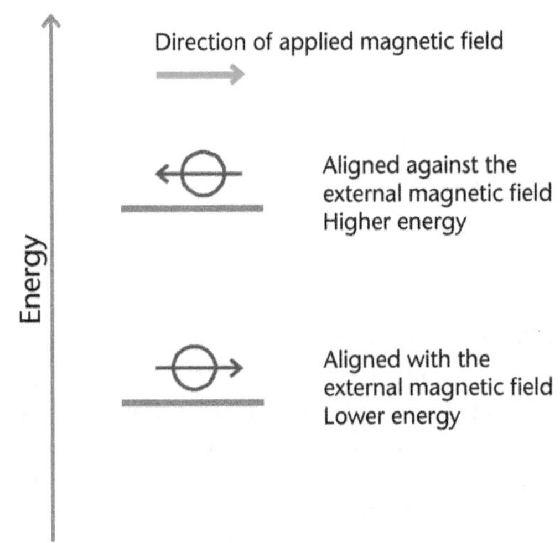

Figure 4 *The nuclear spin (bar magnet) of an atom can align either with an external magnetic field (lower energy) or against it (higher energy)*

If a molecule in a strong magnetic field is irradiated with radio frequency electromagnetic waves, the nuclei of some of the atoms can absorb the radio waves and move from the low-energy to the high-energy state. These absorptions, called **resonances**, occur at different energies depending upon the surrounding environment of the atom. The different resonance energies can then be used to identify atoms, count them and work out their positions in the molecule relative to other atoms. It is this behaviour that leads to the production of an NMR spectrum.

In practice, instead of keeping the external magnetic field constant and changing the radio frequency until resonance occurs, we keep the radio frequency constant and change the external magnetic field.

13.2 PROTON (^{1}H) NMR SPECTROSCOPY

The hydrogen atom (^{1}H) is particularly useful for investigation by NMR because of the large number of hydrogen atoms in almost all organic compounds. This is often referred to as proton NMR because the nucleus of this atom is a single proton.

Not all the ^{1}H nuclei in an organic sample will resonate at the same magnetic field strength for a particular radio frequency. ^{1}H nuclei that have different neighbouring atoms (said to have different **chemical environments**) absorb at slightly different external field strengths. The different environments are said to cause a **chemical shift** of the absorption. If the value of the external field is recorded as the different resonances occur, a spectrum, known as an NMR spectrum, can be produced, as in Figure 5 (the horizontal scale is the chemical-shift δ-scale in units of parts per million, ppm; see later for an explanation of this scale).

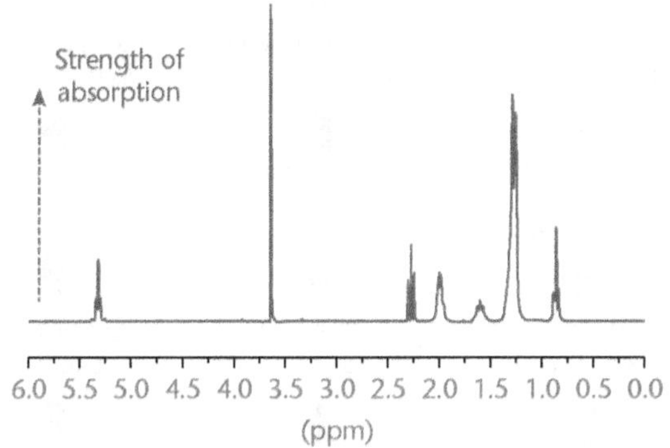

Figure 5 *The ^1H NMR spectrum of biodiesel. ^1H nuclei in different chemical environments resonate at different chemical shifts (horizontal scale).*

The ^1H nuclei in bromoethane have two distinct chemical environments and will produce two resonances. The H's of the CH_2 group (red in Figure 6) next to the bromine atom are in a different chemical environment from the H's of the CH_3 group (blue).

```
    H   H
    |   |
H — C — C — Br
    |   |
    H   H
```

Figure 6 *Equivalent ^1H nuclei in bromoethane*

Worked example

How many different ^1H chemical environments occur in 1-bromopropane?

```
    H   H   H
    |   |   |
H — C — C — C — Br
    |   |   |
    H   H   H
```

There are three. The two in red are the same, the two in blue are the same and the three in green are the same. The ^1H NMR spectrum would have three resonances.

Chemical shifts, in ppm, are related to the electron density *near* the resonating nucleus. If the electron density around the resonating nucleus is low as a result of bonding to an electronegative group of atoms or a delocalised system, the nucleus is said to be 'deshielded' and the resonance occurs at a higher ppm value. For example, the ^1H's in a CH_3 group attached to another carbon atom resonate at approximately 1 ppm, whereas if attached to an oxygen atom they resonate around 4 ppm. If the nucleus is next to an electropositive group then the nucleus is 'shielded' and appears at lower ppm values (Figure 7).

Preparation of samples for NMR spectroscopy

Samples are investigated in dilute solution. This separates the sample molecules from each other, preventing them from interacting and causing very complex absorptions.

The choice of solvent is important. When investigating ^1H atoms, tetrachloromethane (CCl_4) or deuterated trichloromethane ($CDCl_3$) is commonly used because these are very powerful solvents for organic compounds and do not contain ^1H atoms. This means that they do not resonate and so do not interfere with the ^1H NMR spectrum of the sample.

During the production of an NMR spectrum, tetramethylsilane (TMS) (Figure 8) is mixed with the sample. This is added to provide a reference point to which the NMR spectrometer is tuned. The magnetic field is adjusted until the ^1H nuclei of TMS resonate: this is given a chemical-shift value of 0.

TMS is used for these reasons:

- Silicon has a very low electronegativity. As a result, the hydrogen nuclei in TMS resonate at a field strength well above that of any ^1H nuclei in common organic molecules.
- It gives one strong, sharp, easily detected absorption because the absorption is caused by the combined effects of 12 equivalent ^1H atoms (equivalent atoms are those in identical chemical environments, usually due to symmetry within the molecule).

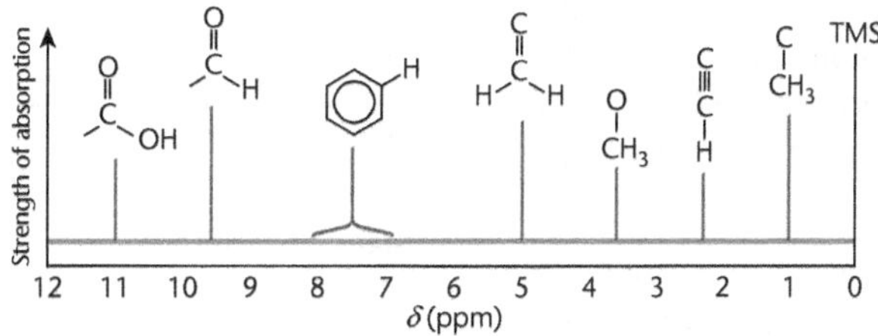

Figure 7 *Chemical shifts of ^1H nuclei (in ppm) of some common functional groups with TMS as a reference*

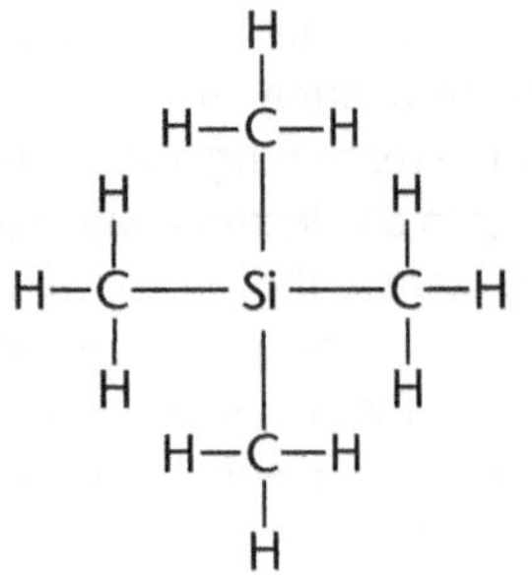

Figure 8 Tetramethylsilane (TMS) is used as a reference point to calibrate the spectrum. The value of delta is zero. It has 12 equivalent protons in the same environment that give an intense peak.

- TMS is non-toxic and cheap.
- It does not react with the sample.
- TMS is easily separated from the sample molecule because it has a low boiling point.

The δ-scale in NMR spectroscopy

The chemical shifts of ^1H atoms in a sample molecule are measured and tabulated relative to the TMS reference absorption, which is given the value zero on a scale called the δ-scale. The value of the external magnetic field that causes a particular proton to resonate depends on the radio frequency that the NMR spectrometer uses. This means that chemical shifts would vary from machine to machine, making comparisons difficult. The use of a reference compound (TMS) and a scale for chemical shift without units (the δ-scale) avoids this problem. Because chemical shifts on the δ-scale are small, we multiply the actual differences by 10^6 and quote the units of the scale as parts per million (ppm).

Low-resolution ^1H NMR spectra

A low-resolution NMR spectrum of ethanol (Figure 10) shows three absorptions (A, B and C) because the ethanol molecule contains three sets of ^1H atoms, each in a different chemical environment. Signal A is produced by the three equivalent ^1H atoms in the CH_3 group, signal B by the two equivalent ^1H atoms in the CH_2 group and signal C by the single ^1H atom in the OH group. Notice that signal C has the largest chemical shift because the ^1H atom is directly bonded to an electronegative oxygen atom. Signal B has a larger chemical shift than A because the CH_2 group is nearer to the electronegative oxygen atom than the CH_3 group is.

The strengths of the absorptions are proportional to the number of equivalent ^1H atoms causing the absorption. The strengths of the absorptions are

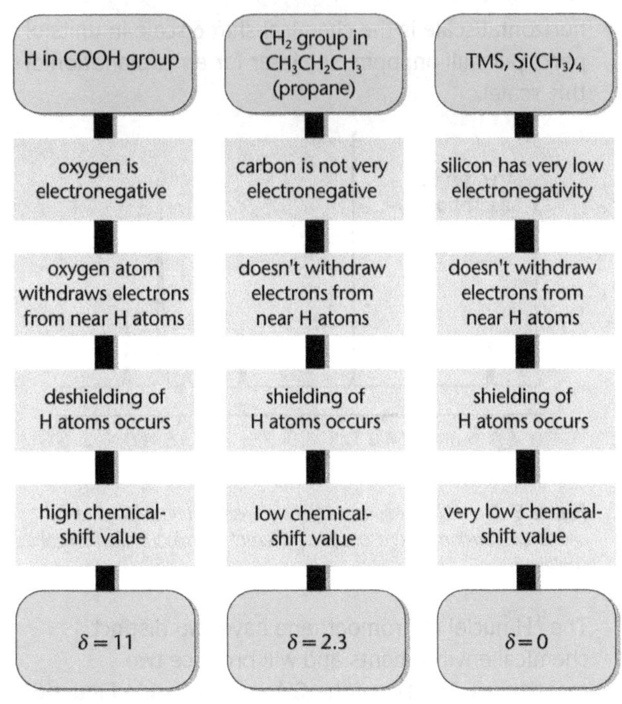

Figure 9 Explanation of chemical shifts

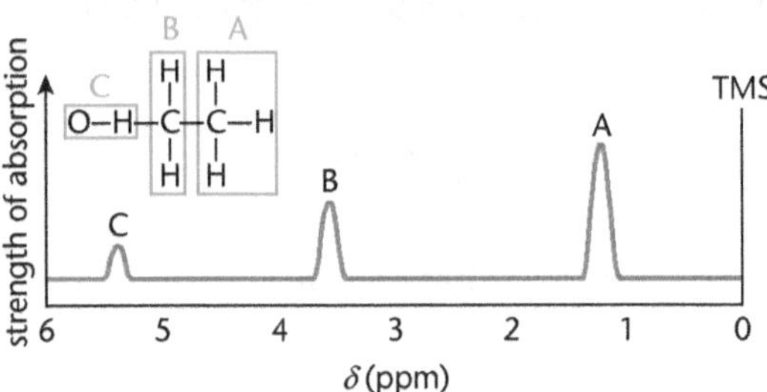

Figure 10 A low-resolution ^1H NMR spectrum of ethanol

measured by the area under each absorption peak. Hence, the areas of absorptions A, B and C in the spectrum of ethanol are in the ratio of 3 : 2 : 1. In modern spectrometers these are measured electronically and superimposed digitally or graphically on the main spectrum (blue text in Figure 11). This is called the **integrated spectrum**.

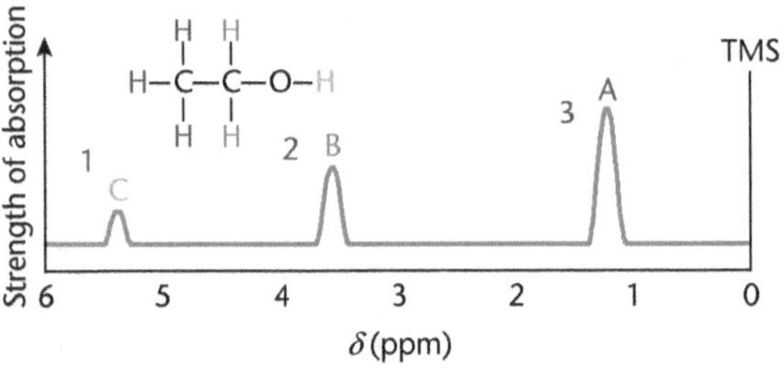

Figure 11 The distances between the plateaux in the integrated spectrum represent the areas under the absorption peaks. The ratio of these distances gives the ratio of the numbers of ^1H atoms in each equivalent group.

QUESTIONS

1. Explain why the three hydrogen atoms of the CH_3 group in ethanol are chemically equivalent.
2. Deduce the number of different chemical environments for the ^1H nuclei and hence the number of absorptions in the low-resolution NMR spectra of:
   a. benzene
   b. propane
   c. propanal
   d. propanone
   e. ethanoic acid
   f. 2-methylpropanol.
3. For compounds b and c in Question 2, deduce the ratios of the areas under the absorptions.
4. Why does the hydrogen atom of an aldehyde group

   absorb at a much higher chemical shift than the hydrogen atom of an alkene group?

5. Without looking at tables of NMR chemical-shift values, predict which of the three following $-CH_2$ groups would occur at the highest chemical shift and which of them at the lowest chemical shift: $-CH_2NH_2$, $-CH_2F$, $-CH_2OH$.

High-resolution ^1H NMR spectra

When examined with a more sensitive spectrometer, some of the basic signals in the ^1H NMR spectrum of ethanol are split into groups of signals. The CH_3 signal (A in Figure 12) is split into three, producing what is called a **triplet**, while the CH_2 signal (B) is split to form a **quartet**. The OH signal (C) is not split – it appears as a **singlet**. This splitting of the absorptions is caused by the influence of ^1H atoms bonded to neighbouring atoms, and the influence is called a **coupling effect**.

Coupling in high-resolution ^1H NMR spectra

Each spinning ^1H nucleus generates a slight magnetic field. When a particular ^1H nucleus resonates in an applied magnetic field, the actual magnetic field that

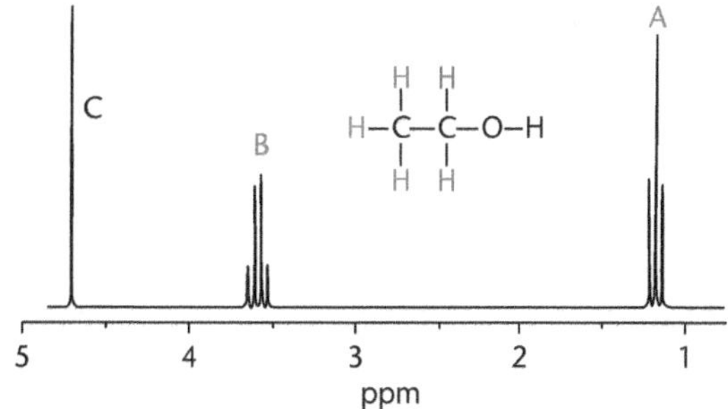

Figure 12 *The high-resolution spectrum of ethanol, showing the coupling effect*

acts on it is the sum of the applied field and the fields from all its neighbours. Thus the ^1H atoms are linked through space (**coupled**) by the interactions of their neighbours (Figures 13 and 14).

The magnetic field from a single neighbouring ^1H nucleus on the next carbon along the chain (Figure 13) may act with or against the applied magnetic field. There is a 50 : 50 chance of either. This means that the three equivalent ^1H nuclei of a CH_3 group will resonate either at a slightly lower applied field or at a slightly higher applied field. The end result is that the original resonance is split into a doublet in a ratio of 1 : 1.

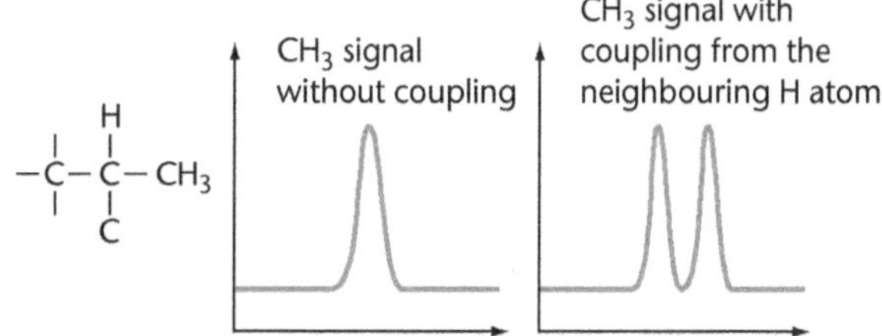

Figure 13 *Coupling to one neighbouring H atom leads to a doublet*

For two equivalent neighbouring ^1H atoms, their magnetic fields could be *both* with the applied field, or *both* against it, or *one with while the other is against*. This means that the three equivalent ^1H nuclei of the CH_3 group are coupled to the two neighbours in three different ways. The result is a triplet. The intensities of each of the peaks that make up the triplet are in the ratio 1 : 2 : 1. These are the relative probabilities of the two neighbours' fields adding with, cancelling out or adding against the applied field (Table 1).

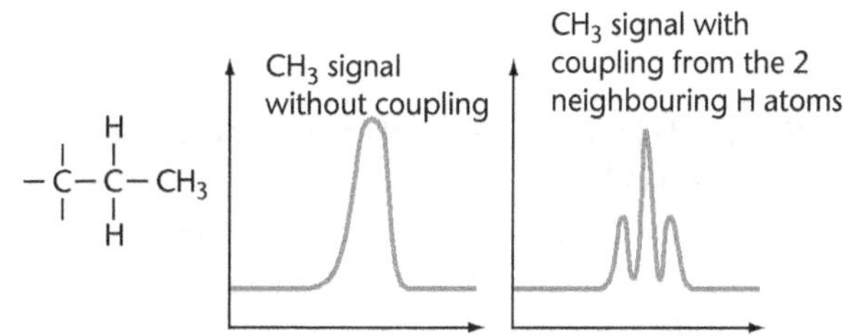

Figure 14 *Coupling to two neighbouring H atoms leads to a triplet*

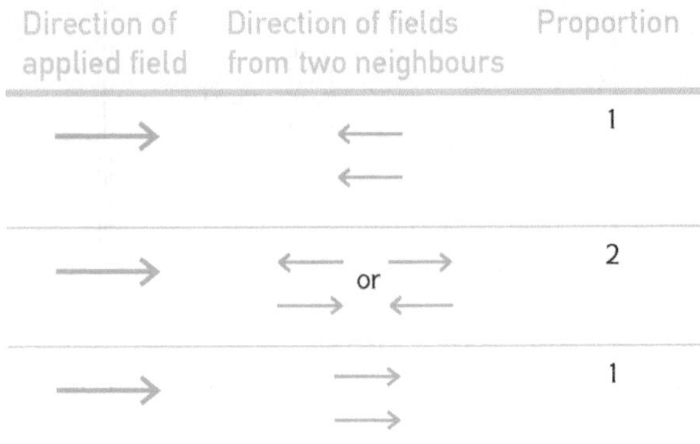

Direction of applied field	Direction of fields from two neighbours	Proportion
→	← ←	1
→	← → or → ←	2
→	→ →	1

Table 1 *Triplet signals are formed in a ratio of 1 : 2 : 1*

Coupling occurs only between H atoms on *adjacent* carbon atoms. Because the magnetic fields involved are so weak, coupling with 'next-door-but-one' neighbours is negligible and can be ignored. Equivalent H atoms *do not* couple with each other.

Table 2 summarises the pattern of significant couplings, all of which can be summarised by the $n + 1$ rule, which states the following:

The NMR absorption of a proton that has n equivalent neighbouring protons is split into n + 1 peaks.

Number of equivalent neighbouring (coupled) ^1H atoms	Splitting effect	Resulting signal	Ratio
1	into 2 signals	doublet	1:1
2	into 3 signals	triplet	1:2:1
3	into 4 signals	quartet	1:3:3:1
n	into $n + 1$ signals	$n + 1$ peaks	

Table 2 *Coupling patterns*

QUESTIONS

6. The ^1H NMR spectrum of ethyl ethanoate is shown in Figure 16.
   a. Referring to H atoms, how many different chemical environments are there in ethyl ethanoate?

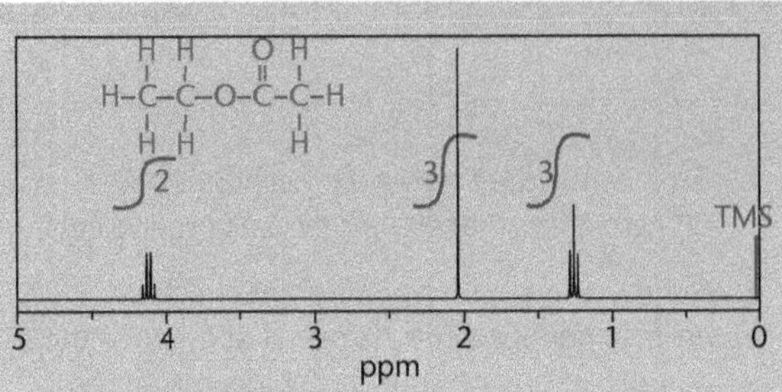

Figure 16 *^1H NMR spectrum of ethyl ethanoate. Each integrated trace $^3\int$ indicates the number of hydrogen atoms in that particular environment.*

   b. Using integration *only* (the areas under the peaks), identify the resonance produced by the CH_2 group. State why the signal is split, and explain the splitting observed using the $n + 1$ rule.
   c. Identify the resonances associated with the CH_3 groups. Which one is which? Justify your answer by referring to:
      i. the chemical shift
      ii. the coupling in the signals.

Coupling of ^1H nuclei can occur with H atoms on two different *adjacent* carbon atoms. For example, the CH_2 signal in propane (blue in Figure 17) is observed as a heptet because it has six neighbouring equivalent H atoms ($n + 1$ rule), three on either side in two equivalent CH_3 groups. This is associated with the symmetry of the propane molecule. The CH_3 groups (red) produce identical triplets by coupling with the CH_2 group.

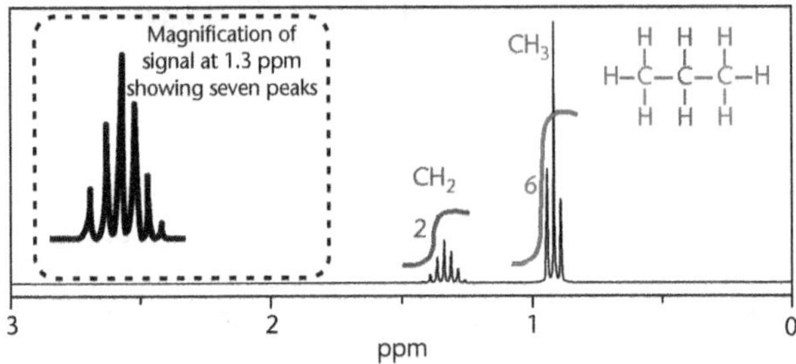

Figure 17 *^1H NMR spectrum of propane*

QUESTIONS

7. Two isomers, isomer 1 and isomer 2 in Figure 18, were studied by ^{1}H NMR spectroscopy.

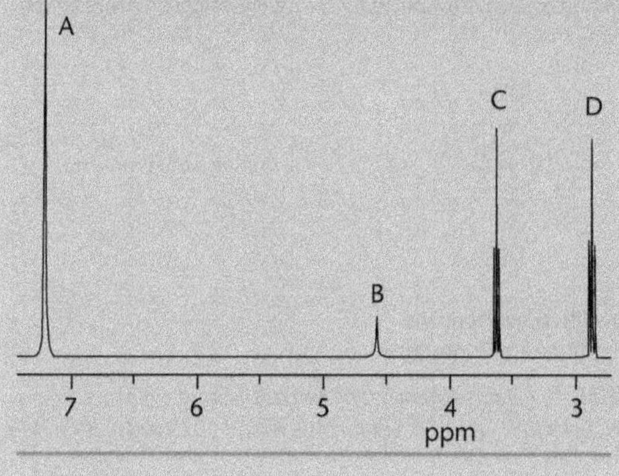


```
     H H                      H     H
     | |                      |     |
(Ph)-C-C-O-H           (Ph)-C-O-C-H
     | |                      |     |
     H H                      H     H
   Isomer 1                 Isomer 2
```

Figure 18 ^{1}H *NMR of an isomer*

a. Which of the isomers produced the spectrum shown in Figure 18?

b. The spectrum has not been integrated. Predict the ratio of the areas under the peaks A, B, C and D.

c. Explain the position and splitting of the peak C.

d. D_2O was added to the NMR sample and the peak B disappeared. Explain this observation.

8. The ^{1}H NMR spectra of two isomeric bromides are shown in Figure 19.

a. Match each isomer to its ^{1}H NMR spectrum.

b. Explain the reasons why the quartet (resonance A) in spectrum A is at a higher chemical shift than the quartet (resonance D) in spectrum B.

c. Predict the ratio of the measured areas under the peaks D, E and F.

```
    H O    H H           H       Br H
    | ||   | |           |       |  |
 Br-C-C-O-C-C-H       H-C-O-C-C-C-H
    |      | |           |   || |  |
    H      H H           H   O  H  H
      Isomer 1              Isomer 2
```

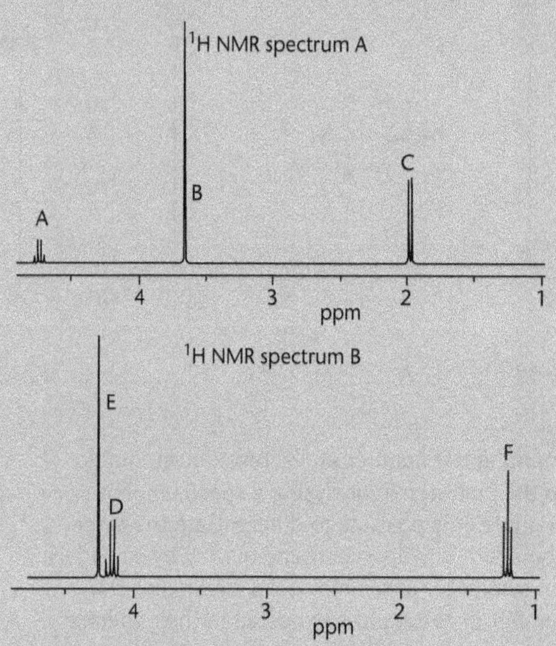

Figure 19 ^{1}H *NMR of two isomers*

13.3 CARBON (^{13}C) NMR SPECTROSCOPY

Although we cannot use ^{12}C nuclei in NMR, we can use the isotope ^{13}C. This isotope has a low natural abundance (1.1%), which means that the probability of two ^{13}C atoms being bonded to one another is very low. Consequently, coupling between two adjacent ^{13}C atoms is not observed and ^{13}C spectra are much easier to analyse than ^{1}H spectra, consisting only of a series of singlet resonances.

Type of carbon	Typical ppm range
Saturated C–C	0–50
Saturated C–O	50–100
Aromatic or C = C	100–160
Carbonyl C = O	160–220

Table 3 *Typical ranges of* ^{13}C *resonances for different types of carbon atom*

Carbon atoms in different chemical environments will give resonances at different chemical shifts in a ^{13}C spectrum. As with ^{1}H NMR spectroscopy, the resonances of carbon atoms attached to electronegative elements occur at higher chemical shifts, as do those of aromatic and alkene carbon atoms. The chemical-shift scale in ^{13}C NMR typically ranges from 0 to 200 ppm (Table 3), and we again use TMS as a reference point at 0 ppm. The ^{13}C spectrum of ethanol consists of two resonances, with the resonance at higher chemical shift (A in Figure 20) assigned to the carbon atom attached to the electronegative oxygen atom. Unlike the case in ^{1}H NMR spectroscopy, it is not possible to determine how many carbons each resonance represents using integration.

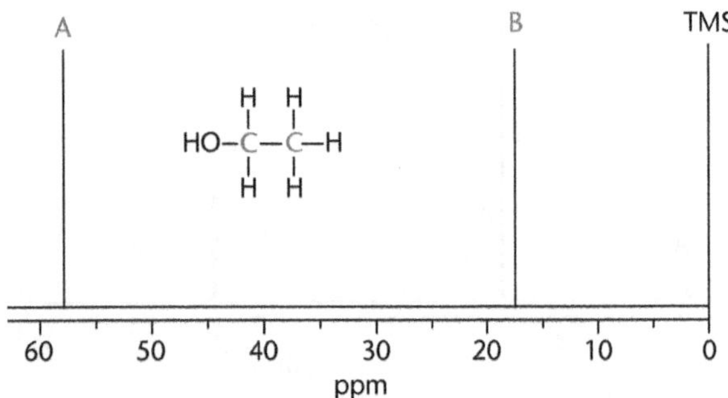

Figure 20 *The ^{13}C spectrum of ethanol*

Counting the number of ^{13}C resonances should be the first step in analysing a spectrum. For example, it is possible to differentiate the three isomers of dihydroxybenzene quickly by considering the symmetry of the molecules and hence the number of resonances expected in their spectra (Figures 21 and 22).

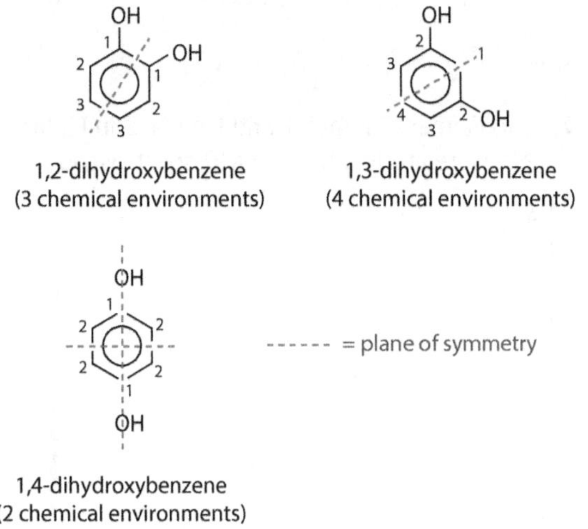

1,2-dihydroxybenzene
(3 chemical environments)

1,3-dihydroxybenzene
(4 chemical environments)

1,4-dihydroxybenzene
(2 chemical environments)

------ = plane of symmetry

Figure 21 *The symmetry of the molecules dictates how many different carbon chemical environments will be observed in ^{13}C NMR spectra*

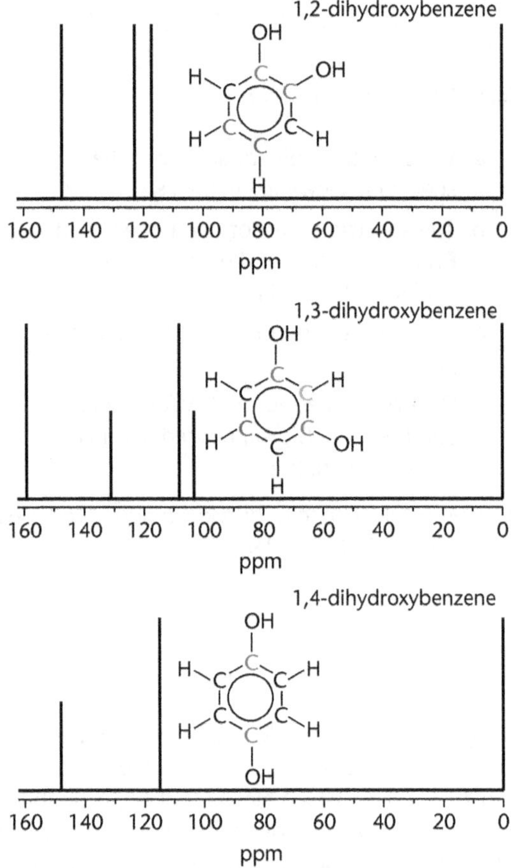

Figure 22 *The ^{13}C NMR spectra of the three isomers of dihydroxybenzene. The relative heights of the peaks in a spectrum indicate the number of carbons in each different chemical environment.*

QUESTIONS

9. Deduce the number of different chemical environments of the ^{13}C nuclei and hence the number of absorptions in the ^{13}C NMR spectra of the following:
   a. benzene
   b. propane
   c. propanal
   d. propanone
   e. ethanoic acid
   f. 2-methylpropanol
   g. 1,4-dimethylbenzene
   h. 1,3-dichlorobenzene.

10. You have been given four different samples of alcohols with the formula $C_4H_{10}O$.
    a. Draw the four alcohol isomers of $C_4H_{10}O$.
    b. For each isomer, deduce the number of different chemical environments expected in the ^{13}C NMR spectrum.
    c. The ^{13}C NMR spectra of two of the isomers are shown in Figure 23. Deduce which of the two isomers produced spectra 1 and 2.

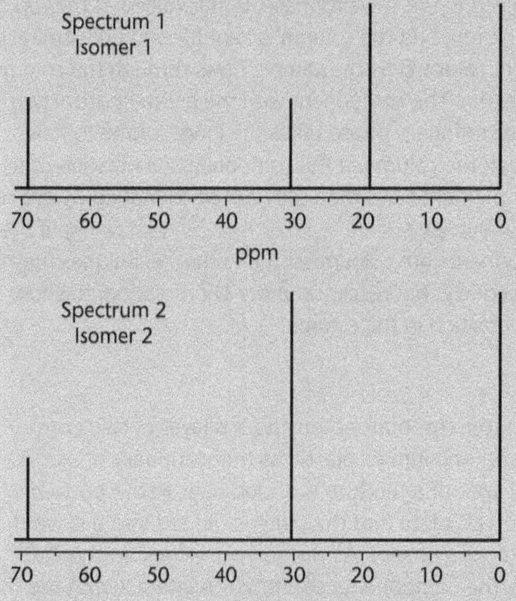

Figure 23 *The ^{13}C NMR spectra of isomers 1 and 2 of $C_4H_{10}O$*

    d. The two remaining isomers were analysed by ^1H NMR spectroscopy. The ^1H NMR spectrum of one of these remaining isomers, isomer 3, is shown in Figure 24. The ratio of the areas under each resonance is given as numbers above the resonances. Based upon the integration, deduce the structure of this isomer.

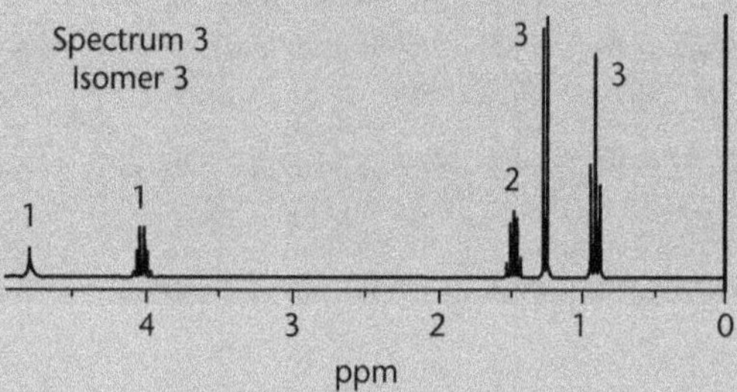

Figure 24 *The ^1H NMR spectrum of isomer 3 of $C_4H_{10}O$*

    e. Explain the splitting of the doublet resonance at 1.25 ppm in spectrum 3.
    f. When a drop of D_2O was added to isomer 3 and the ^1H NMR spectrum obtained, the singlet at 4.75 ppm was absent. Suggest a reason for this.
    g. Assign each of the resonances A, B, C and D in the ^{13}C spectrum (Figure 25) of the remaining isomer to the carbon atoms in isomer 4.

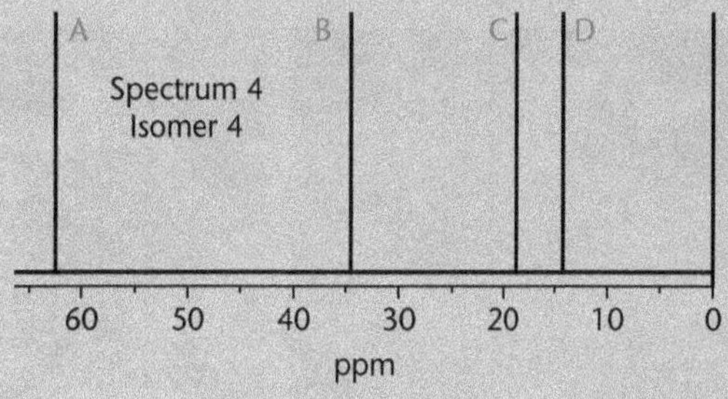

Figure 25 *The ^{13}C NMR spectrum of isomer 4 of $C_4H_{10}O$*

KEY IDEAS

- ^1H and ^{13}C NMR can be used to analyse organic molecules. Each different chemical environment of a ^1H or ^{13}C atom is responsible for a different resonance in the corresponding spectrum.
- In ^1H NMR the signal intensities (areas under the peaks) are proportional to the number of hydrogen atoms in the group responsible for the signal. This is not the case in ^{13}C NMR spectroscopy.
- In ^1H NMR each signal may be split as a result of coupling with neighbouring atoms. In ^{13}C NMR, coupling is not observed.
- In ^1H NMR, if there are n equivalent neighbouring ^1H atoms, this causes an NMR signal to be split into $n + 1$ peaks.

13.4 CHROMATOGRAPHY

Chromatography is a technique that enables the separation of mixtures. Different types of chromatography include paper chromatography, thin-layer chromatography (TLC), column chromatography, gas–liquid chromatography (GLC) (Figure 26) and high-performance liquid chromatography (HPLC). All make use of the principle that components in a mixture when dissolved in a fluid will flow through another material (the **stationary phase**) at varying rates. Separation depends upon how the components interact with the stationary phase (their retention) and how soluble they are in the fluid.

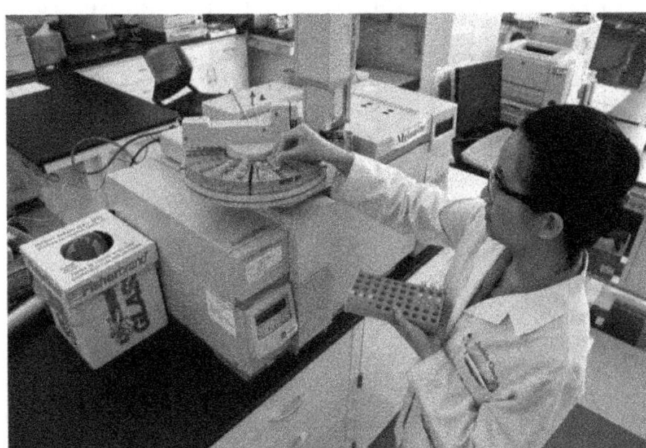

Figure 26 This research chemist is using a gas–liquid chromatography machine to measure melamine levels in food samples

Column chromatography

The foundation for all chromatographic techniques was column chromatography. It was developed in the early 1900s by Mikhail Tsvet to separate plant pigments, and his arrangement is still used today.

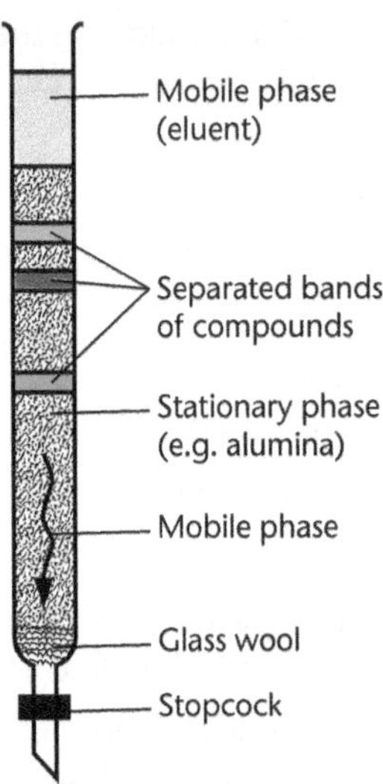

Figure 27 Column chromatography, showing the separation of coloured compounds

In column chromatography, an inert solid, called the stationary phase (usually powdered silica gel or alumina), is placed in the column with a liquid solvent phase, called the **mobile phase** (Figure 27). The sample mixture, dissolved in the solvent phase, is introduced at the top of the column, and the column is kept topped up with fresh solvent (**eluent**) as the sample flows through the column via gravity. The component with the greatest attraction to the stationary phase takes the longest time to flow through the column. If the components are coloured, as plant pigments are, then they can be identified by eye or by R_f value (see chapter 11 of Year Student Book). If the components are colourless, then other techniques may be used (e.g. fluorescence under UV radiation) to show their position in the column.

Thin-layer chromatography

Thin-layer chromatography uses a layer of silica on glass, aluminium or plastic as the stationary phase. A small spot of a mixture is added near to the bottom of the TLC plate and the plate is dipped into a solvent (the mobile phase). As the solvent moves up the TLC plate, the components of a mixture interact with the stationary phase differently and move up the plate at varying rates. The TLC plate is removed when the solvent has nearly reached the top of the plate, and the compounds are visualised using fluorescence under UV radiation or by a chemical staining technique (for example, using ninhydrin; see *chapter 11 of Year 2 Student Book*).

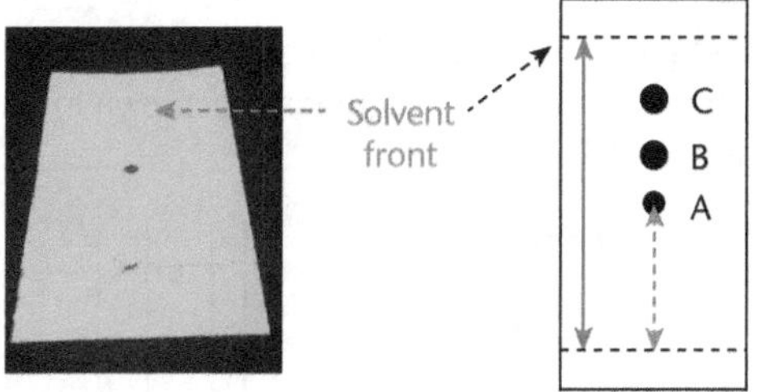

Figure 28 *A TLC plate visualised under a UV light showing one spot fluorescing, indicating a pure compound, and a schematic of a TLC plate showing three different components (A, B and C) in the mixture*

Each component in the mixture will have a unique retention factor (R_f value), which is calculated by dividing the distance the compound moves by the distance moved by the solvent. The Rf value of spot A in fig 28 can be calculated using this formula:

$$R_f \text{ spot A} = \frac{\text{distance moved by compound A}}{\text{distance moved by solvent}}$$

Gas–liquid chromatography

In GLC the mobile phase is an inert gas, such as dry nitrogen or helium, and the stationary phase is usually diatomaceous earth coated with a non-volatile liquid. The stationary phase is packed into a long coiled tube and placed in a heated oven (Figure 29). For GLC to be used, the sample must be either a gas or a volatile liquid at the temperature of the oven. The sample is injected into the column through a self-sealing disc, and the vapour formed is carried through the stationary phase using the inert-gas mobile phase.

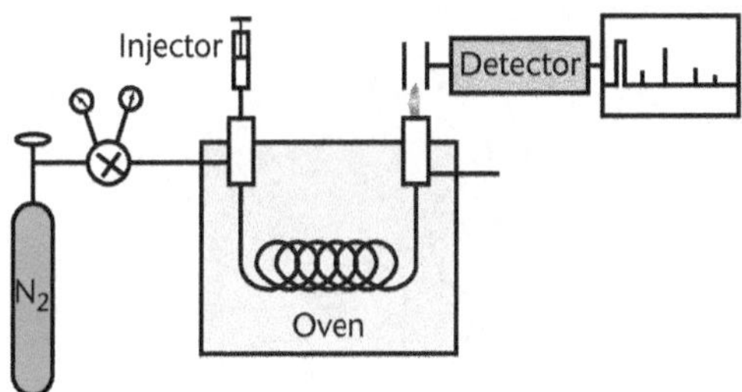

Figure 29 *Schematic diagram of a gas–liquid chromatograph*

The temperature of the stationary phase can be varied to optimise the separation of the mixture in the sample. The time taken to pass through the column is called the **retention time**. This depends on the nature of the solute, the volatility of the solute, the nature of the stationary and mobile phases, and the attraction between the solute and the stationary and mobile phases. The retention time can be compared with standard reference values to identify the compound.

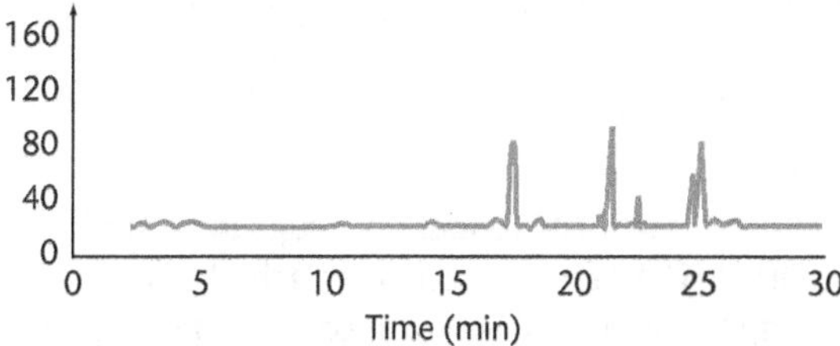

Figure 30 *A typical GLC chart recording of a mixture. Each peak represents a different component of the mixture and the unique retention time can be determined by reading the horizontal scale.*

As the components of the mixture leave the column they can be detected by either thermal conductivity or, more commonly, flame ionisation. In the latter, the outlet gas is mixed with hydrogen and air and burned to produce ions. These ions allow a current to be transmitted, which is then converted to a signal on a chart recorder (Figure 30). The relative sizes (i.e. areas) of the peaks are related to how much of each compound is present in the mixture.

QUESTIONS

11. Would oxygen be a good mobile phase in gas–liquid chromatography? Justify your answer.

12. A typical GLC chromatogram is shown in Figure 31. It contains four components, A, B, C and D.

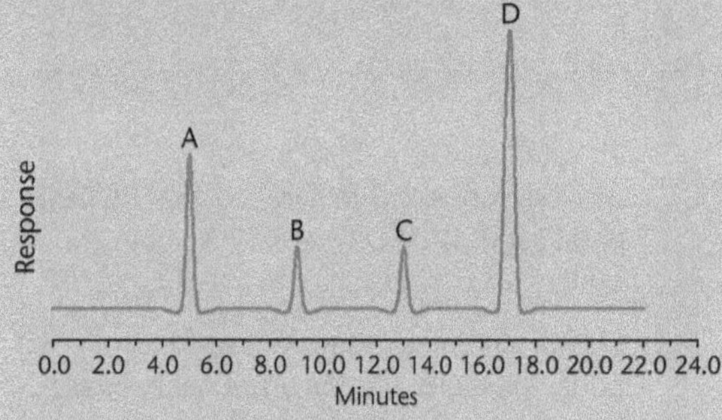

Figure 31 *Chromatogram of mixture*

a. What is the retention time of compound A?
b. Which compound is present in the greatest quantity in the mixture?
c. Which compounds were present in equal amounts?
d. Which compound had the strongest interaction with the stationary phase?

ASSIGNMENT 1: ANALYSIS OF A POISON

Gas chromatography is a technique often used by forensic scientists to identify drugs in blood and urine. The machine can be attached to a mass spectrometer, so as each component leaves the chromatograph it can have its mass and fragmentation pattern checked and compared with library standards.

A 45-year-old man has been rushed to hospital. He had complained of a headache and taken some paracetamol. This made him worse and he very quickly vomited and fell into a coma. The police have provided you with the bottle of paracetamol that he used and it still contains some tablets.

Questions

A1. You first analyse the tablets by gas chromatography (Figure A1).

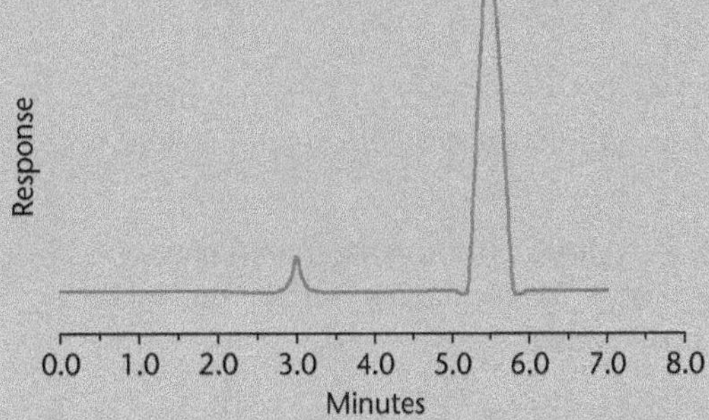

Figure A1 *GLC chromatogram of tablets obtained from police*

The standard retention time of paracetamol is 5.5 minutes. Using the GLC data, suggest TWO conclusions about the tablets.

A2. Column chromatography was used to purify the tablets. Name a stationary phase typically used in column chromatography.

A3. Two compounds were isolated after chromatography. The first to be eluted from the column is compound A and the second is compound B. The ^{13}C NMR spectra of both compounds are shown in Figure A2.

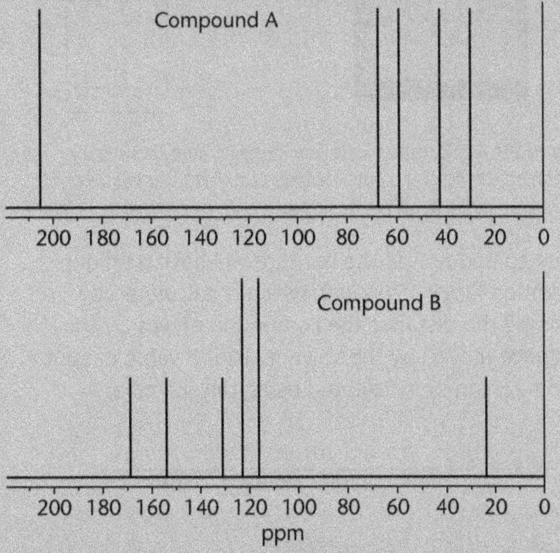

Figure A2 *^{13}C NMR of compounds A and B*

a. Which compound contains an aromatic ring?

b. What type of functional group is responsible for the resonance at 205 ppm in compound A?

c. The structure of paracetamol is shown in Figure A3. Which compound, A or B, is paracetamol? Justify your answer.

O
H_3C NH
OH
Paracetamol

Figure A3

A4. The ^{1}H NMR spectrum of compound A is shown in in Figure A4. How many different ^{1}H chemical environments are there?

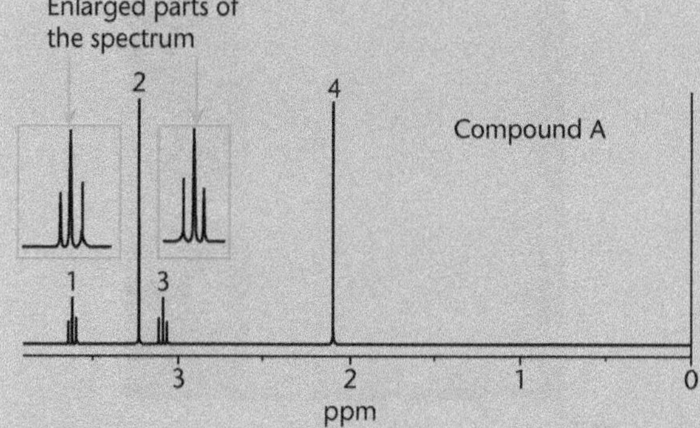

Figure A4

```
  H   H       O   H   H
  |   |       ||  |   |
H—C———C———O———C———C———C—H
  |   |           |   |
  H   H           H   H
            X

  H       O   H   H   H
  |       ||  |   |   |
H—C———O———C———C———C———C—H
  |           |   |   |
  H           H   H   H
            Y

  H   O   H   H       H
  |   ||  |   |       |
H—C———C———C———C———O———C—H
  |       |   |       |
  H       H   H       H
            Z
```

Figure A5

A5. Mass spectrometry determined that the molar mass of compound A was 102 and the formula $C_5H_{10}O_2$. Using the ^{1}H NMR spectrum (Figure A4), determine which of the isomers **X**, **Y** or **Z** (Figure A5) is compound A. Justify your answer and explain why peak 3 is a triplet.

KEY IDEAS

- Chromatography is a technique that allows the separation of mixtures.
- Column chromatography and thin-layer chromatography both use a solid stationary phase and a liquid mobile phase.
- Gas–liquid chromatography uses a liquid stationary phase (adsorbed onto a solid) and a gaseous mobile phase.
- Separation depends upon a balance of how the components interact differently with the stationary phase and how soluble they are in the mobile phase.

REQUIRED PRACTICAL ACTIVITY 12: APPARATUS AND TECHNIQUES

(PS 1.2, PS 3.2, PS 4.1, AT a, AT i, AT k)

Separation of species by thin-layer chromatography (TLC)

This practical activity gives you the opportunity to show that you can:

- apply knowledge to practical contexts
- use thin-layer chromatography
- use laboratory apparatus to record a range of measurements
- process and analyse data.

Apparatus

Thin-layer chromatography (TLC) uses a layer of silica, typically on glass, aluminium or plastic, as the stationary phase. The latter two layers are commercially available in large sheets, which can be cut carefully to the required size with scissors. Solutions of samples to be analysed are added (spotted) onto the TLC plate using a capillary tube. The plate is developed in a covered developing chamber containing solvent. The developing chamber may be commercially available or, alternatively, a beaker covered with a watch glass can be used. Once developed the TLC plate is visualised, normally by using a UV light.

Techniques

When analysing medicine tablets may need to be ground in a pestle and mortar. A solution of the sample to be analysed is prepared. Typically a small amount (about 0.1 g) of the sample is dissolved in about 0.5 cm^3 of a volatile solvent. A TLC plate is prepared with a small nick cut in the side to mark the position of the sample. This is where the sample will be added. Do not touch the TLC plate with your fingers, use forceps to handle it or hold it only by the edges. A capillary tube is placed in the solution of sample and a small amount of solution is drawn up the capillary. The small drop of sample is then added to the plate by touching the capillary to the plate (Figure P1). The plate is then allowed to dry in the air. For best results the sample needs to be concentrated, add a drop of sample then dry it before repeating this several times.

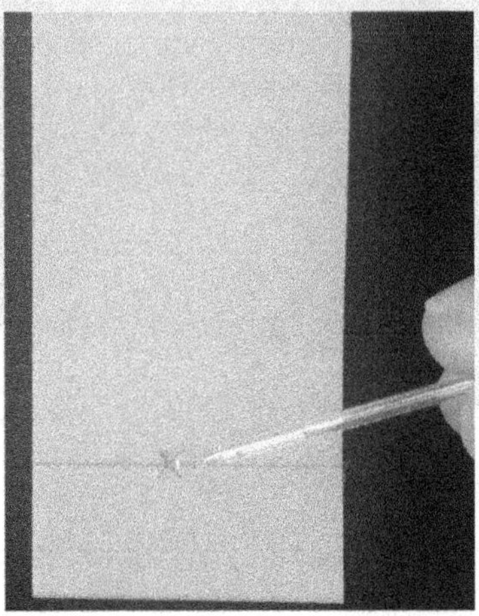

Figure P1 *The sample is added to the TLC plate using a capillary tube*

The TLC plate is placed in the developing tank and solvent added, making sure its level is below the pencil line (Figure P2). When the solvent front has nearly reached the top of the plate the TLC plate is removed from the developing tank and the position of the solvent front recorded with a pencil line. The plate can be visualised by placing under a UV light. Care must be taken not to look at the UV light directly as this will cause damage to the eyes. The position of any visualised spots can be recorded using a pencil.

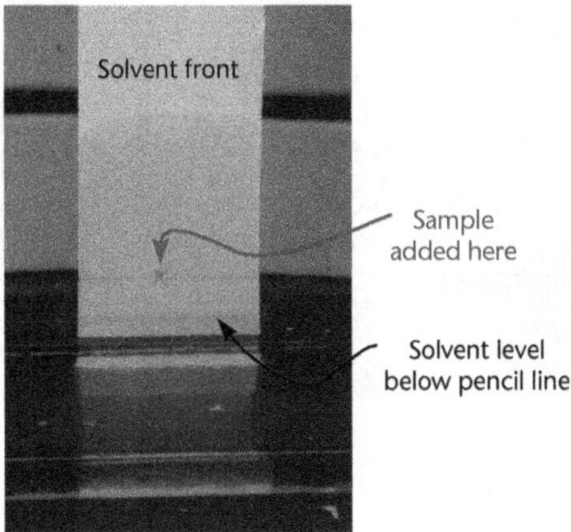

Figure P2 *Solvent moves up the TLC plate by capillary action*

The spots visualised on a TLC plate can then be analysed and the R_f of each spot determined and compared with authentic samples.

Questions

A student was analysing some commercial painkillers. Consider the TLC plate shown in Figure P3. Sample A was pure paracetamol and sample B was pure ibuprofen.

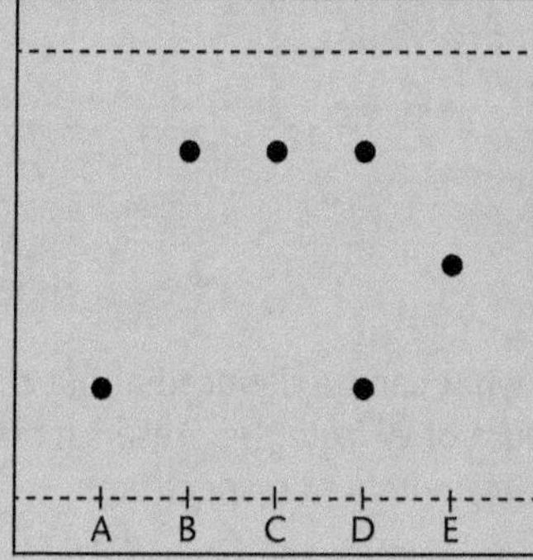

Figure P3 Developed TLC plate from experiment

P1. Calculate the R_f of paracetamol (sample A) using Figure P3.

P2. Sample C was Nurofen. What is the painkiller in Nurofen?

P3. What can you conclude about samples D and E?

P4. Which of the drugs has the strongest interaction with the silica stationary phase of the TLC plate?

When an alcohol was analysed by TLC, it was found to have an R_f of 0.3 when ethyl ethanoate was used as a solvent. A student wished to oxidise this alcohol to an aldehyde with potassium dichromate(VI); however, they were not sure how long the reaction would take. Every 1 hour they took a small quantity of the reaction mixture and analysed it by TLC (Figure P4).

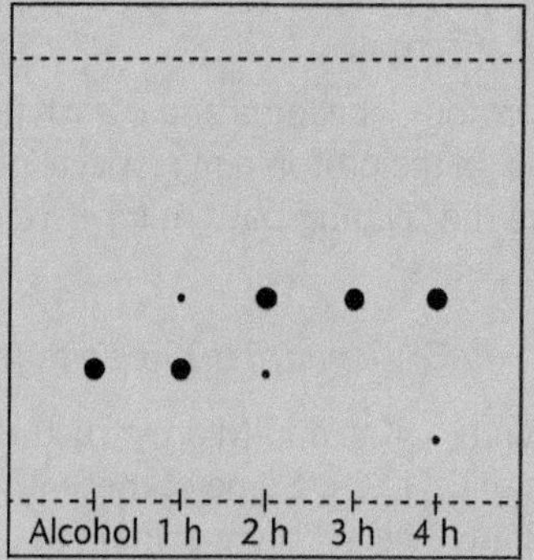

Figure P4 The oxidation reaction analysed over 4 hours

P5. Explain the appearance of the TLC plate for samples taken at 1 hour and 2 hours.

P6. When should the reaction be stopped to provide the highest yield of aldehyde?

P7. Explain what is happening in the reaction mixture after 4 hours.

PRACTICE QUESTIONS

1. Consider this compound:

```
        CH3
  a     |                  b
H3C — C — C — CH2 — CH2 — C — OH
        |    ||             ||
        OH   O              O
```

   a. Predict the number of peaks in its proton n.m.r. spectrum.

   b. The protons labelled a and b each produce a peak in the proton n.m.r. spectrum. Name the splitting pattern for each of these peaks.

AQA January 2008 Unit 4 Question 4

2. Compounds J, K, L and M are structural isomers of $C_4H_{10}O_2$. Some of these isomers are ethers. Ethers contain the C–O–C linkage. Isomers J, K, L and M can be distinguished using proton n.m.r. spectroscopy and infra-red spectroscopy.

   a. The substance TMS is used as a standard in recording proton n.m.r. spectra. Draw the structure of TMS and give two reasons why it is used as a standard.

   b. State the number of peaks in the proton n.m.r. spectrum of isomer J, $CH_3OCH_2CH_2OCH_3$.

   c. i. Isomer K has five peaks in its proton n.m.r. spectrum:

      $\overset{a}{C}H_3\overset{b}{C}H_2OCH_2CH_2OH$

      Predict the splitting pattern of the peaks due to the protons labelled a and b.

      ii. Identify the wavenumber of an absorption which would be present in the infra-red spectrum of K but which would not be present in the infra-red spectrum of J.

AQA January 2007 Unit 4 Question 4

3. This question concerns four isomers, W, X, Y and Z, with the molecular formula $C_5H_{10}O_2$.

   a. The proton n.m.r. spectrum of W shows 4 peaks. This table gives the chemical shifts, δ values, for each of these peaks, together with their splitting patterns and integration values:

δ (ppm)	2.18	2.59	3.33	3.64
Splitting pattern	singlet	triplet	singlet	triplet
Integration value	3	2	3	2

   State what can be deduced about the structure of W from the presence of the following in its n.m.r. spectrum.

      i. The singlet peak at δ = 2.18.

      ii. The singlet peak at δ = 3.33.

      iii. Two triplet peaks.

      iv. Hence, deduce the structure of W.

   b. The infra-red spectrum of X is:

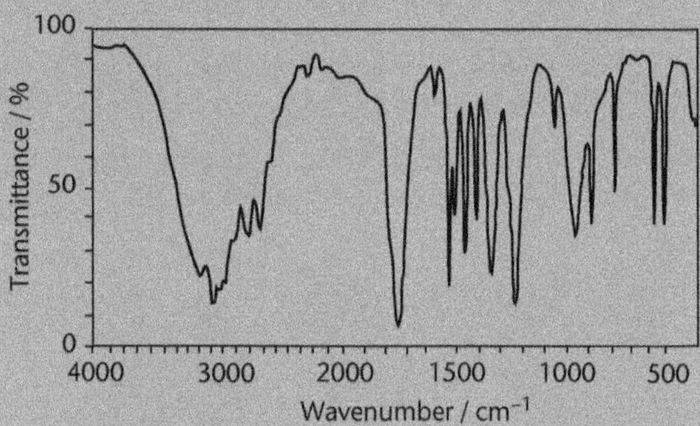

      i. What can be deduced from the broad absorption centred on 3 000 cm^{-1} in the infra-red spectrum of X?

      ii. Given that the proton n.m.r. spectrum of X contains only two peaks with the integration ratio 9:1, deduce the structure of X.

AQA June 2005 Unit 4 Question 4

4. The infrared spectrum (Figure Q1) and the ^1H NMR spectrum (Figure Q2) of compound **R** with molecular formula C_6H_{14} are shown.

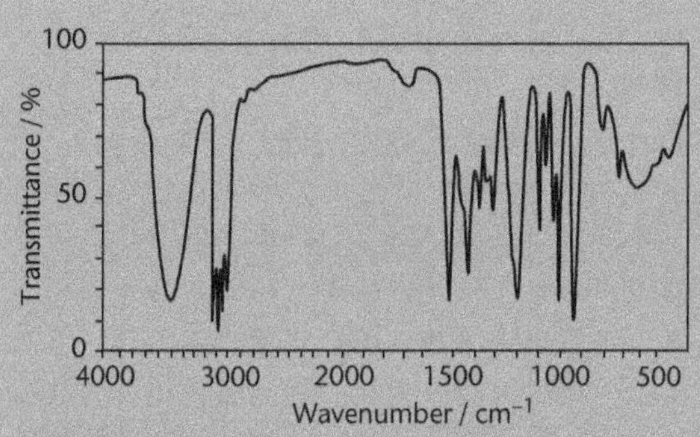

Figure Q1

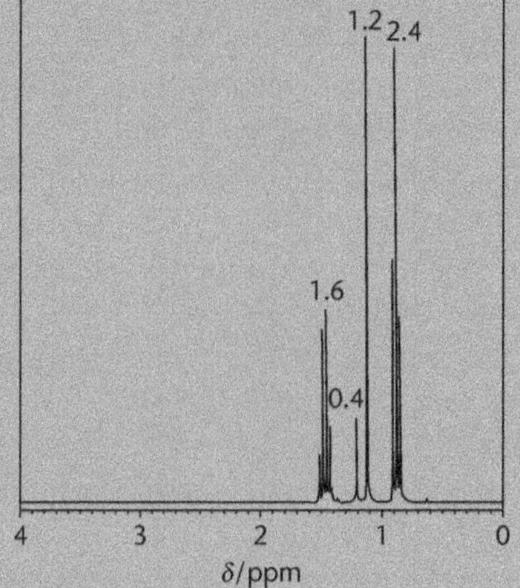

Figure Q2

The relative integration values for the NMR are shown on Figure Q2.

Deduce the structure of compound R by analysing Figures Q1 and Q2. Explain each stage in your deductions.

Use Table Q1 and Table Q2:

Bond	Wavenumber/cm^{-1}
N—H (amines)	3300–3500
O—H (alcohols)	3230–3550
C—H	2850–3300
O—H (acids)	2500–3000
C≡N	2220–2260
C=O	1680–1750
C=C	1620–1680
C—O	1000–1300
C—C	750–1100

Table Q1 *Infrared absorption data*

Type of proton	δ/ppm
ROH	0.5–5.0
RCH_3	0.7–1.2
RNH_2	1.0–4.5
R_2CH_2	1.2–1.4
R_3CH	1.4–1.6
R–C(=O)–C(H)–	2.1–2.6
R–O–C(H)–	3.1–3.9
RCH_2Cl or Br	3.1–4.2
R–C(=O)–O–C(H)–	3.7–4.1
R(–)C=C(–)H	4.5–6.0
R–C(=O)H	9.0–10.0
R–C(=O)–O–H	10.0–12.0

Table Q2 *^{1}H NMR chemical shift data*

AQA Chemistry Specimen Paper 2 2015 Question 10

5. In 2008, some food products containing pork were withdrawn from sale because tests showed that they contained amounts of compounds called dioxins many times greater than the recommended safe levels.

Dioxins can be formed during the combustion of chlorine-containing compounds in waste incinerators. Dioxins are very unreactive compounds and can therefore remain in the environment and enter the food chain. Many dioxins are polychlorinated compounds such as tetrachlorodibenzodioxin (TCDD) shown in Figure Q3.

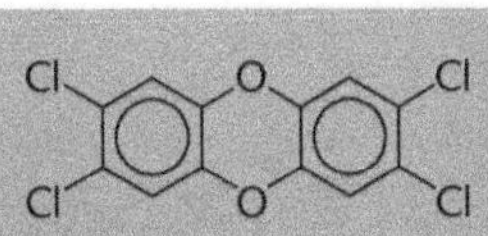

Figure Q3

In a study of the properties of dioxins, TCDD and other similar compounds were synthesised. The mixture of chlorinated compounds was then separated before each compound was identified by mass spectrometry.

a. Fractional distillation is **not** a suitable method to separate the mixture of chlorinated compounds before identification by mass spectrometry. Suggest how the mixture could be separated.

b. The molecular formula of TCDD is $C_{12}H_4O_2Cl_4$. Chlorine exists as two isotopes ^{35}Cl (75%) and ^{37}Cl (25%).

Deduce the number of molecular ion peaks in the mass spectrum of TCDD and calculate the *m*/*z* value for the most abundant molecular ion peak.

c. Suggest **one** operating condition in an incinerator that would minimise the formation of dioxins.

d. TCDD can also be analysed by ^{13}C n.m.r.

i. Give the formula of the compound used as the standard when recording a ^{13}C spectrum.

ii. Deduce the number of peaks in the ^{13}C n.m.r. spectrum of TCDD.

AQA June 2010 Question 4

6. Organic chemists use a variety of methods to identify unknown compounds. When the molecular formula of a compound is known, spectroscopic and other analytical techniques are used to distinguish between possible structural isomers. Use your knowledge of such techniques to identify the compounds described below.

Use the tables of spectral data on the Data Sheet where appropriate.

Each part below concerns a different pair of structural isomers.

Draw **one** possible structure for each of the compounds **A** to **J**, described below.

a. Compounds **A** and **B** have the molecular formula C_3H_6O.

A has an absorption at 1715 cm^{-1} in its infrared spectrum and has only one peak in its ^1H n.m.r. spectrum.

B has absorptions at 3300 cm^{-1} and at 1645 cm^{-1} in its infrared spectrum and does not show *E–Z* isomerism.

b. Compounds **C** and **D** have the molecular formula C_5H_{12}.

In their ^1H n.m.r. spectra, **C** has three peaks and **D** has only one.

c. Compounds **E** and **F** are both esters with the molecular formula $C_4H_8O_2$.

In their ^1H n.m.r. spectra, **E** has a quartet at δ = 2.3 ppm and **F** a quartet at δ = 4.1 ppm.

d. Compounds **G** and **H** have the molecular formula $C_6H_{12}O$.

Each exists as a pair of optical isomers and each has an absorption at about 1700 cm^{-1} in its infrared spectrum. **G** forms a silver mirror with Tollen's reagent but **H** does not.

e. Compounds **I** and **J** have the molecular formula $C_4H_{11}N$ and both are secondary amines. In their ^{13}C n.m.r. spectra, **I** has two peaks and **J** has three.

AQA January 2010 Question 7

7. Atenolol is an example of the type of medicine called a beta blocker. These medicines are used to lower blood pressure by slowing the heart rate. The structure of atenolol is Figure Q4.

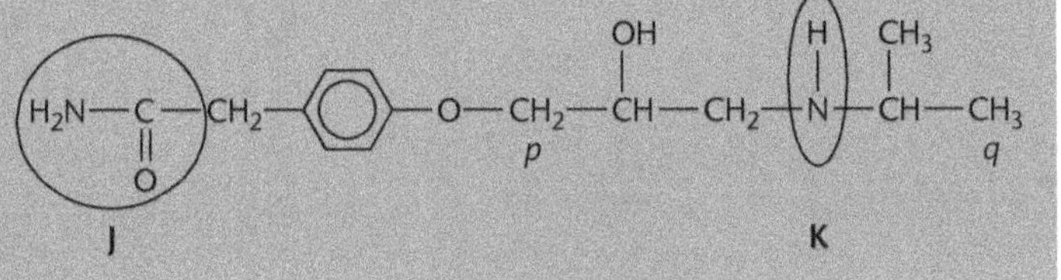

Figure Q4

a. Give the name of each of the circled functional groups labelled **J** and **K** on the structure of atenolol shown above.

b. The ^{1}H n.m.r. spectrum of atenolol was recorded.

One of the peaks in the ^{1}H n.m.r. spectrum is produced by the CH_2 group labelled *p* in the structure of atenolol.

Use the Data Sheet to suggest a range of δ values for this peak. Name the splitting of the peak.

c. N.m.r. spectra are recorded using samples in solution.

The ^{1}H n.m.r. spectrum was recorded using a solution of atenolol in $CDCl_3$.

i. Suggest why $CDCl_3$ and not $CHCl_3$ was used as the solvent.

ii. Suggest why $CDCl_3$ is a more effective solvent than CCl_4 for polar molecules such as atenolol.

d. The ^{13}C n.m.r. spectrum of atenolol was recorded.

Use the structure of atenolol given to deduce the total number of peaks in the ^{13}C n.m.r spectrum of atenolol.

e. Part of the ^{13}C n.m.r. spectrum of atenolol is shown in Figure Q5. Use this spectrum and the Data Sheet, where appropriate, to answer the questions which follow.

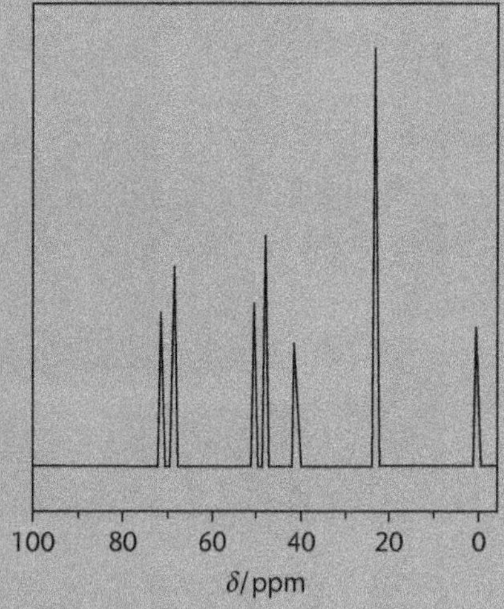

Figure Q5

i. Give the formula of the compound that is used as a standard and produces the peak at δ = 0 ppm in the spectrum.

ii. One of the peaks in the ^{13}C n.m.r. spectrum shown in Figure Q5 is produced by the CH_3 group labelled *q* in the structure of atenolol. Identify this peak in the spectrum by stating its δ value.

iii. There are three CH_2 groups in the structure of atenolol. One of these CH_2 groups produces the peak at δ = 71 ppm in the ^{13}C n.m.r. spectrum, Figure Q5. Draw a circle around this CH_2 group in the structure of atenolol shown in Figure Q6.

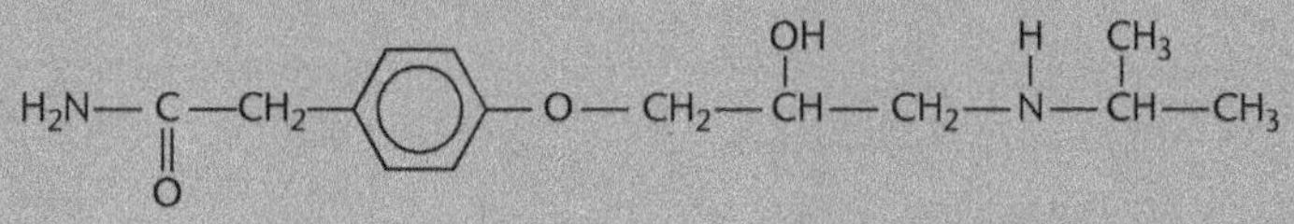

$H_2N-C(=O)-CH_2-C_6H_4-O-CH_2-CH(OH)-CH_2-NH-CH(CH_3)-CH_3$

Figure Q6

AQA January 2011 Question 5

14 ELECTROCHEMICAL CELLS

PRIOR KNOWLEDGE

You will already have studied equilibria (*Chapter 2 of Year 2 Student Book*) and redox chemistry (*Chapter 10 of Year 1 Student Book*).

LEARNING OBJECTIVES

In this chapter you will learn about redox reactions and equilibria. You will learn about batteries and fuel cells. You will be able to calculate the output voltage of an electrochemical cell and predict the direction of a redox reaction.

(Specification 3.1.11)

Redox reactions are central to all batteries – from disposable zinc/carbon batteries, powering low-voltage digital devices, through the lithium ion rechargeable batteries that power tablets and smartphones, to the large batteries that power the electrics in modern vehicles. The need for portable sources of electric current is met by batteries in which redox reactions involving metal ions take place.

When a large amount of current is required, as in the case of electric vehicles, batteries cannot store enough electricity to match the mileage achieved by internal combustion engines. Fuel cells are an excellent alternative, where the energy is stored in the form of a liquid (methanol) or gas (hydrogen) and converted to an electric current by means of a redox reaction.

14.1 OXIDATION STATES

When a metal, M, reacts with a nonmetallic element, X, electrons are transferred from the metal to the nonmetal:

$M \rightarrow M^{n+} + ne^-$

$X + ne^- \rightarrow X^{n-}$

These two half equations represent the redox (reduction-oxidation) reaction between M and X.

Atoms of the metal M are oxidised to positively charged ions, M^{n+}, when n electrons are transferred away (sometimes said to be 'lost').

Atoms of the non-metal X are reduced by gaining n electrons to form negatively charged ions, X^{n-}.

When these equations for the transfer of electrons are written separately, they are called **half-equations** (see *Chapter 10 of Year 1 Student Book*).

Remember the memory aid OILRIG:

- **O**xidation **I**s **L**oss of electrons
- **R**eduction **I**s **G**ain of electrons.

14.2 HALF-REACTIONS

Cells

In cells, a redox reaction is used to produce current in an external circuit. Cells use separated metal/metal-ion solutions, which are connected by an electrolyte. To make a battery, cells are connected together to produce a large enough potential difference and current for the task required such as powering a motor vehicle.

Figure 1 *The cells of this electric vehicle are being recharged using solar power. This not only cuts out urban pollution but also eliminates the pollution caused when electricity is generated from nonrenewable fuels.*

To understand how chemical reactions produce a voltage, we first look at what happens when a metal strip is dipped into a solution of one of its salts. Some of the metal atoms give up electrons and dissolve to form metal ions, leaving behind electrons on the metal strip.

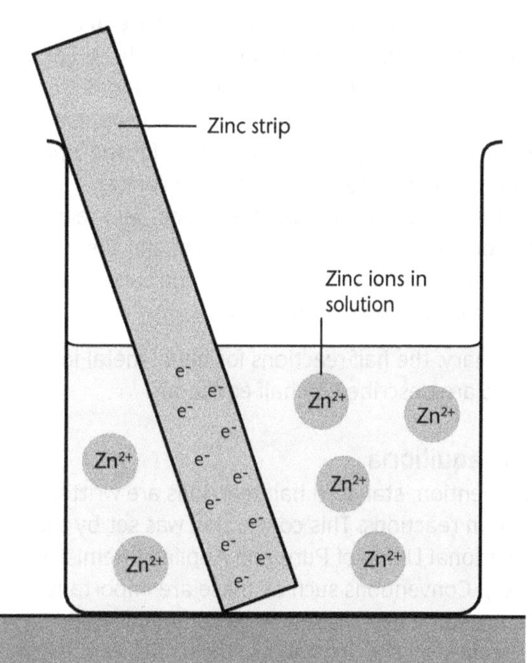

Figure 2 *Zinc rod in zinc salt solution*

Consider a strip of zinc dipping into a solution containing zinc ions (Figure 2).

For zinc ions leaving the metal strip, the half-equation is

$Zn(s) \rightarrow Zn^{2+}(aq) + 2e^-$

The electrons remain on the surface of the metal.

However, metal ions in the solution may recombine with these electrons to re-form metal atoms. The half-equation for this is

$Zn^{2+}(aq) + 2e^- \rightarrow Zn(s)$

The greater the excess of charge on the metal strip (in other words, the more electrons on the surface), the more likely it is that metal ions will form atoms again. An equilibrium is set up, where the rate of formation of metal *ions* equals the rate of formation of metal *atoms*:

$$Zn^{2+}(aq) + 2e^- \underset{\text{zinc atoms oxidised}}{\overset{\text{zinc ions reduced}}{\rightleftharpoons}} Zn(s)$$

This is an example of a **dynamic equilibrium**. At equilibrium, the negatively charged electrons that remain on the metal strip set up a **potential difference** (voltage) between the metal and the solution. The greater the tendency of the metal to produce ions, the greater is the potential difference at equilibrium.

Some metals give up electrons and dissolve in a solution of their ions more readily than others. For example, zinc tends to give up electrons and dissolve in a solution of its ions more readily than copper. At equilibrium, the potential difference for the zinc/zinc-ion system is greater than for the copper/copper-ion system. For copper and zinc, very few metal ions actually end up in solution, and the equilibrium in each of the half-equations above lies well over to the right in both cases.

In summary, the half-reactions for metal/metal-ion systems are described by half-equations.

Redox equilibria

By convention, standard half-reactions are written as reduction reactions. This convention was set by the International Union of Pure and Applied Chemistry (IUPAC). Conventions such as these are important, as they enable information to be communicated consistently by chemists across the world, whether they are researchers working worldwide or students studying in UK schools or colleges.

For example, the half-reaction for the zinc/zinc-ion system is written in the IUPAC convention as follows:

$Zn^{2+}(aq) + 2e^- \rightleftharpoons Zn(s)$

That is, reduction of zinc ions to zinc atoms.

Electrochemical cells: Zn/Cu

Half-reactions in a metal/metal-ion system produce a potential at the electrode. In a cell, the two electrodes are immersed in solutions of their own salts (e.g. $CuSO_4$ and $ZnSO_4$). The two solutions are connected via a salt bridge and the two metal electrodes are joined via an electric circuit.

Electrons flow when two different half-cells, such as Zn/Zn^{2+} and Cu/Cu^{2+}, are connected to complete a circuit. The zinc metal (Figure 3) has a greater build-up of negative charge at its surface than the copper has. This means that the zinc electrode has a more negative **electrode potential**. Relative to the zinc, the copper has a less negative electrode potential, so the copper is said to be the positive electrode.

The difference in electrode potential, the electromotive force (**e.m.f.**), is a measure of the force that moves the electrons around the circuit. The bigger the difference in electrode potential and the more cells connected in series (see the opening page of this chapter), the greater the e.m.f.

Cells have a vast range of uses and can be made using different combinations of metals and numbers of cells, so they can have different electrode potentials appropriate to their uses.

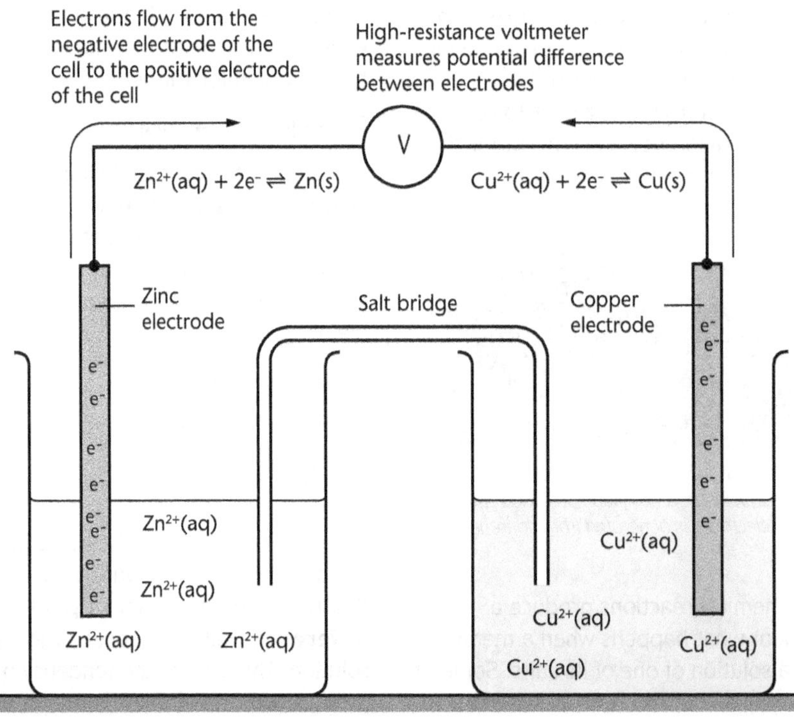

Figure 3 *Zinc/copper electrochemical cell*

QUESTIONS

1. Write out half-reactions for the following so that they obey the IUPAC convention:
   a. magnesium metal (Mg) in equilibrium with magnesium ions (Mg^{2+})
   b. iron(II) ions in equilibrium with iron(III) ions
   c. chlorine gas (Cl_2) in equilibrium with chloride (Cl^-) ions.

The two half-reactions for the zinc/copper cell can be combined to give the overall equation. Electrons flow around the circuit from the *more* negative electrode to the *less* negative electrode. With the two half-reactions written according to the IUPAC convention, the overall equation is obtained by subtracting the more negative (zinc) half-equation from the less negative (copper) one:

$$Cu^{2+}(aq) + 2e^- \rightleftharpoons Cu(s)$$

$$-\ (Zn^{2+}(aq) + 2e^- \rightleftharpoons Zn(s))$$

$$Cu^{2+}(aq) + 2e^- - Zn^{2+}(aq) - 2e^- \rightleftharpoons Cu(s) - Zn(s)$$

Rearranging, this gives

$$Zn(s) + Cu^{2+}(aq) \rightleftharpoons Cu(s) + Zn^{2+}(aq)$$

This is the same reaction as would be predicted from the electrochemical series (see the end of Section 14.3), so that when zinc metal is put in copper sulfate solution, we can write

$$Zn(s) + CuSO_4(aq) \rightleftharpoons ZnSO_4(aq) + Cu(s)$$

Thus, zinc forms zinc ions, and copper ions form metallic copper. Conventionally, the zinc electrode is referred to as 'negative' and the copper electrode as 'positive'.

Notice that the circuit in Figure 3 is completed by a **salt bridge**. The two half-reactions need to be kept separate, yet they still need to be connected by a **conductor**. The salt bridge provides an ionic connection between the two ionic solutions. The ions are free to move in the bridge, so charge is transferred through the bridge solution and this keeps each compartment of the cell electrically neutral. The salt bridge in Figure 3 allows electrons to flow from the negative zinc electrode to the positive copper electrode.

Typically, a salt bridge contains a solution of a salt such as potassium chloride or potassium nitrate. A salt bridge solution can be set in agar jelly and held in a glass tube with a porous plug at each end. In commercial cells, the bridge jelly is held in an absorbent material.

KEY IDEAS

- When a metal is placed in a solution of its ions, some of the metal atoms form ions and go into solution, resulting in a slight build-up of electrons on the metal.
- The build-up of charge on the metal electrode produces an electrode potential between the metal and its solution.
- The equilibrium between the metal and its ions is called a half-reaction. Half-reactions are examples of redox reactions.
- Half-equations are written as reductions according to the IUPAC convention, for example $M^{n+} + ne^- \rightleftharpoons M(s)$.
- Two different half-reactions can be connected using a salt bridge to form an electrochemical cell. There is a potential difference (or e.m.f.) between the two electrodes of the cell.

REQUIRED PRACTICAL 8: APPARATUS AND TECHNIQUES
MEASURING THE E.M.F. OF AN ELECTROCHEMICAL CELL

(AT j and k)

Doing experiments to measure the e.m.f. of an electrochemical cell gives you the opportunity to show that you can:

- Set up electrochemical cells and measure voltages.
- Safely and carefully handle solids and liquids, including corrosive, irritant, flammable and toxic substances.

Apparatus

To set up an electrochemical cell you need:

- Two containers, e.g. two 100 cm^3 beakers.
- A salt bridge to connect the two containers.

  This can be made by lightly pushing a cotton wool plug into one end of a plastic tube, filling the tube with a suitable conducting solution, e.g. 2 mol dm^{-3} NaCl, and finally plugging the other end of the tube with cotton wool. The prepared tube can be flexed into a U-tube so that it can connect the two beakers. Alternatively the salt bridge could be made in a similar way using a glass U-tube.
- A meter to record the e.m.f., e.g. a digital or high impedance voltmeter, with two electrical leads to connect to the voltmeter at one end and crocodile clips at the other end to connect to the electrodes.

In addition to this apparatus you will need samples of metals to be investigated and 1.0 mol dm^{-3} solutions of suitable salts of the metals. Metals that could be used include pairs taken from this list: copper, zinc, titanium, iron, calcium, lithium and silver.

Technique

You need to assemble an electrochemical cell consisting of two different metals, A and B.

1. Clean a piece of A, e.g. copper, and a piece of B, e.g. zinc, using emery paper or fine grade sandpaper and then degrease the pieces using some cotton wool and propanone.
2. Connect A to an electrical lead and place in a 100 cm^3 beaker with about 50 cm^3 of 1 mol dm^{-3} solution of a salt of A, e.g. 1 mol dm^{-3} $CuSO_4$ solution. Make sure the connection is not in or touching the solution.
3. Connect B to another electrical lead and place it into a 100 cm^3 beaker with about 50 cm^3 of 1 mol dm^{-3} solution of a salt of B, e.g. 1 mol dm^{-3} $ZnSO_4$ solution. Again, make sure the connection does not dip into the solution.
4. Join the two beakers with a salt bridge.
5. Connect the two electrical leads to a voltmeter and read off the voltage.

A diagram of the set-up is given in Figure 3 (page 212).

QUESTIONS

P1. Why are the pieces of metal cleaned using abrasive paper and then propanone?

P2. How would you minimise the risks when using propanone to clean the metal pieces?

P3. Why is a salt bridge used when constructing an electrochemical cell?

P4. To make a standard electrochemical cell, 1 mol dm^{-3} solutions of the two metal salts are used. What other conditions are needed?

P5. Describe how you could investigate the effect of temperature on the e.m.f. of an electrochemical cell.

P6. You are given four metals: copper, zinc, silver and lead. Describe how you would find out experimentally which two metals make the electrochemical cell with highest e.m.f.

14.3 ELECTRODE POTENTIALS

Measuring electrode potentials

The position of an equilibrium is affected by factors such as temperature and the concentration of the solution. Because the two half-reactions that make up a cell are both in equilibrium, cell potentials can only be compared if they are measured under standard conditions, and against a standard half-reaction. Some factors affecting the cell potential are:

- the concentration of ions in each half-reaction
- temperature
- pressure if gases form part of the cell
- cell current.

To produce standardised values, cell potentials are measured (Figure 4) under standard conditions using a high-resistance voltmeter. The conditions for measuring are identified in Figure 5, and the values measured in volts are called **standard cell (electrode) potentials**, symbol $E^\ominus$.

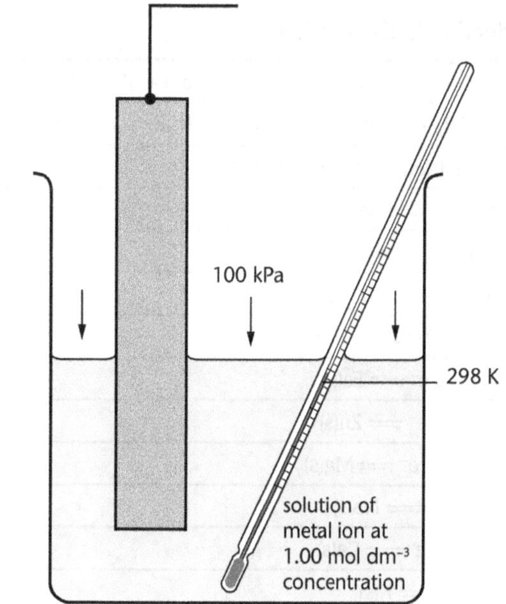

Figure 5 Conditions for measuring standard cell potentials

Figure 4 Measuring electrode potentials in the laboratory

It is not possible to measure the potential of a single electrode. Only potential *differences* can be measured, so it is necessary to define a standard against which potential differences can be measured.

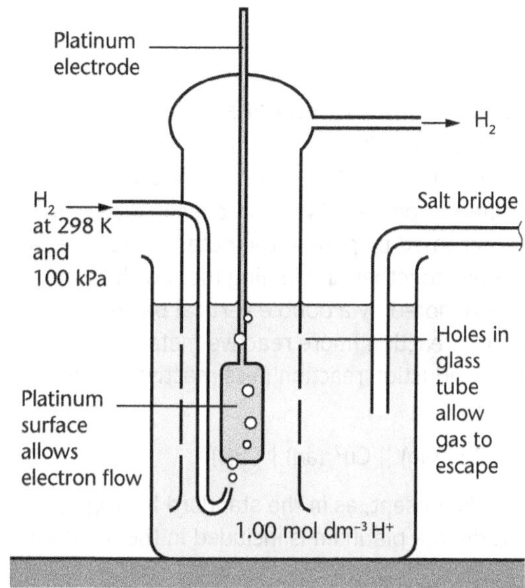

Figure 6 Standard hydrogen electrode

Standard hydrogen electrode

All potentials are measured relative to the **standard hydrogen electrode** (SHE), operating under standard conditions (Figure 6). This is assigned an electrode potential $E^\ominus = 0$.

The cell consists of a platinum electrode with hydrogen gas bubbling over its surface. The electrode is dipped in a solution containing hydrogen ions at a concentration of 1 mol dm^{-3}. The purposes of the platinum electrode are to provide a nonreacting (inert) metal electrical contact and to act as a sink or source for electrons, thereby allowing hydrogen molecules to reach equilibrium with hydrogen ions. The half-reaction for this cell is

$$2H^+(aq) + 2e^- \rightleftharpoons H_2(g)$$

Table 1 lists some combinations of different metal/metal-ion half-reactions and the e.m.f. each produces.

Reduction half-equation	$E^\ominus$/V
$MnO_4^-(aq) + 8H^+(aq) + 5e^- \rightleftharpoons Mn^{2+}(aq) + 4H_2O(l)$	+1.51
$Cr_2O_7^{2-}(aq) + 14H^+(aq) + 6e^- \rightleftharpoons 2Cr^{3+}(aq) + 7H_2O(l)$	+1.33
$O_2(g) + 4H^+(aq) + 4e^- \rightleftharpoons 2H_2O(l)$	+1.23
$Ag^+(aq) + e^- \rightleftharpoons Ag(s)$	+0.80
$Cu^{2+}(aq) + 2e^- \rightleftharpoons Cu(s)$	+0.34
$2H^+(aq) + 2e^- \rightleftharpoons H_2(g)$	0.00
$Pb^{2+}(aq) + 2e^- \rightleftharpoons Pb(s)$	−0.13
$Fe^{2+}(aq) + 2e^- \rightleftharpoons Fe(s)$	−0.44
$Zn^{2+}(aq) + 2e^- \rightleftharpoons Zn(s)$	−0.76
$Mg^{2+}(aq) + 2e^- \rightleftharpoons Mg(s)$	−2.37
$Na^+(aq) + e^- \rightleftharpoons Na(s)$	−2.71
$Ca^{2+}(aq) + 2e^- \rightleftharpoons Ca(s)$	−2.87
$K^+(aq) + e^- \rightleftharpoons K(s)$	−2.92
$Li^+(aq) + e^- \rightleftharpoons Li(s)$	−3.04

Table 1 *Standard electrode potentials*

Convention for writing cells

Electrodes are written in a conventional form where a single vertical bar | represents a boundary between two different phases. Two electrodes in a cell can be represented by putting the notations for the two electrodes together and joining them with a salt bridge, denoted by a double vertical bar ||. The oxidation reaction (more reactive metal) is on the left and the reduction reaction (less reactive metal) is on the right:

$Zn(s) \mid Zn^{2+}(aq) \parallel Cu^{2+}(aq) \mid Cu(s)$

If a gas is present, as in the standard hydrogen electrode, the platinum is included in the notation:

$Pt(s) \mid H_2(g) \mid H^+(aq)$

Standard electrode potentials

Following on from above, these are defined as follows.

The standard electrode potential, $E^\ominus$, is the difference in potential between a given electrode under standard conditions and the standard hydrogen electrode.

Some values for standard electrode potentials are given in Table 1. The series of standard electrode potentials forms part of the **electrochemical series**. Electrodes that have more negative potentials have a greater tendency to form positive ions.

QUESTIONS

2. Using data from Table 1, write the correct notation for the following cells:
   a. a zinc electrode in zinc sulfate solution connected to a lead electrode in lead nitrate solution
   b. a zinc electrode in zinc sulfate solution connected to an SHE
   c. a copper electrode in copper(II) sulfate solution connected to a platinum electrode in a solution of iron(II) and iron(III) ions.

Summary

The strongest reducing agents lose electrons easily and have more negative potentials.

The strongest oxidising agents accept electrons easily and have more positive potentials.

Half-reactions with more negative potentials correspond to electron loss (oxidation) reactions and go readily from right to left.

Half-reactions with more positive potentials correspond to electron gain (reduction) reactions and go readily from left to right.

KEY IDEAS

- The standard conditions for measuring electrode (cell) potentials are concentration, 1.00 mol dm^{-3}; temperature, 298 K; pressure, 100 kPa (where gases are involved); and zero current.
- Electrode potentials are measured relative to an arbitrary standard hydrogen electrode (SHE), for which $E^\ominus$ = 0.0 V.
- A list of reduction electrode potentials forms part of the electrochemical series.

14.4 CALCULATING CELL POTENTIALS

Standard electrode potentials are used to calculate standard cell potentials (or the e.m.f.) across electrochemical cells. We can determine standard cell potentials using the overall equation for the cell reaction written as a spontaneous change. For example, in the zinc/copper cell, the zinc is a more reactive metal than the copper. Its electrode potential is therefore more negative. The cell is written

$Zn(s) \mid Zn^{2+}(aq) \parallel Cu^{2+}(aq) \mid Cu(s)$

more reactive metal	less reactive metal
less positive	more positive

The cell potential is calculated by subtracting the *left-hand* electrode potential from the *right-hand* one, so that

$E^{\ominus}_{cell} = E^{\ominus}_{right} - E^{\ominus}_{left}$

For the cell reaction to be *spontaneous*, $E^{\ominus}_{cell}$ must be positive. For the zinc/copper cell, $E^{\ominus}_{cell}$ will be positive if the standard electrode potential of the $Zn^{2+} \mid Zn$ electrode is subtracted from the standard electrode potential of the $Cu^{2+} \mid Cu$ electrode:

$E^{\ominus}_{cell} = +0.34\ V - (-0.76\ V)$

$E^{\ominus}_{cell} = +1.10\ V$

(using figures from Table 1).

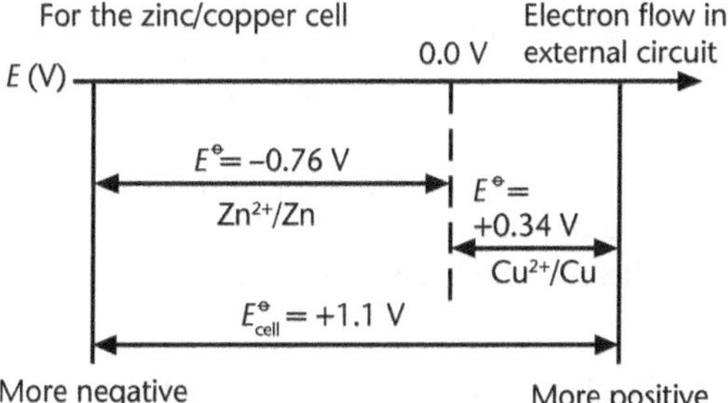

Figure 7 *Calculating standard cell potentials*

Figure 7 gives a diagrammatic treatment of this calculation, which is for a positive value and a negative value. Figure 8 shows calculations of cell potentials for two negative values and for two positive values.

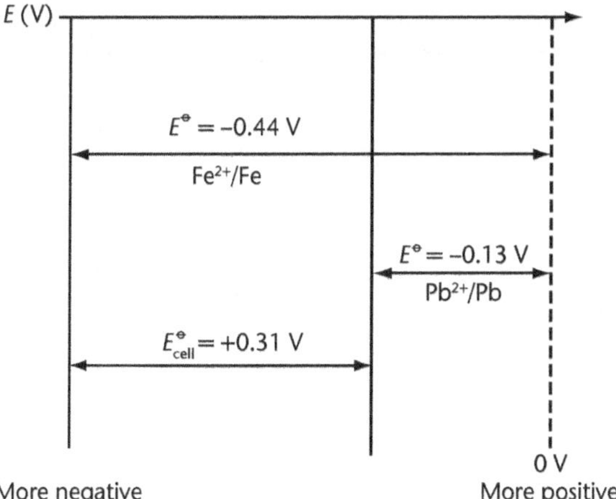

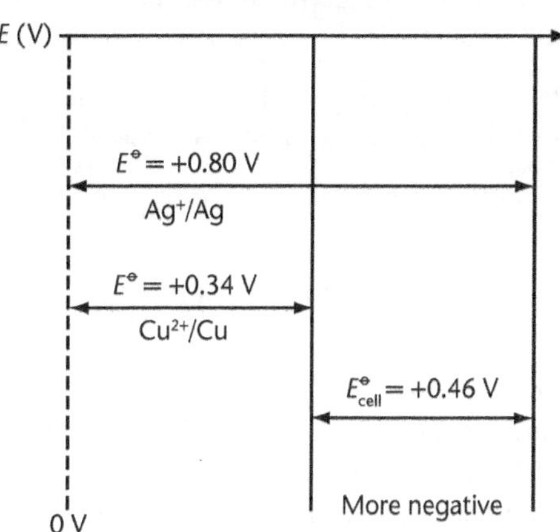

Figure 8 *Calculating standard cell potentials for (a) Fe/Pb and (b) Ag/Cu*

QUESTIONS

3. If you were choosing two metal electrodes for a cell to give a high voltage, which ones would you select from Table 1, based on potential difference? Why?
4. What will happen to the equilibrium in the zinc/zinc-ion system if the concentration of ions in the solution is increased?
5. a. Draw a diagram like Figure 7 for the zinc/silver cell.
   b. Calculate the standard cell potential for this cell.
   c. Use Table 1 to calculate the cell e.m.f. using different combinations of the electrodes Mg^{2+}/Mg, Zn^{2+}/Zn and Ag^{+}/Ag.

KEY IDEAS

- Standard electrode potentials of half-reactions can be used to calculate standard cell potentials (the e.m.f.) across electrochemical cells.
- We can determine standard cell potentials by subtracting the left-hand electrode potential from the right-hand one:

  $E^{\ominus}_{cell} = E^{\ominus}_{right} - E^{\ominus}_{left}$
- Cell reactions are spontaneous if $E^{\ominus}_{cell}$ is positive. For this to happen, the more negative electrode potential is written on the left.

- We can determine standard cell potentials by using a diagrammatic representation of the cell.
- The electrochemical series applies to half-reactions involving nonmetals as well as to metal/metal-ion systems.

14.5 PREDICTING REACTION DIRECTION

The direction of redox reactions can be predicted by using standard electrode potentials. In Table 1, the standard electrode potential is a measure of how readily the species in question will accept electrons and be reduced. The oxidised species in a half-reaction with a more positive potential will accept electrons more readily than will the oxidised species in a half-reaction with a more negative potential.

When two half-reactions are put together:

- the more positive system will gain electrons (be reduced), and
- the more negative system will lose electrons (be oxidised).

This is an important rule to remember. For example, the half-reaction

$Cl_2(g) + 2e^- \rightleftharpoons 2Cl^-(aq)$, $E^\ominus = +1.36$ V

has a more positive electrode potential than the half-reaction

$Br_2(l) + 2e^- \rightleftharpoons 2Br^-(aq)$, $E^\ominus = +1.07$ V

so Cl_2 will accept electrons from Br^- (Figure 9), and the Cl_2 will oxidise Br^- ions to Br_2 and will itself form Cl^- ions when reduced.

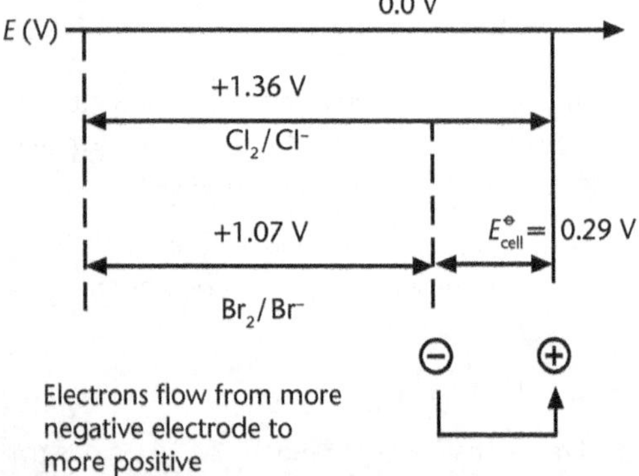

Figure 9 *Predicting direction of reaction between chlorine and bromide ions*

Figure 9 shows how the direction of redox reactions can be predicted using the potentials of half-reactions from the electrochemical series. Table 2 shows some standard potentials for nonmetals.

Worked example

Write a redox equation for a chlorine/bromine cell.

Step 1. Write the more negative (less positive) half-reaction as an oxidation:

$2Br^-(aq) \rightleftharpoons Br_2(l) + 2e^-$

Step 2. Write the more positive half-reaction as a reduction:

$Cl_2(g) + 2e^- \rightleftharpoons 2Cl^-(aq)$

Step 3. Balance the number of electrons being transferred in each equation if necessary.

Step 4. Combine ('add together') the two half-reactions:

$$2Br^-(aq) \rightleftharpoons Br_2(l) + 2e^-$$

$$Cl_2(g) + 2e^- \rightleftharpoons 2Cl^-(aq)$$

$$2Br^-(aq) + Cl_2(g) + 2e^- \rightleftharpoons Br_2(l) + 2e^- + 2Cl^-(aq)$$

The two electrons on each side of the new equation balance out, so they can be struck out from the equation (if this is not the case you need to go back to Step 3):

$2Br^-(aq) + Cl_2(g) + 2e^- \rightleftharpoons Br_2(l) + 2e^- + 2Cl^-(aq)$

The redox equation for the combination of chlorine gas and bromine ions is therefore

$2Br^-(aq) + Cl_2(g) \rightleftharpoons Br_2(l) + 2Cl^-(aq)$

(This is borne out in the laboratory.)

Reduction half-equation	$E^\ominus$/V
$F_2(g) + 2e^- \rightleftharpoons 2F^-(aq)$	+2.87
$H_2O_2(aq) + 2H^+(aq) + 2e^- \rightleftharpoons 2H_2O(l)$	+1.78
$Cl_2(g) + 2e^- \rightleftharpoons 2Cl^-(aq)$	+1.36
$Br_2(l) + 2e^- \rightleftharpoons 2Br^-(aq)$	+1.07
$I_2(s) + 2e^- \rightleftharpoons 2I^-(aq)$	+0.54
$2SO_2(aq) + 2e^- \rightleftharpoons S_2O_4^{2-}(aq)$	+0.40
$O_2(g) + 2H_2O(l) + 4e^- \rightleftharpoons 4OH^-(aq)$	+0.40
$2H^+(aq) + 2e^- \rightleftharpoons H_2(g)$	0.00

Table 2 *Standard electrode potentials for nonmetals*

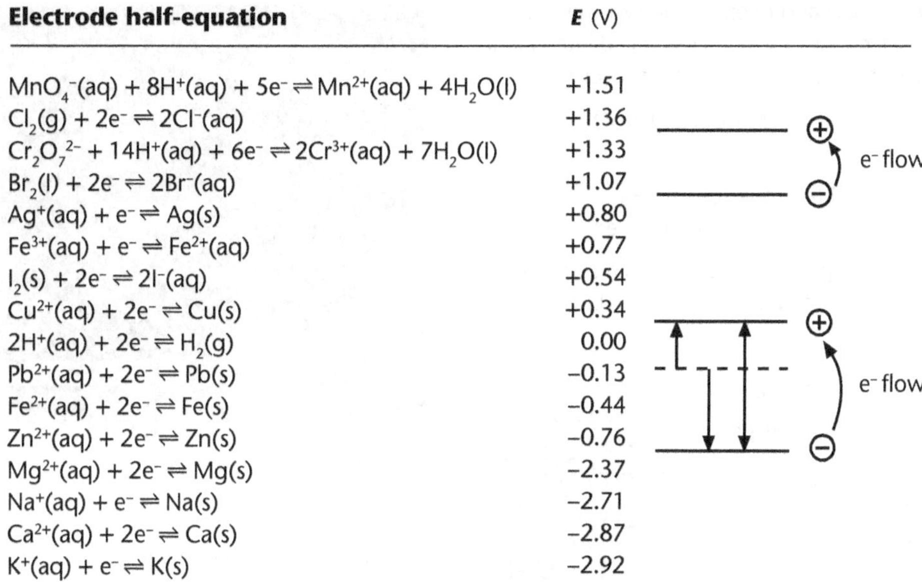

Electrode half-equation	E (V)
$MnO_4^-(aq) + 8H^+(aq) + 5e^- \rightleftharpoons Mn^{2+}(aq) + 4H_2O(l)$	+1.51
$Cl_2(g) + 2e^- \rightleftharpoons 2Cl^-(aq)$	+1.36
$Cr_2O_7^{2-} + 14H^+(aq) + 6e^- \rightleftharpoons 2Cr^{3+}(aq) + 7H_2O(l)$	+1.33
$Br_2(l) + 2e^- \rightleftharpoons 2Br^-(aq)$	+1.07
$Ag^+(aq) + e^- \rightleftharpoons Ag(s)$	+0.80
$Fe^{3+}(aq) + e^- \rightleftharpoons Fe^{2+}(aq)$	+0.77
$I_2(s) + 2e^- \rightleftharpoons 2I^-(aq)$	+0.54
$Cu^{2+}(aq) + 2e^- \rightleftharpoons Cu(s)$	+0.34
$2H^+(aq) + 2e^- \rightleftharpoons H_2(g)$	0.00
$Pb^{2+}(aq) + 2e^- \rightleftharpoons Pb(s)$	−0.13
$Fe^{2+}(aq) + 2e^- \rightleftharpoons Fe(s)$	−0.44
$Zn^{2+}(aq) + 2e^- \rightleftharpoons Zn(s)$	−0.76
$Mg^{2+}(aq) + 2e^- \rightleftharpoons Mg(s)$	−2.37
$Na^+(aq) + e^- \rightleftharpoons Na(s)$	−2.71
$Ca^{2+}(aq) + 2e^- \rightleftharpoons Ca(s)$	−2.87
$K^+(aq) + e^- \rightleftharpoons K(s)$	−2.92

Figure 10 *Electrode potential chart*

Predicting made easy

The electrochemical series and the standard electrode potentials of the corresponding half-reactions can be used to predict the direction of chemical reactions. The series forms an 'electrode potential chart' (Figure 10) and, by following simple rules, the direction of reactions and cell potential can be determined. The cell potential is given by the difference in $E^\ominus$ between the two half-equations.

Steps

Step 1. Draw horizontal lines against the two half-equations you are interested in.

Step 2. Mark with a minus sign the one that is more negative.

Step 3. Mark with a plus sign the one that is more positive.

Step 4. Mark the direction of 'electron flow' (from the minus sign to the plus sign).

Step 5. The 'electron flow' will produce a reduction reaction in the half-reaction marked with the plus sign, and an oxidation reaction in the half-reaction marked with the minus sign.

QUESTIONS

6. Use electrode potentials to explain why iodine will not displace bromine from a solution containing bromide ions. Use Figure 9 to help you.
7. **a.** Use the electrode potentials in Table 1 to determine the e.m.f. of the Li | MnO_2 lithium cell.
   b. Predict the reaction for the Li | MnO_2 cell.
8. Use the electrode potentials in Tables 1 and 2 to answer the following, and explain each of your answers:
   a. Which metal will displace hydrogen from an acid: zinc or copper?
   b. Will bromine oxidise iron(II) to iron(III)?
   c. Will iodine oxidise iron(II) to iron(III)?
   d. A common redox titration is that of acidified potassium manganate(VII) with an iron(II) solution. Will acidified manganate(VII) oxidise iron(II)?

14.6 LITHIUM ION CELLS

A lithium ion cell (Figure 11) is a type of rechargeable cell where lithium ions move from the negative electrode (carbon, graphite C) to the positive electrode (CoO_2) during discharge and from the positive electrode to the negative one during charging. Lithium ion batteries use electrodes in which Li^+

ions are allowed to flow and to enter and exit the solid structure of the electrodes by a process called intercalation. During discharge, the half-reactions are as follows:

Positive electrode: $Li^+ + CoO_2 + e^- \rightleftharpoons LiCoO_2$

Negative electrode: Li (in graphite C) $\rightleftharpoons$
Li^+ + graphite C + e^-

This means that during discharge, there is a reduction of Co^{4+} to Co^{3+} and an oxidation of metallic Li to Li^+.

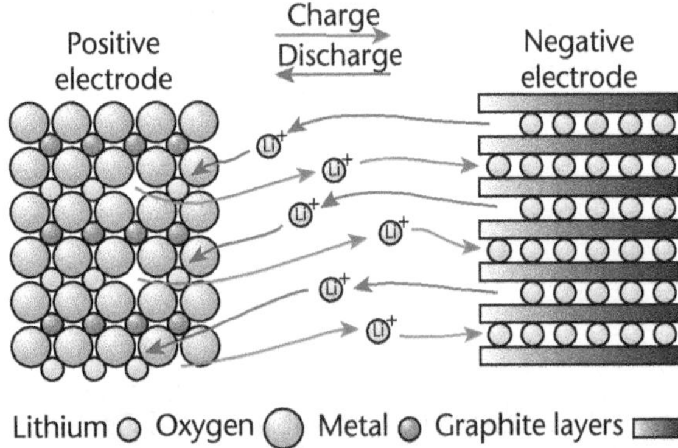

Figure 11 *Schematic of a lithium ion battery. Li⁺ migrates between the two electrodes and fills vacancies in the electrode crystal structure by a process called intercalation.*

14.7 FUEL CELLS

A **fuel cell** (Figure 12) produces electricity by using a fuel (on the negative electrode side) and an oxidant (on the positive electrode side), which react in the presence of an electrolyte. Generally, the reactants flow in and the products flow out, while the electrolyte remains in the cell. So, fuel cells can operate virtually continuously as long as the necessary flows are maintained. There are no moving parts, so they are very reliable.

Typical fuels are methanol, CH_3OH, and hydrogen, H_2. The product of the redox reaction between H_2 and O_2 is water, so a hydrogen fuel cell has no carbon emissions, but storing hydrogen gas is a challenge in itself. Methanol is a liquid and therefore easier and safer to store, but the products of the redox reaction

Figure 12 *A typical fuel cell in a car*

between methanol and oxygen are water and carbon dioxide, a greenhouse gas.

The catalyst is typically made of a platinum group metal or alloy. A hydrogen ion exchange membrane fuel cell and how it works is shown in Figure 13.

The e.m.f. produced by a hydrogen ion exchange membrane fuel cell is only 0.40 V, so the efficiency needs to be as high as possible to match the output from silver | zinc or Li | SO_2 batteries. Increasing the cell surface area leads to increased current from each cell. One of the major advantages of fuel cells is the lightness of the components. Even with their smaller e.m.f., fuel cells could match the energy density (energy per unit of mass) of other systems.

The electrochemical reactions in a fuel cell

On the negative electrode side of a fuel cell, hydrogen diffuses to the catalyst, where it later dissociates into hydrogen ions and electrons (Figure 13). These hydrogen ions often react with oxidants. The hydrogen ions are conducted through the membrane to the positive electrode, but the electrons travel in an external circuit. On the positive electrode catalyst, oxygen molecules react with electrons (which have travelled through the external circuit) and hydrogen ions to form water. Any excess gases are recycled, so water is the only waste product.

In a fuel cell, the typical reactions at the negative and positive electrodes, respectively, are as follows:

$H_2(g) \rightarrow 2H^+(aq) + 2e^-, \quad E^\ominus = 0.00\ V$

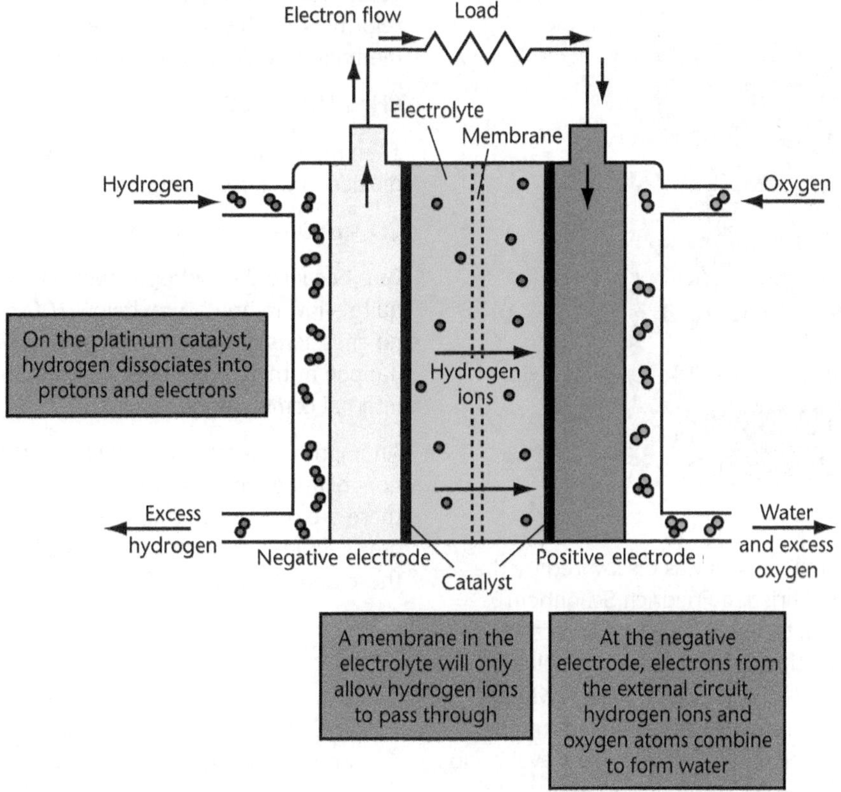

Figure 13 *How a proton exchange membrane fuel cell works*

$O_2(aq) + 2H_2O + 4e^- \rightarrow 4OH^-(aq)$, $E^\ominus = +0.40$ V

To maintain the balance of electrons in the reduction and oxidation processes, the reactions use up twice as much hydrogen as oxygen.

In a combined system, for example when solar cells provide electricity, these reactions can be used to electrolyse water for reuse as a fuel:

$2H_2O \rightarrow 2H_2 + O_2$

$H_2O \rightleftharpoons H^+ + OH^-$

So, overall, we can write this as follows:

$2H^+ + 2e^- \rightarrow H_2 \quad 2OH^- \rightarrow 2OH^\bullet + 2e^-$

$2H^+ + 2e^- \rightarrow H_2 \quad 2OH^\bullet \rightarrow H_2O + O^\bullet$

$O^\bullet + O^\bullet \rightarrow O_2$

$4e^-$ used by forming $2H_2$ $4e^-$ released by forming O_2

QUESTIONS

9. Why does increasing the surface area not increase the voltage obtained from the cell?
10. Use reduction potentials to calculate the minimum voltage needed to electrolyse water to form hydrogen and oxygen.
11. Which gas is evolved at the cathode (the negative electrode, which supplies the electrons) during the electrolysis of water?
12. For the electrolysis of water, balance both sets of equations in terms of electrons to show that twice as much hydrogen as oxygen is produced.

ASSIGNMENT 1: FUEL CELLS IN TRANSPORTATION

(PS 1.1, 1.2)

Figure A1 A London fuel cell bus

The principle of the fuel cell was discovered by the German scientist Christian Friedrich Schönbein in 1838. Based on this work, the first fuel cell was developed by the Welsh scientist Sir William Robert Grove in 1845. The 1966 General Motors *Electrovan* was the first attempt at an automobile powered by a hydrogen fuel cell. It could travel at up to 70 mph for 30 seconds. Today, 100 mph and a range of 300–500 miles are possible. Fuel cells are being developed for cars and for public transport.

Hydrogen fuel cells emit only water as a waste product during use. However, carbon dioxide is produced as a by-product during the majority of hydrogen production. This is because, commercially, the most common method for producing bulk quantities of hydrogen is from natural gas by steam reforming. In this reaction, steam reacts with methane to yield carbon monoxide and hydrogen:

$$CH_4 + H_2O \rightarrow CO + 3H_2$$

Then the carbon monoxide is converted to carbon dioxide and more hydrogen:

$$CO + H_2O \rightarrow CO_2 + H_2$$

But, because the hydrogen fuel cell operates at quite a low temperature, below 100 °C, there are no emissions of oxides of nitrogen (NO_x), which happen at the high temperatures associated with internal combustion engines.

An important feature of fuel cells is that they are nonpolluting, and research scientists believe that there are dozens of other uses no one has thought of yet. Scientists will try in the future to find uses for these and other types of fuel cells.

Questions

A1. How does the previous paragraph illustrate the difference between scientific principles and technological advancement?

A2. What would be the advantages of a fuel cell for a bus?

A3. Why do combustion engines produce the pollutants NO_x?

A4. What are the benefits and risks associated with fuel cells?

ASSIGNMENT 2: A SOLAR RECHARGEABLE AIRCRAFT

(PS 1.1, 1.2; MS 0.0)

AeroVironment, an American company based in California, has been developing prototypes for solar rechargeable aircraft (SRAs) since the early 1980s. *Pathfinder* (Figure A1) is a recent addition to a line of prototypes for use in monitoring weather and relaying data transmitted through the atmosphere (in mobile communications). *Pathfinder* can also act like a **geostationary satellite**, but much closer to Earth.

The aircraft is solar powered during the day, but at night, until a technological solution is found, an SRA is still dependent to some extent on electrochemical cells for its navigational lights, for example. Electrochemical cells were used during tests of the aircraft to save on building expensive solar cell arrays.

According to an engineer working on the research project, 'When we started work on *Pathfinder*, we did some calculations with $E^\ominus$ values to get an idea of the cells that would give us a large voltage. But potential isn't everything. We needed to consider how much energy could be stored per kilogram of cell (energy density), how quickly it could be released safely (power density), and the cell had to be rechargeable.'

During the developmental stages, engineers investigated electrode potentials for a variety of

Figure A1 *The Pathfinder prototype in flight. The craft has a takeoff distance of just 24 metres, less than its own wing span! The 'flying wing' has reached an altitude of 15 385 m, and can travel at 24 kilometres per hour.*

cells, including Ag | Zn, Li | MnO_2 and Li | SO_2 cells. Now they have settled on a combined fuel cell with electrochemical cells that are charged by the solar panels during the daytime.

The eternal aeroplane is now a reality. The cost is only one-tenth of that of putting a conventional satellite in position, because it does not need an expensive rocket launch. As well as studying weather systems, there is great interest in monitoring crops and potential drought areas. Ocean currents can be mapped, marine traffic can be monitored and oil spills can be tracked.

Questions

A1. Researchers worldwide need to use a standard notation system. Write out half-reactions that obey the IUPAC convention for the following:

a. zinc metal (Zn) in equilibrium with zinc ions (Zn^{2+})

b. manganese(II) ions in equilibrium with manganese(IV) ions in acidic solution

c. oxygen gas (O_2) in equilibrium with hydroxide (OH^-) ions in aqueous solution.

Explain what would happen to the electrode potential of a Zn^{2+} | Zn electrode if the Zn^{2+} concentration [Zn^{2+}] was increased.

A2. a. Write the correct notation for electrodes that have the following half-reactions:

i. $Zn^{2+}(aq) + 2e^- \rightleftharpoons Zn(s)$

ii. $Li^+(aq) + e^- \rightleftharpoons Li(s)$

iii. $H^+(aq) + e^- \rightleftharpoons \frac{1}{2} H_2$.

b. What special purpose does the reaction in **a iii** have?

c. What conditions are used for standard electrode potentials?

A3. Write the correct notation for the following cells:

a. a zinc electrode in zinc sulfate solution connected to a silver electrode in silver sulfate solution

b. a zinc electrode in zinc sulfate solution connected to an SHE, which is represented by Pt(s) | H_2(g) | H^+(aq).

A4 a. The cell used in the *Pathfinder* prototype for test flights was a zinc | silver cell. Give one reason why this cell was chosen in preference to the zinc | copper cell. (Use Table 1 to help you.)

b. Draw a diagram like Figure 7 for the zinc | silver cell.

c. Calculate the standard cell potential for this cell.

d. The potential of the Li | SO_2 cell is +3.43 V. Give two advantages of this cell over the Zn | Ag cell.

A5. Predict what would happen (if anything) in the following:

a. Zn(s) with Ag_2SO_4(aq)

b. Ag(s) with $ZnSO_4$(aq)

c. I_2(g) with Br^-(aq)

d. Br_2(g) with I^-(aq).

Explain your reasoning in each case.

PRACTICE QUESTIONS

1. The table below shows some standard electrode potentials.

	$E^\ominus$(V)
$Fe^{3+}(aq) + e^- \rightarrow Fe^{2+}(aq)$	+0.77
$Cr^{3+}(aq) + e^- \rightarrow Cr^{2+}(aq)$	−0.41
$Fe^{2+}(aq) + 2e^- \rightarrow Fe(s)$	−0.44
$Zn^{2+}(aq) + 2e^- \rightarrow Zn(s)$	−0.76
$Cr^{2+}(aq) + 2e^- \rightarrow Cr(s)$	−0.91

a. Predict the products, if any, when the following substances are mixed. In each case use $E^\ominus$ values from the table to explain your answer.

i. iron metal with aqueous zinc(II) ions

ii. aqueous iron(III) ions with aqueous chromium(II) ions

b. Calculate the e.m.f. of the following standard cell and deduce an equation for the overall cell reaction.
$Zn(s) \mid Zn^{2+}(aq) \parallel Cr^{3+}(aq), Cr^{2+}(aq) \mid Pt$

AQA June 2007 Unit 5 Question 3a–b

2. Use the data in the table below, where appropriate, to answer the questions which follow.

Standard electrode potentials	$E^\ominus$(V)
$Fe^{3+}(aq) + e^- \rightarrow Fe^{2+}(aq)$	+0.77
$Cl^2(g) + 2e^- \rightarrow 2Cl^-(aq)$	+1.36
$2BrO_3^-(aq) + 12H^+(aq) + 10e^- \rightarrow Br_2(aq) + 6H_2O(l)$	+1.52
$O_3(g) + 2H^+(aq) + 2e^- \rightarrow O_2(g) + H_2O(l)$	+2.08
$F_2O(g) + 2H^+(aq) + 4e^- \rightarrow 2F^-(aq) + H_2O(l)$	+2.15

Each of the above can be reversed under suitable conditions.

a. i. Identify the most powerful reducing agent in the table.

ii. Identify the most powerful oxidising agent in the table.

iii. Identify **all** the species in the table which can be oxidised in acidic solution by $BrO_3^-(aq)$.

b. The cell represented below was set up.
$Pt \mid Fe^{2+}(aq), Fe^{3+}(aq) \parallel BrO_3^-(aq), Br_2(aq) \mid Pt$

i. Deduce the e.m.f. of this cell.

ii. Write a half-equation for the reaction occurring at the negative electrode when current is taken from this cell.

iii. Deduce what change in the concentration of $Fe^{3+}(aq)$ would cause an increase in the e.m.f. of the cell. Explain your answer.

AQA June 2006 Unit 5 Question 5

3. Where appropriate, use the standard electrode potential data in the table below to answer the questions which follow.

	$E^\ominus$(V)
$Zn^{2+}(aq) + 2e^- \rightarrow Zn(s)$	−0.76
$V^{3+}(aq) + e^- \rightarrow V^{2+}(aq)$	−0.26
$SO_4^{2-}(aq) + 2H^+(aq) + 2e^- \rightarrow SO_3^{2-}(aq) + H_2O(l)$	+0.17
$VO^{2+}(aq) + 2H^+(aq) + e^- \rightarrow V^{3+}(aq) + H_2O(l)$	+0.34
$Fe^{3+}(aq) + e^- \rightarrow Fe^{2+}(aq)$	+0.77
$VO_2^+(aq) + 2H^+(aq) + e^- \rightarrow VO^{2+}(aq) + H_2O(l)$	+1.00
$Cl_2(aq) + 2e^- \rightarrow 2Cl^-(aq)$	+1.36

a. From the table above select the species which is the most powerful reducing agent.

b. From the table above select

i. a species which, in acidic solution, will reduce $VO_2^+(aq)$ to $VO^{2+}(aq)$ but will **not** reduce $VO^{2+}(aq)$ to $V^{3+}(aq)$,

ii. a species which, in acidic solution, will oxidise $VO^{2+}(aq)$ to $VO_2^+(aq)$.

c. The cell represented below was set up under standard conditions.

$Pt \mid Fe^{2+}(aq), Fe^{3+}(aq) \parallel Tl^{3+}(aq), Tl^+(aq) \mid Pt$

Cell e.m.f. = + 0.48 V

i. Deduce the standard electrode potential for the following half-reaction.

$Tl^{3+}(aq) + 2e^- \rightarrow Tl^+(aq)$

ii. Write an equation for the spontaneous cell reaction.

AQA June 2005 Unit 5 Question 4a–c

4. Use the standard electrode potential data given in the table below, where appropriate, to answer the questions which follow.

	$E^{\ominus}$(V)
$V^{3+}(aq) + e^- \rightarrow V^{2+}(aq)$	−0.26
$SO_4^{2-}(aq) + 4H^+(aq) + 2e^- \rightarrow H_2SO_3(aq) + H_2O$	+0.17
$VO^{2+}(aq) + 2H^+(aq) + e^- \rightarrow V^{3+}(aq) + H_2O(l)$	+0.34
$O_2(g) + 2H^+(aq) + 2e^- \rightarrow H_2O_2(aq)$	+0.68
$Fe^{3+}(aq) + e^- \rightarrow Fe^{2+}(aq)$	+0.77
$VO_2^+(aq) + 2H^+(aq) + e^- \rightarrow VO^{2+}(aq) + H_2O(l)$	+1.00
$2IO_3^-(aq) + 12H^+(aq) + 10e^- \rightarrow I_2(aq) + 6H_2O(l)$	+1.19
$MnO_4^-(aq) + 8H^+(aq) + 5e^- \rightarrow Mn^{2+}(aq) + 4H_2O(l)$	+1.52

Each of the above can be reversed under suitable conditions.

a. The cell represented below was set up under standard conditions.

$Pt \mid H_2SO_3(aq), SO_4^{2-}(aq) \parallel Fe^{3+}(aq), Fe^{2+}(aq) \mid Pt$

i. Calculate the e.m.f. of this cell.

ii. Write a half-equation for the oxidation process occurring at the negative electrode of this cell.

b. The cell represented below was set up under standard conditions.

$Pt \mid H_2O_2(aq), O_2(g) \parallel IO_3^-(aq), I_2(aq) \mid Pt$

i. Write an equation for the spontaneous cell reaction.

ii. Give **one** reason why the e.m.f. of this cell changes when the electrodes are connected and a current flows.

iii. State how, if at all, the e.m.f. of this standard cell will change if the surface area of each platinum electrode is doubled.

iv. State how, if at all, the e.m.f. of this cell will change if the concentration of IO_3^- ions is increased. Explain your answer.

AQA January 2005 Unit 5 Question 3a–b

15 PERIOD 3 ELEMENTS AND AQUEOUS CHEMISTRY OF INORGANIC IONS

PRIOR KNOWLEDGE

You will already have studied atomic structure and the different types of shells and subshells of electrons, and learned about coordinate (dative) covalent bonding (*Chapters 1 and 3 of Year 1 Student Book*). You will also understand the Periodic Table, periodicity, and the properties and bonding of elements in Period 3 (*Chapter 4 of Year 1 Student Book*), and be able to determine oxidation states of atoms (*Chapter 10 of Year 1 Student Book*).

LEARNING OBJECTIVES

In this chapter you will learn about the preparation and structures of the oxides of Period 3 elements and about their reactions with water, acids and bases. You will be able to list the general properties of transition metals and their complex ions, in particular their metal–aqua complexes. You will understand why some metal–aqua complexes are more acidic than others, and use a range of test-tube reactions to identify various metal ions.

(Specification 3.2.4, 3.2.5.1, 3.2.6)

Plants need magnesium. There is a magnesium ion at the centre of the chlorophyll molecule, which is vital for photosynthesis. As a complex molecule, chlorophyll illustrates how atoms (in this case, nitrogen) with lone pairs of electrons can form coordinate bonds by donating a lone pair to empty subshells available on the central ion. As well as magnesium, plants need iron and other elements such as cobalt and manganese. Plants extract these nutrients from the soil, so equilibria are set up between aqueous solutions in the plant cells and aqueous solutions in the soil. The positions of these equilibria will depend on the ligands attached to the central metal ions and, importantly, on the pH of the soil water. Changing the soil pH will affect any water ligands attached to the metal ions, and this will affect how well the plant can take up nutrients.

In this chapter you will see how metal ions behave in different aqueous solutions, and how they interact in solution at different pH values.

15.1 PROPERTIES OF PERIOD 3 ELEMENTS AND THEIR OXIDES

Reaction of sodium and magnesium with water

When sodium is put into water, it reacts violently, producing hydrogen and a solution of sodium hydroxide. The reaction is highly exothermic, releasing a large amount of energy. This causes the sodium to melt and heats the water (Figure 1):

$2Na(s) + 2H_2O(l) \rightarrow 2NaOH(aq) + H_2(g)$

This reaction can be written as an ionic equation:

$2Na(s) + 2H_2O(l) \rightarrow 2Na^+(aq) + 2OH^-(aq) + H_2(g)$

Figure 1 *Sodium reacts with water to form aqueous sodium hydroxide and hydrogen*

Sodium hydroxide is a strong base. It dissolves in water, dissociating completely to give a solution containing only $Na^+(aq)$ and $OH^-(aq)$ ions. The solution is strongly alkaline, with a pH of approximately 13.

Compared with sodium, magnesium has a smaller atomic radius and a higher ionic charge, and it has two delocalised electrons. This results in stronger forces holding the magnesium lattice together. The greater forces of attraction mean that it is much less reactive than sodium. The reaction with water is still very exothermic, but because the activation energy for the reaction is high, magnesium must be strongly heated to start it. Water is heated to form steam, which is passed over the hot magnesium (Figure 2). The products are hydrogen and magnesium oxide:

$Mg(s) + H_2O(g) \rightarrow MgO(s) + H_2(g)$

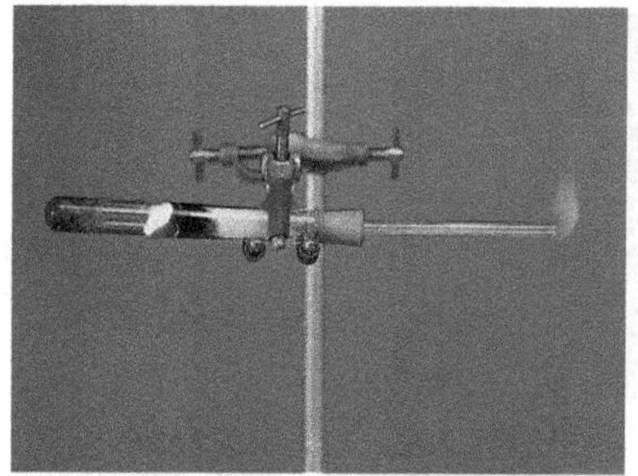

Figure 2 *The reaction of magnesium with steam*

Formation of oxides of sodium, magnesium, aluminium, silicon, phosphorus and sulfur

The Period 3 elements from sodium to sulfur react directly with oxygen. They usually form an oxide with the Period 3 element in its highest possible oxidation state (see Table 1).

The metallic elements Na, Mg and Al are all highly reactive. When heated in oxygen they all glow brightly during reaction (Figures 3–6). The equations for the reactions are

$4Na(s) + O_2(g) \rightarrow 2Na_2O(s)$

$2Mg(s) + O_2(g) \rightarrow 2MgO(s)$

$4Al(s) + 3O_2(g) \rightarrow 2Al_2O_3(s)$

Figure 3 *Sodium burns in oxygen with an orange flame*

Figure 4 *Sodium oxide is a white solid powder*

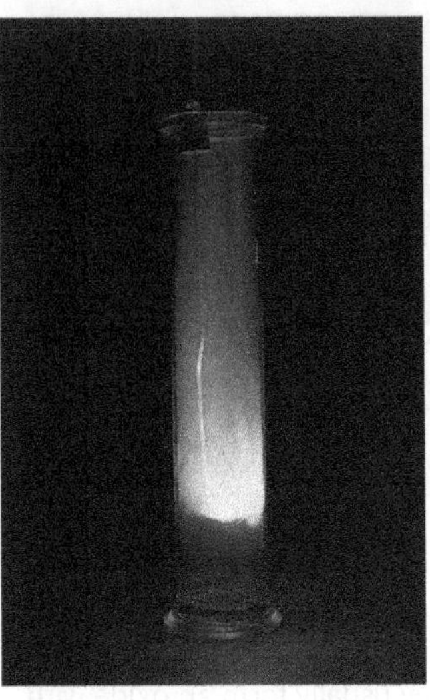

Figure 5 Magnesium ribbon burns in oxygen with a white flame. Magnesium oxide is a white solid

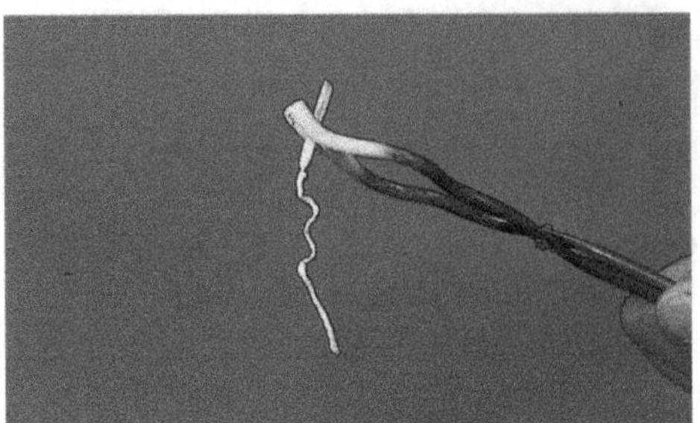

Figure 6 Aluminium burns in oxygen to form aluminium oxide, a white solid powder

The oxides of Na, Mg and Al have ionic lattices. Sodium and magnesium oxides are basic when dissolved in water (see later), and aluminium oxide is **amphoteric**, meaning that it can act as both an acid and a base (Table 1).

Element	Na	Mg	Al	Si	P	S	
Formula of oxide	Na_2O	MgO	Al_2O_3	SiO_2	P_4O_{10}	SO_2	SO_3
State at 25 °C	solid	solid	solid	solid	solid	gas	liquid
Melting point /K	1 548 (sublimes)	3 125	2 345	1 883	853 > 1 atm	200	290
Electrical conductivity when molten	good	good	good	none	none	none	none
Structure	giant ionic	giant ionic	giant ionic	giant molecule	simple molecule	simple molecule	simple molecule
Adding water	reacts and forms hydroxide ions in solution	slightly soluble, dissolved oxide forms a few hydroxide ions in solution	insoluble but amphoteric	insoluble but acidic	acidic; reacts and gives H^+ ions in solution	acidic; reacts and forms weak acid H_2SO_3 with a few H^+ ions in solution	acidic; reacts and forms strong acid H_2SO_4 with H^+ ions in solution
Typical pH of aqueous solution of oxide	13	8	7, i.e. does not dissolve	7, i.e. does not dissolve	2	3	1

Table 1 The properties of oxides in Period 3

The nonmetallic elements silicon, phosphorus and sulfur all react with oxygen. Their oxides are molecular compounds with covalent bonding. White phosphorus spontaneously catches fire and burns in air (Figure 7) (the other form, red phosphorus, also reacts but less vigorously), sulfur initially forms SO_2 (Figure 8) but further oxidation to SO_3 is slow unless a vanadium catalyst is used (the contact process), so it does not always use its highest possible oxidation state, as the other elements do. The equations for the reactions of silicon, phosphorus and sulfur are:

$Si(s) + O_2(g) \rightarrow SiO_2(s)$

$4P(s) + 5O_2(g) \rightarrow P_4O_{10}(s)$

$S(s) + O_2(g) \rightarrow SO_2(g)$

$2SO_2(g) + O_2(g) \rightarrow 2SO_3(g)$

All these oxides form acidic solutions in water.

Figure 7 *Phosphorus burns in air to give phosphorus(V) oxide, P_4O_{10}, a white solid powder*

Figure 8 *Sulfur burns in oxygen with a blue flame to give a colourless gas*

QUESTIONS

1. How does the character of bonding change across the Period 3 oxides?
2. Using Table 1, explain the trends in electrical conductivity of the molten oxides across Period 3.

Properties of the oxides of sodium, magnesium, aluminium, silicon, phosphorus and sulfur

The melting points of the oxides are shown in Figure 9. Melting points are an indication of the forces of attraction between atoms, ions or molecules. The bonding in these oxides can be grouped into three types:

- ionic oxides with giant lattice structures
- covalent oxides with giant lattice structures (sometimes called giant molecules or **macromolecules**)
- covalent oxides that have small molecules.

The forces between ions tend to be stronger than the forces between molecules (intermolecular bonds such as weak van der Waals forces or dipole–dipole interactions). Ionic oxides and covalent oxides with giant lattice structures have higher melting points than simple covalent oxides (Figure 9).

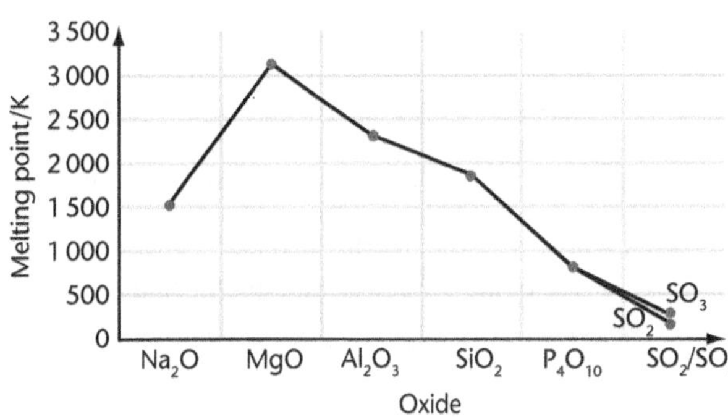

Figure 9 *Melting points of Period 3 oxides*

Ionic oxides

For ions with higher charges, there will generally be a greater force of attraction between ions, which leads to a stronger bond. For the ions Na^+ and Mg^{2+}, the increasing ionic charge and the decreasing size of the ions give increasing electrostatic attractive forces and higher melting points on going from Na_2O to MgO. However, the greater covalent character (due to distortion of the electron densities of the ions) in Al_2O_3 leads to a slightly lower melting point than for MgO.

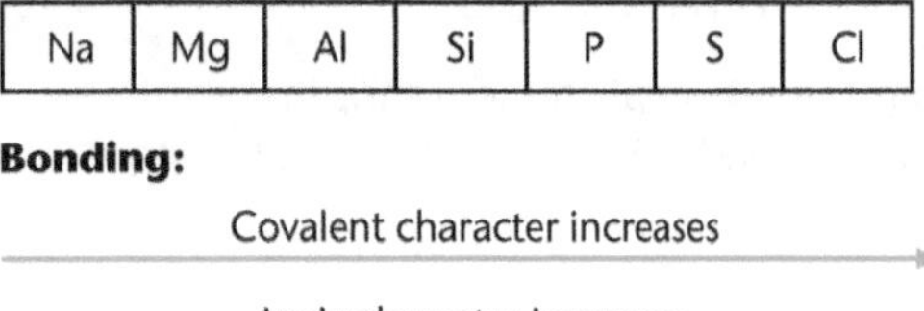

Figure 10 Bonding types in Period 3 oxides

Covalent oxides with giant structures

Silicon dioxide has a giant structure with covalent bonding (Figure 11). The covalent bonds are extremely strong (although not as strong as ionic interactions). This gives the relatively high melting point of a covalent oxide with a giant structure.

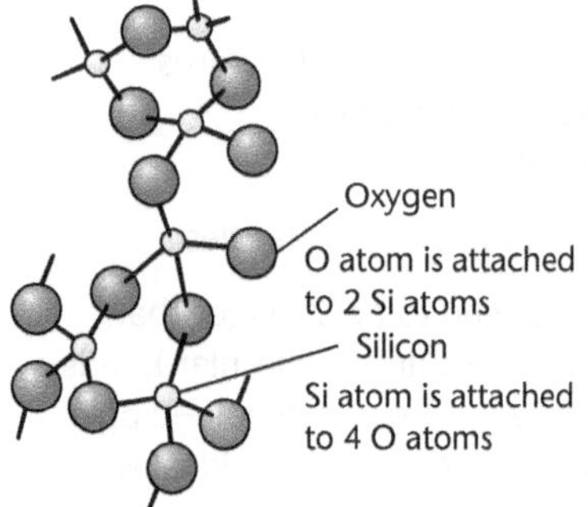

Figure 11 Part of the giant covalent structure of silicon dioxide

Covalent oxides that have small molecules

Moving further across Period 3, after SiO_2, the melting points decrease significantly because the compounds are made up of simple covalent molecules, with weak intermolecular forces between them. Sulfur dioxide, SO_2, consists of simple discrete molecules, so its melting point and boiling point are low. It is a gas at room temperature. Sulfur trioxide, SO_3, is also a gas at room temperature.

Phosphorus(V) oxide, P_4O_{10}, has a larger molecule than SO_2, so there are stronger van der Waals forces of attraction between the molecules and it has a higher melting point (Figure 12).

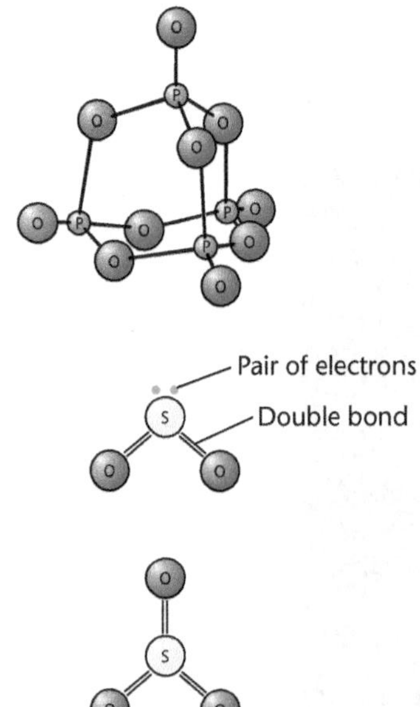

Figure 12 Structures of phosphorus and sulfur oxides

QUESTIONS

3. Suggest why sodium fluoride has a lower melting point (1266 K) than magnesium fluoride (1534 K).
4. Look at Figure 10 and explain how the structures and bonding in the oxides of silicon and sulfur produce such a difference in their melting points.
5. Complete the following table:

Element	Formula of oxide	Type of bonding	Equation for formation of oxide with oxygen
Sodium			
Phosphorus			
Aluminium			

Reactions of the oxides of sodium, magnesium, aluminium, silicon, phosphorus and sulfur with water

Ionic oxides

Both sodium oxide and magnesium oxide are basic oxides.

Sodium oxide, Na_2O, is very soluble in water. It reacts to give a solution of sodium hydroxide (see earlier):

$Na_2O(s) + H_2O(l) \rightarrow 2NaOH(aq)$

Magnesium oxide, MgO, is only slightly soluble in water because of its high lattice energy compared with that of Na_2O:

$MgO(s) + H_2O(l) \rightarrow Mg(OH)_2(aq)$

As only a small amount of MgO dissolves, the concentration of O^{2-} ions is low and, therefore, so is the concentration of the OH^- ions that form. This means the solution is only slightly alkaline, having a pH of only 8.

Aluminium oxide (Al_2O_3) is insoluble in water, so no OH^- ions are formed. The water remains at pH 7.

Covalent oxides with giant structures

Silicon dioxide, SiO_2, is a stable macromolecule and is insoluble in water, and so the pH remains neutral.

Covalent oxides that are small molecules

The oxides of phosphorus, P_4O_{10}, and sulfur, SO_2 and SO_3, are classified as acidic oxides because they dissolve in water to give acidic solutions (Figure 13). The equations for the reactions are

$P_4O_{10}(s) + 6H_2O(l) \rightarrow 4H_3PO_4(aq)$

$SO_2(g) + H_2O(l) \rightarrow H_2SO_3(aq)$

$SO_3(g) + H_2O(l) \rightarrow H_2SO_4(aq)$

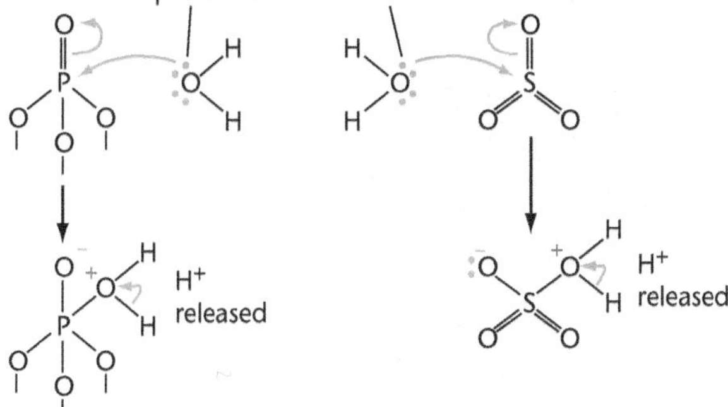

Figure 13 *Hydrolysis of covalent oxides: phosphorus(V) and sulfur(VI) oxides*

The acids dissociate in water to give solutions of hydrogen ions, $H^+(aq)$.

Sulfuric acid is a strong acid. It dissociates fully in aqueous solution:

$H_2SO_4(aq) \rightarrow 2H^+(aq) + SO_4^{2-}(aq)$

Phosphoric acid and sulfuric(IV) acid are both weak acids. They do not dissociate completely in solution. Instead they exist in dynamic equilibria:

$H_2SO_3(aq) \rightarrow H^+(aq) + HSO_3^-(aq)$

$H_3PO_4(aq) \rightarrow H^+(aq) + H_2PO_4^-(aq)$

In both cases, further ionisation can happen.

QUESTIONS

6. Explain how the pH values of aqueous sodium oxide, magnesium oxide and aluminium oxide are related to electronegativity.
7. Draw the three-dimensional structures of P_4O_{10} and SiO_2. When added to water, which oxide gives the more acidic solution and why?
8. Write an equation showing how magnesium oxide reacts with water.

Reactions of the oxides of sodium, magnesium, aluminium, silicon, phosphorus and sulfur with acids and bases

The basic oxides (Na_2O and MgO) react with acids, while the acidic oxides (P_4O_{10}, SO_2 and SO_3) react with bases.

Reaction of ionic oxides with acids:

$Na_2O(s) + H_2SO_4(aq) \rightarrow Na_2SO_4(aq) + H_2O(l)$

$Na_2O(s) + 2HCl(aq) \rightarrow 2NaCl(aq) + H_2O(l)$

$MgO(s) + H_2SO_4(aq) \rightarrow MgSO_4(aq) + H_2O(l)$

$MgO(s) + 2HCl(aq) \rightarrow MgCl_2(aq) + H_2O(l)$

Reaction of covalent oxides with bases:

$P_4O_{10}(s) + 12NaOH(aq) \rightarrow 4Na_3PO_4(aq) + 6H_2O(l)$

$SO_2(g) + 2NaOH(aq) \rightarrow Na_2SO_3(aq) + H_2O(l)$

$SO_3(g) + 2NaOH(aq) \rightarrow Na_2SO_4(aq) + H_2O(l)$

Aluminium oxide reacts with solutions of strong bases such as NaOH(aq) and with strong acids such as H_2SO_4(aq). We say that it is amphoteric. The bonds in aluminium oxide have both ionic and covalent character, explaining its amphoteric properties.

The equations for the reactions are the following:

In acid:

$Al_2O_3(s) + 3H_2SO_4(aq) \rightarrow Al_2(SO_4)_3(aq) + 3H_2O(l)$

or (as an ionic equation)

$Al_2O_3(s) + 6H_3O^+(aq) + 3H_2O(l) \rightarrow 2[Al(H_2O)_6]^{3+}(aq)$

In alkali:

$Al_2O_3(s) + 2NaOH(aq) + 3H_2O(l) \rightarrow 2NaAl(OH)_4(aq)$

or (as an ionic equation)

$Al_2O_3(s) + 2OH^-(aq) + 3H_2O(l) \rightarrow 2Al(OH)_4^-(aq)$

Overall:

$$[Al(OH)_4]^- \xleftarrow{\text{with alkali}} Al_2O_3 \xrightarrow{\text{with acid}} [Al(H_2O)_6]^{3+}$$

behaves as an acid   behaves as a base

Because silicon dioxide, SiO_2, exists as a large covalent molecule it does not react with acids. However, it does react with hot concentrated alkaline solutions to give sodium silicate:

$SiO_2(s) + 2NaOH(aq) \rightarrow Na_2SiO_3(aq) + H_2O(l)$

QUESTIONS

9. Which oxide of the Period 3 elements is classed as an amphoteric oxide? Write equations showing how it reacts with H_2SO_4, HCl and KOH.
10. P_4O_{10} and SO_3 are classified as acidic oxides. What does this mean? Write equations showing how they react with NaOH.
11. Using your knowledge of how sodium reacts with water, write an equation for the reaction of potassium with water.
12. Write equations for the reaction of aluminium oxide with hydrochloric acid (a mineral acid) and sodium hydroxide (an alkali).

Stretch and challenge

13. Selenium is an element in Group 16 of the Periodic Table below sulfur. The reaction between selenium and oxygen produces an oxide of formula SeO_2. Predict the molecular formula of the compound formed when SeO_2 is dissolved in water. Write an equation for this reaction and predict whether the product is acidic or basic.
14. Oxidation of aluminium gives a thin layer of aluminium oxide on the surface of the metal. Suggest a reason for why this layer protects aluminium from further oxidation in moist air.

KEY IDEAS

- The type of bonding in the oxides of Period 3 elements determines their chemical characteristics.
- The ionic character of the oxides decreases from left to right across Period 3.
- The basic character of the oxides in water decreases from left to right across Period 3.
- Sodium and magnesium have basic oxides, aluminium oxide is amphoteric, and the oxides of silicon, phosphorus and sulfur are acidic.

15.2 REACTIONS OF IONS IN AQUEOUS SOLUTION

When ionic compounds dissolve in water, the lattice breaks up and the ions become free to move in solution. They become hydrated aqua ions (see *Section 1.3 in Chapter 1 of Year 2 Student Book*).

Cations have a positive charge. They are attracted to the negative end of the polar water molecules. Anions have a negative charge. They are attracted to the positive end of the water molecules. Further water molecules are attracted and form weak bonds with the water molecules held most closely to the ion. A hydration shell forms (Figure 14). The number of water molecules in the shell is called the hydration number.

When ions move through a solution, the hydration number may vary.

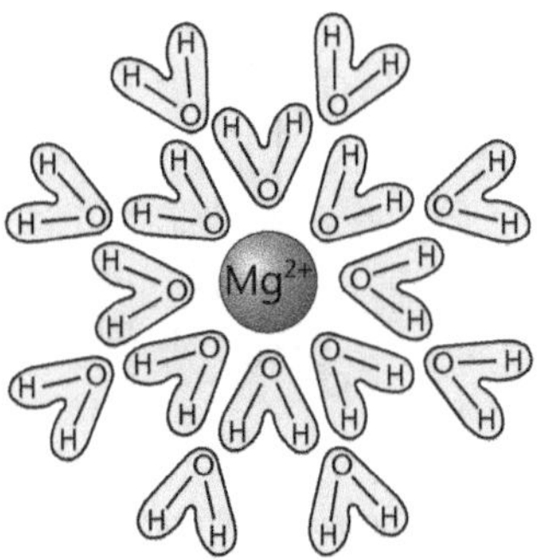

Figure 14 *Hydration shell of a magnesium ion, $Mg^{2+}(aq)$*

Hydrated transition metal ions

The immediate hydration spheres of some metal ions, in other words, those water molecules bonded directly to the metal ion, have a characteristic coordination number and geometry (Figures 15 and 16). This is especially true for transition metal ions. Most commonly the coordination number is 6 and the geometry is octahedral.

A lone pair of electrons from a water molecule forms a coordinate bond (dative covalent bond) with an unoccupied d orbital of the metal ion. Water acts as a Lewis base and a ligand (see *Chapter 16 of Year 2 Student Book*) and the metal ion acts as a Lewis acid.

Figure 15 *The structure of a hexaaqua metal complex with coordination number 6. The charge on the central ion may be 2+ or 3+.*

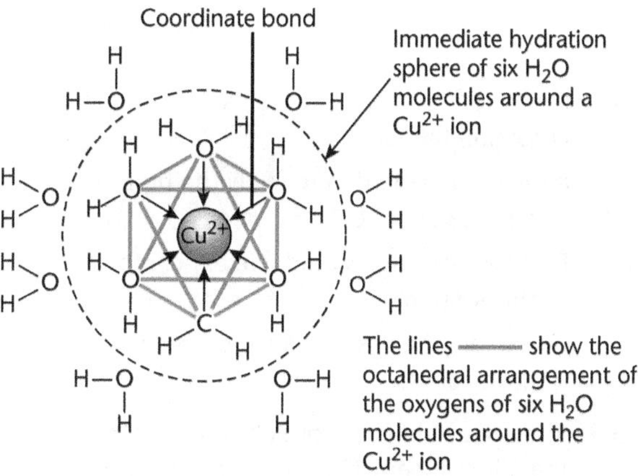

Figure 16 *The structure of $[Cu(H_2O)_6]^{2+}$. Six water molecules surround a copper(II) ion in an octahedral arrangement.*

Hydrolysis of metal–aqua ions gives acidic solutions

Anhydrous aluminium chloride, for example, dissolves in water to produce hexaaquaaluminium(III) ions:

$$AlCl_3 + 6H_2O \rightarrow [Al(H_2O)_6]^{3+} + 3Cl^-$$

The solution is acidic because a proton is transferred from a bonded water molecule to another water molecule that is not bonded:

$$[Al(H_2O)_6]^{3+} + H_2O \rightleftharpoons [Al(H_2O)_5OH]^{2+} + H_3O^+$$

The aluminium ion pulls electron density away from the O–H bond in the coordinated water, weakening the bond. This allows a proton (a H^+ ion) to break away to form H_3O^+. Notice that this is an equilibrium reaction. $[Al(H_2O)_6]^{3+}$ behaves as a weak acid (*Chapter 4 of Year 2 Student Book*).

All metal–aqua ions behave as weak acids if the charge on the metal ion is +2 or +3:

$$[M(H_2O)_6]^{X+} + H_2O \rightleftharpoons [M(H_2O)_5OH]^{(X-1)+} + H_3O^+$$

This is sometimes described as a hydrolysis reaction. Further dissociation of other bonded water molecules can happen, but to a much lesser extent.

The acidity of the solution depends on the position of the equilibrium. The further it lies to the right, the more acidic the solution (the higher the concentration of H_3O^+). This equilibrium can be quantified by an equilibrium constant K_a, the dissociation constant.

For example, for the general reaction of metal–aqua ions with a 2^+ charge,

$$[M(H_2O)_6]^{2+} + H_2O \rightleftharpoons [M(H_2O)_5OH]^+ + H_3O^+$$

The equilibrium constant for the dissociation of one bonded water molecule is given by

$$K_c = \frac{[[M(H_2O)_5(OH)]^+][H_3O^+]}{[[M(H_2O)_6]^{2+}][H_2O]}$$

Since the water is in a large excess, we can assume that its concentration remains constant. This means that we can write the acid dissociation constant K_a as

$$K_a = \frac{[[M(H_2O)_5(OH)]^+][H_3O^+]}{[[M(H_2O)_6]^{2+}]}$$

Because of the magnitudes of the numbers it is often easier to work with pK_a than with K_a itself, where pK_a is given by the expression

$$pK_a = -\log_{10} K_a$$

For $[M(H_2O)_6]^{3+}$, K_a varies between 10^{-2} and 10^{-5} (pK_a = 2 to 5). These ions are weak acids, and solutions typically have pH 3 (Figure 17).

For $[M(H_2O)_6]^{2+}$, K_a varies between 10^{-6} and 10^{-11} (pK_a = 6 to 11). These ions are very weak acids, and solutions typically have pH 6.

For $[M(H_2O)_6]^+$, the dissociation is negligible. These ions are not acidic, and solutions are neutral, pH 7.

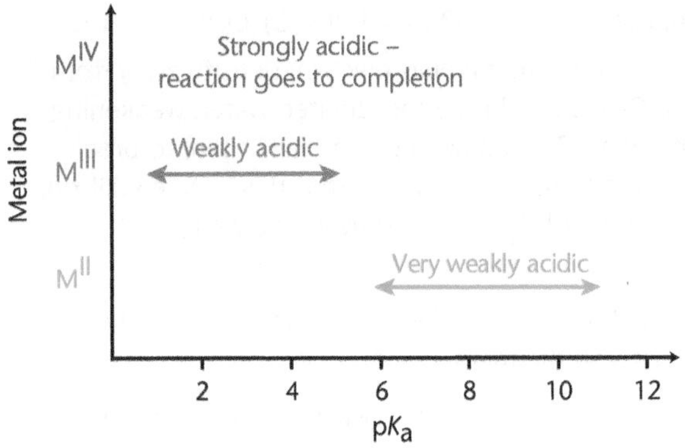

Figure 17 *pK_a values for metal ions*

If an alkali such as aqueous sodium hydroxide is added to a solution of hexaaqua ions, H_3O^+ ions are removed from the solution and the equilibrium moves to the right to replace the H_3O^+ ions removed:

$$H_3O^+ + OH^- \rightarrow 2H_2O$$

If an acid is added, the equilibrium will move to the left to remove H_3O^+ ions from the system, and more metal–hexaaqua ions are produced (Figure 18).

Add acid

$$[M(H_2O)_6]^{3+} + H_2O \rightleftharpoons [M(H_2O)_5(OH)]^{2+} + H_3O^+$$

Add base

Figure 18 *The equilibrium can be shifted by the addition of an acid or base*

The properties of metal ions that affect the of acidity of their aqua ions in solution are:

- the charge on the metal ion
- the size of the metal ion.

The larger the charge on the metal, the greater the attraction of the electrons of the oxygen, leading to weakening of the O–H bond. This explains why $[M(H_2O)_6]^{3+}$ complex ions are stronger acids than $[M(H_2O)_6]^{2+}$ ions.

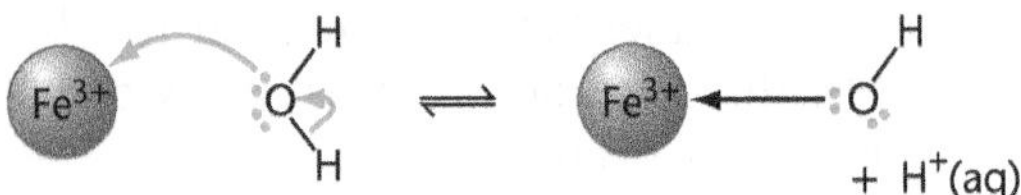

Figure 19 *Schematic diagram showing hydrolysis*

Metal ions carrying the same charge but of different sizes have differing strengths of attraction for electrons in the O–H bonds of water. The greater ionic charge/size ratio (Table 2), the stronger the attraction for the electrons and, consequently, there is more dissociation, producing a more acidic solution. However, the ionic charge is more significant than the size in determining overall acidity.

Figure 20 *Ionic charge/size ratio*

Element	Charge	Ionic radius/nm	Charge/ size ratio
Na	1+	0.95	1.1
Mg	2+	0.65	4.7
Al	3+	0.50	6.0

Table 2 *Charge/size ratio for the elements Na, Mg and Al*

QUESTIONS

15. An aqueous solution contains chromium(III) ions.

   a. Write an equation to show the first equilibrium of Cr^{3+} in water.

   b. What pH value would you expect for this system?

   c. Explain the reasons for the pH you have chosen.

16. When Cu^{2+} ions are dissolved in water the following equilibrium is set up.

$$[Cu(H_2O)_6]^{2+} + H_2O \rightleftharpoons [Cu(H_2O)_5(OH)]^+ + H_3O^+$$

   a. Does this equilibrium lie to the right or the left?

   b. What would happen to the equilibrium if dilute HCl was added to the solution?

   c. What would happen to the equilibrium if dilute NaOH was added to the solution?

KEY IDEAS

- +2 and +3 metal–aqua ions hydrolyse in aqueous solution.
- The pH of a solution of M^{3+} aqua ions is lower than the pH of a solution of M^{2+} aqua ions of the same concentration.
- The acidity of solutions of metal ions is decided predominantly by the charge, but also the size of the metal ion.

Reactions of aqua ions with alkalis

Alkalis are bases that dissolve in water to give solutions that contain the hydroxide ion, $OH^-(aq)$. Reactions of aqua ions with alkalis can produce insoluble metal hydroxides (Figure 22 and Table 3).

If hydroxide ions are added to a solution of a metal–aqua complex, the equilibrium moves further to the right and, when sufficient $OH^-(aq)$ has been added, an insoluble metal hydroxide forms.

This can be illustrated by the reaction of hexaaquacopper(II) ions with $OH^-(aq)$. In aqueous solution, the equilibrium

$$[Cu(H_2O)_6]^{2+} + H_2O \rightleftharpoons [Cu(H_2O)_5(OH)]^+ + H_3O^+$$

lies well over to the left.

Addition of $OH^-(aq)$ shifts the equilibrium to the right (Le Chatelier's principle). Further addition of $OH^-(aq)$ precipitates hydrated copper(II) hydroxide, $[Cu(H_2O)_4(OH)_2]$:

$$[Cu(H_2O)_5(OH)]^+ + OH^- \rightarrow [Cu(H_2O)_4(OH)_2] + H_2O$$

A blue solid, $[Cu(H_2O)_4(OH)_2]$, precipitates from solution. This is not an equilibrium. The reaction goes to completion, though it can be reversed by the addition of an acid, $H^+(aq)$.

$[Cu(H_2O)_4(OH)_2]$ is hydrated copper(II) hydroxide. When it dries it produces copper(II) hydroxide, $Cu(OH)_2$.

The overall reaction may be shown by the equation

$$[Cu(H_2O)_6]^{2+} + 2OH^- \rightarrow [Cu(H_2O)_4(OH)_2] + 2H_2O$$

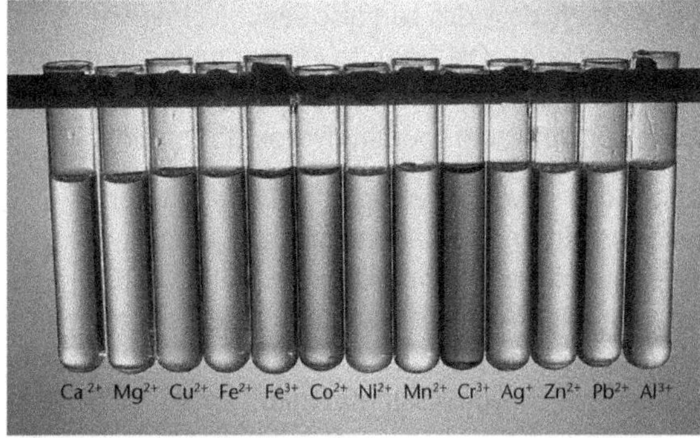

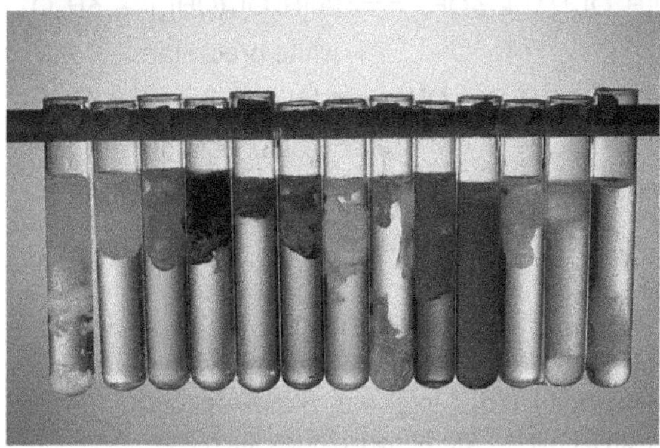

Figure 21 *Aqueous sodium hydroxide can be used in qualitative analysis, because it gives characteristic coloured solutions (upper tubes) and precipitates (lower tubes) with aqueous metal ions*

A similar process occurs for other metal–aqua complexes with the general formula $[M(H_2O)_6]^{2+}$. For example, addition of $OH^-(aq)$ to hexaaquairon(II) produces a green precipitate of iron(II) hydroxide:

$$[Fe(H_2O)_6]^{2+} + 2OH^- \rightarrow [Fe(H_2O)_4(OH)_2] + 2H_2O$$

This also happens when $OH^-(aq)$ is added to metal–aqua complexes with the general formula $[M(H_2O)_6]^{3+}$. For example, when aqueous sodium hydroxide is added to $[Fe(H_2O)_6]^{3+}$ a similar set of reactions can take place:

$$[Fe(H_2O)_6]^{3+} + H_2O \rightleftharpoons [Fe(H_2O)_5(OH)]^{2+} + H_3O^+$$
$$[Fe(H_2O)_5(OH)]^{2+} + H_2O \rightleftharpoons [Fe(H_2O)_4(OH)_2]^+ + H_3O^+$$
$$[Fe(H_2O)_4(OH)_2]^+ + OH^- \rightarrow [Fe(H_2O)_3(OH)_3] + H_2O$$

Aqua complex	Hydroxide	Colour of precipitate
$M^{2+}(aq)$		
$[Cu(H_2O)_6]^{2+}$	$[Cu(H_2O)_4(OH)_2]$	Light blue
$[Fe(H_2O)_6]^{2+}$	$[Fe(H_2O)_4(OH)_2]$	Green
$M^{3+}(aq)$		
$[Fe(H_2O)_6]^{3+}$	$[Fe(H_2O)_3(OH)_3]$	Brown
$[Al(H_2O)_6]^{3+}$	$[Al(H_2O)_3(OH)_3]$	White

Table 3 *Differently coloured precipitates formed by the addition of sodium hydroxide solution to metal ions can be used to identify the metal*

Most metal hydroxides can also react further with excess hydroxide, $OH^-(aq)$, to form complex ions with a negative charge (anionic complexes). Some, however, require concentrated sodium hydroxide solution.

When sodium hydroxide solution is added to an aqueous solution of an aluminium salt a white precipitate of aluminium hydroxide, $[Al(H_2O)_3(OH)_3]$, is formed initially. As more sodium hydroxide is added, the precipitate dissolves to give a colourless solution containing tetrahydroxoaluminate(III) ions, $[Al(OH)_4]^-$:

$$[Al(H_2O)_6]^{3+} + 3OH^- \rightleftharpoons [Al(H_2O)_3(OH)_3] + 3H_2O$$

white precipitate

$$[Al(H_2O)_3(OH)_3] + OH^- \rightleftharpoons [Al(OH)_4]^- + 3H_2O$$

colourless solution

$$[Al(H_2O_6)]^{3+} \rightleftharpoons [Al(H_2O)_3(OH)_3] \rightleftharpoons [Al(OH)_4]^-$$

acidic neutral alkaline

The equilibrium reactions can be reversed. When dilute acid is added to $[Al(OH)_4]^-$ a white precipitate of $[Al(H_2O)_3(OH)_3]$ forms, which dissolves when more acid is added to give a colourless solution of $[Al(H_2O)_6]^{3+}$. Metal hydroxides such as $[Al(H_2O)_3(OH)_3]$ that can react with both acids and alkalis are called **amphoteric**.

QUESTIONS

17. Why is aluminium hydroxide $[Al(H_2O)_3(OH)_3]$ classed as amphoteric?

18. Write the chemical equations for the following reactions.

a. Aqueous Fe^{2+} ions with aqueous sodium hydroxide.

b. Hexaaquacopper(II) ions with aqueous sodium hydroxide.

c. $Al(OH)_4^-$ with excess aqueous hydrochloric acid.

19. Consider the equilibrium

$$[Fe(H_2O)_6]^{3+} + H_2O \rightleftharpoons [Fe(H_2O)_5(OH)]^{2+} + H_3O^+$$

pale violet brown

A series of changes take place on addition of different solutions to this equilibrium. Explain the changes that take place in each of the following, using equations in each case.

a. Adding dilute hydrochloric acid changes the colour of the above solution from brown to pale violet.

b. Adding dilute sodium hydroxide solution changes the colour of the solution from pale violet to brown.

c. Adding excess sodium hydroxide solution gives a brown precipitate, which is insoluble in 2 mol dm^{-3} sodium hydroxide solution.

Reactions with ammonia solution

Similar reactions occur if aqueous ammonia is added to metal–aqua ions. This is because ammonia solution is alkaline on account of the equilibrium

$$NH_3(aq) + H_2O(l) \rightleftharpoons NH_4^+(aq) + OH^-(aq)$$

The hydroxide ions that are formed in the equilibrium precipitate the metal as a hydroxide:

$$[Cu(H_2O)_6]^{2+} + 2NH_3 \rightarrow [Cu(H_2O)_4(OH)_2] + 2NH_4^+$$

$$[Fe(H_2O)_6]^{2+} + 2NH_3 \rightarrow [Fe(H_2O)_4(OH)_2] + 2NH_4^+$$

Even though ammonia is a weak base, the concentration of OH^- is sufficient to shift the equilibrium to the right to allow the precipitate to form.

If the ammonia is in excess, most transition metal hydroxides react further to form soluble ammine complexes (see *Chapter 16 in Year 2 Student Book*). For example, reacting a blue solution of hexaaquacopper(II) with 2 moles of aqueous ammonia gives a pale blue precipitate of copper hydroxide; however, when excess ammonia is added, the precipitate dissolves to give a deep blue solution of tetraamminebisaquacopper(II) ions. The substitution of the water ligand by ammonia in transition metal complex ions also leads to a colour change:

$$[Cu(H_2O)_6]^{2+} + 2NH_3 \rightleftharpoons [Cu(OH_2)(H_2O)_4] + 2NH_4^+$$

blue pale blue

$$[Cu(H_2O)_6]^{2+} + 4NH_3 \rightleftharpoons [Cu(NH_3)_4(H_2O)_2] + 4H_2O$$

blue blue-violet tetraamminebisaquacopper(II) ion

Reaction of hexaaquaaluminium(III) with excess ammonia does not form an ammine complex, so it is considered insoluble in aqueous ammonia.

ASSIGNMENT 1: LANDFILL SITES CAN LEAD TO CONTAMINATION OF SOILS

(PS 1.2)

Rubbish is buried in landfill sites and microorganisms decompose the contents, mainly into methane and carbon dioxide and a liquid, called leachate. Metal ions present in the rubbish can become hydrated and dissolve in the leachate. Before the 1970s landfill sites were not regulated, and the leachate can leak into the surrounding soil and nearby watercourses.

Figure A1 A landfill site

Questions

A1. The leachate in a landfill site was found to contain high concentrations of Cu^{2+} and Fe^{3+} ions. Write the equation for the hydrolysis of $Cu^{2+}(aq)$ and $Fe^{3+}(aq)$ in water.

A2. Why are these reactions called hydrolysis reactions?

A3. Explain why hydrolysis is more significant with Fe^{3+} than with Cu^{2+}.

A4. State how hydrolysis will affect the pH of the leachate.

A5. Describe a chemical test that you could undertake in the laboratory to confirm the presence of Cu^{2+} ions. Write equations for the chemical reactions that take place during the test.

A6. A clear sample of green leachate was extracted from a landfill site. Reaction with aqueous ammonia solution produced a green precipitate that slowly turned brown in air. Identify the metal ions present in the leachate. Why does the precipitate slowly turn brown in air?

Reactions with carbonates

Carbonates, such as sodium carbonate, can also be used to precipitate metal hydroxides from solution. Several different reactions are possible, depending on the oxidation state of the metal.

In metal–aqua ions with the general formula $[M(H_2O)_6]^{3+}$, the oxidation state of the metal is III (or +3). The metal–aqua ions hydrolyse as follows:

$$[M(H_2O)_6]^{3+} + H_2O \rightleftharpoons [M(H_2O)_5(OH)]^{2+} + H_3O^+$$

If carbonate ions are present and the concentration of H_3O^+ produced by hydrolysis of the metal–aqua ions is sufficient, the carbonate ions form carbon dioxide. This is evolved as a gas, shifting the equilibrium to the right:

$$2H_3O^+ + CO_3^{2-} \rightarrow CO_2 + 3H_2O$$

As with the addition of sodium hydroxide and of ammonia solution, $[M(H_2O)_6]^{3+}$ ions will react to give the neutral metal hydroxide $[M(H_2O)_3(OH)_3]$. The metal hydroxide forms as a precipitate, rather than the metal carbonate. The overall equation is therefore

$$2[M(H_2O)_6]^{3+} + 3CO_3^{2-} \rightarrow 2[M(H_2O)_3(OH)_3] + 3CO_2 + 3H_2O$$

In metal–aqua ions with the general formula $[M(H_2O)_6]^{2+}$, the oxidation state of the metal is II (or +2). Solutions of these ions are only very weakly acidic, with a low equilibrium concentration of H_3O^+. This concentration is too low to react with a carbonate and produce carbon dioxide gas. Therefore, the equilibrium is not shifted sufficiently to the right to lead to the formation of the metal(II) hydroxide. Instead, the metal(II) carbonate is formed; these carbonates are not very soluble in water, and precipitate from solution:

$$[M(H_2O)_6]^{2+} + H_2O \rightleftharpoons [M(H_2O)_5(OH)]^+ + H_3O^+$$

$$\underset{\text{pale green solution}}{[Fe(H_2O)_6]^{2+}} + CO_3^{2-} \rightleftharpoons \underset{\text{green precipitate}}{FeCO_3} + 6H_2O$$

$[Cu(H_2O)_6]^{2+} + CO_3^{2-}$ blue solution → $CuCO_3 + 6H_2O$ green-blue precipitate

A summary of the reactions of metal–aqua ions with hydroxide, ammonia and carbonate is presented in Table 4.

	Base added				
	OH^-, small amount	OH^-, excess	NH_3, small amount	NH_3, excess	CO_3^{2-}
Aqueous M(II) ion solution					
Fe(II), green, $[Fe(H_2O)_6]^{2+}$	Green precipitate, $Fe(OH)_2$	Does not dissolve	Green precipitate, easily oxidised by air – turns to brown $Fe(OH)_3$	Green precipitate dissolves to give pale brown solution – turns brown in air	Green participate, $FeCO_3$
Cu(II), blue, $[Cu(H_2O)_6]^{2+}$	Pale blue precipitate, $Cu(OH)_2$	Does not dissolve	Pale blue precipitate, $Cu(OH)_2$	Deep blue solution, $[Cu(NH_3)_4(H_2O)_2]^{2+}$	Green–blue precipitate, $CuCO_3$
Aqueous M(III) ion solution					
Fe(III), violet, $[Fe(H_2O)_6]^{3+}$ (appears brown due to hydrolysis)	Brown precipitate, $[Fe(H_2O)_3(OH)_3]$	Does not dissolve	Brown precipitate, $[Fe(H_2O)_3(OH)_3]$	Does not dissolve	Brown precipitate of hydroxide, $[Fe(H_2O)_3(OH)_3]$, and CO_2 evolved
Al(III), colourless	White precipitate, $Al(OH)_3$	Dissolves to form colourless solution, $[Al(OH)_4]^-$	White precipitate, $Al(H_2O)_3(OH)_3$	Does not dissolve	White precipitate of hydroxide, $Al(OH)_3$, and CO_2 evolved

Table 4 *Summary of the reactions of metal–aqua ions with hydroxide, ammonia and carbonate*

QUESTIONS

20. Why does $[Fe(H_2O)_6]^{2+}$ give $FeCO_3$ on reaction with aqueous sodium carbonate but $[Fe(H_2O)_6]^{3+}$ gives $[Fe(H_2O)_3(OH)_3]$?

KEY IDEAS

- Adding strong alkalis to transition metal salts gives hydroxide precipitates.
- Metal hydroxides that can react with both acids and alkalis are amphoteric.
- Adding acids or alkalis to solutions containing hydrolysis equilibria shifts the equilibria.
- Metal(III) ions in an excess of strong alkali give soluble complex ions containing the hydroxo ligand.
- Metal(II)–aqua ions give precipitates of carbonates on addition of sodium carbonate solution.
- Metal(III)–aqua ions give precipitates of hydroxides and carbon dioxide gas on addition of sodium carbonate solution.

ASSIGNMENT 2: MINING LEACHATE AND THE EFFECT ON THE ENVIRONMENT

(PS 1.1, PS 1.2, PS 2.1, AT k)

Water is an essential resource for mining and other metal-manufacturing processes, so watercourses have been contaminated with heavy metals such as copper, silver and lead by leaching. Contaminated land can often be 'reclaimed' by growing plants which are tolerant of high concentrations of metals and can remove them from the soil.

Figure A1 *There may be contamination of this site by heavy metals. It is easy to see if there is discoloured water, but the site may need further testing to determine the extent of the contamination.*

Questions

A1. The water in some pools around a copper mine is clear and blue. Give a chemical explanation for the water's appearance.

A2. The following experiments were carried out with water from the pools.

Experiment 1

i. Ten drops of the pool water were added to a test tube.

ii. Ten drops of sodium carbonate solution were added and the test tube was gently shaken.

Experiment 2

i. Ten drops of the pool water were added to a test tube.

ii. Ten drops of aqueous ammonia were added and the test tube was gently shaken. A blue precipitate was observed.

iii. After standing for 5 minutes, the precipitate dissolved to give a blue solution.

a. What would you observe in experiment 1?

b. What is the formula of the blue precipitate observed in experiment 2?

c. Write chemical equations that show what is occurring in the two experiments.

d. What are the hazards associated with aqueous ammonia? What safety precautions would you take when using aqueous ammonia?

A3. Old industrial sites are often referred to as 'brownfield' sites. Why might companies be wary of developing on these sites?

A4. Two different types of plant were identified growing near an abandoned copper mine. Five plants of each type were removed from different areas around the site and the copper content of their leaves analysed.

Plant species A (mg of copper per kg of leaves)	Plant species B (mg of copper per kg of leaves)
18	16
100	57
150	101
16	37
206	126

Table A1 *Amounts of copper found in different plant species*

Suggest one reason why there are large differences in the amounts of copper found in plants of the same species.

A5. Which plant would you advise someone to cultivate to decontaminate soil contaminated with copper?

A6. Hydrangeas are plants that are particularly sensitive to the pH of the soil in which they grow. If the soil is acidic their flowers are blue, but in alkaline soil they are pink. By reference to transition metals, can you suggest a reason why some soils are more acidic than others?

A7. A garden's soil was slightly alkaline. A gardener noticed that while most of his hydrangea flowers were pink, there was one plant near a metal gate post that grew blue flowers. Explain this observation.

Stretch and challenge

A8. At low pH, nearly all metals are more soluble than in neutral water. Generally, soft water contains more aluminium ions (dissolved from soil and rocks) than does hard water.

Most plumbing in houses is made from copper pipe. Explain why there are higher amounts of dissolved copper in drinking water in a soft water area than in a hard water area. Illustrate your answer by writing equations for the chemical reactions occurring.

REQUIRED PRACTICAL ACTIVITY 11: APPARATUS AND TECHNIQUES

(PS 1.1, PS 1.2, PS 2.1, AT b, AT d, AT k)

Carry out simple test-tube reactions to identify transition metal ions in aqueous solution

This practical activity gives you the opportunity to show that you can:

- Use a water bath.
- Use laboratory apparatus for a variety of techniques, including qualitative tests for transition metal ions.
- Safely and carefully handle solids and liquids, including corrosive, irritant, flammable and toxic substances.

Apparatus

Qualitative tests to identify transition metal ions in aqueous solution are carried out in a similar fashion to those described in *Chapter 12 of Year 1 Student Book* and in *Chapter 6 of Year 2 Student Book*. If the sample that is being tested is a solid, then an aqueous solution will have to be prepared. Dissolve a small quantity of the solid in a beaker with deionised water (not tap water), stirring with a glass rod if necessary. Label the beaker.

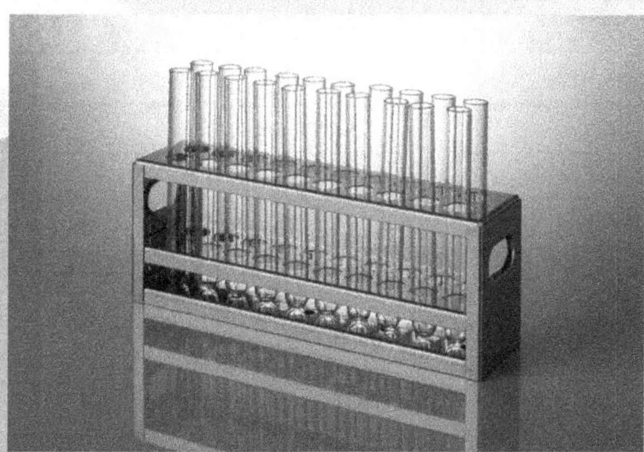

Figure P1 *If you are carrying out more than one test, then a test-tube rack is necessary*

Generally, qualitative tests such as these are carried out in a test tube or a boiling tube. It is important that these tubes are clean to avoid contamination, which would lead to a false result. It is also important that any solutions that are used are transferred to the test tube with a clean dropping pipette to avoid contamination. The test tubes should be labelled and stored in a test tube rack.

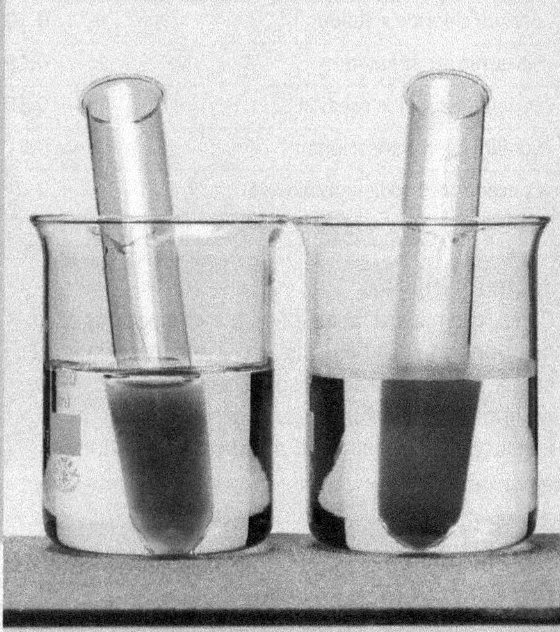

Figure P2 *Warming a test reaction by placing the test tube in a beaker of warm water*

It may be necessary to warm the mixture of reagents in the test tube in order for the test to be carried out. In this case it is convenient to rest the test tube carefully in a beaker of warm water (Figure P2).

Reagents are usually stored in labelled bottles. If you are using silver nitrate solution, this will be stored in a dark glass bottle as it is light sensitive. The common reagents used to identify transition metal ions and common anions are listed below, together with their hazards.

Reagent	Concentration/mol dm^{-3}	Hazard at this concentration
Dilute ammonia solution	2.0	Irritant
Concentrated ammonia solution	14.4	18M concentrated ammonia is Corrosive and Very Toxic to the Environment. 14M is Corrosive and Toxic to the Environment.
Dilute hydrochloric acid	0.40	Irritant
Barium chloride solution	0.10	Harmful
Silver nitrate solution	0.10	Irritant
Sodium hydroxide solution	< 0.50	Irritant
Sodium carbonate solution	0.5	No hazard classification
Concentrated sodium hydroxide solution	2.0	Corrosive

Techniques

Check the hazard labels of all the compounds and solutions you will be using and use appropriate safety measures and personal protective equipment. Add the reagents according to instructions carefully and avoid contamination.

It is not normally required to measure volumes accurately for qualitative tests. If the solution needs to be heated, it is convenient to use a hot water bath. Record all observations carefully; note particularly any colour change, any precipitate formation and any gas evolution.

QUESTIONS

P1. How does the concentration of sodium hydroxide solution affect its hazard warning?

P2. Why is it necessary to dissolve samples for testing in deionised water and not tap water?

P3. Aqueous solutions of three transition metal salts ($FeSO_4$, $CuCl_2$ and $Fe(NO_3)_3$) have been provided and the following observations made upon testing:

Sample	Colour of initial solution	Dilute NaOH(aq) added	Na_2CO_3(aq) added
A	Green	Green precipitate	Green precipitate
B	Blue	Blue precipitate	Green–blue precipitate
C	Brown	Brown precipitate	Brown precipitate and CO_2 evolved

a. Match each sample (A, B and C) with the transition metal salt. Write equations to show how each hexaaqua metal ion reacts with dilute aqueous sodium hydroxide.

b. Describe what you would observe if 10 drops of aqueous silver nitrate solution were added to each of the solutions A, B and C in separate test tubes.

Stretch and challenge

P4. A ruby red solution of a chromium salt was provided. It was known to be either chromium(II) chloride, chromium(III) nitrate or chromium(III) sulfate. Two tests were carried out and observations recorded.

a. Upon reaction with aqueous $BaCl_2$ a white precipitate was observed.

b. Upon reaction with aqueous sodium carbonate a green precipitate was observed, as well as evolution of CO_2 gas.

Using these observations, deduce the structure of the chromium salt provided and explain your reasoning.

PRACTICE QUESTIONS

1. a. i. Name the main type of bonding in each of the oxides MgO and P_4O_{10}.
   ii. Explain how the type of bonding in P_4O_{10} can be predicted by a consideration of electronegativity.

   b. Write equations for the reaction of Na_2O and of SO_2 with water.

   c. Write an equation for the reaction of MgO with dilute hydrochloric acid.

   d. Write an equation for the reaction of P_4O_{10} with an excess of aqueous sodium hydroxide.

AQA June 2007 Unit 5 Question 4c–f

2. State what is observed when separate samples of sodium oxide and phosphorus(V) oxide are added to water. Write equations for the reactions which occur and, in each case, state the approximate pH of the solution formed.

AQA June 2005 Unit 5 Question 7b

3. Describe the trend in pH of the solutions formed when the oxides of the Period 3 elements, sodium to sulfur, are added separately to water. Explain this trend by reference to the structure and bonding in the oxides and by writing equations for the reactions with water.

AQA March 1999 CH01 Question 6b

4. a. Write equations to show what happens when the following oxides are added to water and predict approximate values for the pH of the resulting solutions.
   i. sodium oxide
   ii. sulfur dioxide

   b. What is the general relationship between bond type in the oxides of the Period 3 elements and the pH of the solutions which result from addition of the oxides to water?

NEAB June 1997 CH01 Question 6

5. a. Magnesium oxide and sulfur dioxide are added separately to water. In each case describe what happens. Write equations for any reactions which occur and state the approximate pH of any solution formed.

   b. Write equations for two reactions which together show the amphoteric character of aluminium hydroxide.

AQA June 2006 Unit 5 Question 7c–d

6. State what you would observe after addition of the following reagents to separate aqueous solutions containing $[Cr(H_2O)_6]^{3+}$ ions. In each case give the formula of the chromium containing product.
   i. an excess of NaOH(aq)
   ii. Na_2CO_3(aq)

AQA June 2007 Unit 5 Question 3d

7. a. Explain why the atomic radii of the elements decrease across the Period 3 from sodium to chlorine.

   b. Explain why the melting point of sulfur (S_8) is greater than that of phosphorus (P_4).

   c. Explain why sodium oxide forms an alkaline solution when it reacts with water.

   d. Write an equation for the reaction of phosphorus(V) oxide with an excess of sodium hydroxide solution.

AQA Specimen Paper 1 (7405/1) Question 2

8. a. A co-ordinate bond is formed when a transition metal ion reacts with a ligand. Explain how this co-ordinate bond is formed.

   b. Describe what you would observe when dilute aqueous ammonia solution is added dropwise, to excess, to an aqueous solution containing copper(II) ions. Write equations for the reactions that occur.

AQA Specimen Paper 1 (7405/1) Question 8 parts 1–2

9. a. Magnesium oxide, silicon dioxide and phosphorus(V) oxide are white solids but each oxide has a different type of structure and bonding. State the type of bonding in magnesium oxide. Outline a simple experiment to demonstrate that magnesium oxide has this type of bonding.

b. By reference to the structure of, and the bonding in, silicon dioxide, suggest why it is insoluble in water.

c. State how the melting point of phosphorus(V) oxide compares with that of silicon dioxide. Explain your answer in terms of the structure of, and the bonding in, phosphorus(V) oxide.

d. Magnesium oxide is classified as a basic oxide. Write an equation for a reaction that shows magnesium oxide acting as a base with another reagent.

e. Phosphorus(V) oxide is classified as an acidic oxide. Write an equation for its reaction with sodium hydroxide.

AQA Chemistry Unit 5 June 2013 Question 4

10. This question is about test-tube reaction of some ions in aqueous solution. For each reaction in parts a. to c., state the colour of the original solution. State what you would observe after the named reagent has been added to the solution. In each case, write an equation for the reaction that occurs.

a. Sodium hydroxide solution is added to a solution containing $[Fe(H_2O)_6]^{3+}$ ions.

b. An excess of ammonia is added to a solution containing $[Cu(H_2O)_6]^{2+}$ ions.

c. Sodium carbonate solution is added to a solution containing $[Al(H_2O)_6]^{3+}$ ions.

AQA Chemistry Unit 5 Jan 2013 Question 5b–d

11. A chemical company has a waste tank of volume 25 000 dm^3. The tank is full of phosphoric acid (H_3PO_4) solution formed by adding some unwanted phosphorus(V) oxide to water in the tank. A 25.0 cm^3 sample of this solution required 21.2 cm^3 of 0.500 mol dm^{-3} sodium hydroxide solution for complete reaction. Calculate the mass, in kg, of phosphorus(V) oxide that must have been added to the water in the waste tank.

AQA Chemistry Unit 5 Feb 2010 Question 8c

16 TRANSITION METALS

PRIOR KNOWLEDGE

You will already have studied thermodynamics (*Chapter 1 of Year 2 Student Book*), the aqueous chemistry of inorganic compounds and the general properties of transition metal elements (*Chapter 15 of Year 2 Student Book*), and redox chemistry (*Chapter 10 of Year 1 Student Book*). You should also understand the different types of stereoisomerism (*Chapter 5 of Year 1 Student Book*), including optical isomerism, chemical equilibria (*Chapter 9 of Year 1 Student Book*) and the chemistry of electrochemical cells (*Chapter 14 of Year 2 Student Book*).

LEARNING OBJECTIVES

In this chapter you will learn about the different types of ligands that can bond to transition metals, as well as the shapes that complex ions can form. You will be able to draw the *cis–trans* and optical isomers of metal complex ions and understand how colour arises in transition metal compounds. You will learn about the variable oxidation states of transition metals and how they can act as heterogeneous and homogeneous catalysts.

(Specification 3.2.5.2, 3.2.5.3, 3.2.5.4, 3.2.5.5, 3.2.5.6)

Transition metal complexes are essential to life. The efficiency of oxygen transport relies on the formation and dissociation of oxygen–iron(II) porphyrin complexes in mammals and oxygen–copper(II) haemocyanin complexes in marine invertebrates. *Cis*-platinum(II) complexes are a powerful tool in chemotherapy, owing to their ability to bind DNA strands and affect replication in cancerous cells.

The large availability of binding sites on transition metals is ideal for catalysis, where a metal–reagent intermediate lowers the activation energy of a given reaction and therefore makes it happen under mild conditions. Catalytic converters based on transition metals are currently fitted to both diesel and petrol vehicles, where they promote both the oxidation of carbon monoxide and uncombusted hydrocarbons and the reduction of nitrogen oxides.

Complexes of platinum(II) and iridium(III) with conjugated ring-type ligands show stable, bright light emission when incorporated into low-voltage electronic circuits. A new generation of full-colour displays based on organic LEDs (OLEDs, or Organic Light Emitting Diodes) relies on these exciting new molecules.

Complexes of ruthenium(II) show intense absorption bands in the visible region of the spectrum. This unique feature has prompted their application in dye-sensitised solar cells, which are proving a more efficient alternative to traditional silicon photovoltaics in low-light conditions, as found in northern Europe.

16.1 GENERAL PROPERTIES OF TRANSITION METALS

The **transition metal** elements are found in the central d block of the Periodic Table (Figure 1). The first transition series, in Period 4 of the Periodic Table, contains the elements from scandium to zinc. The Period 4 elements have common properties:

- They form complex ions.
- Their ions are coloured.
- They show catalytic activity.
- Their oxidation states are variable.

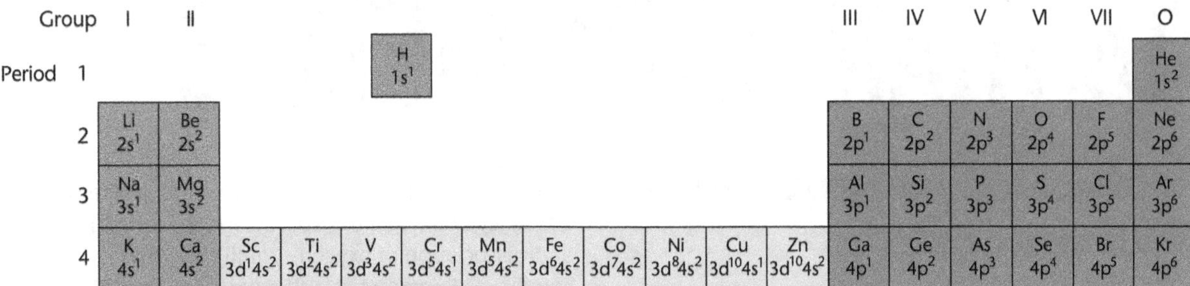

Figure 1 *Periods 1 to 4 of the Periodic Table*

A transition metal is defined as an element that has an incomplete d subshell either in the element or in one of its ions. The properties of transition elements are directly related to the electronic structures of their atoms.

The 4s subshell is at a lower energy than the 3d subshell and fills up first (Figure 2). Chromium and copper can promote a 4s electron to the d subshell and this gives rise to a half-filled and a fully filled d shell, respectively, which are stabilised. If electrons occupy the 3d subshell, the 4s subshell increases to a higher energy level. This means that, when transition metal atoms react, they lose the 4s electrons first.

The normal ion formed in scandium compounds is Sc(III). This has no electrons in the d orbital – its electron configuration is [Ar]$3d^0 4s^0$ and so scandium is not considered a transition metal. Similarly, zinc

Z	Element	Electron configuration	Electron spin diagram															
			1s	2s	2p			3s	3p			3d					4s
21	Sc	$1s^2 2s^2 2p^6 3s^2 3p^6 3d^1 4s^2$	↑↓	↑↓	↑↓	↑↓	↑↓	↑↓	↑↓	↑↓	↑↓	↑					↑↓
22	Ti	$1s^2 2s^2 2p^6 3s^2 3p^6 3d^2 4s^2$	↑↓	↑↓	↑↓	↑↓	↑↓	↑↓	↑↓	↑↓	↑↓	↑	↑				↑↓
23	V	$1s^2 2s^2 2p^6 3s^2 3p^6 3d^3 4s^2$	↑↓	↑↓	↑↓	↑↓	↑↓	↑↓	↑↓	↑↓	↑↓	↑	↑	↑			↑↓
24	Cr	$1s^2 2s^2 2p^6 3s^2 3p^6 3d^5 4s^1$	↑↓	↑↓	↑↓	↑↓	↑↓	↑↓	↑↓	↑↓	↑↓	↑	↑	↑	↑	↑	↑
25	Mn	$1s^2 2s^2 2p^6 3s^2 3p^6 3d^5 4s^2$	↑↓	↑↓	↑↓	↑↓	↑↓	↑↓	↑↓	↑↓	↑↓	↑	↑	↑	↑	↑	↑↓
26	Fe	$1s^2 2s^2 2p^6 3s^2 3p^6 3d^6 4s^2$	↑↓	↑↓	↑↓	↑↓	↑↓	↑↓	↑↓	↑↓	↑↓	↑↓	↑	↑	↑	↑	↑↓
27	Co	$1s^2 2s^2 2p^6 3s^2 3p^6 3d^7 4s^2$	↑↓	↑↓	↑↓	↑↓	↑↓	↑↓	↑↓	↑↓	↑↓	↑↓	↑↓	↑	↑	↑	↑↓
28	Ni	$1s^2 2s^2 2p^6 3s^2 3p^6 3d^8 4s^2$	↑↓	↑↓	↑↓	↑↓	↑↓	↑↓	↑↓	↑↓	↑↓	↑↓	↑↓	↑↓	↑	↑	↑↓
29	Cu	$1s^2 2s^2 2p^6 3s^2 3p^6 3d^{10} 4s^1$	↑↓	↑↓	↑↓	↑↓	↑↓	↑↓	↑↓	↑↓	↑↓	↑↓	↑↓	↑↓	↑↓	↑↓	↑
30	Zn	$1s^2 2s^2 2p^6 3s^2 3p^6 3d^{10} 4s^2$	↑↓	↑↓	↑↓	↑↓	↑↓	↑↓	↑↓	↑↓	↑↓	↑↓	↑↓	↑↓	↑↓	↑↓	↑↓

Figure 2 *Electronic configurations of the elements from scandium to zinc*

forms Zn(II) compounds with the configuration [Ar]$3d^{10}4s^0$ and because the d subshell is complete, it is also not considered a transition metal. Therefore only the elements from titanium to copper are considered transition metals.

QUESTIONS

1. Write out the electronic configurations for:
   a. Fe
   b. Fe^{2+}
   c. Fe^{3+}.

KEY IDEAS

- Transition metals contain an incomplete d subshell of electrons in an atom or an ion.
- All transition metals have common properties.

16.2 SUBSTITUTION REACTIONS

Transition metal ions in water solutions form coordination complexes with water. Complexes with water ligands are called metal–aqua ions and may be represented as $Co^{2+}(aq)$, $Cu^{2+}(aq)$ etc.

In a complex, the number of bonds formed between the metal ion and lone pairs from the ligands is called the coordination number.

QUESTIONS

2. Identify the coordination number of the metals in the following complex ions:
   a. $[Co(NH_3)_6]^{2+}$
   b. $[Co(NH_3)_6]^{3+}$
   c. $[Cu(CN)_4]^{3-}$
   d. $[Ag(CN)_2]^-$.

Ligands are molecules or ions which can share an electron pair with a metal ion to form a coordination complex. The reaction of the replacement of one or more ligands is called ligand substitution. NH_3 and H_2O are neutral molecules of similar size, which have an electron pair on the nitrogen and the oxygen atom, respectively.

The reactivity of divalent (2+) metal–aqua ions from the fourth period increases from Mn^{2+} to Cu^{2+}. Ligand substitution between water and ammonia occurs without change of coordination number. Ligand substitution can be complete, when all ligands are replaced, or incomplete, when only some of the ligands are replaced. $[Cu(NH_3)_4(H_2O)_2]^{2+}$ is energetically more stable than complexes with either six water or six ammonia molecules, and therefore the substitution of a Cu^{2+} aqua complex with ammonia is incomplete.

The reaction of ligand substitution is reversible and is indicated by a double arrow, indicating it can occur either way. The overall reaction of $Cu^{2+}(aq)$ with NH_3 is made up of four separate equilibrium reactions:

1. $[Cu(H_2O)_6]^{2+} + NH_3 \rightleftharpoons [Cu(NH_3)(H_2O)_5]^{2+} + H_2O$
2. $[Cu(NH_3)(H_2O)_5]^{2+} + NH_3 \rightleftharpoons [Cu(NH_3)_2(H_2O)_4]^{2+} + H_2O$
3. $[Cu(NH_3)_2(H_2O)_4]^{2+} + NH_3 \rightleftharpoons [Cu(NH_3)_3(H_2O)_3]^{2+} + H_2O$
4. $[Cu(NH_3)_3(H_2O)_3]^{2+} + NH_3 \rightleftharpoons [Cu(NH_3)_4(H_2O)_2]^{2+} + H_2O$

Each ligand substitution reaction has an equilibrium constant, K_c.

Equilibrium 1:

$$K_{c1} = \frac{\left[\left[Cu(NH_3)(H_2O)_5\right]^{2+}\right][H_2O]}{\left[\left[Cu(H_2O)_6\right]^{2+}\right][NH_3]}$$

Equilibrium 2:

$$K_{c2} = \frac{\left[\left[Cu(NH_3)_2(H_2O)_4\right]^{2+}\right][H_2O]}{\left[\left[Cu(NH_3)(H_2O)_5\right]^{2+}\right][NH_3]}$$

and so on. Square brackets indicate the equilibrium concentrations in mol dm^{-3} of ions or molecules in aqueous solution. Since water is the solvent and in a large excess, its concentration is assumed to be constant.

The equations can be simplified to give a dissociation constant of the complex, K_d. For example,

$$K_{d1} = \frac{\left[\left[Cu(NH_3)(H_2O)_5\right]^{2+}\right]}{\left[\left[Cu(H_2O)_6\right]^{2+}\right][NH_3]}$$

This is the same assumption and simplification that is used to derive an acid dissociation constant K_a (*Chapter 4 of Year 2 Student Book*). The formation constant, K_f, is the reciprocal of the complex dissociation constant:

$$K_f = \frac{1}{K_d}$$

Halide ions (F^-, Cl^-, Br^- and I^-) are negatively charged ligands that also can share their electron pair with a metal ion, but they are larger in size than water or ammonia. Metal ions of the fourth period such as Cu^{2+}, Fe^{3+} and Co^{2+} are too small to coordinate six halide ions. As a result, the ligand substitution of water with Cl – from HCl involves a change in coordination number from 6 to 4:

$$[Cu(H_2O)_6]^{2+} + 4Cl^- \rightleftharpoons [CuCl_4]^{2-} + 6H_2O.$$

Note that the complex is now negatively charged as a result of the coordination of four chloride ions to one copper(II) ion. Only four fit around because chloride ions are bigger than water molecules.

Ethylenediamine ($H_2NCH_2CH_2NH_2$) and ethanedioate (oxalate) $(C_2O_4)^{2-}$ have two electron pairs each and are called bidentate ligands (meaning with two teeth), as opposed to monodentate ligands (with one tooth) such as ammonia and water. Ligands can have more than two electron pairs, in which case they are called multidentate. Ethylenediaminetetraacetate, $EDTA^{4-}$, and sarcophagine, SAR (Figure 3), have six electron pairs to share with a transition metal ion. Multidentate ligands are also called chelating agents, as they form very stable complexes with transition metal ions.

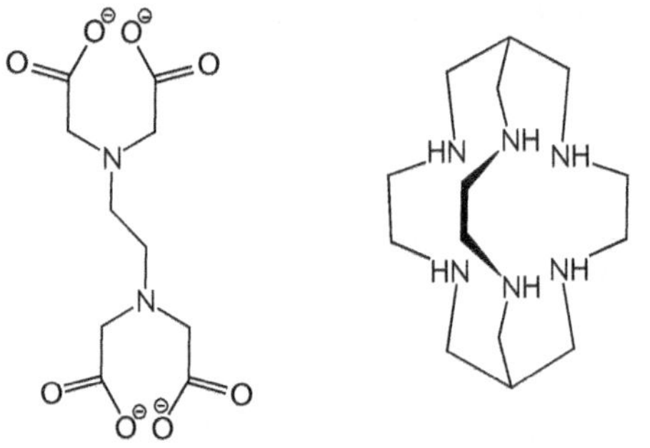

Figure 3 *Skeletal structures of (left) ethylenediaminetetraacetate, EDTA⁴⁻, and (right) sarcophagine, SAR. In EDTA⁴⁻ the two Ns and two of the –O's bond to a metal ion and in SAR six Ns bond to a metal ion.*

All chemical reactions are governed by the second law of thermodynamics, and K_f is proportional to the inverse of the free energy of the reaction:

$$\Delta G^\ominus = \Delta H^\ominus - T\Delta S^\ominus$$

where $\Delta G^\ominus$ is the Gibbs free energy of the reaction, $\Delta H^\ominus$ is the enthalpy change, T is the absolute temperature in kelvin and $\Delta S^\ominus$ is the entropy change. The feasibility of a reaction happening depends on the magnitudes of the two energy terms $\Delta H^\ominus$ and $\Delta S^\ominus$ (see *Chapter 1 of Year 2 Student Book*).

The reaction of ligand substitution with sarcophagine,

$$[Co(NH_3)_6]^{2+} + SAR \rightleftharpoons [Co(SAR)]^{2+} + 6NH_3$$

has a high formation constant. A high value of K_f indicates the forward reaction is thermodynamically favoured and a low value indicates the reverse reaction is favoured. Similarly, the reaction of ligand substitution with EDTA has a high formation constant.

$$[Co(NH_3)_6]^{2+} + EDTA \rightleftharpoons [Co(EDTA)]^{2+} + 6NH_3$$

The enthalpy content when Co^{2+} is bonded to a molecule of sarcophagine is similar to that when it is bonded to six molecules of ammonia. So the enthalpy change $\Delta H^\ominus$ for the reaction is small. However, the entropy change $\Delta S^\ominus$ is very different. The forward reaction is between one ion and one molecule, producing one ion and six molecules. So the entropy change has a high positive value (the system has become more disordered). Therefore, the term $-\Delta S^\ominus$ is highly negative. In contrast, the term for the reverse reaction is highly positive. The forward reaction is an entropy-driven reaction.

Red cells in mammals contain a protein called haemoglobin, which transports oxygen to all tissues via the bloodstream. Each haemoglobin (Hb) molecule contains four chelating agents, called haem groups, each coordinated to an Fe^{2+} ion. Fe^{2+} is also coordinated by one histidine amino acid of the protein and one molecule of water, which is replaced by O_2 in the pulmonary alveoli by ligand substitution. The reaction is an equilibrium:

$$Hb(H_2O) + O_2 \rightleftharpoons Hb(O_2) + H_2O$$

From the equilibrium constant equation it is clear that reducing the concentration (pressure) of oxygen results in a lower concentration of $Hb(O_2)$, which accounts for altitude sickness.

Haemoglobin can react with other ligands that disrupt oxygen transport. Carbon monoxide, CO, can replace oxygen in haemoglobin and is therefore a poisonous gas. The formation constant of Hb(CO) is 210 times higher than that of $Hb(O_2)$.

QUESTIONS

3. Assign positive or negative entropy to the following reactions of ligand substitution:
   a. $[Cu(H_2O)_6]^{2+} + 4Cl^- \rightleftharpoons [CuCl_4]^{2-} + 6H_2O$
   b. $[Ni(en)_3]^{2+} + 4Cl^- \rightleftharpoons [NiCl_4]^{2-} + 3en$
   ('en' is an abbreviation for ethylenediamine)
   c. $[Co(NH_3)_6]^{2+} + EDTA^{4-} \rightleftharpoons [Co(EDTA)]^{2-} + 6NH_3$
4. Write the overall equilibrium constant for the following reactions in water:
   a. $[Cu(H_2O)_6]^{2+} + 4Cl^- \rightleftharpoons [CuCl_4]^{2-} + 6H_2O$
   b. $[Co(NH_3)_6]^{2+} + 4Cl^- \rightleftharpoons [CoCl_4]^{2-} + 6NH_3$
5. Death from carbon monoxide poisoning occurs when the concentration of Hb(CO) is three times that of $Hb(O_2)$. Calculate the corresponding concentration of CO in the air in ppm, knowing the O_2 concentration is 20%.

KEY IDEAS

- A ligand is a molecule or ion that can form a coordinate bond to a metal by donating a pair of electrons.
- A complex ion is a metal atom surrounded by ligands.
- Complexes form by ligand displacement reactions.
- Ligand displacement reactions are dynamic equilibria that can be described by equilibrium constants.

16.3 SHAPES OF COMPLEX IONS

Transition metal complexes are arranged in octahedral symmetry if the coordination number is 6; they are tetrahedral or square planar if the coordination number is 4, and linear if the coordination number is 2 (Figure 4). The size of the ligand has an effect on the coordination number and shape (symmetry) of the complex.

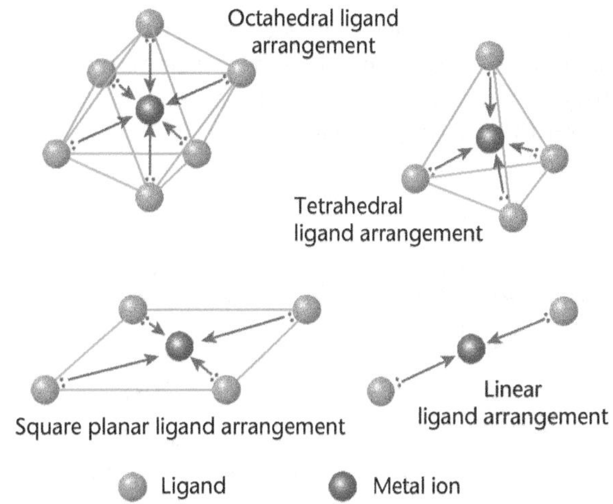

Figure 4 *Symmetry of metal complexes*

Octahedral complexes

Water, ammonia and cyanide are small monodentate ligands and six can fit around a central metal ion, forming an octahedral complex. Octahedral complexes with two (A, B) or three (A, B, C) different ligands can exist as *cis* or *trans* isomers, depending on the position of the coordinating ligands around the metal (Figure 5).

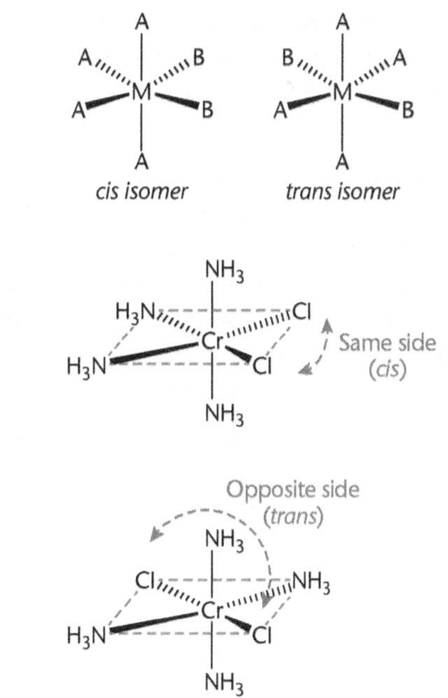

Figure 5 *Cis and trans isomers of octahedral complexes*

For example, $[Cr(NH_3)_4Cl_2]^+$ exists as two isomers, where the chloride ligands can be on the same side (*cis*) or opposite sides (*trans*) of the complex.

An octahedral complex with bidentate ligands can exist as a pair of enantiomers as their mirror images are not superimposable, for example $[Ni(NH_2CH_2CH_2NH_2)_3]^{2+}$ (Figure 6).

Figure 6 *Pairs of enantiomers in octahedral complexes*

Tetrahedral and square planar complexes

With larger ions such as chloride ions, only four ligands can fit around the central metal ion, giving a tetrahedral complex as the preferred geometry.

Complexes of large metal ions with coordination number 4 prefer a square planar geometry, for example cisplatin, which has two Cl^- ligands and two NH_3 ligands.

In a square planar complex, the ligands can be arranged in a *cis* or a *trans* configuration. In the *cis* configuration the A ligands are adjacent, and in the *trans* configuration the A ligands are opposite each other with respect to the metal ion (Figure 7). Since the complex is planar, this *cis–trans* isomerism is similar to *E–Z* isomerism in alkenes.

The square planar complex *cis*-$[Pt(NH_3)_2Cl_2]$ (Figure 8), commonly called cisplatin, a commonly used chemotherapy drug to treat many different cancers. The *cis* symmetry means that the two chloride ligands can be displaced by DNA bases on the same strand. The metal-bound DNA strand can no longer replicate and the cancer cell dies.

The complex ion $[Cu(NH_3)_4(H_2O)_2]^{2+}$ (Figure 9) is often described as square planar, but it also has two water ligands at a greater distance than the ammine ligands, forming a distorted octahedral structure.

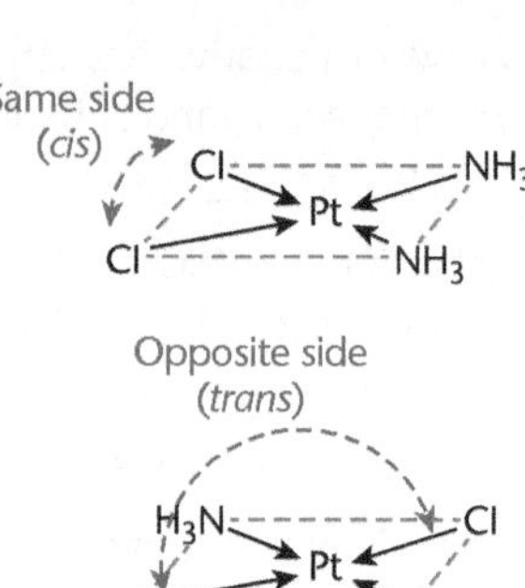

Figure 7 *Cis and trans isomers of square planar complexes*

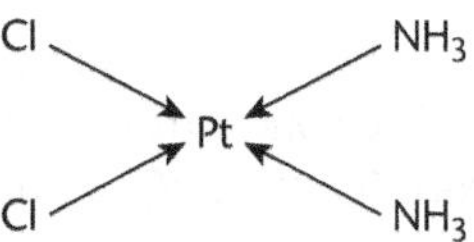

Figure 8 *Structure of cisplatin*

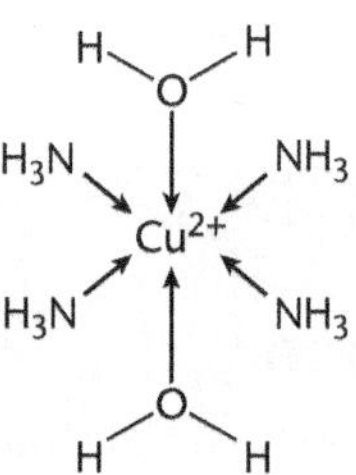

Figure 9 *Structure of* $[Cu(NH_3)_4(H_2O)_2]^{2+}$

Linear complexes

Some transition elements, such as Ag(I) and Cu(I), form complexes with a coordination number of 2. These are linear complexes. An example is $[Ag(NH_3)_2]^+$ (Figure 10), the complex formed in Tollens' reagent, used in the test to distinguish between aldehydes and ketones. This will react with compounds that are easily oxidised, to form metallic silver. This property is used in the silver mirror test to distinguish between ketones and aldehydes.

$$\left[H_3N \longrightarrow Ag \longleftarrow NH_3\right]^+$$

Figure 10 *Structure of* $[Ag(NH_3)_2]^+$

Dilute ammonia is added to silver nitrate solution until the precipitate of Ag_2O, which is formed initially, just redissolves. The solution formed, called Tollens' reagent, contains the soluble $[Ag(NH_3)_2]^+$ ion. When Tollens' reagent is warmed with an aldehyde, the aldehyde is oxidised to an acid and the silver(I) ion is reduced to silver, which forms a silver mirror on the surface of the container (Figure 11):

$$CH_3CHO + H_2O + 2Ag^+ \rightarrow CH_3COOH + 2H^+ + Ag$$

Ketones are not so easily oxidised; they do not form a silver mirror on the surface of the container, and so can be readily distinguished from aldehydes.

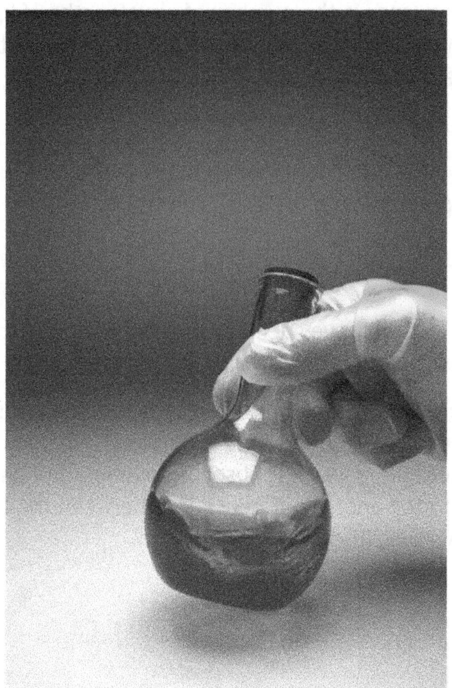

Figure 11 *In the presence of aldehydes, Tollens' reagent is reduced to metallic silver*

QUESTIONS

6. Give the bond angles in
   a. octahedrally shaped complexes
   b. tetrahedrally shaped complexes.
7. Predict the shape of the following molecules or ions:
   a. $[Co(NH_3)_6]^{2+}$
   b. $[CoCl_4]^{2-}$
   c. $[Ag(NH_3)_2]^+$.
8. Draw the two isomers of octahedral $[Co(NH_3)_4(Cl)_2]^+$.
9. Which isomer of $[Cu(NH_3)_4(H_2O)_2]^{2+}$ is drawn in Figure 9?

Stretch and challenge

10. The ethanedioate (or oxalate) ligand is a bidentate ligand.
    a. What type of isomerism is exhibited by the complex ion shown in Figure 12?
    b. Draw the other isomer.

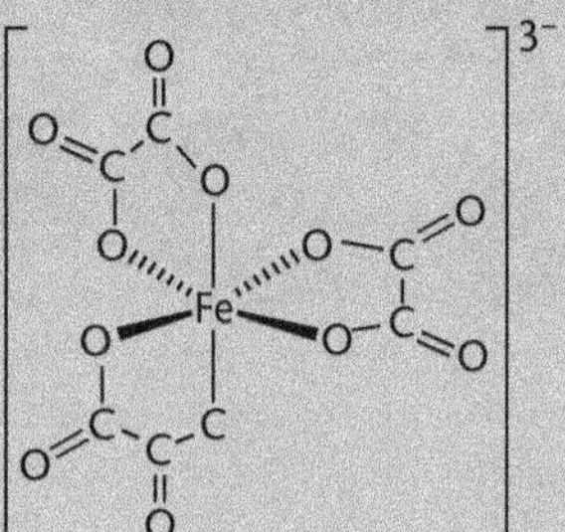

Figure 12 *Structure of the trisoxalatoferrate(III) ion*

16.4 FORMATION OF COLOURED IONS

A typical property of transition metal compounds is that they are coloured. Colour is produced when some parts of the visible spectrum are absorbed and others are reflected. The haem complex in haemoglobin is red and is responsible for the red colour of blood. If the oxygen attached to the haemoglobin (making oxyhaemoglobin) is replaced by carbon monoxide, carboxyhaemoglobin is formed, which has a darker red colour, a sign of carbon monoxide poisoning.

The colours of transition metal compounds depend on the electronic configuration of the metal ion.

The electron configuration for any element can be worked out using the Periodic Table. So, from the Periodic Table, the s, p, d notation for chromium is

$1s^2 2s^2 2p^6 3s^2 3p^6 3d^5 4s^1$

This can also be written as $[Ar]3d^5 4s^1$.

QUESTIONS

11. Write the electron configuration of
    a. nickel (atomic number 28)
    b. manganese (atomic number 25).

Figure 13 Paint pigments made from transition metal compounds are coloured because they each absorb a particular range of the frequencies of light in the visible spectrum, and reflect others

How does absorption produce colour?

Many chemical compounds are coloured (Figure 13). Light is electromagnetic radiation in the visible region of the electromagnetic spectrum.

When light falls on a coloured solid, some wavelengths are absorbed and others are reflected. The reflected wavelengths are what we see.

When light falls on a coloured solution, some wavelengths are absorbed and others pass through. The wavelengths that pass through are what we see (Figure 14).

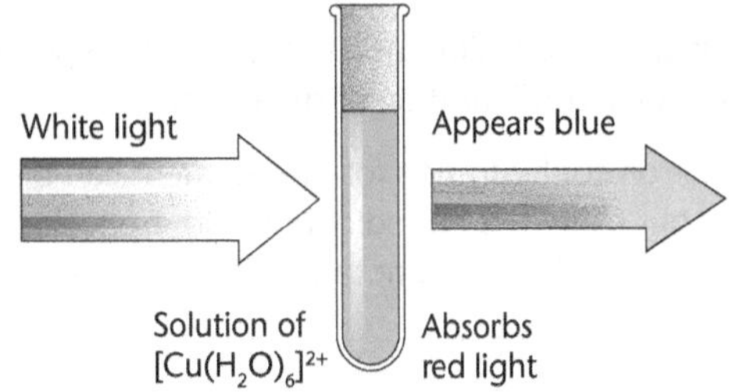

Figure 14 Absorption of light by a coloured solution

The visible region of the electromagnetic spectrum covers the wavelength range from 400 nm to 800 nm. Violet has the shortest wavelength (highest energy) and red the longest wavelength (lowest energy) of visible light. Ultraviolet (UV) is the portion of the electromagnetic spectrum with wavelengths shorter than 400 nm. Infrared (IR) is the portion of the electromagnetic spectrum with wavelengths longer than 800 nm. Both ultraviolet and infrared are invisible to the human eye.

In 1900, Max Planck proposed that energy can only be transferred (absorbed or emitted) in definite amounts, called **quanta**. Each amount of energy corresponds to a particular **frequency** of radiation. The frequency is the number of wavelengths of light passing a particular point in a second. The equation for the relationship is

$$\Delta E = h\nu$$

where ΔE is the energy difference, ν is the frequency of the radiation and h is Planck's constant, or

$$\Delta E = \frac{hc}{\lambda}$$

where c is the wave speed (the speed of light) and λ is the wavelength.

If an electron in an atom, ion or molecule absorbs the right amount of energy, it is promoted from a lower to a higher energy level. It absorbs an amount of energy equal to the energy difference, ΔE, between the two energy levels (Figure 15).

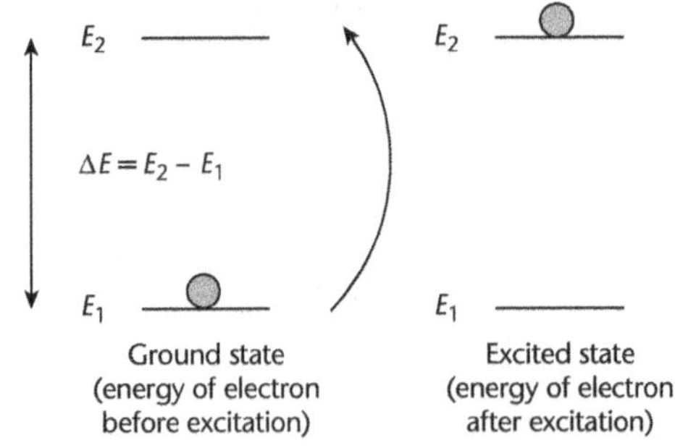

Figure 15 An electron can be excited (moved to a higher energy level) if it absorbs energy equal to the energy difference between the two levels

Colour and transition metal compounds

In a first-row transition metal atom (Ti–Cu), the electrons in the five 3d orbitals have the same energy. However, when the atom forms a complex ion the ligands 'split' the d orbitals into two groups. This is due to electrons in the ligand repelling electrons in 3d orbitals which are in close proximity.

The 3d orbitals are 'split' into two levels, one of higher and one of lower energy.

The colour of transition metal complex ions is due to the absorption of light with energy that can excite an electron from a 3d orbital of lower energy to one of higher energy.

For example, cobalt chloride dissolved in water is pink. The ions present are $[Co(H_2O)_6]^{2+}$. They are octahedral. The pink colour shows that radiation from the blue region of the visible spectrum has been absorbed.

Cobalt chloride dissolved in concentrated hydrochloric acid is blue. The ions present are $[CoCl_4]^{2-}$. They are tetrahedral. The blue colour shows that radiation from the red region of the visible spectrum has been absorbed.

Radiation in the blue region of the visible spectrum has higher energy than radiation in the red region.

The factors that affect the value of ΔE are:

- the ligand (its size and the strength of the ligand–metal bond in the complex)
- the shape of the complex
- the coordination number
- the oxidation state of the metal in the central ion.

Ligands may be classified as:

- strong-field ligands – those that induce a large ΔE, e.g. CN^-, CO and $P(C_6H_5)_3$
- weak-field ligands – those that induce a small ΔE, e.g. NH_3, H_2O and Cl^-.

ASSIGNMENT 1: INVESTIGATING COLOURED IONS

(PS 1.1, 2.1, 3.3; MS 0.0, 0.1, 1.1)

You have been asked to investigate some coloured transition metal complex ions. The instructions tell you to:

1. Prepare 10 cm^3 of 0.1 mol dm^{-3} aqueous solutions of copper(II) chloride and cobalt(II) chloride.
2. Divide each into two 5 cm^3 portions in separate test tubes.
3. Use a dropping pipette to add concentrated hydrochloric acid drop by drop to (a) 5 cm^3 of 0.1 mol dm^{-3} aqueous copper(II) chloride and (b) 5 cm^3 of 0.1 mol dm^{-3} aqueous cobalt(II) chloride until you observe a colour change. The solutions should be stirred during the addition.
4. Repeat step 3 using 5 mol dm^{-3} ammonia solution.

Questions

A1. You are provided with copper(II) chloride-2-water, $CuCl_2.2H_2O(s)$, and cobalt(II) chloride-6-water, $CoCl_2.6H_2O(s)$. Describe how you would make 10 cm^3 of 0.1 mol dm^{-3} aqueous solutions of copper(II) chloride and cobalt(II) chloride.

A2. Describe the hazards of using

a. concentrated hydrochloric acid

b. 5 mol dm^{-3} ammonia solution.

What precautions should be taken to minimise risk when using them?

A3. Describe the structure of the metal ions in aqueous solution.

A4. Below are a student's observations when she carried out steps 3 and 4. Explain these observations.

a. Addition of concentrated hydrochloric acid to aqueous copper(II) chloride changed the colour from blue to green. Adding greater quantities changed the colour further to yellow. All changes were gradual.

b. Addition of concentrated hydrochloric acid to aqueous cobalt(II) chloride changed the colour from pink to blue. The change was gradual.

c. Addition of 5 mol dm^{-3} ammonia solution to aqueous copper(II) chloride changed the colour from blue to a much deeper (more intense) blue. The change was gradual.

d. Addition of 5 mol dm^{-3} ammonia solution to aqueous cobalt(II) chloride changed the colour from pink to blue. The change was gradual.

Changing the ligands

If a transition metal ion is dissolved in water, the lone pairs on the water molecules are attracted to the positive metal ion. The best way for these ligands to fit around the ion is in an octahedral arrangement. If the ligand is changed (Figure 16), the value of ΔE is also changed.

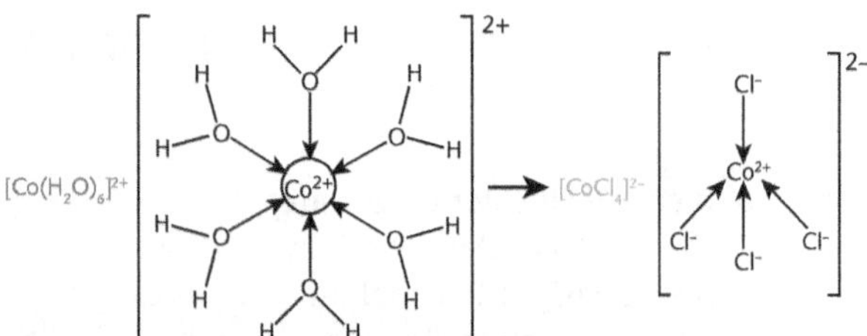

Figure 16 *$[Co(H_2O)_6]^{2+}$ (octahedral) changing to $[CoCl_4]^{2-}$ (tetrahedral)*

Changing the oxidation state

Changing the oxidation state of a given element changes the number of electrons in the d levels. This will alter the value of ΔE. Table 1 summarises some examples.

QUESTIONS

12. Which end of the spectrum is more likely to be absorbed by an ion with a large energy split?

Changing the ligand, but not the coordination number		Changing the ligand and the coordination number	Changing the oxidation state	
$[Cr(H_2O)_6]^{3+}$	$[Cr(NH_3)_6]^{3+}$	$[Cu(H_2O)_6]^{2+}$	$[Fe(H_2O)_6]^{2+}$	$[Fe(H_2O)_6]^{3+}$
red–violet	purple	blue	green	pale violet
octahedral	octahedral	octahedral	octahedral	octahedral
$[Cu(H_2O)_6]^{2+}$	$[Cu(NH_3)_4(H_2O)_2]^{2+}$	$[CuCl_4]^{2-}$	$[Cr(H_2O)_6]^{3+}$	$[Cr(NH_3)_6]^{2+}$
blue	deep blue	yellow	red–violet	blue
octahedral	octahedral	tetrahedral	octahedral	octahedral

Table 1 *Examples of factors affecting colour*

Water and chloride ions cause the ligand and the coordination number to change, but with Co^{2+} ions there is no change in oxidation state. With cobalt chloride paper, this colour change is used to detect the presence of water (Figure 17).

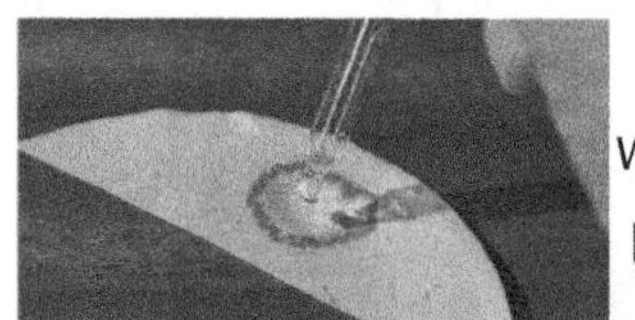

Water present	Water absent
$[Co(H_2O)_6]^{2+}$	$[CoCl_4]^{2-}$
pink	blue

Figure 17 *Cobalt chloride paper before and after the addition of water. $[Co(H_2O)_6]^{2+}$ absorbs blue, green and yellow, so it is pink. $[CoCl_4]^{2-}$ absorbs orange, red and pink, so it is blue.*

QUESTIONS

13. Which ligand, CN^- or H_2O, produces a complex which absorbs light at higher frequency?
14. Why does the colour change if the ligand is changed?
15. If $[Cu(H_2O)_6]^{2+}$ is treated with excess cyanide ions, CN^-, it will go through a series of reactions and eventually form the complex ion $[Cu(CN)_4]^{3-}$.
    a. Give the oxidation state of the copper in the two complexes above.
    b. Write the electronic configuration of the copper in each of these complexes.
    c. The aqua complex is blue and the cyano complex is colourless. Explain this change in terms of electronic configuration.

Analysis using colour

The amount of light absorbed by a coloured solution depends on the number of ions it interacts with, so it will be affected by

- the nature of the ion (which relates to ΔE)
- the concentration of the solution
- the distance the light has to travel through the solution (the path length).

The more light that is absorbed, the less that is transmitted (Figure 18).

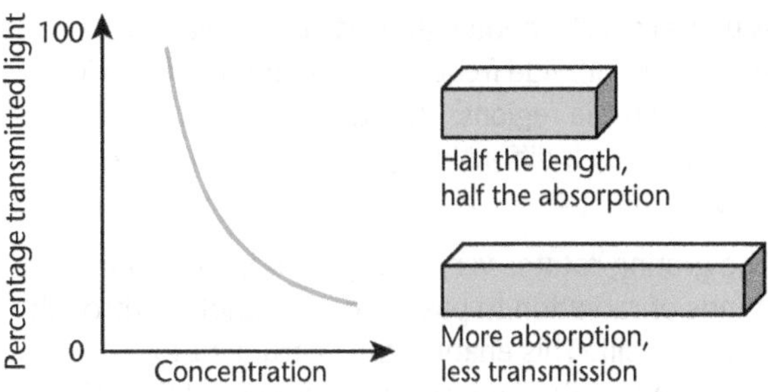

Figure 18 *The effect of path length and concentration on light absorption*

If a solution is more concentrated, more ions are present in a given volume and more will interact, so the colour will be more intense. If the light has to travel a greater distance, there will again be more ions to interact with the light.

Ultraviolet/visible spectrophotometry

The instrument used to investigate the colour of solutions, including those of transition metal complex ions, is called a **spectrophotometer** (Figure 19). It uses visible or ultraviolet radiation, which it shines through the sample. The detector measures the radiation that passes through the solution. From this, the instrument calculates the amount absorbed (the absorbance) and displays this on a meter or as a graph.

If the nature of the coloured ion in solution and the path length are fixed, the concentration in a sample can be determined by comparing it with standard solutions.

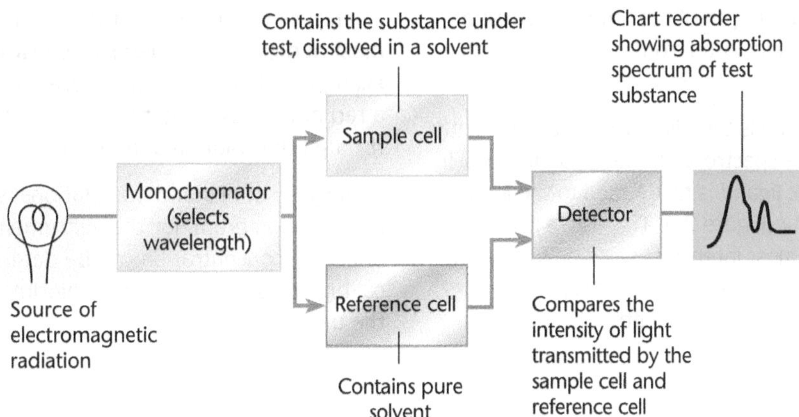

Figure 19 *Scheme of an ultraviolet/visible spectrophotometer*

A typical spectrophotometer has two radiation sources, to provide frequencies in both the ultraviolet and the visible regions. The various frequencies are separated by a diffraction grating. This produces a spectrum.

The grating rotates very slowly, allowing narrow bands of radiation to pass one after another through a narrow slit. This enables the instrument to measure the absorbance for radiation within each band. The narrower the range of wavelengths in a band, the more precise the measurement by the instrument. The instrument plots the absorbance for each band against the average wavelength of the band and displays this on a computer screen (Figure 20).

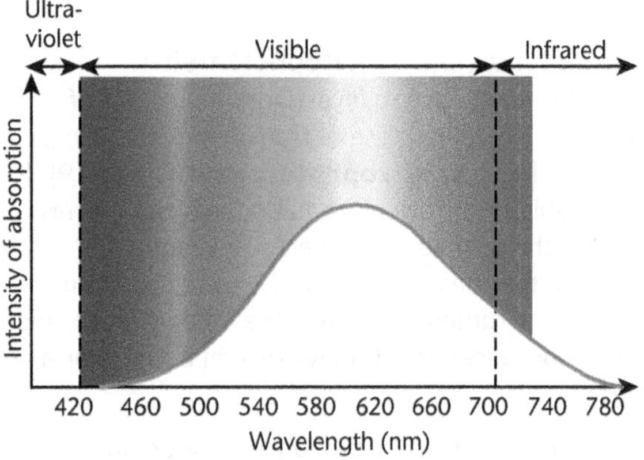

Figure 20 *An absorption spectrum for a blue solution of a complex metal ion*

Spectrophotometers may be used to determine the concentration of transition metal ions in aqueous solution. The wavelength at which the absorbance is greatest is used. A sample is placed in the spectrophotometer and the absorbance measured at the wavelength of maximum absorption. Its concentration is calculated from a calibration graph.

Sometimes the solution is too dilute to give a sufficiently intense colour for the spectrophotometer to measure. In such cases a suitable ligand is first added to the ion to give an intense colour (Figure 21). The visible range is scanned to find the most intense absorption frequency, and then a suitable range of frequencies is passed through a solution of fixed path length.

Figure 21 *SCN^- gives an intense red colour with Fe^{3+}, so it is used frequently for analysing Fe^{3+} compounds*

QUESTIONS

16. Why does the colour of a solution become paler if water is added?

17. What is the wavelength of the peak absorption in Figure 20?

Colorimetry

A simpler instrument that can be used to measure the absorption of radiation is the **colorimeter**. This uses a lamp as a source of white light, which passes through a filter to produce light of one colour. This colour will be the one that the sample will absorb the most and is called its **complementary colour**. For example, a blue solution will absorb red, and therefore a red filter is used, so that only red light passes through the solution and maximum absorption occurs.

Usually, a set of standard solutions is prepared to give a calibration graph for the instrument, and then the unknown concentration can be determined from the calibration graph, using the colorimeter reading for the unknown.

ASSIGNMENT 2: RATE OF SUBSTITUTION

(PS 1.1, 2.2, 3.1; MS 0.0; 1.1; 2.3; 2.4; 3.2; 3.3)

The Lambert–Beer law relates the absorbance to the concentration of a coloured complex in solution. You do not need to recall this law, it is used here as an example of the mathematics of such problems. The relationship is given by the equation

$A = \varepsilon c l$

where A = absorbance, ε = molar extinction coefficient, c = concentration (mol dm^{-3}) and l = path length (distance travelled by radiation through the solution).

In an experiment, UV/visible spectrophotometry was used to investigate the rate of this ligand exchange reaction:

$[M(H_2O)_6]^{2+} + HCl \rightleftharpoons [MCl(H_2O)_5]^{+} + H_3O^{+}$

The initial concentration of $[M(H_2O)_6]^{2+}$ in the reaction mixture was 0.44 mol dm^{-3}. The reaction was monitored after 60 seconds, 180 seconds, 240 seconds and 300 seconds by collecting 0.1 cm^3 and diluting it in 100 cm^3 of water to stop the reaction. The sample was placed in a sample container (called a cuvette). This had an internal width of 1 cm, so the path length was 1 cm. Radiation at the wavelength of maximum absorbance was passed through each diluted sample and the absorbance recorded.

Time/s	Absorbance
60	0.0081
120	0.0167
180	0.0279
240	0.0368
300	0.0430

Table A1 *Absorbance of diluted samples*

The molar extinction coefficient of $[MCl(H_2O)_5]^{+}$ at its wavelength of maximum absorbance is 165 dm^3 mol^{-1} cm^{-1}.

Questions

A1. Calculate the concentration of $[MCl(H_2O)_5]^{+}$ in each of the samples taken. Remember that each sample was diluted before analysis.

A2. Plot a graph of the concentration of $[MCl(H_2O)_5]^{+}$ in solution against time in seconds.

A3. Calculate the rate of the reaction in mol dm^{-3} s^{-1}.

A4. Estimate the time taken for half of the initial complex to react.

A5. Assuming the reaction is first order, that is, rate = $k_r[M(H_2O)_6]^{2+}$, calculate the rate constant k_r.

KEY IDEAS

- The colour of ions in solution depends on which part of the visible spectrum is being absorbed.
- The energy of the radiation absorbed depends on the type of ligand: strong-field or weak-field.
- The frequency of the radiation absorbed is given by the relationships $\Delta E = h\nu$ and $\Delta E = hc/\lambda$.
- The energy of the radiation also depends on the element and its oxidation state.
- The concentration of ions can be determined using UV/visible spectrophotometry.

16.5 VARIABLE OXIDATION STATES

Changing oxidation state

One of the properties of transition metals is that they can have variable **oxidation states**. When metals react, they transfer electrons, with those of higher energy being transferred first. For the transition metals, these are the 4s electrons. This gives a commonly occurring oxidation state of +2 for these metals. However, transition metals can form compounds in which the transition metal has other oxidation states; for example, iron can form Fe^{2+} or Fe^{3+} compounds.

When a transition metal or an ion of it is oxidised, it forms an ion in a higher oxidation state. The other reactant is reduced (gains electrons) and changes to a lower oxidation state. This is a redox reaction (see *Chapter 14 of Year 2 Student Book*).

Metallic zinc is a good reducing agent. It reacts with dilute acid to form Zn^{2+} ions and releases electrons for the reduction:

$Zn \rightarrow Zn^{2+} + 2e^-$

We can see this process in the reactions of many transition elements. If you take the highest oxidation state of chromium, Cr(VI), you can form lower oxidation states using zinc and hydrochloric acid as a reducing agent (Table 2). Air must be excluded from the Cr^{2+} species, otherwise oxidation will occur, giving Cr^{3+}. The oxidation states of chromium change in the presence of HCl when it is used as an acid. Therefore, in Table 2, $[CrCl_2(H_2O)_4]^+$ (green) is the complex, not $[Cr(H_2O)_6]^{3+}$ (blue).

Oxidation state	+6	+3	+2
Chromium ion	$Cr_2O_7^{2-}$	$[CrCl_2(H_2O)_4]^+$	$[Cr(H_2O)_6]^{2+}$
Colour in aqueous solution	Orange	Green	Blue

Table 2 *Oxidation states of chromium. The $Cr_2O_7^{2-}$ ion can be reduced using zinc and hydrochloric acid.*

QUESTIONS

18. a. Write a balanced redox equation for Zn reducing Cr(VI) to Cr(III).
    b. Write a balanced redox equation for Zn reducing Cr(III) to Cr(II).
    c. Write a balanced redox equation for $O_2(g)$ oxidising Cr(II) to Cr(III).

When hydrochloric acid is used with zinc for the reduction, the Cl^- ion acts as a ligand, donating to the Cr^{3+} ion. With sulfuric acid (Figure 22), the complex ion is still green because both SO_4^{2-} and water act as ligands. $[Cr(H_2O)_6]^{3+}$, which is red–violet, is not formed. The isomers of $CrCl_3(H_2O)_6$ are shown in Table 3.

Molecular formula	Structural formula	Colour
$CrCl_3(H_2O)_6$	$[Cr(H_2O)_6]^{3+}$ $3Cl^-$	Violet
$CrCl_3(H_2O)_6$	$[Cr(H_2O)_5Cl]^{2+}$ $2Cl^-$ H_2O	Light green
$CrCl_3(H_2O)_6$	$[Cr(H_2O)_4Cl_2]^+$ Cl^- $2H_2O$	Dark green

Table 3 *Isomers of $CrCl_3(H_2O)_6$*

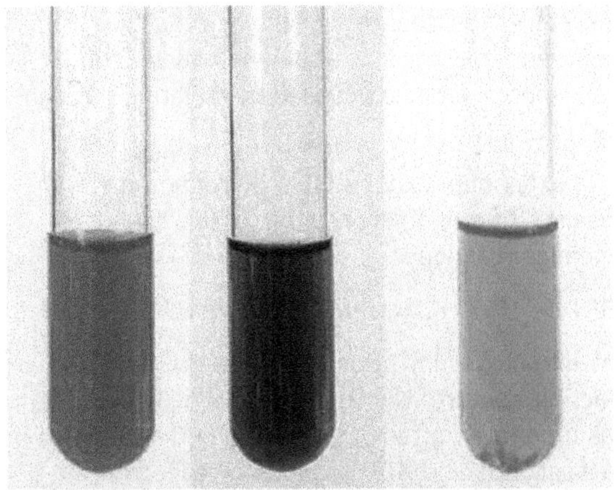

Figure 22 *If granulated zinc and 1 mol dm^{-3} sulfuric acid are added to a solution of potassium dichromate(VI) (in the absence of air), the chromium is reduced and the solution changes colour from orange to blue*

Worked example

The equation for the overall redox reaction can be shown as follows. Writing the half-equations for

$Cr_2O_7^{2-}(aq) + 8e^- \rightarrow 2Cr^{2+}(aq)$

and

$Zn(s) \rightarrow Zn^{2+}(aq) + 2e^-$

gives

$Cr_2O_7^{2-}(aq) + 8e^- + 14H^+ \rightarrow 2Cr^{2+}(aq) + 7H_2O(l)$

$Zn(s) \rightarrow Zn^{2+}(aq) + 2e^-$

Balancing the electron transfer gives

$Cr_2O_7^{2-}(aq) + 8e^- + 14H^+ \rightarrow 2Cr^{2+}(aq) + 7H_2O(l)$

$4Zn(s) \rightarrow 4Zn^{2+}(aq) + 8e^-$

Adding these two half-equations gives

$Cr_2O_7^{2-}(aq) + 8e^- + 14H^+ \rightarrow 2Cr^{2+}(aq) + 7H_2O(l)$

$4Zn(s) \rightarrow 4Zn^{2+}(aq) + 8e^-$

$Cr_2O_7^{2-}(aq) + 14H^+ + 4Zn(s) \rightarrow 2Cr^{2+}(aq) + 7H_2O(l) + 4Zn^{2+}(aq)$

Changing redox properties

The effect of ligands on the ease of oxidation can be shown with cobalt.

In aqueous solution, the oxidation of $[Co(H_2O)_6]^{2+}$ to $[Co(H_2O)_6]^{3+}$ is not normally possible. However, in alkaline solution a precipitate of $Co(OH)_2$ forms initially. This is readily oxidised to $Co(OH)_3$ by air, at the surface or dissolved in the solution. An oxidising agent such as H_2O_2 (hydrogen peroxide) will also do this. Similarly, if an excess of concentrated ammonia solution is added the initial precipitate of $Co(OH)_2$ dissolves to form the pale brown complex $[Co(NH_3)_6]^{2+}$. Again, this is oxidised readily by air or H_2O_2. This reaction produces the yellow complex hexaammine cobalt(III).

Another ion that can be oxidised by this method is Cr(III). First, the chromium(III) ions are reacted with sodium hydroxide to give $Cr(OH)_3(aq)$:

$[Cr(H_2O)_6]^{3+} + 3OH^- \rightarrow [Cr(H_2O)_3(OH)_3]$

green precipitate

This precipitate dissolves in an excess of sodium hydroxide solution, giving a deep green solution of $[Cr(OH)_6]^{3-}$:

$[Cr(H_2O)_3(OH)_3] + 3OH^- \rightarrow [Cr(OH)_6]^{3-}$

When H_2O_2 is added, $[Cr(OH)_6]^{3-}$ is oxidised to CrO_4^{2-}:

$2[Cr(OH)_6]^{3-} + 3H_2O_2 \rightarrow 2CrO_4^{2-} + 2OH^- + 8H_2O$

yellow

The yellow chromate(VI) ion is formed. Chromate(VI) can be converted to dichromate(VI) by simply adding acid:

$2CrO_4^{2-}(aq) + 2H^+(aq) \rightarrow Cr_2O_7^{2-}(aq) + H_2O(l)$

Chromium has its highest oxidation state of +6 in the two complex ions CrO_4^{2-} and $Cr_2O_7^{2-}$. The position of the equilibrium

$2CrO_4^{2-} + 2H^+ \rightarrow Cr_2O_7^{2-} + H_2O$

depends on the pH of the solution. In acidic solution, the equilibrium lies to the right, so if H^+ is added, the equilibrium as written will shift from left to right. In a solution of high pH, for example if OH^- is added to $Cr_2O_7^{2-}$, the equilibrium as written below shifts to the right:

$2Cr_2O_7^{2-} + 2OH^- \rightarrow 2CrO_4^{2-} + H_2O$

Another example of where a transition metal ion in a low oxidation state, in an alkaline solution, is readily oxidised to a higher oxidation state is iron(II) being oxidised to iron(III). Aqueous iron(II) ions must be stored as an acidified solution, because any air present will oxidise the solution to iron(III). This process is very rapid if alkali is added to the solution. If all air is excluded from the solution (including dissolved oxygen in the solution), a white precipitate is formed.

Normally, when OH^- is added to Fe^{2+} ions, a 'dirty' green solution is formed because oxidation is taking place, giving a complex mixture of compounds. If the solution is left standing, the precipitate becomes darker and a brown precipitate of hydrated Fe_2O_3 is formed, especially at the surface of the solution where it is in contact with the atmosphere.

QUESTIONS

19. Demonstrate that there is no change in oxidation state in converting $CrO_4^{2-}(aq)$ to $Cr_2O_7^{2-}(aq)$.

KEY IDEAS

- Transition metals have variable oxidation states.
- An element in different oxidation states has differently coloured ions.
- The ease of oxidation depends on pH and the nature of the ligand.

16.6 REDOX TITRATIONS

Potassium manganate(VII) titrations

Potassium permanganate contains the manganate (VII) ion, which is a strong oxidising agent and can be used in titrations to estimate the amount of iron(II) ions in solution (Figure 23).

In these titrations, the manganate(VII) is the oxidising agent and is reduced to $Mn^{2+}(aq)$. The iron is the reducing agent and is oxidised to $Fe^{3+}(aq)$. The reaction mixture must be acidified, and so excess acid is added to the iron(II) ions before the reaction begins. If insufficient acid is present, the brown solid MnO_2 will be formed, and MnO_4^- to Mn^{4+} is only a $3e^-$ change and has a different stoichiometry. The acid used must not react with the manganate(VII) ions, so the acid normally used is dilute sulfuric acid. Acids such as hydrochloric acid are not used because the chloride ions in the solution can be oxidised to chlorine.

The acid must:

- be a strong acid (one that is fully dissociated), because a high concentration of hydrogen ions is needed
- not be an oxidising agent, because it may react with the reductant and affect the titration results
- not be a reducing agent, because it may be oxidised by the manganate(VII) ions and affect the titration results.

We choose dilute sulfuric acid because it is a strong acid and the dilute acid does not oxidise under these conditions.

We do not choose:

- hydrochloric acid, because it can be oxidised to chlorine by the manganate(VII) ions
- nitric acid, because it is an oxidising agent and may oxidise the substance being analysed
- concentrated sulfuric acid, because it may oxidise the substance being analysed
- ethanoic acid, because it is a weak acid, so the concentration of hydrogen ions will be insufficient.

Worked example

To find the stoichiometry for the reaction, we follow the usual steps:

Complete the two half-equations:

$$MnO_4^-(aq) + 5e^- + 8H^+(aq) \rightarrow Mn^{2+}(aq) + 4H_2O(l)$$

$$Fe^{2+}(aq) \rightarrow Fe^{3+}(aq) + e^-$$

Balance the electrons:

$$MnO_4^-(aq) + 5e^- + 8H^+(aq) \rightarrow Mn^{2+}(aq) + 4H_2O(l)$$

$$5Fe^{2+}(aq) \rightarrow 5Fe^{3+}(aq) + 5e^-$$

Add the two half-equations:

$$MnO_4^-(aq) + 5e^- + 8H^+(aq) \rightarrow Mn^{2+}(aq) + 4H_2O(l)$$

$$5Fe^{2+}(aq) \rightarrow 5Fe^{3+}(aq) + 5e^-$$

$$MnO_4^-(aq) + 8H^+(aq) + 5Fe^{2+}(aq) \rightarrow Mn^{2+}(aq) + 4H_2O(l) + 5Fe^{3+}(aq)$$

Potassium permanganate acts as its own indicator. As the purple potassium permanganate solution is added to the titration flask from a burette, it reacts rapidly with the $Fe^{2+}(aq)$. The manganese(II) ions have a very pale pink colour, but they are present in such a low concentration that the solution looks colourless. As soon as all the iron(II) ions have reacted with the added manganate(VII) ions, a pink tinge appears in the flask due to an excess of manganate(VII).

Figure 23 *Titration of iron(II) with manganate(VII) ions*

ASSIGNMENT 3: CALCULATING THE AMOUNT OF IRON(II) IN AN IRON TABLET

(PS 1.1, 2.1, 2.3, 3.2, 4.1; MS 0.0, 0.2, 1.1, 2.3)

The NHS says 'Iron is an essential mineral, with several important roles in the body. For example, it helps to make red blood cells, which carry oxygen around the body.' A man needs 8.7 mg a day and a woman needs 14.8 mg a day.

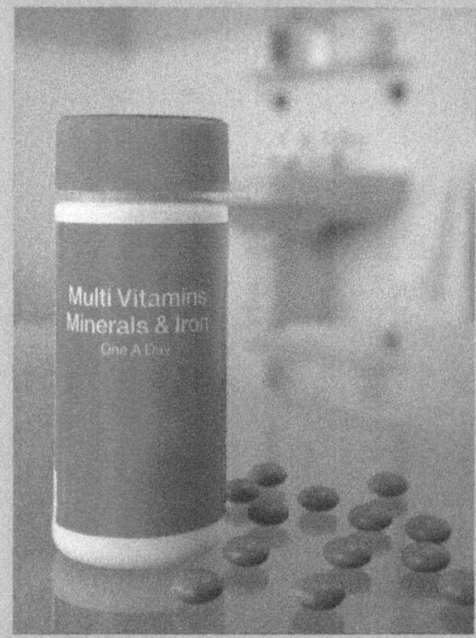

Figure A1 *An iron supplement*

Most people get the iron they need from their daily diet. However, sometimes they cannot get sufficient and so take iron supplements, often in the form of tablets (Figure A1). The tablets contain iron(II) salts.

The manufacturers of these tablets carry out analyses as part of their quality control procedures. One technique used is a redox titration. The amount of iron is determined by titration with manganate(VII) solution. One or more tablets are taken as samples from each batch manufactured.

- *Procedure.* An iron tablet is weighed and dissolved in dilute sulfuric acid, and the solution is titrated with 0.02 mol dm^{-3} potassium manganate(VII) solution.
- *Quality control.* A tablet must contain 11.2 to 11.6% by mass of iron.

Figure A2 *The endpoint when MnO^{4-}(aq) is being added in a manganate(VII) titration is shown by the first permanent pink tinge to the solution in the flask*

Here are some data from the analysis of two batches of tablets.

Batch 1:

	Mass of tablet/g	Titre/cm^3
Tablet 1a	0.850	17.4
Tablet 1b	0.845	17.1

Batch 2:

	Mass of tablet/g	Titre/cm^3
Tablet 2a	0.845	16.5
Tablet 2b	0.855	16.9

Questions

A1. Write the balanced equation for the reaction of manganate(VII) ions with iron(II) ions in acidic solution.

A2. For a tablet of mass *m* g and a titre of *V* cm^3, show how to calculate the percentage by mass of iron in the tablet, using these steps to guide you:

a. the number of moles of MnO_4^-(aq) in the titre solution

b. the number of moles of Fe^{2+}(aq) in the solution of the tablet

c. the mass of Fe^{2+} in the tablet (relative atomic mass of Fe = 56)

d. the percentage by mass of iron in the tablet.

A3. Use the expression you derived in A2 to calculate the percentage by mass of iron in each of the tablets analysed.

A4. Which batch meets the quality control requirements?

A5. The burette used can measure volumes to $\pm 0.03\ cm^3$. The electronic balance used can measure masses to ± 0.001 g.

a. Calculate the margin of error in the result you obtained for tablet 1a.

b. Explain why the margin of error is the same for each of the tablets analysed.

A6. Explain how the reliability of the analysis of a batch could be improved.

Potassium dichromate(VI) titrations

Like the manganate(VII) ion, the dichromate(VI) ion can be used to find the amount of iron in iron tablets. Dichromate(VI) is a powerful oxidising agent when it changes from the +6 oxidation state in the dichromate(VI) ion, $Cr_2O_7^{2-}$, to the +3 oxidation state in Cr^{3+}:

$$Cr_2O_7^{2-}(aq) + 14H^+(aq) + 6e^- \rightarrow 2Cr^{3+}(aq) + 7H_2O(l)$$

This reacts with iron(II) ions:

$$6Fe^{2+}(aq) \rightarrow 6Fe^{3+}(aq) + 6e^-$$

The colour change for this titration is from orange to bluish green. To give a more visible endpoint, the indicator sodium diphenylaminesulfonate is used. This turns from colourless to purple at the endpoint.

Worked example

An iron tablet, weighing 0.960 g, was dissolved in dilute sulfuric acid. A titre of 28.5 cm^3 of 0.0180 mol dm^{-3} potassium dichromate(VI) solution was needed to reach the endpoint. What is the percentage by mass of iron in the tablet? Again, this can be calculated using the correct equation for the redox reaction and the relevant formulae.

One mole of dichromate(VI) ions oxidises six moles of iron(II) ions, and the overall equation is

$$6Fe^{2+}(aq) + Cr_2O_7^{2-}(aq) + 14H^+ \rightarrow 6Fe^{3+}(aq) + 2Cr^{3+}(aq) + 7H_2O(l)$$

The number of moles of $Cr_2O_7^{2-}$ used in the titration to reach the endpoint is given by

$$\text{number of moles} = \frac{28.5 \times 0.0180}{1000} = 5.13 \times 10^{-4} \text{ moles}$$

$$\text{Moles of iron(II)} = 6 \times 5.13 \times 10^{-4} = 3.078 \times 10^{-3} \text{ moles}$$

$$\text{Mass of iron(II)} = 56 \times 3.078 \times 10^{-3} = 0.1724 \text{ g}$$

The percentage by mass of iron in the tablet is given by

$$\text{percentage by mass} = \frac{0.1724 \times 100}{0.960} = 18.0\%$$

QUESTIONS

20. The balanced redox equation for the reaction of $Cr_2O_7^{2-}(aq)$ with $Fe^{2+}(aq)$ is

$$Cr_2O_7^{2-}(aq) + 14H^+(aq) + 6Fe^{2+}(aq) \rightarrow 2Cr^{3+}(aq) + 6Fe^{3+}(aq) + 7H_2O(l)$$

Use your knowledge of oxidation states to show that this is correct.

21. A sample of iron wire of mass 2.225 g was dissolved in dilute sulfuric acid to give a solution containing Fe(II) ions and was made up to 250 cm^3 in a volumetric flask. Then 25.0 cm^3 of this solution was acidified and titrated against a 0.0185 mol dm^{-3} solution of potassium dichromate(VI). The iron solution needed 31.00 cm^3 of dichromate(VI). Use the following steps to calculate the percentage of iron metal in the iron wire.

a. Calculate the number of moles of dichromate(VI) in 31.0 cm^3 of a 0.0185 mol dm^{-3} solution.

b. From the redox equation, write down the number of moles of iron(II) reacting with one mole of dichromate(VI).

c. Calculate the number of moles of iron(II) in the 25.0 cm^3 sample.

d. Calculate the number of moles of iron(II) in the flask.

e. Calculate the mass of iron(II) in the flask (made from 2.225 g of iron wire). [A_r(Fe) = 56.]

f. Calculate the percentage of iron in the iron wire.

General sequence for redox titration calculations

The following sequence can be used for all redox titrations when the reductant and its oxidation product are known:

Step 1. Write the half-equations for oxidant and reductant.

Step 2. Deduce the equation for the overall reaction.

Step 3. Calculate the number of moles of manganate(VII) or dichromate(VI) used.

Step 4. Calculate the ratio of moles of oxidant to moles of reductant from the redox equation.

Step 5. Calculate the number of moles in the sample solution of reductant.

Step 6. Calculate the number of moles in the original solution of reductant.

Step 7. Determine either the concentration of the original solution or the percentage of reductant in a known quantity of sample.

QUESTIONS

22. In a titration, 25.0 cm³ of a sodium sulfite solution needs 45.0 cm³ of 0.0200 mol dm⁻³ potassium manganate(VII) solution to reach the endpoint. What is the concentration of the sodium sulfite solution?

23. Some ethanedioic acid-2-water (mass 2.145 g) was dissolved in water and diluted to 250 cm³ in a volumetric flask. Then 25.0 cm³ of this solution was titrated with potassium manganate(VII) solution and needed 35.0 cm³ to oxidise the acid solution. Calculate the concentration of the potassium manganate(VII) solution.

KEY IDEAS

- For calculations in redox titrations, (a) write half-equations, (b) balance electron transfer and (c) add these balanced half-equations.
- The commonly used oxidants MnO_4^- and $Cr_2O_7^{2-}$ must be acidified.
- For solutions (with molar concentration in mol dm^{-3} and volume in dm^3):

$$\text{Number of moles} = \frac{\text{volume} \times \text{molar concentration}}{1000}$$

- For masses:

$$\text{Number of moles} = \frac{\text{mass}}{M_r}$$

or

$$\text{Number of moles} = \frac{\text{mass}}{A_r}$$

16.7 CATALYSTS

The way in which catalysts work was explained in *Chapter 8 of Year 1 Student Book*. The key is their ability to form a transition state with one of more of the reactants and, in doing so, provide an alternative pathway of lower activation energy (Figure 24).

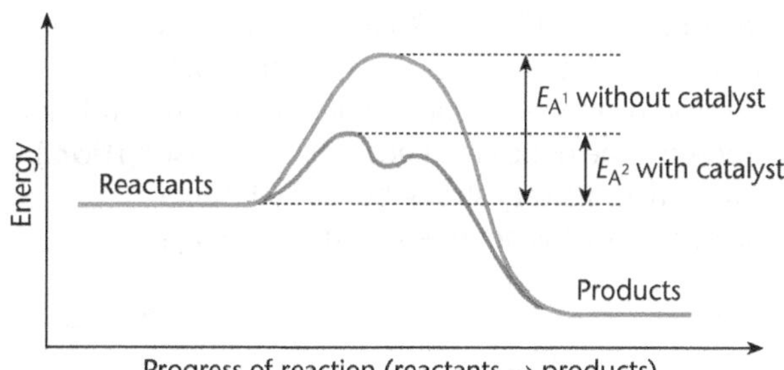

Figure 24 *Energy profiles for a catalysed and an uncatalysed reaction*

While a catalyst affects the rate of a chemical reaction, it does not alter the equilibrium position. It speeds up both the forward and the reverse reactions equally.

In most cases, a catalyst will be used to speed up a chemical reaction. However, some catalysts, called inhibitors or negative catalysts, slow down chemical reactions.

Heterogeneous catalysis

Transition metals have many applications as catalysts. They are examples of heterogeneous catalysts. Reactions happen on the surface of the metal, typically involving reactants in the gas phase, though they may also be in the liquid phase.

In heterogeneous catalysis, at least one of the reactants binds to the metal's surface using available orbitals by a mechanism similar to ligand donation. This process is called **adsorption**. It is in this new 'state' that the reactant is more likely to undergo a given reaction. Adsorption of a reactant onto a metal surface can speed up a reaction for the following reasons:

- It can weaken bonds within the reactant molecule, reducing the activation energy.
- It can cause a reactant molecule to break up into more reactive fragments, again reducing the activation energy.
- It can hold a reactant in a particular position, increasing the chance of a favourable collision.
- It can give a higher concentration of one reactant on the catalyst surface, increasing the chance of a favourable collision with another reactant.

The strength of the bonding between the metal and the reactant is important in determining the suitability of a catalyst for a particular reaction. Metal atoms on the surface of the catalyst need to form bonds with reactant gas molecules that are strong enough to hold the reactant in position while it reacts with other molecules (Figures 25 and 26). However, if the bond is too strong, the product molecule will not be released by the metal catalyst and the reaction will not proceed. (The opposite of adsorption is **desorption**.) Tungsten forms very strong bonds with some molecules, so it is not often used as a catalyst.

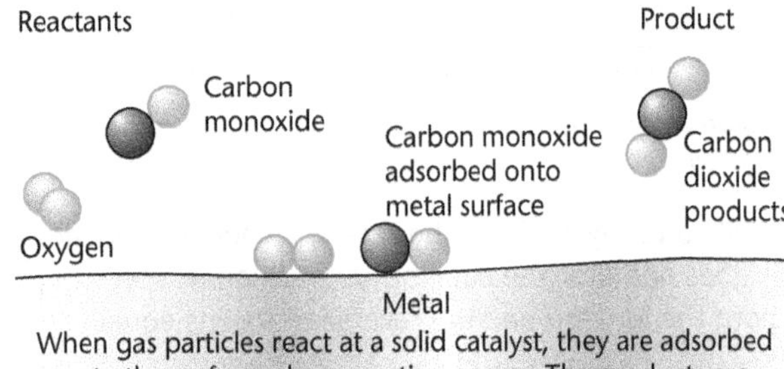

Figure 25 *Adsorption of gases on the surface of a catalytic converter*

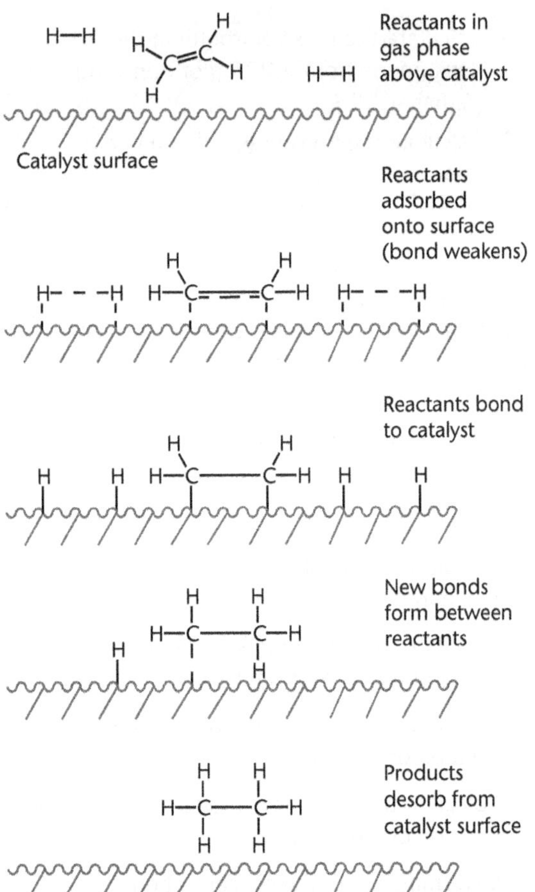

Figure 26 *Hydrogenation at a nickel catalyst surface*

Weak adsorption also results in poor catalysis. Silver forms very weak bonds with molecules, so it is usually unable to hold onto the gas long enough for a reaction to take place, although it is used in the manufacture of epoxyethane. Good catalysts include palladium, rhodium and platinum, but unfortunately they can be expensive.

To minimise costs, a cheap support medium (called a substrate) is often coated with a thin layer of the expensive metal catalyst. The support material is often a ceramic. The higher the catalyst's surface area, the more active sites (places where the reactions happen) it provides and the more effective it is (Figure 27).

Another way of maximising the surface area of the catalyst in contact with the reactants is to use a fluidised bed (Figure 28). When gases are blown through a very fine powder, the powder 'floats' on the gas, separating the catalyst particles, so that all the surface of the catalyst is available for reactions.

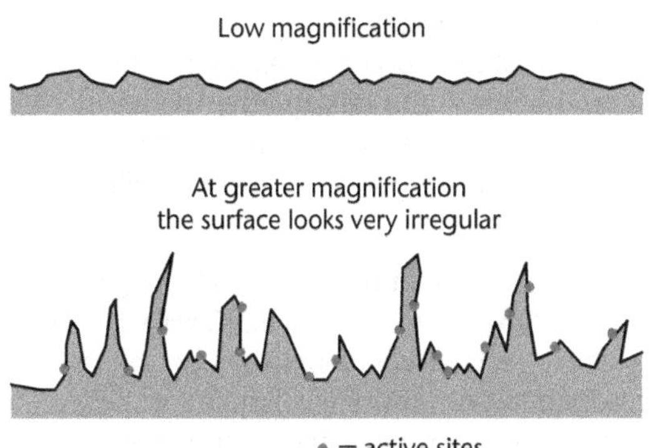

Figure 27 *The surface of a catalyst*

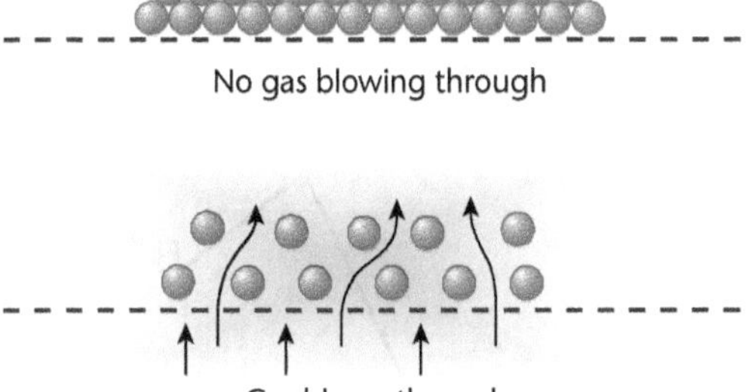

Figure 28 *A fluidised catalytic bed*

QUESTIONS

24. Why do you think the coating is deliberately applied so that its surface is not smooth?

Catalyst poisoning

Sometimes unwanted gases adsorb strongly on a catalyst, 'blocking' the active sites and reducing the catalyst's effectiveness. This is called poisoning. In the Haber process, it is vital that traces of sulfur and carbon monoxide are removed as these poison the iron catalyst.

Catalytic converters on cars contain a mixture of the metals palladium, platinum and rhodium, coated onto cerium oxide. These remove unwanted products of combustion. If the exhaust emissions contain sulfur dioxide, this gas will also adsorb onto the catalyst. The sulfur dioxide is adsorbed very strongly and it 'blocks' the active sites on the catalyst, reducing its effectiveness. All petrol contains some sulfur, but the lower the sulfur content achieved during the refining process, the better. To help overcome sulfur dioxide poisoning, manufacturers of catalytic converters mix in aluminium oxide with the catalyst. The aluminium oxide 'stores' the sulfur oxides under oxidising (normal running) conditions, and converts them to hydrogen sulfide under reducing (accelerating) conditions. This removes the sulfur periodically, so that it does not permanently poison the catalyst. This is why the emissions from catalytic converters occasionally smell of hydrogen sulfide.

Industrial processes

Many industrial processes involve the use of catalysts under a variety of conditions. When a mixture of hydrogen and carbon monoxide in the ratio 2 : 1 is passed over the catalyst chromium(III) oxide, Cr_2O_3, under high pressure and at high temperature, methanol is formed.

Two of the most important industrial processes in the economy of any industrialised nation are the manufacture of ammonia and the manufacture of sulfuric acid. Both involve equilibria, and for each process it is vital to obtain the maximum possible output in the shortest possible time at the lowest possible cost. A catalyst is used to increase the rate of reaction, allowing a much lower temperature to be used, yet maintaining sufficient output for the process to be cost-effective.

Haber process

The **Haber process** is an industrial method for the manufacture of ammonia (NH_3). An iron catalyst is used in the Haber process:

$$N_2(g) + 3H_2(g) \xrightarrow{Fe} 2NH_3(g)$$

The iron is mixed with aluminium oxide and potassium oxide, which act as promoters. The promoters are present in smaller amounts than the iron, and improve the efficiency of the catalyst. The hydrogen for this reaction is obtained from methane, so trace amounts of steam and carbon monoxide are found as impurities in the hydrogen. If the carbon monoxide was allowed to remain in the gas mixture, it would poison the catalyst by forming an iron carbonyl compound, so it must be removed. The carbon monoxide is removed by heating with an excess of steam in a two-stage process, first with an iron oxide catalyst and then with a zinc/copper catalyst. The products are carbon dioxide, which is easier to remove from the mixture, and hydrogen, which is used in the process.

Contact process

The **contact process** is an industrial method for the manufacture of sulfuric acid, H_2SO_4. A key step in the manufacture is the oxidation of sulfur dioxide to sulfur trioxide:

$2SO_2(g) + O_2(g) \rightarrow SO_3(g)$

The reactant mixture is passed over a vanadium(V) pentoxide catalyst, V_2O_5. This has replaced platinum even though platinum increases the reaction rate more. The reason is that V_2O_5 is cheaper and less prone to poisoning by impurities.

Its catalytic properties are linked to its ability to exist in more than one oxidation state. In V_2O_5, the oxidation state of vanadium is +5. V_2O_5 reacts with SO_2 and is reduced to VO_2, where the vanadium is in the +4 oxidation state. Sulfur is oxidised from the +4 state in SO_2 to +6 in SO_3. VO_2 is oxidised back to V_2O_5 by oxygen.

The vanadium(V) oxide catalyst takes part in the reaction, but is unchanged at the end:

$V_2O_5(s) + SO_2(g) \rightarrow 2VO_2(s) + SO_3(g)$

+5 +4

$4VO_2(s) + O_2(g) \rightarrow 2V_2O_5(g)$

+4 +5

KEY IDEAS

- A heterogeneous catalyst is in a different phase from the reactants; for example, there may be a solid *metal* catalyst and *gaseous* reactants.
- In heterogeneous catalysis, reaction occurs at the surface of the catalyst.
- Many transition metals are good catalysts.
- The strength of the bond formed between the reactant and the catalyst must allow both adsorption of reactant molecules and desorption of product molecules to occur, if the catalyst is to be effective.
- Different metal atoms form bonds of different strengths with reactants.
- Catalysts are poisoned if active sites are blocked.
- Catalysts are unchanged in their chemical composition at the end of the reaction.

Homogeneous catalysts

Homogeneous catalysis occurs when the reactants and the catalyst are in the same phase. The ability of transition metal ions to act as catalysts is often linked to a transition metal's ability to form ions in different oxidation states.

An example of an ion that behaves as a homogeneous catalyst is the hexaaquacobalt(II) ion, $[Co(H_2O)_6]^{2+}(aq)$. Under suitable reaction conditions the Co^{2+} ion is easily oxidised to Co^{3+}, which can form temporary intermediates in, for example, the reaction between hydrogen peroxide and sodium potassium tartrate,

$Na^+ \ {}^-OOCCH(OH)CH(OH)COO^- \ {}^+K$

Cobalt(II) ions form a pink complex with water molecules.

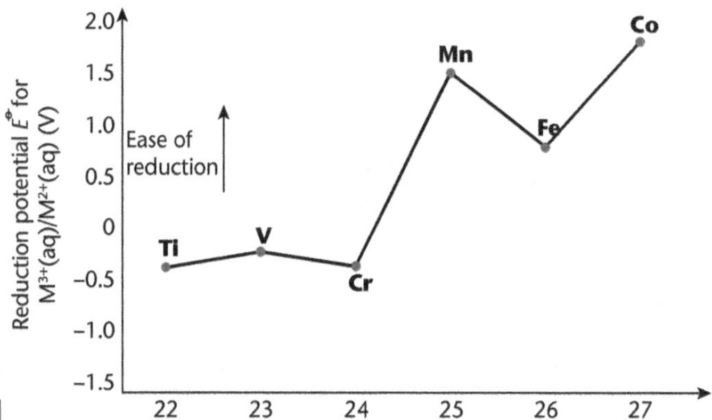

Figure 29 *Reduction potentials of M^{3+}/M^{2+} hexa-aqua complexes of period 4 transion metals, from Ti to Co.*

The reduction of Co(III) to Co(II) is favourable (Figure 29). With H_2O as ligands, reduction from Co(III) to Co(II) can occur spontaneously, but not the oxidation of Co(II) to Co(III). A powerful oxidising agent is needed to overcome the reduction potential. However, some ligands can lower the reduction potential sufficiently for a mild oxidising agent to produce the change from Co(II) to Co(III). Here is an example.

If cobalt(II) ions are added to a solution of sodium potassium tartrate and hydrogen peroxide, the cobalt ions form an intermediate complex with the tartrate. In this intermediate, the cobalt(II) ions are more easily oxidised to cobalt(III) by the hydrogen peroxide. (Changing the ligands changes the electrode potential for oxidation of Co(II) to Co(III).)

A green cobalt(III) tartrate complex forms. The cobalt(III) ions in the complex are then able to oxidise the tartrate, to produce carbon dioxide gas and a carbonyl compound (Figure 30), and Co(III) is reduced back to the pink Co(II) complex $[Co(H_2O)_6]^{2+}$. Colour changes often accompany a change in oxidation state of transition metals, and the colour change reveals the catalytic ability of cobalt in this reaction.

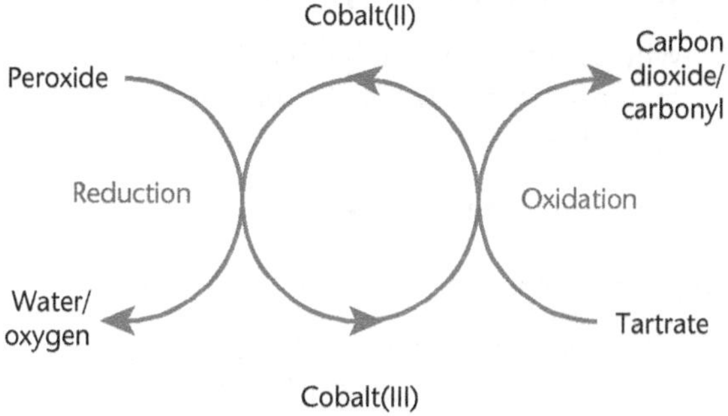

Figure 30 *Catalysis of the reaction between hydrogen peroxide and tartrate ions by cobalt ions*

Another reaction that involves homogeneous catalysis is the oxidation of iodide ions by peroxodisulfate(VI) ions,

$$S_2O_8^{2-} + 2I^- \rightarrow I_2 + 2SO_4^{2-}$$

The reaction is quite slow even though it is energetically favourable. Both ions are negatively charged, so they are unlikely to make fruitful collisions with each other. However, if iron(II) ions are added to the reaction, the rate is much quicker. The positive Fe^{2+} ions make effective collisions with the negative peroxodisulfate ions and the iron(II) is oxidised to iron(III), which rapidly oxidises the iodide ions to iodine. In this redox reaction, the iron(III) is reduced to iron(II). This then continues the catalysis:

$$2Fe^{2+} + S_2O_8^{2-} \rightarrow 2Fe^{3+} + 2SO_4^{2-}$$

$$2Fe^{3+} + 2I^- \rightarrow 2Fe^{2+} + I_2$$

$$S_2O_8^{2-} + 2I^- \rightarrow I_2 + 2SO_4^{2-}$$

The Fe^{2+} ions do not appear in the final equation, because they are catalysts.

Autocatalysis

When manganate(VII) is titrated with a warmed acidified solution of ethanedioate ions, $C_2O_4^{2-}$, the reaction is quite slow initially and, during the first addition of manganate(VII), the purple colour is slow to decolourise. When more manganate(VII) is added, however, the solution immediately turns colourless and continues to do so until the endpoint is reached.

The reaction is catalysed by the Mn^{2+} ion, which is formed during the reaction.

To balance the electrons, $2MnO_4^-(aq)$ reacts with $5C_2O_4^{2-}(aq)$. Then, adding the two half-equations and cancelling gives

$$2MnO_4^-(aq) + 8H^+(aq) + 5C_2O_4^{2-}(aq) \rightarrow 2Mn^{2+}(aq) + 10CO_2(g) + 4H_2O(l)$$

The reaction does not speed up until some Mn^{2+} ions have been formed. The catalysis of a reaction by one of its products is called **autocatalysis**.

This reaction is slow initially because both the oxidant and the reductant are negatively charged, so they are unlikely to make fruitful collisions. However, the positive Mn^{2+} ions can react with MnO_4^- ions to form Mn^{3+} ions:

$$4Mn^{2+} + MnO_4^- + 8H^+ \rightarrow 5Mn^{3+} + 4H_2O$$

The Mn^{3+} ions can then react with $C_2O_4^{2-}$ ions to liberate CO_2 and re-form Mn^{2+} ions, which can then continue the autocatalysis:

$$2Mn^{3+} + C_2O_4^{2-} \rightarrow 2Mn^{2+} + 2CO_2$$

QUESTIONS

25. a. Write the half-equation for the reaction of Mn(VII) to Mn(II).

b. Write the half-equation for the reaction of $C_2O_4^{2-}$ to $2CO_2$.

c. Why is the manganate(VII)/ethanedioate reaction an example of homogeneous catalysis?

KEY IDEAS

- Homogeneous catalysis proceeds via an intermediate (or intermediates).
- Transition metal ions taking part in homogeneous catalysis usually go through a temporary change in oxidation state.
- Autocatalysis occurs when one of the products catalyses the reaction.

ASSIGNMENT 4: CATALYSTS AT WORK

(PS 1.2)

Oil refining

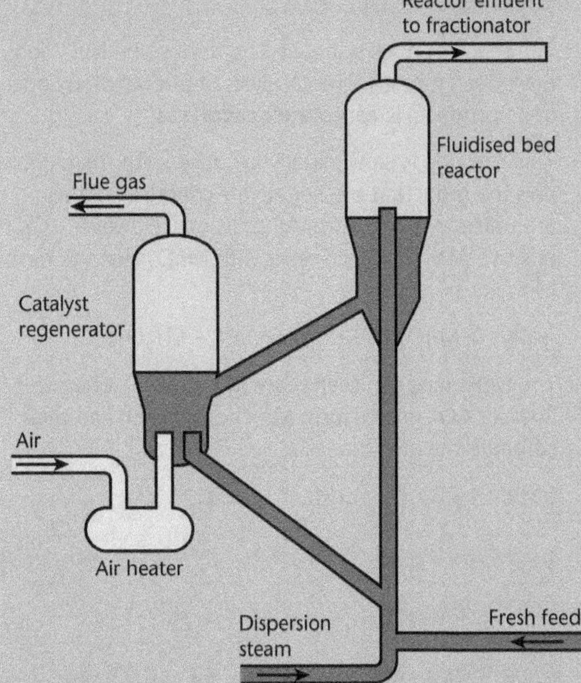

Figure A1 *A catalytic cracker used in oil refining*

A catalytic cracker takes a number of feedstocks, including heavy gas oil, treated fuel oil and residue from the lubricant treatment plant. The feedstock is mixed with a hot zeolite catalyst and passes up through the reaction vessel. The long-chain hydrocarbons are split into shorter chains using the catalyst and moderately high temperatures (400–500 °C). The main product is ethane, C_2H_6; the C_5 to C_8 hydrocarbons go into the petrol blend. The catalyst flows back into the regenerator on the left, where it is reheated to burn off carbon ready for another round of catalysing. An individual zeolite crystal is barely visible to the naked eye, but it has a large surface area owing to its shape. Each crystal flows around the cracker and regenerator along with billions of other crystals. They are supported on a bed of air and behave like a fluid.

Questions

A1. Why are feedstocks recycled and cracked?

A2. Why does the carbon that builds up on the surface of the zeolite have to be burned off?

A3. Why is the catalyst fluidised?

Catalytic converters

Catalytic converters have proven to be reliable devices and have been successful in reducing noxious emissions from exhaust pipes. However, they may have some adverse environmental impacts in use. There is a requirement for the engine to run 'richer' so that there is balance between reduction and oxidation. The manufacture of catalytic converters requires palladium and/or platinum. A portion of the world's supply of these precious metals is produced near the Russian city of Norilsk, with significant negative environmental effects.

Figure A2 *The palladium and platinum deposits at Norilsk, Russia, lie at a depth of between 500 m and 1500 m. The high-grade sulfide ores can be high in nickel and/or copper, and may contain up to 32% copper. Annual production currently includes about 3 000 000 kg of palladium and 21 300 kg of platinum.*

Questions

A4. Give an environmental advantage related to air quality of using a catalytic converter. What environmental problem associated with vehicle emissions do these devices **not** solve?

A5. What might the negative environmental effects of platinum and palladium production include?

Catalysts for taste

Catalysts for pollution control form a very important part of the industrial use of catalysts, but some catalytic materials have very different uses. The food industry makes significant use of catalysts, especially nickel. This is used particularly for hydrogenating oils to make fats. Often these catalysts catalyse reactions that stop at a very precise stage of hydrogenation, before taste or texture or both are ruined.

Many foods are now manufactured from vegetable oils. Butter, chocolate and ice cream used to be all-dairy products, and so contained animal fat. Oils and fats are very similar chemically. Vegetable oils contain long chains of carbon atoms; oils contain a higher proportion of carbon–carbon double bonds (unsaturated groups) than fats do, and are better for consumers' health. Oils can be hydrogenated to make them into solids for use in foods such as chocolate by converting the double bonds to single bonds. The catalyst is very finely divided nickel, deposited on small particles of an inert carrier material, which can be filtered out. Some chocolate is made from hydrogenated vegetable oils. The catalyst is nickel and is mixed with the oil in the reactor.

The temperature for the hydrogenation reaction of oils is critical and must be controlled to within 1 °C, or the number of double bonds converted will not be correct. If the melting point of chocolate is incorrect, the fat will not release its flavour quickly enough and there will be no flavour burst. This is why the extent of hydrogenation must be controlled very carefully.

To really enjoy eating a chocolate bar, the melting point has to be just right so you get that cooling, luxurious texture from the melting chocolate that makes it so enjoyable.

Questions

A6. Why is nickel called a heterogeneous catalyst?

A7. Why is it important that the nickel is finely divided?

A8. Why would increasing the proportion of double bonds in a molecule reduce the melting point?

A9. Why are vegetable oils considered healthier than animal fats?

PRACTICE QUESTIONS

1. One characteristic property of transition metals is variable oxidation state.

   a. For each of the following processes, write two equations to show how the transition metal catalyst reacts and is reformed. Identify the different oxidation states shown by the transition metal catalyst in each process.

      i. the Contact Process catalysed by vanadium(V) oxide

      ii. the oxidation of ethanedioate ions by acidified potassium manganate(VII), autocatalysed by Mn^{2+}(aq) ions.

   b. Cobalt(II) ions cannot easily be oxidised to cobalt(III) ions in water. Suggest why this oxidation can be carried out in aqueous ammonia and identify a suitable oxidising agent.

   c. Metal ions $\mathbf{Q}^{2+}$ in acidified aqueous solution can be oxidised by aqueous potassium dichromate(VI).

      In a titration, an acidified 25.0 cm^3 sample of a 0.140 mol dm^{-3} solution of $\mathbf{Q}^{2+}$(aq) required 29.2 cm^3 of a 0.040 mol dm^{-3} solution of potassium dichromate(VI) for complete reaction.

      Determine the oxidation state of the metal **Q** after reaction with the potassium dichromate(VI).

AQA June 2007 Unit 5 Question 6

2. A 0.263 g sample of impure iron, containing an unreactive impurity, was reacted with an excess of hydrochloric acid. All of the iron in the sample reacted, evolving hydrogen gas and forming a solution of iron(II) chloride. The volume of hydrogen evolved was 102 cm^3, measured at 298 K and 110 kPa.

The percentage, by mass, of iron in the sample can be determined using either the volume of hydrogen produced or by titrating the solution of iron(II) chloride formed against a standard solution of potassium dichromate(VI).

a. i. Write an equation for the reaction between iron and hydrochloric acid.

ii. Calculate the number of moles of hydrogen produced in the reaction.

iii. Use your answers to parts **a i** and **ii** to determine the number of moles of iron and the mass of iron in the original sample.

(If you have been unable to complete part **a ii** you should assume the answer to be 4.25×10^{-3} mol. This is not the correct answer.)

iv. Calculate the percentage of iron in the original sample.

b. i. Write half-equations for the oxidation of Fe^{2+} and for the reduction of $Cr_2O_7^{2-}$ in acidic solution, and use these to construct an overall equation for the reaction between these two ions.

ii. The number of moles of iron in the sample was determined in part **a iii**. Use this answer to calculate the volume of a 0.0200 mol dm^{-3} solution of potassium dichromate(VI) which would react exactly with the solution of iron(II) chloride formed in the reaction.

(If you have been unable to complete part **a iii** you should assume the answer to be 3.63×10^{-3} mol. This is not the correct answer.)

iii. Explain why an incorrect value for the number of moles of iron(II) chloride formed would have been obtained if the original solution had been titrated with potassium manganate(VII).

AQA June 2006 Unit 5 Question 1

3. a. Explain why the reaction between sodium ethanedioate, $Na_2C_2O_4$, and potassium manganate(VII) in acidified aqueous solution is initially slow but gradually increases in rate. Write equations to illustrate your answer.

b. State what is meant by the term ***active site*** as applied to a heterogeneous catalyst.

Explain how the number of active sites can be increased for a given mass of catalyst. The efficiency of a heterogeneous catalyst often decreases during use. Explain, using a specific example, why this happens.

AQA June 2006 Unit 5 Question 9

4. a. State and explain the effect of a catalyst on the rate and on the equilibrium yield in a reversible reaction.

b. Explain the terms *heterogeneous* and *active sites* as applied to a catalyst. Give **two** reasons why a ceramic support is used for the catalyst in catalytic converters in cars.

Explain how lead poisons this catalyst.

c. In aqueous solution, Fe^{2+} ions act as a homogeneous catalyst in the reaction between I^- and $S_2O_8^{2-}$ ions. Give **one** reason why the reaction is slow in the absence of a catalyst.

Write equations to show how Fe^{2+} ions act as a catalyst for this reaction.

AQA June 2005 Unit 5 Question 5

5. a. Complete the electronic arrangement of the Co^{2+} ion.

b. Give the formula of the cobalt complex present in an aqueous solution of cobalt(II) sulfate and state its colour.

c. i. When a large excess of concentrated aqueous ammonia is added to an aqueous solution of cobalt(II) sulfate, a new cobalt(II) complex is formed. Give the formula of the new cobalt(II) complex and state its colour.

ii. Write an equation for the formation of this new complex.

d. When hydrogen peroxide is added to the mixture formed in part **c**, the colour of the solution darkens due to the formation of a different cobalt complex. Identify this different cobalt complex and state the role of hydrogen peroxide in its formation.

AQA January 2005 Unit 5 Question 6

6. a. In the Haber Process for the manufacture of ammonia, the following equilibrium is established in the presence of a heterogeneous catalyst.

$N_2(g) + 3H_2(g) \rightarrow 2NH_3(g)$

Identify the heterogeneous catalyst used in this process.

A heterogeneous catalyst can become poisoned by impurities in the reactants.

Give one substance which poisons the heterogeneous catalyst used in the Haber Process and explain how this substance poisons the catalyst.

b. State what is observed when an excess of aqueous ammonia reacts with an aqueous iron(II) salt. Write an equation for this reaction.

AQA January 2005 Unit 5 Question 9

ANSWERS TO IN-TEXT QUESTIONS

1 THERMODYNAMICS

1. When a lattice dissociates, ionic bonds are broken. This is an endothermic process in which energy is transferred from the surroundings to the substance.

2. Pressure, 100 kPa; temperature, 298 K.

3. $\Delta_f H^\circ = -796\ \text{kJ mol}^{-1}$

4. **a.** Because there is a change from one shell to another.

b. Energy must be supplied to overcome the attractive forces between the positively charged nucleus and the negatively charged electrons.

5. For element X, there is a large increase in ionisation enthalpy after the third electron has been removed. This indicates that the atom is in Group 3. For similar reasons element Y is in Group 4 and element Z is in Group 6.

6. Energy has to be supplied to break the bonds between the atoms.

7. The potassium atom is smaller than rubidium and therefore has fewer inner electron shells to screen the nucleus from the delocalised electrons.

8. As the halogen atoms become larger, the forces holding the atoms together in the molecules become weaker. The shared electron pair is attracted less strongly by the nuclei because of the greater shielding by the larger number of inner electrons.

9. Adding one electron to an atom of sulfur releases energy (exothermic). However, adding a second electron is an endothermic process because the repulsive force between the electron and the negatively charged ion, $S^-(g)$, must be overcome.

10. **a.** Enthalpy of atomisation of potassium

b. 1st electron affinity of oxygen

c. 2nd electron affinity of oxygen

d. Enthalpy of formation of potassium oxide

11.

$$2NaHCO_3(s) \xrightarrow{\Delta H_r} Na_2CO_3(s) + CO_2(g) + H_2O(l)$$

$\Delta H_1 \nearrow$ $\qquad\qquad$ $\nearrow \Delta H_2$

$$2Na(s) + H_2(g) + 2C(s) + 3O_2(g)$$

$$\Delta H_1 + \Delta H_r = \Delta H_2$$

$$\Delta H_r = \Delta H_2 - \Delta H_1 = -1810.0 - (-1901.6) = +91.6\ \text{kJ mol}^{-1}$$

12. Each O–H bond is polar because of the electronegativity difference between H and O. The overall effect is to make the molecule polar. The repulsion between two pairs of electrons increases in the order bonding pair–bonding pair < bonding pair–lone pair < lone pair–lone pair.

13. Oxygen in water molecules bonds to cations, and hydrogen in water molecules bonds to anions.

14. The strength of attraction between oppositely charged particles decreases as the distance between them increases.

15. Water molecules attached to the outer part of the hydrated ion are held weakly and are constantly in motion, breaking free and becoming associated with other hydrated ions. While the immediate shell of water molecules often contains a fixed number of molecules, the total number varies at any one time.

16. a. $MgCl_2$ and $SrCl_2$.

b. KCl and RbCl.

2 RATE EQUATIONS

1. a. The reactant is used up fastest at the start of the reaction when its concentration is greatest. At this point the slope of the curve is at its steepest.

b. For the same reasons, the rate at which the product is formed is fastest at the start: product formation rate decreases as the reaction proceeds.

2. a. Order with respect to A = 0 and B = 2

b. Order with respect to A = 1 and to B = 1

c. Order with respect to A = 2 and to B = 1

d. Order with respect to A = 0 and B = 0

3. a. rate = $k[X][Y]^2$

b. rate = $k[H_2O]^2$

c. rate = $k[A]^2[B]^2[C]$

4. a. Overall order of reaction = 2

b. Overall order of reaction = 0

c. Overall order of reaction = 2

d. Overall order of reaction = 1

e. Overall order of reaction = 3

5. a. Rate constant k = rate/[A][B] = 0.05

b. $mol^{-1}\ dm^3\ s^{-1}$

c. No effect

d. Increasing temperature increases the value of the rate constant

6. a. Rate = $k[H_2O_2]^2$

b. $mol^{-1}\ dm^3\ s^{-1}$

c. Rate constant $k = 0.048/(1.2)^2 =$ 0.033 $mol^{-1}\ dm^3\ s^{-1}$ (to 2 significant figures)

7. a. From first two experiments, keeping $[OH^-]$ constant and tripling $[CH_3CH_2Br]$ triples the rate; therefore, order with respect to CH_3CH_2Br = 1. From experiments two and three, keeping $[CH_3CH_2Br]$ constant and tripling $[OH^-]$ triples the rate; therefore, order with respect to OH^- = 1.

b. rate = 1.55×10^{-6} mol $dm^{-3}\ s^{-1}$

8. a. Order with respect to ethanal = 1

b. Order with respect to hydrogen ions = 2

9. Consistent with the rate equation: $C + E \rightarrow X$ (slow) then $X + D \rightarrow F + G$ (fast)

10. a. Rearranging equation: $E_A/RT = \ln A - \ln k$, and therefore $E_A = (\ln A - \ln k)RT$
Substituting values given $E_A = (2.20 - 1.22) \times 8.31 \times 298 = 2430$ J mol^{-1} (to 3 significant figures) = 2.43 kJ mol^{-1}

b. $\ln k = 2.2 - (2430/8.31 \times 400) = 1.47$, therefore k = 4.35 mol $dm^{-3}\ s^{-1}$

11. a.

$1/T\ (K^{-1})$	$\ln k$ (s)
0.00360	−10.4
0.00336	−7.7
0.00325	−6.4
0.00314	−5.3

b.

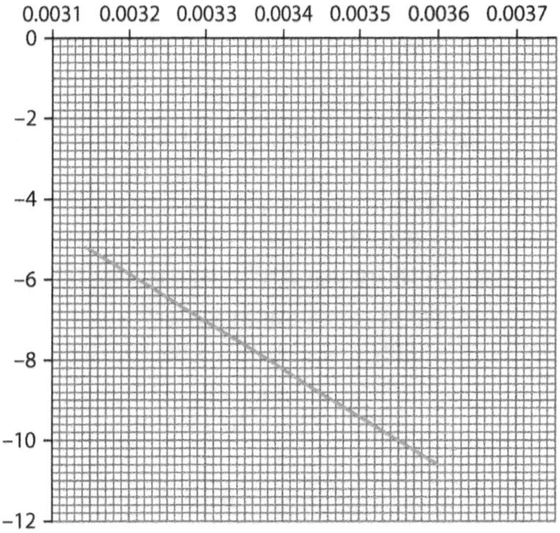

0.0031 0.0032 0.0033 0.0034 0.0035 0.0036 0.0037
0
−2
−4
−6
−8
−10
−12

c. Gradient of straight line = $-(10.4 - 5.3)/(0.0036 - 0.00314) = -11\ 090 = -E_A/R$
$E_A = -11\ 090 \times -8.31 = 92\ 100$ J mol^{-1} (to 3 significant figures) = 921 kJ mol^{-1}

3 EQUILIBRIUM CONSTANTS

1. Mole fraction of A = $\dfrac{40}{200} = \dfrac{1}{5}$

2. Ratio is 0.12 : 0.88 = 1 : 7.3

3. Total pressure = $\dfrac{30}{0.15}$ = 200 kPa

4. a. $K_p = \dfrac{P_{CO}P_{NO_2}}{P_{CO_2}P_{NO}}$

b. $K_p = \frac{P_{NO_2}{}^2}{P_{N_2O_4}}$

c. $K_p = \frac{P_{H_2O}{}^2}{P_{H_2}{}^2 P_{O_2}}$

d. $K_p = \frac{P_{CO_2} P_{H_2O}{}^2}{P_{CH_4} P_{O_2}}$

5. a. 7500 – (3000 + 2500) = 2000 kPa

b. 7500 × 0.15 = 1125 kPa

c. $\frac{1500}{7500} = 0.2$

d. 1 – (0.2 + 0.2) = 0.6

e. Mole fraction of hydrogen = 0.55; partial pressure of hydrogen = 7500 × 0.55 = 4125 kPa.

6. a. Mole fractions: 1/6 nitrogen, 1/2 hydrogen, 1/3 ammonia.
Partial pressures: nitrogen 7500 × 1/6 = 1250 kPa, hydrogen 7500 × 1/2 = 3750 kPa, ammonia 7500 × 1/3 = 2500 kPa.

b. $K_p = \frac{P_{NH_3}{}^2}{P_{N_2} P_{H_2}{}^3} = \frac{2500^2}{1250 \times 3750^3} = 9.5 \times 10^{-8}$

c. kPa^{-2}

7. a. $H_2(g) + F_2(g) \rightleftharpoons 2HF(g)$

b. Number of moles at equilibrium: H_2 = 1 – 0.15 = 0.85; F_2 = 2 – 0.15 = 1.85; HF = 0.3.
Total number of moles are equilibrium = 0.85 + 1.85 + 0.3 = 3.0 moles.
Mole fraction of HF at equilibrium = 0.3/3.0 = 1/10.

c. Partial pressure at equilibrium: H_2 = 1 – 0.15 = 0.85; F_2 = 2 – 0.15 = 1.85; HF = 0.3.

$$K_p = \frac{(0.3 \times 1.5 \times 10^6)^2}{(0.85 \times 1.5 \times 10^6) \times (1.85 \times 1.5 \times 10^6)}$$

$$= \frac{0.3}{0.85 \times 1.85} = 0.19$$

8. a. $2CO(g) + O_2(g) \rightleftharpoons 2CO_2(g)$

b.

	CO	O_2	CO_2
Initial number of moles	2.0	1.0	0.0
Change in number of moles	$-x$	$-0.5x$	$+x$
Number of moles at equilibrium	$2.0 - x$	$1.0 - 0.5x$	x

2.57

Total number of moles at equilibrium = $(2.0 - x) + (1.0 - 0.5x) + x = 3.0 - 0.5x$

Mole fraction of CO_2 at equilibrium = $\frac{P_{CO_2}}{P_{total}} = \frac{100}{300}$

Therefore, $\frac{100}{300} = \frac{1}{3} = \frac{X}{0.3 - 0.5X}$

$3.0 - 0.5x = 3x$

$3.0 = 3x + 0.5x = 3.5x$

Therefore, $x = \frac{3.0}{3.5} = 0.86$

and total number of moles at equilibrium = 3.0 – 0.43 = 2.57

Partial pressure of carbon monoxide = mole fraction × total pressure = $\frac{1.14}{2.57} \times 300 = 133$ kPa

Partial pressure of oxygen = mole fraction × total pressure = $\frac{0.57}{2.57} \times 300 = 67$ kPa

Partial pressure of carbon dioxide = mole fraction × total pressure = $\frac{0.86}{2.57} \times 300 = 100$ kPa

$$K_p = \frac{P_{CO_2}{}^2}{P_{CO}{}^2 P_{O_2}} = \frac{100^2}{133^2 \times 67} = 8.4 \times 10^{-3}\ kPa^{-1}$$

4 ACIDS AND BASES

1. a. $HCl(aq) + KOH(aq) \rightarrow KCl(aq) + H_2O(l)$
$H+(aq) + OH^-(aq) \rightarrow H_2O(l)$

b. $H_2SO_4(aq) + 2NaOH(aq) \rightarrow 2NaCl(aq) + 2H_2O(l)$
$2H+(aq) + 2OH^-(aq) \rightarrow 2H_2O(l)$

2. a. The hydrogens in methane are held by covalent bonds between elements with similar electronegativities, so there is no polarisation of the C–H bond. In HCOOH one of the hydrogens is attached to an oxygen atom, an element with a high electronegativity. The difference in electronegativity means there is a polarisation of the O–H bond and it dissociates more easily, releasing H^+ (H_3O^+) ions.

b. $HCOOH(aq) + H_2O(l) \rightleftharpoons HCOO^- + H_3O^+(aq)$

3. a. $CuO(s) + H_2SO_4(aq) \rightleftharpoons CuSO_4(aq) + H_2O(l)$
Base Acid

b. $NH_4{}^+(aq) + OH^-(aq) \rightleftharpoons NH_3(aq) + H_2O(l)$
Acid Base

c. $CH_3COO^-(aq) + H_3O^+(aq) \rightleftharpoons CH_3COOH(aq) + H_2O(l)$
Base Acid

4. **a.** $-\log_{10} 0.2 = 0.70$

b. $-\log_{10}(1.2 \times 10^{-2}) = 1.92$

c. $-\log_{10} 6.7 \times 10^{-5} = 4.17$

5. $pH = -\log_{10}[H^+] = -\log_{10} 2.0 = -0.30$

6. $$K_a = \frac{[H^+][CH_3(CH_2)_2COO^-]}{[CH_3(CH_2)_2COOH]}$$

7. **a.** $[H^+] = 10^{-pH} = 10^{-5.49} = 3.24 \times 10^{-6}$ mol dm^{-3}

b. $[H^+] = 10^{-2.75} = 1.78 \times 10^{-3}$ mol dm^{-3}

8. $[H^+] = \sqrt{(\text{acid concentration} \times K_a)} = \sqrt{(0.01 \times 1.34 \times 10^{-5})} = 3.66 \times 10^{-4}$ mol dm^{-3}
pH = 3.44

9. $pK_a = 4.20$; $K_a = 10^{-4.20} = 6.31 \times 10^{-5}$ mol dm^{-3}
$[H^+] = \sqrt{(\text{acid concentration} \times K_a)} = \sqrt{(0.150 \times 6.31 \times 10^{-5})} = 3.08 \times 10^{-3}$ mol dm^{-3}
pH = 2.51

10. $pK_a = 4.86$; $K_a = 10^{-4.86} = 1.38 \times 10^{-5}$ mol dm^{-3}
pH = 3.56; $[H^+] = 10^{-3.56} = 2.75 \times 10^{-4}$ mol dm^{-3}
Acid concentration = $[H^+]^2/K_a = (2.75 \times 10^{-4})^2/1.38 \times 10^{-5} = 0.00548$ mol dm^{-3}

11. A neutral solution is one in which $[H^+] = [OH^-]$.

12. **a.** When the temperature rises, it shifts the position of equilibrium in the direction of the endothermic change. $[H^+]$ increases.

b. Since $[H^+]$ increases and $pH = -\log_{10}[H^+]$, then pH decreases.

13. **a.** 0.15 mol dm^{-3} KOH; $[OH^-] = 0.15$ mol dm^{-3};
$[H^+] = 10^{-14}/0.15$; $pH = -\log_{10}(10^{-14}/0.15) = 13.2$.

b. 0.05 mol dm^{-3} NaOH; $[OH^-] = 0.05$ mol dm^{-3};
$[H^+] = 10^{-14}/0.05$; $pH = -\log_{10}(10^{-14}/0.05) = 12.7$.

c. 0.20 mol dm^{-3} $Ba(OH)_2$; $[OH^-] = 0.40$ mol dm^{-3};
$[H^+] = 10^{-14}/0.40$; $pH = -\log_{10}(10^{-14}/0.04) = 13.6$.

14. **a.** NaOH with pH 14.30; $[H^+] = 5.10 \times 10^{-15}$;
$[OH^-] = 10^{-14}/5.10 \times 10^{-15} = 1.96$ mol dm^{-3}.

b. KOH with pH 13.70; $[H^+] = 2.00 \times 10^{-14}$;
$[OH^-] = 10^{-14}/2.00 \times 10^{-14} = 0.500$ mol dm^{-3}.

c. $Ba(OH)_2$ with pH 12.50; $[H^+] = 3.16 \times 10^{-13}$;
$[OH^-] = 10^{-14}/3.16 \times 10^{-13} = 0.0316$ mol dm^{-3}.
Therefore, concentration of $Ba(OH)_2 = 0.0316/2 = 0.0158$ mol dm^{-3}.

15. **a.** **i.** Methyl orange.

ii. Phenolphthalein.

iii. None suitable.

b. **a**

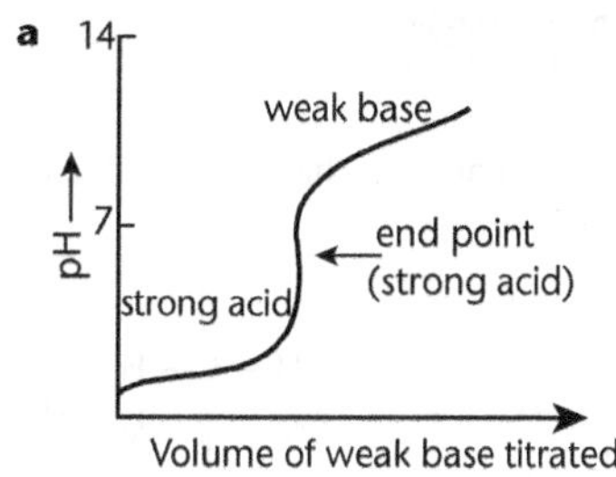

b

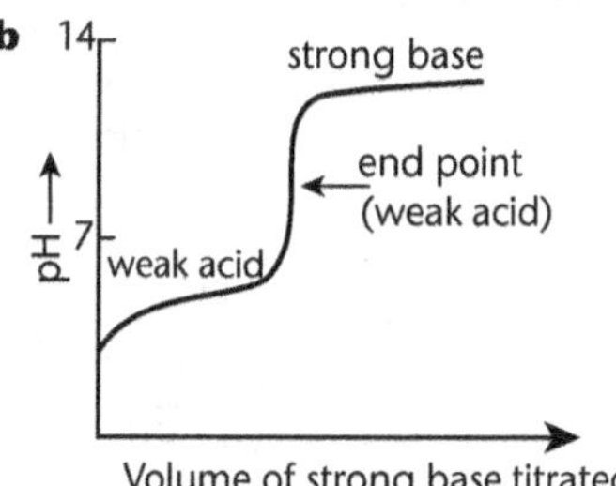

c

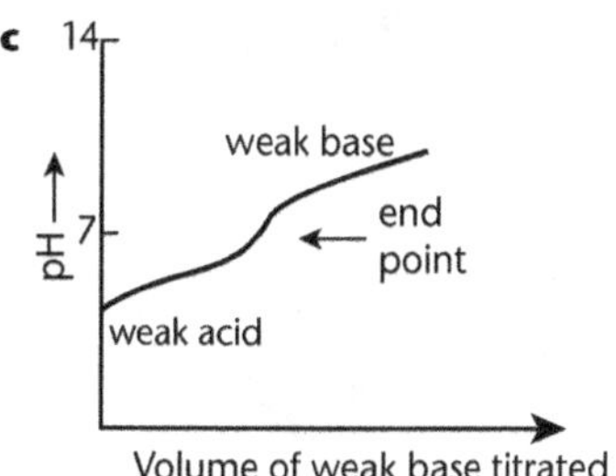

16. **a.** NH_3 is a weak base:
$NH_3(aq) + H_2O\,(l) \rightleftharpoons NH_4{+}(aq) + OH^-(aq)$
The salt NH_4Cl provides a supply of NH_4^+ ions. If H^+ ions are added to the buffer solution the ions will react with NH_3 to produce NH_4^+ ions, thereby removing H^+ ions from the solution:
$NH_3(aq) + H^+(aq) \rightleftharpoons NH_4^+(aq)$
If OH^- ions are added to the buffer they will react with NH_4^+ ions to produce NH_3, thereby removing OH^- ions from solution:
$NH_4^+(aq) + OH^-(aq) \rightleftharpoons NH_3(aq) + H_2O(l)$

b. $$[H^+] = K_a \times \frac{[CH_3CH_2COOH]}{[CH_3CH_2COO^-]}$$

$= 1.3 \times 10^{-5} \times 0.05/0.02 = 3.25 \times 10^{-5}$
$pH = -\log_{10}(3.25 \times 10^{-5}) = 4.49$

17. $$[H^+] = K_a \times \frac{[CH_3CH_2COOH]}{[CH_3CH_2COO^-]}$$

No. of moles of $CH_3CH_2COOH = 25.0 \times 2/1000 = 5 \times 10^{-2}$

No. of moles of $CH_3CH_2COO^- = 20.0 \times 1.5/1000 = 3 \times 10^{-2}$

$[H^+] = 1.34 \times 10^{-5} \times (5 \times 10^{-2})/(3 \times 10^{-2}) = 2.23 \times 10^{-5}$

$pH = -\log_{10} [H^+] = 4.65$

5 OPTICAL ISOMERISM

1. Each circled carbon atom is chiral if it is attached to four DIFFERENT groups.

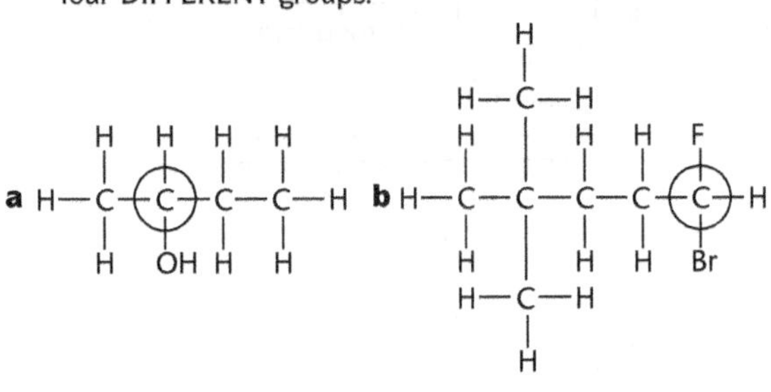

c

d

2. a CH_2ClBr

No

b $CH_3\overset{*}{C}HClBr$

Yes

c

No

d

Yes

3. a

Mirror

b

Mirror

c

Mirror

d

Mirror

4. **a.** There are two isomers of heptane that exhibit optical isomerism. The two are 3-methylhexane and 2,3-dimethylpentane. The chiral centres are illustrated by an asterisk.

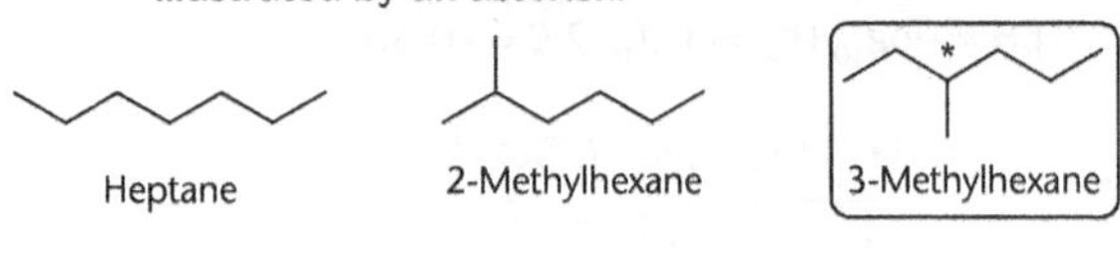

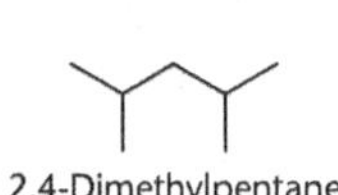

2,2-Dimethylpentane

2,3-Dimethylpentane

2,4-Dimethylpentane

3,3-Dimethylpentante

3-Ethylpentane

2,2,3-Trimethylbutane

b.

5. There are eight.

Cholesterol

6 ALDEHYDES AND KETONES

1. **a.**

$$CH_3CH_2CHO + HCN \longrightarrow CH_3CH_2CH(OH)CN$$

b.

$$CH_3CH_2COCH_3 + HCN \longrightarrow CH_3CH_2C(OH)(CH_3)CN$$

c.

$$CH_3CH_2CH_2CH_2COCH_3 + HCN \longrightarrow CH_3CH_2CH_2CH_2C(OH)(CH_3)CN$$

2. 2-Hydroxybutanenitrile, 2-hydroxy-2-methylbutanenitrile, 2-hydroxy-2-methylhexanenitrile

3. They all contain chiral centres.

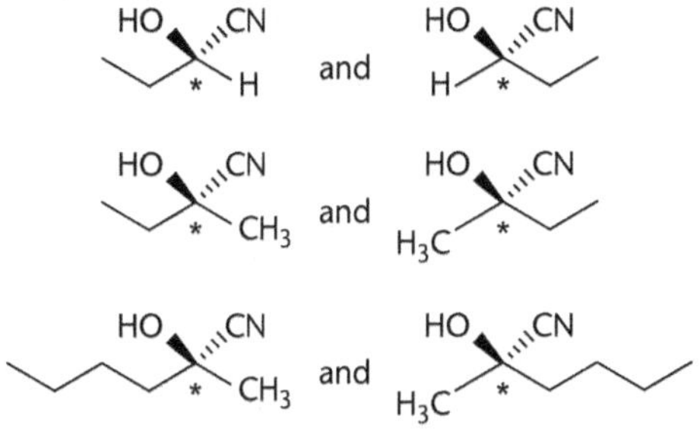

HO, CN, * H and HO, CN, H *

HO, CN, * CH_3 and HO, CN, H_3C *

HO, CN, * CH_3 and HO, CN, H_3C *

4. **a.** OH

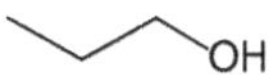

b. OH

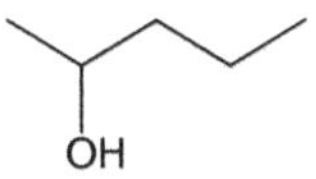

c. H, O

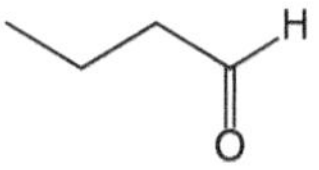

5. **a.** $NaBH_4$ in water.

b. $:H^-$

c.

H_3C–CH_2–C(=O)–CH_3 → 2[H] → H_3C–CH_2–CH(OH)–CH_3

H_3C–CH_2–CH_2–CH=O → 2[H] → H_3C–CH_2–CH_2–CH_2–OH

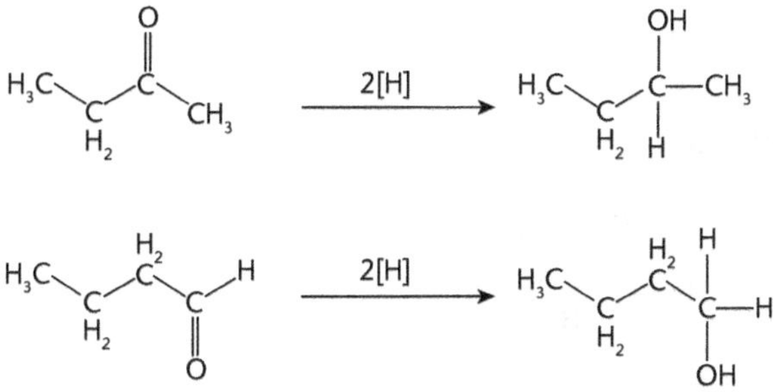

d. The hydride ion acts as a nucleophile, so this is an example of a nucleophilic addition reaction.

6.

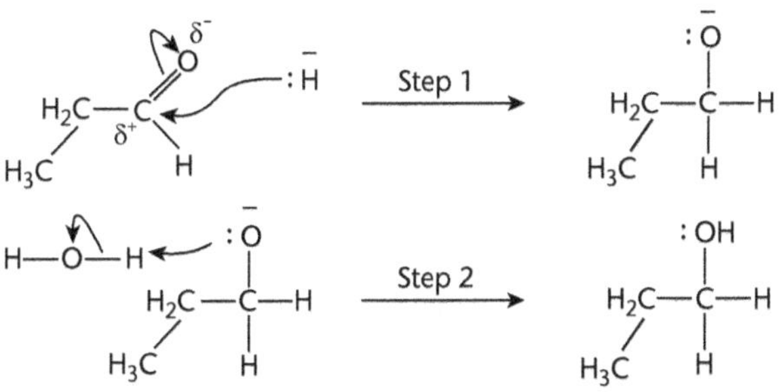

Step 1

Step 2

7 CARBOXYLIC ACIDS AND DERIVATIVES

1. Methanoic acid < ethanoic acid < benzoic acid.

2. **a.** propyl butanoate

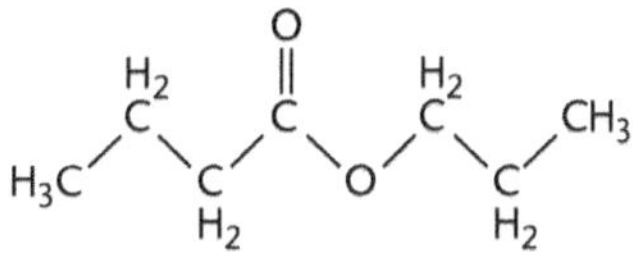

b. *N*-Butyl ethanamide

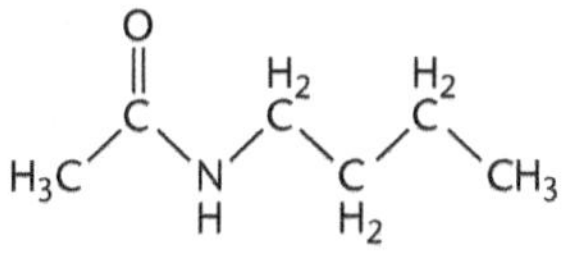

c *N*-Ethyl butanamide

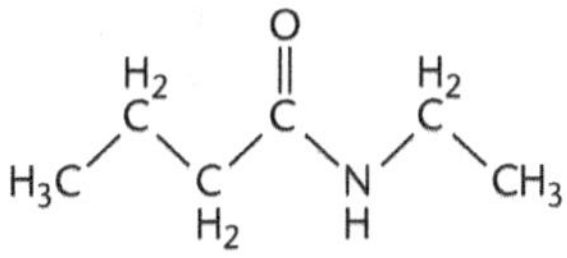

d. 2-Methyl-5-chloro-pentanamide

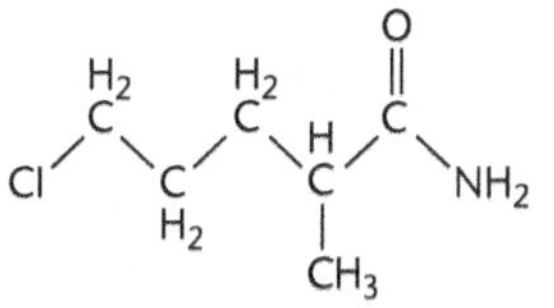

3.

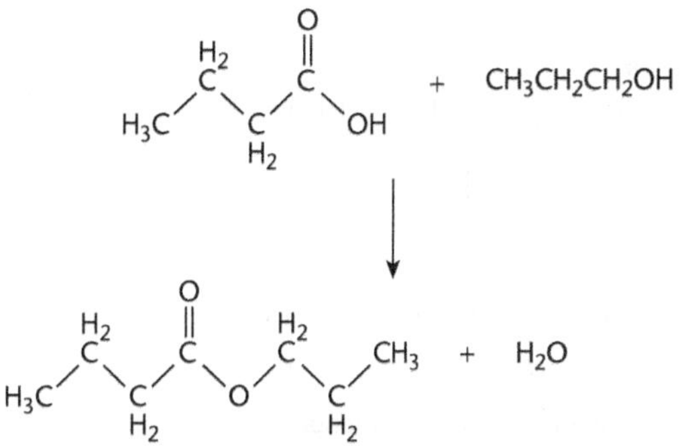

$CH_3CH_2CH_2COOH$ + $CH_3CH_2CH_2OH$ → $CH_3CH_2CH_2COOCH_2CH_2CH_3$ + H_2O

Propyl butanoate

4.

Banana

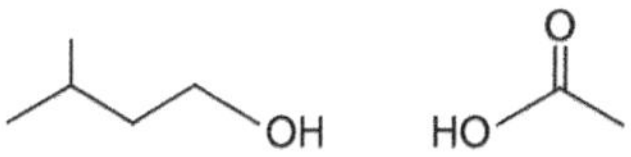

Rum

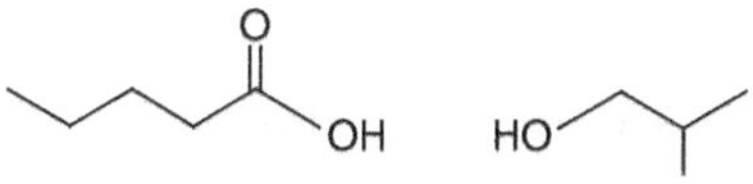

Peach

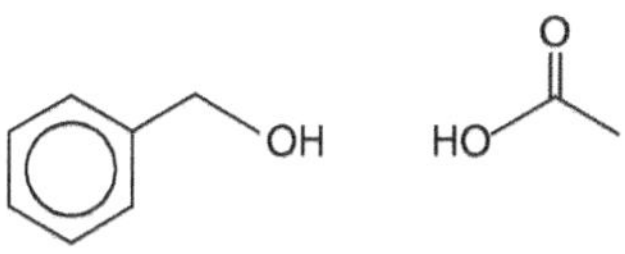

5. a. H_3C–CH_2–CH_2–$CH(CH_2CH_3)$–CH_2–OH

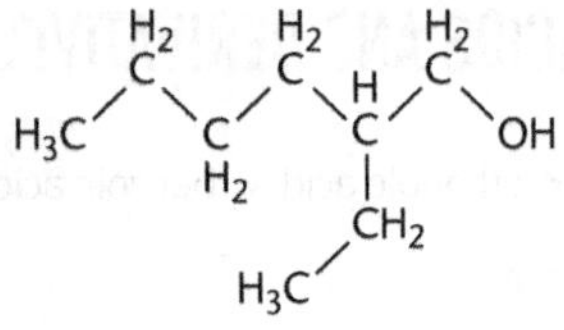

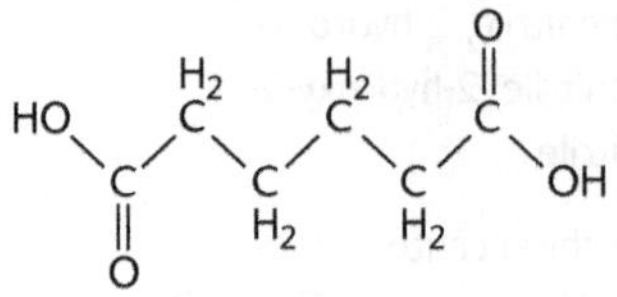

b. HO–C(=O)–CH_2–CH_2–CH_2–C(=O)–OH

c.

2 H_3C–CH_2–CH_2–$CH(CH_2CH_3)$–CH_2–OH

+

HO–C(=O)–CH_2–CH_2–CH_2–C(=O)–OH

↓

H_3C–CH_2–CH_2–CH_2–$CH(CH_2CH_3)$–CH_2–O–C(=O)–CH_2–CH_2–CH_2–C(=O)–O–CH_2–$CH(CH_2CH_3)$–CH_2–CH_2–CH_2–CH_3 + $2H_2O$

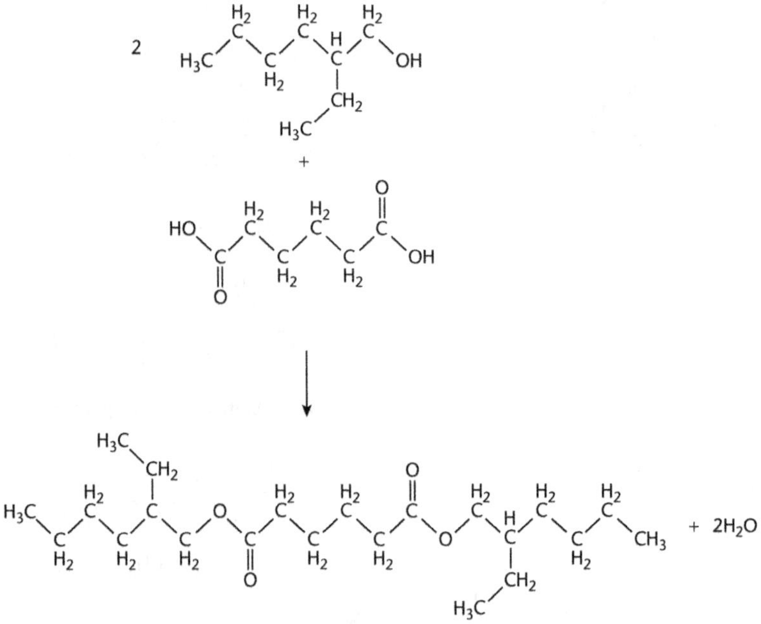

6. a

CH_3—C(=O)—OCH_2CH_3 + H_2O

↓

CH_3—C(=O)—OH + CH_3CH_2OH

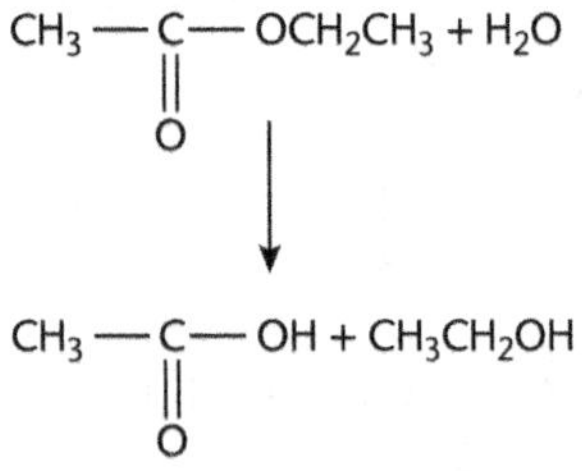

Ethanoic acid Ethanol

b

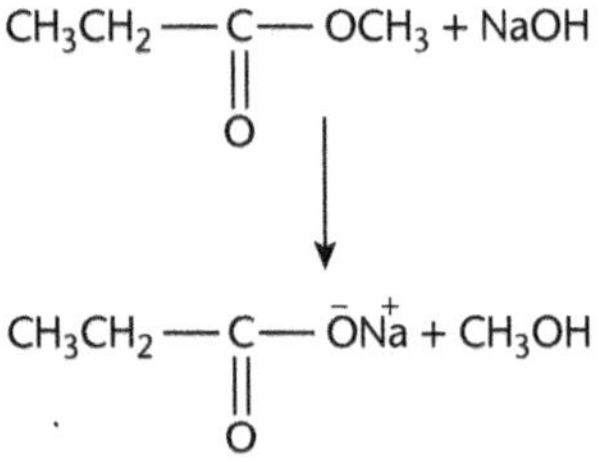

CH_3CH_2—C(=O)—OCH_3 + NaOH

↓

CH_3CH_2—C(=O)—$\bar{O}\overset{+}{Na}$ + CH_3OH

Sodium propanoate Methanol

7. a. H_3C–CH_2–CH_2–C(=O)–Cl

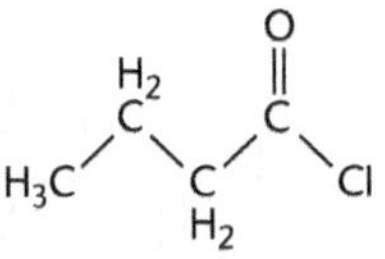

b. H_3C–CH_2–CH_2–C(=O)–O–C(=O)–CH_2–CH_2–CH_3

c. H_3C–CH(Cl)–CH_2–CH(CH_3)–C(=O)–Cl

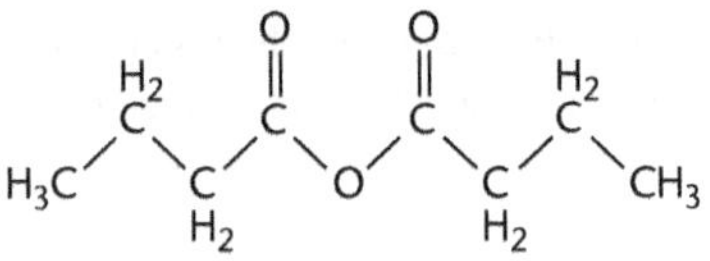

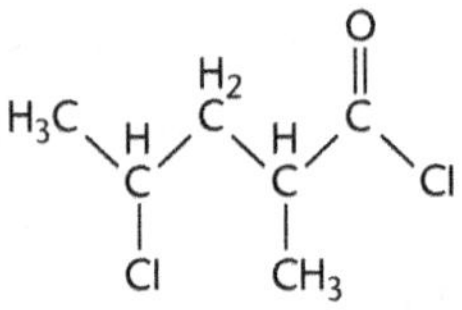

8. a.

$H_3C-C(=O)-OH$

Ethanoic acid

b.

$H_3C-CH_2-C(=O)-NH_2$ + HCl

Propanamide

c.

$H_3C-CH_2-CH_2-C(=O)-NH-CH_2-CH_3$

N-Ethyl butanamide

$H_3C-CH_2-CH_2-C(=O)-OH$

Butanoic acid

9. a.

Addition

Elimination

Deprotonation

$+ \bar{O}COR$

R = ethyl group

b.

Addition

Elimination

Deprotonation

$+ Cl^-$

c.

Addition

Elimination

Deprotonation

$+ \bar{O}CO$

R = butyl group

10 a. Reaction of ethanoyl chloride with water is a violent exothermic reaction producing HCl gas.

b. Reaction with ethanol is equally violent and also produces HCl gas.

c. Reaction with ammonia is also very violent, producing ammonium chloride.

8 AROMATIC CHEMISTRY

1. It would decolourise orange bromine solution or purple potassium permanganate solution. Also consider any electrophilic addition reaction.

2. (1) Benzene undergoes substitution, not addition reactions.
(2) The bond energy of hydrogenation of benzene (–208 kJ mol^{-1}) is less than that of the hypothetical cyclohexatriene (3 × –119 kJ mol^{-1}), which means that benzene is more stable than if it had three separate double bonds.
(3) The carbon–carbon bond lengths have been shown by X-ray crystallography to be all the same, whereas double bonds would be shorter than single bonds.

3. 1,4–Diethylbenzene and 1,2–dibromobenzene.

4. **a.** OH / CH_3 (4-methylphenol)

b.

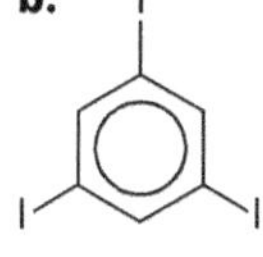

c. OH / NO_2 (4-nitrophenol)

5.

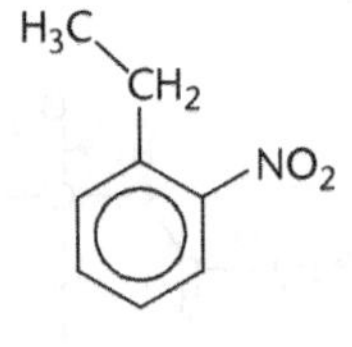

2-Nitroethylbenzene 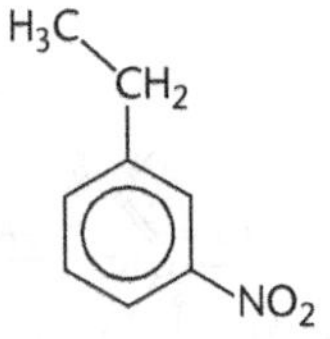 3-Nitroethylbenzene

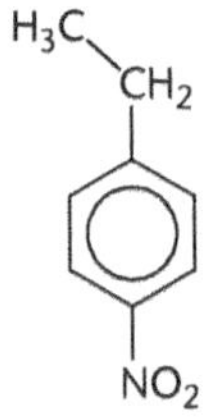

4-Nitroethylbenzene

6. Step 1: $AlCl_3$ and CH_3CH_2COCl.
Step 2: Zn/HCl or Ni/H_2.

7. Electrophilic substitution.

8.

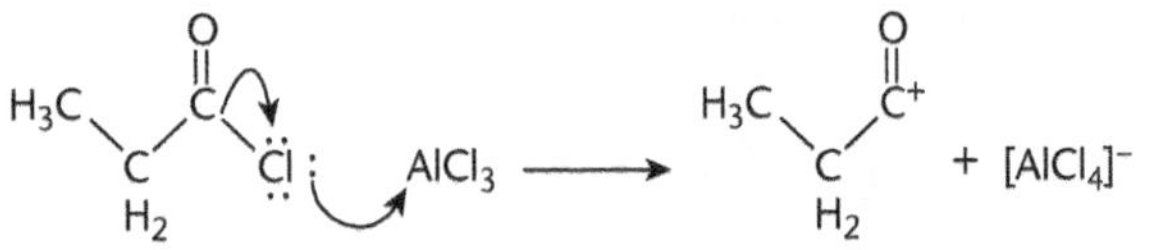

H_3C–CH_2–$C(=O)$–Cl + $AlCl_3$ ⟶ H_3C–CH_2–$C^+(=O)$ + $[AlCl_4]^-$

Electrophile

9 AMINES

1. Dopamine (primary amine), benzedrex (secondary amine), acetylcholine (quaternary ammonium salt).

2. **a.** $CH_3CH_2CH_2CH_2$–NH–CH_2CH_3

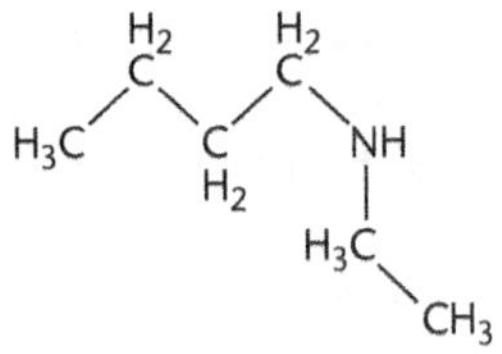

b. $CH_3CH_2CH_2$–N(CH_3)–CH_2CH_3

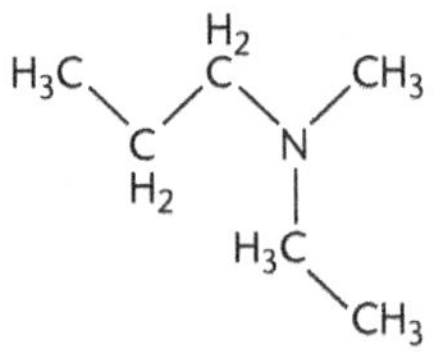

c. $CH_3CH_2CH_2CH_2$–N(CH_3)–CH_3

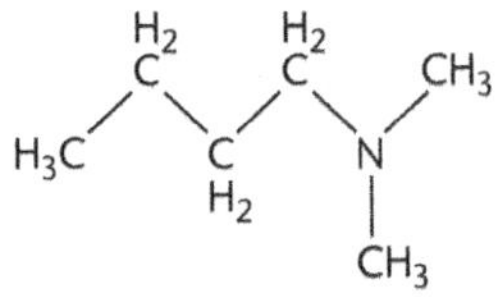

3. **a.** *N*-Methyl-2,2-dimethylbutylamine.

b. *N*,*N*-Diethylethylamine.

4. *trans*-3-Penten-2-amine.

5.

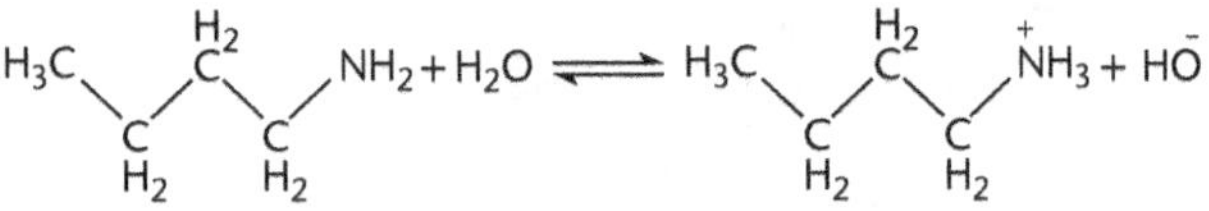

$$CH_3CH_2CH_2CH_2NH_2 + H_2O \rightleftharpoons CH_3CH_2CH_2CH_2\overset{+}{N}H_3 + H\overset{-}{O}$$

Butylamine will be more basic than phenylamine. The alkyl group in butylamine is electron donating, making the lone pair more negative. The lone pair in phenylamine is delocalised into the benzene ring, making it less basic.

6. **a.** Bromoethane.

b. 2-Bromopropane.

c. 1,6-Dibromohexane.

7. Diethylamine (*N*-ethylethylamine), triethylamine (*N*,*N*-diethylethylamine) and tetraethylammonium ion (*N*,*N*,*N*-triethylethylammonium ion).

8. excess $ClCH_2CH_2CH_2CH_2CH_2CH_2CH_2CH_3$ + NH_3

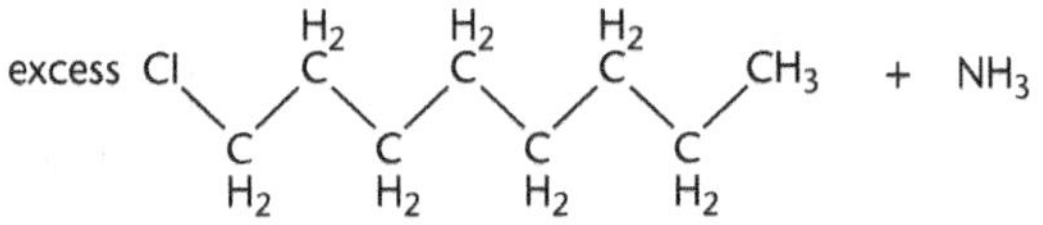

1-Chlorooctane

9. 2-Bromobutane + KCN → 2-methylbutanenitrile
2-Methylbutanenitrile + $LiAlH_4$ →
2-methylbutylamine.

10. No, because the required amine has the NH_2 group bonded midway along the carbon chain, whereas the nitrile reduction introduces the group at the end of the chain.

11. **a.** Poor reaction. The high electron density of the delocalised electron cloud of the benzene ring repels electron-rich nucleophiles such as ammonia. The aromatic ring is an electron-attracting group. The lone pairs of the halogen atom are delocalised towards the benzene ring. This has the effect of shortening and strengthening the C–Br bond, making it less reactive than in an aliphatic halogenoalkane.

b. Good reaction. The reduction will lead to one product in high yield.

c. Poor reaction. The primary amine product is still nucleophilic and can react further, and mixtures of secondary and tertiary amines and quaternary ammonium salts are inevitably produced.

d. Good reaction. The reduction will lead to one product in high yield.

12.

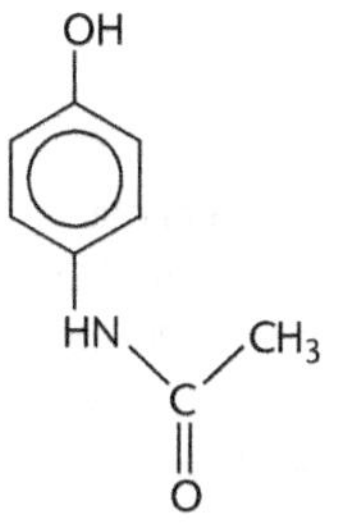

13.

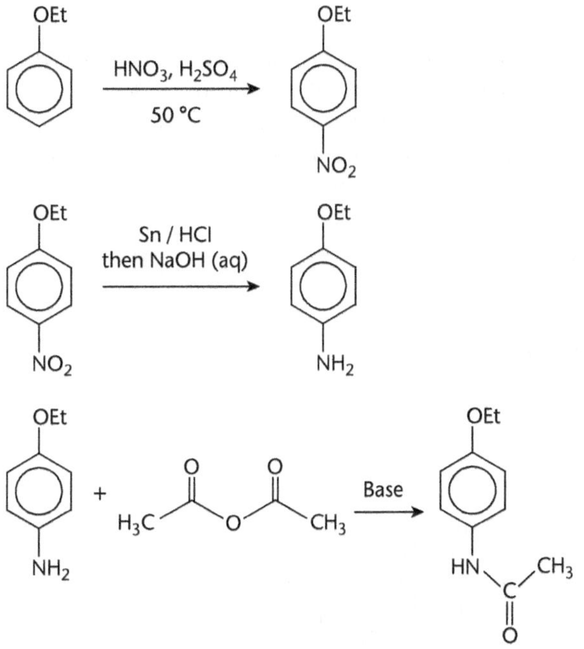

HNO_3, H_2SO_4, 50 °C

Sn / HCl then NaOH (aq)

Base

Note that in the last stage the use of ethanoyl chloride and a base would also be acceptable.

10 POLYMERS

1. a.

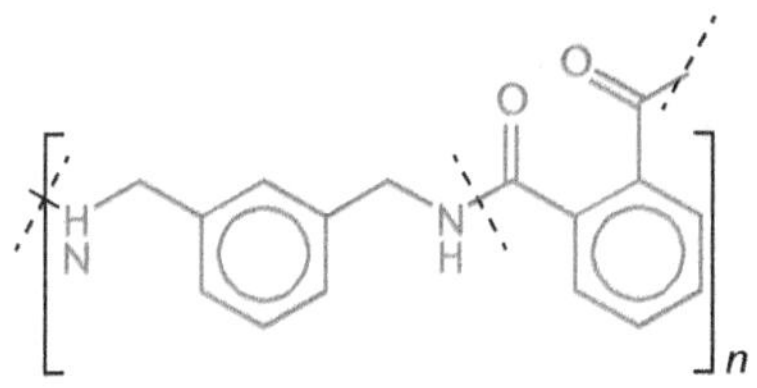

Monomers

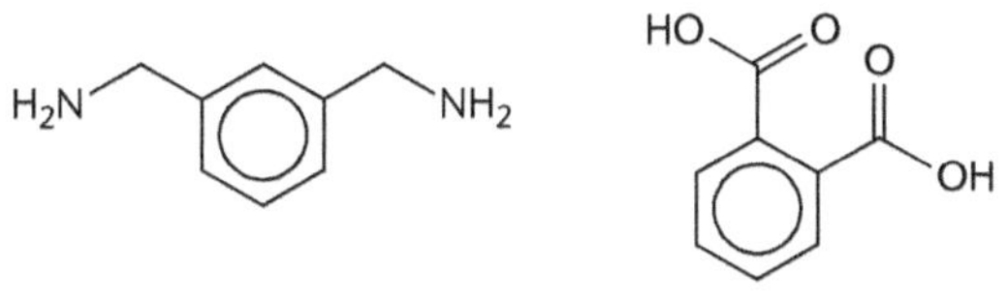

b.

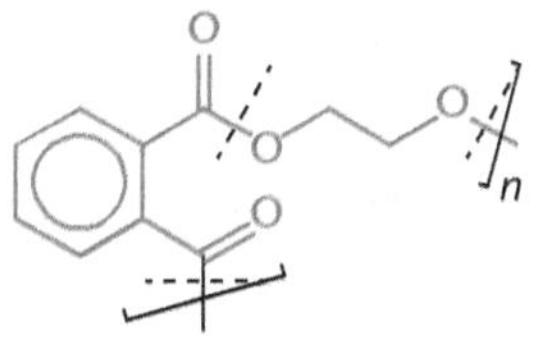

Monomers

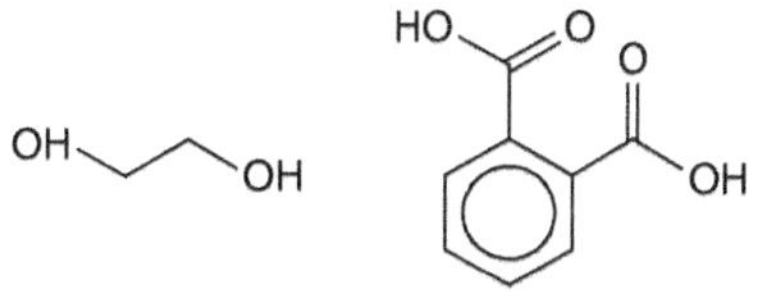

c.

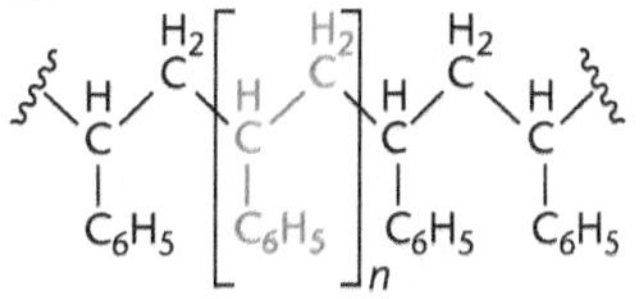

Monomer

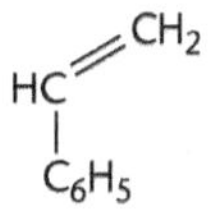

d.

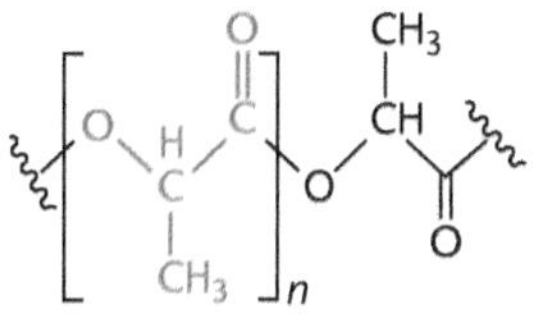

Monomer

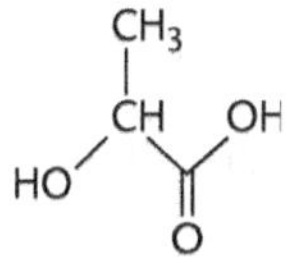

2.

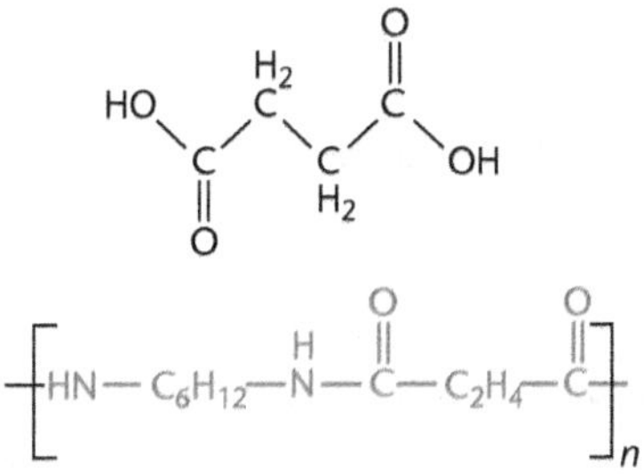

3. a.

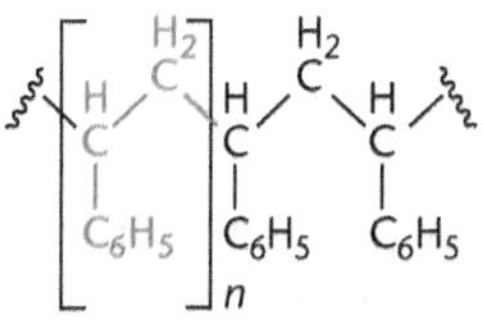

Addition polymer

b. Condensation polymer

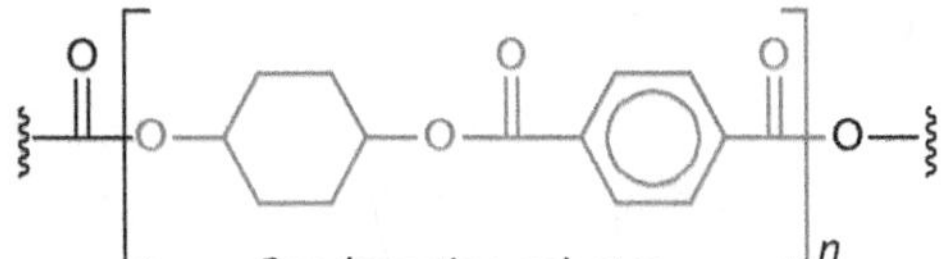

c. Condensation polymer

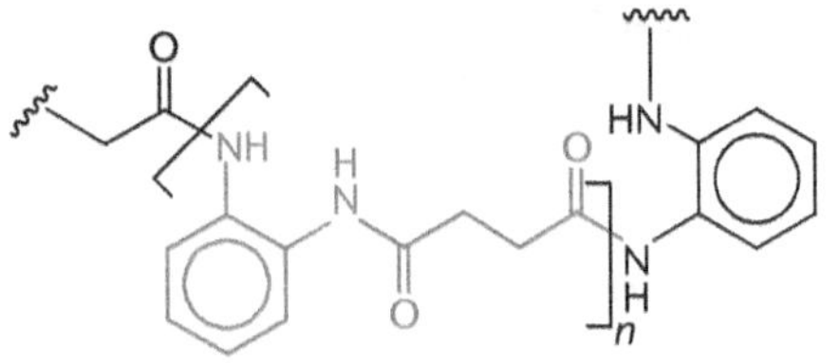

d. Condensation polymer

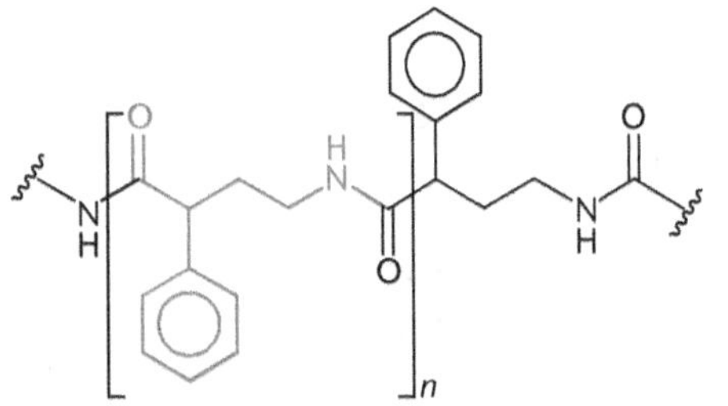

4. a.

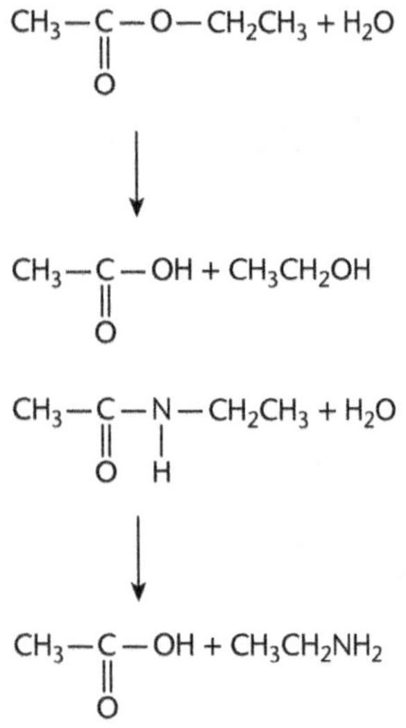

$$CH_3{-}C(=O){-}O{-}CH_2CH_3 + H_2O \rightarrow CH_3{-}C(=O){-}OH + CH_3CH_2OH$$

$$CH_3{-}C(=O){-}NH{-}CH_2CH_3 + H_2O \rightarrow CH_3{-}C(=O){-}OH + CH_3CH_2NH_2$$

b. Hydrolysis

c. Long-chain polyester and polyamide plastics will be broken down by repeated hydrolysis reactions at the ester or amide links.

5. Recycling conserves diminishing resources of oil. It reduces emissions compared with landfill and incineration. Suitable landfill sites are rapidly being used. Plastics take a long time to degrade. Landfill sites can be unstable in terms of emissions. Incineration can produce toxic emissions and contribute to global warming.

6. *Advantages:* Monomers are derived from a sustainable source rather than limited petrochemical sources. Because monomers are obtained from plants which grow by using up CO_2, the carbon footprint of polymers would be lower than that of conventional petrochemical-derived polymers. Condensation polymers would be biodegradable. Biodegraded or composted polymers could be used as fertiliser for next season's crops.

Disadvantages: Growing plants to produce monomers means there is less land available to grow food crops. Extraction of monomers from plants might be expensive. Processing of materials will still require fossil fuels as an energy source.

11 AMINO ACIDS, PROTEINS AND DNA

1. a. $H_2N{-}CH_2{-}COOH$

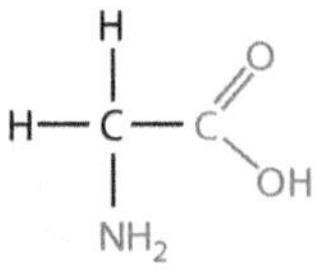

b. $H_2N{-}C^5H_2{-}C^4H_2{-}C^3H_2{-}C^2H_2{-}C^1OOH$

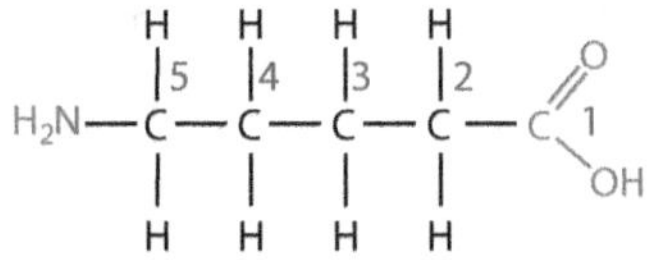

2. 4-Aminobutanoic acid.

3. It does not have a chiral carbon atom, i.e. it has no carbon atom with four different groups bonded to it.

4.

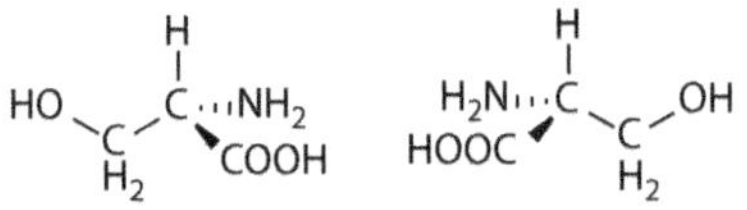

5. Two (highlighted by asterisks).

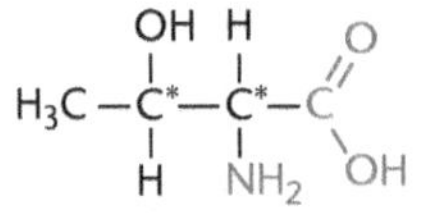

$$H_3C{-}C^*H(OH){-}C^*H(NH_2){-}COOH$$

Threonine

6. The L-isomer.

7.

$$HOOC-CH_2-NH_2 + HOOH-CH(CH_3)-NH_2$$

$$\downarrow$$

$$HOOC-CH_2-NH-C(=O)-CH(CH_3)-NH_2$$

or $+ H_2O$

$$HOOC-CH(CH_3)-NH-C(=O)-CH_2-NH_2$$

8. The sequence of α-amino acids linked together in the protein chain.

9. H-bonds.

10. The tertiary structure is the overall three-dimensional shape of the protein. Two cysteine side chains can react together to form a covalent disulfide bond which holds different parts of the protein together, maintaining the desired shape of the protein.

11. a. R_f for large spot = 2.1/5 = 0.42 (alanine); R_f for small spot = 1.8/5 = 0.36 (glycine).

b. It is a catalyst used to hydrolyse the peptide bond.

c. Spray ninhydrin onto the plate. The ninhydrin reacts with the amine groups of the amino acids, giving a blue colour (heat might be required).

12. Enzymes are proteins that catalyse specific chemical reactions.

13. A catalyst lowers the activation energy for a reaction by providing an alternative route where at least one intermediate is formed. The rate of reaction increases because the activation energy is lowered.

14. a. The reactant on which the enzyme acts to form the product.

b. The position in the enzyme where the substrate binds and undergoes reaction to form the product.

c. A molecule that blocks the active site so that the natural substrate cannot enter, thus stopping the natural reaction.

15. The enzyme active site has a unique three-dimensional shape, meaning that only certain molecules can bind to it.

16. H-bonding interactions, electrostatic (ionic) interactions or induced dipole–dipole/van der Waals interactions.

17. Enzymes are made of chiral α-amino acids, and so the active site itself may be stereospecific and bind only one enantiomer of a substrate. In this case only enantiomer 2 can bind.

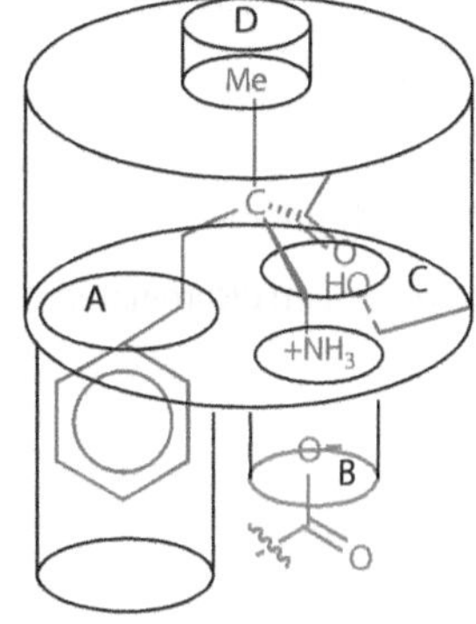

A. Large pocket, van der Waals
B. Electrostatic (ionic) interaction
C. H-bonding between OH and C=O lone pair
D. Can accept a small methyl group only

18. 3-TCCAGGTG-5

19.

The adenine–uracil (AU) base pair

20. Nucleotide, nitrogen, phosphorus, base, phosphate, 2′-deoxyribose, five, thymine, two intermolecular.

21.

$H_3N \rightarrow Pt$ (Cl), H_3N, $:\ddot{O}:$ (H, H)

22. It could bond to two guanines on different strands.

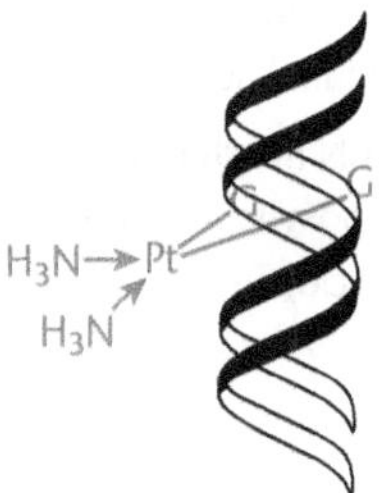

23. Structurally, they all have two molecules of an amine bonded to platinum via coordination (dative bonds). The amines are cis in arrangement to each other.

24. Other drugs can be given to decrease side effects. Chemotherapy is given in rounds where the patient has time to recover between doses.

If a patient has severe side effects the outlook can be poor. This is because the level of drug that is tolerated may be too low to kill the cancer.

12 ORGANIC SYNTHESIS

1. (0.5 × 0.4 × 0.75) × 100% = 15%

2. **a.** Excess hot acidified potassium dichromate(VI).

$CH_3CH_2(OH)CH_3 + [O]$

$$\downarrow$$

$$CH_3CH_2{-}\underset{\underset{O}{\|}}{C}{-}CH_3 + H_2O$$

b. CH_3COOH and concentrated sulfuric acid catalyst; heat.

$$CH_3CH_2CH_2OH + CH_3COOH \longrightarrow$$

$$CH_3CH_2CH_2{-}O{-}\underset{\underset{O}{\|}}{C}{-}CH_3 + H_2O$$

c. Concentrated sulfuric acid; heat.

$CH_3CH_2CH_2CH_2OH \rightarrow CH_3CH_2CH{=}CH_2 + H_2O$

d. $LiAlH_4$ in ethoxyethane.

$CH_3CH_2CH_2COOH + 4[H] \rightarrow CH_3CH_2CH_2CH_2OH + H_2O$

e. Excess ammonia and ethanol; heat and pressure.

$CH_3CH_2Br + 2NH_3 \rightarrow CH_3CH_2NH_2 + NH_4Br$

3. **a.** Alkene to secondary alcohol (H_2O and H_3PO_4 catalyst, high temperature).
Secondary alcohol to ketone (excess acidified potassium dichromate and sulfuric acid catalyst).

b. Alkane to bromoalkane (bromine and UV light). Bromoalkane to primary amine (excess concentrated ammonia in ethanol solvent; heat).

c. Halogenoalkane to nitrile (KCN in ethanol solution; heat). Nitrile to carboxylic acid (heat with dilute aqueous sulfuric acid).

4. **a.**

$$CH_3{-}CH{=}CH_2 \xrightarrow[H_3PO_4]{H_2O} CH_3{-}\underset{\underset{OH}{|}}{CH}{-}CH_3$$

$$\xrightarrow[H^+]{K_2Cr_2O_7} CH_3{-}\underset{\underset{O}{\|}}{C}{-}CH_3$$

b.

$$CH_3CH_2OH + 2[O] \xrightarrow[\text{excess}]{Cr_2O_7^{2-}/H^+ \text{ in}} CH_3CH_2COOH + H_2O$$

$$CH_3COOH + CH_3CH_2OH \xrightarrow[H_2SO_4 \text{ catalyst}]{} CH_3COOCH_2CH_3 + H_2O$$

c.

$$C_6H_6 + HNO_3\text{(Conc.)} \xrightarrow[50\ °C]{\text{Conc. } H_2SO_4} C_6H_5NH_2 + H_2O$$

$$C_6H_5NO_2 + 6[H] \xrightarrow{Sn/HCl} C_6H_5NH_2 + 2H_2O$$

5. **Route 1** increases the number of carbons by one.

$CH_2{=}CH_2 + HBr \rightarrow CH_3CH_2Br$

$$CH_3CH_2Br + KCN \xrightarrow[\text{Ethanol}]{\text{Heat}} CH_3CH_2CN$$

$$CH_3CH_2CN + 2H_2O \xrightarrow[H_2SO_4]{\text{Heat}} CH_3CH_2COOH + NH_3$$

Product: propanoic acid.

Route 2:

$$CH_2{=}CH_2 \xrightarrow[\text{high temperature}]{H_2O \text{ catalytic } H_3PO_4} CH_3CH_2OH$$

$$CH_3CH_2OH \xrightarrow[\text{catalytic } H_2SO_4]{\text{Excess } K_2Cr_2O_7,} CH_3COOH$$

Note that oxidation of a primary alcohol to a carboxylic acid proceeds via the aldehyde.

Product: ethanoic acid.

6. The atom economy is the fraction of the mass of the starting materials that become products and is calculated as follows:

$$\frac{\text{molecular mass of desired product}}{\text{sum of molecular masses for all reactants}} \times 100$$

It is a measure of the amount of waste products in a process.

7. **a.** Synthesis 1: A to D = (0.96 × 0.62 × 0.76) × 100% = 45%. Synthesis 2: E to D = (0.75 × 0.99 × 0.81) × 100% = 60%. Synthesis 2 is more efficient.

b. To make 1 mole of product D via synthesis 1 requires 1/0.45 = 2.22 moles of A = 2.22 × £10 = £22.20.
To make 1 mole of product D via synthesis 2 requires 1/0.6 = 1.67 moles of A = 1.67 × £12 = £20.00.
Synthesis 2 is more cost-efficient.

c. Synthesis 1 requires HCN gas, which is highly toxic, while synthesis 2 requires dilute HCl. The other steps are common to both. Synthesis 2 is less hazardous.

d. Synthesis 2 because it is cheaper and high-yielding and involves less dangerous reagents.

8. a.

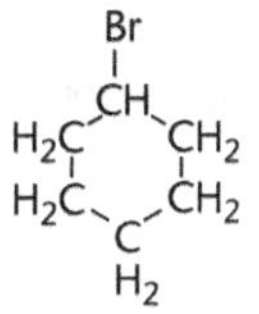

b. Aqueous HBr.

c. Reduction.

d.

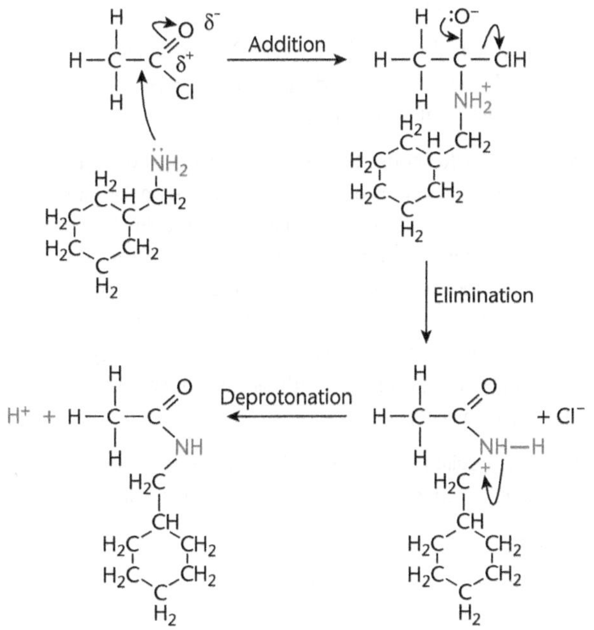

Addition

Elimination

Deprotonation

9. a. 4-Nitromethylbenzene.

b. Nitration can occur in the 2, 3 or 4 position giving rise to three isomeric products.

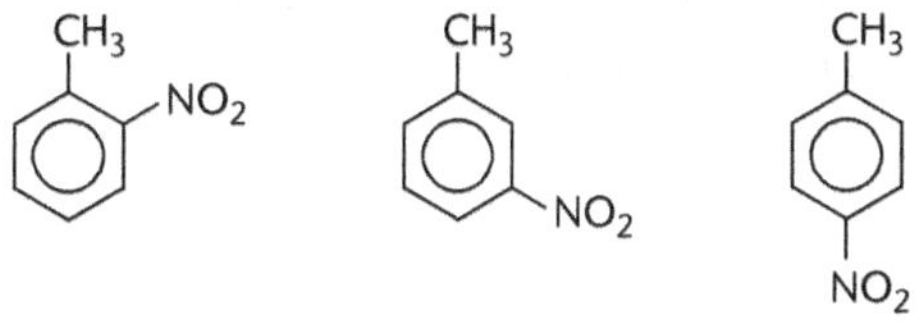

CH_3 NO_2

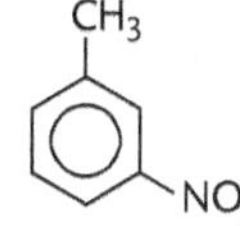

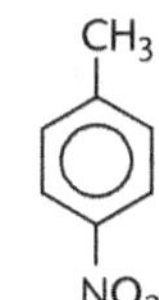

c. Electrophilic substitution (nitration).

d.

Reduction.

e.

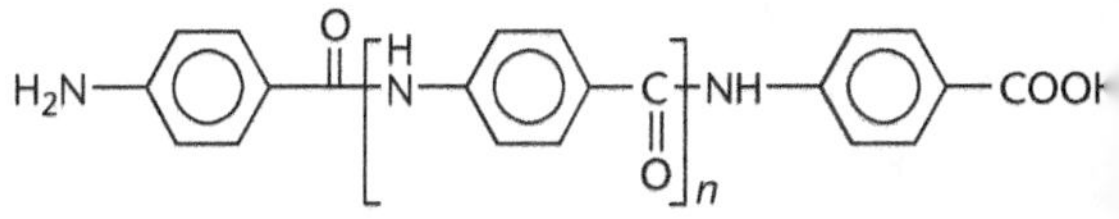

f. Condensation polymer.

13 NMR AND CHROMATOGRAPHY

1. Each H atom is bonded to the same carbon.

2. a. 1

b. 2

c. 3

d. 1

e. 2

f. 4

3. Propane 3 : 1, propanal 3 : 2 : 1.

4. The electronegative oxygen atom near to the aldehyde hydrogen atom causes the hydrogen nucleus to resonate in a higher ppm range.

5. $-CH_2F$ highest (the most electronegative atom, F, is attached to CH_2); $-CH_2NH_2$ lowest (the least electronegative atom, N, is attached to CH_2).

6 a. 3

b. 4.1 ppm. Split owing to coupling with neighbouring CH_3. $n + 1$ rule = quartet.

c. i. The singlet at 2 ppm is at a higher ppm than the triplet at 1.25 ppm. So the singlet at 2 ppm is next to the more electronegative C=O group.

ii. The triplet at 1.25 ppm is coupled to a neighbouring CH_2 group, but the singlet at 2 ppm is not coupled to any neighbouring groups.

7. a. 1

b. 5 : 1 : 2 : 2

c. The triplet means that the group is next to a CH_2 group. Out of the two triplet (CH_2) groups it has the higher ppm value and so must be next to the electronegative oxygen.

d. B is from the OH group. The H atom can exchange with the D atom in D_2O. The D atom does not give a signal in the ^1H NMR spectrum.

8. **a.** A = isomer 2, B = isomer 1

b. A = C–H next to the electronegative bromine atom and the C=O group. So it has a higher ppm value than D, which is from a C–H just next to an O atom.

c. 2 : 2 : 3

9. **a.** 1

b. 2

c. 3

d. 2

e. 2

f. 3

g. 3

h. 4

10. **a.**

H_3C–CH_2–CH_2–CH_2–OH ; $(H_3C)_2CH$–CH_2–OH ; H_3C–C(OH)(CH_3)–CH_3 ; HO–CH(CH_3)–CH_2–CH_3

b.

H_3C–CH_2–CH_2–CH_2–OH (4) ; $(H_3C)_2CH$–CH_2–OH (3) ; H_3C–C(OH)(CH_3)–CH_3 (2) ; HO–CH(CH_3)–CH_2–CH_3 (4)

c. Spectrum 1 =

$(H_3C)_2CH$–CH_2–OH

Spectrum 2 =

H_3C–C(OH)(CH_3)–CH_3

d.

HO–CH(CH_3)–CH_2–CH_3

e. It is a doublet as there is coupling to the CH group (n + 1 rule)

HO–CH((CH_3))–CH_2–CH_3 — coupling to 1 H atom

f. It is the OH group. The H atom can exchange with the D atom in D_2O. The D atom does not give a signal in the ^1H NMR spectrum.

g. Based upon how far away the carbons are from the electronegative O atom, we have

H_3C (D) – CH_2 (C) – CH_2 (B) – CH_2 (A) – OH

11. No. The gas must be inert, but oxygen can cause compounds to burn and react.

12. **a.** 5 minutes

b. D

c. B and C

d. D – it takes the longest time to elute from the column.

14 ELECTROCHEMICAL CELLS

1. **a.** $Mg^{2+} + 2e^- \rightleftharpoons Mg$, **b.** $Fe^{3+} + e^- \rightleftharpoons Fe^{2+}$, **c.** $Cl_2 + 2e^- \rightleftharpoons 2Cl^-$

2. **a.** Zn(s) | Zn^{2+}(aq) || Pb^{2+}(aq) | Pb(s), **b.** Zn(s) | Zn^{2+}(aq) || H^+(aq) | H_2(g) | Pt(s), **c.** Pt(s) | Fe^{2+}(aq) | Fe^{3+}(aq) || Cu^{2+}(aq) | Cu(s).

3. You would choose two electrodes which gave you as large an e.m.f. as possible, for example an Ag^+(aq) | Ag(s) cell with a Li^+(aq) | Li(s) cell. In reality you would need to consider many other factors as well, such as mass (lower mass is preferred), cost (the cheaper the materials and construction costs, the better) and chemical hazards (e.g. reactivity of electrode chemicals with air and water, and their toxicity).

4. The equilibrium will move from left to right towards zinc to reduce the number of zinc ions in solution.

5. **a.**

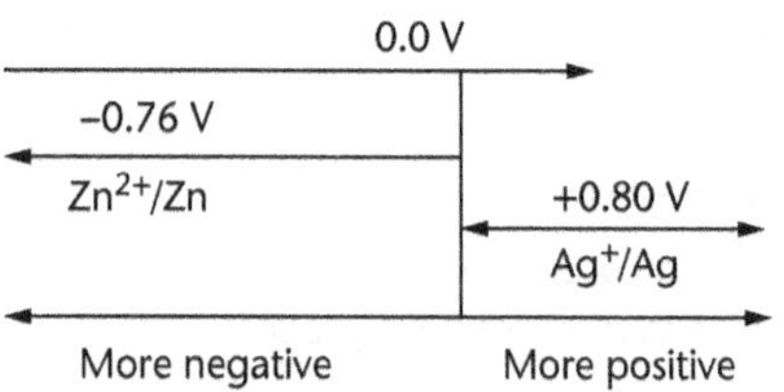

b. $+0.80 - (-0.76)$ V = 1.56 V.

c. A cell of electrodes Mg^{2+}/Mg and Zn^{2+}/Zn produces an e.m.f. of 1.61 V (difference between −2.37 and −0.76). A cell of electrodes Zn^{2+}/Zn and Ag^{+}/Ag produces an e.m.f. of 1.56 V (difference between −0.76 and +0.80). A cell of electrodes Mg^{2+}/Mg and Ag^{+}/Ag produces an e.m.f. of 3.17 V (difference between −2.37 and +0.80).

6. For iodine to displace bromine from solution the following two half–reactions must occur:

$$I_2(s) + 2e- \rightleftharpoons 2I^-(aq),\ E^\circ = +0.54\ V$$

$$2Br^-(aq) \rightleftharpoons Br_2(l) + 2e^-,\ E^\circ = -1.07\ V$$

The sum of these two half-reactions is $I_2(s) + 2Br^-(aq) \rightleftharpoons 2I^-(aq) + Br_2(l),\ E^\circ = -0.53$ V.

For this reaction to be spontaneous E° must be positive. Therefore iodine does not displace bromine from solution.

7. a. For a spontaneous cell reaction to occur E° must be positive, so for the Li | MnO_2 cell $E^\circ = +1.23 - (-3.03) = +4.26$ V.

b. To work out the reaction for the cell, write the more negative half-reaction as an oxidation, and the more positive half-reaction as a reduction. Then balance the number of electrons in each half-reaction and add the two together:

$2Li \rightleftharpoons 2Li^+ + 2e^-$
$MnO_2 + 4H^+ + 2e^- \rightleftharpoons Mn^{2+} + 2H_2O$
$2Li + MnO_2 + 4H^+ \rightleftharpoons 2Li^+ + Mn^{2+} + 2H_2O$

8. a. Zinc, because Zn^{2+}/Zn has a more negative electrode potential than H^+/H_2 so that electrons flow from the zinc half-reaction to the hydrogen ions in the acid, producing hydrogen gas molecules.

b. Yes. Fe^{3+}/Fe^{2+} has a more negative electrode potential than Br_2/Br^- so electrons flow towards Br_2/Br^-. This oxidises iron(II) ions to iron(III).

c. No. I_2/I^- has a more negative electrode potential than Fe^{2+}/Fe so electrons flow towards Fe^{2+}/Fe. This reduces iron(III) ions to iron(II).

d. Yes. Fe^{3+}/Fe^{2+} has a more negative electrode potential than $MnO_4^-,H^+/Mn^{2+}$.

9. The voltage depends on the reactants used (and their electrode potentials), not on their amounts.

10. 0.4 V.

11. Hydrogen.

12. $2H^+ + 2e^- \rightarrow H_2$
$4OH^- \rightarrow 2H_2O + O_2 + 4e^-$
To balance, need to double H^+ equation to give:
$4H^+ + 4e^- \rightarrow 2H_2$
Therefore, for each mole of oxygen produced, 2 moles of hydrogen are produced.

15 PERIOD 3 ELEMENTS AND AQUEOUS CHEMISTRY OF INORGANIC IONS

1. Sodium oxide has the largest difference in electronegativity values (for the Period 3 elements), so Na_2O will have the greatest ionic character. Mg has a greater nuclear charge, and so a greater attraction for the electrons on the O^{2-} ions. This produces a less ionic/more covalent character. At SiO_2, the electronegativity difference between the two atoms is small and so the electrons are shared – this tendency will increase across the period.

2. Only Na_2O, MgO and Al_2O_3 conduct electricity when molten. This is because their bonding is ionic. When the oxides are molten, the ions are free to conduct electricity. The other oxides are covalent solids and so will not conduct electricity.

3. The melting point is affected by the force of attraction between the positive and the negative ions. In the fluorides, Mg^{2+} has a greater ionic charge than Na^+, so there is a greater force of attraction between ions, and more energy is needed to separate them.

4. The melting point of silicon dioxide is relatively high for a covalent compound because the structure is macromolecular and is held together by covalent bonds. The oxides of sulfur have low melting points and are gases at room temperature because they comprise simple covalent molecules with weak intermolecular forces between them.

5.

Element	Formula of oxide	Type of bonding	Equation for formation of oxide with oxygen
Sodium	Na_2O	Ionic	$4Na(s) + O_2(g) \rightarrow 2Na_2O(s)$
Phosphorus	P_4O_{10}	Covalent	$4P(s) + 5O_2(g) \rightarrow P_4O_{10}(s)$
Aluminium	Al_2O_3	Ionic	$4Al(s) + 3O_2(g) \rightarrow 2Al_2O_3(s)$

6. O^{2-} ions cannot exist in water, so they combine with H_2O molecules to form OH^- ions. If we look at the M–O–H system, then the M–O bond will be weakest for Na–O–H and will increase in strength in the order Na → Mg → Al. The weaker the M–O bond, the greater will be the number of OH^- ions produced, so the pH will be higher. In addition, the solubility of the oxides decreases in the order Na → Mg → Al, so fewer OH^- ions will be released into the water, and so the pH will be lower.

7.

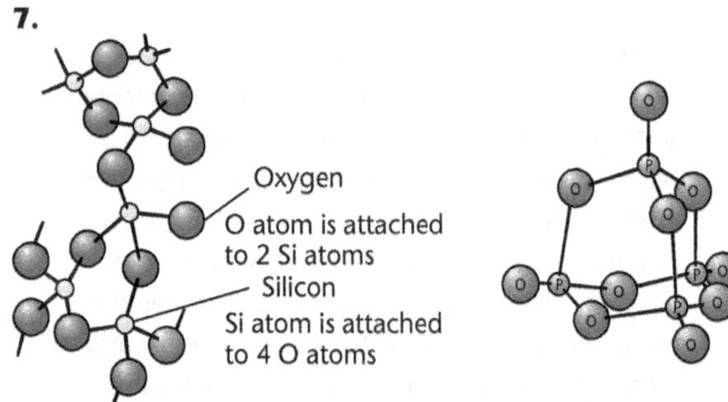

SiO_2 is insoluble in water but the more covalent P_4O_{10} dissolves to give phosphoric acid: $P_4O_{10}(s) + 6H_2O(l) \rightarrow 4H_3PO_4(aq)$. The more electronegative P atom causes ionisation, to give $P–O^-$ and H^+.

8. $MgO(s) + H_2O(l) \rightarrow Mg(OH)_2(aq)$

9. Al_2O_3
$Al_2O_3(s) + 3H_2SO_4(aq) \rightarrow Al_2(SO_4)_3(aq) + 3H_2O(l)$
$Al_2O_3(s) + 6HCl(aq) \rightarrow 2AlCl_3(aq) + 3H_2O(l)$
$Al_2O_3(s) + 2KOH(aq) + 3H_2O(l) \rightarrow 2KAl(OH)_4(aq)$

10. They form acids when dissolved in water.
$P_4O_{10}(s) + 12NaOH(aq) \rightarrow 4Na_3PO_4(aq) + 6H_2O(l)$
$SO_3(g) + 2NaOH(aq) \rightarrow Na_2SO_4(aq) + H_2O(l)$

11. $2K(s) + 2H_2O(l) \rightarrow 2KOH(aq) + H_2(g)$

12. $Al_2O_3(s) + 6HCl(aq) \rightarrow 2AlCl_3(aq) + 3H_2O(l)$ or
$Al_2O_3(s) + 6HCl(aq) + 9H_2O(l) \rightarrow 2[Al(H_2O)_6]^{3+}(aq) + 6Cl^-(aq)$
$Al_2O_3(s) + 2NaOH(aq) + 3H_2O(l) \rightarrow 2[Al(OH)_4]^-(aq) + 2Na^+(aq)$

13. H_2SeO_3
$SeO_2(g) + H_2O(l) \rightarrow H_2SeO_3(aq)$, acidic

14. Aluminium oxide is not soluble in water, so it is not easily removed from the surface. The thin layer blocks oxygen from diffusing to the surface and reacting with the aluminium metal.

15. **a.** $[Cr(H_2O)_6]^{3+} + H_2O \rightleftharpoons [Cr(H_2O)_5(OH)]^{2+} + H_3O^+$

b. pH 3–6

c. The highly polarising 3+ ion attracts electrons from the metal–oxygen bond and therefore weakens the oxygen–hydrogen bond in the ligand. This releases some H^+ ions, forming H_3O^+ ions, producing acidity and lowering the pH value below 7.

16. **a.** Left

b. It would move further to the left.

c. It would move to the right.

17. It can react with both acids and bases.

18. **a.** $[Fe(H_2O)_6]^{2+} + 2OH^- \rightarrow [Fe(H_2O)_4(OH)_2] + 2H_2O$

b. $[Cu(H_2O)_6]^{2+} + 2OH^- \rightarrow [Cu(H_2O)_4(OH)_2] + 2H_2O$

c. $[Al(OH)_4]^- + H^+ + 3H_2O \rightarrow [Al(H_2O)_3(OH)_3]$
$[Al(H_2O)_3(OH)_3] + 3H^+ \rightarrow [Al(H_2O)_6]^{3+}$

19. **a.** Adding H^+ ions drives the equilibrium to the left, from the brown $[Fe(H_2O)_5(OH)]^{2+}$ complex to the pale violet $[Fe(H_2O)^6]^{3+}$ complex.

b. Adding OH^- ions means they will react with H^+ ions (forming H_2O) and remove H^+ ions from solution. The equilibrium will shift from left to right replace these H^+ ions, and produce a brown colour.

c. Adding excess OH^- ions will send the equilibrium as far right as is feasible and a brown precipitate of $Fe(H_2O)_3(OH)_3$ forms.

20. Because $[Fe(H_2O)_6]^{2+}$ ions produce only a very weakly acidic solution, there are very few H_3O^+ ions at equilibrium. Upon addition of carbonate ions, there will not be a sufficient concentration of H_3O^+ to release carbon dioxide gas and the equilibrium will not be moved sufficiently to the right to lead to the formation of iron(II) hydroxide. Instead, $FeCO_3$ is formed as a precipitate. $[Fe(H_2O)_6]^{3+}$ is more acidic and the higher concentration of H_3O^+ reacts with the carbonate to give CO_2, water and $[Fe(H_2O)_3(OH)_3]$.

16 TRANSITION METALS

1. **a.** $1s^22s^22p^63s^23p^63d^64s^2$,
b. $1s^22s^22p^63s^23p^63d^6$,
c. $1s^22s^22p^63s^23p^63d^5$

2. **a.** 6, **b.** 6, **c.** 4, **d.** 2

3. **a.** Positive, **b.** Negative, **c.** Positive

4. **a.** $[[CuCl_4]^{2-}][H_2O]^6/[[CU(H_2O)_6]^{2+}][Cl^-]^4$
b. $[[CoCl_4]^{2-}][NH_3]^6/[[Co(NH_3)_6]^{2+}][Cl^-]^4$

5. 2857 ppm
$[O^2]$ = 20% = 200 000 ppm. Therefore, [CO] = 200 000/210 = 952.3 ppm. Death occurs at 3 × 952.3 = 2857 ppm]

6. **a.** 90°, **b.** 109.5°

7. **a.** Octahedral, **b.** Tetrahedral, **c.** Linear

8. *Cis* and *trans*

9. *Trans* isomer.

10. **a.** Optical enantiomers

b.

11. **a.** [Ar] $3d^8 4s^2$, **b.** [Ar] $3d^5 4s^2$

12. High energy, short wavelength, high frequency – violet end of the visible spectrum.

13. H_2O (higher in the spectrochemical series and forms an octahedral complex ion).

14. The difference in energy between the split d orbitals changes.

15. **a.** $[Cu(H_2O)_6]^{2+} = +2$, $Cu(CN)_4]^{3-} = +1$

b. $[Cu(H_2O)_6]^{2+}$ = [Ar]$3d^9$, $[Cu(CN)_4]^{3-}$ = [Ar]$3d^{10}$

c. In $Cu(H_2O)_6]^{2+}$ not all the d orbitals are occupied, so the photons in the visible region of the spectrum can be absorbed and colour is produced. $[Cu(CN)_4]^{3-}$ has all its d orbitals occupied, so the absorption is not in the visible region and so the substance is not coloured.

16. Absorption of colour is caused by photons interacting with the ions present in solution, so if the solution is diluted there is a lower concentration of ions, and therefore fewer interactions as the light passes through it. This will result in a less intense (paler) appearance but the actual colour will be unchanged.

17. Between 610 and 620 nm.

18. **a.** $3Zn + Cr_2O_7^{2-} + 14H^+ \rightarrow 3Zn^{2+} + 2Cr^{3+} + 7H_2O$
b. $Zn + 2Cr^{3+} \rightarrow Zn^{2+} + 2Cr^{2+}$
c. $4Cr^{2+} + O_2 + 4H^+ \rightarrow 4Cr^{3+} + 2H_2O$

19. $Cr_2O_7^{2-}$: Cr (2 × +6) = +12, O (7 × −2) = −14, overall charge = +12 − 14 = −2; CrO_4^{2-}: Cr (+6), O (4 × −2) = −8, overall charge = +6 − 8 = −2.

20. The equations for the two half–reactions are
$Cr_2O_7^{2-} + 14H^+ + 6e^- \rightarrow 2Cr^{3+} + 7H_2O$ and
$Fe^{2+} \rightarrow Fe^{3+} + e^-$
Balancing the electron transfer gives $6Fe^{2+} \rightarrow 6Fe^{3+} + 6e^-$
The overall equation is
$Cr_2O_7^{2-} + 14H^+ + 6Fe^{2+} \rightarrow 2Cr^{3+} + 6Fe^{3+} + 7H_2O$
1 mol of dichromate(VI) reacts with 6 mol of iron(II) ions.

21. **a.** 5.735×10^{-4} mol, **b.** 6, **c.** 3.44×10^{-3} mol, **d.** 3.44×10^{-2} mol, **e.** 1.9264 g, **f.** 86.58%

22. Moles of MnO_4^- used:
$45.0 \times 0.0200/1000 = 9.0 \times 10^{-4}$ mol
The balanced half–equations give this full equation:
$MnO_4^-(aq) + 5e^- + 8H^+(aq) \rightarrow Mn^{2+}(aq) + 4H_2O(l)$

$SO_3^{2-}(aq) + H_2O(l) \rightarrow SO_4^{2-}(aq) + 2e^- + 2H^+$

$2MnO_4^-(aq) + \cancel{10e^-} + 5SO_3^{2-}(aq) + 6H^+(aq) \rightarrow$
$2Mn^{2+}(aq) + 5SO_4^{2-}(aq) + \cancel{10e^-} + 3H_2O(l)$

1 mol of manganate(VII) reacts with 5/2 mol SO_3^{2-} ions, so

Moles of $SO_3^{2-} = 5/2 \times 9.0 \times 10^{-4} = 2.25 \times 10^{-3}$ mol (in 25.0 cm^3)

Concentration of $SO_3^{2-} = 1000 \times 2.25 \times 10^{-3}/25 = 9.00 \times 10^{-2}$ mol dm^{-3}

23. Ethanedioic acid-2-water is $(COOH)_2.2H_2O$ (M_r = 126) and in water it behaves as the ethanedioate ion $C_2O_4^{2-}(aq)$.
The balanced half-equations give this full equation:

$MnO_4^-(aq) + 5e^- + 8H^+(aq) \rightarrow Mn^{2+}(aq) + 4H_2O(l)$
$C_2O_4^{2-}(aq) \rightarrow 2CO_2(g) + 2e^-$

$2MnO_4^-(aq) + \cancel{10e^-} + 5C_2O_4^{2-}(aq) + 16H^+(aq) \rightarrow$
$2Mn^{2+}(aq) + 10CO_2(g) + \cancel{10e^-} + 8H_2O(l)$

1 mol of $C_2O_4^{2-}$(aq) reacts with 2/5 mol of manganate(VII), so:

Moles of $(COOH)_2.2H_2O$ (to give $C_2O_4^{2-}$(aq)) = 2.145/126 = 1.702 × 10^{-2} mol (dissolved in 250 cm^3)

Moles of $(COOH)_2.2H_2O$ in 25.0 cm^3 = 1.702 × 10^{-3} mol

Moles of MnO_4^- used = 2 × 1.702 × 10^{-3}/5 = 6.81 × 10^{-4} mol

Concentration of MnO_4^- = 1000 × 6.81 × 10^{-4}/35.0 = 0.0195 mol dm^{-3}

24. To give a greater surface area and increase the number of active sites.

25. **a.** $MnO_4^-(aq) + 5e^- + 8H^+(aq) \rightarrow Mn^{2+}(aq) + 4H_2O(l)$

b. $C_2O_4^{2-}(aq) \rightarrow 2CO_2(g) + 2e^-$

c. Homogeneous because both reactants are in the same phase.

GLOSSARY

2-deoxyribose The sugar component in the side chains of DNA; derived from the pentose sugar ribose by the replacement of a hydroxyl group with a hydrogen atom.

Absolute standard entropy See Standard entropy

Acid A substance that donates protons in a reaction.

Active site A region on an enzyme that binds to a protein or other substance during a reaction.

Acylation A substitution reaction in which an acyl group (right) substitutes for another group.

Addition polymer Many molecules of a monomer form one large molecule of polymer. No other substances are formed. Ethene forms poly(ethene) by addition polymerisation.

Adsorption The process in which (usually) a gas bonds to the surface of a solid catalyst. The gas (or its products) is released after reaction occurs.

α-helix A secondary structure of proteins, characterised by a single, spiral chain of amino acids stabilised by hydrogen bonds.

Amphoteric Having both acidic and basic properties. For example, aluminium oxide is an amphoteric oxide. It forms salts both with acids and with alkalis.

Anionic detergent (anionic surfactant) Cleaning agent in which the long chain is an anion.

Aramids A family of nylons containing aromatic rings e.g. Kevlar™. They have particular strength.

Autocatalysis The ability of one of the products of a reaction to catalyse the reaction producing it. In autocatalysis the initial reaction rate increases, as more catalyst is produced.

Azo Containing two adjacent nitrogen atoms between carbon atoms.

Azo dye A coloured compound formed from a reaction of benzene diazonium chloride with another group with significant delocalisation.

Base A substance that accepts protons in a reaction.

Base pair A pair of complementary bases in a double-stranded nucleic acid molecule.

Bifunctional A compound with two functional groups that can react with each other.

Born–Haber cycle A cycle of reactions used for calculating the lattice energies of ionic crystalline solids.

β-pleated sheet A secondary structure found in proteins in which hydrogen bonds are formed between two parts of the protein chain that can be far apart.

Carbonyl group A functional group composed of a carbon atom double-bonded to an oxygen atom: C=O; found in, among others, aldehydes and ketones.

Carboxylic acid groups Organic acids having the general formula RCOOH. Their names end in -oic acid. Ethanoic acid has the formula CH_3COOH.

Cationic surfactant A cation that will act at a surface reducing surface tension.

Chemical environment Neighbouring atoms surrounding a particular atom producing differing NMR absorptions.

Chemical shift The position, relative to the proton absorption of tetramethylsilane, where a nucleus absorbs in an NMR spectrum.

Chemotherapy The use of drugs to treat cancer.

Chiral A molecule where a central carbon atom (the chiral atom) is attached to four different groups.

Chromophore A functional group that causes an organic molecule to be coloured. Examples are the nitro ($-NO_2$) and azo (C–N=N–C) groups.

Colorimeter An instrument that measures the absorption of a range of radiation.

Complementary colour A colour that a sample will absorb the most.

Complementary strand Either of the two chains that make up a double helix of DNA, with corresponding positions on the two chains being composed of a pair of complementary bases.

Condensation polymer A polymer formed in a reaction where a simple molecule such as water or ammonia is eliminated.

Condensation reaction A reaction in which two or more organic molecules (e.g. an alcohol and an acid) are linked to form a larger organic molecule (e.g. an ester) by elimination of a small molecule such as water, hydrogen chloride or methanol. Overall, it is an addition reaction followed by an elimination reaction.

Conductor A substance that will allow heat or electricity to pass through it easily.

Contact process The process used to make sulfuric acid from sulfur, oxygen and water.

Coupled Two atoms in a molecule are coupled when the magnetic field experienced by one is altered by the effect of the magnetic field created by the other.

Coupling A chemical reaction in which two molecules join together.

Coupling effect The interaction between the nuclear spins of neighbouring atoms in a molecule.

Delocalisation energy The extra stability in a compound produced by delocalisation of the electrons.

Delocalised Electrons that are not located at one particular atom, but are free to move between all atoms in the structure. Examples of materials with delocalised electrons are metals, graphite and benzene.

Denature To produce a structural change in a protein or nucleic acid that results in the reduction or loss of its biological properties.

Desorption The process in which a substance (usually a gas) is released from the surface of a solid catalyst following reaction.

Dipeptide A compound formed when two amino acids react together eliminating a molecule of water.

Dynamic equilibrium A stage in a reaction where the forward reaction equals the backward reaction so that there is no net change in the concentration of the substances involved in the reaction.

E.m.f. (electromotive force) The e.m.f. for a cell is:
$E^{\ominus}_{cell} = E^{\ominus}_{RHS} - E^{\ominus}_{LHS}$
For an electrochemical cell or battery the e.m.f. is the output voltage. Strictly, e.m.f. is the cell potential measure when zero-current flows.

Electrochemical series A list of half-reactions and their electrode potentials. The half-reactions are written as reductions. The series can contain half-reactions involving metals and non-metals.

Electrode potential The potential of an electrode measured relative to the Standard Hydrogen Electrode (SHE), under standard conditions.

Electrophile Molecules and groups attracted by regions of negative charging (the name means 'electron-loving').

Electrophoresis A method used in clinical and research laboratories for separating molecules according to their size and electrical charge.

Eluent A substance used as a solvent in separating materials in elution.

Emulsification A process in which an emulsion is formed, which is a liquid containing fine droplets of another liquid without forming a solution.

Enantiomers Isomers formed in a molecule with a chiral carbon atom. They rotate plane polarised light.

Enthalpy of lattice dissociation The enthalpy change when one mole of lattice is broken up to produce gaseous ions an infinite distance apart.

Enthalpy of lattice formation The enthalpy change when one mole of a crystalline compound is formed from gaseous ions scattered an infinite distance apart.

Entropy (S) Entropy is a measure of the amount of disorder in a system. Gases have higher entropy than solids because the particles in a gas are more randomly arranged (disordered) than in a solid. All chemical reactions and physical processes involve an overall increase in the entropy for the universe (system and surroundings). For an individual system there may be a decrease in entropy: e.g. the reaction $2Mg(s) + O_2(g) \rightleftharpoons 2MgO(s)$ involves a decrease in entropy. However, the overall entropy for a system and its surroundings will increase. The oxidation of magnesium by oxygen gas produces heat which increases the entropy of the surroundings, and for the overall universe.

Enzyme inhibitor A molecule that binds to an enzyme active site and decreases its activity.

Enzyme–substrate complex The intermediate formed when a substrate molecule interacts with the active site of an enzyme.

Esterification Formation of an ester from an acid and an alcohol.

Fatty acid Consists of a carbon chain with a carboxylic acid group at one end. These are part of fat and oil molecules.

Feasibility Whether or not a physical or chemical change could take place spontaneously.

Fehling's solution Reagent producing brick-red copper(I) oxide in the presence of an aldehyde group.

First ionisation energy The energy required to move the first electron from an atom in its gaseous state.

First-order reaction A reaction whose rate is proportional to the concentration of a reactant. Rate = $k[A]^x$ where $x = 1$.

Frequency (of radiation) Number of wavelengths of light passing a particular point in one second.

Fuel cell Cell producing electricity by using fuel reacting with an oxidant.

Geostationary satellite A satellite is geostationary if it moves in a geosynchronous orbit, i.e. it moves in such a way that it remains in a fixed position relative to Earth. Most communications satellites are geostationary.

Haber process Manufacturing process for the production of ammonia from nitrogen and hydrogen.

Half equation Either of two equations that describe each half of a redox reaction.

Heterogeneous Relating to two or more phases.

Homogeneous Relating to only one phase.

Integrated spectrum A series of peaks that represent the areas under NMR peaks. These are equivalent to the number of protons in various groups.

Ionic equation An equation showing only ions that change in a reaction.

Isoelectric pH The pH at which an amino acid exists as a zwitterion.

Lattice Giant regular structure formed by an ionic compound.

Lewis acid An electron pair acceptor.

Lock and key hypothesis A scientific analogy that states that only the correctly sized key fits in the lock; the key refers to a substrate and the lock refers to an enzyme.

Macromolecule A very large molecule.

Magnetic field The region surrounding a magnetic north or south pole in which attractive and repulsive forces are felt.

Mobile phase The liquid in chromatography that moves through the solid medium and carries the sample.

Mole fraction The number of moles of a substance divided by the total number of moles in the mixture.

Monomer A molecule that can react with many other similar molecules to build up a large molecule, a polymer, e.g. the monomer ethene gives rise to the polymer poly(ethene).

Neutralisation reaction A reaction in which an acid and a base react to form a salt and water only.

Nuclear spin A property of nuclei with odd atomic numbers or mass numbers, behaving as if they were bar magnets.

Nucleophilic addition across the C = O bond An addition reaction where a nucleophile donates an electron pair to an electron-deficient atom to form a new molecule.

Nucleophilic substitution A chemical reaction in which one nucleophile replaces another in a molecule. For example, in the reaction of bromoethane with alkali, the nucleophilic hydroxide ion replaces the bromide ion in the bromoethane molecule: $C_2H_5Br + OH^- \rightarrow C_2H_5OH + Br^-$

Nucleotide Forms the basic structural unit of nucleic acids such as DNA; consists of a nucleoside linked to a phosphate group.

Optical isomers Compounds whose molecules, though alike in every other way, are mirror images of each other.

Order of reaction The proportionality of the rate to the concentration of reactants. Rate = k[A]x where x = the order of reaction.

Oxidation state The charge that an element would have if it were totally ionically bonded. For an ion, it is the charge on the ion. In a covalent compound, it is the theoretical number assigned to each atom in a molecule if it were an ionic compound. For example, in water the oxidation state of hydrogen is + 1 and that of oxygen is −2, even though water is covalently bonded. Oxidation state can change in a redox reaction. The oxidation state of elements is zero.

PH scale A measure of the acidity or alkalinity of solutions. $pH = -\log_{10}[H+]$.

Plasticiser A substance added to a plastic in order to increase its flexibility.

Polynucleotide A linear polymer composed of many nucleotide units, constituting a section of a nucleic acid molecule.

Potential difference The difference between two electrode potentials in a cell.

Primary structure A continuous chain of repeated peptide links.

Proton acceptor A substance that accepts protons in a reaction.

Proton donor A substance that donates protons in a reaction.

Quanta Single packets of energy in light photons.

Quartet A group of four signals in the ratio 1:3:3:1 produced when a set of equivalent protons with three equivalent neighbouring protons in the molecule undergoes NMR resonance.

Racemate (racemic mixture) A 50:50 mixture of optical isomers, where the rotation effects on plane polarised light cancel each other out.

Rate The relative speed of progress or change of something variable.

Rate equation Rate = $k[A]^x$ where x = the order of reaction.

Rate-determining step The slowest step in any sequence of intermediate stages. This will determine the rate of reaction.

Residue The material remaining after distillation, evaporation or filtration; may also refer to an atom or a group of atoms that forms part of a molecule, such as a methyl group.

Resonance The natural vibrational frequency of a bond when subjected to IR radiation or the protons when subjected to a radio frequency radiation.

Retention time The time taken to pass through a GLC column; depends upon the nature of and attraction between the solute and the stationary and mobile phases and the volatility of the solute.

Salt bridge An electrolyte solution (e.g. saturated potassium chloride or potassium nitrate in agar jelly) that allows movement of ions between two half-reactions of an electrochemical cell which are in separate electrode compartments. The salt bridge completes the electrical circuit within the cell.

Saponification The process of forming a soap by the hydrolysis of a fat or oil, usually with sodium or potassium hydroxide.

Second ionisation energy The enthalpy change when one mole of electrons is removed from one mole of singly charged ions to produce doubly charged ions.

Secondary structure A helical shape produced when a polyamide chain forms hydrogen bonds between the C=O and N-H.

Singlet A signal produced when a set of equivalent protons with no neighbouring protons in the molecule undergoes NMR resonance.

Spectator ions Ions present in a solution that do not take part in the reaction.

Spectrophotometer An instrument used to carry out spectroscopy – the analysis of a compound by detecting its response to electromagnetic radiation.

Standard cell (electrode) potential The potential of an electrode measured relative to the Standard Hydrogen Electrode (SHE), under standard conditions.

Standard enthalpy of formation The energy absorbed when one mole of a substance is formed from its elements in their standard states.

Standard entropy An absolute measure of entropy, based on zero entropy at zero Kelvin.

Standard hydrogen electrode (SHE) The standard reference electrode (or half-reaction) for measuring the electrode potentials of cells. The SHE is arbitrarily assigned an electrode potential of 0 V when operating under standard conditions. The cell consists of hydrogen gas at 1 bar bubbling over an electrode of finely divided platinum, dipped into a solution of 1 mol dm^{-3} hydrochloric acid.

Starting material The chemicals used at the start of organic synthesis.

Stationary phase The solid used in GLC; it is usually diatomaceous earth or kieselghur (the ground remains of very small plant skeletons).

Stereoisomers Isomers that have the same molecular formula and structural formula but different arrangements of their atoms in space. Optical and *E-Z* geometrical isomers are stereoisomers.

Stereospecific Describes reactions that give products with a particular arrangement of atoms in space.

Strong acid An acid that dissociates fully in aqueous solution.

Substrate A support medium designed to hold expensive, finely divided catalyst material, and to maximise the surface area of a catalyst.

Tertiary structure The overall three-dimensional shape of a protein.

Thin-layer chromatography A technique for the analysis of liquid mixtures using chromatography.

Tollens' reagent A mild oxidising agent that can be used in testing for aldehydes.

Transesterification The process of exchanging the alkoxy group of an ester compound by another alcohol; often catalysed by the addition of an acid or base.

Transition metal Any of the set of metallic elements occupying the central d block of the Periodic Table.

Tri-ester A compound formed when a carboxylic acid reacts with a trihydric alcohol e.g. glycerol.

Triplet A group of three signals in the ratio 1:2:1 produced when a set of equivalent protons with two equivalent neighbouring protons in the molecule undergoes NMR resonance.

Weak acid An acid that does not dissociate fully in water.

INDEX

T

U

V

W

Y

Z

ACKNOWLEDGEMENTS

The Publishers gratefully acknowledge the permissions granted to reproduce copyright material in this book. Every effort has been made to contact the holders of copyright material, but if any have been inadvertently overlooked, the Publisher will be pleased to make the necessary arrangements at the first opportunity.

Practical work in chemistry

p2: left: bikeriderlondon/ Shutterstock; right Lisa S./ Shutterstock; p3: top: bogdanhoda/ Shutterstock; bottom: phloxii/ Shutterstock; p4 top: Decha Thapanya/Shutterstock; bottom: Yenyu Shih/Shutterstock

Chapter 1

p5 background: Shutterstock/ Lisa S.; p19: Science Photo Library; p23 left: Shutterstock/Everett Historical; right: LAWRENCE MIGDALE/ SCIENCE PHOTO LIBRARY;

Chapter 2

p29 background: Shutterstock/ Bertold Werkmann; p34: ANDREW LAMBERT PHOTOGRAPHY/ SCIENCE PHOTO LIBRARY;

Chapter 3

p49 background: Shutterstock/ Juriah Mosin; p50 left: Science Photo Library ; right: Shutterstock/ andrey_l; p57 top: Wikimedia Commons; bottom: Wikimedia Commons;

Chapter 4

p59 background: Shutterstock/ Click and Photo; p61: ANDREW LAMBERT PHOTOGRAPHY/ SCIENCE PHOTO LIBRARY; p63 top: ANDREW LAMBERT PHOTOGRAPHY/SCIENCE PHOTO LIBRARY; bottom: ANDREW LAMBERT PHOTOGRAPHY/ SCIENCE PHOTO LIBRARY; p64: Joerg Beuge/Shutterstock; p67: Flickr Creative Commons/G Xianfu; p77 top left: Wikimedia Commons

Chapter 5

p83 background: Shutterstock/ Mugurel E; p87: PHILIPPE BENOIST/LOOK AT SCIENCES/ SCIENCE PHOTO LIBRARY

Chapter 6

p92 background: Shutterstock/ Dream79; p96 left: ANDREW LAMBERT PHOTOGRAPHY/ SCIENCE PHOTO LIBRARY; right: ANDREW LAMBERT PHOTOGRAPHY/SCIENCE PHOTO LIBRARY

Chapter 7

p103 background: Shutterstock/ anat chant; p107 left: Shutterstock/ Yulia Myron; right: Shutterstock/ Andrii Bielov; p119: ANDREW LAMBERT PHOTOGRAPHY/ SCIENCE PHOTO LIBRARY

Chapter 8

p125 background: Shutterstock/ Artsci

Chapter 9

p135 background: Shutterstock/ molekuul.be

Chapter 10

p148 background: Shutterstock/ somsak nitimongkolchai; p151: Shutterstock/ Chones; p153: Shutterstock/ Ecuadorpostales; p156: Shutterstock/ Warut Chinsai

Chapter 11

p161 background: Shutterstock/ royaltystockphoto.com; p161: Shutterstock/ molekuul.be; p166: Wikimedia Commons; p173: Wikimedia Commons; p177: RAMON ANDRADE 3DCIENCIA/ SCIENCE PHOTO LIBRARY

Chapter 12

p183 background: Shutterstock/ taviphoto; p183: Shutterstock/ Promotive

Chapter 13

p191 background: Shutterstock/ Semnic; p191: PATRICE LATRON/ LOOK AT SCIENCES/SCIENCE PHOTO LIBRARY; p200: FOOD & DRUG ADMINISTRATION/SCIENCE PHOTO LIBRARY

Chapter 14

p210 background: Shutterstock/ hfng

Chapter 15

p226 background: Shutterstock/ meaofoto; p237: Shutterstock/Dr. Morley Read; p241: Shutterstock/ kai keisuke

Chapter 16

p245 background: Shutterstock/ Adam J; p251: CHARLES D. WINTERS/SCIENCE PHOTO LIBRARY; p261: Shutterstock/ Monkey Business Images